D0435722

A
DICTIONARY
FOR
PSYCHOTHERAPISTS

Also by Richard D. Chessick, M.D., Ph.D.

Agonie: Diary of a Twentieth Century Man (1976)

Intensive Psychotherapy of the Borderline Patient (1977)

Freud Teaches Psychotherapy (1980)

How Psychotherapy Heals (1969, 1983)

Why Psychotherapists Fail (1971, 1983)

A Brief Introduction to the Genius of Nietzsche (1983)

Psychology of the Self and the Treatment of Narcissism (1985)

Great Ideas in Psychotherapy (1977, 1987)

The Technique and Practice of Listening in Intensive Psychotherapy (1989)

The Technique and Practice of Intensive Psychotherapy (1974, 1983, 1991)

What Constitutes the Patient in Psychotherapy (1992)

A
DICTIONARY
FOR
PSYCHOTHERAPISTS

DYNAMIC CONCEPTS IN
PSYCHOTHERAPY

Richard D. Chessick, M.D., Ph.D.

JASON ARONSON INC.
Northvale, New Jersey
London

Production Editor: Judith D. Cohen

This book is set in 10 pt. Bem by Lind Graphics of Upper Saddle River, New Jersey, and printed and bound by Haddon Craftsmen of Scranton, Pennsylvania.

Library of Congress Cataloging-in-Publication Data

Chessick, Richard D., 1931–
    A dictionary for psychotherapists : dynamic concepts in
psychotherapy / Richard D. Chessick.
        p.   cm.
    Includes bibliographical references and index.
    ISBN 0-87668-338-3
    1. Psychotherapy—Dictionaries.   2. Psychotherapy—Encyclopedias.
I. Title.
    [DNLM: 1. Psychotherapy—dictionaries.   WM 13 C524d]
RC475.7.C48   1993
616.89′14′03—dc20
DNLM/DLC
for Library of Congress   92-23967

Manufactured in the United States of America. Jason Aronson Inc. offers books and cassettes. For information and catalog write to Jason Aronson Inc., 230 Livingston Street, Northvale, New Jersey 07647.

This book is dedicated to my wife

MARCIA

On the occasion of our fortieth year of married life together.

Love:

1. The passion between the sexes.
2. Kindness; good-will; friendship.
3. Courtship.
4. Tenderness; parental care.
5. Liking; inclination to . . .
6. Object beloved.
7. Lewdness.
8. Unreasonable liking.
9. Fondness; concord.
10. Principle of union.
11. Picturesque representation of love.
12. A word of endearment.
13. Due reverence to God.
14. A kind of thin silk stuff.

Samuel Johnson
Dictionary of the English Language

Contents

◆

Preface

One of the most neglected great books of the Western world is *A Dictionary of the English Language,* first published in 1755. The author, the genius Samuel Johnson, introduced this work by stating, "He that undertakes to compile a Dictionary, undertakes that, which, if it comprehends the full extent of his design, he knows himself unable to perform. Yet his labours, though deficient, may be useful, and with the hope of this inferior praise, he must incite his activity and solace his weariness" (p. xiii). Reddick (1990) outlines in detail the enormous dedication and enterprise that Johnson devoted to this extraordinary accomplishment.

In this dictionary for psychotherapists, with the ideal of Samuel Johnson hovering unattainably above me, I attempt to address the same difficulty that he (1773) describes:

> When I took the first survey of my undertaking, I found our speech copious without order, and energetic without rules; wherever I turned my view, there was perplexity to be disentangled, and confusion to be regulated; choice was to be made out of boundless variety without any established principle of selection; adulterations were to be detected, without a subtle test of purity; and modes of expression to be rejected or received, without the suffrages of any writers of classical reputation or acknowledged authority. [p. iii]

Setting out to produce a practical guide for the use of experienced psychotherapists, as well as mental health professionals in various stages of their training, I decided to render it as much in narrative form as possible. The approach of this dictionary is designed so that the reader may look up any term he or she finds puzzling by reference to the simple alphabetical order of the book or in the table of contents, while at the same time a dedicated clinician or student who wishes an overview of practical problems in psychotherapy can read the book from cover to cover because of its format. A name index has also been included at the end for those who wish to examine the contributions of any individual thinker to our discipline, but I have restricted the selection of famous names to some of those who are often cited in current unresolved issues.

In devising this format, I have made no effort to be inclusive of the innumerable terms and the infinite variety of their usage in our field, but rather to express, on the basis of thirty-five years of clinical experience, the way I have used these terms and to provide the best or optimal understanding that I may convey to the practicing psychotherapist. In discussing the various concepts involved, I have elected to stay with clinical material and avoid long and tedious abstract or theoretical metapsychological controversies. I have necessarily been selective, choosing those terms from the psychiatric, psychoanalytic, medical, philosophical, and artistic vocabulary that have immediate practical significance. In so doing, I hope to offer the comprehensive reader a large number of useful clinical ideas that are suggested by the terms I have emphasized in this dictionary. The aim would be not only to improve and sharpen the vocabulary of the practicing psychotherapist, but also to provide the clinician with the everyday practical use of this terminology. I hope this will facilitate the actual practice of the art and craft of psychotherapy as well as instruct student mental health professionals. These choices and my approach lead me to share Johnson's (1773) concern:

> That part of my work on which I expect malignity most frequently to fasten, is the *Explanation*; in which I cannot hope to satisfy those, who are perhaps not inclined to be pleased, since I have not always been able to satisfy myself. To interpret a language by itself is very difficult. . . . When the nature of things is unknown or the notion unsettled and indefinite, and various in various minds, the words by which such notions are conveyed, or such

things denoted, will be ambiguous and perplexed. [p. vii]

Some of the pioneer attempts at a dictionary for mental health professionals are those by Eidelberg (1968), English and English (1958), Fodor and Gaynor (1950), and more recently Walrond-Skinner (1986). I have leaned more at times on certain other specialized texts, such as those by Rycroft (1968), Laplanche and Pontalis (1973), Moore and Fine (1990), Campbell (1989), and Hinshelwood (1989).

Rycroft (1968) lists some of the "linguistic stumbling-blocks" to gaining entry to the psychoanalytic literature. The use of abstract explanatory concepts while describing facts leads to a misuse of jargon and a writing of case histories with reported facts presented only through a theoretical haze. This makes it impossible for the reader to grasp in everyday language the material presented, which might then have been explained in some other way. Technical jargon can easily be used to construct theories that are consistent and intellectually satisfying, "not because they really explain the facts but because the definitions of the technical terms interlock beautifully" (p. xi). Jargon often is used to conceal ignorance. Psychiatrists, according to Rycroft, "following a long-established medical tradition, are more often guilty of this form of unconscious deception than are the analysts, the procedure or trick being to translate the patient's complaint into Greek and then assure him that his troubles are due to an illness with an outlandish and exotic name" (p. xii).

In the preparation of a dictionary, an important objective is what Basch (1973) has called "expression" (p. 47) and Langer (1962) "the presentation of an idea, usually by the proper and apt use of words" (p. 78). Unfortunately, instead of a common language, there exists an "increasing psychoanalytic diversity . . . a pluralism of theoretical perspectives, of linguistic and thought conventions, of distinctive regional, cultural, and language emphases" (Wallerstein 1988, p. 5). To make matters even more complex, Moore and Fine (1990) point out Freud's conceptual inconsistency and poetic word play, leading to an ambiguity and flexibility in his writings "that enabled him to say several different things at the same time. . . . Freud communicated his concepts via consummate use of vivid and emotionally compelling language. . . . He did not adhere to precise definitions of technical terms" (p. xxi). Furthermore, the translation of Freud by Strachey in the mid-1960s consistently replaced Freud's affect-laden everyday German words with a more scientific-sounding terminology and changed Freud's dynamic concepts into "static, passive" ones (p. xxi). Strachey apparently believed that he had improved on and presented a definitive version of Freud's thinking, but there is considerable controversy on that subject at the present time (Ornston 1985).

Anyone wishing to explore these matters more fully and with greater scholastic rigor is referred to Moore and Fine's glossary (1990) for psychoanalytic terms and concepts, and to Campbell's fine psychiatric dictionary (1989). The latter is presented in the format of a typical medical dictionary, offering relatively brief definitions and discussions, and not written in a narrative form. The former is more technical and carefully geared to the psychoanalyst or psychoanalytically oriented psychotherapist who wishes to gain some metapsychological depth in this terminology, and it provides references for even further investigation in detail. Laplanche and Pontalis (1973) offer a less useful compendium, which traces psychoanalytic terminology from a more European orientation, and includes concepts that are obsolete. The major value of their work is for those interested in the terminology of various psychoanalytic movements, but it will not be very helpful to the everyday practicing clinician.

This book is intended for the clinician. In the immortal prose of Samuel Johnson (1773):

> To have attempted much is always laudable, even when the enterprise is above the strength that undertakes it: To rest below his own aim is incident to every one whose fancy is active, and whose views are comprehensive; nor is any man satisfied with himself because he has much, but because he can conceive little. . . . Thus it happens, that in things difficult there is danger from ignorance, and in things easy from confidence; the mind, afraid of

greatness, and disdainful of little-
ness, hastily withdraws herself from
painful searches, and passes with
scornful rapidity over tasks not adequate to her powers, sometimes too
secure for caution, and again too
anxious for vigorous effort; sometimes idle in a plain path, and sometimes distracted in labyrinths, and
dissipated by different intentions.
[pp. ix–xi]

> Richard D. Chessick, M.D., Ph.D.
> Evanston, Illinois

References

Basch, M. (1973). Psychoanalysis and theory
formation. *Annual of Psychoanalysis*
1:39–52.

Campbell, R. (1989). *Psychiatric Dictionary.*
New York: Oxford University Press.

Eidelberg, L. (1968). *Encyclopaedia of Psychoanalysis.* New York: The Free Press.

English, H. B., and English, A. C. (1958). *A
Comprehensive Dictionary of Psychological
and Psychoanalytical Terms.* New York:
David McKay.

Fodor, N., and Gaynor, F. (1950). *Freud: Dictionary of Psychoanalysis.* New York:
Philosophical Library.

Hinshelwood, R. (1989). *A Dictionary of Kleinian Thought.* London: Free Association
Books.

Johnson, S. (1773). *A Dictionary of the English
Language.* Beirut, Lebanon: *Librairie Du
Liban,* 1978.

Langer, S. (1962). Problems in techniques of
psychoanalytic validation and progress.
In *Psychoanalysis as a Science,* ed. E.
Pumpian-Mindlin. Stanford, CA: Stanford University Press.

Laplanche, J., and Pontalis, J. (1973). *The Language of Psychoanalysis.* Trans. D. Nicholson-Smith. New York: W. W. Norton.

Moore, B., and Fine, B. (1990) *Psychoanalytic
Terms and Concepts.* New Haven: Yale
University Press.

Ornston, D. (1985). Freud's conception is different from Strachey's. *Journal of the
American Psychoanalytic Association*
33:379–412.

Reddick, A. (1990). *The Making of Johnson's
Dictionary 1746–1773.* New York: Cambridge University Press.

Rycroft, C. (1968). *A Critical Dictionary of Psychoanalysis.* New York: Basic Books.

Wallerstein, R. (1988). One psychoanalysis or
many? *International Journal of Psycho-
Analysis* 69:5–21.

Walrond-Skinner, S. (1986). *A Dictionary of
Psychotherapy.* London: Routledge &
Kegan Paul.

Acknowledgment

◆

I wish to thank Ms. Elizabeth Grudzien for her loyal and tireless assistance in obtaining the references necessary for this book and her hard work on the many tasks required in preparing the manuscript. I also wish to thank Ms. Wanda Sauerman for patiently and promptly typing and retyping the many drafts and items required. This work could not have been produced without the encouragement of Dr. Jason Aronson and the invaluable, conscientious, and reliable help of Ms. Norma Pomerantz, Ms. Judy Cohen, and Ms. Carol McKenna on the staff of Jason Aronson Inc., and above all, the tolerance, loving devotion, and forbearance of my wife, Marcia. Thank you.

A

ABANDONMENT NEUROSIS

This is an excellent term with which to begin a dictionary for psychotherapists. The concept of the "neuroses of abandonment" was introduced by Odier (1956) in a book entitled *Anxiety and Magic Thinking,* which deserves more attention than it has received. Odier regarded the anxiety of the patients we call "borderline" today as directly proportional to the amount of insecurity in early childhood, producing regression to the prelogical stage of infantile thinking. He described this magic thinking in detail as involving (a) objectification of fear: "Whatever threatens me is wicked, whatever protects me is good"; (b) objectification of anger—toward animistic malevolent objects as chosen; and (c) identification with the aggressor. The "objectification" is the magical defense, which places the anxiety and fear and anger outside the psyche onto external objects, as in phobias, or onto fantasy objects, as in nightmares and religious preoccupations or guru-inspired cults.

In the neuroses of abandonment, the anxiety is objectified onto a human being instead of a cosmic image or a transitional object—a human being who is then given the power of creating or abolishing abandonment, insecurity, or helplessness. This individual is seen as all-powerful, sometimes benevolent, sometimes malevolent. In this situation, the oscillation between love and hate, security and insecurity, dependency and paranoia, and the rapid transitions from euphoria to depression, all as a function of minor provocations or reassurances from the chosen object, lead to the typical picture of the borderline patient and the common phenomena described as part of narcissistic object relations.

The purpose of this magical thinking, according to Odier, is as a defense against the recurrence of deception, the fear of the feeling of abandonment arising from early, mostly preoedipal childhood experiences. Leuba (1949) introduced rather metaphorically the concept of a "phobia of penetration," which means the fear in each living being of being penetrated and destroyed. He depicted by this concept an elementary fear and threat to the integrity of the body, "the fear of the cut-up body," and believed that all manifestations of this fear are identical with the concept that Odier called "primary phobias" that lie at the basis of the neuroses of abandonment.

The clinician should remember that behind many of these psychoanalytic and psychiatric concepts as they appear in psychotherapy lies the fear of the four major calamities of childhood: loss of the love object, loss of the mother's love, fear of castration, and guilt that demands punishment (Brenner 1982). These are usually telescoped together in our clinical work as the patients present their material, and it is only with careful exploratory study that we are able to ascertain what is fundamental and what represents regression.

References

Brenner, C. (1982). *The Mind in Conflict.* New York: International Universities Press.

Leuba, J. (1949). Introduction à l'étude clinique du narcissisme. *Revue Française de Psychoanalyse* 13:456.

Odier, C. (1956). *Anxiety and Magic Thinking.* New York: International Universities Press.

ABREACTION

This represents the discharge of emotion that was attached to a previously repressed memory as it emerges into the consciousness. Abreaction was originally thought to be therapeutic in itself and was a central concept in the early days of psychoanalysis. Even today we recognize that a therapeutic effect can occur through the partial discharge of painful emotions, which allows for a desensitization to them. Abreaction was originally induced using the process of hypnosis by Breuer and Freud, and the best reference on the subject is Breuer and Freud's (1893–1895) *Studies on Hysteria.*

Freud thought that abreaction, whether it was brought about by hypnosis or simply by the therapist's persuasion, would cure hysterical symptoms through a kind of purging or catharsis analogous to cleaning out an abscess. It is no longer a central goal in psychotherapy or psychoanalysis (Caper 1992). The entire approach of using hypnosis in psychotherapy for anything but the most superficial symptom removal is to be thought of as questionable, except in experimental or research situations.

Abreaction is sometimes a goal of brief psychotherapies, especially in treating a posttraumatic stress disorder and focusing on the discussion and reliving of the experience.

References

Breuer, J., and Freud, S. (1893–1895). Studies on hysteria. *Standard Edition* 2:1–335.

Caper, R. (1992). Does psychoanalysis heal? A contribution to the theory of psychoanalytic technique. *International Journal of Psycho-Analysis* 73:283–292.

ABSTINENCE

Samuel Johnson (1773) defines abstinence as the "forbearance of any thing" (p. 12), or the forbearance of necessary food. He reminds us of Shakespeare's line in *Love's Labor Lost:* "And abstinence engenders maladies." This term is often confused and used in several ways. The literal meaning of the term is simply the denying of gratification. For example, in the area of drug dependency, the state of being without the drug is a state of abstinence. Thus, withdrawal symptoms are sometimes called the "abstinence syndrome."

In psychoanalytic treatment the term came to be employed by Freud (1915) in his recommendation that the treatment be carried out in a state of abstinence, implying that since the symptoms were gratifying, a level of frustration should be preserved as optimal for a treatment response. The analyst came to be enjoined even more by subsequent psychoanalytic authorities to oppose those activities and pleasures of the patient that drained off anxiety by giving pleasure. This led to confusion because some therapists understood it to mean that the patient should even be asked to refrain from all personal sexual activity during the therapy.

The proper meaning of the rule of abstinence as it is used in uncovering psychotherapy is that, unless it is done for a very specific purpose, the therapist should not deliberately gratify the patient to any significant degree during the treatment. It does not refer to having the therapist command the patient to abstain from nonharmful gratifications outside the therapy office.

Unfortunately, the so-called rule of abstinence has never been made clear and lends itself to use by a sadistic therapist or a therapist who has some sort of countertransference problem to justify unreasonable withholding from the patient. If this is carried to an extreme, it produces an iatrogenic narcissism, the withdrawal of the patient into a self-contained grandiosity, which often gets the patient labeled as a narcissistic personality disorder. Even more unfortunately, it can lead to serious acting out behavior by borderline patients who cannot contain their rage at the therapist's distance and coldness.

I think what Freud meant is that the therapist should maintain a benign neutrality in his or her work with a patient. This means treating the patient as one would treat any human being who is a guest in one's home or one's office, but it should be kept in mind that this is a formal guest, not a member of one's family. There is an almost absolute contraindication to any form of physical contact with patients for any reason whatsoever except in the most extreme emergency situations. In my supervisory experience psychotherapists have engaged in an unfortunate plethora of physical contact, such as hugging, massaging, or hand holding, all of which definitely violates the rule of abstinence. Any form of physical contact with patients inevitably stirs up a host of desires, transferences, and countertransferences, and must be regarded as countertransference acting out by the therapist regardless of the rationalization employed, and regardless of the amount of clamor coming from the patient for gratification.

The avoidance of gratification in the transference fosters regression and facilitates the emergence, recognition, and understanding of the transference. It follows that in supportive psychotherapy, where one's goal is simply to make the patient feel better, the therapist does a good deal more gratifying by explanations, teaching, and verbal activity than in a psychoanalytic treatment. There is no agreement as to how much abstinence is optimal in a treatment, but it is usually individualized to fit the situation of the patient at any given time. An important part of the art of psychotherapy is to neither overgratify nor undergratify the patient so as to avoid the pitfalls of each of these countertransference mistakes.

This is not as difficult as it sounds, in spite of Freud's ambiguity of the concept, because it depends largely on the successful personal psychoanalysis of the therapist. One of the most common causes of destructive or stalemated psychotherapies is a lack of sufficient thorough and deep personal psychoanalysis of the therapist, and it is in the area of abstinence and gratification that these difficulties often begin. Patients present us with innumerable pitfalls and seductions in order to reenact their neuroses with us, and it is our responsibility as therapists to be sufficiently free of our personal difficulties so as to be able to maintain a neutral stance, equidistant from the id, ego, and superego of the patient. This does not imply or justify discourteous or insensitive language, prolonged or unnatural silences, or rude behavior on the part of any therapist. See Dewald (1992) for a traditional description and defense of the psychoanalytic concept of abstinence as it is currently employed in clinical treatment.

References

Dewald, P. (1992). The "rule" and role of abstinence in psychoanalysis. In *The Technique and Practice of Psychoanalysis: A Memorial Volume to Ralph R. Greenson,* ed. A. Sugarman, R. Nemiroff, and D. Greenson, pp. 135–157. Madison, CT: International Universities Press.

Freud, S. (1915). Observations on transference love (Further recommendations on the technique of psycho-analysis III). *Standard Edition* 12:159–171.

Johnson, S. (1773). *A Dictionary of the English Language.* Beirut, Lebanon: Librairie du Liban, 1978.

ACTING OUT

This term is not to be used, as it often is in everyday language, to label what the therapist considers to be misbehavior on the part of the patient. Although it is used by many authors in different ways, it does have a basic technical meaning, which was first delineated by Freud (1913). Freud writes, "The patient does not *remember* anything of what he has forgotten or repressed, but *acts* it out. He reproduces it not as memory but as an action; he *repeats* it without, of course, knowing that he is repeating it" (p. 150).

It is essential that the therapist have a clear grasp of acting out, because this type of resistance probably represents the clearest danger to any psychotherapy and can easily break up a treatment. The acting out patient does not confine conflicts within himself or herself but externalizes them rather directly. The inability to internalize and confine one's conflicts is what Bird (1957) calls the "pathognomonic functional defect," which distinguishes the acting out patient from all other people. This developmental defect, he says, comes out of a failure of the ego of the child and of the mother to move apart. What we experience in psychotherapy is not so much the predominantly acting out patient, but acting out as it occurs as resistance during the process of psychotherapy of a patient who does not significantly and continuously act out. These are the conditions under which a psychotherapy can suddenly and unexpectedly be threatened with destruction.

Acting out as a resistance in psychotherapy may occur as a response to an interpretation, especially a wild interpretation or an interpretation that has been made prematurely or without sufficient preparation. An example of this can be found in any supervisory experience with neophyte therapists. For instance, a therapist who deals too quickly with and vigorously offers interpretations of a schizophrenic patient's affect hunger or starvation for love and affection may find the patient responding by sudden hyperphagia: the patient begins to eat voraciously day and night or, alternately, may suddenly refuse to eat and actually go into a state of starvation or anorexia. What has happened is that rather than having to deal with the unbearably painful feelings of starvation for love aroused by the neophyte, the patient switches the whole arena to the gastrointestinal tract and then acts out either the starvation or intense defenses against the wish to take in, by dramatic behavior relating to the gastrointestinal tract.

So-called borderline patients when they act out tend to do so very dramatically and can often get themselves into a great deal of difficulty before the therapist is even aware of it. Considerable acting out with a third person may occur before the patient can finally be persuaded that this is really a shift of fantasies away from the therapy, which are then acted out and produce a draining of affects that belong in the therapy situation.

Acting out represents the partial discharge of drive tensions, achieved by responding to the present situation as if it were the situation that originally gave rise to the drive demand; thus it is a displacement of behavioral response from one situation to another. The character structure of a person may be thought of as a set of habitual patterns of reaction that develops as a result of conflict between the drives and the frustrating outer world. This originates in the family situation but may be preserved throughout life as a typical method of reacting to any stress or frustration. There is no insight into these behavior patterns; the important issue is not whether it occurs in or out of the analyst's office (when it occurs in the analyst's office it is sometimes called "acting in") but to discover what is reproduced in the action rather than remembered and verbalized (see Boesky 1982).

In very primitive preoedipal disorders it may not be possible for the patient to verbalize what is being reproduced in the action, and it may be necessary for the therapist to help articulate this with the patient. Some of these early preverbal situations can produce very bizarre action patterns that seem totally irrational to both the patient and the therapist.

The presence of such extraordinary behavioral patterns, whether on a microscopic or macroscopic level, should alert the therapist to the possibility that he or she is dealing with an early preoedipal disorder.

It is best to use the term "acting out" to represent the equivalent of a transference—the patient avoids understanding the transference by acting it out outside the office or acting it in inside the office. This should be distinguished from the behavior of impulsive character disorders, but the terms are frequently used in an overlapping fashion and also confused with labeling what the therapist considers simply to be bad behavior on the part of the patient.

Etchegoyen (1991) emphasizes that, "Acting out characteristically places the analyst in a compromising situation, which always creates strong countertransference conflicts" (p. 700). It should be kept in mind, as he emphasizes, that acting out is often an effort to make the analyst blunder, to interfere with his or her competence, or to constitute an attack on the frame or setting in which the psychoanalytic process goes on. Etchegoyen concludes, "The transference goes towards the object; the acting out distances itself from the object" (p. 701).

References

Bird, B. (1957). A specific peculiarity of acting out. *Journal of the American Psychoanalytic Association* 5:630–647.

Boesky, D. (1982). Acting out. *International Journal of Psycho-Analysis* 63:39–55.

Etchegoyen, R. (1991). *The Fundamentals of Psychoanalytic Technique*. Trans. P. Pitchon. New York: Karnac Books.

Freud, S. (1913). Remembering, repeating and working through. *Standard Edition* 12:147–156.

ACTION THOUGHT

Kohut (1977) introduced the clinical concept of action thought, which represents steps made by the patient who is healing a disorder of the self along the path of achieving psychological equilibrium. It consists of action patterns, creatively initiated by the patient on the basis of actual talents, ambitions, and ideals, but to be further modified and perfected in order to provide a reliable means of establishing the postanalytic maintenance of a stable psychoeconomic equilibrium in the narcissistic sector of the personality. Such activity should not be expected to dissolve as a consequence of correct interpretation and does not represent regressive or defensive behavior, but rather constitutes a forward movement. Lack of recognition of the forward nature of this movement is experienced by the patient as an empathic lapse.

The sequence described (Kohut 1977) in the case of Mr. M., of an action sequence from playing the violin, to befriending an adolescent boy, to opening a writing school, is an excellent description of action thought as clinically observed. A similar form of action thought has to take place as the patient gradually develops a more effective empathic matrix of selfobjects that reflects the patient's improvement in the cohesion of the self and the internal integration of archaic narcissistic structures.

Reference

Kohut, H. (1977). *Restoration of the Self.* New York: International Universities Press.

ACTIVE TECHNIQUE

This represents a notorious variation in psychoanalytic technique introduced by Ferenczi, in which the analyst no longer concentrates on an expectant attitude characterized by free-floating attention and in preparation for interpretations, but rather formulates injunctions and prohibitions with regard to certain behavior by the patient. This behavior may refer to what is happening within the treatment or outside of it if such behavior is procuring satisfaction. The active technique also includes placing a time limit on the treatment in certain cases.

The definitive statement of this technique was presented in a monograph by Ferenczi and Rank (1986), which first appeared in 1924, and brought down considerable vilification on both authors. Their suggestions included taking on certain roles with patients and attempting to convert the analysis into a new affective experience for the patient. At one point Ferenczi experimented with actually kissing and holding patients, but he abandoned such extreme measures and recognized that they were counterproductive (see FERENCZI).

Unfortunately, Ferenczi has been condemned for his experimentation without recognition that he was responding to Freud's insistence on the specificity of interpretation as the curative factor in psychoanalysis; these days we would be inclined to agree with Ferenczi that there is an emotional experience that takes place between the patient and the doctor which has an important effect on the treatment. The extent and centrality of this effect remains a matter of considerable debate (Chessick in press).

Ferenczi and Rank (1986) downplay the intellectual aspects of explanation and interpretation in psychoanalytic therapy and stress the importance of repeating crucial relationships in the treatment under the influence of the repetition compulsion. At times they advocate an "active" form of intervention on the part of the analyst, even hypnosis or suggestion, in the service, as they see it, of facilitating this repetition. This "active therapy" for the ostensive purpose of facilitating feelings and emotions in the treatment was correctly perceived by their contemporaries as a major divergence from standard psychoanalytic technique, fraught with problems of countertransference acting out.

There are some fascinating comments about narcissistic countertransference contained in their monograph. For example, they warn of the "development of a kind of narcissistic countertransference which provokes the person being analyzed into pushing into the foreground certain things which flatter the analyst and, on the other hand, into suppressing remarks and associations of an unpleasant nature in relation to him" (pp. 41–42). The authors even stress that failures in analysis can be attributed to the narcissism of the patient as a consolation for the analyst, since "it is not difficult to find proofs in his behavior and thoughts for the narcissism of the patient" (p. 42).

References

Chessick, R. (in press). What brings about change in psychoanalytic treatment. *Psychoanalytic Review.*

Ferenczi, S., and Rank, O. (1986). *The Development of Psychoanalysis,* trans. C. Newton. Madison, CT: International Universities Press.

ACTUAL NEUROSIS

This term is included because it is still found occasionally in the literature, although nobody currently pays much attention to the concept. It was used by Freud to denote disorders that were neurotic but not psychoneuroses. The cause of actual neuroses was thought due to an unhealthy sex life the patient was actually leading at the time he or she appeared in the clinical consulting room (the German word *aktual* means "present-day"). This is contrasted by Freud with the psychoneuroses, which have their etiologic nucleus in the unresolved childhood Oedipus complex. The basis of the actual neuroses was thought by Freud to be somatic, a damming up of sexual toxins that led to the symptoms the patient complained of, such as neurasthenia with its classical signs of fatigue, headache, various gastrointestinal disturbances, paresthesias, and so forth.

Freud did not believe the actual neuroses were amenable to psychoanalytic treatment. He (1895) divided the actual neuroses into "neurasthenia proper," which he believed due to inadequate or "abnormal discharge of sexual excitation" as in masturbation, and "anxiety neurosis," which he thought due to the blockage of sexual discharge and the deflection of sexual toxins into morbid anxiety, as in the practices of abstinence or *coitus interruptus.*

Reference

Freud, S. (1895). On the grounds for detaching a particular syndrome from neurasthenia under the description anxiety neurosis. *Standard Edition* 3:87–117.

ADAPTATION

Samuel Johnson (1773) defines adaptation as the act of fitting one thing to another, or "the fitness of one thing to another" (p. 27). This apparently simple term is much more tricky than it appears and has led to considerable controversy. The implication is that fitting or conforming to the environment is an advantageous change; furthermore, that the end result of successful adaptation is normal adjustment, whereas maladjustment represents a failure in adaptation. This was a central tenet of the work of Hartmann (1958), which initiated the so-called United States school of ego psychology. Hartmann, by stressing the importance of adaptation as a goal of ego functioning, attempted to create the foundation of a general psychoanalytic psychology of the normal as well as the abnormal individual, and moved psychoanalytic theory a step closer to emphasizing primary object relations and becoming more of a two-person theory (Greenberg and Mitchell 1983).

The whole concept came under considerable attack from Lacanians and other continental psychoanalysts, who argued that this was a United States travesty of psychoanalysis, in which fitting into the culture was given too much emphasis and the uncovering of repressed unconscious conflicts was deemphasized. It also became a rallying point for Marxists, who opposed U.S. ego psychology and challenged whether adaptation to a "sick" culture or a repressive society could be taken as a mark of mental health. There has been a gradual reduction of emphasis on the importance of adaptation as a goal in psychoanalytic therapy.

References

Greenberg, J., and Mitchell, S. (1983). *Object Relations in Psychoanalytic Theory.* Cambridge, MA: Harvard University Press.

Hartmann, H. (1958). *Ego Psychology and the Problem of Adaptation.* New York: International Universities Press.

Johnson, S. (1773). *A Dictionary of the English Language.* Beirut, Lebanon: Librairie du Liban, 1978.

ADHESIVENESS OF THE LIBIDO

This concept was introduced by Freud to account for failures in psychoanalysis in which there was such a strong binding of libido to various complexes or infantile objects that enormous or heroic effort was needed to remove such a tangle if it could be removed at all. It was one of the factors referred to by Freud (1937) as a cause of interminable analysis, and it has the unfortunate history of being used as an excuse for failure of treatment. Adhesiveness is thought of as a certain psychical inertia and implies the flow of libido as a liquid. Indeed, Freud's entire metapsychological system has been characterized as a hydrodynamic model (Peterfreund and Schwartz 1971), which is a correct depiction. If the phrase "adhesiveness of the libido" is not obsolete, it should be. One can still find it used with serious intent, however, in the work of Guntrip (1968).

References

Freud, S. (1937). Analysis terminable and interminable. *Standard Edition* 23:209-254.

Guntrip, H. (1968). *Schizoid Phenomena, Object Relations and the Self.* New York: International Universities Press.

Peterfreund, E., and Schwartz, J. (1971). *Information, Systems, and Psychoanalysis.* New York: International Universities Press.

AFFECT

There is considerable controversy about the precise metapsychological meaning of "affect," a general term for feelings and emotions; Samuel Johnson defines affect as passion. It is not necessary to think of affect as quite that powerful, so any feelings accompanying an idea or mental representation are properly characterized as affects. What is also important, of course, is the clinical situation where no affect appears, a situation sometimes referred to as "flatness" of affect. This may be characteristic of schizophrenia, as Bleuler (1911) thought, or it may occur in such conditions as depression and the obsessional neuroses. In the latter, affect is separated from ideation and only the ideation appears in the content of consciousness. In certain borderline patients the opposite may be true.

The debate over the metapsychological meaning of affect continues even today (Lester 1980), for example in the argument as to whether there is such a thing as unconscious affect. Freud's original idea was that the nuances of affect were added by the preconscious when unconscious ideation rose into the conscious mind, and that seems to be a satisfactory clinical working definition.

References

Bleuler, E. (1911). *Dementia Praecox or the Group of Schizophrenias,* trans. J. Zinkin. New York: International Universities Press, 1950.

Lester, E. (1980). New directions in affect theory. *Journal of the American Psychoanalytic Association* 30:197–211.

AFTER-EDUCATION

Freud (1940) described psychoanalysis as a form of after-education. This is a concept which seems to run contrary to Freud's usual, more formal insistence that interpretation is the central curative factor in psychoanalytic therapy. It remains controversial today to what extent interpretation is curative and to what extent the after-educational or corrective emotional experience process is primary as curative in psychotherapy. The traditional theoretical idea is that the more a psychoanalysis approaches the pure ideal, the more interpretation becomes central. In forms of supportive psychotherapy, after-education is central.

The psychotherapist should never forget that no matter how hard he or she attempts to not influence the patient, there is always a tremendous after-education that goes on in any intensive psychotherapy or even psychoanalysis. The clinical situation calls forth a transference that renders the patient quite suggestible; it is this suggestibility that makes it so difficult to evaluate the data of any psychoanalytic treatment. So Jungians hear Jungian material, Adlerians hear Adlerian material, Freudians hear evidence for Freud's theories, Kohutians hear about the self, and so on. The effect of all this should be to make us more humble and less inclined to criticize our colleagues when they have theoretical positions that are different from our own.

Reference

Freud, S. (1940). An outline of psychoanalysis. *Standard Edition* 23:141–208.

AGENT

Samuel Johnson (1773) defines the agent as "he that possesses the faculty of action" (p. 47). Freud often used the term "agency" or "system" to designate the substructures of his psychical apparatus. It is important to keep in mind that the ego and the superego are to be regarded as agents rather than material parts of a machine. They represent a series of functions or psychic activities and not little men operating levers and pulleys inside the head, as they are so often misleadingly employed in the literature.

Furthermore, the agency "ego" is the sum total of its various functions and in this manner is different from the sense of self. Confusion occurred because Freud never made this differentiation, referring to "ego" and "self" by the same term (see EGO).

References

Johnson, S. (1773). *A Dictionary of the English Language.* Beirut, Lebanon: Librairie du Liban, 1978.

AGGRESSIVE DRIVE

Every practicing clinician encounters enormous amounts of aggression pouring out of their patients in various forms, either active or passive, direct or indirect, displaced or disguised. The question of the origin of all this aggression is one of the most hotly debated issues in the literature today. Whether there is such a thing as an aggressive drive in contrast to the sexual drive, a duality that more or less satisfied U.S. ego psychologists, or whether the aggressive drive represents the outward manifestations of primary masochism or the death instinct as the Kleinians

propose, remains an almost impossible argument to resolve (Chessick 1992). Other authors, such as Kohut (1977), maintain that aggression, when it appears, is a breakdown product of the sense of self and that there is no primary aggressive drive in the personality (see FRAGMENTATION and SELF PSYCHOLOGY).

Considerable research has managed to produce a series of conflicting theories and hypotheses on the topic. For the purposes of the practicing clinician, the main choice is between the traditional psychoanalytic view that there is an aggressive drive and the view of self psychology that the appearance of aggression signals that the self is in danger of fragmentation or has fragmented. This is a clinical decision that will have to be made by each therapist after prolonged immersion in the material and considerable self-scrutiny.

Aggression also must be distinguished by clinicians from assertiveness, which is a more forward-moving and constructive form of behavior. The goal of aggression is destruction of the object and, as Freud (1930) pointed out, there is considerable narcissistic gratification in the outpouring of pure aggression. Although it was Adler who introduced the concept of an aggressive drive in 1908, it is in the theories of Melanie Klein that primary masochism and secondary sadism reach their central importance.

There are over 200 definitions of aggression in the literature. The clinician should keep in mind that when we speak of an aggressive drive in our therapeutic work, we are referring to hate and destruction and not an attenuated form of it, which would only represent derivatives of the aggressive drive. These derivatives, as they are seen clinically, can range from withholding, irritation, anger, and resentment, to the extremes of tantrums, fury, and murderous rage. Dealing with this poses one of the most difficult, if not the most difficult, tasks of intensive psychotherapy. Collusion between the patient and therapist to avoid these derivatives in the negative transference is a frequent cause of the need for reanalysis and of acting out.

References

Chessick, R. (1992). The death instinct revisited. *Journal of the American Academy of Psychoanalysis* 20:3–28.

Freud, S. (1930). Civilization and its discontents. *Standard Edition* 21:59–145.

Kohut, H. (1977). *Restoration of the Self.* New York: International Universities Press.

AIM INHIBITION

Freud (1915) said that every instinct has a source, aim, and object. When the aim of the drive is inhibited, we say that a partial manifestation of the drive shows itself in our clinical work. A typical example of this is represented by friendships, or so-called platonic love, or domestic affection between relatives. If the aim of the drive was not inhibited in these situations, friendships would be overtly sexual, platonic love would be consummated, and incest would be ubiquitous.

The aim of an instinct is the activity by which the drive or impulse achieves gratification or discharge. A maximum of pleasure takes place when there is discharge, in a fully uninhibited, sudden fashion, of a dammed up powerful instinctual drive. So the program of human life is the program of the pleasure principle, according to Freud.

When aim inhibition occurs, a qualification of the discharge and a diminution of the pleasure involved must take place. We find this to occur frequently in clinical situations where patients, first tentatively and sometimes timidly, aim their instinctual drives at us in seeking gratification. Only with the help of interpretation can the full power of these drives be released in the transference situation. The converse is also true: when a patient very early in treatment releases the full power of these drives in a transference situation to the therapist, we are almost invariably dealing with a disabled or defective ego that is not functioning properly. The exception to this is a patient who has already had one or two psychoanalyses and is now in a reanalysis; in such a patient, the capacity for regression in the service of the ego sometimes has been highly developed.

For the most part, however, clinicians should be extremely wary of patients who begin therapy with massive discharges of affect and powerful attempts to utilize the therapist as a source of gratification. These are very difficult and disturbed patients. Their transferences are often labeled "archaic" and give rise to serious countertransference problems.

There could be no culture and no civilization and no orderly process of psychotherapy if there were no substantial aim inhibition of the drives going on all the time. This is one of the reasons addicted patients claim that nothing gives them the same satisfaction as the powerful "high" of their addictive substances, and in this sense they are correct. We must remember that, in asking addicted patients to give up their addiction, we are asking them to live a life that is not nearly as immediately pleasurable as the one they had, but which, of course, is not nearly as self-destructive.

Reference

Freud, S. (1915). Instincts and their vicissitudes. *Standard Edition* 14:109–140.

ALEXITHYMIA

This term, like the phrase "adhesiveness of the libido" (see ADHESIVENESS OF THE LIBIDO) carries the danger of being used as an excuse for the failure of a psychotherapy. Krystal (1982) introduced it to characterize those patients who are unable to articulate their emotions or to distinguish among them. It was originally outlined in a paper by Sifneos (1975), but Krystal has utilized it in explaining the difficulty in the psychotherapy of addictive or psychosomatic patients.

There definitely seems to be a subgroup of patients who have difficulty in articulating their affects. This appears to be part of some sort of mentation disturbance in which their mind works primarily without conscious fantasies, and with thoughts concentrated on daily external events or pragmatic operative maneuvers involving actions and reactions of ordinary trivial life. All this is recited in monotonous detail by the patient, and it seems somewhat akin to the vague concept of a lack of psychological-mindedness.

Whether it actually represents a genetic problem to be found in the addictions and psychosomatic disorders, or an ego defect, or a compromise formation formed in the preoedipal period is the issue that remains unresolved. Those psychiatrists who tend to be biologically oriented, of course, see it as an actual neurological problem, whereas those who are more psychoanalytically oriented regard it as either a developmental ego defect or a compromise formation with a better prognosis. In my clinical experience, the latter point of view is usually correct.

References

Krystal, H. (1982). Alexithymia and the effectiveness of psychoanalytic treatment. *International Journal of Psychoanalytic Psychotherapy* 9:353–388.
Sifneos, P. (1975). Problems of psychotherapy of patients with alexithymic characteristics and physical disease. *Psychotherapy and Psychosomatics* 26:65–70.

ALLON, THE (STRAUS) (SEE ALSO PHANTOM LIMB)

All of the revisions of psychoanalytic theory since the time of Freud have attempted to overcome the problem of psychoanalysis as a solipsistic doctrine. Freud attempted to build a two-person psychology out of a solipsistic metapsychology. Erwin Straus (1891–1975), the pioneer German phenomenologist-psychiatrist (see PHENOMENOLOGY), was one of the first to recognize this. He (1966) insists, "Significant phenomena of psychic life must remain inaccessible to psychological understanding when psychologists define their sphere of investigation too narrowly—with regard to purposive, calculated activity and scientific knowledge only" (p. 5). He (1958) emphasizes the basic "axioms of everyday life" (p. 146), in which we experience the Other in a multimodal fashion, a common "something," as Aristotle put it, using all the senses.

Straus insists there cannot be a separation of the I from the Other as assumed in traditional Cartesian epistemology, and he (1958) claims that a "reaching-out beyond oneself, thus attaining to the *Other*—which reveals itself thereby as the *Other*—is the basic phenomenon of sensory experience, a relationship which cannot be reduced to anything in the physical world" (p. 147). Like Husserl (1970), he warns us of the mathematization of nature in the sciences and attempts to lead us back to lived experience, especially in a phenomenological analysis of our relationship to the Other. The epistemology of Freud's psychoanalysis, the "narrow" natural sciences epistemology, causes much to be lost, according to Straus (1958): "Lost is the possibility of grasping the phenomena, so essential in one's relation to the *Other*,

of contact, distance, direction, freedom, and constraint" (p. 148).

Straus offers an interesting application of his concept of our relationship to the Other and of "deformation" in his brief discussion of schizophrenia, which he views as resting on a fundamental alteration of one's relation to the Other. For Straus, "*Hallucinations originate in the medium of distorted modalities.* They appear at points where the I–world relations are pathologically transformed" (p. 162), although the causes of pathological alterations can be many and diverse. Straus's concentration on the I–Other relationship that the patient's conscious phenomena represent characterizes his approach and distinguishes it from traditional psychoanalysis. In his study of hallucinations he turned to the phenomenology of sensory experience, which had been largely ignored in work with schizophrenic patients. He (1966) called this "aesthesiology," attempting to reinstate the forgotten meaning of "aisthesis" (p. 259). The objective of Straus's (Straus and Griffith 1970) aesthesiology is to present sensory experience freed from traditional prejudices, and I believe his success in doing so accounts for the freshness and impact of his clinical demonstrations (which I personally experienced).

A more formal way to conceive this is in Straus's (1966) complaint that "the misapprehensions of objectivistic psychology originate principally in its efforts to comprehend the organism moving itself as if it were a body moved. Thus, it encounters the other one as an *object*" (p. 57). But, "we live in the present; we comprehend in the perfect" (p. 57). That is to say, for Straus the present is something that "becomes" in time, and accounting for sensing and lived movement rests on maintaining the crucial contact with the primary situation of "the spatiotemporal unity that characterizes our immediate and lived rapport with the world" (p. 58).

Straus's (1966) well-known paper "The Upright Posture," originally published in 1952, concludes, contra Freud, that there is no basis to claim priority for the drives and that the "rational" is as genuine a part of human nature as the "animal." Modern U.S. psychoanalytic theory has moved away from emphasis on drives, but there is no agreement on what has priority in humans, or why. Straus (1966) claims in this paper that, contrary to Freud's metapsychology, he makes clinical experience his point of departure and does not regard the typical patient "as an apparatus but as an experiencing creature" (p. 256). Consistent with that approach, Straus (1965) elsewhere presents some experimental material from which he concludes that the distance between seeing and thinking cannot be reduced to the difference of certain cerebral functions: "In sensory experience we are in direct contact with things; they stand before us and we before them. In thinking the relation is an indirect one; the noema mediates between the thinker and the target of his imagination" (pp. 282–283). This viewpoint mixes together several philosophical positions and explains why Straus is so hard to classify (Spiegelberg 1972).

In an essay on psychiatry and philosophy Straus (Straus et al. 1969) summarizes his views in this way: "The object of psychiatric action is not primarily the brain, the body, or the organism; it should be integral man in the uniqueness of his individual existence as this discloses itself—independently of the distinction between healthy and sick—in existential communication" (p. 2). This difficult essay, first published in 1963, deals with the fact that I and another person do not encounter each other in a void. We do not confront one another immediately as ego and another ego. So a discussion of my relation to the Other, which mediates between us, must accompany if not precede a discussion of our communicative relationship.

Straus uses the term "the Allon" to distinguish the fact that when he speaks of the Other he is not denoting a particular isolated human or a particular thing separate from the experiencing subject. The Allon represents the relationship of the individual to the whole of which he or she is a part, so the Allon is present even for someone who is alone. In applying this, for example, to a study of visual perception, the Allon encompasses whatever the situation might be that the individual finds himself or herself in visually. Straus writes, "The meaning of 'mine' is determined in relation to, in contraposition to, the world, the Allon, to which I am nevertheless a party. The meaning of 'mine' is not comprehensible in the unmediated antithesis of I and not-I, own and strange, subject and object, constituting I and constituted world. Everything points to the fact that separateness and union originate in the same ground" (p. 29).

It is very significant in the practice of psychotherapy that, as Straus points out, "our relation to the Allon is a dialectical one, a contraposition or connection in separation. The visible does not belong to an external world from which we are separated by an impassable gulf" (p. 33). So Straus would say that the natural sciences epistemology used in psychiatry and psychoanalysis has replaced the axioms of everyday life by abstract constructs, yet it is the naive realism of everyday life through which the living reach an understanding among themselves and an understanding of the evidences of the past.

The concept of the Allon becomes rather mysterious, since, as Straus conceives of it, "in the dialectic of accessibility and remoteness, of hiddenness and openness, the Allon remains enigmatic" (p. 46). Here, one is reminded of Heidegger's concept of the simultaneous concealing and revealing of Being, which is what I think Straus had in mind. More evidence for Heidegger's influence appears when Straus remarks, "In our relationship to the Allon the whole reveals itself only in fragments. The fragments, comprehended as such, refer beyond themselves to still other fragments and to the constantly present background of the as yet indeterminate whole. We always find ourselves encircled

by a spatial and a temporal horizon, which, however open, remains a boundary that excludes what lies beyond it" (p. 49). I think Straus's concept of the I–Other or the I–Allon relationship is precisely what has been left out in the training of psychiatrists and psychoanalysts in the past, and does not receive the recognition that it deserves. His ten theses (Straus 1966, pp. 268–274) on the Allon well repay their careful study by clinicians.

Straus (1958) explains that "the actual moment, the changing Now of my becoming, is determined with reference to the *Other,* by which I am affected" (p. 152). This Other, which Straus sometimes uses synonymously with "the world," although it is a unit, shows itself composed of a manyness of things and divided into a variety of aspects. This idea becomes even more complex when we speak of the relationship of two individuals to each other. As Straus teaches, we cannot understand that relationship without reference to a "Third," which represents the Other, or Allon; it is this Allon that is the milieu in which we are immersed inextricably, thrown into it, to use the language of Heidegger. So we can never totally perceive the Other, and only with various senses can we perceive variegated aspects or perspectives on it. At the same time, we are immersed in it, which explains the curious simultaneous separateness and attachment in our relationship to the Other.

It is phenomenological analysis (see PHENOMENOLOGY) that reveals "the manyness of modalities"

(Straus 1958, p. 155) in which the Other is shown in shifting aspects and perspectives, and it is such analysis that effectively demonstrates the reductiveness of the traditional epistemology of psychoanalysis. This is true whether we use Freud's drive theory or whether we use object relations theory, since the latter reduces the internalizations of the parent figures as object representations without reference to the Allon, in which both the baby and the parent are immersed and separated simultaneously. When the relationship to the Other is distorted in one modality or another, what appears phenomenologically as hallucinations are simply the patient's descriptions of these distortions. Straus (1958) explains that an early pathological disturbance of one's relation to the Other, "so alters direction, distance, and boundary, that the *Other* appears as it were, in new aspects" (p. 162). In his most sophisticated study of the Other, Straus seeks to demonstrate our relationship to the Allon primarily on the basis of his phenomenological analysis of visual sensation and human locomotion and motility.

References

Husserl, E. (1970). *The Crisis of European Sciences and Transcendental Phenomenology,* trans. D. Carr. Evanston, IL: Northwestern University Press.

Spiegelberg, H. (1972). *Phenomenology in Psychology and Psychiatry: A Historical Introduction.* Evanston, IL: Northwestern University Press.

Straus, E. (1958). Aesthesiology and hallucinations. In *Existence: A New Dimension in Psychiatry and Psychology,* ed. R. May, E. Angel, and H. Ellenberger, pp. 139–169. New York: Basic Books.

——— (1965). The expression of thinking. In *An Invitation to Phenomenology: Studies in the Philosophy of Experience,* ed. J. Edie. Chicago: Quadrangle Books.

——— (1966). *Phenomenological Psychology: The Selected Papers of Erwin Straus,* trans. E. Eng. New York: Basic Books.

Straus, E., and Griffith, R., eds. (1970). *Aisthesis and Aesthetics: The Fourth Lexington Conference on Pure and Applied Phenomenology.* Pittsburgh, PA: Duquesne University Press.

Straus, E., Natanson, M., and Eye, H. (1969). *Psychiatry and Philosophy.* New York: Springer-Verlag.

ALLOPLASTIC

The terms "alloplastic" and "autoplastic adaptation," introduced by Alexander (1930), refer to a patient's lifestyle. A patient who uses predominantly autoplastic adaptation employs intrapsychic mechanisms of defense, such as those that typically appear in the psychoneuroses, whereas a patient who uses alloplastic forms of adaptation tends to act out and repeat conflicts with others in the environment. Patients can be arranged according to their forms of adaptation, with those who are mostly alloplastic at one end of the spectrum and those who are mostly autoplastic at the other. These descriptive terms can be used to trace early characterological compromise formations, but there are also possibly constitutional factors involved.

Reference

Alexander, F. (1930). The neurotic character. *International Journal of Psycho-Analysis* 11:292–311.

ALPHA-FUNCTION

This concept constitutes part of a rather obscure and fanciful but fascinating epistemology invented by the Kleinian psychoanalyst Wilfred Bion (1967). In the infant, experience is generated from raw sense data by meeting with some preexisting expectations. Together these constitute a meaningful conception. The alpha-function is the conversion of this raw sense data as it combines with the preexisting expectations into meaningful integrated experiences. On some occasions, however, there is a failure of the alpha-function, with the result that particles of "undigested" sense data accumulate. These are beta elements (Hinshelwood 1989). So the alpha-function represents the process involved in taking raw sense data and generating out of it mental contents that have meaning and can be used for thinking. These resulting products of alpha-function are what Bion calls alpha elements. The failure of alpha-function causes an accumulation of beta elements, which are then, according to Bion, expelled by the process of projective identification (see PROJECTIVE IDENTIFICATION).

From my point of view, what is important in this for psychotherapists is Bion's concept that the mother's alpha-function has to assimilate these projected beta elements and convert them into alpha elements, which the baby can then take back by the process of introjection (see INTROJECTION). This has significant ramifications for psychother-apy. The patient projects raw, unintegrated beta elements onto the therapist, whose calm, neutral, anxiety-free attitude enables him or her to assimilate, understand, and interpret this material. The patient is then able to introject the assimilated material in a "digested" form, which contributes to his or her development and ego integration. Another name for this is the "toilet function" of the analyst, which, using Kleinian terminology, is an important factor in healing through psychotherapy (see REVERIE).

Readers tend to be put off by the metaphorical or obscure language of Bion and many of the neo-Kleinians. However, there are some concepts buried in this obscurity that are very important and bring us to the cutting edge of the nonverbal interaction and communication that goes on in intensive psychotherapy.

References

Bion, W. (1967). *Second Thoughts: Selected Papers on Psycho-Analysis.* London: Heinemann.

Hinshelwood, R. (1989). *A Dictionary of Kleinian Thought.* London: Free Association Books.

ALTRUISM

The French philosopher Auguste Comte (1798–1857) coined the term "altruism" as representing living for the sake of others. There is clearly a moral judgment involved in the use of the term, since altruistic individuals are considered to be ethically superior to those who are narcissistic. Freud did not believe there was such a thing as altruism and argued that in some manner all so-called altruistic behavior brings gratification of various derivatives of instinctual drives, either directly or vicariously. Anna Freud (1946) identified an important defense, which she called "a form of altruism," that represents vicarious gratification by an altruistic surrender to the needs of another individual.

The question of whether or not there is such a motive or impulse as genuine altruism ultimately resolves itself into the question of the basic nature of humans and how it is formed (Chessick 1992). Freud, of course, conceived of humans as primarily instinct-driven and pleasure seeking; theologians have attempted to find a divine aspect to humans with a higher ethical valance. This controversy has been one of the sources of repeated condemnations of the psychoanalytic point of view and raises the issue of the "politics" of psychoanalysis (Frosh 1987). It is not of great importance to the practicing clinician, except that the clinician should be warned not to interpret altruistic behavior as primarily pleasure seeking unless there is a very unusual definite indication to do so. A patient may experience such interpretations of altruistic behavior as wounding and demeaning, which may lead to a rupture of the empathic bond between the patient and the therapist with the production of rage, which is then sometimes mislabeled as the rage that was hidden under the allegedly defensive altruistic behavior.

References

Chessick, R. (1992). *What Constitutes the Patient in Psychotherapy*. Northvale, NJ: Jason Aronson.

Freud, A. (1946). *The Ego and the Mechanisms of Defense*. New York: International Universities Press.

Frosh, S. (1987). *The Politics of Psychoanalysis*. New Haven, CT: Yale University Press.

AMBIVALENCE

Bleuler (1911) used this term to describe the coexistence of contradictory emotions toward the same object, most commonly the coexistence of love and hate. He believed that it was one of the fundamental signs of schizophrenia, but actually it is universal. In the group of schizophrenias ego functioning is poor, so that the extremes of the ambivalence appear more rapidly and more clearly in the clinical material, whereas in the average individual these extremes are well hidden and often repressed, so only derivatives of them show in the conscious mind.

In our clinical work we observe how ambivalence causes great suffering for patients with obsessional neuroses who continuously attempt to balance the two sides of the ambivalence that appear in their consciousness, whereas in most neuroses one or the other of these sides is more or less repressed. Ambivalence must be distinguished in clinical work from having a mixture of feelings toward someone on the basis of a mixture of experiences with that person. Ambivalence is not based on a realistic assessment; unfortunately, the term has lost its precision and is often used vaguely to refer to a mixture of feelings that arise on a realistic basis.

In regarding ambivalence as one of the fundamental symptoms of schizophrenia, Bleuler differentiated among emotional ambivalence, intellectual ambivalence, and ambivalence of the will. Freud (1912) borrowed the term from Bleuler to account for the phenomenon of negative transference when it is found side by side with an affectionate transference, both directed simultaneously toward the same person.

This concept is central to the work of Melanie Klein (see KLEIN), since love for the primary maternal object is inseparable from the wish to destroy it on the basis of the dual instinct theory and leads to splitting at the very beginning of life with subsequent projective identification. This in turn leads to the paranoid-schizoid position that Klein considered universal in the first few months of life.

In our clinical work the importance of ambivalence when it appears rests on how central it is to a patient's preoccupations; a schizophrenic or obsessional patient is especially prone to suffer from an incapacity due to this ambivalence. When ambivalence appears in the transferences of a psychoneurotic patient, it is important to clear away the resistances to the manifestations of these emotions, so that the patient may experience them in a more fundamental form and deal with the nuclear infantile conflicts where ambivalence first originates.

References

Bleuler, E. (1911). *Dementia Praecox or the Group of Schizophrenias,* trans. J. Zinkin. New York: International Universities Press, 1950.

Freud, S. (1912). The dynamics of the transference. *Standard Edition* 12:97–108.

ANACLITIC

Freud (1914) distinguished between narcissistic and anaclitic object choice. The term "anaclitic" comes from the Greek verb ἀνακλίνω (*anaklinō*), which literally means "to lean one thing on another." Narcissistic object choice occurs when a person chooses an object on the basis of some real or imagined similarity to himself or herself, while anaclitic object choice is manifest when it is based on the pattern of childhood dependency. Thus anaclitic object choice attempts to bring back a lost mother and precedes developmentally any narcissistic object choice. The latter is a form of secondary narcissism in which the person chosen to love resembles one's own self. For example, in certain cases of homosexuality, the object chosen is the child-self, who is then treated the way the homosexual wishes his or her mother to treat him (see HOMOSEXUALITY).

To avoid confusion, it is important to understand that, for Freud, in early development omnipotent primary narcissism comes first; then, due to inevitable frustration, anaclitic object choice occurs, with the mother as the first object. Narcissistic object choice, when it appears clinically, represents a form of secondary narcissism, a regression in which, as Freud said, the person loves what he himself is or was, what he would like to be, or someone thought of as a part of himself (see NARCISSISM).

Reference

Freud, S. (1914). On narcissism: an introduction. *Standard Edition* 14:67–102.

ANALYTIC THERAPY

Analytic therapy, or psychoanalytically informed psychotherapy, is based on a paid professional relationship undertaken by the patient for the purpose of the relief of mental suffering. The patient pays for the treatment in good faith in order to assume (a) that the psychotherapist has had a thorough training in diagnostic and treatment techniques, and (b) that the psychotherapist has had a thorough personal psychoanalysis that will maximally ensure against countertransference acting out and enable the psychotherapist to listen to what the patient is trying to communicate without being disturbed by the clamor of the therapist's needs. Only psychoanalytic therapy can offer this fundamental setting, in which the roots of the patient's pathology can then unfold for examination and working through. If symptom removal is attempted, primarily under the influence of some sort of relationship, this is known as supportive psychotherapy. If the focus is on allowing the transference to develop and interpreting it when it does so, then the usual uncovering techniques that define the psychoanalytic approach can be used.

Only the psychoanalytic method offers an escape from conscious or unconscious collusion with the patient to avoid facing the truth of the patient. This method requires special techniques and capacities in the psychotherapist in order to let the material emerge in a relatively undisturbed fashion and to facilitate the development of transference manifestations. Once a proper empathic relationship has been established, it is primarily in the interpretation of these transference manifestations that the patient gains insight into the roots of his or her mental suffering and the basic functioning of his or her character. Transference interpretations, beginning with the contributions from both the therapist and the patient, eventually allow valid reconstructions of the patient's early relationships and character formation.

The alteration of character that results from transference interpretations and reconstructions of the past is then tested by the patient, first on the therapist and then on others in the outside world. Through new experiences a gradual modification and correction takes place on the basis of this testing, known as "working through." In uncovering or analytic psychotherapy, due to limitations of time, we often deal with derivatives of the basic or nuclear transferences. As a result, we must be satisfied with partial results or improvement in only certain sectors of the patient's living; usually these are the sectors the patient has identified as in need of immediate treatment. In psychoanalysis, we hope for a more general and deeper change in the patient's character, which also leads to a greater capacity to deal with unforeseen problems that arise in the future as well as with the inevitable new problems that accompany subsequent stages of life.

Analytic therapy should be sharply distinguished from "analytical psychology," the Jungian theoretical system, which minimizes the influence of sexual factors in emotional disorders and stresses mystical or quasi-religious influences.

ANXIETY

Samuel Johnson (1773) defines anxiety as the trouble of the mind about some future event or "in the medical language, lowness of spirits with uneasiness of the stomach" (p. 89). By the late eighteenth century it was clear that there was a relationship between anxiety and depressive sensations. For the practicing clinician today, the important distinction is between the fear of some real external danger and anxiety, which may be thought of as an irrational fear of some anticipated event. This irrational fear is based on the great calamities that comprise the terrors of childhood: loss of the mother or parenting object, loss of the love of the mother or parenting object, castration, and guilt that demands punishment. The symptoms of anxiety

are well known and the concept has been used by continental thinkers to represent a sort of existential malaise. The symptoms of acute anxiety form one clinical extreme and shade off to the symptoms of a generalized discomfort and malaise at the other end of the spectrum.

Freud's earliest explanation for anxiety was that it represented the transformation of dammed up sexual toxins that were not being properly discharged. He (1926) revised this in a very significant paper, in which he presents his so-called signal theory of anxiety, vitally important to understanding the formation, diagnosis, and treatment of neurotic and character disorders. It is interesting that Freud does not discuss anxiety in psychotic patients but confines his theoretical work on the subject to the neuroses. In the signal theory he contends that anxiety motivates the ego to inhibit or repress when there is conflict with the id, conflict with the superego, or problems within the ego itself. When the ego is opposed to an instinctual process in the id, "it has only to give a *signal of unpleasure* in order to obtain its object with the aid of that almost omnipotent institution, the pleasure principle" (p. 92). Brenner (1982) claims that the signal of unpleasure that initiates repression can be either anxiety, if the fear is of something that has not yet taken place, or depression, if the conviction is that it has already taken place, but this constitutes a significant controversial revision of Freud's signal theory.

According to Freud, the ego borrows energy cathected to the instinct that is to be repressed and uses this energy for the purpose of releasing unpleasure, which Freud equates with a feeling of anxiety. This unpleasure then mobilizes psychic functions along the pleasure principle and sets the ego's mechanisms of defense into action, beginning with repression and utilizing others if repression is not sufficient. Thus if the ego successfully represses the instinct, we learn nothing; we find out about this repression only from those cases in which the repression has more or less failed. In the event of failure of the repression, a substitute formation occurs, very much reduced, displaced, and inhibited, which is no longer clearly recognizable as a satisfaction. This is a symptom. A symptom, then, is a sign of, and a substitute for, an instinctual satisfaction that has been forbidden direct gratification—it is a consequence of the process of repression.

Anxiety is thus conceived of by Freud as a signal by the ego of a situation of a danger, and subsequently obviated by the ego's doing something to avoid that situation or to withdraw from it. Symptoms are the ultimate result of attempting to remove the danger situation emerging from within, whose presence was originally signaled by the generation of anxiety.

There are many forms of anxiety used descriptively in the literature, such as castration anxiety, separation anxiety, depressive anxiety, persecutory anxiety, neurotic anxiety, and psychotic anxiety. These are essentially descriptive terms and do not imply any theory of the origin of anxiety. See Compton (1972a,b) for a complete review of the topic.

A subclass of the anxiety disorders is currently known as the panic disorders (see PANIC DISORDER), which are thought by some authors to have an organic origin. There remains considerable controversy as to whether panic disorders should be treated by psychoanalysis or by a combination of psychopharmacology and psychotherapy. Silber (1989) reports a case of panic attacks experienced during the course of analysis which had a psychological component that proved "amenable to understanding and amelioration in a classically conducted analysis" (p. 362). He reminds us that panic attacks, at least in part and in some patients, have an important psychological antecedent and therefore should not be explained exclusively in physiological or pharmacological terms, nor treated with an exclusively biological orientation.

References

Brenner, C. (1982). *The Mind in Conflict.* New York: International Universities Press.

Compton, A. (1972a). A study of the psychoanalytic theory of anxiety: I. The development of Freud's theory of anxiety. *Journal of the American Psychoanalytic Association* 20:3–44.

———— (1972b). A study of the psychoanalytic theory of anxiety: II. Developments in the theory of anxiety since 1926. *Journal of the American Psychoanalytic Association* 20:341–394.

Freud, S. (1926). Inhibitions, symptoms, and anxiety. *Standard Edition* 20:77–175.

Johnson, S. (1773). *A Dictionary of the English Language.* Beirut, Lebanon: Librairie du Liban, 1978.

Silber, A. (1989). Panic attacks facilitating recall and mastery: implications for psychoanalytic technique. *Journal of the American Psychoanalytic Association* 37:337–364.

APHANISIS

Ernest Jones (1948) used this term to represent the disappearance of sexual desire in the context of his inquiries into feminine sexuality. He had in mind the idea that the fear of castration was simply a concrete expression of a more basic or general fear of "aphanisis," which involves a kind of total destruction or wiping out of the psyche involving a loss of all capacity for pleasure, especially sexual pleasure. This is to be distinguished from anhedonia, which is a descriptive term that represents the inability to experience any kind of pleasure whatsoever and is more related to the depressive disorders rather than to castration anxiety.

It is perhaps helpful to remember that the original Greek term ἀφάνισις (*aphanisis*) is a noun that designates the getting rid of something or the destruction of something. The clinical use of this term was an attempt by Jones to find a common basis for the sexual development of boys and girls rather than simply the castration complex that is related more specifically to the loss of the penis. Jones was never comfortable with Freud's theory of the psychosexual development of women (see FEMALE PSYCHOLOGY).

Reference

Jones, E. (1948). *Papers on Psycho-Analysis.* Baltimore: Williams & Wilkins.

ARCHAIC TRANSFERENCES AND EGO STATES

Something is called archaic when it stems from a primitive condition or era. In the past psychiatrists emphasized the archaic modes of thinking and expression in the schizophrenias; an important theory of the understanding of schizophrenia was offered by Arieti (1974) based on his concept of "paleological thinking" in schizophrenia. This approach to schizophrenia has been largely abandoned as research into the subject has progressed.

Clinicians today are more interested in "archaic ego states," which are attributed to the early stages in the development of the ego. The well-known "oceanic feeling" discussed by Freud (1930) was provided by the author Romain Rolland (1866–1944) and involves an indissoluble bond between the self and the external world, which Rolland thought was the basis of religious experience but Freud insisted was a manifestation of an archaic ego state. The transitional phenomena of Winnicott (1953) and the selfobject phenomena of Kohut (1971) are examples of archaic ego or self states used as a descriptive term.

Perhaps of the greatest importance for clinicians, however, is the concept of archaic transferences, which have been discussed by Gedo (1977), myself (Chessick 1989), and others. The problem in the treatment of the borderline or difficult patient lies in the extreme stress it places on the therapist to deal with disruptions, acting out, archaic transference challenges, and the many incessant reality problems that keep impinging on the patient's chaotic life. The archaic transference presents a situation in which the patient demands an immediate response from the therapist. It is fraught with difficulties. If the therapist is silent, the patient becomes enraged at his or her "rudeness" in not offering an answer to his or her demand. But obviously any definitive answer to the demand based on the material would be the wrong answer and would be met with objections, denials, and possibly even an irrational enraged situation.

The question of how to respond to archaic transference challenges is very thorny. In the management of difficult patients one should provide only direct gratification when forced to do so in order to preserve the therapy. Even then there is a limit to the direct gratification that can be provided. This is discussed most poignantly by Freud (1905) in his postscript to the case of Dora. The rule of abstinence (see ABSTINENCE) should be followed as much as possible, even with difficult patients, and the therapist should not step out of the analytic stance any more than is absolutely necessary. It goes without saying that the therapist should never step out of an ethical stance regardless of the circumstances, as this is always countertransference acting out on the part of the therapist and always contraindicated.

A transference is archaic if the patient has no insight into the difference between the therapist and the parenting object, so that the demand is for immediate gratification and no amount of explanation or discussion will suffice. In this sense it is not a typical transference in which libidinal or aggressive drives cross the repression barrier and are aimed at the object of the therapist. Rather, it is an intrapsychic amalgamation of the therapist's self with the patient's self, in which the therapist is experienced as an extension of the patient and expected to yield to total control. All psychotherapists who work with a variety of patients are the aim of these archaic transferences from time to time; furthermore, they are often the cause of serious countertransference acting out with disruptions and destructive events in both the lives of the patients and the therapists. The proper management of the archaic transference is one of the hardest and most important tasks to learn in the art and craft of intensive psychotherapy.

References

Arieti, S. (1974). *Interpretation of Schizophrenia,* 2nd ed. New York: Basic Books.

Chessick, R. (1989). *The Technique and Practice of Listening in Intensive Psychotherapy.* Northvale, NJ: Jason Aronson.

Freud, S. (1905). Fragment of an analysis of a case of hysteria. *Standard Edition* 7:3–122.

——— (1930). Civilization and its discontents. *Standard Edition* 21:59–145.

Gedo, J. (1977). Notes on the psychoanalytic management of archaic transferences. *Journal of the American Psychoanalytic Association* 25:787–803.

Kohut, H. (1971). *The Analysis of the Self.* New York: International Universities Press.

Winnicott, D. (1953). Transitional objects and transitional phenomena. In *Collected Papers,* pp. 229–242. New York: Basic Books, 1958.

"AS-IF" PERSONALITY

This refers to a classical paper by Deutsch (1965), in which she designated persons that today would probably be labeled borderline personality disorders. These individuals seem to fit into any situation, creating an illusion of conviction and involvement, whereas in reality there is an absence of depth and emotional experience. The importance of this kind of disorder is that if it is not properly identified by the clinician, a miscarriage of the psychotherapy takes place. A patient appears to be cooperating and stabilizing with therapeutic progress until, as time passes, the therapist realizes that nothing is really happening and the patient has not achieved any change at all in his or her actual life. Deutsch thought of the "as-if" personality as a type of schizoid individual who behaves as though he or she had normal emotional responses to situations but actually is empty. Today we think of such patients more in terms of narcissistic personality disorders or, with Kohut, as disorders of the self.

The "as-if" personality represents an extreme caricature of Riesman and colleagues' (1955) "other-directed" personality. Although the patient appears outwardly amiable, he or she has no identity of his own and is not capable of forming any genuine emotional attachment to people or moral principles. While there is a poverty of object relationships and again the central issue seems to revolve around narcissism, no obvious defect in reality testing is present; in fact, the "as-if" personality may become a very successful politician or administrator.

References

Deutsch, H. (1965). Some forms of emotional disturbances and their relationship to schizophrenia. In *Neuroses and Character Types,* pp. 262–281. New York: International Universities Press.

Riesman, D., Denney, R., and Glazer, N. (1955). *The Lonely Crowd.* New York: Doubleday.

AUTHENTIC

The terms "authentic" and "inauthentic" are used by a variety of continental philosophers and psychologists in different ways. The concept was originally introduced by Heidegger (1962) as one of two ways of living in the world. In the inauthentic manner one has "concern" for people as things or objects (the word "concern" in Heidegger has no moral connotation and merely implies Kierkegaardian interestedness or curiosity). In authentic living there is a binding with people by devotion to common causes, which Heidegger called "solicitude," that is achieved by "resolve."

Heidegger claimed that this solicitude is what has been lost in our age. In place of it, inauthentically, we have relationships with people based on what he called (a) competitiveness, which sets us apart from each other; (b) publicness, which suppresses the exceptional by an obsession with promoting a "well-rounded" personality; (c) average ness—what one ought to do to fit in; and above all, (d) adaptation, which later gave ammunition for considerable attack from some continental psychoanalysts on the U.S. psychoanalytic ego-psychology school with its central aim of adaptation. Heidegger claimed that all such inauthentic relationships result in our age in "fallenness" into the "they" or public world, which relieves one of personal responsibility by such arguments as "Everybody does it," or, "I was just following orders."

This concept of inauthentic and authentic existence was emphasized by Sartre, who utilized it to distinguish between acts that are done in good faith and those based on bad faith. Inauthentic behavior is usually interpreted by psychotherapists as defensive behavior, with the implication that the patient's real feelings and motives are other than the patient realizes or that the patient was insincere and in bad faith in order to avoid confronting some aspect of the situation or of the patient, which would have led to anxiety (see also FALSE SELF).

These are all descriptive terms and are interchangeable; they have no metapsychological or psychodynamic basis. The problem with the use of the terms "authentic" and "inauthentic" is that they carry a moral connotation. Calling someone "inauthentic" has a pejorative tone, and it is best if psychotherapists leave these issues to philosophers. When a patient begins complaining that he or she feels "inauthentic" or is leading an "inauthentic" life, this should be heard by the therapist as a complaint of malaise under which there are hidden, important psychodynamic conflicts. To respond to these complaints with discussions of existential issues is to respond to manifest content and to enter into a collusion with the patient to avoid the unfolding and interpretation of the transference and the investigation of the infantile conflicts that are plaguing the patient's current adult life.

Reference

Heidegger, M. (1962). *Being and Time,* trans. J. Macquarrie and E. Robinson. New York: Harper & Row.

AUTOEROTISM, AUTOEROTICISM

Autoerotism was introduced by Havelock Ellis in 1889 to refer to a form of sexual behavior in which the subject obtained satisfaction solely through the recourse to his or her own body and needing no outside object. The usual example of autoerotic behavior is masturbation. Freud (1905) made use of the term to describe infantile sexuality. He regarded earliest infantile sexual behavior as attaining satisfaction without resorting to an external object, so that the instinct is not directed toward other people but obtains satisfaction from the subject's own body. This implies that there is no inborn ready-made path that directs the newborn toward a predetermined object. It represents an archaic stage before the formation of the ego.

When the ego has formed, primary narcissism occurs, in which the libidinal object is the unified image of the body or the ego. But autoerotism is an archaic stage preceding this convergence of the component instincts on the ego. Freud claimed that the autoerotic instincts are there from the beginning and converge on the various zones of the body in a primal state before the ego has formed.

This distinction was gradually abandoned by Freud, who came to feel that there was a state of primary narcissism from the beginning of life. He then used the definition of autoerotism simply in the first sense given above, namely, the use of one's own body for sexual gratification. There is some confusion in Freud's views as to whether there is an autoerotic libidinal stage as contrasted to adult sexual activity, which involves object choice. Freud loosely thought of a developmental line from autoerotism through narcissism to adult object love, but the concept of autoerotism as a sharply demarcated stage in time came from Karl Abraham (1916).

The confusion in this concept comes from the fact that in using autoerotism as a description of getting pleasure from one's own body, we are making a descriptive definition that is observable, whereas the definition of it as a stage in development is inferential regarding the infant's disregard of external objects. The question of whether the infant is or is not born oriented toward external objects is one of the basic and fundamental sources of disagreement among psychoanalytic theorists. The

general trend at the current time is to believe that such an orientation is indeed inborn, in contrast to Freud's idea that it develops only along a line in which fundamental object relatedness is not primary. So-called object relations theorists such as Fairbairn (1954) insist that the infant is mother-related from the very beginning; it is object seeking, not pleasure seeking.

The controversy remains as to (a) whether autoerotism is primary and makes no distinction between the self and the nonself, paying little heed to the external environment or to other individuals who are present there; (b) whether narcissism is the primary state, in which others are perceived simply as an extension of the self and all libido is directed upon the self; or (c) whether object love is the primary state, as subsequent theorists have declared. In narcissism the infant takes its own body as a love object so that the ego or the "I" is recognizable, whereas autoerotism comes before that time, if indeed it represents a phase in development, when no distinction is made between the self and the nonself.

For the clinician the use of autoerotism as a developmental stage is unnecessary and a complex unverifiable theoretical speculation. It is best to restrict the use of this concept to the descriptive definition and to keep in mind that autoerotic behavior takes place at any stage of life and simply represents a statement of how the given individual is obtaining pleasure at any given time. This deprives the term of any sort of metapsychological depth and reduces its importance substantially, which I think is a good idea. The term auto-eroticism is sometimes used inter-changeably with autoerotism.

References

Abraham, K. (1916). The first pregenital stage of the libido. In *Selected Papers on Psycho-analysis,* trans. D. Bryan and A. Strachey, pp. 248–279. New York: Basic Books, 1954.

Fairbairn, W. (1954). *An Object Relations Theory of the Personality.* New York: Basic Books.

Freud, S. (1905). Fragment of an analysis of a case of hysteria. *Standard Edition* 7:3–122.

B

BAD OBJECT

A loose terminological usage of part and whole objects pervades the Kleinian literature, sometimes referring to representations and sometimes referring to the object itself. The use of the term "bad" has a special meaning in metapsychology. It can qualify either part objects, such as the breast or the penis, or whole objects, such as mother or father, or representations or images of either part or whole objects. This was made specific and more precise by Kernberg (1976, 1980), who emphasized the "splitting" process early in development in which representations are divided into "good" and "bad" (see SPLITTING). The "bad" self and object representations imply that they are frustrating, hateful, frightening, malevolent, and persecuting, all borrowed from Klein's original notions. The source of these bad objects, according to Klein, is the sadistic aggression of the death instinct originally turned on the infant but deflected for self-preservative purposes onto these "all bad" objects. For Kernberg in his early work, an excess of constitutional aggression invested these split-off bad objects with their negative valence; in his later work early experiences pro-duced the negative valence. The point is that a postulated splitting occurs early in life into "all good" and "all bad" self and object representations, which are kept separate until around six to eight months, the second subphase of Mahler's separation-individuation stage.

For Kernberg (1976) the first month of life is relatively undifferentiated. By the second to the sixth or eighth month the infant forms images or representations or constellations that are "all good" and separate from those that are "all bad." However, in this period between the second month and the sixth to eighth month there is no distinction between self and object representations, either under the "good" or "bad" group. Near the end of this stage, from the sixth to ninth month, however, the representations are differentiated between those of the self and the object, both under the "good" group and the "bad" group. Then, in the period of six to eight months to one and a half to three years, the "good" and "bad" self representations are combined into a group of self representations and divided from the object representations, which are similarly combined. This division permits object constancy to occur. From the end of the third year to the end of the oedipal phase, the split "good" and "bad" self representations are integrated and neutralized into a total self representation; similarly, the split "good" and "bad" object representations are integrated into a total object representation.

If this integrative process does not occur, according to Kernberg, the patient has the potential to be stuck in what he calls a borderline personality organization. Such a patient readily projects the "all bad" self and object representations onto the therapist and reacts accordingly. This is the process of projective identification that Kernberg says accounts for the clinical phenomena seen with the borderline patient.

References

Kernberg, O. (1976). *Object Relations Theory and Clinical Psychoanalysis.* New York: Jason Aronson.

———— (1980). *Internal World and External Reality.* New York: Jason Aronson.

BASIC FAULT

This term was used by Balint (1952) to depict what are commonly referred to as patients whose difficulties are preoedipal and for whom the Oedipus complex is not the nucleus of their neuroses. Such patients include the well-known character disorders, borderline personalities, addicts, schizophrenics, and so forth, all of whom need what Balint called a "new beginning" in therapy, or what Fromm-Reichmann (1950) called patients who need an experience and not an explanation in their treatment. The concept of "basic fault" was a way station toward the gradual recognition in the middle of the present century that many of the patients we see in psychotherapy have disorders that do not primarily arise in the oedipal phase of development and are different from Freud's classical psychoneuroses.

Balint hoped to treat these patients by allowing a benign regression to occur until the patient reached what he called an "arglos" state. In such a state the analyst could literally correct the basic fault by an appropriate humane encounter with the patient. A modern version of this in much more sophisticated terminology was developed by Kohut (see SELF PSYCHOLOGY).

References

Balint, M. (1952). *Primary Love and Psycho-Analytic Technique.* New York: Liveright.
Fromm-Reichmann, F. (1950). *Principles of Intensive Psychotherapy.* Chicago: University of Chicago Press.

BASE, SUPERSTRUCTURE

These are Marxist terms that refer to the hypothesis that human personality, culture, and history are all a function of the means of production. The economics of a given culture, which represents the means of production employed by that culture, was designated as the "base" by Marx. From it arise the history and characteristics of the given culture as well as the personality of the individuals who live in that culture, including their philosophy, ethics, and religion. All of this was designated by Marx as the "superstructure." The importance of Marxist contentions for psychotherapists is that one must indeed keep in mind the influence of the particular economic system under which one lives on the formation of the personality of the patients with whom one works. One must also keep in mind the influence of this economic base on one's self and one's practice of psychotherapy (see Chessick 1992).

After 1844 Marx concentrated on economics, which culminated in his controversial masterpiece *Capital* in 1867. But already in 1844 he saw capitalist economics as establishing an alienated form of social intercourse and argued that private property, greed, and selfish materialism are a product of this alienation. Marx maintained that this is not natural to humans. He viewed the human as a "species-being," a notion he borrowed from the philosopher Ludwig Feuerbach (1804–1872). Wood (1981) gives an excellent discussion of the problem of alienation and the importance of species consciousness as it appears in the work of Marx.

For the purposes of psychotherapists, Marx's (1963) *Economic and Philosophical Manuscripts* of 1844 is most significant. In this work he visualizes a change in the capitalist system as producing a better sort of human being, creative and altruistic, and with more autonomy, because he thought of human psychology to a large extent as the product of the economic base. He argued, following Hegel, that there was no immutable nature in humans, only various potentials. These were the potential for self-determination, autonomy, and choices; the potential of sociality—man as a species being—because all human activity has a social dimension and humans can empathize and cooperate; and the potential for aesthetic enjoyment and the capacity for disinterested contemplation. Marx claimed that the actualization of these wonderful potentials was interfered with by the economic base of our culture, capitalism.

The sense of "alienation," which comes up so often in psychotherapy as a complaint by patients, was first stressed by Hegel, who thought of it as a separation from identification with the World Spirit. Subsequently, Feuerbach argued that we are alienated when we believe in any extra-human entity, including a World Spirit, a view just the opposite of Hegel. Both Hegel and Feuerbach thought alienation needed to be overcome by correcting intellectual error, but Marx believed that one must change the world and remove disabling social institutions in order to remove alienation, not just give intellectual interpretations. This is obviously of great interest to psychotherapists for many reasons. Also, it parallels the contemporary argument whether intensive psychotherapy or psychoanalysis functions primarily through cognitive insights provided by interpretations alone or through some kind of actual change in the patient directly brought about by the experience with the therapist (see Chessick in press).

References

Chessick, R. (1992). *What Constitutes the Patient in Psychotherapy*. Northvale, NJ: Jason Aronson.

———— (in press). What brings about change in psychoanalytic treatment. *Psychoanalytic Review*.

Marx, K. (1963). *Early Writings,* trans. T. Bottomore. New York: McGraw-Hill.

Singer, P. (1980). *Marx*. New York: Hill & Wang.

Wood, A. (1981). *Karl Marx*. London: Routledge & Kegan Paul.

BEATING FANTASY (SEE ALSO MASOCHISM)

Freud's (1919) classic paper entitled "A Child Is Being Beaten" discussed beating fantasies accompanying masturbation. According to Freud, in the girl such fantasies go through three stages of development. In the first stage, the father is beating a sibling; next, he beats the girl herself. Finally, he beats the other children again, but these are boys and need not be siblings. Beating fantasies accompanying masturbation in the boy, according to Freud, develop in two stages. In the first stage, the father beats the boy; in the second, the mother beats the boy. Freud believed these fantasies to originate from an incestuous attachment to the father. The boy evades the threat of homosexuality by transforming the beating father into the beating mother, while the girl in fantasy becomes a boy and derives masochistic pleasure from what on the surface appears to be a sadistic beating fantasy.

More generally, in beating fantasies the fantasizer may identify with either the person doing the beating or the person being beaten, or both. The person doing the beating has a role that is usually connected with phallic aggression or sadism, while the person being beaten has an unconscious role of passivity and feminine masochism.

Certainly sibling rivalry is expressed in these fantasies, but the fact that they are masturbatory indicates a deeper incestuous origin. In my clinical experience, girls and women do not always go to the third stage to achieve masturbatory satisfaction but can complete masturbation to orgasm with the fantasy of being directly beaten by their father or other male figures, or, when the transference has developed, by the therapist.

It is of historical interest, as discussed by Young-Bruehl (1988), that Anna Freud's paper on "Beating Fantasies and Daydreams," which resumes the topic of her father's paper, may be a self-description. This was apparently an important masturbatory theme for her, and she was in "analysis" with her father at the time the paper was written. Young-Bruehl suggests that one of the cases reported in Freud's classic paper (the fifth) was that of his daughter. Perhaps some day when more documents are released we will understand the mind-boggling relationship between Freud and his daughter, analyst and analysand, a lot better. As in contemporary cases, the masturbatory beating fantasies of

Anna Freud offer us a tantalizing clue but insufficient material by themselves to reach any conclusions.

References

Freud, S. (1919). A child is being beaten. *Standard Edition* 17:175–204.

Young-Bruehl, E. (1988). *Anna Freud: A Biography*. New York: Summit.

BEYOND INTERPRETATION (GEDO)

With this title, John Gedo (1979) offers his own psychoanalytic metapsychology based on his notion of self-organization and arising from his study of preoedipal disorders. This begins a series of explorations on Gedo's (1981, 1986, 1988) part in the study of patients who present archaic demands based on preoedipal problems. According to him, these are compensatory efforts to patch over developmental deficits, actual skills that the patient lacks. He calls these an accumulation of functional handicaps produced by early developmental vicissitudes. Gedo (1981) believes that the treatment of this is beyond interpretation: "In such cases, psychoanalysis must be attempted to correct the structuralization of maladaptive patterns" (p. 57), a kind of repair job applied to the early maladaptive practices.

Gedo (1986) says that Freud's structural theory is applicable only from the latter half of the second year of life, at the earliest. This is a function of the acquisition of imaging capacity in which the mental self and representational intelligence, in Piaget's terms, gradually take over. But underlying this are the archaic phases of infantile organization with derivatives that are not necessarily ever encoded in linguistic communications. Gedo (1986) points out, in his discussion of various psychosomatic disorders and psychophysiological dysfunctions characteristic of archaic or borderline states, "Adequate behavior depends on a variety of psychological skills, beyond those of perception and cognition, for pathology of this kind comes about when primary bodily experiences are not *assimilated* into the individual's set of acknowledged personal aims" (p. 175).

Gedo (1988) refers to deficiencies caused by any failure to learn adaptively essential skills as a form of apraxia. He adds that organic damage is not implied in his use of this term, although in my clinical experience, especially in the psychotherapy of patients with epilepsy, this problem is especially pronounced in patients with concomitant organic problems. Whether adaptive skills are lacking due to maturational lag, constitutional factors, inadequate nurture, or a combination of these is not the relevant issue in understanding the psychopathology. For patients with apraxia, Gedo (1988) views therapy as a "technology of instruction" (p. 9). People get into difficulty not only from certain behaviors produced by the repetition of certain response patterns established in infancy or early childhood but also from maladaptive or troublesome types of conduct that result from apraxia—"failure, for whatever reason, to acquire essential psychological skills" (p. 17). The demonstration of these skills to the patients Gedo calls "beyond interpretation"; he considers this remedial education as vital, since "even remediable instances of disorders in thought, communication, learning, planning, affectivity, or the regulation of tensions will not respond to the resolution of intrapsychic conflicts—disorders of this type require a variety of interventions that psychoanalysts have hitherto regarded as 'nonanalytic' educational measures" (p. 28) (see AFTEREDUCATION).

Gedo (1988) insists that his noninterpretative interventions are not simply direct instruction but also concentrate on reconstructing the childhood circumstances that prevented the acquisition of the proper skills in the first place, such as the identification with a sick parent, anxiety about progress, a need to safeguard autonomy through rejecting external influences, grandiosity (in which the person feels so perfect that he or she has no need for skills), and too much frustration and disappointment in the caretaker. The identification with a sick parent may produce "focal disorders" (p. 188) in thinking because the parent identified with suffered from the same handicaps, a common clinical situation. Obsessional thinking for Gedo can be due to an apraxia in planning behavior, due to a situation in which planning behavior "is drawn into the arena of a toddler's struggles about complying with parental expectations or resisting them" (p. 197).

In every case, according to Gedo,

apparent apraxias appearing in psychoanalytic treatment must be labeled as either a temporary regression, an apraxia and ignorance of the rules of communication, or an identification with bizarre caretakers. The primary apraxias will require a variety of interventions "beyond interpretation," as Gedo (1988) explains it, "designed to correct deficiencies in psychological skills resulting from unfavorable developmental vicissitudes and transcending the matter of learning to forego the use of defensive operations. In this sense, the model technique designed to deal with the transference neuroses, that of promoting 'ego dominance' in the areas of unresolved intrapsychic conflict" (p. 213), that is, classical psychoanalysis, is not sufficient.

References

Gedo, J. (1979). *Beyond Interpretation.* New York: International Universities Press.

———— (1981). *Advances in Clinical Psychoanalysis.* New York: International Universities Press.

———— (1986). *Conceptual Issues in Psychoanalysis: Essays in History and Method.* Hillsdale, NJ: Analytic Press.

———— (1988). *The Mind in Disorder: Psychoanalytic Models of Pathology.* Hillsdale, NJ:

BION (SEE REVERIE)

BIPOLAR SELF

Kohut's books, *The Restoration of the Self* (1977) and *How Does Analysis Cure?* (1984), contain his final views stressing the two "poles" of the supraordinate concept: bipolar self.

These two poles are ambitions, derived from the grandiose self and its strivings for exhibitionistic ambitious acclaim and mirroring; and *guiding ideals* and the pursuit of them, derived from internalization of the idealized parent imago. In psychotherapy one pole may be strengthened to compensate for defects in the other, a process known as functional rehabilitation of the self. Defensive structures (such as common fantasies of sadistically enforced control and acclaim) may develop to mask defects, and more hopeful compensatory structures (such as the more constructive pursuits of goals and accomplishments) may make up for weakness at one pole by strengthening the other. So, curative process for Kohut is now thought of as either filling a defect in the self by transmuting internalizations in the transference or strengthening the compensatory structures by making them functionally reliable, realistic, and autonomous, which would not constitute a cure in classical psychoanalysis.

For children of 8 months to 3 years of age, Kohut postulates a normal, intermediate phase of powerful narcissistic cathexis of the grandiose self (a grandiose exhibitionistic image of the self) and the idealized parent imago (the image of an omnipotent selfobject with whom fusion is desired). These psychic formations are gradually internalized and integrated within the psychic structure. As a result of appropriate minor disappointments, the grandiosity is integrated at around 2 to 4 years of age (Kohut 1977); it forms the nuclear ambitions pole of the self, driving the individual forward, and derives mainly from the relationship with the mother. In Kohut's final theory, "the psychology of the self in the broader sense," the self and ego are separated and the internalized grandiose self is thought to form the nuclear ambitions pole of the self.

At 4 to 6 years of age (Kohut 1977), at the height of the oedipal phase, the idealized parent imago, which derives from both parents, is also internalized and integrated. In Kohut's earlier theory, it was thought of as an infusion of both the superego and the ego with the love and admiration originally aimed at the idealized parent imago, which then serves as a vital internal source of self-esteem and the basis of the ego-ideal aspect of the superego (see EGO IDEAL). This ego-ideal forms a system toward which the person aspires; thus the individual is driven from below by nuclear ambitions and pulled from above by the ego-ideal. In the psychology of the self in the broader sense, the consolidation of the idealized parent imago forms the other pole of the self, the nuclear ideals pole. This notion of the bipolar self is the crucial concept of the psychology of the self (see SELF PSYCHOLOGY).

References

Kohut, H. (1977). *Restoration of the Self.* New York: International Universities Press.
_____ (1984). *How Does Analysis Cure?* Chicago: University of Chicago Press.

BORDERLINE

What is a borderline patient? Signals to watch for at the start of therapy are a sense of entitlement, magical expectations or thinking, an impaired differentiation between fantasy and reality, episodes of anger and suspicion with no sense of humor, and fears of rejection or hints of paranoia. There are no pathognomonic symptoms of a borderline personality, and no consensus on characteristic metapsychology, dynamics, or precise stage of failure in development exists. It is the quality of the therapist's ongoing experiences with the patient that is key to the diagnosis, which introduces an unavoidable controversy about establishing the diagnosis in some cases where *DSM-III-R* criteria are not immediately apparent (Chessick 1982).

It is not necessary to insist that all borderline patients are arrested at one specific point or stage in development. The borderline condition arises as a consequence of the first three years of a disastrous and disappointing ambience in the mother-child interaction combined with genetic or constitutional factors, which is then complicated by the inevitable failure of an appropriate solution to the Oedipus complex. The role of the father is also very important. It is not necessary in practical clinical work to have recourse to a highly complex theory of object relations in dealing with the day-to-day treatment, although the temperament and cognitive functioning of some therapists may require such an elaborate theoretical structure to enhance their own sense of understanding of the patient. I question the value of speculations based on adult patient material as to what kind of psychodynamic processes and images occur in the mind of the 1- or 2-year-old child.

It is a mistake not to take into consideration that a patient must undergo all developmental phases by the time he or she comes into treatment; certainly failures of the later phases because of a faulty foundation or structure are also going to affect the symptomatology and behavior of the patient. I am unable to agree that there is a specific metapsychological entity called borderline personality organization. I am not convinced there will be much further theoretical understanding of the borderline patient because I am not convinced that it constitutes an independent autonomous entity; the value of the concept lies in the clinical descriptive diagnosis with the implications of poor ego functioning and consequent special requirements for a proper therapeutic approach.

It is very misleading to label any patient one does not understand as "borderline." For example, a patient reacting with rage to a gross empathic failure on the part of the therapist is showing neither a transference nor a borderline personality organization, but rather is responding appropriately to deep disappointment. Borderline patients especially react with angry disruption or suicidal behavior to therapies that they intuitively recognize are inappropriate to their intense personal suffering, such as certain types of counseling or so-called touching and feeling treatments; these reactions are not simply manifestations of psychopathology but rather represent an increase in desperation and disappointment in yet another encounter with lack of empathy and inappropriate misunderstanding of the patient's basic needs by a parental figure.

I have no objections to the use of the *DSM-III-R* criteria for research purposes or to form a starting point in the establishment of the diagnosis, but in clinical practice, as generally agreed, it is rare that patients who have these *DSM-III-R* criteria do not also have criteria for other forms of personality disorder at the same time. There is a definitive diagnostic difference between the borderline patient and some character disorders on the descriptive criterion that in the latter, one set of well-known characterologic features consistently predominates the clinical picture in a relatively rigid and all-pervasive way; thus we have the obsessive compulsive character, the narcissistic character, the hysterical character, and so forth. In the borderline patient, however, as I (Chessick 1975, 1983) have pointed out, any variety of neurotic or quasi-psychotic, psychosomatic, or sociopathic symptoms, in any combination or degree of severity, may be part of the initial presenting complaint. Either a bizarre combination of such symptoms may cut across the standard nosology, or the relative preponderance of any symptom group is frequently changing or shifting. The borderline patient may present either a very chaotic or stormy series of relationships with a variety of people or a bland and superficial but relatively stable set of relationships. Vagueness of complaint or even an amazingly smooth or occasionally socially successful personality may be encountered. Careful investigation reveals a poverty of genuine emotional relationships sometimes well hidden behind even an attractive and personable social facade.

The capacity for reality testing and ability to function in work and social situations are not as catastrophically impaired in borderline patients as in schizophrenics, although the degree of functioning may vary from time to time and may be quite poor. On the whole, these patients are able to maintain themselves, sometimes raise families, and otherwise fit more or less into society. Although their functioning is more impaired than narcissistic personalities, they do not present as isolated drifters, chronic hospital or long-term prison cases, totally antisocial personalities, or chronic addicts. They have, however, often tried everything and may present a variety of sexual deviations, but they are not functionally paralyzed by these or by their various symptoms or anxieties for very long periods of time. Borderline patients suffer from an unpleasant but relatively stable and enduring condition. They may experience what appear to be transient psychotic episodes either for no apparent reason or as a result of stress, alcohol, drugs, improper psychotherapy, and so on, but they do not remain psychotic for long. They snap out of it and often learn what will snap them out of it and administer a self-remedy, which sometimes consists of dangerous acting out.

One is usually compelled to be more active in the psychotherapy of borderline patients than in the treatment of many other conditions. For example, one must often actively inquire what is going on outside therapy hours. The fact that the therapist is interested in the patient's real everyday life, although it can be viewed as a form of gratification, also constitutes a form of limit setting. In general, the therapist must have a great deal of flexibility to work with borderline patients and must learn to suit the treatment to each patient, not each patient to the treatment. Careful listening often tells us what a patient needs in the way of treatment and what a patient can and cannot tolerate. If we follow this, we will have as smooth and workable a relationship as possible and also demonstrate that we have some empathy with that patient's fears and anxieties.

It is extremely important for the structure of the treatment to be flexible and reasonable; above all, it has to make sense to the patient. If borderline patients can even vaguely understand the reason for the structure and the limitations, although they may still fight against the framework of the treatment they will not be basically impeded by it. Such patients do very badly if structure is simply imposed on them by fiat without discussion and if the therapist is unwilling to negotiate.

The first pitfall in dealing with the archaic transferences (see ARCHAIC TRANSFERENCES) of these patients is the danger of the therapist's panic. Flamboyant acting out often stirs up countertransference hatred manifested by fears of patient suicide or malpractice litigation. It looks as if the patient is exploding, and unless the therapist has a dynamic grasp of what is going on, he or she can be stampeded into doing something radical or into getting rid of the patient.

The second pitfall is therapist impatience. The therapist must be willing to sit sometimes for years with a borderline patient while he or she gradually catalyzes the rebuilding of ego structure. Many therapists simply don't want to do this, as it is stressful, tedious, and painstaking work that can be ungratifying for long periods of time. Borderline patients tend to set up in external reality the kinds of situations they need to have occurring. Sometimes they are quite expert at this, and the therapist gets sucked into playing various kinds of roles, depending on the projection assigned to the therapist. This leads to serious chronic countertransference problems.

When the raging begins, it is usually impossible to argue a borderline patient out of his or her accusations. If on careful objective assessment it turns out that the accusations are correct—and this sometimes happens—then the therapist needs to self-correct and sometimes apologize. If the accusations are based on distortions or projection, the proper approach to this is a calm, nonanxious, patient, nonretaliatory stance, with eventual interpretation of what is happening. It is this consistent stance that provides the basic ambience of the treatment. Any disruption of it interrupts the subliminal soothing that is always going on in a well-conducted treatment of a borderline patient. No matter how much the therapist may wish to get away from this in his or her theoretical conceptions, the ambience or subliminal soothing the therapist provides coming from consistency, reliability, and integrity—the ambience of the therapist's office; the therapist's personality; the deep inner attitude toward patients that cannot be faked—supports the basic motor that permits the psychotherapy of the borderline to go forward.

Sometimes the rage of a borderline patient is stirred up directly by frustration of the need for omnipotent control of everything; sometimes the rage is a secondary phenomenon to paranoid projection or an intense transference. In a sense such patients are correct when they predict that all human relationships will end up badly for them, with disappointment and dislike coming from everyone around them. Elsewhere I (Chessick 1972) have discussed this as externalization in the borderline patient. A patient responds selectively to the negative aspects of significant people and develops a case or *dossier* based on selective negative perceptions for expecting attack from all sides—which then justifies a preemptive strike. The chronic calculated attacks on the therapist's defects, if not interpreted, can easily lead to countertransference acting out on the part of the therapist, even to the point of directly or indirectly getting rid of the patient. This is quickly used as "proof" by the patient of his or her expectation of apparently unprovoked betrayal and abandonment.

Psychotherapists of borderline patients painfully experience the intensity of a patient's effort to manipulate them into validating his or her projections. The therapists feel the inner conflict as they struggle against this manipulation. The most benign therapist approaching the borderline patient in a raging archaic transference finds himself or herself transformed into a horrible monster very quickly by the patient's selective perception. Unless the therapist is aware of this danger, the tendency is either to retaliate or to quarrel with the patient's extremely unflattering portrayal. This sudden transformation of the therapist into a horrible monster can occur at any time in the treatment, even when there seems to be a good working alliance. It often leads to therapist discouragement and burnout, with a lingering sense of depression and injured self-esteem.

The clinical phenomena must be studied to see what the therapist is actually doing with the patient regardless of the theoretical model that the therapist professes to follow. For example, the technique of Kohut (see SELF PSYCHOLOGY), in which the idealization of the therapist is permitted over a long period of time so that the full transference involving the search for the idealized parent imago is permitted to develop, can easily be used by an untrained or untreated therapist as an excuse to permit a flattering kind of worship and massage the narcissism of the therapist. Conversely, the technique of Kernberg, in which more confrontation goes on, can be used by the therapist to act out hostility and aggressiveness and to produce chaos, or even a sort of counterprojective identification.

Meticulous attention to the details of the interaction is the best starting point in dealing with patients who are subject to explosions of rage in the treatment. What is important is not the therapist's minor empathic failures per se, but the way in which they are experienced by the patient. The patient uses these minor empathic failures to relive a dreadful interpersonal experience in a protective effort to further demonstrate the need for distancing in interpersonal relationships. What the therapist should be listening for in the psychotherapy is how the patient is experiencing the interaction with the therapist and in what context these experiences are being placed within the patient's preexisting patterns. It is only after the therapist has been able to establish this information with the patient that he or she can begin asking why these experiences are placed in a particular context.

The most common fantasies the therapist may see emerging from the unconscious of the borderline patient are not oedipal fantasies but narcissistic fantasies and fantasies of rage and of world and self-destruction. The acting out of conscious deriva-tives of such rage and of world and self-destruction fantasies endangers the very life of the patient; the acting out of disavowed narcissistic fantasies often renders the patient poorly adapted and causes great difficulties in interpersonal relationships.

At the deepest point of the treatment these core narcissistic and destructive fantasies emerge and are worked through, not by giving the patient a metapsychological explanation, but by allowing such fantasies to emerge into the light, studying their genesis, and showing the patient how the acting out of such fantasies interferes with aims and goals in life. The borderline disorder is similar to the narcissistic disorder in that narcissistic transferences and fantasies often appear, but is different from the narcissistic personality disorder in that the intensity of the raging, fear, mistrust, and annihilation fantasies is much greater.

References

Chessick, R. (1972). Externalization and existential anguish. *Archives of Psychiatry* 27:764–770.

_____ (1975). The borderline patient. In *American Handbook of Psychiatry*, ed. S. Arieti, 2nd ed., pp. 808–819. New York: Basic Books.

_____ (1982). Intensive psychotherapy of a borderline patient. *Archives of General Psychiatry* 39:413–422.

_____ (1983). Problems in the intensive psychotherapy of the borderline patient. *Dynamic Psychotherapy* 1:20–32.

BOREDOM

It may surprise the psychotherapist to find the term "boredom" listed in a dictionary for psychotherapists, but actually it is an important form of countertransference. When the therapist finds himself or herself "bored" with the patient's hour or the patient's material, it means that something has gone wrong. Kleinians tend to interpret therapist boredom as the result of negative projective identification, in which they view the patient as projecting in such a way as to interfere with the therapist's mental processes, reduce the material to meaningless, and produce a vacuous interpersonal field. All psychotherapists have had the experience of boredom with certain types of patients or with certain patients when they produce certain types of material, and as a function of how a particular patient expresses himself or herself. The danger of interpreting boredom as a function of a patient's negative projective identification is that it tends to put the blame for the situation on the patient.

Whenever I sense countertransference, I try to look at myself first (see Chessick 1990). When I feel bored with a patient, I usually am not understanding the patient's material, not as a result of the process of negative projective identification, but because the patient is arousing anxiety or hostility in me, or because some extraneous matter is distracting my attention. Self-analysis of boredom often reveals that underneath it is a state of instinctual tension (Fenichel 1954). As nicely summarized by Moore and Fine (1990), "Boredom has been interpreted as arising from a defensive struggle against unacceptable fantasies and impulses in which the ideational content of the impulse is repressed but the tension achieves affective representation" (p. 35). I suggest that the psychotherapist apply this to himself or herself when feeling bored with a patient.

The converse is true when the patient quizzically inquires as to whether the therapist is bored by him or her. When a patient speaks of "boring" the therapist, the therapist should keep in mind the double meaning of the term. In Samuel Johnson's (1773) dictionary, the usage of the term "bore" is exclusively related to an aggressive drilling for the purpose of making a hole in something!

References

Chessick, R. (1990). Self analysis: fool for a patient? *Psychoanalytic Review* 77: 311–340.

Fenichel, O. (1954). *Collected Papers,* vol. 1. New York: Norton.

Johnson, S. (1773). *A Dictionary of the English Language.* Beirut, Lebanon: Librairie du Liban, 1978.

Moore, B., and Fine, B. (1990). *Psychoanalytic Terms and Concepts.* New Haven, CT: Yale University Press.

BOUNDARY SITUATIONS (SEE LIMIT SITUATIONS)

BULIMIA, EATING DISORDERS

The origin of this term is from the classical Greek, the words βούς (*bous*), meaning ox, and λιμός (*limos*), meaning hunger. Thus, the person with what Samuel Johnson (1773) calls bulimy has an enormous appetite, which Johnson considered to be often attended with fainting and coldness of the extremities. The problem of bulimia nervosa, as it is called, which is a variant of anorexia nervosa characterized by self-induced vomiting or purging following binge eating, is an increasingly common clinical picture encountered by psychotherapists. During the eating binges a large amount of food is ingested in a short period of time. This is usually followed by a depressed mood, self-criticism, and self-induced vomiting or purging. Sometimes the patient uses dangerous chemicals like ipecac to induce vomiting or destructive laxatives to induce purging. Between binges the patient is often anorexic, on a strict diet, and preoccupied with exercise to the point of a pathological obsession. This condition may be accompanied by stealing, sexual promiscuity, and stormy interpersonal relationships, in contrast with the classical anorexia nervosa, which is usually found in a more withdrawn individual.

The psychological link underlying the whole spectrum of the eating disorders from superobesity to anorexia is stressed by Wooley and Wooley (1980) and many other authors. Shainess (1979) vividly describes that link in psychoanalytic terms: "I feel convinced that the unconscious fantasies connected with food are that it is poison. The patient is trapped between the need to eat and to sustain life, and the paranoid projection in relation to food. . . . the anorexic feels full after a few bites, while the obese always has room for more, no matter how much has been eaten" (pp. 230–231). The efforts not to eat are seen as a phobic avoidance of poison, while overeating represents the need to retain food-as-mother, says Shainess. One obese patient of mine regularly referred to binge eating of bags of cookies as eating "bags of garbage," and clearly distinguished this from her ordinary and normal eating pattern.

In all the cases, the whole eating pattern is disorganized, and the relationship of child to mother is acted out over food. The dramatic eating disorder, whether through "alimentary orgasms," masochistic infliction of self-starvation or unpleasant compulsive stuffing, or the binge-purge guilt and restitution circle, drains off the rage and paranoia (more or less) and focuses the patient's attention away from the empty, depleted self and onto preoccupation with gastro-intestinal-tract sensations. In this manner, some sort of sense of being alive is maintained. So on top of the depleted and fragmented nuclear core, the patient has built various protective rituals and soothing activities, which, in the case of the eating disorders, sometimes permit the patient to function in society.

At the same time, the patient must deal with the massive narcissistic rage or unconscious sadism. For example, Offenkrantz and Tobin (1974) discuss such a patient as a "depressive character" and emphasize the great unconscious rage at important objects who are not providing the patient with what he or she unconsciously needs—a rage that often gets turned on the therapist. Under this lies an anaclitic depression characterized by depletion and a hopelessness that sufficient gratification will ever be possible.

The classical psychodynamics of anorexia in young women have long been known to include the impairment of development arising from an early unsuccessful mother–daughter relationship. The adolescent girl, faced with feminine individuation and threatened by the loss of dependency on the family, responds to the conflict in these cases by regression to an infantile maternal relationship with unconscious craving for blissful eating experiences. This is denied in the drama that is carried out by an oscillation between eating and severe dieting; the pursuit of thinness usually represents an act of hostile and defiant compliance by the patient against the mother.

It is clear from clinical experience that the eating disorders protect the patient from unbearable affects, which then do appear if the eating disorder is stopped. It is the extremely negative self-image and self-hatred—or in Kohut's terms, the depleted self with the disintegration product of narcissistic rage—that precede the development of the eating disorder. This intrapsychic psychopathology forms the foundation for the various eating disorders, which then develop when the ten-

sion becomes unbearable, the faulty preoedipal self-soothing system becomes overwhelmed, and the self threatens to fragment or actually does so.

In my clinical experience the most serious problem in the intensive psychotherapy of an eating disorder is not that of a schizophrenic loss of reality testing, as Bruch (1973) suggests, but of a deep characterologic depression often with core paranoid features—manifested by a derogatory self-image, cynicism, and hopelessness and reinforced by the long-standing nature of the condition—as well as a profound narcissistic rage that begins to show itself as the eating disorder itself is corrected. Thus a long and difficult intensive psychotherapy is to be expected because we are dealing with a profound preoedipal disorder characterized by severe early structural defects.

References

Bruch, H. (1973). *Eating Disorders: Obesity, Anorexia Nervosa, and the Person Within.* New York: Basic Books.

Johnson, S. (1773). *A Dictionary of the English Language.* Beirut, Lebanon: Librairie du Liban, 1978.

Offenkrantz, W., and Tobin, A. (1974). Psychoanalytic psychotherapy. *Archives of General Psychiatry* 39:593–606.

Shainess, N. (1979). The swing of the pendulum—from anorexia to obesity. *American Journal of Psychoanalysis* 39:225–235.

Wooley, S., and Wooley, O. (1980). Eating disorders: obesity and anorexia. In *Women and Psychotherapy*, ed. A. Brodsky and R. Hare-Muslin, pp. 135–158. New York: Guilford.

C

Cannibalistic

The term "cannibalistic" was given to Abraham's (1954) second oral stage of development, the so-called oral-sadistic stage. It is used by analogy with cannibalism and represents fantasies supposed to occur with active oral incorporation. The connotation is that of the hostile, sadistic aspects of oral introjection or incorporation. This term is used very loosely in the literature and has tended to fall out of favor because it speculates about the kinds of fantasies infants have when introjection or incorporation goes on, and it draws a questionable analogy between the literal cannibalistic behavior of certain primitive peoples and the alleged fantasies in the mind of an infant.

Reference

Abraham, K. (1954). *Selected Papers on Psychoanalysis,* trans. D. Bryan and A. Strachey. New York: Basic Books.

Castration Anxiety

This well-known aspect of Freud's theory of sexuality pertains especially to his view that all men and male children are liable to anxiety over the possibility of their castration. It refers usually not to castration in its literal sense but to the fear of the loss of the penis or, at a more general level, to the loss of the masculine role.

Women, of course, cannot suffer from castration anxiety in this sense, but classical theory assumes they have a "castration complex," referring to their sense of being "castrated" and lacking in a fundamental part (see FEMALE PSYCHOLOGY). The awareness of this lack, which occurs when a little girl first observes a penis, is sometimes referred to as "castration shock" and was believed by Freud (1925) to cause the little girl to enter into the Oedipus complex. To say the least, the issue of whether the lack of a penis per se is a central one in the developmental psychology of women is highly debatable. Certainly Freud (1923, 1925) was wrong in his devaluation of the importance of vaginal sensations in prepubertal girls; at times he did seem to recognize the importance of social and cultural factors in so-called penis envy, which refers more to the oppressed status of women in our culture than to their actual lack of a bodily organ.

Freud thought the little boy's basic fear was of being castrated by his father, but Melanie Klein (1932) believed there was a forerunner of castration anxiety based on sadistic pregenital phases. At any rate, castration anxiety represents an important part of oedipal fantasies and together with the associated emotions constitutes what is known as the "castration complex."

In psychotherapeutic work it should be kept in mind that castration anxiety can be precipitated by everyday events that may have the same significance, such as the loss of a job, loss of a tooth, or even humiliating experiences or situations where a man has not acted in a way socially determined to be masculine and is ridiculed for this fact. The problem of a castration complex carries with it an early fantasy process in the child that arises out of the child's puzzlement over the anatomical difference between the sexes. In psychoanalytic work it is crucial to try to uncover these early fantasy processes because they often have a decisive effect on the later life of the patient.

Understanding the psychology of women hinges on one's opinions about the importance of their castration complex and the significance of it in determining their behavior as a way of denying or overcoming their sense of castration (see FEMALE PSYCHOLOGY). The so-called masculine protest of Adler was a way of describing the woman's refusal to accept the feminine role and the sense of castration; Freud considered such a refusal to lead to psychopathology. I believe any efforts to explain away the behavior of a woman on the basis of such speculation to be both demeaning and misleading unless the analyst can demonstrate, after a study over years of time of the unfolding of the patient's transference, that the early fantasy process of the specific woman patient involved did indeed manifest a castration complex. There are some cases in which this seems to be evident, but the danger of misinterpreting the striving of any oppressed group for justice and equality on the basis of wild psychoanalysis should always be kept in mind; psychotherapy and psychoanalysis should never be allowed to be used as a tool for oppression or to force adaptation to a pathological culture.

References

Freud, S. (1923). The infantile genital organization. *Standard Edition* 19:141–145.

———— (1925). Some psychical consequences of the anatomical distinction between the sexes. *Standard Edition* 19:243–258.

Klein, M. (1932). *The Psychoanalysis of Children.* London: Hogarth.

CATHEXIS

This imprecise term was coined by Freud when he was thinking of quanta of energy attached to certain ideation; it is used less and less in the literature, since the tendency is to move away from Freud's hydrodynamic model of metapsychology. Cathexis represents the conscious or unconscious attachment of emotional feeling and significance to an idea or person. Laplanche and Pontalis (1973) tell us that "cathexis" is the rendering of Freud's *Besetzung* by James Strachey in 1922 using the

Greek word κατέχειν (katechein), meaning to occupy or hold fast. Freud did not like this choice. A typical use of *Besetzung* in German is to denote the occupation by a military force of a town or territory; but there are many connotations of the term, and some authors (Cheshire and Thoma 1991) argue it should remain untranslated.

Although it is technically difficult to defend, in clinical practice we do see phenomena that can be conceptualized as the cathexis of the ego, the cathexis of certain fantasies or wishes, and the cathexis of objects— with a consequent shifting of libidinal and aggressive energies as cathexis is bound or unbound during the therapeutic process. It is this common clinical phenomena that Freud was trying to articulate when he used the term *Besetzung,* perhaps having in mind military occupation or the removal of troops from various positions. Decathexis would be the withdrawal of cathexis. Anticathexis or countercathexis would be energy used in a conflict against the originally cathected ego, fantasy, or object. This kind of description is known as the "economic" viewpoint, and is not much favored today, although as a metaphor I think it has clinical value.

References

Cheshire, N., and Thoma, H. (1991). Metaphor, neologism and "open texture": implications for translating Freud's scientific thought. *International Review of Psycho-Analysis* 18:429–455.

Laplanche, J., and Pontalis, J. (1973). *The Language of Psychoanalysis,* trans. D. Nicholson-Smith. New York: Norton.

CENSOR

The "censor" was one of Freud's early formulations before the structural theory and labels the mental agency responsible for dream distortion and repression in his early topographic formulations. I include it here because it is sometimes forgotten that there are not one but two censors in topographic theory. One censor is between the unconscious and preconscious and another is between the preconscious and conscious. In our therapeutic work we deal primarily with the censor between the preconscious and the conscious. As preconscious material is allowed into the conscious by the second censor, earlier derivatives are allowed from the unconscious into the preconscious by the first. These concepts have been replaced by the structural theory, in which censorship has been relegated as one of the ego functions.

For example, Rangell (1989) has emphasized the ego function of unconscious choice and decision about what material to allow into the conscious. The ego unconsciously evaluates, plans, and executes action, in his view. Sartre (1973) opposes the entire notion of a "censor" as "bad faith." (For details, see Chessick 1984, 1985.) One's theoretical decision on this matter will greatly affect how one conducts psychotherapy.

References

Chessick, R. (1984). Sartre and Freud. *American Journal of Psychotherapy* 38:229–238.

_____ (1985). *Psychology of the Self and the Treatment of Narcissism.* Northvale, NJ: Jason Aronson.

Rangell, L. (1989). Action theory within the structural view. *International Journal of Psycho-Analysis* 70:189–203.

Sartre, J. (1973). *Being and Nothingness,* trans. H. Barnes. New York: Washington Square Press.

CHARACTER

"Character" is defined by Samuel Johnson (1773) as "a mark; a stamp; a representation" (p. 300). That is to say, it is a descriptive term that represents the sum of the consistently displayed personality traits and habitual modes of response an individual uses. A character defense would involve personality traits that serve an unconscious defensive purpose. A "defense transference" represents the personality characteristics presented by the patient at the beginning of treatment that are used typically by that patient to defend himself or herself against the pressure of unconscious drives potentially aimed at the analyst and that will emerge later in the treatment as the defense transference drops away.

The features of a personality or character disorder and the current official nosology are discussed in *DSM-III-R* and will not be reviewed here. It is a judgmental diagnosis implying that the patient's habitual patterns of reaction are maladaptive and limiting, often provoking the very responses from the people around that the patient was most concerned to avoid. Character traits are typically ego syntonic in contrast to neurotic symptoms, which are ego dystonic.

The old term "character neurosis" denoted a situation in which the neurosis manifested itself by character traits rather than neurotic symptoms, but this term has not achieved general acceptance. I think one of the reasons for this is that a character neurosis was thought to be based primarily on an infantile Oedipus complex, whereas most thinking about personality disorders today emphasizes the preoedipal features in their formation. The concept of personality disorder is fundamentally a social diagnosis made by people other than the patient, and a variety of classifications of character disorders or personality disorders have appeared in the literature.

One's personality or character must be understood as a "readout" displaying compromise formations made by the ego between the demands of the id, the superego, and external reality. So character traits are a mixture of drive derivatives, defenses, and superego components. They may be thought of as developing over time out of the attempt to resolve intrapsychic conflict. There is also a growing body of evidence that genetic and constitutional factors play an important role as supplying potentials that may or may not be used by each individual in the development of character traits. Although the classic papers on the formation of character are by Freud (1908, 1916), there is general agreement that his formulations represent to some extent an oversimplification. The therapist should avoid the "wild analysis" of character traits by reference to the various libidinal stages of development; such interpretations are the mark of an amateur (see WILD PSYCHOANALYSIS).

References

Freud, S. (1908). Character and anal erotism. *Standard Edition* 9:167–175.
_____ (1916). Some character types met with in psychoanalytic work. *Standard Edition* 14:309–333.
Johnson, S. (1773). *A Dictionary of the English Language.* Beirut, Lebanon: Librairie du Liban, 1978.

COMPLEMENTAL SERIES

Freud develops the clinically important notion of complemental series. He begins by asking whether neuroses are exogenous or endogenous illnesses; that is, are they the inevitable result of a particular constitution, or the product of certain detrimental or traumatic experiences in life? Freud maintains that a series of cases could be presented that vary in the amount of each of these factors, so that in some, constitutional factors seem overwhelmingly important, while in others the detrimental experiences seem to be the primary determinant of the formation of the neuroses. This notion was originally presented as the "etiological equation" in Freud's earliest works. However, in *Introductory Lectures on Psychoanalysis* (1916) it is discussed at some length, and several examples of complemental series are offered.

In addition to the complemental series formed by cases involving constitutional or biological factors on the one hand, and detrimental or traumatic experiences on the other, we have a series formed of those cases in which the intensity and pathogenic importance of infantile experiences are primary, and of those cases in which later adult experiences of an overwhelming destructive nature are clearly the major factor in the formation of the neurosis. Still another series is formed by those cases in which the destructive events in infancy, such as parental seduction, really happened, and by those cases based on the psychic fantasies during the early years that have no basis in fact.

The notion of complemental series is extremely useful in understanding the breadth of Freud's view. For example, even the thorny problem of the group of schizophrenias can be explained as a complemental series of cases: in some, it seems clear that a major constitutional or biological factor is at work; in others, there is ample evidence for profound detrimental and environmental factors in childhood. Freud's viewpoint leaves room for all types of cases and offers a neat integration of the psychological and the biological. Similarly, we know that any adult can be broken down and forced into neurotic symptomatology if sufficient psychic trauma is applied; this unfortunate empirical information fits into the second complemental series described above.

Perhaps the most interesting is the third complemental series, in which some neurotics allow the psychic reality of their infantile fantasies to influence their entire lives. Freud does not explain why this might be so, but it is perhaps related to his obsolete concept of the adhesiveness of the libido (see ADHESIVENESS OF THE LIBIDO), which he defined as the tenacity with which the libido adheres to particular trends and objects, an independent factor varying from individual to individual. The causes of such adhesiveness are unknown but probably represent a biological or constitutional factor. Not only is this adhesiveness of the libido of great significance in understanding the etiology of neuroses, but it is a factor encountered in the intensive psychotherapy of all disorders, since there seems to be a remarkable variation in the timetable with which a patient can work through and free up from certain infantile positions and attachments. Awareness and an understanding of the individual patient's timetable is extremely important, for attempts to hurry psychotherapy increase resistance and interfere with the treatment.

Reference

Freud, S. (1916). Introductory lectures on psychoanalysis. Lecture 22. *Standard Edition* 16:339–357.

COMPULSION TO REPEAT

This is one of the most remarkable and inexplicable tendencies of the human mind that seems to show itself inevitably in psychoanalytic treatment. It refers to the universal tendency of individuals to repeat in their lives distressing or even painful situations without realizing they are doing so, or even understanding they are bringing about the recurrence and repeating in their current situation the worst times from their past. This has been attributed to some kind of urge to mastery (Hendrick 1948), although Freud (1920) attributed it to the death instinct. As a rule of thumb in psychotherapy, one should always ask, if the patient is involved in a difficult or unpleasant situation either outside the treatment or with the therapist, what is being repeated.

Transference is an important manifestation of the compulsion to repeat (see TRANSFERENCE). Indeed, Freud's (1914) early use of the concept was to point out how the patient repeats behavior with a doctor that was characteristic of earlier experiences. In this way, repetition can be thought of as a way of remembering. Repetition substitutes for the articulation of forgotten memories; therefore, in unraveling the compulsion to repeat, one should end up with early memories and core fantasies that have been long forgotten. This extraordinary process of the compulsion to repeat is ungratifying, and Freud (1920) did not believe it could be explained by the pleasure principle; hence he thought it was stemming from "beyond the pleasure principle."

References

Freud, S. (1914). Remembering, repeating and working through. *Standard Edition* 12:145–156.
_____ (1920). Beyond the pleasure principle. *Standard Edition* 18:3–64.

Hendrick, I. (1948). *Facts and Theories of Psycho-analysis.* New York: Knopf.

CONSCIOUSNESS

Samuel Johnson (1773) defines "conscious" as "endowed with the power of knowing one's own thoughts and actions" (p. 397). "Consciousness" remains one of the most difficult and controversial of all the concepts discussed in this book. We know that consciousness is a state that can be contrasted to being asleep and is centered on self-awareness, allegedly differentiating humans from animals. Freud thought of consciousness as a sense organ that could perceive internal mental events and discriminate them from external perceptions, a function he termed reality testing. The tendency in classical psychoanalytic work has been to minimize the importance of consciousness and to assume that conscious phenomena are derivatives or compromise formations stemming from unconscious factors. This stands in sharp contrast to the phenomenologic point of view, which attempts to approach human behavior and expression by meticulous analysis of the conscious phenomena without making assumptions about underlying processes. The emphasis or lack of emphasis on conscious phenomena sharply differentiates so-called existential psychiatry and psychoanalysis from Freud's work.

In his topographical theory Freud depicted consciousness as the function of the system Pcpt.-Cs., which he thought of as lying on the "periphery" of the psychical apparatus. I (Chessick 1980) believe that Freud's (1950) famous "Project for a Scientific Psychology" floundered on the difficulty of explaining consciousness from his neuronal theory, just as today the argument over consciousness is a crucial one in the field of artificial intelligence and poses the classical mind-brain problem in philosophy (McGinn 1991; see MIND). Freud believed that the system Pcpt.-Cs. had free and mobile energy which could be attached to certain mental contents—this was his notion of attention and explained how the preconscious became conscious. An evanescent attention cathexis determines what is conscious at any given time. Moore and Fine (1990) state, "Consciousness is dependent on and influenced by the individual's present situation and past history, including such factors as motivation, affect, memory, and knowledge" (p. 46). So consciousness is a subjective experience, which lends itself to the phenomenological approach (Husserl 1913; see PHENOMENOLOGY).

Obviously consciousness may be altered by various factors such as sleep, organic illness, and drugs. The *DSM-III-R* (American Psychiatric Association 1987) dissociative disorders often present with an altered state of consciousness.

References

American Psychiatric Association (1987). *Diagnostic and Statistical Manual of Mental Disorders (Third Edition-Revised): DSM-III-R.* Washington, DC: American Psychiatric Association.

Chessick, R. (1980). *Freud Teaches Psychotherapy.* Hillsdale, NJ: Analytic Press.

Freud, S. (1950). Project for a scientific psychology. *Standard Edition* 1:283–397.

Husserl, E. (1913). *Ideas: General Introduction to Pure Phenomenology.* Trans. W. Gibson. New York: Macmillan, 1952.

Johnson, S. (1773). *A Dictionary of the English Language.* Beirut, Lebanon: Librairie du Liban, 1978.

McGinn, C. (1991). *The Problem of Consciousness: Essays Towards a Resolution.* Oxford, England: Blackwell.

Moore, B., and Fine, B. (1990). *Psychoanalytic Terms and Concepts.* New Haven, CT: Yale University Press.

CONSCIOUSNESS RAISING

Consciousness raising, the attempt to elevate an individual's awareness of himself or herself and to better recognize the individual's needs and special problems in the particular culture or family environment in which he or she dwells, has become popular these days. Although it is a central function of various discussion groups, it may be traced back to Marxist efforts to encourage class consciousness among the proletariat as a prelude to the anticipated revolutionary changes in society. Even today consciousness raising is an extremely important psychotherapeutic process, although it is not primarily psychoanalytic in nature. Still, I doubt if it is possible to do intensive psychotherapy with a patient without some consciousness raising taking place. Certainly women become more aware of the kinds of pressures on them in society and from their families, and men become more aware of their passive and receptive needs. Similarly, if there are healthy developmental alterations in an individual, that person may become more conscious of the needs of the underprivileged and economically disadvantaged groups in society.

It is not conceivable to me how the therapist's preconceptions and value system can be kept completely opaque to a patient during the process of intensive psychotherapy or psychoanalysis, regardless of what is thought of as the ideal situation. One glance at any therapist's office, including Freud's (Engelman 1976), makes that obvious. The apparent contrast, at least in some areas, between the assumed healthy attitudes of the properly psychoanalyzed therapist toward various oppressed groups and on other subjects such as the value of military operations, and on those assumptions the patient has simply taken in from our violent culture constitutes a form of consciousness raising, whether the therapist intends it or not.

Reference

Engelman, E. (1976). *Berggasse 19: Sigmund Freud's Home and Offices, Vienna 1938.* New York: Basic Books.

CONSTRUCTION (SEE RECONSTRUCTION)

CONTAINER (SEE REVERIE)

CONVERSION

In this process a physical symptom replaces an unconscious

psychic complex. It is a generally unsatisfactory concept because it leaves unexplained the so-called mysterious leap from the mental to the physical. My approach to conversion symptoms when they occur in psychotherapy or are the presenting symptoms is to regard them as substitutes for the expression of compromise formations by the ego that might otherwise be articulated in language. Conversion symptoms, then, are a form of language, and by uncovering the unconscious fantasy processes underlying the conversion symptoms one converts them into articulated language (see LACAN).

There is a genetic or constitutional propensity to the formation of conversion symptoms. It is often argued that conversion symptoms appear more in rural and uneducated populations, but I have also seen them in some highly sophisticated and educated metropolitan individuals. Conversion is a defense mechanism that operates unconsciously and removes anxiety that would otherwise be present before the compromise formation has taken place. For this reason, patients with conversion symptoms often show the classical *belle indifférence*. The symptoms may be very minor or extremely dramatic, and almost any organ system can be involved. The tendency is for the striated musculature to be used in conversion symptoms, but cases involving smooth musculature and even the cardiovascular system are reported. The treatment for such patients is far more difficult than was originally believed. Although the symptoms may be temporarily re-

moved by hypnosis or narcosynthesis, other symptoms soon take their place. Some of Breuer and Freud's (1893–1895) classical cases of conversion hysteria were probably borderline or schizotypal personality disorders.

Reference

Breuer, J., and Freud, S. (1893–1895). Studies on hysteria. *Standard Edition* 2:1–335.

CORRUPTION

Psychoanalysts have not paid sufficient attention to the development of corruption as it manifests itself not only in their patients and their societies but in themselves. Corruption as discussed here is not the inevitable physical decay and death of body tissue. It is the corruption of one's ego-ideals under the vicissitudes of life.

Technically speaking, corruption represents the vicissitudes of the progressive withdrawal of narcissistic libido from cathexis of the ego-ideal and back to a cathexis of the ego itself, analogous to Freud's (1914) concept of secondary narcissism, in which narcissistic libido is withdrawn from objects and replaced in the ego (see NARCISSISM and LIBIDO). The cause of this withdrawal, as in the situation of Freud's secondary narcissism, is progressive narcissistic wounding out of the disappointments encountered in the vicissitudes of life and in an attempt to prevent further pain.

The ego-ideal shrivels under the

impact of reality, which punishes all but the most talented or lucky individuals for their attempts to live up to it. A similar phenomenon accounts for the decline of "Cultures" into "Civilizations" and then into chaos and barbarism, as described by Spengler (1926, 1962). The ego-ideal of a culture is set by its founders, such as the early Greeks or the American colonists.

Spengler was not aware of the profound significance of narcissistic wounding and attributed the decline of cultures to an inherent botanical organicity, borrowing from the romantic philosophy of Goethe. Hutchins (1968), who was not psychoanalytically oriented (Ashmore 1989) described the corruption of an individual in moralistic and Aristotelian terminology. But when the ego-ideal is divested of its narcissistic libido, there is consequently less and less motivation to live up to it, since there is less and less gratification when an identification with the ego-ideal has been achieved.

Spengler (1962) considered the "megapolis" as the worst feature of what he called "Civilization," a decadent phase of each "Culture." He forecast larger and larger cities, which he conceived of as being laid out for 20 million inhabitants and covering vast areas of the countryside. He gave many examples of the development of these megapolises in history and concluded that the end of all these cities was inevitably the same. After the city, beginning as a primitive barter center, develops to its zenith as a Culture city—which for Spengler was the ideal—a line of

inevitable corruption begins. Gradually it balloons into a world city or megapolis, which then undergoes an inevitable decline and ends with a handful of nomads camping in the ruins.

Spengler prophesied that (white male) Western Europe would lose its world hegemony and that Western Culture, like all other cultures, would go under. For Spengler, each Culture has its own new possibilities of self-expression that arise, ripen, decay, and never return. These Cultures grow with the same superb aimlessness as the flowers of the field, a romantic concept that Spengler borrowed from Goethe, who, in his holistic or organic ideal of nature, described plants and animals developing in the same fashion.

As Spengler (1962) put it, the problem of the "Decline of the West" is the problem of Civilization. There is an organic succession in which Civilization is the inevitable destiny of each Culture; "Civilizations are the most external and artificial states of which a species of developed humanity is capable" (p. 24). As an example of the change from Culture to Civilization, he discussed the shift from the Greeks to the Romans: "The Romans were barbarians who did not *precede* but *closed* a great development" (p. 24). Spengler continued, "Unspiritual, unphilosophical, devoid of art, clannish to the point of brutality, aiming relentlessly at tangible successes, they stand between the Hellenic Culture and nothingness" (p. 24). He attempted to demonstrate an inevitable line of development in human groups culminating in Civilization, in which "appears this type of strong-minded, completely nonmetaphysical man" (p. 25). This type of individual represents "Civilization," a late phase of the decline of every Culture.

Spengler (1962) claimed that the transition from Culture to Civilization occurred in the Western world in the nineteenth century, just as it occurred for the Greek classical world in the fourth century B.C. When this happens, he wrote, "in place of a type-true people, born of and grown on the soil, there is a new sort of nomad, cohering unstably in fluid masses, the parasitical city dweller, traditionless, utterly matter-of-fact, religionless, clever, unfruitful, deeply contemptuous of the countryman. . . . The world-city means cosmopolitanism in place of 'home.' . . . To the world-city belongs not a folk but a mob" (p. 25).

Heidegger (1962) later took up this concept of "home" when he drew the distinction between the planet on which we dwell as an ancient landscape and background providing a context for everyday life, and an inauthentic existence marked by "turbulence" and exerting a whirlpool effect, pulling individuals in the world city into a frenzy of what one of my North Shore patients called "shopping and lunching." Or, as Spengler (1962) put it, there is "the reappearance of *panem et circenses* in the form of wage-disputes and sports stadia—all these things betoken the definite closing down of the Culture and the opening of a quite new phase of human existence" (p. 26). This, Spengler claimed, helps us to com-

prehend the great crisis of the present. The hallmark of Civilization today, Spengler insisted, in contrast to the Culture of yesterday, is the way in which rhetoric and journalism serve money, which represents the power of Civilization: "It is the money-spirit which penetrates unremarked the historical forms of the people's existence" (pp. 26–27) in a Civilization. More generally, "The energy of culture-man is directed inwards, that of civilization-man outwards" (p. 28), so that there is an expansive tendency, "a doom, something daemonic and immense, which grips, forces into service, and uses up the late mankind of the world-city stage, willy-nilly, aware or unaware" (p. 28). There has been a line of development in the Western world that leaves us as a civilized, not a Gothic or Rococo, people: "We have to reckon with the hard cold facts of a *late* life, to which the parallel is to be found not in Pericles' Athens but in Caesar's Rome" (p. 31).

As it happened in the fourth century B.C. for the classical world and in the nineteenth century for the Western world, there developed the great world cities with the provinces relegated to the background. Culture cities like Florence, Nuremberg, Bruges, and Prague became provincial towns. In this shift from Culture to Civilization, argued Spengler (1926), cosmopolitanism replaces home, cold matter of fact replaces reverence for tradition and age, scientific irreligion replaces the old religion of the heart, society replaces the state, and natural rights replace hard-earned rights. In short, "Any high ideal of life becomes largely a question of money" (p. 33).

His argument that Western culture shifted to civilization in the 1800s is buttressed by the historian Johnson (1991), who gives an extremely detailed description of the period from 1815 to 1830 in which the so-called modern age began, an age of technology that Spengler would define as the civilization phase of Western culture. Spengler concluded his first volume by predicting that a spiritual crisis will involve Europe and America.

Some civilizations do not always disappear, and certain ones, like India and China, may last indefinitely in their decadent form. Spengler also conceded that cultures can perish through external assault, as when the Spaniards invaded the Western Hemisphere and destroyed the old Mexican world. In his concept of "pseudomorphosis," a culture too close to a stronger culture can perish by what he called "spiritual damage." Thus, for example, Russian culture was deformed by the intrusions of Faustian culture, first in Peter the Great's reforms and again in the Bolshevik revolution. Whereas Russian culture is what Spengler called a "flat-plane culture," characterized by low-lying buildings and nondiscriminating brotherhood, as in the novels of Dostoevsky, the ancient Egyptian culture is a one-dimensional world, its architecture predominantly a corridor enclosed in masonry, and moving down a narrow and inexorably prescribed life path.

Like Hegel (1976), Spengler explained that each philosophy expresses only its own time. Spengler (1926), not Heidegger, introduced the importance of longing and dread, a "trickling-away" (p. 78) that we feel in the present as our dread of mortality; death as a frontier, inexorable and irreversible. Spengler contended that this "enigma of time" (p. 79) runs through all creativity and philosophy, a theme made famous by Heidegger (1962).

Spengler (1962) saw a similar inevitable line of corruption in the development of philosophy, correctly forecasting the current trend toward Rorty's (1979, 1982) pragmatics, neo-Marxist criticism, and hermeneutics (see HERMENEUTICS). He (1962) concluded that we cannot help it "if we are born as men of the early winter of a full Civilization, instead of on the golden summit of a ripe Culture, in a Phidias or a Mozart time. Everything depends on our seeing our own position, our *destiny*, clearly, on our realizing that though we may lie to ourselves about it, we cannot evade it" (p. 34).

The noted educator Robert Maynard Hutchins (1968) struggled with a similar and perhaps more familiar line of decline and growth of corruption in the individual. In a lecture to college graduates from the University of Chicago, he explained:

> I am not worried about your economic future. I am worried about your morals. My experience and observation lead me to warn you that the greatest, the most insidious, the most paralyzing danger you will face is the danger of corruption. Time will corrupt you. Your

friends, your wives or husbands, your business or professional associates will corrupt you; your social, political, and financial ambitions will corrupt you. The worst thing about life is that it is demoralizing. [p. 1]

As Hutchins put it, " 'Getting on' is the great American aspiration. And here the demoralizing part comes in; the way to get on is to be 'safe,' to be 'sound,' to be agreeable, to be inoffensive, to have no views on important matters not sanctioned by the majority, by your superiors, or by your group" (p. 2).

Hutchins points out that by helping students learn to think, universities tend to make them resistant to pressure, propaganda, or reward, and to make them dissatisfied and want to do something to improve the conditions under which people live. Proper education, which forms university graduates into independent individuals, causes problems in "getting on" and in fact, as Hutchins explains, they may not even be interested in getting on. Yet everybody now is afraid, writes Hutchins presciently in 1935. He continues:

> We are convinced that by knowing the right people, wearing the right clothes, saying the right things, holding the right opinions, and thinking the right thoughts, we shall all get on; we shall all get on to some motion-picture paradise, surrounded by fine cars, refreshing drinks, and admiring ladies. So persuasive is this picture that we find politicians during campaigns making every effort to avoid saying anything; we find important people

condoning fraud and corruption in high places because it would be upsetting to attack it. [p. 2]

Hutchins concludes with an exhortation to the graduates of the university to not let "practical" people tell them they should surrender their ideals because they are impractical. He begs them, "Do not be reconciled to dishonesty, indecency, and brutality because gentlemanly ways have been discovered of being dishonest, indecent, and brutal" (p. 4), and he urges them to take a stand now when they are graduating, before time corrupts them.

The explanation of this inevitable decline in both cultures and individuals can be more sophisticated and depth-psychological now than it was in the days of Spengler, Heidegger, and Hutchins. The problem of life lies in the necessity to withstand the inevitable narcissistic wounding that occurs as a function of the vicissitudes of every person's existence and of the existence of a Culture as it struggles to manifest itself in a world of Civilizations. As this wounding through disappointment occurs, there is a shriveling of the soul that Freud (1914) called secondary narcissism, a tendency of the libidinal investment in objects to be withdrawn into the self; this takes place not only as a consequence of inevitable narcissistic wounding but even as the consequence of the anticipation of narcissistic wounding, such as recognizing one's inevitable physical decline and death, which in our youth-oriented culture bring scorn and indifference. Hence we observe the typical phenomenon of elderly people who frequently lose interest in the problems of others and become extremely preoccupied with themselves, their finances, and their innumerable physical complaints.

This progresses to a withdrawal of libidinal investment in the ego-ideal, so that in the final stage of our typically corrupted individual we observe also a cynicism, a rage, and a Scroogelike mentality, what Erikson (1959) called despair rather than integrity. He explains, "Such a despair is often hidden behind a show of disgust, a misanthropy, or a chronic contemptuous displeasure with particular institutions and particular people—a disgust and displeasure which . . . only signify the individual's contempt of himself" (p. 98). People vary in their capacity to withstand this decaying process, as a function of their capacity to withstand narcissistic wounding or, as Kohut (1971) would put it, as a function of the basic cohesiveness of their selves.

Similarly, in Civilization we observe the development of the big-city dweller described by Spengler, who has withdrawn libidinal investment from neighboring people as well as from any sort of humanistic, philosophical, spiritual, or religious ideals. As this individual steps nonchalantly around the homeless street beggars, he or she marks what is usually described as the Alexandrian phase of culture. In this form, or Civilization, art becomes gigantic, morals flexible, and religious observances perfunctory. Cosmopolitan tastes, populist standards, and esoteric cults predominate. High and low fashions or fads come and go with amazing rapidity, and extremes of feminism appear, including hatred of men and confusion in gender roles to the point of denying even biologically obvious differences.

Massie (1991) has described in great detail certain crucial and representative individuals and the general populace of the British and German Civilizations of the twenty-five or thirty years before the actual outbreak of World War I. His work demonstrates the theses of both Spengler and Hutchins quite dramatically. The unfortunate link between the decline of individuals and the decline of cultures is that the individuals with power in cultures are already in the stage of the personal decline of their ideals, and therefore are more likely to accept rather than resist the corruption and disintegration of the springtime values of the Culture and of the individual that are taking place. Hence the public elects banal mediocrities again and again who symbolize the corrupt status of the ego-ideal and who hasten rather than oppose further decline.

We should never forget that in psychoanalytic work we transmit to our patients and our students the status of our value system, whether we wish to do so or not, so this problem is of immediate personal concern to every individual who deals with the psychological problems of another person. An extreme example is found in the disintegration of psychoanalysis in France into quarreling schisms, schools, and counterschools, as the history of Lacan and his followers and enemies and ever-changing alliances dramatically entails (Roudinesco 1990, Turkle 1978). A less flamboyant but still sad and unfortunate example is that of "The New York Psychoanalytic Civil War" described by Frosch (1991), a turmoil marked by "personal differences, power struggles, and ideological differences" (p. 1058). The effect of this on the students and patients of the eminent psychoanalysts involved is quite significant and is well documented in *The Freud–Klein Controversies* (King and Steiner 1991), a record of the crisis situation in the British Psycho-Analytical Society shortly after Freud's death in 1939.

Personal narcissistic and other investments may underly apparent "scientific disagreements" in the field. Stein (1991) points out that countertransference (see COUNTERTRANSFERENCE) has a hitherto unrecognized important further source, "deriving from the utilized theory of the analyst. This countertransference may occur independently of the patient's motivation and independently of the internal dynamics of the analyst" (p. 326). King and Steiner (1991) tell us:

Overtly, controversy was mainly couched in terms of scientific differences of opinion about what was considered to be accepted psychoanalytical theory and technique, as formulated by Freud, and what view of it should be taught to students of psychoanalysis or included in public lectures by analysts representing the Society. Inevitably, these issues also masked deeper ones to do with who should decide these questions, and

therefore, which individuals and groups held power in the Society. [p. 9]

Following Steiner (1985), there is much to be learned from an examination of the power struggles and narcissistic investments demonstrated in the Freud–Klein controversies for those who are involved in the current power structures and hierarchies of organized psychiatry and psychoanalysis. There may be an inevitable development of corruption. This can occur both in the individual and in the Culture, from a springtime of optimism to a winter of cynicism and despair. It is extremely important for every therapist to examine his or her position on this corruption scale, because this position is transmitted and has an effect on the ego-ideal of the patient. The lack of explicit attention paid to one's ideals and values and one's motivation to live up to them and sacrifice for them will have an important subliminal effect on the treatment process.

References

Ashmore, H. (1989). *Unseasonable Truths: The Life of Robert Maynard Hutchins.* Boston: Little, Brown.

Erikson, E. (1959). *Identity and the Life Cycle.* New York: International Universities Press.

Freud, S. (1914). On narcissism: An introduction. *Standard Edition* 14:67–102.

Frosch, J. (1991). The New York psychoanalytic civil war. *Journal of the American Psychoanalytic Association* 39:1037–1064.

Hegel, G. (1976). *Hegel's Philosophy of Right,* trans. T. Knox. London: Oxford University Press.

Heidegger, M. (1962). *Being and Time,* trans. J.

Macquarrie and E. Robinson. New York: Harper & Row.

Hutchins, R. (1968). To the graduating class, 1935. In *No Friendly Voice,* pp. 1–4. New York: Greenwood Press.

Johnson, P. (1991). *The Birth of the Modern: World Society 1815–1830.* New York: Harper Collins.

King, P., and Steiner, R. (eds.). (1991). *The Freud–Klein Controversies.* London and New York: Tavistock/Routledge.

Massie, R. (1991). *Dreadnought: Britain, Germany, and the Coming of the Great War.* New York: Random House.

Rorty, R. (1979). *Philosophy and the Mirror of Nature.* Princeton, NJ: Princeton University Press.

——— (1982). *Consequences of Pragmatism.* Princeton, NJ: Princeton University Press.

Roudinesco, E. (1990). *Jacques Lacan & Co.: A History of Psychoanalysis in France, 1925–1985.* Chicago: University of Chicago Press.

Spengler, O. (1926). *The Decline of the West.* Vol. 1: *Form and Actuality,* trans. C. Atkinson. New York: Knopf.

——— (1962). *The Decline of the West,* trans. C. Atkinson. New York: Knopf.

Stein, S. (1991). The influence of theory on the psychoanalyst's countertransference. *International Journal of Psycho-Analysis* 72:325–334.

Steiner, R. (1985). Some thoughts about tradition and change arising from an examination of the British Psycho-analytical Society's controversial discussions (1943–1944). *International Review of Psycho-Analysis* 12:27–71.

Turkle, S. (1978). *Psychoanalytic Politics: Freud's French Revolution.* New York: Basic Books.

COUNTERTRANSFERENCE

Countertransference reactions have a very important impact on the process of psychotherapy. The whole subject is controversial and poorly understood, and the reader will have to be satisfied with a variety of definitions and conflicting attempts at clarification of the situation (Baum 1969–1970). Singer (1970) points out that countertransference seems to appear "when the therapist is made anxious by the patient, when he fears feelings and ideas which therapeutic investigation may arouse in him, and when his desire to avoid anxiety and its dynamic roots force him into assuming defensive attitudes" (p. 296). These defensive attitudes interfere with genuine therapeutic understanding of the patient. Dewald (1976) conceives of the psychoanalytic process as involving a new model of interpersonal interaction. Countertransference leads to disruption when the analyst's response repeats that of the parents and repetition rather than a new experience prevails.

In the broadest terms, countertransference is best thought of as a manifestation of the therapist's reluctance to know or learn something about himself or herself. It is a reflection of a wish to remain oblivious to certain facets of the psyche and to allow unresolved intrapsychic conflicts to remain buried. This powerful counterforce can move the therapist to quite hostile behavior against patients. The hostility, which can be either overt or covert, may be expressed in acts of omission or commission or in irrational "friendliness" or irrational annoyance or anger. In fact, McLaughlin (1981) suggests dropping the term "countertransference" entirely as it assumes that the analyst was pushed by the patient from his or her usual neutral "wise" state. He suggests the term "analyst's transferences," to stress the shared adventure of two humans together. Similarly, Brenner (1985) sees no need for the term "countertransference," which for him simply is the transference of the analyst in an analytic situation. The set of compromise formations "that being an analyst is," involving these drives and defenses against them, allows normal analytic functioning; when these shift due to various circumstances, analytic work is helped or hindered.

According to Singer (1970), countertransference reactions can be grouped roughly into three categories: (a) reactions of irrational "kindness" and "concern," (b) reactions of irrational hostility toward the patient, and (c) anxiety reactions by the therapist to the patient. All of these may occur in waking life or in the dreams or fantasies of the therapist.

Probably the most quoted study of countertransference is by Racker (1968), who tried to understand the deep infantile and possibly neurotic roots of countertransference reactions in some very controversial ways utilizing Kleinian theory. Hunt and Issacharoff (1977) review his important contribution. Racker points out that the significance given to countertransference depends on two misfortunes that it generates: (a) countertransference may distort or hinder the perception of unconscious processes in the patient by the therapist; and (b) countertransference may not interfere with the therapist's perception of what is going on, but it

may impair the interpretive capacity of the therapist. So the manner, behavior, tone of voice, form of the interpretations, even the attitude toward the patient consciously or unconsciously may be vastly influenced by countertransference. A patient's complaint of the tone, manner, or voice of the therapist is not always a manifestation of transference to the therapist. It may instead represent the patient's perception of a countertransference problem in the therapist, for, as Arlow (1985) reminds us, "much as we observe and study the patients, the patients do the same to us. They observe our reactions, often in order to ascertain what they can do to provoke gratification of their infantile strivings" (p. 172).

An understanding of countertransference is vital to the success of psychotherapy. It is usually defined in two limited ways or in one or more general fashion (Greenson 1978). The most limited definition of countertransference is that it consists of a set of therapist transference reactions, in the form of fantasies, feelings, thoughts, and behavior, to the transference manifestations and the transference neurosis of the patient. The formal psychoanalytic definition in use today usually amends this to include therapist transference reactions—involving, of course, the significant persons in the therapist's childhood—to any aspect of the patient's personality, including the patient's transference (Reich 1973).

The most general definition of countertransference is the total reaction of the therapist, both the transference or the realistic reaction, to all aspects of the patient's transference and general personality. Kernberg (1975) pointed out that the early appearance of such totalistic or global countertransference in an intense—and usually uncomfortable—form is typical in the treatment of borderline patients. An extreme example of this is the countertransference hatred described by Maltsberger and Buie (1974), which can develop in the treatment of borderline, psychotic, and suicidal patients. Thus totalistic countertransferences tend to develop as a response to intense archaic transferences, although Winnicott (1958) argues that some hate is always present in latent form in all countertransference to all patients; it becomes a problem especially in the treatment of more psychotic types of patients and a great strain on the analyst of such patients. Chediak (1979), however, prefers to call these "counterreactions" rather than countertransferences.

Therapists should be aware of their reactions to the realistic aspects of the patient's personality, and of their transference reactions to the patient, with focus on what aspects of the patient have stirred up countertransference. The purpose of this is neither to act out nor to share countertransference problems with the patient but to determine what aspects of the patient are producing the countertransference, for the purpose of further understanding. It is nonsense to burden the patient with countertransference problems, especially those aspects of countertransference that are the therapist's transference to the patient. This is

exploitation of the patient and belongs in the personal therapy of the psychotherapist. Racker (1968) and others have distinguished between a "countertransference structure," a "countertransference neurosis," and a "countertransference character disturbance." The countertransference structure is a consistent and relatively permanent aggregate of feelings, fantasies, and ways of reacting that develop in the therapist as a response to the transference and the personality of the patient over a long period of psychotherapy (Tower 1956).

A countertransference neurosis (Greenson 1978) is said to occur when the patient becomes more important to the therapist than anyone else in his or her life. Except possibly in certain situations involving the psychotherapy of schizophrenics, as suggested by Searles (1965), the countertransference neurosis is almost always pathological and can be very dangerous. Racker (1968) interprets the countertransference neurosis mainly as an oedipal phenomenon, but this is subject to considerable debate. In my experience it appears as a manifestation of impaired ego functioning in the therapist, an impairment that can occur for many reasons. Arlow (1985) gives three typical situations that evoke or foster countertransference: (a) a fixed identification with the patient due to a correspondence of unconscious wishes and fantasies; (b) fantasies and wishes of the analyst evoked by the patient's wishes and fantasies, such as the patient's wish to be rescued and the analyst's wish to rescue; and (c) the analytic setting, which offers tempting opportunities for the analyst to gratify narcissistic needs.

Just as we differentiate among patients between neuroses and character disturbances, and their various corresponding transferences, so we can differentiate countertransference neuroses and countertransference character disturbances, although this rarely appears in the literature. Countertransference character disturbances involve the therapist's character. His or her countertransference character disturbance is analogous to the patient's character defenses. Thus the countertransference character disturbance in the therapist would involve certain forms of behavior and a general interpersonal approach to the patient, suggesting that the patient was someone significant in the therapist's past life who called forth this general character pattern in the therapist. It is sometimes very difficult to spot this, but it is *very* important and does not get nearly the attention it deserves. Many failures in psychotherapy can be traced to unconscious countertransference character disturbances.

A variety of authors (see Menninger 1958) have discussed the signals that indicate the presence of a countertransference problem (see also EXIT LINE). After establishing a particular structure and routine of procedure with each patient, the therapist should carefully examine any departures from the routine because they may well be related to countertransference (Langs 1979). This includes the decision to offer ancillary psychopharmacological agents and other modalities. Even the most mature and well-analyzed psychotherapist is going to have important countertransference reactions to patients over a period of time (Reich 1973). A countertransference structure, as defined above, *always* appears in long-term intensive psychotherapy.

The difference between the novice and the experienced psychotherapist is that the experienced psychotherapist is constantly on the lookout for the countertransference and the countertransference structure, becomes aware of it when it occurs, engages in continuous self-analysis, keeps countertransference in check by not permitting the acting out of countertransference feelings, and holds it in abeyance or even utilizes it for the purpose of the psychotherapy.

In attempting to identify countertransference, therapists must apply the same standards of honest and forthright self-appraisal to themselves that they expect of their patients. When a countertransference problem is severe, the therapist may have to consider at least one of three alternatives. The first of these, and the simplest, is to keep therapeutic interventions and activity at a minimum for a short period of time while busily working through countertransference problems in self-analysis. A general rule is that if the therapist feels anxious with the patient, interpretations or therapeutic interventions should not be made, since they almost invariably will be meant to allay the therapist's own anxiety. If self-analysis is not successful, as a second alternative the therapist ought to consult a colleague. My experience has been that a consultation is extremely helpful and important in dealing with countertransference. A great many cases of personal disaster, suicide, sexual acting out, failure, and stalemate in psychotherapy could have been prevented if the therapist had had the courage to get a consultation from a respected colleague at the point he or she became aware of countertransference manifestations. If after this the therapist feels chronically anxious or otherwise disturbed with a patient, as a third alternative he or she should consider further personal psychoanalysis.

I insist on two maxims regarding behavior toward one's patients as the "categorical imperatives" of psychotherapy. These serve as a check on countertransference acting out: Never be either exploitative or retaliative toward your patients, and always behave as you would toward a guest in your home with your spouse present. I have seen cases where a famous maxim from Benjamin Franklin's *Poor Richard's Almanac,* had it been followed, would have saved a disaster in the psychotherapy: "Do not do that which you would not have known"—that is to say, do not behave with the patient in psychotherapy in such a way that you would be unwilling to have it generally broadcast and known to your colleagues. Here lies a third important imperative to serve as a check on countertransference acting out in psychotherapy.

Countertransference should not be thought of as intrinsically negative. It only becomes negative and interferes in psychotherapy when it is not correctly recognized and handled. The aim of the therapy of the therapist is not to remove the possibility of all countertransference reactions but to make the therapist capable of being aware of these reactions and of dealing appropriately and maturely with them. Sometimes these reactions, if studied objectively, can lead to further information and data about the patient. If the therapist notices a countertransference reaction and analyzes this, he or she may become aware that something the patient is doing or saying is producing countertransference. The therapist may not have been aware previously of the message or communication the patient was trying to send. Instead of listening, the therapist has been reacting—suffering from a countertransference reaction. In this sense, countertransference can be thought of as a resistance to uncovering and remembering. The analysis of countertransference in the therapy brings the reward of knowing and understanding new material.

Kohut (1971) described the typical countertransference responses to the mirror and idealizing transferences encountered in narcissistic personality disorders (and also in other preoedipal disorders or patients who have defensively regressed to such transferences). The typical countertransference to the idealizing selfobject transferences occurs through the mobilization of the therapist's archaic grandiose self, leading to an embarrassed defensive "straight-arming" of the patient by denial of the idealization in various ways. Typical countertransference reactions to mirror transferences are boredom, lack of involvement with the patient, inattention, annoyance, sarcasm, a tendency to lecture the patient out of counterexhibitionism, or an attempt to gain control of the therapy by exhortation, persuasion, and so on.

Gunther (1976), utilizing self psychology, explains countertransference phenomena as aimed at restoring narcissistic equilibrium in the therapist, which is endangered especially in preoedipal cases by archaic demands of the patient. This valuable concept can help explain countertransference fantasies and unethical behavior on the part of narcissistically depleted therapists and therapists with narcissistic personality disorders. In my supervisory experience, narcissistic disequilibrium problems are the most common generators of countertransference, although it is not possible to judge from supervision whether these problems defend against deeper unresolved infantile sexual conflicts.

Wolf (1985) stresses the regression of both the patient and the analyst in psychoanalytic treatment, and the defenses against this regression. The analyst regresses as a consequence of the demand for evenly hovering attention in place of customary ways of thinking and the constraint placed by the procedure on ordinary self-expression of the analyst. This can lead to what self psychologists call self-state anxiety

in the analyst. But it can also have favorable consequences, including stronger motivation to remain empathically in tune with the patient and some idealization of the patient. The latter is experienced by the patient as a confirmation of his or her unrealized potential and as a stimulus to live up to it. Thus countertransference is not necessarily pathology and can be a positive force in the treatment, leading to better cohesion of the self of the patient and, when worked through, for the analyst. Wolf (1985) claims, "The analytic process involves both participants—they both get analyzed, so to speak" (p. 282).

The interaction of the transference of the patient and the countertransference structure of the therapist is probably one of the basic and most important factors in healing through psychoanalytic psychotherapy. A parallel struggle goes on throughout the process of psychotherapy in both patient and psychotherapist. In the patient there is a struggle between the forces of resistance and the innate biological and psychological forces toward health and toward mastering neurotic conflicts. In the therapist there is a struggle arising from the stimulus of the personality and transference of the patient. A struggle occurs between the desire to understand and interpret the transference properly and the tendency to misunderstand and misinterpret the transference out of countertransference problems. The patient must fight to overcome the forces of the resistance. The therapist must struggle within to understand and master the forces of the countertransference structure, which always interfere with correct understanding of and interpretations to the patient.

These coexisting struggles are central in determining the outcome of psychotherapy. They also explain this oft-repeated remark: In every psychotherapy the therapist "learns" from the patient. The therapist expands his or her boundaries of human understanding, increases in maturity, and achieves further ego integration. Conversely, unanalyzed negative countertransference experiences over a prolonged period can produce what Wile (1972) calls "therapist discouragement," an irrational pessimism regarding one's therapeutic work and personal life. This leads to premature termination of therapy cases, even the abandonment of the profession itself, the susceptibility to new fads and shortcut active techniques, or an irrational overoptimism and overconfidence in one's powers of healing. Perhaps worst of all, "Deprived of his sense of purpose and value in what he is doing, the therapist may turn to his patient for compensatory reassurance and affirmation" (Wile 1972, p. 52).

References

Arlow, J. (1985). Some technical problems of countertransference. *Psychoanalytic Quarterly* 54:164–174.

Baum, O. (1969–1970). Countertransference. *Psychoanalytic Review* 56:621–637.

Brenner, C. (1985). Countertransference as compromise formation. *Psychoanalytic Association* 54:155–163.

Chediak, C. (1979). Counter-reactions and countertransference. *International Journal of Psycho-Analysis* 60:117–129.

Chessick, R. (1985). Psychoanalytic listening II. *American Journal of Psychotherapy* 39: 30–48.

Dewald, P. (1964). *Psychotherapy*. New York: Basic Books.

———— (1976). Transference regression and real experience in the psychoanalytic process. *Psychoanalytic Quarterly* 45: 213–230.

Greenson, R. (1978). Loving, hating, and indifference to the patient. In *Explorations in Psychoanalysis,* pp. 505–518. New York: International Universities Press.

Gunther, M. (1976). The endangered self: a contribution to the understanding of narcissistic determinants of countertransference. *Annual of Psychoanalysis* 4:201–224.

Hunt, W., and Issacharoff, A. (1977). Heinrich Racker and countertransference theory. *Journal of the American Academy of Psychoanalysis* 5:95–106.

Kernberg, O. (1975). *Borderline Conditions and Pathological Narcissism.* New York: Jason Aronson.

Kohut, H. (1971). *The Analysis of the Self.* New York: International Universities Press.

Langs, R. (1979). *The Therapeutic Environment.* New York: Jason Aronson.

Maltsberger, J., and Buie, D. (1974). Countertransference hate in the treatment of suicidal patients. *Archives of General Psychiatry* 39:625–633.

McLaughlin, J. (1981). Transference, psychic reality, and countertransference. *Psychoanalytic Quarterly* 50:639–664.

Menninger, K. (1958). *Theory of Psychoanalytic Technique.* New York: Basic Books.

Racker, H. (1968). *Transference and Countertransference.* New York: International Universities Press.

Reich, A. (1973). *Psychoanalytic Contributions.* New York: International Universities Press.

Searles, H. (1965). *Collected Papers.* New York: International Universities Press.

Singer, E. (1970). *Key Concepts in Psychotherapy.* New York: Basic Books.

Tower, L. (1956). Countertransference. *Journal of the American Psychoanalytic Association* 4:224–255.

Wile, D. (1972). Negative countertransference and therapist discouragement. *Interna-*

*tional Journal of Psychoanalysis & Psycho-
therapy* 1:36–67.

Winnicott, D. (1958). Hate in the countertransference. In *Collected Papers,* pp.
194–203. New York: Basic Books.

Wolf, E. (1985). The search for confirmation:
technical aspects of mirroring. *Psychoanalytic Inquiry* 5:271–282.

CURATIVE FANTASY

Ornstein and Ornstein (1977),
utilizing self psychology rather than
the traditional view, stress the "curative fantasy" with which the patient
begins treatment, the wish to have
the past undone and made up for.
When this is activated in the treatment, there occurs an interaction or
engagement with the therapist, and
the therapist's responses are crucial.
According to these authors, the therapist must help curative fantasies
emerge and deal with the guilt over
them, allowing them to transform
and mature. What is curative are not
primarily nonspecific "physicianly
vocation" elements in the treatment,
but the increased unfolding of archaic curative fantasies, the wish to
use the therapist as a selfobject
(Kohut 1977), and the hope for a
"new beginning" (Balint 1968). The
curative fantasy motivates the patient toward recovery out of the assumption that the treatment will
compensate for everything by
bringing power, skills, and success.

The interpretation of this fantasy
depends on one's theoretical orientation. For example, some would relate
it to infantile instinctual aims seeking
satisfaction in the transference, similar to Freud's discussion of a cure by
love. Ornstein and Ornstein, from
the point of view of self psychology,
focus on the patient's new hopes
that, due to the fear of disappointment, are defended against. This is
experienced by the analyst as "resistance." A patient may need to set up
rejecting situations, despite his or her
wish to be accepted, as a defense
against the possibility of disappointment. Attempting to get the patient
to face his or her hostility when these
fantasies are disappointed and when
projection takes place implies that
the patient is unlovable and that
something is fundamentally wrong
with the patient. Such interpretations, according to Ornstein and
Ornstein, just retraumatize the patient. The rage must be accepted as
appropriate to the patient's experienced reality, as a response to an experienced injury due to the disappointed wish for unconditional
success, acceptance, power, and
skills. For self psychologists, empathic acceptance, followed by understanding, followed by interpretation remains crucial in analytic cure
(Kohut 1984).

References

Balint, M. (1968). *The Basic Fault: Therapeutic
Aspects of Regression.* London: Tavistock.

Kohut, H. (1977). *The Restoration of the Self.*
New York: International Universities
Press.

———— (1984). *How Does Analysis Cure?* Chicago: University of Chicago Press.

Ornstein, P., and Ornstein, A. (1977). On
the continuing evolution of psychoanalytic psychotherapy: reflections and
predictions. *Annual of Psychoanalysis* 5:
329–370.

D

DASEIN

Heidegger (1962) introduced this term to represent what is characteristic about the being of humans, "being-there." This differentiates his notion of human being from previous theories that postulated some sort of fixed essence or substance or "human nature" to members of our species. Sartre (1973) popularized this by maintaining, in his famous saying, that "existence precedes essence." Heidegger insisted what was characteristic of humans was that they presented a "clearing" in which Being might present itself; it is *Dasein* that asks the question, Why is there something rather than nothing at all? At other times Heidegger (1977) speaks of *Dasein* as the "shepherd of Being," and his conceptions of it become increasingly mystical and poetic.

But Heidegger did not consider himself an existentialist. He was preoccupied with the nature of Being, and his investigation of human being (*Dasein*) was primarily for the purpose of attaining some understanding of Being. He later gave up this approach because he felt that any active investigation would defeat itself and that an attitude of passive openness is required for Being to manifest itself, a form of medita-

tive—as opposed to calculative—thinking. He claimed that certain poets, such as Hölderlin, gathered in the manifestations of Being and proclaimed "the Holy" (Richardson 1974). Existentialists ignored all this and concentrated on *Dasein* and human freedom, emphasizing that humans could make their own essence and were not born with some sort of fixed nature. Psychotherapists have not given sufficient thought to how their assumptions on this issue affect their approach to patients (Chessick 1992).

References

Chessick, R. (1992). *What Constitutes the Patient in Psychotherapy.* Northvale, NJ: Jason Aronson.

Heidegger, M. (1962). *Being and Time,* trans. by J. Macquarrie and E. Robinson. New York: Harper & Row.

———— (1977). Letter on humanism. In *Basic Writings,* ed. D. Krell, pp. 189–242. New York: Harper & Row.

Richardson, W. (1974). *Heidegger: Through Phenomenology to Thought,* 3rd ed. The Hague, Netherlands: Martinus Nijhoff.

Sartre, J-P. (1973). *Being and Nothingness,* trans. H. Barnes. New York: Washington Square Press.

DEATH INSTINCT

The first draft of *Beyond the Pleasure Principle* was completed in May

1919 by the 63-year-old Freud during a period of famine and deprivation. Although Austria was impoverished and ruined by World War I and its aftermath, Freud seemed to experience a resurgence of his creative powers. From the clinical manifestations of the repetition compulsion he evolved a biological metatheory of the life and death instincts. The death instinct was a silent force, and biological phenomena of the most diverse sort were all explained as manifestations of its striving to restore the inorganic state from which life had emerged. Life was maintained against this force by the opposing power of Eros. The death instinct was seldom invoked in a clinical context except to account for unusual states of instinctual "defusion," when destructive energies could be observed in "pure culture" (Freud 1923). In *Beyond the Pleasure Principle,* Freud (1920) delineates a certain symmetry between Eros and the death instinct but leaves the impression that the death instinct is more powerful.

Freud elaborated on the death instinct in subsequent writings (1927, 1930, 1933a,b, 1940), postulating the drive source of aggression to be the death instinct turned outwards. In *Civilization and Its Discontents,* he (1930) added the important clinical point that when the death instinct emerges without any sexual purpose "in the blindest fury of destructiveness, we cannot fail to recognize that the satisfaction of the instinct is accompanied by an extraordinarily high degree of narcissistic enjoyment, owing to its pre-senting the ego with a fulfillment of the latter's old wishes for omnipotence" (p. 121). In the same publication he switches to a different language, poetically envisioning the evolution of civilization as a result of the "battle of the giants" (p. 122), a struggle for the life of the human species between Eros and the death instinct.

Three years later, Freud (1933b) wrote, "The theory of the instincts is so to say our mythology. Instincts are mythical entities, magnificent in their indefiniteness. In our work we cannot for a moment disregard them, yet we are never sure that we are seeing them clearly" (p. 95). But here, using the language of metapsychology, Freud specifically characterizes the death instinct as primary masochism and points out that it seems to be necessary for us to destroy some other thing or person in order not to destroy ourselves, so as to guard against our primary impulse to self-destruction. In that same year Freud (1933a), now 77 years old, wrote to Einstein depicting this impulse as striving to bring every living creature to ruin and to reduce life to its original condition of inanimate matter. In his (1940) final writing on the death instinct he proposes an additional dualism, contrasting individual death, which occurs through some portion of the death instinct remaining permanently within until at length it succeeds in doing the individual to death, with the death of the species, which dies of an unsuccessful struggle against the world because it cannot adapt to external changes.

The ambiguity of Freud's concept appears in the shifting emphasis on different aspects of it. Primary masochism implies a fundamental aggressive drive component, with the destructiveness originally turned inward and actively directed against the organism itself. More mysteriously, a conservative force that wishes to bring the organism to die in its own fashion implies a less directly destructive aspect; it tones down the aggressive component and envisions a sort of magnetic force, pulling the organism to a natural disintegration and death in a quieter manner, although this may be a very powerful pull indeed. But usually it is the primary masochism aspect that is emphasized as the source of human aggression and destructiveness.

One difficulty in accepting the death instinct may be traced to Freud's (1915) contention that "our unconscious . . . does not believe in its own death" (p. 296), because we cling in our unconscious to archaic beliefs in immortality and omnipotence. Recently, however, Litman (Brooks 1988) disagreed with Freud's contention, claiming it is contradicted by the dreams of suicidal patients; furthermore, none of the presenters at a psychoanalytic meeting on this topic "conceptualized masochism as resulting from a purely instinctual need of the masochist or as a particular vicissitude of the aggressive drive" (p. 20).

In *Beyond the Pleasure Principle,* Freud (1920) defines an instinct as "an urge inherent in organic life to restore an earlier state of things" (p. 36). After reflecting rhetorically on "the mysterious masochistic trends of the ego" (p. 14), he later concludes, "It is as though the life of the organism moved with a vacillating rhythm. One group of instincts rushes forward so as to reach the final aim of life as swiftly as possible; but when a particular stage in the advance has been reached, the other group jerks back to a certain point to make a fresh start and so prolong the journey" (pp. 40–41).

A more definitive statement occurs in Section 4 of Freud's (1923) *The Ego and the Id.* Here he sometimes refers to the death instinct as a "class of instincts" (p. 40) that he calls "the death instincts" (p. 46), and he declares that sadism is the representative of the death instincts. He explains that the "death instincts are by their nature mute" (p. 46) and discusses the various clinical phenomena that appear as the two classes of instincts fuse with each other or regressively defuse. In melancholia, however, "What is now holding sway in the superego is . . . a pure culture of the death instinct" (p. 53). Finally, in *An Outline of Psychoanalysis,* Freud (1940), now 84 years old, alternately uses the term "destructive instinct" and "death instinct" to refer to the same group of basic instincts in contrast to the Eros group. He adds,

> So long as that instinct operates internally, as a death instinct, it remains silent; it only comes to our notice when it is diverted outwards as an instinct of destruction. It seems to be essential for the preservation of the individual that this diversion should occur; the muscular appa-

ratus serves this purpose. When the superego is established, considerable amounts of the aggressive instinct are fixated in the interior of the ego and operate there self-destructively. [p. 150]

Here Freud's thinking seems clear; he is thinking of the death instinct as a destructive, aggressive, sadistic assault on the organism that may be diverted outward or stored in the superego. The silent pull toward the inorganic state is deemphasized.

Yet Freud in this work also writes,

The core of our being, then, is formed by the obscure *id,* which has no direct communication with the external world and is accessible even to our own knowledge only through the medium of another agency. Within this id the organic *instincts* operate, which are themselves compounded of fusions of two primal forces (Eros and destructiveness) in varying proportions. [p. 197]

Here two mysterious primal forces again appear, which, when fused in various degrees, make up the biological instincts. Similarly, in *Analysis Terminable and Interminable,* Freud (1937) denotes the "instinct of aggression or of destruction according to its aims, and which we trace back to the original death instinct of living matter" (p. 243). In this paper he cites the Greek philosopher Empedocles and refers to Eros and the death instinct as "primal instincts," leaving it ambiguous as to whether and how the primal instincts or forces generate secondary instincts or derivatives, and implying some sort of hierarchy of instincts or forces.

This ambiguity pervades Freud's thinking, as evidenced in his (1933a) letter to Einstein in which he writes, "The death instinct turns into the destructive instinct when, with the help of special organs, it is directed outwards, onto objects" (p. 211). In this letter, Freud says the death instinct strives to reduce life to its original condition of inanimate matter; furthermore, some portion of the death instinct, even when part of it is turned outward and made into the destructive instinct, "remains operative *within* the organism" (Freud's emphasis). Freud again refers to his theory of primal instincts as "a kind of mythology" (p. 211). As Jones (1957) points out, "These principles or instincts were by now assuming something of a transcendental significance" (p. 275) for Freud. Indeed, Freud's (1937) contrast between the "cosmic phantasy" of Empedocles and his own theory claiming "biological validity" mentioned above seems to collapse.

This became an important source of error. The concept of primal instincts can only be adduced in a theoretical context since it is a metaphysical or transcendental concept; when concretized it becomes, unfortunately, akin to "vitalism" in biology (Gedo 1986). No evidence of a clinical or empirical nature could serve to either decisively establish or disprove the existence of such primal instincts, which are of a different epistemological order. Some writers have even suggested that the sudden death of one of Freud's daughters, the onset of his cancer, and the death of his favorite grandson were sources for Freud's preoccupation with the death instinct, but it has been established that *Beyond the Pleasure Principle* was drafted in 1919, several months before the first of these events and four years before the other two (Gay 1988, Jones 1957). Still, as Gay (p. 395) points out, the term "death drive" entered his correspondence a week after the death of his daughter. Surely these events influenced Freud's elevation of the death instinct to a primal force and his coming to regard it as a "fact."

It is often overlooked that the theory of the primal instincts, as Bibring (1941) explains, was founded on an essentially changed concept of instinct:

> According to it, instinct was not a tension of energy which impinged upon the mental sphere, which arose from an organic source and which aimed at removing a state of excitation in the organ from which it originated. It was a directive or directed "something" which guided the life processes in a certain direction. The accent was no longer upon the production of energy but only upon the function of determining a direction. [p. 128]

What results is an ambiguous and vague concept of "the death instincts which seek to cancel out tensions, the instincts of destruction at work within, aggressiveness directed outwards, the trend toward a state of rest (the Nirvana principle) and the inclination to suffer" (pp. 129–130) all forming a related group, in contrast to the life instincts.

As I have discussed in detail elsewhere (see Chessick 1992), by the death instinct concept Freud was trying to link the tendency toward the reduction of tension within the organism, masochistic and sadistic clinical phenomena, the repetition compulsion, the conservative trend toward a state of rest, sleep, and death, the amazing inclination for suffering and self-destruction seen in severe melancholias, and perhaps his own personal agonies (cancer and the loss of his loved ones). It was conceived during the European self-destructive horror of World War I and its aftermath that brought nineteenth-century optimism to an end, as Nietzsche had predicted. In fact, there is a distinct echo of Nietzsche to be found in Freud's (1919) paper on "The 'Uncanny,'" published in the year he drafted *Beyond the Pleasure Principle,* in which he refers to "the constant recurrence of the same thing" (p. 234) and the "daemonic character" (p. 238) of certain aspects of the mind.

References

Bibring, E. (1941). The development and problems of the theory of the instincts. *International Journal of Psycho-Analysis* 22:102–131.

Brooks, R. (1988). Report on scientific meeting "Masochism: Current Considerations." *Bulletin of the Southern California Psychoanalytic Institute and Society* 80:19–20.

Chessick, R. (1992). The death instinct revisited. *Journal of the American Academy of Psychoanalysis* 20:3–28.

Freud, S. (1915). Thoughts for the times on war and death. *Standard Edition* 14:273–302.

_____ (1919). The 'uncanny.' *Standard Edition* 17:217–256.

_____ (1920). Beyond the pleasure principle. *Standard Edition* 18:3–64.

_____ (1923). The ego and the id. *Standard Edition* 19:3–66.

_____ (1927). The future of an illusion. *Standard Edition* 21:5–56.

_____ (1930). Civilization and its discontents. *Standard Edition* 21:59–145.

_____ (1933a). Why war? *Standard Edition* 22:197–215.

_____ (1933b). New introductory lectures on psychoanalysis. Ch. 32. *Standard Edition* 22:81–111.

_____ (1937). Analysis terminable and interminable. *Standard Edition* 23:209–253.

_____ (1940). An outline of psychoanalysis. *Standard Edition* 23:141–207.

Gay, P. (1988). *Freud: A Life for Our Time.* New York: Norton.

Gedo, J. (1986). *Conceptual Issues in Psychoanalysis: Essays in History and Method.* Hillsdale, NJ: Analytic Press.

Jones, E. (1957). *The Life and Work of Sigmund Freud 1919–1939: The Last Phase.* New York: Basic Books.

DEFENSE, DEFENSE MECHANISMS (SEE EGO)

DEFUSION

In classical psychoanalytic metapsychology the energy of the aggressive instinct is fused with that of the sexual instinct to provide neutralized energy the ego uses for its purposes, such as operating the mechanisms of defense. When an individual regresses, this unification, fusion, and organization crumble. The result is a freedom of the destructive and sexual instincts in their raw or archaic form, which often leads the patient into trouble. According to the structural theory, defused or "neutralized" energy is also used by the superego. The notion of fusion and defusion of instincts has a wide variety of clinical applications in traditional psychoanalytic metapsychological theory. Details may be found in Nagera (1970).

Reference

Nagera, H. (1970). *Basic Psychoanalytic Concepts on the Theory of Instincts.* New York: Basic Books.

DENIAL, DISAVOWAL, NEGATION

"Denial" is a defense mechanism used by the ego to vitiate a painful experience or aspect of the self. In Kleinian theory it is often followed by splitting and projection, which reinforce the denial. A denial of psychic reality may also be found in the classical Kleinian notion of a manic defense against depressive feelings. Denial is different from negation in that in the latter the perception is still present and experienced but accompanied by an assertion of its negative.

Denial operates unconsciously to resolve emotional conflict and remove the anxiety signal by a mechanism of disavowing those thoughts, feelings, wishes, needs, or reality factors that would otherwise be intolerable to the conscious mind of the individual. Disavowal and denial are often used interchangeably and as translations of the term *Verleugnung.* The use of disavowal was emphasized first in Freud's concept of the little boy's "denial," even after he sees a naked girl, that there are any people who have no penis. Later he (1927) used disavowal especially to understand the case of fetishism. In a very late paper, he (1940a) introduced the notion of a splitting of the ego in order to cast a clearer light on the concept of disavowal. This is also mentioned in his (1940b) final unfinished work.

Nicholson-Smith (1973), in a translator's note, points out that although *Verleugnung* is still widely translated as "denial," he has followed the recommendations of the editors of the *Standard Edition* and has used "disavowal" to resolve an ambiguity in these words (p. 120). Regardless of the semantic details, the importance of denial or disavowal in clinical work is paramount. I am inclined to use denial as an unconscious mechanism, while disavowal has more of a preconscious quality in my clinical thinking and can be more easily brought to the patient's consciousness. This is consistent with Kohut's (1971) notion of a "vertical split" (see SELF PSYCHOLOGY), which I believe is also a form of disavowal. Negation, on the other hand, is a conscious statement of a perception accompanied by a negative term. Thus, for example, a patient claims, "I absolutely never had any wish to see my sister naked."

References

Freud, S. (1927). Fetishism. *Standard Edition* 21:149–157.
———— (1940a). Splitting of the ego in the process of defense. *Standard Edition* 23:271–278.
———— (1940b). An outline of psychoanalysis. *Standard Edition* 23:141–207.
Kohut, H. (1971). *The Analysis of the Self.* New York: International Universities Press.
Nicholson-Smith, D. (1973). Translator's note. In *The Language of Psychoanalysis,* by J. Laplanche and J. Pontalis, p. 120. New York: Norton.

DEPRESSION

It is interesting that the psychological sense of this word is not given in Samuel Johnson's dictionary. In psychiatry depression can be either an emotional state or a diagnosis; the current usage, characteristics, and classifications are listed in *DSM-III-R*. The classical psychoanalytic attempt to understand depression was made by Freud (1917) in "Mourning and Melancholia." It should be kept in mind that in that paper Freud explained he was attempting to understand only a limited subgroup of patients with manifestations of depression. He left room for other varieties, as well as for the possibility of depressions on an organic or biochemical basis.

Any psychotherapist confronted by significant depression today has the obligation to assess the patient for antidepressant medication. This is a malpractice issue, but the psychotherapist should not feel that the use of antidepressant medication is mandatory. Judicious use of medication in this situation is required, as in any medical condition. Psychotherapists who are not thoroughly conversant with the large variety of antidepressant medications on the market, or who have no medical training that would enable them to deal with the side effects of these medications, should *not* take the responsibility of administering them. In my clinical experience there is a substantial qualitative and quantitative difference between the kind of depression one sees in neurotic outpatients and the deep melancholias that are treated in hospitals.

Freud's viewpoint was that depression arises when an ambivalently loved object is lost. The loved part of the object is introjected into the superego and the hated part into the ego; the superego then chastises the ego and the individual feels the emotional experience of melancholia. Moore and Fine (1990) view the breakdown of the regulation of self-esteem as perhaps a universal feature in depression. This may result from "loss of an object by death, hurt, neglect, or disappointment. Other causes include disillusionment over an idealized cause, failure to live up to ego ideals, or a sense of helplessness and powerlessness in the face of insurmountable odds" (p. 53). One sees from this current official psychoanalytic definition the considerable shift from and enlargement of the early formulations of depression and the emphasis on preexisting narcissism or narcissistic disorders.

There is a vast literature on depression. For example, Jacobson (1971) claims that aggression is a crucial result of the infant's experience of helplessness. She views ambivalence as arising from this and sees it as central to the predisposition to depression. The lack of the moth-

er's empathy, she explains, lowers the child's self-esteem and produces aggressive conflicts. Frustration leads to rage, which leads to aggressive attempts to gain gratification. When this fails, aggression is turned toward the self-image, with the resultant loss of self-esteem, a conflict between the wishful self and the failing, depleted self. This leads to the mood expressed in depression, an intersystemic conflict whose severity depends on the intensity of the hostility and the severity and duration of disappointment.

Milrod (1988) views the simplest depression as arising from a narcissistic injury in which there is a gap between the view of the self and the image of what one wishes to be. The self representation falls to critical levels below the wished-for self-image. Narcissistic supplies from the ego are cut off, and libidinal cathexis of the self representation is replaced by a hostile cathexis, instigated by the self-critical function of the ego: "I am a failure." In a second type of depression, as described by Milrod, the self representation falls short of ethical values. Here there is guilt, and the superego cuts off libidinal cathexis and replaces it with a hostile cathexis of the self representation. Depression results if it becomes a mood state: "I am bad and deserve to be punished." This is intersystemic, in contrast to the former type of depression Milrod describes, which is intrasystemic.

In formulating a third type of depression, Milrod says that the ambivalently loved object is a source of narcissistic supply and is essential to the individual. Loss of this object or its love precipitates the depression. Milrod argues that so-called morality in depression is restitutive and not fundamental and disagrees with Brenner's (1982) view of depression as a basic affect. For Brenner, depression is a signal, whereas for Milrod, it emerges out of conflict and is not a signal. Instead, the diminished sense of self-worth is fundamental. Depression follows a narcissistic blow, which, if it evolves to a mood state, can be a clinical problem. If it does not evolve, it is felt as self-criticism, which can be constructive. Aggression lies beneath all depressive states. Such depressive states can be defended against by self-hate, denial, projection, elation, obsessional activity to bind the hostility, obsessional character formation, self-pity, and a veering of aggression off to the world, giving the patient a paranoid flavor.

Davis (1976) wisely refers to Bibring's (1953) concept of the state of helplessness as the starting point in depression. This helplessness is from the ego's sense of powerlessness and failure against superior powers and of being doomed to the "inescapable fate of being lonely, isolated, or unloved" (p. 23). There is an affect of emptiness like hunger, due to a narcissistic wound. An inner pressure to work and fight on prevails, although the patient would rather rest passively; the patient must live up to the demands of strongly held narcissistic aspirations. Davis deemphasizes the role of anger and focuses on a rapid and sudden narcissistic wounding as most causative in depression.

Stone (1986) emphasizes the preeminent importance of an archaic characterologic core in depression manifesting pathological narcissism, ambivalent morality, and a sadistic superego. Depression is frequently precipitated by a narcissistic wound in a patient who has a rigid ego-ideal and cannot modify his or her goals or give them up. The patient cannot adapt to failure without disastrous loss of self-esteem. There is a rigid maladaptive pursuit of certain goals due not only to the ego-ideal but to narcissistic aggressive components in the original ambitious thrust, which adds an obstinate and uncompromising quality to the patient's activities. All these factors operate synergistically along with an oral aggressive impatience, a narcissistic grandiose self, a sensitivity to criticism, an undue readiness for severe disappointment, and an unbridgeable gulf between the acceptance of defeat and reality.

References

Bibring, E. (1953). The mechanism of depression. In *Affective Disorders: Psychoanalytic Contributions to Their Study,* ed. P. Greenacre, pp. 13-48. New York: International Universities Press.

Brenner, C. (1982). *The Mind in Conflict.* New York: International Universities Press.

Davis, G. (1976). Depression: some updated thoughts. *Journal of the American Academy of Psychoanalysis* 4:411–424.

Freud, S. (1917). Mourning and melancholia. *Standard Edition* 14:237–258.

Jacobson, E. (1971). *Depression.* New York: International Universities Press.

Milrod, D. (1988). A current view of the psychoanalytic theory of depression. *Psychoanalytic Study of the Child* 43:83–99. New Haven, CT: Yale University Press.

Moore, B., and Fine, B. (1990). *Psychoanalytic*

Terms and Concepts. New Haven, CT: Yale University Press.

Stone, L. (1986). Psychoanalytic observations on the pathology of depressive illness: selected spheres of ambiguity or disagreement. *Journal of the American Psychoanalytic Association* 34:329–362.

DEPRESSIVE POSITION

This term is included here to differentiate it from "depression," with which it is often confused. A thorough treatment of it may be found in Hinshelwood (1989). Briefly, according to Melanie Klein (1975), this position is reached around the fourth month of life and is gradually overcome in the course of the first year, although it may recur at any time when losses occur. It is ushered in by the development of the cognitive capacity of the infant to perceive the mother as a whole object, making it harder to split and project parts of the mother or to incorporate projected parts once more, as is characteristic of the earlier or "paranoid" position. Libidinal and hostile instincts are now focused on the same object, leading to depressive anxiety caused by the possibility of the infant annihilating and destroying the mother as a result of sadistic impulses toward her. Various defenses are constructed against this anxiety, according to Klein, either manic defenses or the deflection or inhibition of the sadism.

Later in life, when there are inevitable object losses, this depressive anxiety is reactivated and the depressive position is worked through once more. According to Klein, this may lead to either a failure in working through and a regression back to the paranoid position (see KLEIN) or a successful reworking with even maturation and improvement in the individual's functioning. The classic paper in which Melanie Klein outlined the depressive position may be found in her (1975) collected writings, originally published in 1935. The best introduction to the work of Klein may be found in Segal (1974); a more general introduction to the life and work of Melanie Klein by Segal (1979) is also useful. Grosskurth (1986) has provided a readable biography, and Petot (1990, 1991) offers a detailed advanced study of the development of her controversial concepts and theories.

References

Grosskurth, P. (1986). *Melanie Klein: Her World and Her Work.* New York: Knopf.

Hinshelwood, R. (1989). *A Dictionary of Kleinian Thought.* London: Free Association Books.

Klein, M. (1975). *The Writings of Melanie Klein,* vol. 1. London: Hogarth Press.

Petot, J. (1990). *Melanie Klein. Volume 1: First Discoveries and First System, 1919–1932.* Madison, CT: International Universities Press.

—— (1991). *Melanie Klein. Volume 2: The Ego and the Good Object, 1932–1960.* Madison, CT: International Universities Press.

Segal, H. (1974). *Introduction to the Work of Melanie Klein.* New York: Basic Books.

—— (1979). *Melanie Klein.* New York: Viking.

DESIRE

In contrast to the simple definition by Samuel Johnson (1773) of "desire" as an "eagerness to obtain or enjoy," this term in the hands of Hegel and subsequently Lacan attained considerable importance. Johnson quotes John Locke as saying, "*Desire* is the uneasiness a man finds in himself upon the absence of any thing, whose present enjoyment carries the idea of delight with it" (p. 520).

It is in Hegel's (1807) original conception of the evolution of self-consciousness that we come across the more modern technical concept of the desiring mind. In Hegel's view, "To desire something is to wish to possess it—and thus not to destroy it altogether—but also to transform it into something that is yours, and thus to strip it of its foreignness" (Singer 1983, p. 57). For Hegel, self-consciousness cannot exist in isolation and needs an object from which to differentiate itself. Desire arises because self-consciousness needs an external object; thus desire is an unsatisfactory state for self-consciousness. Self-consciousness is doomed to be permanently unsatisfied and its object, according to Hegel, must be another self-consciousness. In language that is not technical, this is a way of saying that in order to see oneself, one needs a mirror. Furthermore, Hegel contends that self-consciousness requires the context of social interaction and could never develop in a child growing up in total isolation. Whether this explication is what Hegel had in mind in his murky prose remains controversial in the literature; what is significant is that the intimate relationship between one's self-consciousness and that self-consciousness of the other is at the center of the definition of the desire that was adopted by Lacan (1977). Even Ricoeur (1940) relabeled Freud's psychoanalysis as the "semantics of desire."

Lacanians (see LACAN) think of desire as arising from the primordial "demand of the brute," when the separation from the mother occurs and human self-consciousness develops. For Lacanians, desire is to be the desired of the other, a rough approximation of what Hegel had in mind in his discussion of the evolution of self-consciousness. Since initially the infant subject wishes to be the object of the mother's desire, Lacan uses the phallus as the signifier of that basic desire that arises out of the primary split between mother and infant: "In order to insure himself of his mother's presence and her complete affective support, the child unconsciously seeks to be that which can best gratify her. He seeks to make himself exclusively indispensable" (Lemaire 1977, p. 87).

References

Hegel, G. (1807). *Phenomenology of Spirit,* trans. A. Miller. Oxford, England: Clarendon Press, 1977.

Johnson, S. (1773). *A Dictionary of the English Language.* Beirut, Lebanon: Librairie du Liban, 1978.

Lacan, J. (1977). *Écrits: A Selection,* trans. A. Sheridan. New York: Norton.

Lemaire, A. (1977). *Jacques Lacan,* trans. D. Macey. London: Routledge & Kegan Paul.

Ricoeur, P. (1940). *Freud and Philosophy.* New Haven, CT: Yale University Press.

Singer, P. (1983). *Hegel.* New York: Oxford University Press.

DIALOGUE, DIALOGISM (BAKHTIN)

Holquist (1990) claims that Bakhtin (1895–1975) never used the term "dialogism," but this master thinker, who led a harsh life under the Soviet system, continued in spite of it all to think and rethink the nature of dialogue. For him the self and the other exist not as separate entities but in a dialogic relationship at a particular moment in space and time, a sort of relativistic self-psychology. As illustrated best in Dostoevsky's novels, he believed, the self is a triad: a center, a not-center, and the relation between them. Similarly, a dialogue is composed of an utterance, a reply, and the relation between the two. The latter is the most important, because without it the utterance and the reply would have no meaning. This makes the self of the analyst of coequal importance in determining the meaning and shape of the dialogue with the patient, and even in determining the "self" of the patient as it is experienced by the analyst, and vice versa.

An important issue is presented by the noted Bakhtin scholar Todorov (1992): whether human existence is or is not originally social and whether or not it can be reduced to its biological dimension without being deprived of the characteristics that make it human. Bakhtin (1989), in his "dialogism" theory takes an extreme view in which he sees the human personality as entirely produced by the social whole. When To-

dorov says that Bakhtin (contrary to Freud) conceives of the unconscious as not preceding language, he is stating the same thesis as that held by Lacan.

Another crucial issue in Todorov's review of Bakhtin's theories is whether the "utterances" (as Bakhtin calls them, to emphasize the social nature of discourse) that constitute the transference in the psychoanalytic dialogue are a product of the present and current situation between therapist and patient or whether the transference, as Arlow (1985) in the extreme opposite view would say, is the attempt on the part of the patient to impose a reenactment of an infantile fantasy on the patient–analyst relationship. My position is that it is probably a varying combination of both depending on the patient, the analyst, and the phase of analysis they are in, and that would separate my view from the view of Bakhtin.

Todorov says that according to Bakhtin, the psychological approaches of Dostoevsky and Freud are incompatible. I do not know whether Bakhtin actually believed this or not, but Freud (1929) recognized Dostoevsky to be the great psychologist he certainly was, and in rereading his two major novels (1990, 1992) one certainly can become even more directly aware, especially in the wonderful, newly available translations, of Dostoevsky's capacity to plumb the psychological depths of his characters. Freud did not like Dostoevsky personally (he said he had enough of neurotics in his consulting room) and he disagreed with Dostoevsky's moral solutions, but he recognized Dostoevsky's creative genius and deep intuitive insight into neurotics and character disorders.

If Bakhtin says, as Todorov (1992) insists, "At the bottom of man we find not the Id but the other," (p. 33), many psychoanalysts would respond that we cannot separate the Id from the other, thus holding a kind of intermediate position not so far from Klein. Klein pointed out over and over again that the infant's aggressive drives were projected and then reintrojected, so that there occurs quickly in life a continual intrapsychic confusion between what constitutes the original aggressive drives and what constitutes the projected and reintrojected object representations. This poses a problem that one encounters clinically all the time and that I find quite baffling, to the point where I have ceased to attempt to separate out the archaic persecutory object representations from the archaic drives. Indeed, Freud's "drive theory" has few adherents today.

It is certainly true as Todorov (pp. 41–43) quotes Bakhtin that utterances are different than propositions because utterances are in the context always of an interpersonal relationship. There is nothing really new in this, but here again Bakhtin's naivete is showing because he says in this quote that, "Discourse is oriented toward the person addressed, oriented toward what that person is." Discourse is certainly oriented toward the person addressed, but perhaps it is better to say it is oriented toward what one has as a representation of the person addressed, and this representation comes from the life history and compromise formations of the individual who is producing the utterance or discourse. Understanding this would give depth to Bakhtin's increasingly popular but ambiguous theories. The crucial premise of his "dialogism" theory, that every utterance is also related to previous utterances, creating intertextual or dialogical relations, is very important. But how is this much different than Lacan's concept of language he borrowed from Saussure?

Bakhtin's later work seems to become increasingly vague and metaphysical (see Holquist 1990 for details). It is certainly astute, and perhaps Bakhtin gets the credit for having first articulated it, to say that the intonation, affective tonality, and values of the parents give rise to the words and forms that constitute the first images in the mind of the child. But it is another thing to say that, "life by its very nature is dialogic" (Bakhtin 1989, p. 293). Booth points out in his introduction (p. xxi) to Bakhtin's (1989) book that there is disagreement about the extent to which Bakhtin's unsystematic system is religious or metaphysical. His tendency to think away from the concept of private or autonomous individuality to the extreme of an essentially irreducible multi-centeredness or "polyphony" of human life is valuable, but it leaves the question of whether there is anything else that constitutes the human beside the cultural forces. The fact that humans are not isolated countable units does not necessarily imply that they are nothing but products of the collective, a concept that Marxist-Leninists held, but which was not even held by the early Marx (1963), who believed that although man was a species-being as Feuerbach claimed, there were certain aspects that were universally and essentially human besides what is formed by the culture.

I do not agree with the extreme postmodernist or even deconstructionist positions, but hold a more moderate view in between the Cartesian and the Bakhtin view of the subject. At least this is what I gather about Bakhtin's view after wading through what the translator (Bakhtin 1989) of his work calls "the repetitiousness, disorganization, and reliance on neologisms" (p. xxvi). But it is valuable also to emphasize the translator's comment, "Two speakers must not, and never do, completely understand each other; they must remain only partially satisfied with each other's replies, because the continuation of dialogue is in large part dependent on neither party knowing exactly what the other means" (p. xxxii). This certainly has application to our work. Schafer (1992) has emphasized Bakhtin's dialogism in his approach to psychoanalytic theory.

I will not discuss Bakhtin's actual analysis of Dostoevsky except to disagree with him on two major points. First, I do not think Dostoevsky has generated a whole new form of the novel, which according to Bakhtin, was equaled only by Dante. Bakhtin's description of Dostoevsky's work as polyphonic (allowing the characters to stand independently against the author), and his emphasis on the constant appearance of doubles and interior dialogue in which characters examine each other and in a sense have an equal representation with that of the author is accurate, but is that new in literature? Can we not find, for example, the same genius in Shakespeare? What about the famous soliloquies? Some scholars even present arguments that Homer's *Odyssey* represents a tale of self-exploration and self-development. The difference, of course, as Bakhtin says, is that in real life there is no resolution at the end and the truth about an individual remains polyphonic and unintegrated. Is this not similar to Lacan? How would one apply this to the work of psychoanalysis? Could an argument be made that the reason no resolution takes place in many of Dostoevsky's most important characters is because they remain neurotic to the very end? In this sense Dostoevsky is being true to reality in portraying a whole variety of neurotics as he does in his incomparable fashion, but is it wise to extrapolate this to all humans?

My second disagreement is with Bakhtin's (1989) insistence that "there is no causality in Dostoevsky's novels, no genesis, no explanations based on the past, on the influences of the environment or of upbringing, and so forth. Every act a character commits is in the present, and in this sense is not predetermined; it is conceived of and represented by the author as free" (p.

29). This is wrong. In the new translations there are innumerable passages in which Dostoevsky discusses causality and the role of the environment, as well as temperament or what today would be called the organic or biological genetic background of the individual. The whole centerpiece of *The Brothers Karamazov* rests on the famous Karamazov extremes of passion which are present in their own unique way in each of the characters! Even the villagers are made to comment on this problematic "Karamazov temperament" which is Dostoevsky's way of portraying the internal struggle that the ego must constantly endure among its three harsh masters as vividly described later in metapsychological terms by Freud (1929). Each person solves this struggle continuously and in their own unique way; some solutions are seriously maladaptive (neurotic) and some are creative or socially valuable. Most are neither.

References

Arlow, J. (1985). The concept of psychic reality and related problems. *Journal of the American Psychoanalytic Association* 33:521–535.

Bakhtin, M. (1989). *Problems of Dostoevsky's Poetics,* ed. C. Emerson. Minneapolis: University of Minnesota Press.

Dostoevsky, F. (1990). *The Brothers Karamazov,* trans. R. Pevear and L. Volokhonsky. New York: Vintage Books.

_____ (1992). *Crime and Punishment,* trans. R. Pevear and L. Volokhonsky. New York: Vintage Books.

Freud, S. (1929). Dostoevsky and parricide. *Standard Edition* 21:175–196.

_____ (1933). New introductory lectures on psycho-analysis. *Standard Edition* 22: 57–80.

Holquist, M. (1990). *Dialogism: Bakhtin and His World.* New York: Routledge.

Kohut, H. (1978). *The Search for the Self.* New York: International Universities Press.

Marx, K. (1963). *Early Writing.* New York: McGraw-Hill.

Schafer, R. (1992). *Retelling A Life: Narration and Dialogue in Psychoanalysis.* New York: Basic Books.

Todorov, T. (1992). *Michail Bakhtin: The Dialogical Principle,* trans. W. Godzich. Minneapolis: University of Minnesota Press.

DIRECT ANALYSIS

Rosen (1953) borrowed this term from Federn (1952) to describe his remarkable but now largely forgotten technique of intensive psychotherapy of schizophrenic patients. He contended that many times in the treatment of such patients his unconscious knew more than he did as the therapist, so he simply let it lead him wherever necessary. His crucial technique of treatment was to view the therapist as a loving, omnipotent protector and provider for the patient, since the patient is under heavy psychic threat and, according to Rosen, has for the most part become an infant. Rosen believed that this catastrophic collapse was due to unconsciously malevolent mothering received by the patient; the antidote was thus benevolent mothering. He postulated that the unconscious of the infant is cognizant of whether or not the mother has an unconscious that makes it possible for her to be benevolent. This theory is very important and has many ramifications for psychotherapy. For example, Nacht (1988) stated, "What matters is what the analyst is rather than what he says" (p. 106). (See Nacht [1962] for a further discussion).

In Rosen's technique the therapist begins by trying to convince the patient that he or she is trying to help and understand, and actually wishes to give the patient what the patient cannot get alone—benevolent mothering. The therapist must have the deepest possible knowledge of the unconscious and must be thoroughly psychoanalyzed. Rosen himself put in ten hours a day for two months and another four hours a day for seven months with one schizophrenic patient. He argued that the definition of recovery is not simply living outside an institution but achieving enough emotional maturity to withstand the ordinary blows of life. Rosen used a variety of shocking behaviors with the patient, as well as shocking statements, in an effort to "shake things up," that is, to draw attention from the patient's interior preoccupations. In cases that had reached a standstill he even tried to initiate important therapeutic movement forward or backward by finding some sort of wedge into the psychosis by taking control of the patient literally, including at times wrestling the patient to the ground.

Rosen's treatment procedures were observed by a number of first-rate psychiatrists who were quite impressed by them. Later it became apparent that the improvement Rosen dramatically obtained did not prove to be lasting; however, what Rosen did demonstrate is that even the most regressed and deteriorated schizophrenic patients may be reached and may respond to intensive psychotherapeutic treatment administered by a thoroughly psychoanalyzed therapist.

References

Federn, P. (1952). *Ego Psychology and the Psychoses.* New York: Basic Books.

Nacht, S. (1962). The curative factors in psychoanalysis. *International Journal of Psycho-Analysis* 43:206–211.

_____ (1988). Symposium on essentials of psychoanalytic cure. M. Osman, and N. Tabachnick, reporters. *Psychoanalytic Review* 75:185–215.

Rosen, J. (1953). *Direct Analysis.* New York: Grune & Stratton.

DREAMS

Although Freud considered dreams to be the "royal road to the unconscious," there is considerable debate and discussion about the meaning of dreams, and differing opinions over the use of dream analysis in psychotherapy and psychoanalysis even today. We know that dreaming is a normal universal phenomenon, and considerable research indicates that rapid eye movements (REMs) in certain stages of sleep accompany dreaming. This research tells us that about 50 percent of the night sleep of an infant is occupied by REM sleep and dreaming, but this percentage diminishes in adulthood to about 20 minutes out of every 90 spent sleeping.

The great classic that opened the door to the introduction of dreams into psychiatric treatment was of course by Freud (1900), with some emendations in later papers (Freud 1901, 1917). Freud divided the dream into the manifest content as it was related by the patient and the latent content, which consisted of the urge to fulfill a wish and its mental representation. A dream therefore needed to be interpreted in depth from the manifest content down to an articulation of the wish that was fulfilled in the dream in a disguised or distorted fashion. This disguise Freud labeled the dream work, characterized by displacement, condensation, substitution with the use of symbols, and a secondary elaboration in which the dream was linked together in some sort of story or action. Displacement and condensation are generally considered the most important aspects of the dream work. Freud labeled the precipitating stimulus to the dream as the day residue, elements from daily life that stirred up through derivative connections certain unconscious wishes or thoughts in the dreamer that press up for expression. These erotic and aggressive infantile drives are expressed in a disguised way and discharged through that expression, thus enabling the dreamer to continue to sleep. As Freud pointed out, the function of the dream is to permit sleep to continue.

Freud's (1900) original work on the interpretation of dreams was preoccupied primarily with demonstrations and illustrations of how the manifest content of the dream through free association can be decoded to reveal the latent content, the unconscious infantile dream wishes that are expressed (see FREE ASSO-CIATION). The dreams that Freud used as examples are mostly his own, which carried the problem that Freud did not always properly interpret his own dreams, and in some instances refused to carry the interpretation past a certain limit because of personal reticence. There has been a vast literature (Grinstein 1980) on Freud's dreams as they are revealed in his master work. Psychoanalysts eagerly picked up Freud's dream interpretation technique and in the early days of the discipline spent a great deal of time analyzing their patients' dreams and the dreams of each other. This mutual dream analyzing among pioneer psychoanalysts led to considerable hostility at times.

Sharpe (1951) wrote a classic monograph in 1937 illustrating the standard use of dreams in psychoanalytic practice in the first quarter of the twentieth century. It is a thorough review, although it contributes little that is new. French and Fromm (1964) presented quite a radical approach to dream interpretation, in which they concentrated on the reactive motive to the infantile wish. They believed that the thought processes behind dreams are rational and were more interested in why the infantile wish was disturbing to the dreamer than in the wish itself. Their work represented a transition, focusing more on ego functions as they are revealed in dream analysis than on the nature of the id wishes themselves. These authors recognized that every dream has many meanings, but, they pointed out, each dream rests on a focal conflict along with other "subfocal" conflicts. The focal conflict is the most cathected meaning. These conflicts are interpersonal and involve adaptation, but the current conflicts over interpersonal adaptations are derivatives of the past. Using a theory of thought processes that has not been accepted, the authors concluded with a focus on the patient's ego.

Altman (1969) gives an excellent review of the use of dream interpretation in classical psychoanalysis with many examples and comments about technique. His book, he says, is for trained analysts, but it illustrates the extraordinary selectivity that is used in the interpretation of dreams, even in psychoanalysis. Rothstein (1987) presents a current collection of arguments about dream interpretation. One of the issues that is unresolved deals with the so-called self-state dream of Kohut in self psychology. All of the authors in Rothstein's work disagree with Kohut on self-state dreams, which I will now discuss.

Kohut's (1977) self psychology emphasizes "disintegration anxiety," which typically occurs as a result of the failure of a selfobject to live up to demands, severe narcissistic wounding, or the danger of uncontrolled regression in intensive psychotherapy (see SELF PSYCHOLOGY). It is clinically different in both dreams and experienced phenomena from the classical signal anxiety in Freud's structural theory, which is based on castration fear or fear of separation. It is not related to the fear of the loss of love, but rather to the fear of disintegration of the sense of self (see FRAG-MENTATION), which would essentially result in a psychosis in consequence of the loss of an intense archaic enmeshment with the selfobject. It is vague, cannot be pinned down by clinical questioning, cannot be expressed in detail, and is not attached to any one situation.

In self-state dreams (Kohut 1977), which announce such anxiety, associations lead nowhere. The analyst should not challenge the patient's explanations of this anxiety (a different approach from that taken with classical castration anxiety) as these provide a tension-reducing intellectual structure. Instead of fault-finding or arguing with the patient's explanations, it is best to concentrate on finding the narcissistic wound that touched off the anxiety and then explaining the sequence to the patient.

The self-state dream has been the target of strong disapproval by some critics of self psychology. Kohut (Lichtenberg and Kaplan 1983) attempts to directly address this problem, which arose out of a misunderstanding of a short passage from *The Restoration of the Self* (Kohut 1977, pp. 109–110). It is not true that such dreams are interpreted only from the manifest contents. Associations are not ignored. Kohut points out that the clue to the self-state dream is that associations lead nowhere: "At best they provide us with further imagery that remains on the same level as the manifest content of the dream" (Lichtenberg and Kaplan 1983, p. 402). It is most critical that the analyst's understanding of the state of the patient's self, as depicted in the imagery of self-state dreams, be accurate because "only when an analysand feels that the state of his self has been accurately understood by the selfobject analyst will he feel sufficiently secure to go further" (p. 406). Pressing the patient for further associations in order to emerge with dynamic-genetic conflict-based interpretations will be experienced by the patient as an empathic failure and will generate rage and "resistances." Kohut does admit that most dreams are not self-state (p. 404) and must be pursued in the traditional way.

It should be noted that some biological psychiatrists currently dispute Freud's entire theory of the function of dreams and substitute for it various versions of a neurophysiological discharge theory. This view began with Aristotle.

In my clinical experience the best approach to dreams in psychotherapy is a function of the amount of time that is available in the treatment and the length of the dream. In a psychoanalysis, a short dream lends itself to the flow of free associations and a rather thorough analysis of wherever they lead; in an intermittent, once-weekly psychotherapy, a long dream may not be able to be studied, except in a most superficial manner. The psychotherapist should always be aware that the presentation of a long dream that takes up much of a session can be a defensive maneuver by the patient's unconscious to preempt the time and make discussion of serious current issues impossible.

In general, it is wise to follow the lead of the patient's associations after telling a dream and to fit the dream material with whatever is the current transference situation in the treatment. It is especially prudent to avoid interpretations based on the use of symbols, which often sounds to the patient like a form of quackery or popular psychology. Most interpretations offered by patients of their own dreams should be viewed with suspicion, but it is important to take them seriously and not humiliate the patients by ignoring them. Certainly some dreams do seem to be representative of the patient's state of impending disintegration, and as such are a warning and a cry for help.

The art of dream interpretation and its proper use in intensive psychotherapy or psychoanalysis is one of the most important crafts that the psychotherapist has to learn; it requires a thorough capacity on the part of the therapist to analyze his or her own dreams as a consequence of a successful psychoanalysis. An excellent review of the classical psychoanalytic theory of dreams may be found in Nagera (1969).

References

Altman, L. (1969). *The Dream in Psychoanalysis.* New York: International Universities Press.

French, T., and Fromm, E. (1964). *Dream Interpretation.* New York: Basic Books.

Freud, S. (1900). The interpretation of dreams. *Standard Edition* 4,5:1–627.

_____ (1901). On dreams. *Standard Edition* 5:630–686.

_____ (1917). A metapsychological supplement to the theory of dreams. *Standard Edition* 14:217–235.

Grinstein, A. (1980). *Sigmund Freud's Dreams.* New York: International Universities Press.

Kohut, H. (1977). *The Restoration of the Self.* New York: International Universities Press.

Lichtenberg, J., and Kaplan, S., eds. (1983). *Reflections on Self Psychology.* Hillsdale, NJ: Analytic Press.

Nagera, H. (1969). *Basic Psychoanalytic Concepts on the Theory of Dreams.* New York: Basic Books.

Rothstein, A., ed. (1987). *The Interpretation of Dreams in Clinical Work.* Madison, CT: International Universities Press.

Sharpe, E. (1951). *Dream Analysis: A Practical Handbook for Psycho-Analysts.* London: Hogarth Press.

DRIVE (SEE ALSO DEATH INSTINCT)

This term was sometimes used in place of "instinct" in psychoanalytic theory because "instinct" in biology implies a genetic sequence of behavior that is triggered by certain stimuli. It stands on the border of the somatic and the psychic; the biological needs of the organism generate certain tensions for discharge, which are reflected on the psychological level by mental representations in the unconscious. Freud's term *Trieb* was translated by Strachey in the *Standard Edition* of Freud's work, however, as "instinct," and no useful purpose is served to try to distinguish between instinct and drive in psychoanalytic theory as Freud presented it. The preface to the *Standard Edition* gives Strachey's (1966) reasons for the use of the term "instinct": "There seems little doubt that, from the standpoint of modern biology, Freud used the word 'Trieb' to cover a variety of different concepts" (p. xxv). For that reason, Strachey sees no advantage in translating *Trieb* into a word that is not an English word, since "drive," he says, could not be found in the Oxford English Dictionary.

Controversy continues about whether the concept of drives or instincts has to be retained at all; a number of alternative metapsychologies have been developed without it, whereas traditional psychoanalysts still use it in their metapsychological thinking. I contend that one's keeping or replacing drive theory has a lot to do with one's basic beliefs about the nature of humans. For example, modern research raises the question of whether infants are primarily a bundle of drives or are born with the capacity and the need for object relationships. Many psychoanalysts today have embraced object relations theories of one form or another in place of drive theory (see OBJECT RELATIONS THEORY), citing both their clinical experience and results from infant research. On the other hand, the historically proven primacy of human lust and aggression makes Freud's theory seem quite plausible. The matter remains unresolved.

Reference

Strachey, J. (1966). General preface. In *Standard Edition of the Complete Psychological Works of Sigmund Freud* 1:xiii–xxvi. London: Hogarth Press.

E

EATING DISORDERS (SEE BULIMIA)

EGO, EGO-IDEAL, SUPEREGO (SEE ALSO ID AND SUPEREGO)

Many aspects of Freud's (1923) *The Ego and the Id* are important in the practice of intensive psychotherapy. This work is Freud's basic presentation of the structural theory of the mind, a radical revision of his earlier "topographic" theory. Of special interest is Freud's description of the relation of the ego to the id as analogous to a rider on horseback. The rider has to hold in check the superior strength of the horse "with this difference, that the rider tries to do so with his own strength while the ego uses borrowed forces," and often a rider, "if he is not to be parted from his horse, is forced to guide it where it wants to go" (p. 25)—so sometimes the ego must transform the id's will into action as if it were the ego's own wish.

The traditional goal of psychotherapy is to uncover the unconscious and help the ego to sublimate and control the power of the id while dealing with the superego and reality. There is a limit to how much one can accomplish that in turn depends on how much one can help the ego to sublimate, utilize, and control id energy. This activity of the ego has a drive-channeling function. The ego also has a drive-curbing function—this represents the ego, or rider off the horse. In an atmosphere of appropriate soothing, structures in the preoedipal ego acquire form. For self psychologists, this is a consequence of transmuting microinternalizations and the gradual integration of the archaic, grandiose self (see SELF PSYCHOLOGY).

In the early phases of development, Freud (1923) explains, "the character of the ego is a precipitate of abandoned object-cathexes and . . . contains the history of those object-choices" (p. 29). The condition of identification is a major one under which the id can give up its object, according to Freud, and in the early years of life the separation from objects requires a precipitation of identifications with the lost objects in the ego. In an extremely important clinical passage Freud reminds us that if there are too many object identifications in the ego, "too numerous, unduly powerful and incompatible with one another" (p. 30), a pathological outcome will not be far off.

As a consequence of the different identifications becoming cut off from one another by resistances, a disruption of the ego may occur; at least, conflicts between the various identifications can take place. Furthermore, as Freud points out, the effects of the first identifications made in earliest childhood will be most general and lasting. It follows that any psychotherapy aiming to produce major changes in the ego must struggle with these earliest identifications.

In Freud's theory the ego is that part of the id that has been modified by the direct influence of the external world—it is first and foremost a body ego, an extension of the surface differentiation between the body and the rest of the world. It is ultimately derived from body sensations, especially those springing from the surface of the body; Freud liked to regard it as a mental projection of the surface of the body, akin to the famous cortical homunculus of the neuroanatomists in describing the projection of the pyramidal tract fibers on the cerebral cortex.

The ego comes into being by the rhythmical and phase-appropriate appearance of the mother administering to the infant's needs. This produces the beginning perception that a source outside the infant has the capacity to protect it from overstimulation and unpleasure; consequently, the initial anxiety of being overwhelmed from within by painful stimuli becomes replaced by anxiety regarding the appearance or disappearance of the mother (see STIMULUS BARRIER). A phase-appro-priate appearance and disappearance can enable the ego to set up an identification with the mother; drive-channeling mechanisms develop so that gradually a delay in the mother's appearance can be tolerated and eventually the process of separation-individuation can occur. However, until the time of the Oedipus complex, the ego remains quite primitive and limited in the variety of mechanisms at its disposal (see OEDIPUS COMPLEX).

The most important psychotherapeutic consequence of the structural theory that emerged out of the genius of Freud's old age was to place the ego in the limelight of psychotherapy, especially as the site of anxiety. In the structural theory, the main concern of psychotherapy is to relieve the ego's suffering under the pressures of three harsh masters—the id, the superego, and the external reality—by reducing these pressures and helping the ego to acquire strength. Ellenberger (1970) explains:

> As a consequence of these new theories, the focus of Freudian therapy shifted from the analysis of the instinctual forces to that of the ego, from the repressed to the repressing. Analysis of defenses would necessarily uncover anxiety, and the task of the analyst was now to dispel the excess of anxiety and to strengthen the ego, so that it could face reality and control the pressure of drives and the superego. [p. 517]

The fact that the mechanisms of defense operating within the ego and the need for punishment are often not accessible to consciousness forced the revision in Freud's thinking from the topographic to the structural theory of the mind. The cruel, relentless, even destructive attitude of the superego toward the individual is, in many cases, very striking and may be entirely unconscious in the patient. Aggressive energy is borrowed from the id by the superego and channeled into the superego's cruelty and destructiveness, all of which may go on outside the consciousness. In certain cases, the superego may gain the position of a tyrannical power over the rest of the personality and proceed in the slow or even dramatic process of subjugating and destroying the individual.

According to Freud's theory, the precursors of the superego are not very relevant; the superego is seen predominantly as the heir of the resolution of the Oedipus complex, and the firm consolidation of the mind into ego, id, and superego occurs at the point of the resolution of the Oedipus complex, followed by latency identifications and the consolidation process of puberty. The exact details of this consolidation remain somewhat in dispute, but the important clinical point is that before the age of 4 to 6, when the Oedipus complex becomes central, one cannot speak of a significant superego or of an internalized behavior-regulating system unless, like the Kleinians, one introduces a major modification of Freud's thought.

To review briefly Freud's conceptions of the superego and ego-ideal, we might begin with his (1914) paper "On Narcissism," written before the structural theory was presented. Here Freud proposed two psychic agencies that function to preserve for the ego a sense of self-esteem. The first agent, or ego-ideal, represents the series of achievements that, if they can be reached, lead to a state of imagined infantile perfection and narcissistic bliss. Freud differentiated this agent from the agent that observed the real achievements and compared them with the ideal standards. In *Introductory Lectures on Psychoanalysis,* Freud (1916) considered this self-criticizing faculty to be the same as the dream censor and as belonging to the ego, not the superego.

In *Group Psychology and the Analysis of the Ego* (1921), the separateness of the "conscience" and ego-ideal from the ego begins to appear in Freud's thinking; here he conceives of the possibility of the ego-ideal-conscience as coming into conflict with the rest of the ego, even raging with a critical cruelty against the ego. The extent of this cruelty, which can function unconsciously, was a major motivation for the development of the structural theory.

Freud always considered the development of the superego primarily to be a consequence of the resolution of the Oedipus complex. He increasingly emphasized the punitive and cruel aspects of the superego rather than its benign, loving aspect. In *Inhibitions, Symptoms and Anxiety,* he (1926) portrayed the threat from the superego as an extension of the castration threat. Finally, in *New Introductory Lectures on Psychoanalysis,* he (1933) viewed the superego as an internalized parental authority dominating the ego through punishment and threats of withdrawal of love. The apparent paradox of the clinically observed contrast between the harshness of the superego imitation of the parents and the gentleness of the parents in real life was explained through the borrowing by the superego of the child's own hostility to the prohibiting parent. Thus the superego is always thought of as having a direct connection to the id and as able to drain aggression from the id by turning it upon the ego.

The classic work on the mechanisms of defense employed by the ego is by Anna Freud (1946) (see FREUD, ANNA). The signal of anxiety sets these mechanisms of defense in action (Freud 1926). As Anna Freud elaborates, this is sometimes felt as superego anxiety, "objective" anxiety (such as that of infantile fantasies and bodily fears, e.g., of castration), dread of the strength of the instincts, or disruption of the ego's need for synthesis and harmony in adult life. According to Anna Freud, the purpose of analysis is to make the mechanisms of defense conscious so that the original impulses may come through and the patient can deal with them in a more adult way. A preliminary stage of defense would involve denial in fantasy, word, or act, or simply restriction and withdrawal from the field of activities and experiences. Anna Freud mentions the more sophisticated defenses of identification with the aggressor and a form of altruism or "altruistic surrender" of one's own instinctual impulses in favor of other people, such as that illustrated in Rostand's famous play, *Cyrano de Bergerac*. There

are also defenses motivated by the fear of the strength of the instincts as manifested in the typical phenomena of puberty. These characteristic adolescent defense mechanisms are asceticism, intellectuality, and new object "loves" taking place through identification.

The ego defense mechanism of introjection represents a totalistic phenomenon in which one takes in the ambivalently loved object (see INTROJECTION). It then functions inside as an introject. This is a more basic process than identification, in which only a certain aspect of the personality of the object is taken in (see IDENTIFICATION). Healthy adolescents identify but rarely introject. The ego is victorious, says Anna Freud, when its defense mechanisms effect their purpose, to avoid anxiety and transform the instincts so even in difficult circumstances some gratification is secured. It is the task of the ego to establish a harmonious relation between the id, the superego, and the outer world. This allows us to speak roughly of "ego strength" depending on how well the task has been accomplished.

Freud never differentiated clearly between "ego" and "self." It was Hartmann (1950) who distinguished the libidinal cathexis to the ego, which represents a narcissistic ego cathexis; the libidinal cathexis to the self (or self representation), which represents narcissism; and the libidinal cathexis to the soma, or body, which is clinically manifest as hypochondriasis. The focus in psychoanalytic theory shifted from the id (1897–1923), in which authoritative id interpretations were made to the patient, to the ego (1923 and thereafter), in which the emphasis was on the interpretation of the ego as it often unconsciously functioned in defenses and resistances. A vast and detailed "ego psychology" literature arose on these topics, especially in the United States.

In Hartmann's (1950, 1958) work, the ego was thought to also contain primary and secondary autonomous functions, as well as intrapsychic self and object representations and identifications. A secondary autonomous function is one that has become separated from its instinctual origins and over which the ego now has a certain dominance and can use it in the service of adaptation. The ego is the executive organ of the reality principle and is ruled by secondary process thought. In Freud's thinking, it developed from the id, but in Hartmann's conceptions the ego developed from separate ego *anlage*.

Hartmann (1958) introduced the notion of the conflict-free ego sphere. This is based on inborn ego apparatuses and represents ego processes outside the realm of conflicts. A change of function of the mechanisms of defense enables them to shift into the conflict-free sphere in the service of adaptation. Thus for Hartmann we have primary autonomous ego functions, which have been so from the beginning and develop from inborn apparatuses, and ego functions that have gained secondary autonomy after being used in the service of dealing with intrapsychic conflict. Hartmann believes there to be a rank order of ego func-

tions that decisively affect a person's stability and effectiveness.

The most accurate current thinking about the ego conceives of it as the sum of certain mental functions, including perception, memory, and the mechanisms of defense. The critical task of the ego is to mediate between the three harsh masters and form compromises in order to resolve intrapsychic conflict as efficiently as possible. These compromises, beginning early in life, determine all of an individual's significant choices and personality traits. Whatever emotions, thoughts, or behaviors that are experienced by the ego as unacceptable and foreign to the self are known as "ego-dystonic" or "ego-alien." An example of this would be various neurotic symptoms that trouble individuals and bring them into treatment. Thoughts, behaviors, or affects that are acceptable are known as "ego-syntonic." An example of this would be an individual's personality characteristics that he or she accepts or is even unaware of. In work with character disorders we often have to make certain personality characteristics that were ego-syntonic, ego-dystonic. This often involves undoing the disavowal of the consequences of certain previously ego-syntonic behavior patterns. These behavior patterns, like all choices and symptoms, are compromises formed by the ego early in life.

References

Ellenberger, H. (1970). *The Discovery of the Unconscious: The History and Evolution of Dynamic Psychiatry.* New York: Basic Books.

Freud, A. (1946). *The Ego and the Mechanisms of Defense.* New York: International Universities Press.

Freud, S. (1914). On narcissism: an introduction. *Standard Edition* 14:67–102.

———— (1916). Introductory lectures on psychoanalysis. *Standard Edition* 15:3–239.

———— (1921). Group psychology and analysis of the ego. *Standard Edition* 18:67–143.

———— (1923). The ego and the id. *Standard Edition* 19:3–66.

———— (1926). Inhibitions, symptoms and anxiety. *Standard Edition* 20:77–175.

———— (1933). New introductory lectures on psychoanalysis. Ch. 31. *Standard Edition* 22:57–80.

Hartmann, H. (1950). Comments on the psychoanalytic theory of the ego. In *Essays on Ego Psychology*, pp. 113–141. New York: International Universities Press, 1964.

———— (1958). *Ego Psychology and the Problem of Adaptation.* New York: International Universities Press.

EGO CONSCIOUSNESS, EGO EXPERIENCE, EGO FEELING

Federn (1952) pointed out that the ego was more than simply the sum total of the usual ego functions that psychoanalysts talk about: "The ego, however, is more inclusive; more especially it includes the subjective psychic experience of these functions with a characteristic sensation" (p. 61). He labeled this subjective experience the ego experience (*Icherlebnis*), the ego's experience of itself.

This phenomenon cannot be clearly explained. As long as the ego functions normally, one may ignore or be unaware of its functioning. To use Federn's metaphor, normally there is no more awareness of the ego than the air one breathes; only when respiration becomes burdensome is the lack of air recognized. The subjective ego experience includes "the feeling of unity, in continuity, contiguity, and causality, in the experiences of the individual" (Federn 1952, p. 6). In waking life the sensation of one's own ego is omnipresent, but it undergoes continuous changes in quality and intensity.

Federn attempted to distinguish within the subjective ego experience between ego feeling (*Ichgefühl*) and ego consciousness (*Ichbewusstsein*). Ego consciousness represents an enduring consciousness and knowledge that our ego is continuous and persistent, despite interruptions by sleep or unconsciousness, because we "know" intuitively that processes within us, even though they may be interrupted by forgetting or unconsciousness, have a persistent origin within us, and that our body and psyche belong permanently to our ego. Ego consciousness involves our conviction of the continuity of our person in respect to time, space, and causality. Our sense of ego consciousness plays a central role in the argument of Kant's *Critique of Pure Reason.* Ego consciousness in the pure state remains only when there is a deficiency in ego feeling. Thus the mere empty knowledge of oneself is already a pathological state known as estrangement or depersonalization.

In contrast, ego feeling

is the totality of feeling which one has of one's own living person. It is the residual experience which persists after the subtraction of all ideational contents—a state which, in practice, occurs only for a very brief time.... Ego feeling, therefore, is the simplest and yet the most comprehensive psychic state which is produced in the personality by the fact of its own existence, even in the absence of external or internal stimuli. [Federn 1952, pp. 62–63]

Ego feeling is the constantly present sensation of one's own person, the ego's own perception of itself.

Federn maintained that ego feeling is quite different from mere knowledge of one's self or of consciousness of the ego at work; it is primarily a feeling or sensation, normally taken for granted. Remarkably, Federn pointed out, and he certainly had not read Heidegger's (1962) comment that German and Greek were the only languages for philosophy, that the classical Greek language, in contrast to English, is necessary to get an intuitive verbal concept of ego feeling. This is because in the classical Greek language there is a middle voice, a neutral objectless form. The middle voice implies action involving one's self and not passing over to other objects. In English the middle voice is expressed by certain intransitive phrases such as I grow, I drive, I live, I prosper, I develop, I perish, I age, I die.

Our intuitive conviction or grasp or foreknowledge of the Being of humans comes from our inner ego feeling. Our inner sense of existence, of being alive, our capacity to develop a state of relatedness to both the human and nonhuman environ-

ment (Searles 1960) and of life having some sense of meaningfulness, require a healthy development of ego feeling. This in turn requires what Winnicott has described as good-enough mothering. (See also Chessick 1991 for a discussion of the origin of our sense of Being.)

To avoid confusion, note that Freud (1917) used the same term "ego feeling" (*Ichgefühl*), in *Mourning and Melancholia,* but he used it to mean something akin to self-esteem, which is quite different. There is an overlap between Federn's concept of ego feeling and Kohut's (1971) "sense of self," although they are not employed in compatible theoretical systems.

References

Chessick, R. (1991). The unbearable obscurity of being. *American Journal of Psychotherapy* 45:576–593.

Federn, P. (1952). *Ego Psychology and the Psychoses.* New York: Basic Books.

Freud, S. (1917). Mourning and melancholia. *Standard Edition* 14:237–258.

Heidegger, M. (1962). *Being and Time,* trans. J. Macquarrie and E. Robinson. New York: Harper & Row.

Kohut, H. (1971). *The Analysis of the Self.* New York: International Universities Press.

Searles, H. (1960). *The Nonhuman Environment in Normal Development and Schizophrenia.* New York: International Universities Press.

EMPATHY

Does empathy have a healing power, or is it simply a mode of observation? If a person feels understood empathically by another person, does this exert a healing effect? If so, how are we to describe this healing effect metapsychologically?

When we take the position of another person, our imagination moves from ourselves into the other person. We may experience certain changes in our own muscles and actual physical posture (Chessick 1965). To empathize does not mean that the individual must experience physical sensations; empathy can be physical, imaginative, or both. Fenichel (1945) quotes Reik, who maintained that empathy consists of two acts, "(a) an identification with the other person, and (b) an awareness of one's own feelings after the identification, and in this way an awareness of the object's feelings" (p. 511).

Katz (1963) along with Reik (1949) presented some metapsychologically imprecise and intuitive definitions and discussions of empathy. Katz discusses the fielding of signals through a "kind of inner radar" that works from cues in the conversation or impressions we received. Reik (1949) explains that "in order to comprehend the unconscious of another person, we must, at least for a moment, change ourselves into and become that person. We only comprehend the spirit whom we resemble" (p. 361).

Perhaps no other author before Kohut emphasized the importance of empathy as much as Harry Stack Sullivan. He never really defined the term but spoke of empathy developing through "induction" and postulated that the tension of anxiety present in the mothering one "induces" anxiety in the infant. The process by which this induction takes place is referred to as a manifestation of an interpersonal process, which Sullivan called empathy. He (1953) also introduced the term "empathic linkage," meaning a situation in which two people are linked in such a way that one induces a feeling in the other.

Fromm-Reichmann (1950) offered a dramatic clinical example of the empathic process. She explained how "some empathic notion for which I cannot give any account" made her turn back toward a patient, with consequences that later marked the beginning of successful therapy of that patient. This example, like Sullivan's definition, leaves empathy as a rather mysterious intuitive process and demonstrates empathy by the presence of a response in the therapist that can be observed by the patient or by an observer. Fromm-Reichmann (1950) insisted that empathy between the patient and therapist is crucial to psychotherapy: "The success or failure of psychoanalytic psychotherapy is, in addition, greatly dependent upon the question of whether or not there is actually an empathic quality between the psychiatrist and the patient" (p. 62).

All seem to agree that the use of empathy in psychotherapy calls for a pendulumlike action alternating between subjective involvement and objective detachment. Traditional analysts refer to this as a regression in the service of the ego when it is used toward specific goals. When the good empathizer regresses in the service of the ego, that person engages in a playful kind of activity, inwardly imitating events in the life of the patient. The activity is regressive only in the sense that it calls for a relaxed and unstructured experience associated with the fantasy of the child or the poetic license of the artist. The therapist must then be able to swing back to an objective and detached relationship in order to make clinical use of the information gained through the empathic process.

Long before Kohut, Fliess (1942) explained that the skill of the therapist depends on the ability "to step into [the patient's] shoes, and to obtain in this way an inside knowledge that is almost first-hand. The common name for such a procedure is empathy" (pp. 212–213). Levine (1961) claimed that empathy, if handled correctly, leads to a type of immediate comprehension of the patient's problems, a comprehension superior to the intellectual variety of understanding.

French and Fromm (1964) discussed "empathic thinking" in dream interpretation, stressing "empathic understanding" as a direct intuitive communication between the unconscious of the patient and that of the therapist. The patient evokes in the therapist "an empathic sense of what is going on" in the unconscious of the patient. French and Fromm pointed out that there must then occur a translation from this empathic understanding into a language suitable for scientific analysis. This translation is called "conceptual analysis" by these authors, and thus we have again the pendulumlike action described above.

Kohut (1984) posits three functions for empathy: (1) it is the indis-pensable tool of psychoanalytic fact finding; (2) it expands the self to include the other, constituting a powerful psychological bond between individuals in order to counteract man's destructiveness against his fellows; and (3) it arises out of the self-object matrix, becoming the accepting, confirming, and understanding human echo evoked by and needed by the self as a psychological nutriment without which human life could not be sustained. In this shift from his primary definition of empathy as a mode of observation or psychoanalytic fact-finding to the other functions of empathy, Kohut caused the greatest controversy.

Kohut (1971) distinguishes between empathy and intuition. He defines intuitions as simply the same as any other reactions and judgments of a rational sort except that they occur much faster. What appears to be an intuitive grasp of a situation is really a speeded-up series of rational decisions, such as those one may observe when a master chess player glances at the board and quickly sees the right move. This process fundamentally differs from vicarious introspection as a mode of observation.

A brief discussion of the current scientific status of empathy is presented by Goldberg (1983). He points out that there is a division in the psychoanalytic literature on the role of empathy in psychoanalysis. One view, although agreeing that empathy may be desirable, sees it as a relatively rare and unreliable phenomenon, fraught with the dangers of error due to countertransference. The other sharply contrasting view sees empathy as a common and universal mode of communication between people. Hartmann (1927) at an early date objected strongly to this latter approach in psychoanalytic work and claimed that it was unscientific and unreliable. But Goldberg concludes that "empathy seems to have a therapeutic effect when it is sustained" (p. 168), and he concurs with Kohut's placing of empathy in a central position in psychoanalysis.

The entire subject of the role of empathy within the psychoanalytic situation as conceived by various authors is reviewed by Levy (1985). He complains of the "multiple and different meanings" (p. 369) Kohut gave to empathy. He warns of the transference gratifications involved in Kohut's positing a therapeutic factor of major import besides the analyst's interpretations. Shapiro (1974, 1981; Leider 1984) claims that he does not even know what empathy is and views it as a form of animism that would destroy psychoanalysis as a science.

The German word *Einfühlung* was used in the late nineteenth century to describe aesthetic perception and was translated into English as "empathy." It was defined as "a tendency to merge the activities of the perceiving subject with the qualities of the perceived object," as quoted from Paget in 1913 by Reed (Lichtenberg, Bornstein, and Silver 1984a, p. 7). Reed gives seven definitions of empathy (pp. 12–13) on the basis of carefully cited quotations. Empathy is:

1. Both knowledge and communication.

2. Simultaneously a capacity, a process, and an expression.
3. An ability to sample others' affects and to be able to respond in resonance to them.
4. A method of data gathering.
5. An inner experience of sharing in and comprehending the psychological state of another person.
6. A special method of perceiving.
7. A means of communication and of nonrational understanding.

Pao (1983) offers still another definition from the Sullivanian viewpoint:

> To make use of one's empathic capacity to understand another person's needs and wants is not a solo activity. It is a process in which the two participants—the one who desires to understand and the one who desires to be understood—must both participate actively. Together, these two participants will gradually set up a more and more intricate "network" of connected communication. [pp. 152–153]

Basch (1983) views empathic understanding as a complex process. He emphasizes vicarious introspection but argues that it is not a subjective or untestable phenomenon. Basch disagrees with Kohut's idea that empathy is curative in itself and insists, more traditionally, that cure is the function of interpretation. Lichtenberg et al. (1984a,b) have devoted two volumes to various studies of empathy, the reader is referred to these for details of the controversy on the topic, which remains quite current. For example, Levy (1985) argues at length that the concept of empathy does not have a spe-

cific technical meaning, involves unconscious material, and is a much
more tricky phenomenon than
Kohut (1977) thought it was. In his
judgment, this makes it too diffuse a
concept on which to build a theory.

References

Basch, M. (1983). Empathic understanding: A
review of the concept and some theoretical considerations. Journal of the American
Psychoanalytic Association 31:101–126.

Chessick, R. (1965). Empathy and love in psychotherapy. American Journal of Psychotherapy 19:205–219.

Fenichel, O. (1945). The Psychoanalytic Theory
of Neurosis. New York: Norton.

Fliess, R. (1942). The metapsychology of
the analyst. Psychoanalytic Quarterly 2:
211–227.

French, T., and Fromm, E. (1964). Dream Interpretation. New York: Basic Books.

Fromm-Reichmann, F. (1950). Principles of In
tensive Psychotherapy. Chicago: University of Chicago Press.

Goldberg, A. (1983). On the scientific status
of empathy. Annual of Psychoanalysis
11:155 159.

Hartmann, H. (1927). Understanding and explanation. In Essays on Ego Psychology, pp.
369–403. New York: International Uni
versities Press, 1964.

Katz, R. (1963). Empathy, Its Nature and Uses.
New York: Glencoe/Free Press.

Kohut, H. (1971). The Analysis of the Self. New
York: International Universities Press.

_____ (1977). The Restoration of the Self. New
York: International Universities Press.

_____ (1984). How Does Analysis Cure? Chicago: University of Chicago Press.

Leider, R. (1984). Panel report on the neutrality of the analyst in the analytic situation. Journal of the American Psychoanalytic
Association 32:573–586.

Levine, M. (1961). Principles of psychiatric
treatment. In The Impact of Freudian Psychiatry, ed. F. Alexander and H. Ross.
Chicago: University of Chicago Press.

Levy, S. (1985). Empathy and psychoanalytic
technique. Journal of the American Psychoanalytic Association 33:353–378.

Lichtenberg, J., Bornstein, M., and Silver, D.,

eds. (1984a). Empathy, Vol. 1. Hillsdale,
NJ: Analytic Press.

_____ (1984b). Empathy, Vol. 2. Hillsdale,
NJ: Analytic Press.

Pao, P. (1983). Therapeutic empathy and the
treatment of schizophrenics. Psychoanalytic Inquiry 3:145–167.

Reik, T. (1949). Listening with the Third Ear.
New York: Farrar, Straus.

Shapiro, T. (1974). The development and distortions of empathy. Psychoanalytic Quarterly 43:4–25.

_____ (1981). Empathy: a critical evaluation.
Psychoanalytic Inquiry 1:423–448.

Sullivan, H. (1953). The Interpersonal Theory of
Psychiatry. New York: Norton.

ENVY (SEE ALSO PENIS ENVY)

Samuel Johnson (1773) defines
envy as the hatred of another for that
person's excellence, happiness, or
success; grieving at any qualities of
excellence in another; maliciously
withholding. It involves a negative
self-assessment accompanied by anger. Freud brought this term into the
psychiatric and popular psychology
vocabulary through his concept of
penis envy, which he considered to
be central in understanding the psychological development of women.
Freud (1925) claims that the girl's
discovery that she has no penis is a
wound to her narcissism, which
leads to a certain sense of inferiority,
jealousy, and the loosening of her
relationship to the mother as a love-
object. Consequently, "whereas in
boys the Oedipus complex is destroyed by the castration complex, in
girls it is made possible and led up to
by the castration complex" (p. 256).
Instead, the little girl turns to the
father for a baby. This leads Freud to

the logical conclusion that the Oedipus complex in girls escapes the fate it meets with in boys—in girls it may be slowly abandoned or dealt with by repression. Freud offers some disparaging remarks about women in this and other papers on the topic.

The psychotherapist should not be misled by Freud's disparaging remarks about women into ignoring his basic description of female sexuality. The little girl is disappointed by the narcissistic blow that she has no penis; she turns out of this disappointment to her father to obtain a baby from him, which in a way substitutes for the lost penis. As Freud explains, a wave of repression of this narcissistic wound and the corresponding wish for a penis occurs at puberty, an event that has the function of doing away with a large amount of the girl's masculine sexuality to make room for the development of her femininity. Along with the blossoming of the feminine orientation, he says, there is a shift in the narcissistic focus on the genitals from the clitoris to the vagina. The existence of this transfer has not been refuted by experimental work on the physiology of the female orgasm, since the transfer is primarily a normal shift in narcissistic emphasis as a function of the development of femininity. All of this is a highly controversial view of female sexual development under intensive review today (see FEMALE PSYCHOLOGY).

As if this controversy were not sufficient, Melanie Klein (1957) also introduced a concept of envy into her theories (see KLEIN). In a paper that caused a sensation when it was introduced entitled "Envy and Gratitude," she declares that envy is primary and constitutional. She writes,

For many years the envy of the feeding breast as a factor which adds intensity to the attacks on the primal object has been part of my analyses. It is, however, only more recently that I have laid particular emphasis on the spoiling and destructive quality of envy in so far as it interferes with the building up of a secure relation to the good external and internal object, undermines the sense of gratitude, and in many ways blurs the distinction between good and bad. [p. 230]

Opponents of Melanie Klein claimed that her postulation of constitutional envy attributed ego capacities and cognitive abilities to an infant that were impossible to verify or even to accept. The argument over the existence of constitutional envy is one of the basic disagreements between Kleinian and Freudian psychoanalysts.

References

Freud, S. (1925). Some psychical consequences of the anatomical distinction between the sexes. *Standard Edition* 19:243–258.

Johnson, S. (1773). *A Dictionary of the English Language.* Beirut, Lebanon: Librairie du Liban, 1978.

Klein, M. (1957). Envy and gratitude. In *Envy and Gratitude and Other Works 1946–1963,* pp. 176–235. New York: Dell.

EROTOGENIC ZONE, EROGENOUS ZONE

Freud (1905) in his early work postulated that from certain areas of the body erotic sensations arose physiologically. He called these "erotogenic zones" and specified the genitals and the mucous membranes surrounding the body openings. Because it is no longer believed that these body zones generate sexual desire but simply are zones of sexual pleasure, they are now more commonly referred to as "erogenous" zones. Any area of the body, however, may become secondarily invested as an erogenous zone besides the oral, anal, and genital areas.

Reference

Freud, S. (1905). Three essays on the theory of sexuality. *Standard Edition* 7:125–243.

EVENLY SUSPENDED ATTENTION

Freud's (1912) technique of listening with "evenly suspended attention" (p. 111) constitutes an effort to avoid prescinding from the patient's material in order to prevent the therapist from making any selection out of preconceived expectations. He wishes to avoid the danger of the therapist's never discovering anything that he or she does not already know, and of distorting what is perceived to fit experience-distant theoretical preconceptions.

The question of whether the therapist really can give such equal notice to everything communicated by the patient has often been raised, but only recently has it been answered increasingly in the negative. Experienced therapists have learned that everyone approaches the data

provided by the patient's free associations and behavior during sessions with a certain mental set, one that is based on either conscious or preconscious personal, theoretical, and philosophical conceptions. This mental set determines what is perceived and what is selected, regardless of the therapist's effort to listen with evenly suspended attention (Goldberg 1987) or to be "neutral." What we learn from the stance of evenly suspended attention is enhanced greatly if therapists are aware of how their preconceptions influence all aspects of their perception of the patient. Many schisms and scholastic disagreements in our field would have been avoided if this had been recognized. (see FREE ASSOCIATION).

References

Freud, S. (1912). Recommendations to physicians practicing psycho-analysis. *Standard Edition* 12:109–120.

Goldberg, A. (1987). Psychoanalysis and negotiation. *Psychoanalytic Quarterly* 56: 109–129.

EXISTENTIAL ANGUISH

It is important to distinguish between "anxiety" as it is used in the clinical psychotherapeutic sense and the "anxiety" or "dread" of Kierkegaard (1946). Kierkegaard's *Angst* is usually translated as "dread," although May (1950) uses "anxiety." Unamuno rendered it as *agonie* and Sartre by *angoisse*; here I am calling it existential anguish. The technical meaning of existential anguish and Freud's signal anxiety are really rather different, and it confuses matters considerably to include both under the term "anxiety." Kierkegaard (May 1950), similar to Freud's discussion of anxiety, views existential anguish developmentally, beginning with the original state of the child. But unlike Freud he does not, in my opinion, really pin down the source of existential anguish developmentally, believing it to be a universal condition related to the freedom and the possibilities of human decisions and choices.

Kierkegaard and many philosophers who followed him have overemphasized the importance of existential anguish in the life of the ordinary, relatively normal human being. But existential anguish does often constitute an extremely important complaint from people who suffer with emotional difficulties. It is a conscious derivative of disturbance of holding and handling in the early stages of infancy, a disturbance that leaves the individual, as Winnicott (1958) says, with a defective sense of Being, a preoccupation with the meaning of life, confusion over his or her own identity, and lack of a place in the panorama of human events.

Existential anguish, if prolonged, can lead to an increasing sense of the hopelessness and meaninglessness of life. Kierkegaard (Jones 1975) gives an excellent description of this sense of "melancholy":

> I feel so dull and completely without joy, my soul is so empty and void that I cannot even conceive what could satisfy it—oh, not even the blessedness of heaven.

It is terrible when I think, even for a single moment, over the dark background which, from the very earliest time, was part of my life. The dread with which my father filled my soul, his own frightful melancholy, and all the things in this connection which I do not even note down.

From a child I was under the sway of a prodigious melancholy, the depth of which finds its only adequate measure in the equally prodigious dexterity I possessed of hiding it under an apparent gayety and *joie de vivre*. [p. 211]

References

Jones, W. (1975). *A History of Western Philosophy: Kant and the Nineteenth Century,* 2nd ed., rev. New York: Harcourt Brace Jovanovich.

Kierkegaard, S. (1946). *The Concept of Dread.* Princeton, NJ: Princeton University Press.

May, R. (1950). *The Meaning of Anxiety.* New York: Ronald Press.

Winnicott, D. (1958). *Collected Papers.* New York: Basic Books.

EXIT LINE

Gabbard (1982) reminds us that the exit line of the patient is designed to leave the analyst with a certain affect state. It may defend against narcissistic injury on the part of the patient, for example, in being told the time of the session is over, and can be motivated by the hope for a hostile triumph to torment the analyst after the patient is gone. Other examples are the "curtain call" exit line, in which the patient shows his or her true self at the end; the "last-second question," in which the patient attempts to catch the analyst off guard and get personal information; and the "stereotyped exit," a character defense against being affected by the analysis. There are also the obvious comments, "I'm glad the session is over," or "I'll collapse out there," or a reparation comment such as, "I'm sorry I gave you a hard time."

An astute psychotherapist should also watch his or her own exit line, which often slips out as the patient leaves and expresses countertransference.

Reference

Gabbard, G. (1982). The exit line: heightened transference–countertransference manifestations at the end of the hour. *Journal of the American Psychoanalytic Association* 30:579–598.

EXTERNALIZATION

Credit for coining the term is usually given to Anna Freud (1965), who described externalization as a subspecies of transference (see TRANSFERENCE). She viewed externalization in child analysis as a process in which the person of the analyst is used to represent one or the other part of the patient's personality structure.

The concept of externalization was expanded by Brodey (1965). In his experience while working with family units, externalization appeared as a mechanism of defense defined by the following characteristics:

1. Projection is combined with the manipulation of reality selected for the purpose of verifying the projection.
2. The reality that cannot be used to verify the projection is not perceived.
3. Information known by the externalizing person is not transmitted to others except as it is useful to train or manipulate them into validating what will then become the realization of the projection.

The psychotherapist feels the intensity of the patient's effort to manipulate him or her into validating projections. He or she feels conflict in the struggle against this manipulation, but behavior that will be used as validation seems the only way to gain a relationship with the patient. The manipulation of the therapist into behavior that is symmetrical to the projection is different from the simple transfer of feelings to a therapist. It implies an interpersonal process. Even the therapist's active denial of the patient's presumption is used by the patient in the service of proving to the patient that the therapist is actually congruent with his or her projective image.

Brodey points out that the therapist of the ego-disturbed patient must become skilled at managing his or her congruence with the patient's projected image. This management is often intuitive and usually very demanding emotionally, since the temptation to yield is strong: "Being a distorted object is much easier than being nonexistent" (p. 169).

Externalization is a combination

of projection followed by selective perception and manipulation of other people for the purpose of verifying the initial projection. Other people are experienced wholly in terms of their value in verifying the initial projection, and only those aspects of other people which have this value are perceived at all. For example, even the most benign therapist approaching the borderline patient may find himself or herself transformed into a horrible monster very quickly by the patient's selective perception (see BORDERLINE). Unless the therapist is aware of this danger, he or she will be inclined either to retaliate or to quarrel with the patient's extremely unflattering image of the therapist, which usually contains a kernel of truth and a direct assault on the therapist's narcissistic conception of himself or herself as a benevolent physician (Chessick 1972).

Giovacchini (1967) emphasizes paradoxical self-defeating behavior with a defensive purpose that is usually the result of externalization. This must be distinguished from self-defeating behavior resulting from a breakdown of the personality. A patient of this type cannot cope with a warm and nonthreatening environment. He or she expects and brings about failure, and adapts to life by feeling beaten in an unpredictable and ungiving world. Giovacchini distinguishes this from a masochistic adjustment and points out the relationship of externalization to the repetition compulsion, on which it is based (see COMPULSION TO REPEAT). Externalization contains a mode of adaptation or adjustment that makes any interaction between the ego and the outer world possible, and characterizes that interaction as doomed to disappointment.

References

Brodey, W. (1965). On the dynamics of narcissism: externalization and early ego development. *Psychoanalytic Study of the Child* 20:165–193. New York: International Universities Press.

Chessick, R. (1972). Externalization and existential anguish. *Archives of Psychiatry* 27:764–770.

Freud, A. (1965). *Normality and Pathology in Childhood*. New York: International Universities Press.

Giovacchini, P. (1967). Frustration and externalization. *Psychoanalytic Quarterly* 36:571–583.

F

FAIRBAIRN (SEE QUASI-INDEPENDENCE)

FALSE SELF (SEE ALSO WINNICOTT)

For R. D. Laing (1969), patients with what he calls "ontological insecurity" substitute dependency on the other for genuine mutuality. The schizoid patient oscillates between merger and isolation, not, as in the normal person, between relatedness and separation (see SCHIZOID). The patient splits into a secret true self and a body associated with a false self. This false self system was borrowed from Kierkegaard's (1946) concept of "shut-up-ness." For Kierkegaard, the "shut-up" is the mute; he or she does not wish to communicate and feels dread if required to do so.

This definitive split becomes a basic and irreversible schizoid style. The patient tries to do everything for himself or herself in isolation. The advantage of this is that it protects the patient from ontological insecurity and the anxieties associated with it. The disadvantage is that it is impossible, since we all need other people; isolation of one's self leads to despair and a sense of emptiness and alienation from the world. Laing (1969) writes, "The more the self is defended this way, the more it is cut off and destroyed" (pp. 80–81).

To get a better understanding of Laing's concept, it is worth comparing three different types of false self systems. In the normal individual, some behavior is mechanical, but the person is not compelled to it and there is no encroachment on spontaneity and no feeling of being lived in contrast to living. In the neurotic individual, such as the hysteric, there is bad faith, as Sartre (1973) calls it. This is a way of life aimed at taboo gratification. The individual "pretends" to himself or herself and to others. The schizoid's false self system, however, is aimed not at gratification but at preservation. It involves hiding fear and hatred, being compulsively compliant, being good, and not making trouble. This compliance poses one of the most difficult defensive systems encountered in psychoanalytic treatment and is often the source of therapeutic stalemate when it is overlooked by the therapist.

References

Kierkegaard, S. (1946). *The Concept of Dread,* trans. W. Lowrie. Princeton, NJ: Princeton University Press.

Laing, R. D. (1969). *The Divided Self.* New York: Pantheon Books.

Sartre, J-P. (1973). *Being and Nothingness,* trans. H. Barnes. New York: Washington Square.

FANTASY (SEE ALSO PHANTASY)

The current controversies about the exact nature and metapsychological status of early fantasy formations have been covered recently in a series of papers (Abend 1990, Dowling 1990, Inderbitziw and Levy 1990, Shane and Shane 1990, Shapiro 1990, Trosman 1990). Suffice it to say here that behind the fixed and organized repressed unconscious fantasies is what Dowling (1990) calls "the blurred, undifferentiated preconceptual thought of early oedipal and preoedipal life," that perhaps includes "sensorimotor or behavioral memories, which arise primarily from preverbal experience and remain influential throughout childhood and adult life" (p. 109). Indeed, sometimes the first clue to such fantasies appears in the patient's behavior rather than in his or her verbalization during the analytic process. These fantasies differ from other unconscious content in "their enduring quality and their organized, story-like quality reflecting the distortions typical of the primary process" and form "dynamically unconscious templates from the childhood past" that "are relatively impervious to new experience" (Interbitziw and Levy 1990, p. 113).

Arlow (1985) stresses that after the age of 6 or 7 everyone has a unique typical repetitive fantasy activity, of which their adult fantasy life reflects derivatives. Even our perception is determined by this crucial unconscious fantasy activity, which forms "the mental set against which the data of perception are perceived, registered, interpreted, remembered, and responded to" (p. 526). These fantasies go through convolutions as the individual develops, and some later editions may even provide defensive distortions of earlier fantasies. Arlow writes:

> In the course of treatment one can observe how the symptoms of the patient's illness, how his life history and his love relations, his character structure and his artistic creations may all represent in different ways derivative manifestations of the persistent unconscious fantasy activity, of the "fantasied reality" that governs the individual's life. [p. 534]

Arlow views the analyst's behavior as a stimulus, as a day residue, but it is through the stimulation of the patient's unconscious fantasy life that the reaction we call transference occurs. Even in the transference, at least at first, we see only derivatives of the persistent unconscious fantasy activity of childhood that governs the individual's life.

I (Chessick, in press) agree with this out of my own clinical experience. At the core of every patient there resides a crucial fantasy activity process interwoven with early infantile experiences to a greater or lesser degree, depending on how traumatic these experiences have been. But, as Arlow (1985) explains, "What constitutes trauma is not inherent in the actual, real event, but rather the individual's response to the disorganizing, disruptive combination of impulses and fears integrated into a set of unconscious fantasies" (p. 533). Certain object relations and self psychology theories tend to minimize the role of this unconscious activity and emphasize the pathogenic effect of real events and interactions. But the individual's experience, explains Arlow (1980), "is usually organized in terms of a few leading unconscious fantasies which dominate an individual's perception of the world and create the mental set by which she or he perceives and interprets her/his experience" (p. 131). Transference is not a repetition of the patient's early interactions with present objects, but expresses derivatives of the patient's persistent unconscious childhood fantasies, the "psychic reality" of these early interactions for the patient.

References

Abend, S. (1990). Unconscious fantasies, structural theory, and compromise formation. *Journal of the American Psychoanalytic Association* 38:61–74.

Arlow, J. (1980). Object concept and object choice. *Psychoanalytic Quarterly* 49: 109–133.

—— (1985). The concept of psychic reality and related problems. *Journal of the American Psychoanalytic Association* 33: 521–535.

Chessick, R. (in press). What brings about change in psychoanalytic treatment. *Psychoanalytic Review*.

Dowling, S. (1990). Fantasy formation: a child analyst's perspective. *Journal of the American Psychoanalytic Association* 38:93–112.

Inderbitziw, L., and Levy, S. (1990). Unconscious fantasy: a reconsideration of the concept. *Journal of the American Psychoanalytic Association* 38:113–130.

Shane, M., and Shane, E. (1990). Unconscious fantasy: developmental and self psychological considerations. *Journal of the American Psychoanalytic Association* 38: 75–92.

Shapiro, T. (1990). Unconscious fantasy: introduction. *Journal of the American Psychoanalytic Association* 38:39–46.

Trosman, H. (1990). Transformations of unconscious fantasy in art. *Journal of the American Psychoanalytic Association* 38: 47–60.

FEE

The subject of the setting and collection of fees in psychotherapy and psychoanalysis has not received the attention it deserves. Eissler (1974) has written the best paper on the topic to date. He recommends that analysts set an initial optimal fee and points out that the analyst's behavior in setting the fee and collecting it is an important indicator to the patient of the professional's attitude toward money. This attitude can be either a function of the analyst's consideration for what is best for the patient or a function of an unresolved narcissistic problem of the analyst. Eissler mentions that younger analysts are especially vulnerable to the latter because they are upwardly mobile and wish to be financially comfortable as soon as possible.

Eissler recommends scrupulous honesty and objects to increasing the fee as indexed to inflation. His paper was written before the more serious inflationary changes in today's economy, so some therapists may legitimately choose to warn the patient at the beginning of treatment that there will be an increase in fee from time to time based on inflation. For example, if there is substantial inflation in a year (over 5 percent), I will increase the fee of a once-a-week patient on an annual basis. But a patient coming three or four times a week should not have the fee increased more than once every three or four years, and this should be done carefully, if at all. The handling of the fee increase is a matter of the personal characteristics of the analyst, but it is an important signal to the patient of whether the analyst really is or is not considering the patient's needs above his or her own.

It is possible for the analyst to err in the other direction, by setting too low a fee. This can be a serious problem because, if the patient is aware that he or she is paying a very low fee as compared to others in treatment, the patient may feel obligated not to get angry at this kindly, benevolent parent figure who is doing this favor. I have had several patients in reanalysis who were unable to express their rage at their previous analysts because the fee was set low and the analysts announced this fact to the patients at the beginning of the sessions. The patients took this as a declaration of benevolence and kindliness and felt throughout the treatment that they could not directly lose their temper; as a result, the analysis floundered. However, if one must err, it is better to set too low rather than a crushingly high fee, and better to lose by the inflation than to raise the fee to hardship levels for the patient.

I believe that in all cases the therapist must be prepared to substantially lower the fee if the patient becomes disabled or suffers financial reverses or burdens that are not the result of acting out or manipulation or provocation but are genuinely beyond the patient's control. This is part of the physicianly vocation (see PHYSICIANLY VOCATION).

Reference

Eissler, K. (1974). On some theoretical and technical problems regarding the payment of fees for psychoanalytic treatment. *International Review of Psycho-Analysis* 1:73–101.

FEMALE PSYCHOLOGY

In the area of classical psychoanalytic theory, no set of concepts has come under as much criticism from clinical and observational experience as Freud's psychoanalytic view of feminine psychology. It is very important for the modern practicing psychotherapist to have a thorough understanding of the issues that are involved.

Although Freud assumed in his early formulations that sexual development in boys and girls was similar (see Table 1), in his later formulations he maintained that the Oedipus complex in the girl was a much more complicated process. According to classical Freudian theory, the divergence between the psychosexual development of the boy and the girl appears early in the phallic phase.

Before then, the girl shares with the boy the passive position in relation to her mother. With the development of motility and locomotion both enter an increasingly active phase, with the emphasis on autonomy and mastery of the object world. At this point, a basic developmental divergence takes place.

The girl has to change not only

Table 1. Freud's Changing Views on Female Sexuality

1. *Unfathomable, But . . .*
    a. 1905: *Three Essays on Sexuality*—"impenetrable obscurity" of erotic life of women (*S.E.* 7, p. 151), but sexuality of little girls is wholly masculine, they undergo a more complex and difficult development; clitoral-vaginal transfer theory introduced (*S.E.* 7, pp. 219–221).
    b. 1923: *The Infantile Genital Organization*—is phallic in both sexes (*S.E.* 19, p. 143), and the processes of the phallic phase unknown in women. But at preoedipal level the polarities are male genital vs. castrated (disavowal introduced p. 143), and only on completion of puberty does it become male, active vs. female, passive.
    c. 1926: *The Problem of Lay Analysis*—"the sexual life of adult women is a 'dark continent' for psychology" (*S.E.* 20, p. 212).
2. *Penis Envy*
    a. 1908: *The Sexual Theories of Children* (*S.E.* 9, pp. 217–218).
    b. 1918: *The Taboo of Virginity* (*S.E.* 11). Bondage and hostility to men.
    c. 1916: *Some Character Types*—stresses injury to narcissism and rage at mother (*S.E.* 14, p. 315).
3. *Less Ego Development (Possibly)*
    a. 1920: *Psychogenesis of a case of homosexuality in a woman*—women are less objective, less lucid, less astute, "but these distinctions are conventional rather than scientific" (*S.E.* 18, p. 154).
4. *Outcome of Oedipus Complex, Including Superego, Is Exactly the Same as Boys*
    a. 1900: *Interpretation of Dreams* (*S.E.* 4, p. 257).
    b. 1916–1917: *Introductory Lectures on Psychoanalysis* (*S.E.* 16, Lect. 21)
    c. 1923: *The Ego and the Id*—"a precise analogy" in character development of males and females as a function of the dissolution of the Oedipus complex (*S.E.* 19, p. 32).
5. *The Outcome Is Different in Women*
    a. 1919: *A Child Is Being Beaten*—not satisfied with the "precise analogy": "the expectation of there being a complete parallel was mistaken" (*S.E.* 17, p. 196).
    b. 1924: *The Dissolution of the Oedipus Complex*—women have less sadism and are more affectionate, connected with "stunted growth of her penis" (*S.E.* 19, p. 179). "It must be admitted, however, that in general our insight into these developmental processes in girls is unsatisfactory, incomplete, and vague" (ibid).
6. *Findings Are Tentative—Final Views*
    a. 1931: *On Female Sexuality* (*S.E.* 21)—stresses importance of preoedipal attachment to the mother and opens investigation of preoedipal period as setting scene for the oedipal.
    b. 1933: *New Series of Lectures*—"Femininity" (*S.E.* 22, Lect. 33)—very depreciating view of women.
7. *Women Are Different and Inferior—Victorian Prejudice*
    a. 1925: *Some Psychic Consequences of Anatomical Differences*—complete reassessment of views, elaborating on 1924 paper. Women have more jealousy (*S.E.* 19, p. 254) and are ethically inferior (pp. 257–258).
    b. 1937: *Analysis Terminable and Interminable*—penis envy "bedrock" (*S.E.* 23).
    c. 1940: *Outline of Psychoanalysis*—patriarchal and condescending views, his final statement (*S.E.* 23, Ch. 7, e.g., p. 194).

her sexual object from the woman or mother to the man or father, but her leading genital zone as well—from the clitoris to the vagina. This stands in sharp contrast to the boy, whose sexual development remains simpler in that his leading genital zone remains the phallus and the sexual object remains a woman. For many years Freudians assumed that the vagina was virtually nonexistent and possibly did not produce sensations until puberty. The sexual life of women was divided, according to classical psychoanalytic theory, into two phases, of which the first has a masculine character and only the second is specifically feminine. In female development there is a process of transition from one phase to the other, to which there is nothing analogous in the male. The matter is further complicated because the clitoris continues to function in later female sexual life in a manner that is quite variable and not satisfactorily understood.

Along with this great difference in genital zones there is another concerning the finding of the object. The girl has her mother as first object, just like the boy; but at the end of her development, the father, a man, becomes the new love object. According to Freud (1925), "*Whereas in boys the Oedipus complex is destroyed by the castration complex, in girls it is made possible and led up to by the castration complex*" (p. 256). Thus the castration complex inhibits and limits masculinity and encourages femininity (see CASTRATION ANXIETY and OEDIPUS COMPLEX).

This is further elaborated in clas-sical theory, where it is postulated that the narcissistic wound in the girl from her discovery of the lack of a penis tends to bring about the giving up of clitoral sexuality for the development of "femininity." The girl's libido slips into a new position; at this point the Oedipus complex begins to play its part. The basic equation is that penis equals child, and for the purpose of getting a child, she now takes her father as love object and the mother becomes the object of her jealousy. She turns to her father, but this attraction to him is secondary to her wish to obtain a baby from him. Whereas in boys the Oedipus complex is destroyed, in girls it escapes this fate because the girl is already castrated. The Oedipus complex may be slowly abandoned or dealt with by repression, or its effects may persist far into a woman's normal mental life.

Thus the girl has an early identification with the active mother that is an initial active (negative) oedipal position. Then the girl turns with the passive aim to the oedipal love object, the father, which forms the passive (positive) oedipal position; this occurs relatively late compared to the boy's active (positive) oedipal position. In turning from the mother to the father, according to this theory, the girl turns from an active to a passive sexual position. Passivity then becomes the normal sexual orientation for the girl. Furthermore, the very recognition of castration, which in the boy brings on the destruction of the Oedipus complex, in the girl brings the Oedipus complex into existence, and no force or circumstance similar to the one that makes the boy renounce his oedipal wishes exists in the situation of the girl.

Blos (1962) explains that as the limitations of physical immaturity, incestuous guilt feelings, and the persistent narcissistic injury experienced in masturbatory activity eventually combine to bring about a decline of the girl's oedipal fantasies and facilitate her entrance into the latency period, so the resolution of the girl's Oedipus complex may not come about until her adolescence or perhaps even later with the birth of a child, or perhaps never at all in any complete fashion.

This theory led with superficial logic to some of Freud's depreciating remarks about the superego in women. Muslin (1971) carefully reviews the entire matter, pointing out that it is not necessary to reach any conclusions about any kind of inferiority of superego function in women from basic psychoanalytic theory. Although the superego of a woman may be unique as compared to the superego of a man, superego functioning is normally similar and effective in both sexes.

Conclusions from Freud's basic postulates about female sexuality involve the three final pathways that feminine sexuality may take: (a) a general revulsion from sexuality, (b) a defiant self-assertiveness in which the girl clings to her threatened masculinity in the hope of getting a penis and to the fantasy of being a man (the so-called phallic woman), and (c) a circuitous development in which the girl takes her father as her object and

finds her way to the feminine form of the Oedipus complex. Only the third path, according to Freud, leads to the final normal female attitude.

Certain additions were made to Freud's basic postulates, some of them even in Freud's lifetime and with his approval. For example, Ruth Mack-Brunswick (Fliess 1948), one of the early female classical psychoanalysts, stressed the anger at the mother that the oedipal girl feels when she discovers that she does not have a penis. The girl abandons the mother as love object with far more embitterment and finality than does the boy; this tremendous anger at the mother, Mack-Brunswick said, is also expressed in feminine masochism. Masochism is seen as a normal part of femininity and a consequence of the defense against the anger of the mother.

A complete exposition of the classical psychoanalytic position on feminine sexuality is to be found in the various works of Helene Deutsch. Several of her papers are reprinted in Fliess's (1948) *Psychoanalytic Reader*; her expanded views are in her two-volume *Psychology of Women* (1944). Deutsch (1973) played an interesting role in the history of the psychoanalytic movement. She explains in her autobiography that "three of Freud's women pupils achieved a certain degree of prominence as 'pioneers in feminine psychology' (that was the phrase Freud used in his writings). These were Ruth Mack-Brunswick, Jeanne Lampl-de Groot, and myself" (pp. 137–138).

Deutsch maintains that parturition constitutes for women the termination of a sexual act that was only inaugurated by coitus. The ultimate gratification of the erotic instinct in women takes place at the point of giving birth. Femininity for Deutsch means the feminine, placid, masochistic disposition in the mental life of women. The basic feminine fantasy, according to Deutsch, is, "I want to be castrated and raped by my father and to have a child by him," a threefold wish of plainly masochistic character. Castration, rape, and parturition are mixed together as basic elements in feminine psychology. The masochistic fantasies and wish for a child are permeated by pleasure tendencies of a masochistic nature. This masochism is a defensive consequence of the bitterness toward the mother generated by the girl's discovery that she has no penis. This wish for castration, rape, and parturition is termed by some authors the masochistic triad in the female.

A whole series of clinical objections has been made to these basic theoretical conceptions about feminine psychology. Gardiner (1955) discusses in detail the subject of feminine masochism and passivity. Is this a need or a culturally enforced tendency in women to repress their aggressiveness more than men? Is it really true that femininity and masochism are inextricably connected, as Deutsch says they are? When the girl begins to accept the fact that her clitoris is an inferior organ and incapable of actively penetrating, the wish may develop passively to receive caresses and stimulation from the love object and eventually, by

way of the father's penis, a child instead of the penis, which has been taken away from her or denied her. But this is hardly a wish for pain or suffering. Gardiner points out that it seems rather a wish for libidinal pleasure that can be achieved passively, and indeed the child experiences receiving pleasure passively in the mother's physical care and caresses during the preoedipal phase. An instinctual wish for a child is then reinforced by the equation penis equals child or child equals penis.

Gardiner also questions Deutsch's (Fliess 1948) concept that parturition is for the woman an orgy of masochistic pleasure. When pain occurs in pregnancy or giving birth, this is a reality and must be suffered for the sake of the result, but it is normally not enjoyed for itself. Also, the pleasure in the sexual act is direct and immediate and except perhaps at defloration and for a short time thereafter, intercourse for the normal woman is without pain. Here the pleasure principle pure and simple is at work. When a normal Oedipus complex develops and there is no regression to the anal-sadistic or oral stage, Gardiner feels we should not expect to find more than a trace of masochism or sadism.

Ash (1971) argues that Freud's concept, femininity implies passivity, was simply a cultural prejudice and nothing more. In the *New Introductory Lectures on Psychoanalysis,* Freud (1933) himself expressed reservations about equating femininity with passivity. In that work his struggle with inner contradictions in his theory becomes especially evident, as he describes how the suppression of women's aggressiveness, which is prescribed for them constitutionally and imposed on them socially, favors the development of powerful masochistic impulses.

These two major objections to Freud's theory—femininity does not have to imply masochism or the wish for masochistic orgy and femininity does not necessarily have to imply passivity—are based on clinical and social observations but do not threaten the basic theory itself; they merely require modifications. Over the past twenty years, however, objections have occurred that threaten Freud's whole theory of feminine psychology. For example, Sherfey (1973) makes an extreme attack on the psychoanalytic concept of female sexuality. Her position consists of three major theses: (a) the early embryo of all human beings is female; (b) by the nature of their physiological structure, women are sexually insatiable; and (c) civilization arose as a means of suppressing the inordinate demands of female sexuality that result from an inherent insatiability. The first thesis challenges the Freudian belief in an embryo that is sexually undifferentiated and therefore bisexual. This is, of course, vital in analytic theory, because Freud assumed that the clitoris served as a residual organ of the masculine element in women. The second and third theses are based on the work of Masters and Johnson (1966). Sherfey takes their work to mean that, from the standpoint of normal physiologic functioning, the more orgasms a woman has, the more she will con-

tinue to have, unless inhibited by fatigue or external repression. Leaning on Masters and Johnson's observations, she throws out the whole concept that the transfer from clitoris to vagina takes place in a normal female sexual development and contends that the forceful suppression of women's inordinate sexual demands has led to the development of civilization.

Fisher (1973) could discover no correlation between the consistency with which women achieved orgasm and their degree of psychological maladjustment; the extent to which their mother and father may or may not have been permissive in sexual matters; their sexual information prior to marriage; their femininity as conventionally defined; or their aggressiveness, passivity, religiosity, or even preference for clitoral versus vaginal stimulation. Furthermore, the length of foreplay, the duration of coitus, and so on, have no consistent correlation with a woman's ability to achieve orgasms regularly. As a matter of fact, Fisher attacks the Freudians for thinking that the woman who prefers vaginal stimulation is more normal or more mature than others, and he emphasizes the importance of male dependability as a determining factor in the woman's orgasmic responses.

Stoller (1973) reviews the whole area of sex research and the methodological problems that it involves, and these are many. The concept of the primacy of the penis has come into doubt. There is no question that male chauvinism is connected to Freud's enthusiasm for the position that men are emotionally, intellectually, and morally superior to women and fitted anatomically with something superior. But Stoller does not feel that the clitoris–vagina transfer theory is refuted by Masters and Johnson.

The women's liberation movement has served a useful function in challenging some of the basic early psychoanalytic tenets about feminine sexual development. Even less extreme advocates have brought under serious question certain basic postulations that were more or less taken for granted until the 1960s, after which, under pressure from feminists, there has been an increasing reassessment of the entire subject. Whether or not motherhood is at the center of female psychology is a clinical question. If it is not, then the whole psychoanalytic theory of feminine development and feminine psychology must be wrong.

Whether or not penis envy is nothing but a reassurance created by frightened males and is only symbolic of realistic justified envy of man's dominant social advantages is a question that also can be resolved clinically. It is possible to fudge on this issue, for example, by arguing that penis envy is only one of several constituent forces at work on the girl that cause her to turn to the father. Penis envy is probably closely related to recent formulations on the vicissitudes of narcissism (see ENVY).

If it is true that anatomical and biological differences do not make important contributions to gender personality traits, then the whole analytic approach to female psychology must be wrong. Again, this is a sociological and clinical issue; but feminists recite over and over again Freud's various snide and demeaning comments about women, implying that since Freud had a prejudice or blind spot against women, the entire psychoanalytic theory of the psychology of women is wrong. This is an ad hominem rather than a clinical argument. Salzman (1967) points out that a tremendous variety of factors goes into the formation of character, and the concept that anatomy is destiny is probably too simplistic a view of character formation. There is an absolutely unsatisfactory ambience about Freud's theory, in that the woman is viewed as an embittered, castrated male rather than a healthy female in her own right (see also Schafer 1974).

The complex problem of gender role has been studied in a number of physiologic, biochemical, and chromosomal ways in recent years. Although the whole matter requires review and restudy, (Chessick 1983, 1984, 1988) there is no agreement at this time that Freud's basic psychoanalytic tenets of female psychology have been disproven by any form of evidence. The entire debate over feminine psychology unfortunately has been very muddled and confused by the issue of who is for or against psychoanalysis as a whole, and by such political issues as women's liberation and radicalism.

These arguments have a long history, starting with the debate between Deutsch, Lampl-de Groot, and Freud, on the one side, and

Horney and Jones, on the other (Fliegel 1973). Freud's later writing on the subject began with his paper "The Dissolution of the Oedipus Complex" (1924), and was answered in a 1924 paper "On the Genesis of the Castration Complex in Women" by Horney (1967). The latter's basic contention was that the girl's oedipal attachment develops out of her intrinsic femininity undergoing its own maturational process, not out of penis envy. The notion of the maturation of intrinsic, innate, internal femininity was not accepted by Freud, and in his next paper, "Some Psychical Consequences of the Anatomical Distinction between the Sexes" (1925), he stuck to his original concept of the importance of penis envy in setting the little girl off on the pathway of the Oedipus complex.

Fliegel (1973) suggests that Horney's thesis of an intrinsic, pleasure-oriented feminine sexuality that undergoes its own vicissitudes of development is practically a mirror image of Freud's (1925) paper. Freud's paper also contains some criticism of Horney, which she did not accept, and she responded in 1926 in a paper entitled "The Flight from Womanhood: The Masculinity Complex in Women as Viewed by Men and Women" (1967), a frankly polemical work that stresses the importance of motherhood envy in men. This paper, which may be thought of as the inception of the women's liberation movement, led to a complete separation between Horney and Freud. Unfortunately, Freud's (1933) final words on feminine psychology also contain some very disparaging antifemale remarks, and his paper "Female Sexuality" (1931) simply recapitulates his theories (see Table 1).

These opposing views carry important theoretical implications. The result of Freud's view is that since women can never really gain a penis, a woman never really gets what she wants and no amount of psychotherapeutic work can ever disguise this fact. In this sense, all psychotherapeutic work with females must be regarded as unfinished and women as unsatisfied (Freud 1937). In contrast to this, Horney argues that it is not correct that penis envy must be accepted with resignation as the end point of treatment. Penis envy, according to Horney, could be found to screen other early losses and privations or deeper feminine wishes and developmental failures in other areas. This is an extremely important clinical debate. A supplement to the 1976 (vol. 24) *Journal of the American Psychoanalytic Association* contains a series of excellent papers that present various aspects of this debate.

References

Ash, M. (1971). Freud on feminine identity and feminine sexuality. *Psychiatry* 34: 322–329.

Blos, P. (1962). *On Adolescence: A Psychoanalytic Interpretation.* New York: Free Press.

Chessick, R. (1983). Marilyn Monroe: Psychoanalytic pathography of a pre-oedipal disorder. *Dynamic Psychotherapy* 1:161–176.

———— (1984). Was Freud right about feminine psychology? *American Journal of Psychoanalysis* 44:355–368.

———— (1988). Thirty unresolved psychodynamic questions pertaining to feminine psychology. *American Journal of Psychotherapy* 42:86–95.

Deutsch, H. (1944). *The Psychology of Women,* 2 vols. New York: Grune & Stratton.

———— (1973). *Confrontations with Myself.* New York: Norton.

Fisher, S. (1973). *The Female Orgasm: Psychology, Physiology, Fantasy.* New York: Basic Books.

Fliegel, Z. (1973). Feminine psychosexual development in Freudian theory. *Psychoanalytic Quarterly* 42:385–406.

Fliess, R. (1948). *The Psychoanalytic Reader.* New York: International Universities Press.

Freud, S. (1924). The dissolution of the Oedipus complex. *Standard Edition* 19:173–179.

———— (1925). Some psychical consequences of the anatomical distinction between the sexes. *Standard Edition* 19:243–258.

———— (1931). Female sexuality. *Standard Edition* 21:223–243.

———— (1933). New introductory lectures on psychoanalysis. *Standard Edition* 22:112–135.

———— (1937). Analysis terminable and interminable. *Standard Edition* 23:209–253.

Gardiner, M. (1955). Feminine masochism and passivity. *Bulletin of the Philadelphia Association for Psychoanalysis* 5:74–79.

Horney, K. (1967). *Feminine Psychology.* New York: Norton.

Masters, W., and Johnson, V. (1966). *Human Sexual Response.* Boston: Little, Brown.

Muslin, H. (1971). The superego in women. In *Moral Values and the Superego Concept in Psychoanalysis,* ed. S. Post, pp. 101–125. New York: International Universities Press.

Salzman, L. (1967). Psychology of the female. *Archives of Psychiatry* 17:195–203.

Schafer, R. (1974). Problems in Freud's psychology of women. *Journal of the American Psychoanalytic Association* 22:459–485.

Sherfey, M. (1973). *The Nature and Evolution of Female Sexuality.* New York: Random House.

Stoller, R. (1973). Sex research and psychoanalysis. *American Journal of Psychiatry* 130:241–251.

FERENCZI, SÁNDOR (1873–1933)

Of all the psychoanalytic pioneers, Sándor Ferenczi perhaps has been the most neglected and most misunderstood, as a result of his controversial quarrels with Ernest Jones. His thought and work is currently undergoing a significant reappraisal, and Ferenczi is emerging as a very important pioneer in the area of understanding countertransference (see COUNTERTRANSFERENCE) and in investigating the non-interpretive aspects of psychoanalytic healing.

Ferenczi was born in Hungary and encountered Freud's *Interpretation of Dreams* as a physician specializing in psychiatry. At the time he read it, he felt revulsion, but there must have been sufficient ambivalence to motivate him to make it a point to meet Freud in Vienna in 1908. There followed a very complex relationship between Freud and Ferenczi that does not do very much credit to either of them. There has not yet been sufficient release of the Freud–Ferenczi correspondence to make any definitive judgments about that relationship, and it remains discussed at length in the literature.

Stanton (1990) describes the astonishing confusion that began with Ferenczi's relationship to a married woman named Gizella. In 1911 Gizella, Ferenczi's lover, sent her daughter Elma for analysis with Ferenczi. Ferenczi ceased to desire Gizella and began lusting for Elma.

Because of this, Elma was then sent for analysis to Freud in 1912. Freud advised Ferenczi against marriage to Elma and also wrote and advised Gizella. In addition, Gizella's other daughter, Magda, later married Ferenczi's younger brother. Elma went to America and got married there; the news of this deeply distressed Ferenczi, who developed serious psychosomatic complaints. Following Freud's advice, he proposed to Gizella, with Freud as an intermediary. When they arrived at the town hall for their wedding ceremony, they were told that Gizella's ex-husband had just died of a heart attack.

As a member of Freud's inner circle of practicing analysts, Ferenczi accompanied Freud to the United States in 1909. In 1910 he acted as Freud's representative at the founding of the International Psychoanalytic Association. He also played an important role in the genesis of Freud's landmark papers on metapsychology, but the tension between them steadily increased. To some extent, this was because of the strange "psychoanalysis" that Ferenczi received from Freud, which actually satisfied neither of them, and Freud's involvement in Ferenczi's love life as described above.

From the 1920s Ferenczi began to experiment with radical changes in psychoanalytic procedure, such as "mutual analysis," so eloquently described in his diary (Ferenczi 1988). This mutual analysis technique was abandoned within a year, but considerable differences remained between Ferenczi and Freud (Hoffer 1991).

Ferenczi's "active technique" consisted of heightening the tension by making demands and prohibitions on patients in stalemated analyses, a technique for which Ferenczi is rather well known and which was described in his monograph with Rank (1986; see ACTIVE TECHNIQUE).

Ferenczi renounced this "active technique" in the mid-1920s and went to the opposite extreme in what he called the "relaxation technique," which is less well known. Here he attempted, as Hoffer (1991) points out, "to gratify the patient's longings without making any demands" (p. 467), because "he took it upon himself to enrich psychoanalytic technique by including the 'positives' which he felt Freud omitted, including 'tact', 'empathy', elasticity, indulgence, warmth, candour and responsiveness, in an egalitarian rather than in an authoritarian atmosphere" (p. 467). These attempts at gratification of the patient and violation of the principle of abstinence (see ABSTINENCE) were severely criticized by Freud, as was Ferenczi's attempt to return, at least partially, to Freud's early seduction theory, in which all the claims of the patient of being traumatized in childhood were essentially taken at face value from the manifest content.

Ferenczi was a warm and loving individual who was willing to experiment with various changes in psychoanalytic technique. Vida (1991) remarks, "Ferenczi was a true forebear of those who have sought to incorporate biological, sociological, and historical data into the psychoanalytic field, to represent more accurately a woman's subjective reality in the theory of her sexuality" (p. 280). A three-volume edition of Ferenczi's papers (1950a,b, 1955) has been published in an unsatisfactory English translation.

A brief review of Ferenczi's work by Gedo (1976) is a recommended starting point for the study of Ferenczi. Gedo emphasizes Ferenczi's concept of the "wise baby," which arose out of Ferenczi's unusual opportunities for the study of very difficult cases; Ferenczi's fame brought him many patients that were considered too difficult for most psychoanalysts. The "wise baby" undergoes a precocious maturity in order to defend against helplessness and the fear of abandonment. Such patients may undergo narcissistic withdrawal or assume a parenting function toward their parents. The problem of treating such patients involves the capacity of the analyst to engender sufficient trust in them before they dare to experience their profound dependency in the analysis.

Ferenczi was concerned with the problem of preoedipal disorders years before the topic became a central one in the psychoanalytic literature. His manipulations of the patient in such techniques as "relaxation therapy" and "mutual analysis" had as a basic aim the attempt to get at the walled off core of the patient's personality. In mutual analysis, physical holding did take place. Such a therapy, involving the patients being allowed to kiss Ferenczi repeatedly, when reported to Freud led to Freud's stern admonition and harmed Ferenczi's reputation. Fe-

renczi himself realized and admitted that such techniques were not successful, and at no time did he allow them to lead to overt genital sexuality. The importance of his experiments today rests on the fact that such techniques shift the focus of the curative aspect of psychoanalysis from interpretation to the transference–countertransference interaction. This "transference–countertransference dynamic" becomes crucial (Stanton 1990):

> The analyst, therefore, had to sense when to "let go," and how to work with the countertransference to promote the dynamic unconscious relationship through which psychoanalysis advanced. There were no hard and fast rules for this, just a warning not "to overstep the right limits in either a positive or negative sense," that is, not to be too "active" in expression of either love or hate for the patient. [p. 147]

References

Ferenczi, S. (1950a). *Sex in Psychoanalysis: The Selected Papers of Sándor Ferenczi, M.D.,* vol. 1, trans. E. Jones. New York: Basic Books.

――― (1950b). *Further Contributions to the Theory and Technique of Psychoanalysis: The Selected Papers of Sándor Ferenczi, M.D.,* vol. 2, trans. J. Suttie. New York: Basic Books.

――― (1955). *Final Contributions to the Problems and Methods of Psychoanalysis: The Selected Papers of Sándor Ferenczi, M.D.,* vol. 3, trans. E. Mosbacher. New York: Basic Books.

――― (1988). *The Clinical Diary of Sándor Ferenczi,* ed. J. DuPont, trans. M. Balint and N. Jackson. Cambridge, MA: Harvard University Press.

Ferenczi, S., and Rank, O. (1986). *The Development of Psychoanalysis.* Madison, CT: International Universities Press, 1925.

Gedo, J. (1976). The wise baby reconsidered. In *Freud: The Fusion of Science and Humanism—The Intellectual History of Psychoanalysis,* ed. J. Gedo and G. Pollock, pp. 356–378. New York: International Universities Press.

Hoffer, A. (1991). The Freud–Ferenczi controversy—a living legacy. *International Review of Psycho-analysis* 18:465–472.

Stanton, M. (1990). *Sándor Ferenczi: Reconsidering Active Intervention.* London: Free Association Books.

Vida, J. (1991). Sándor Ferenczi on female sexuality. *Journal of the American Academy of Psychoanalysis* 19:271–281.

FIFTY-MINUTE HOUR

The 50-minute hour has become an anachronism. Greenson (1974), in a classic article, called our attention to what this means. When the patient comes in at the end of a previous patient's 45 minutes and says, "Doctor, the couch is still warm from your last patient," what does this "assembly-line" procedure do to the ambience of the treatment? Greenson claims that the old-fashioned 50-minute hour was better for both the therapist and the patient; furthermore, that the assembly-line approach causes the patient to start the hour without the therapist. This is because the therapist has had no break from the last patient and is still thinking about the previous session as the new patient begins to talk.

Greenson points out that the only reason for this change in the length of sessions is money. Patients know this and resent it. Greenson argues that analysts who are both financially and emotionally well off tend not to use the assembly-line

procedure. He sees it as an act of hostility to treat patients on such a basis, since it degrades the patient, fatigues the analyst, and kills the pleasure of the work. According to Greenson, back-to-back sessions encourage sadomasochistic transference–countertransference relationships.

There is no question that the 45-minute hour is much more efficient in terms of the use of the therapist's time as measured by financial remuneration. My sense is that either the 50-minute hour or two 45-minute sessions followed by a 15-minute break is the optimal way to see patients. I believe that Greenson is right and that therapists who see patient after patient on a 45-minute basis all day long are displaying unresolved narcissistic problems in the area of money and an unconscious hostility to their patients.

Reference

Greenson, R. (1974). The decline and fall of the fifty-minute hour. *Journal of the American Psychoanalytic Association* 22: 785–791.

FIXATION

Fixation is evidence of failure to progress satisfactorily through the classical phases of libidinal development. It is manifested by the persistent demanding of archaic methods of gratification, immature ways of relating to other people, and the use of primitive types of defenses. Freud (1916) tried to use this concept to explain perversions, in which he felt there was a fixation at some stage of psychosexual development. Later he believed that these fixations were very important in the understanding of neuroses. For example, Freud held that fixation in the anal stage of development was quite important in the obsessive-compulsive disorders.

Freud used the analogy of an army under attack that had to retreat to strong points to defend itself. This symbolized the individual who, overwhelmed with the pressures of adulthood, regresses to the fixation points from childhood. The neurotic symptoms then appear, and represent the conflicts involved at the fixation points in childhood development. That is to say, the neurotic symptom represents a compromise formation between the unacceptable infantile wish stemming from the stage at which the patient is fixated developmentally, the inhibition of that wish, and both punishment and gratification in a disguised form. Freud believed that in the classical psychoneuroses the unresolved Oedipus complex was the fixation point to which the patient regressed, and therefore the symptoms represented the expression of unacceptable oedipal wishes in the compromise formation described above.

The more extreme examples of fixation occur when there is actually a developmental arrest and the patient does not progress at all past the point of fixation. Patients who remain fixated at the oral or anal stage were thought of as having preoedipal disorders, but this attitude has been largely discarded. It is clear that even borderline patients, for example, do go through the oedipal stage on the road to adulthood. All but the most extremely pathological patients have traversed the stages of psychosexual development. A developmental arrest means that the further stages are grossly distorted, in both their presentation and resolution, by derivatives of the fixated stage. For example, a patient who is fixated at a stage of oral sadism will experience the primal scene even during the oedipal period in terms of ferocious cannibalistic activity.

Freud (1905) ties fixation with the theory of the libido and defines it as causing the persistence of anachronistic sexual traits. For example, in perversions the individual seeks particular kinds of activity or else remains attached to certain properties of an object whose importance can be traced to something in the sexual life of his or her childhood. This also implies the importance of childhood trauma, which was paramount in Freud's mind at the time.

Freud was not consistent in his use of the term "fixation." At times he speaks of fixation of a memory or of a symptom; at other times he describes fixation of the libido to or at a certain stage or type of object. What is of clinical importance is whether the given symptomatology of a patient shows a developmental arrest or a regression to an earlier fixation point. The latter represents less psychopathology and has a better prognosis in psychotherapeutic work. It is often very difficult to make this judgment before considerable psychotherapeutic work has taken place because the presenting symptoms may be very dramatic and suggest a developmental arrest by their very intensity; on the other hand, initial dramatic presentations can simply constitute a regression.

References

Freud, S. (1905). Three essays on the theory of sexuality. *Standard Edition* 7:125–243.

———— (1916). Introductory lectures on psychoanalysis. *Standard Edition* 16: 243–496.

FORECLOSURE

In delineating the essential psychopathology of neuroses and psychoses, Lacan (1977, 1978) describes the "paternal metaphor": the father has to be accepted by the mother, or the child will remain subjected to her and cannot fit into the symbolic order. This disaster Lacan calls "foreclosure." The mother's attitude to both the father and the child is critical to the genesis of mental illness. In the normal state, identification with the father liberates the child and provides the child with a secure place in the family and the culture. If foreclosure occurs, the child fails to enter into the symbolic order. The person so constituted remains in nondistinction between the self and the external world, dwelling in the realm of the imaginary—that is, psychosis. In the neuroses there is a disturbed relationship between the imaginary and the symbolic worlds, so that speech and behavior become deformed, represented by neurotic symptoms. In contrast to the psychotic, who lives

in an imaginary world, the neurotic displays what Lacan calls a wish fulfilled but mutilated.

References

Lacan, J. (1977). *Ecrits: A Selection*, trans. A. Sheridan. New York: Norton.

———— (1978). *The Four Fundamental Concepts of Psycho-analysis*, trans. A. Sheridan. New York: Norton.

FORT-DA GAME (GONE-THERE)

Freud (1920) observed his 18-month-old grandson playing a game in which the little boy, throwing a spool connected to a string over the side of his crib, called out *"Fort"* (gone). Then he reeled it back by the use of the string, crying *"Da"* (there). There are at least four different interpretations (Chessick 1992) of this famous incident. For Freud (1920), it represents instinctual renunciation, allowing the boy's mother to go away without protest, in a form of mastery, "beyond the pleasure principle." For R. D. Laing, it is an attempt to establish ontological security. For Kohut, it represents an effort to maintain control over a self-object, which, as it works, leads to a sense of cohesion of the self, triumph, and joy. For Lacan, it is an example of how the child is born into language. The desire for the mother and the frustration of this desire are expressed through verbal sounds, "gone" and "there." Man is constituted by his language, says Lacan, an idea borrowed from Heidegger.

There is a little noticed footnote

in Freud's (1920) "Beyond the Pleasure Principle" (p. 15), in which Freud mentions the child looking at itself in the mirror and then under it (the mirror did not reach to the floor), thus making *itself* disappear. Here absence and presence are being verbalized (*fort-da*), not just the desire to control the mother. This does seem related to Lacan's clever interpretation.

References

Chessick, R. (1992). *What Constitutes the Patient in Psychotherapy*. Northvale, NJ: Jason Aronson.

Freud, S. (1920). Beyond the pleasure principle. *Standard Edition* 18:3–64.

FRAGMENTATION

Kohut's self psychology has been criticized (Schwartz 1978) because it lacks a clear definition of the term "fragmentation." The fragmenting self occurs when the patient reacts to narcissistic disappointments, such as the therapist's lack of empathy, by the loss of a sense of cohesive self. Signs of this are disheveled dress, posture and gait disturbances, vague anxiety, time and space disorientation, and hypochondriacal concerns. In a minor way this occurs in all of us when our self-esteem has been taxed for long periods and no replenishing sustenance has presented itself, or after a series of failures that shake our self-esteem.

The concept of the fragmentation of the self seems to be equated with psychoticlike phenomena, at which time reality contact, even with the therapist, is in danger of being lost. It is characterized as a regressive phenomenon, predominantly autoerotic, a state of fragmented self-nuclei, in contrast to the state of the cohesive self (Kohut 1971). Kohut (1977) emphasizes the signs of fragmentation of the self having to do with the subjective feeling of self-state anxiety and what Freudians would call signs of deteriorating ego function.

In his early work, Kohut (1971) calls fragmentation of the self "dissolution of the narcissistic unity of the self" (pp. 120–121) and explains how it is often accompanied by frantic activities of various kinds in the work and sexual areas, especially in an effort to "counteract the subjectively painful feeling of self-fragmentation by a variety of forced actions, ranging from physical stimulation and athletic activities to excessive work in . . . profession and business" (p. 119). In Kohut's later work, fragmentation of the self seems to be defined by the experiences that it produces (see SELF PSYCHOLOGY).

References

Kohut, H. (1971). *The Analysis of the Self*. New York: International Universities Press.

——— (1977). *The Restoration of the Self*. New York: International Universities Press.

Schwartz, L. (1978). Review of *The Restoration of the Self*. *Psychoanalytic Quarterly* 47:436–443.

FREE ASSOCIATION

Freud gradually developed a technique of free association between 1892 and 1898. Breuer and Freud (1893–1895), in their work using hypnosis, were already attempting to encourage the patient to give voice to all thoughts, without exception. One of their patients called this "chimney sweeping" (p. 30) and actually taught Breuer and Freud to listen while she described her thoughts as they appeared, because these led gradually to the more and more important material. In the atmosphere of *fin de siècle* Vienna it was very unusual for a doctor to listen. The tradition was that the doctor examined the patient and gave instructions, and the idea of listening at length and being interested in every thought that came to a patient's mind was a radical innovation. Unfortunately, today it has again become unusual for doctors to listen.

Free association is extremely difficult because we are all socially trained not to reveal a substantial portion of our thoughts. Some analysts have quipped that when a patient can free associate properly, the analysis is over; a great deal of analytic work consists of dealing with resistances to free association.

The term "free," of course, refers to the patient being asked to suspend conscious control and to express verbally each thought and feeling, as well as sensation, image, and memory, without reservation as it spontaneously occurs. This is sometimes referred to as the fundamental rule of psychoanalysis and requires the patient to overcome the usual conscious embarrassment, fear, shame, and guilt. The interventions of the analyst's interpreting defenses hopefully removes these defenses and allows more material to bubble up into the patient's conscious and be expressed through free association.

Free association is an ideal and can never totally occur. Out of the interaction between the patient and the analyst a certain shaping of the patient's free associations inevitably takes place, since a patient wishes to either please or oppose the analyst, depending on the current state of the transference. This presents one of the most difficult problems in the verification of psychoanalytic hypotheses, because a patient may tend to produce material that verifies any hypothesis that the analyst may put forward. In other situations, the analyst may hear only that material he or she wishes to hear (see EVENLY SUSPENDED ATTENTION). The problem of selecting out of the free associations what is relevant also remains extremely difficult and is central to the craft of psychoanalytic listening.

In my supervisory experience the concept of free association often appears to be abused. For example, it makes no sense to tell a patient who is coming in once a week to report every thought, feeling, and sensation that comes to mind. The patient may obediently fill a session with free association, but the therapist may simply lose contact with where the patient is and what is going on in his or her life. As a general rule of thumb, the less frequently a patient is seen, the more the therapy should be problem oriented and the less free association should be employed. The novice is sometimes fooled in the other direction because the patient may use the request for free association to fill up session after session, even three or four times a week, with disconnected and unintelligible gibberish. This is a form of resistance and does not constitute genuine free association. If the associations seem to be leading nowhere at all, either the analyst is not listening properly or the patient is too anxious or in a state of incipient fragmentation and appropriate interventions need to be supplied.

Reference

Breuer, J., and Freud, S. (1893-1895). Studies on hysteria. *Standard Edition* 2:1-309.

FREUD, ANNA (1895-1982)

Anna Freud, daughter of Sigmund Freud, produced seven volumes of collected works of her own (A. Freud 1972). A recent excellent biography gives a balanced view of her life and work (Young-Bruehl 1988). She shared her father's professional life and the vicissitudes of the psychoanalytic movement in the years between the world wars and afterward. With the Nazi occupation of Austria, Anna Freud fled with her father to England, where she founded the Hampstead War Nurseries for children who had suffered through bombing, indiscriminate evacuation, and billeting. After the war she founded a child therapy clinic, the largest center in the world for the treatment of children and training of child analysts. She was involved in a bitter controversy with followers of Melanie Klein (see KLEIN) over the proper technique for child psychoanalysis (King and Steiner 1991).

Anna Freud became a living legend in psychoanalytic circles, carrying on her father's late-life focus in psychoanalysis on the exploration of the ego. Her most famous work, *The Ego and the Mechanisms of Defense* (1946), constitutes a milestone in the development of psychoanalytic psychotherapy. It elaborates in detail on the ego and the mechanisms of defense, which she felt could be studied through the examination of the resistances presented during psychoanalytic treatment. She reviewed such defense mechanisms as regression, repression, reaction-formation, isolation, undoing, projection, introjection, turning against the self, reversal, and sublimation or displacement of instinctual aims.

Much of her book is devoted to elucidating hitherto poorly understood and rather vague concepts. Preliminary stages of the defense mechanisms are discussed; examples given are denial in fantasy, denial in word and act, and ego restriction (see EGO). Two important types of defenses are investigated at length: identification with the aggressor (crucial in superego formation) and a form of altruism (the altruistic surrender of one's own instinctual impulses in favor of other people). Finally, defenses motivated by fear of the strength of the instincts are illustrated by focusing on the phenomena of puberty, in which a relatively strong id confronts a relatively weak ego.

The battle of puberty is resolved, she said, depending on the strength of the id (which is seen as a physiologic aspect of the individual), the ego's tolerance or intolerance of instincts (which depends on the character formed by the latency period), and the nature and efficacy of the defense mechanisms at the ego's command. This last group of factors is decisive. Certain characteristic adolescent defense mechanisms are discussed in detail, such as asceticism, intellectuality, adolescent object love, and identification. The ego is seen as victorious when its defensive measures effectively avoid anxiety and transform instincts so that even in difficult circumstances some gratification is secured. Thus a harmonious relation between the id, superego, and outer world is established.

Anna Freud begins her important monograph *Difficulties in the Path of Psychoanalysis* (1969) with Freud's suggestion that therapeutic alteration of the ego must be accomplished by the psychotherapist. The ego distortions that hinder analysis are acquired by the individual in his or her earliest defensive struggles against unpleasure. In this tract the importance of a therapeutic normalization of the ego is focused on, but it is left open as to how and in what way this can be accomplished. Anna Freud points out that any attempt to carry analysis from the verbal to the preverbal period of development brings with it practical and technical innovations as well as theoretical implications, many of which are controversial. There is no doubt that this issue is just as pertinent and controversial today.

References

Freud, A. (1946). *The Ego and the Mechanisms of Defense.* New York: International Universities Press.

———— (1969). *Difficulties in the Path of Psychoanalysis.* New York: International Universities Press.

———— (1972). *The Writings of Anna Freud,* 7 vols. New York: International Universities Press.

King, P., and Steiner, R., eds. (1991). *The Freud–Klein Controversies.* New York: Routledge.

Young-Bruehl, E. (1988). *Anna Freud: A Biography.* New York: Summit Books.

FREUD, SIGMUND (1856–1939)

Sigmund Freud's theories and ideas are discussed throughout this dictionary under a variety of headings. For an excellent scholarly biography and review of Freud's life and work, see Gay (1988). The classic work by Jones (1953, 1955, 1957), although biased, is also extremely valuable and informative. Freud was born in Freiberg, Moravia. His parents were Jewish and he was the eldest of seven children from his father's second marriage. His favorite work was in classical physiology and biology, in the strict physico-chemical laboratory of Ernst Brücke, but he was widely read in the classics and was blessed with a photographic memory. He trained to be a neurologist under the pressure of having to support a wife and family. The turning point of his career was a visit to Paris, where he attended the displays of the famous neurologist Charcot, who demonstrated on hypnotized hysterical patients the power of suggestion in symptom removal. Because of his compelling need to be famous he (1896) rather abruptly reported on cases of hysteria to the Vienna medical society, connecting them etiologically to sexual abuse in childhood and claiming the same to be always true of cases, ubiquitous at the time, of female hysteria. This, in addition to his premature publications about cocaine, caused damage to his reputation. He opened his practice, wrote a book on cerebral palsy, and began treating hysterical patients.

Despite his shortcomings and limitations as a man of his Victorian culture, Freud still presents us with a worthwhile model. He was capable of physical courage and amazing stoic endurance even in his later years when he suffered from a painful cancer of the oral cavity, requiring many operations and an irritating prosthesis. He was a man of tremendous energy who combined a boundless capacity for work with the ability to concentrate intensely on one goal. He allied physical courage with moral courage, but his conviction of the truth of his theories was so complete that he did not easily admit contradiction.

Freud lived morally, socially, and professionally according to the highest standards of a man and phy-

sician of his time and status. He was a person of scrupulous honesty and professional dignity. He kept his appointments exactly and set all his activities to a timetable. He was equally punctilious about his appearance; considerable dignity and decorum were expected of professional men in his day, and Freud lived up to these expectations. In many ways he may be said to have lived a life beyond reproach, and in his genuine and human interest in patients, his boundless capacity for work, and his passion to discover the truth, Freud makes a very fine model indeed for anyone who is attempting to do psychotherapy.

Freud went through four phases in his work: first, a search for methodology, culminating in the method of free association; second, a delving into the many ramifications of the unconscious, the preconscious, and the conscious—that is to say, the workings of the mind according to the topographical theory; third, an unfinished development of modern structural metapsychology and ego psychology; and finally, a preoccupation with matters of life and death and the general issues of sociology, anthropology, and philosophy.

As everybody knows, the founder of long-term, intensive psychotherapy and psychoanalysis was Freud, and in this sense all of Freud is worth reading and repeatedly rereading throughout one's career for its historical interest as well as for the innumerable clinical pearls scattered throughout his writings (Chessick 1980). In my experience, the emphasis on actually reading the works of Freud in psychiatric training programs is diminishing at an accelerated pace. This is unfortunate, not only for the loss of clinical knowledge and historical perspective it entails, but also for the loss of an outstanding model of scientific writing.

If Freud had died before 1897 or before the age of 40, he would have achieved at most perhaps a page or two in books on the history of psychiatry. Up to then his work on a theory of the neuroses had culminated in "The Aetiology of Hysteria," published in 1896. His basic thesis was that hysteria is determined by traumatic sexual experiences in childhood, the unconscious memory of which reappears in a symbolic way in the symptoms of the illness. The illness, in turn, can be cured by recalling the memory into consciousness and discharging the associated affect (see ABREACTION). The sexual aspects of these traumata are stressed, and Freud claimed that with amazing frequency patients had been seduced by adults in their immediate environment and that this is often followed by sexual experience with children of the same age. Although Freud proclaimed this theory to be a great discovery, a year later he realized he had been misled by patient fantasies.

Had Freud died at this point, he would have received credit for developing, with the help of Breuer and of his patient Emmy Von N., a method of investigating hysterical symptoms (Breuer and Freud 1893–1895). The method of free association replaced hypnosis in Freud's treatment of hysteria, and ultimately became the fundamental rule of psychoanalysis (see FREE ASSOCIATION).

In 1897 Freud at 41 took one of those rare and incredible turns in life that might be called a turn toward genius. Perhaps the discovery that his whole theory of hysteria was based on a misleading conception, or the death of his father in 1896, or a midlife crisis led Freud to begin his self-analysis through the use of dreams.

The main tenets of depth psychology are Freud's dream theory and his theory of errors, which represent the first two generalizations of the pattern he had worked out for hysteria. These theories were elaborated simultaneously and presented in two of his best-known books, *The Interpretation of Dreams* in 1900 and the *Psychopathology of Everyday Life* in 1901, and were followed by his (1905) epoch-making monograph on sexuality. Western culture has never been the same.

Freud's creative surge began again with "On Narcissism" (1914). This was the first paper following the 1905 monograph in which he modified his instinct theory. (Freud's instinct theory actually went through four phases and caused him a great deal of difficulty and heavy thinking; see INSTINCT). This and the series of five papers that followed it were written essentially to present Freud's notion of metapsychology. In fact, the five papers were conceived of as chapters in a book entitled *Introduction to Metapsychology,* and were written with an amazing burst of creative energy in six weeks during the spring of 1915. Perhaps even more remarkably, Freud wrote five more essays in the next six weeks, which he subsequently destroyed. (A copy of one of these [Freud 1987] was found recently among Ferenczi's papers.) His famous papers and case histories, written during these years, remain mandatory reading for all psychotherapists.

Despite the dreadful living conditions in post–World War I Vienna, Freud in his sixties experienced still another creative surge. In *Beyond the Pleasure Principle* (1920), an attempt is made to give metapsychology its final shape. The notion of the repetition compulsion, of the utmost importance to psychotherapists, is emphasized here. This is the most original clinical contribution in the book. From it, along with other considerations, Freud derives his concepts of the death instinct and primary masochism, which are still very controversial (see DEATH INSTINCT). This set the stage for a basic revision of his thinking, known as the structural theory.

It is best to begin study of the structural theory phase of Freud's work with one of his great masterpieces, *The Ego and the Id* (1923), which describes the "three harsh masters" that the ego has to deal with—reality, the id, and the superego. The concept of the id was borrowed from Groddeck (1923), and the concept of the superego seems closest to Nietzsche (1887) in *The Genealogy of Morals,* but this is a matter of dispute. Freud did not acknowledge a debt to Nietzsche, although he did acknowledge his debt

to Groddeck. With the publication of *The Ego and the Id,* ego psychology became the predominant interest of depth psychology. The final touches were put on this theory in 1926 with the publication of *Inhibitions, Symptoms, and Anxiety* (1926). This work, which some have called one of Freud's most difficult books, was written partly as a refutation of Rank's birth trauma theory and contains the famous signal theory of anxiety (see ANXIETY). As a consequence of all this, the focus in long-term, intensive psychotherapy shifted permanently from the instinctual forces to the analysis of the ego (see EGO and FREUD, ANNA).

References

Breuer, J., and Freud, S. (1893–1895). Studies on hysteria. *Standard Edition* 2:1–309.

Chessick, R. (1980). *Freud Teaches Psychotherapy.* Hillsdale, NJ: Analytic Press.

Freud, S. (1896). The aetiology of hysteria. *Standard Edition* 3:189–221.

—— (1900). The interpretation of dreams. *Standard Edition* 4,5:1–627.

—— (1901). Psychopathology of everyday life. *Standard Edition* 6:1–310.

—— (1905). Three essays on sexuality. *Standard Edition* 7:125–243.

—— (1914). On narcissism: an introduction. *Standard Edition* 14:67–102.

—— (1920). Beyond the pleasure principle. *Standard Edition* 18:3–64.

—— (1923). The ego and the id. *Standard Edition* 19:3–66.

—— (1926). Inhibitions, symptoms, and anxiety. *Standard Edition* 20:77–174.

—— (1987). *A Phylogenetic Fantasy: Overview of the Transference Neuroses,* trans. A. Hoffer and P. Hoffer. Cambridge, MA: Harvard University Press.

Gay, P. (1988). *Freud: A Life for Our Time.* New York: Norton.

Groddeck, G. (1923). *The Book of the It.* New York: Mentor Books, 1961.

Jones, E. (1953). *The Life and Work of Sigmund Freud,* vol. 1. New York: Basic Books.

———— (1955). *The Life and Work of Sigmund Freud,* vol. 2. New York: Basic Books.

———— (1957). *The Life and Work of Sigmund Freud,* vol. 3. New York: Basic Books.

Nietzsche, F. (1887). The genealogy of morals. In *Basic Writings,* trans. and ed. W. Kaufmann, pp. 439–599. New York: Random House, 1968.

FROMM-REICHMANN, FRIEDA (1889–1957)

Frieda Fromm-Reichmann shifted attention from the understanding of the patient to the understanding of the psychotherapist in attempting to clear away the obstacles to psychoanalytic cure and extend the theoretical knowledge of psychoanalysis to the treatment of schizophrenia. Her *Principles of Intensive Psychotherapy* (1950) remains one of the outstanding fundamental texts on the subject, and every other book written on the subject since that time refers extensively back to this work.

Fromm-Reichmann saw psychoanalytic therapy as offered in a "spirit of collaborative guidance." Basing her work on Harry Stack Sullivan's writings, she conceived of treatment as aimed at the solution of difficulties in the growth, maturation, and independence of the patient. The goal is to develop the capacity for mature love—a self-realization in which the patient becomes able to use his or her talents, skills, and powers to his or her satisfaction within a realistic, freely established set of values. She (1959) warned us:

The psychotherapist is expected to be stable and secure enough to be constantly aware of and in control of that which he conveys to his patients in words and mindful of that which he may convey in empathy; that his need for operations aimed at his own security and satisfaction should not interfere with his ability to listen consistently to patients, with full alertness to their communications per se and, if possible, to the unworded implications of their verbalized communications; that he should never feel called upon to be anything more or less than the participant-observer of the emotional experiences which are conveyed to him by his patients. . . . On the surface, these rules seem obvious and easy to follow; yet they are not. . . . In actuality, none of us will be able to live up to all of them. We have to bear in mind that no amount of inner security and self respect protects the psychiatrist from being as much a subject of and vulnerable to the inevitable vicissitudes of life as is everyone else. [p. 86]

Fromm-Reichmann graduated from medical school in Prussia in 1914. During World War I she took care of brain-injured soldiers as a member of the staff of Kurt Goldstein. Under his leadership, she gained a solid foundation in the physiology and pathology of brain function and acquired insights into Goldstein's notion of the "catastrophic reaction" of brain-injured patients that prepared her for an understanding of psychotic panic states. During the 1920s she worked in a sanatorium in Dresden and became a visiting physician at Kraeplin's Psychiatric Clinic in Munich.

Her discovery of Freud's writings led to a turning point in her professional career. She undertook psychoanalytic training and practiced in Heidelberg, establishing a private psychoanalytic sanatorium there; together with her husband Erich Fromm she founded the Psychoanalytic Training Institute of Southwest Germany. Georg Groddeck, who first proposed the term "id," became an important influence in the group of Heidelberg psychoanalysts to which Fromm-Reichmann belonged. When the Nazis overran Germany, Fromm-Reichmann fled to Alsace-Lorraine, Palestine, and finally the United States. An opportunity to test the psychoanalytic treatment of functional psychoses was offered to her at Chestnut Lodge, a sanatorium in Rockwell, Maryland. There she achieved, in the course of the years, surprising results in the treatment of psychoses. At Chestnut Lodge, she became a close friend of Harry Stack Sullivan.

Her work is based on the premise that there is a tendency toward health in every human being, regardless of how seriously mentally disturbed he or she is. Fromm-Reichmann was fully convinced of this idea taken from Harry Stack Sullivan. In her textbook, in some cases the patient is even asked to operate for the time being solely on the therapist's belief that it might be worthwhile to recover. The presence or lack of presence of this inherent tendency toward health and the capacity of the psychotic ego to become altered in psychotherapy remain two of the most important and controversial issues facing modern psycho-

analytic psychotherapists. One of the most interesting facets of this is that older and more experienced therapists tend to be more pessimistic about the extent to which the ego can be basically altered, whereas the younger and more enthusiastic therapists tend to be more optimistic about how thoroughly basic change can take place. This was not true of Fromm-Reichmann, who remained optimistic to the end of her life and wrote beautifully about it.

Her final paper, unfinished, is entitled "On Loneliness" (1959). It stands apart from her other productions because it combines important psychoanalytic insight with an extraordinary aesthetic effect.

Fromm-Reichmann's great contribution was to apply the principles of psychoanalysis and the findings of Harry Stack Sullivan to the clinical practice of intensive psychotherapy with schizophrenics. In addition, she focused more accurately on the meaning of maturity as the capacity to exchange love and success in interpersonal relationships, which in psychoanalytic language represents shifts and alterations in basic ego functions. Finally, she put the responsibility for the success or failure of psychotherapy more heavily on the psychotherapist, on his or her capacity to empathize and listen, which in turn depended on the therapist's own treatment, innate abilities, and education.

References

Fromm-Reichmann, F. (1950). *Principles of Intensive Psychotherapy*. Chicago: University of Chicago Press.
_____ (1959). On loneliness. In *Psychoanalysis*

and Psychotherapy: Selected Papers of Frieda Fromm-Reichmann, ed. D. Bullard, pp. 325–336. Chicago: University of Chicago Press.

FUSION OF HORIZONS

Gadamer (1982) attempted to move entirely away from a natural sciences approach to understanding humans to a hermeneutic approach. He suggested replacing the natural sciences approach, which assumes a subject without preconceptions studying a text, for example, the "objective" psychoanalytic authority studying a patient's narrative of a dream, with an approach realizing that "understanding" always arises out of our preconceptions, our position in a historical tradition. To understand the patient's narrative and associations, then, we must merge or fuse our horizons with the patient and the patient's society, which always yields a new meaning each time there is an encounter between a patient and a doctor, a reader and a text, or an historian and an historical "fact" (see HERMENEUTICS).

These communal horizons channel and constitute individual human experience. It follows, as Gadamer explains, that our self-knowledge is not freely chosen but is actually deeply embedded in culture, history, and our bodily being, aspects that are so pervasive as to be nearly invisible. Gadamer writes, "History does not belong to us, but we belong to it. Long before we understand ourselves through the process of self-examination, we understand ourselves in a self-evident way in the family, society and state in which we live. . . . The self awareness of the individual is only a flickering in the closed circuits of historical life" (p. 245).

In *Truth and Method* (1982), his major work, Gadamer points out how there is a dialectic or mutual influence between the subject of interpretation and the interpreter, in which, as the horizons of each coparticipate, meaning is generated in that particular dyadic pair at that particular time and place. What is known is always known by a knower situated within history and society, and therefore interpretation is always conditioned and influenced by the tradition and the horizon of understanding within which the individual operates. Gadamer proclaims that one should not attempt to overcome the "prejudices" that constitute our sociohistorical vantage point, because no technique and method can ever secure absolute objectivity in interpretation.

Reference

Gadamer, H. (1982). *Truth and Method,* trans. G. Braden and J. Cumming. New York: Crossroad.

G

GADAMER, HANS-GEORG (SEE FUSION OF HORIZONS, HERMENEUTICS, HORIZONS)

GEDO, JOHN (SEE BEYOND INTERPRETATION)

GELASSENHEIT (SERENITY, COMPOSURE)

Bion (1967) advises us to approach each session with a patient without memory, desire, or understanding. He bases this on a kind of faith that the patient will, by projection, place into us whatever important aspects of where he or she is at a given time—whatever important thoughts, feelings, and sensations are in the patient's unconscious at a given time. We are not to interfere with this process by approaching the therapy session with preconceived notions, prejudices, or ambitions as to where the treatment ought to be going (see REVERIE).

This is remarkably similar to Heidegger's concept of *Gelassenheit* (Richardson 1974). In his later work, Heidegger believed that a certain attitude of mind, which he labeled *Gelassenheit*, was needed to get in touch with Being. This is a kind of passive-receptive attitude, in great contrast to the active scientific-empirical approach that we use in trying to understand and interpret nature and which forms the assumed basis of psychiatric treatment today. *Gelassenheit* actually implies, just as in Bion's concept, that if we approach Being actively with a scientific stance, we will be blocked by that very stance from achieving enlightenment.

The importance of these concepts is that they pose an alternative methodology for psychoanalytic treatment. They also presuppose a certain kind of faith that the vital material with which we are trying to make contact will be sent to us in some fashion if we are only properly prepared to receive it. This borders on mysticism and has come under considerable attack; it seems more compatible to the Eastern mind than the Western. An area of investigation is suggested here in which each therapist must come to some personal decisions about how he or she is going to approach a patient.

References

Bion, W. (1967). *Second Thoughts: Selected Papers on Psycho-Analysis.* London: Heinemann.

Richardson, W. (1974). *Heidegger: Through Phenomenology to Thought,* 3rd ed. The Hague, Netherlands: Martinus Nijhoff.

GENITAL STAGE

In *Three Essays on the Theory of Sexuality,* Freud (1905) argued that the genital organization is instituted at puberty and stands in opposition to the polymorphous perversity and autoerotism of infantile sexuality. This gradually became modified in the direction of an equation of infantile and adult genital sexuality, with the so-called phallic stage of infantile genital organization initiating the Oedipus complex (see OEDIPUS COMPLEX). Freud still proclaimed that the definitive genital organization took place in puberty, during which the component instincts are definitively fused, with the pleasure attached to the nongenital erotogenic zones becoming part of the foreplay. To maintain this point of view, the term "genital organization" should be confined to the developmental phase of puberty and the term "phallic phase" to the centering of sexual excitement on the genitals in infantile sexual development.

Moore and Fine (1990) give an excellent review of current controversy involving genitality and the genital stage. Briefly, there seems to be a general consensus that too much emphasis has been placed by practitioners on the importance of the achievement of genital sexuality in a physiological sense and not enough on the value of achieving mutual orgasms with a love partner with whom one is able and willing to share trust and the vicissitudes of life. This has led to a kind of distortion of what it means to be "normal" and probably has contributed to popular and amateur misunderstandings of the goal of psychoanalytic treatment.

References

Freud, S. (1905). Three essays on the theory of sexuality. *Standard Edition* 7:125–243.

Moore, B., and Fine, B. (1990) *Psychoanalytic Terms and Concepts.* New Haven, CT: Yale University Press.

GE-STELL (EN-FRAMING)

This concept is a very important one for psychotherapists. It was introduced by Heidegger (1954) to describe the way human beings are thought of in our age of technology. By his idiosyncratic use of the German word *Ge-stell,* usually translated as En-Framing, he refers to the use of humans as one uses rolling stock in a railroad yard, or raw material, which may be stacked up and stored as a resource that is dispensable and disposable for the purpose of various individuals who are in power. This attitude toward humans, which automatically arises from our age of technology, separates humans from the environment and views the individual as just another object. The extreme consequence of this was the Holocaust.

The issue of *Ge-stell* raises the entire question of what is the best attitude to take toward the patient. Considerable controversy has been generated about the therapist–patient interaction. Should this interaction be viewed as arising from a dyadic process, or as primarily due to transference projections from the patient as an isolated subject onto the relatively "neutral" therapist? These disagreements in the psychoanalytic literature contain basic divergences of philosophical premises (Chessick 1980). The current trend in psychiatry today toward more psychopharmacologic treatment and less psychotherapy is an excellent example of what Heidegger meant by En-Framing in the age of technology.

References

Chessick, R. (1980). Some philosophical assumptions of intensive psychotherapy. *American Journal of Psychotherapy* 34:496–509.

Heidegger, M. (1954). *The Question Concerning Technology and Other Essays,* trans. W. Lovitt. New York: Harper & Row.

GOOD OBJECT (SEE BAD OBJECT)

GRANDIOSE SELF

This term gained prominence in the literature through the work of Kohut (1971, 1977, 1978). In response to stimuli from the environment and due to an epigenetic preprogramming, developmental pathways lead from autoerotism to primary narcissism—in which the infant blissfully experiences the world as being itself—and then, due to inevitable disappointment in such narcissistic omnipotence, to the formation of the grandiose self and the idealized parent imago. The grandiose self carries the conviction of being very powerful, even omnipotent, with a demand for mirroring confirmation by the selfobject; the idealized parent imago attributes all omnipotence to a magical figure, which is then viewed as a selfobject to be controlled and with which to be fused.

By a series of transmuting microinternalizations (see SELF PSYCHOLOGY) in an appropriate environment, the grandiose self becomes incorporated into the ego or self as ambition (in Kohut's [1977] "psychology of the self in the broad sense" it becomes a pole of the bipolar self), a drive or push that can be realistically sublimated and is itself drive-channeling (Kohut 1971), resulting in motivated enthusiastic activity. The idealized parent imago becomes infused into the ego-ideal (or, in the later theory, becomes the other pole of the self), which attracts the individual toward certain goals and performs a drive-curbing function (Kohut 1971). The proper integration of these narcissistic formations leads ultimately by further transformations to a sense of humor, empathy, wisdom, and acceptance of the transience of life, even to creativity within the limitations of the individual.

If the grandiose self is not integrated gradually into the realistic purposes of the ego, derivatives of it are disavowed or it is repressed and persists unaltered in archaic form; the individual then consciously oscillates between irrational overestimation of himself or herself and feelings of inferiority with narcissistic mortification due to the thwarting of ambition.

An important controversy revolves around whether the grandiose self is a normal developmental formation found in all children or whether it represents a pathological formation. Kernberg (1974), influenced by the work of Klein, regards the grandiose self as a pathological structure. He attempts to describe the different qualities of normal infantile narcissism and pathological narcissism, with special emphasis on the difference between the grandiosity of normal children and the grandiosity expressed in pathologically narcissistic adult patients. Kohut (1984) answered this argument. Gedo (1977), although he offers an orientation different from both Kohut and Kernberg (see BEYOND INTERPRETATION), also disagrees with Kernberg's view that the grandiosity primarily defends against rage and aggression.

References

Gedo, J. (1977). Notes on the psychoanalytic management of archaic transferences. *Journal of the American Psychoanalytic Association* 25:787–803.

Kernberg, O. (1974). Contrasting viewpoints regarding the nature and psychoanalytic treatment of narcissistic personalities: a preliminary communication. *Journal of the American Psychoanalytic Association* 22:255–267.

Kohut, H. (1971). *The Analysis of the Self.* New York: International Universities Press.

——— (1977). *The Restoration of the Self.* New York: International Universities Press.

——— (1978). *The Search for the Self,* ed. P. Ornstein. New York: International Universities Press.

——— (1984). *How Does Analysis Cure?* Chicago: University of Chicago Press.

GUILT

It is extremely important in clinical work to have some distinction in mind between "shame" and "guilt." The classic reference on this topic is by Piers and Singer (1953). Both shame and guilt arise from a tension between the ego and the superego. Shame takes place when a person has failed to live up to his or her ego-ideal. An individual feels guilty when he or she has transgressed definitive prohibitions contained in the superego.

The phemonenological experiences of shame and guilt are somewhat different and, of course, are universal. Shame refers more to a kind of narcissistic mortification and produces the various reactions and defenses that an individual uses to deal with narcissistic wounding. Guilt carries with it more fear and anticipation of punishment, and thereby stirs up a different variety of defensive functions.

In more neurotic situations a patient may consciously or unconsciously believe he or she has already carried out a transgression of the superego prohibitions (e.g., hurt a loved one). This often produces either depression or characterologic problems in which the patient seeks pain and punishment. A great many failure neuroses arise out of this. The character type mentioned by Freud (1916) as "those wrecked by success" is explained as related to the patient's unconscious fantasy that success injures a beloved parent.

Guilt produces the common clinical picture of self-mortification and aggression against the self, even to the extent of self-mutilation and suicide. At times one sees reaction formations, as in masochistic characters or individuals who are unable to compete and are excessively submissive and compliant, or a manic sort of defense in which the person deliberately violates and injures everyone. Some patients defend against their guilt by making a career of causing others to feel guilty. The so-called negative therapeutic reaction was thought by Freud (1923) to be based on an unconscious guilt that causes a patient to need the punishment of suffering and therefore prevents him or her from giving up the illness in psychoanalytic treatment (see NEGATIVE THERAPEUTIC REACTION).

None of this should be confused with Kohut's (1978) "guilty man," set off in the psychology of the self against "tragic man." Kohut distinguishes "tragic man," the individual blocked in the attempt to achieve self-realization, from Freud's "guilty man," the individual in conflict over the pleasure-seeking drives and struggling against guilt and anxiety. Guilty man is a concept that refers to the realm of parental responses that the individual receives as a child to single parts of his or her body and single bodily and mental functions. But Kohut points out that there is another realm of parental responses, "attuned to his beginning experience of himself as a larger, coherent and enduring organization, i.e., to him as a self" (pp. 755–756). Individuals with difficulties in this latter realm of parental responses Kohut labels as "tragic man."

References

Freud, S. (1916). Some character-types met with in psychoanalytic work. *Standard Edition* 14:309–333.

_____ (1923). The ego and the id. *Standard Edition* 19.3–66.

Kohut, H. (1978). *The Search for the Self*, ed. P. Ornstein. New York: International Universities Press.

Piers, G., and Singer, M. (1953). *Shame and Guilt*. New York: Norton.

H

HERMENEUTICS

Hermeneutics is usually defined as the art and science of interpretation. It emerged in the seventeenth century as a discipline devoted to establishing the correct interpretation of biblical scripture, with the aim of uncovering and reconstructing the message from God that biblical scripture supposedly contains. The term "hermeneutics" is often traced to Hermes (in Greek mythology, the messenger of the gods—and also the god of cheats, thieves, and gamblers), but the actual etymology of the word is probably from the verb ἑρμηνεύω (hermēneuō), which refers to the explication of meaning and to interpretation. By the end of the eighteenth century hermeneutics began to be expanded to apply to literary texts and historical periods. The German philosopher Wilhelm Dilthey (1831–1911) brought hermeneutics into the service of understanding human motivations and behavior and attempted to introduce it as an alternative "method" to that of the natural sciences, an idea first suggested by the Italian philosopher Giambattista Vico (1668–1744).

There are three general modern uses of the term "hermeneutics," as explained by Messer and colleagues (1988). One of these uses, from Dilthey, emphasizes hermeneutics as a methodological alternative to the natural sciences, an art or science of interpretation especially suitable to the domain of the human sciences. Unlike those human science approaches that attempt to emulate the natural sciences, "methodological hermeneutics" does not strive for "objective facts" but emphasizes meanings as developed by investigators whose activities are inevitably rooted in a given sociohistorical setting. The consequence of this approach is to emphasize the inseparability of fact and value, detail and context, and observation and theory: "Methodological hermeneutics utilizes qualitative description, analogical understanding, and narrative modes of exposition. It de-emphasizes quantification and controlled experimentation, and does not seek a neutral objective vocabulary with which to characterize social phenomena" (p. xiv).

Another use of the term, from Heidegger (1962), is labeled "ontological hermeneutics" and concerns itself with the very basis of human existence. This aspect of Heidegger's work has been developed by Gadamer (1982) and rests on the premise that our fundamental mode of being in the world is that of understanding and interpreting; there is no knowledge free of presuppositions. Human knowing or understanding always is interpretive and always takes place within an at best dimly perceived horizon. This horizon consists, depending on which author one reads, of bodily activities, symbol systems, cultural practices and institutions, or "superstructure" and "base." The consequence of ontological hermeneutics is to call into question the standard Cartesian world view separating a knowing subject from an object of study, a view that carries with it the implication that it is possible to have a neutral subject recording in an unprejudiced fashion observed objective "facts." This view is the fundamental epistemological tenet of nineteenth-century natural science.

A third usage, that of "critical hermeneutics," has a more political and moral aim in that it attempts to reveal the ideological underpinnings of the culture, the intellectual practices, the social institutions, and the prevalent economic system of exchange itself, with the goal of fostering consciousness of these underpinnings. It is hoped this will lead to emancipation from arbitrary forms of political domination and cultural pressures. The assumption behind critical hermeneutics is also that made by Breuer and Freud (1893–1895) in *Studies on Hysteria*: knowledge of one's self will allow the ego to make realistic choices and, in the case of the psychoneuroses, permit freedom from bondage to unconscious childhood conflicts. Habermas (1971) applied this tenet of Freud to a philosophy of self-reflection, in the hope that a useful critical theory and practice could be developed to free human beings from blindly following the social institutions into which they are thrown by the accident of their birth.

The hope is that hermeneutics can function as a corrective to what Heidegger (1954) called the age of technicity and to the modern proclivity to view the natural sciences as models for all forms of inquiry. In some ways it represents a revolt against this technicity: against quantification, objectivism, ahistoricism, and technology, which Heidegger claimed led to a "darkening of the world" in our time. To put it another way, Gadamer (1982) pointed out that to have a method is already to have an interpretation. Hermeneutics forces psychological investigators to confront their false sense of objectivity and epistemological privilege.

Methodological hermeneutics, then, attempts to reform, broaden, and humanize the social sciences; ontological hermeneutics, employing phenomenological methods, seeks truths that are foundational for all inquiry, including science; and critical hermeneutics attempts in particular to reveal sources of domination and coercion by exposing and criticizing the ideological underpinnings of all social practices, including political and scientific activity.

Hermeneutics as a methodology begins with the work of Friedrich Schleiermacher (1768–1834), who proposed that a literary text could not be understood unless one understood the sociocultural context in which the work was created and whatever factors in addition gave rise to and made meaningful the author's productions. It was also Schleiermacher who first described the "hermeneutic circle": since understanding always involves reference to that which is already known, the understanding must operate in a circular, dialectical fashion. A fact never stands on its own, independent from its context and interpreter, but is always partially constituted by them, since it can be evaluated only in relation to a larger theory or argument of which it is a part. Therefore, we go back and forth between the part and the whole as we attempt to understand the given "facts."

From this Dilthey (1978) attempted to develop a method of understanding in human sciences that involved a kind of empathic reliving of the culture or historical epoch that produced whatever was being studied. To put it another way, according to Dilthey a radically different method from that utilized in the natural sciences was required, one based on an empathic identification with the subject under study rather than on an attempt to remain separate and "objective," as one might watch an insect under the microscope. Although Dilthey's theories have been much criticized, they still present a timely debate about whether the psychological study of humans should be carried on in a natural sciences fashion or through the method of hermeneutics and empathy. Authors disagree, some stressing one pole and some the other, and some

trying to make the methods complementary and therefore synergistic—which is very difficult to do because their premises contain a basic epistemological opposition.

For Gadamer (1982), science is perceived as "method," whereas hermeneutics is dialectical and rests on uninterrupted listening. Gadamer hopes to supplement science through the use of hermeneutics in human sciences. This is based on a dissatisfaction with modern "methodology" in the natural sciences. Because all understanding contains prejudices or prejudgments, the scientific method does not guarantee truth. Especially in the human sciences, the knower's own being is involved, a dynamic involvement between the patient we seek to understand and our theoretical preconceptions (see FUSION OF HORIZONS). "Method" does not lead to truth; according to Gadamer, questioning and hermeneutic research lead to a kind of truth. This approach employed by Gadamer leaves us in an unsatisfactory position because it does not really help to explain how truth emerges in a given historical situation. There is a certain self-contradiction in Gadamer's work: How does one know when the truth has been found? What should one do when one has found it? There is a threat of relativism lurking in the hermeneutic circle.

An important aspect of the hermeneutic stance is to listen with wise Heideggerian passivity (see GELASSENHEIT) and to allow the text or patient's narrative to speak to us. What we hear depends on the kind of questions we ask from our vantage point in history. It also depends on our ability to reconstruct the problems that the text or patient narrative is attempting to communicate and to answer. The present is only understandable through the past, with which it has a living continuity. The event of understanding comes when our horizon (see HORIZONS) of historical meanings and assumptions fuses with the horizon within which the text or narrative is placed. At such a moment we enter into an alien world, but at the same time we gather into our own realm, reaching a more complete understanding of ourselves. This assumes that history is a continuity and that what holds us apart in understanding others and texts from the past is ideology, in which there is a failure of communication between the cultures, or the conflict between the powerful ideology of one individual or culture versus the powerful ideology of another.

The "knowledge" that arises from such an investigation is not some sort of immutable truth or essence, but is context-dependent and a function of the "prejudices" that the investigator brings to the investigation.

By assuming that a text is coherent and a narrative has a truth to teach us, by adopting, as Bion later also advocated, a certain goodwill toward the text or narrative, Gadamer limits the arbitrariness of hermeneutic understanding. This crucial stance constitutes a defense of tradition even though tradition may be prejudiced, a standpoint for which

Gadamer has been criticized. To a certain extent Gadamer advocates a conservative form of hermeneutics, in contrast to what Caputo (1987) calls "radical hermeneutics."

Bernstein (1988) points out that it is not possible "to state once and for all, in a rigorous, determinate, and nonvacuous manner, what are or ought to be the standards, criteria, or rules by which interpretations can be epistemically evaluated" (p. 89). This indeed is the central complaint that is made against those who would envision the psychoanalytic process or the dialogue in any dyadic interchange such as psychotherapy as generating meanings that can be best understood by the procedures of hermeneutics rather than approached by the standard methods of natural science. In an effort to solve this problem, Ricoeur (1977, 1981) attempts to validate psychoanalytic interpretations not by the use of the observational sciences but by trying to apply certain criteria: that the interpretation must be consistent with the basic tenets of Freudian theory, must satisfy psychoanalytic rules for understanding the unconscious, must be "mutative" or therapeutically effective, and must be part of an intelligible narrative and not inconsistent with other aspects of the narrative.

Hermeneutics has been attacked from one direction by such natural scientists and empirical philosophers as Grünbaum (1984), and from another direction by authors like Spence (1982), who have emphasized the relativism that it can easily become. In addition, there is a tendency on the part of hermeneuticists to write in a very difficult fashion, using a convoluted prose that is very unfamiliar to U.S. readers. In our pragmatic country we are used to and expect clear and lucid exposition, and we tend to react negatively to jargonistic and continental terminology, especially when it is not clearly defined. The existence of a whole variety of hermeneutic approaches further complicates the issue and often leads to a total rejection of the field by the impatient student of the topic. This is a mistake. For example, one of the finest works combining hermeneutics and the natural science approach is to be found in Ricoeur's (1970) *Freud and Philosophy,* a very difficult book to read (see Chessick 1988), which, although it stresses the centrality of hermeneutics and interpretation in psychoanalysis, leaves the door open for the empirical study of what Ricoeur believes to be Freud's combination of praxis with interpretation.

Diagnoses and formulations in the practice of psychotherapy, if the hermeneutic approach is employed, cannot be viewed as disease entities and natural science "facts," but rather as temporary formations that change with the times, historical eras, cultures, and prevailing prejudices and practices. The problem of a hermeneutic psychiatry would be to steer between the Scylla of naive realism, ignoring the major participation of the culture and the psychotherapist, and the Charybdis of relativism, nihilism, and hopeless skepticism. Much work remains to be done to clarify the role and limi-

tations of hermeneutics and to incorporate it into the clinical practice of psychotherapy, and this work must be done against the prevailing ideology of scientific materialism that characterizes our historical era. A hermeneutic psychiatry offers us the best hope of not losing sight of the methodological horizons that delimit our clinical work, and of widening these horizons to provide further understanding of our patients.

References

Bernstein, R. (1988). Interpretation and its discontents: the choreography of critique. In *Hermeneutics and Psychological Theory,* ed. S. Messer, L. Sass, and R. Woolfolk, pp. 87–108. New Brunswick, NJ: Rutgers University Press.

Breuer, J., and Freud, S. (1893–1895). Studies on hysteria. *Standard Edition* 2:1–309.

Caputo, J. (1987). *Radical Hermeneutics: Repetition, Deconstruction, and the Hermeneutic Project.* Bloomington: Indiana University Press.

Chessick, R. (1988). Prolegomena to the study of Paul Ricoeur's book "Freud and Philosophy." *Psychoanalytic Review* 75: 299–318.

Dilthey, W. (1978). *The Critique of Historical Reason,* trans. M. Ermarth. Chicago: University of Chicago Press.

Gadamer, H. (1982). *Truth and Method,* trans. G. Braden and J. Cumming. New York: Crossroad.

Grünbaum, A. (1984). *The Foundations of Psychoanalysis: A Philosophical Critique.* Berkeley, CA: University of California Press.

Habermas, J. (1971). *Knowledge and Human Interests.* Boston: Beacon.

Heidegger, M. (1962). *Being and Time,* trans. J. Macquarrie and E. Robinson. New York: Harper & Row.

——— (1954). *The Question Concerning Technology and Other Essays,* trans. W. Lovitt. New York: Harper & Row.

Messer, S., Sass, A., and Woolfolk, R., eds. (1988). *Hermeneutics and Psychological The-*

ory: Interpretive Perspectives on Personality, Psychotherapy, and Psychopathology. New Brunswick, NJ: Rutgers University Press.

Ricoeur, P. (1970). Freud and Philosophy: An Essay on Interpretation. New Haven, CT: Yale University Press.

———— (1977). The question of proof in Freud's psychoanalytic writing. Journal of the American Psychoanalytic Association 25:835–872.

———— (1981). Hermeneutics and the Human Sciences, trans. J. Thompson. New York: Cambridge University Press.

Spence, D. (1982). Narrative Truth and Historical Truth. New York: Norton.

HOLDING ENVIRONMENT

The technique of providing an experience or an atmosphere for a patient in psychotherapy, sometimes depicted as "good-enough holding" to emphasize the parallel to the facilitating mother–infant dyad, has been described by Winnicott (1958). A summary of what Winnicott (pp. 285–286) says the therapist has to provide is as follows:

1. A consistent and frequent being at the service of the patient, at a time arranged to suit mutual convenience.
2. Being reliably there, usually on time.
3. For the contracted-for period, keeping awake and being professionally preoccupied with the patient and nothing else (e.g., telephone calls, note taking, tape recorders).
4. The expression of "love" in the positive interest taken and "hate" (as Winnicott calls it) in

the strict start and finish and in the matter of fees.
5. The sincere and dedicated attempt to get in touch with the psychodynamic process of the patient, to understand the material presented, and eventually to communicate this understanding by properly timed and formulated interpretations.
6. A nonanxious approach of objective observation and scientific study, with a concomitant sense of physicianly vocation.
7. Work done in a room that is quiet and not liable to sudden unpredictable sounds and yet not dead quiet; proper lighting of a room, not a light staring in the face and not a variable light.
8. Keeping out of the relationship both moral judgment and any introduction of details of the therapist's personal life and ideas.
9. Avoiding temper tantrums, compulsive falling in love, and so on, and in general being neither hostile and retaliatory nor exploitative toward the patient.
10. Maintaining a consistent, clear distinction between fact and fantasy, so that the therapist is not hurt or offended by an aggressive dream or fantasy; in general, eliminating any "talion reaction" and ensuring that both the therapist and the patient consistently survive the interaction.

In my supervisory experience, these basic precepts are often violated. Some of the raging reactions we see from patients who are labeled borderline are actually a response to the sensed empathic failure of the therapist when a good-enough holding environment is not provided (see BORDERLINE). Providing a good-enough holding environment is especially difficult in public mental health facilities, where there are many interruptions and, most unfortunately, insufficient privacy in the rooms used for therapy. One wonders whether anyone would dare to carry on surgery under such suboptimal conditions unless it were in a battlefield situation, but it is the rule rather than the exception in crowded public clinics for these suboptimal conditions to prevail. Somehow the patient and the therapist are supposed to ignore the effect of these violations on the relationship, the therapeutic alliance, and the production of the patient's material. This is a social problem that, to a great extent, has been simply ignored. It also exerts a subtle pressure on the psychiatrist to rely more on psychopharmacologic agents than on psychotherapeutic listening and interpretation under such conditions (see GE-STELL).

Reference

Winnicott, D. (1958). *Collected Papers.* New York, Basic Books.

HOMOSEXUALITY (SEE ALSO PSEUDO-HOMOSEXUALITY)

The discussion of homosexuality has always been and continues to be unfortunately mired in social issues. Samuel Johnson does not mention the subject in his dictionary. Clearly, the persecution of any group of individuals on the basis of the fact that they differ from the average is simply the acting out of hostile and violent impulses in a socially acceptable milieu and is never to be condoned. An important factor leading to the persecution of homosexuals is repressed homosexuality in the persecutors; thus in many instances the hatred of homosexuals, known as homophobia, has the same dynamics as homosexual panic (see HOMOSEXUAL PANIC). The actual killing of homosexuals is parallel to the violence and assault that takes place when an individual undergoes a homosexual panic, but the persecution of homosexuals has a wider basis because every society always seems to need an "enemy," whether blacks, Jews, homosexuals, or Communists (see DEATH INSTINCT).

The term "homosexual" simply refers to mentation or behavior in which the object of the individual's sexual desire is a person of the same sex. The cause of this, when it appears, is hotly disputed. It is well known that in situations where persons of the opposite sex are unavailable, such as in prisons, homosexuality flourishes. It is also well known that certain societies, such as ancient Greece, condoned homosexuality as a normal form of behavior, especially between men and pubescent boys. Most Western societies have been extremely prejudiced against homosexuality, and it is only recently that the demand for equal rights by homosexuals has become even tolerable to the heterosexual culture.

Freud (1914) distinguished between anaclitic and narcissistic choices of love objects. The anaclitic object choice attempts to bring back the lost mother and precedes developmentally the narcissistic object choice. The latter is a form of secondary narcissism in which the person chosen to love resembles one's own self. In certain forms of homosexuality the object chosen is the child-self who is then treated the way the homosexual wishes his mother to treat him. Some forms represent a type of secondary narcissism in which the person loves what he himself is or was, what he would like to be, or someone once thought of as a part of himself (see NARCISSISM).

In both males and females homosexuality may be active, in which the subject behaves as a man and treats his or her object as though he or she were a female, or passive, in which the subject behaves as a woman and treats his or her object as a man. It may be manifest, latent, aim-inhibited, or sublimated. The whole question of whether such a concept as latent homosexuality refers to anything remains in dispute, since it connotes a certain passivity or submissive behavior toward more powerful males (or females in the case of latent female homosexuality) rather than necessarily to specifically repressed homosexual feelings. It has degenerated to a certain extent into a pejorative term and is best avoided.

Although Freud suggested in various writings that fear of castra-tion, excessive oedipal attachment to the mother, narcissistic object choice, and repressed sibling rivalry with overcompensatory love for the rival were important etiologic factors in male homosexuality, there is much argument as to whether these concepts have ever been of value in the treatment of homosexuals, especially homosexuals who are satisfied with their orientation. The question of whether homosexuality has a genetic or constitutional basis remains open; studies of the subject so far have not been well designed. There are no acceptable general formulations about developmental events that may propel an individual toward homosexual object choice, such as faulty parenting or parental or sibling seduction, although in individual cases these factors may be prominent.

Freud (1905) divided homosexuals into absolute, amphigenic, and contingent. An absolute homosexual is aroused exclusively by a member of his or her own sex and is indifferent or even hostile to the opposite sex. Amphigenic subjects engage in sexual relations with both sexes; this term today is usually replaced with the term "bisexual." This is unfortunate, because Freud correctly postulated that there was a bisexual potential in all humans, but the amphigenic homosexual carries this out, whereas the average individual under normal conditions does not. Contingent homosexuals are individuals capable of accepting homosexual gratification when persons of the opposite sex are unavailable, as in prison situations. There are also individuals whose sexual orientation is heterosexual but who occasionally take part in homosexual activity. In my clinical experience there are individuals whose homosexual activity is confined to what would ordinarily be called foreplay, such as stroking and caressing or occasional mutual masturbation, but who at the same time carry on active genital heterosexual activity. It follows that there is an endless variety of permutations and combinations of heterosexual and homosexual behavior, and it is well known that these permutations and combinations can change over the life of an individual from adolescence to old age. These classifications are therefore strictly descriptive and indicate nothing about etiology or psychodynamics.

The fact of such a variety implies that developmental and environmental factors, regardless of constitutional and genetic factors, play a major role in the individual's specific activities and object choices, and difficulties in the preoedipal or oedipal stages influence the situation in an important fashion. Clinical work certainly indicates that many male homosexual individuals have not satisfactorily traversed the oedipal phase and are often deeply attached to their mother, which makes it very difficult for them to transfer their attachment to other women without suffering from incestuous fantasies. They solve this by changing their orientation from women to men. Fear of castration often contributes to a negative oedipal resolution, with the acting out in homosexual behavior of regression to oral and anal

levels. The homosexual outcome of a negative resolution of the Oedipus complex, however, is related to unresolved preoedipal issues with the mother. But these findings are gathered from the treatment of homosexual patients who are not satisfied with and often wish to change their orientation. Much less is known about patients who are comfortable with their homosexual orientation, and there is no evidence that such patients are in any other areas of life more pathological than the average heterosexual individual. It should be noted that this was already recognized by Freud in 1905.

From the point of view of the therapist, it is clear that each patient must be judged on the basis of his or her individual and unique psychodynamics and family constellation. Patients who are satisfied with their sexual orientation should not be approached with the idea that because of some theoretical norm it is the duty of the therapist to change them; it is much better in psychotherapy to approach patients in the areas where they themselves feel they need help rather than to impose on the patients additional tasks that the patients did not bring into the treatment. Therapists who have prejudices against homosexuals should clearly not work with such patients and should refer them elsewhere. In my opinion, however, there is no evidence that homosexuals should be treated exclusively by homosexual therapists, any more than blacks should be treated by black therapists, Jews by Jewish therapists, and so forth. It is the individual personality of the therapist or psychoanalyst that counts the most, not these more or less superficial features.

There is even less understanding of female homosexuality, or lesbianism. In addition to the dynamics described above, the female homosexual partner is sometimes thought of as providing the mothering that the patient did not receive, or the homosexual activity becomes the acting out of a blissful symbiotic relationship that attempts to deny the oedipal conflict. The latter dynamic involves not the replacement of the mother for the purposes of substituting for what was not received but rather a denial that the daughter hates the mother in the oedipal situation and an acting out of the defensive fantasy of a blissful symbiosis with the mother.

In my clinical experience the father has an important role in the development of homosexuality. Often the father of the male homosexual is a rather passive or remote figure who presents a very poor idealization prospect. In the language of self psychology, for example, there is an early and phase-inappropriate disappointment in idealization of the father, and the homosexuality represents a search for an appropriate male idealization figure. In the development of female homosexuality there is not only the conscious or unconscious encouragement of dependency on the part of the mother or the mother's depreciation of the girl's body, but also a father who shows contempt and criticism toward men and/or toward the girl and her body, which may lead the girl

away from heterosexual interests. There are many difficulties in living that may precipitate the appearance of homosexual behavior in women, such as disappointing love experiences or stress situations that are intolerable, which in turn precipitate a regression to the yearning for a symbiosis with the preoedipal mother. All of this remains for exploration and is of great clinical importance.

References

Freud, S. (1905). Three essays on the theory of sexuality. *Standard Edition* 7:125–243.
_____ (1914). On narcissism: an introduction. *Standard Edition* 14:67–102.

HOMOSEXUAL PANIC

An attack of severe anxiety based on the stirring up of unconscious conflicts involving homosexuality was labeled in previous literature as homosexual panic, a term that is not used as much as it should be today. The importance of this concept lies in the fact that a significant number of physical assaults on psychiatrists are the result of homosexual panic. Sometimes this is precipitated by a male psychiatrist attempting to interview a male patient in a very small room or attempting to do a physical examination on such a patient in isolated conditions. What happens in these circumstances is that the patient's unconscious homosexual urges are stirred up by the situation or by the behavior of the therapist, and this produces unbearable anxiety in the patient. In the worst case scenario, the patient may deal with the unacceptable homoerotic urges by the dynamics described by Freud (1911) in the case of Schreber. Briefly, the patient unconsciously thinks, "I do not love him, I hate him, because he persecutes me." The result of this is to destroy and eliminate the persecutor, which in turn removes the patient's source of anxiety.

It follows that when the therapist is confronted with growing anxiety in a patient, one of the considerations ought to be whether the therapist is utilizing an environment or engaging in behavior that might be stirring up homosexual anxiety. It is the mark of the amateur to ignore this until the patient explodes.

According to Campbell (1989), Kempf in 1920 described this situation, which became known as Kempf's disease. Besides physical violence, the patient may display delusions, hallucinations, and depression, and may even commit suicide. Homosexual panics can be precipitated by the loss of a member of the same sex to whom the subject is emotionally attached, or by a variety of other conditions that reduce the capacity of the ego to hold unacceptable desires in repression, such as fatigue or illness. Sometimes it is precipitated by failures in heterosexual courting or performance, and traditionally it was described as often heralding the onset of schizophrenia. It is more frequent in males than in females but may be seen in both sexes, especially these days when there is such a blurring of social roles and gender identity.

References

Campbell, R. (1989). *Psychiatric Dictionary*. New York: Oxford University Press.

Freud, S. (1911). Psycho-analytic notes on an autobiographical account of a case of paranoia (dementia paranoides). *Standard Edition* 12:3–82.

HORIZONS

According to Heidegger (1962), human being always involves a context or cultural totality within which experience occurs that is labeled, alternatively, "ground," "horizon," or "clearing." This horizon is the essential concept of modern hermeneutics (see HERMENEUTICS) because it undercuts the Cartesian opposition of subject and object and is the very condition or possibility of anything at all appearing or being known. According to Heidegger, the horizon involves the customs, institutions, and language of a given culture, not the idiosyncratic perspectives of isolated individuals.

Gadamer (1982) attempted to move away from a natural sciences approach to understanding humans by the use of hermeneutic theory, an approach realizing that "understanding" arises out of our preconceptions, our position in historical tradition. To understand the patient's narrative and associations, we must merge or fuse our horizons with the patient and his or her culture or society (see FUSION OF HORIZONS).

These communal horizons channel and constitute individual

human experience. It follows, as Gadamer explains, that our self-knowledge is not freely chosen but actually deeply imbedded in our culture, history, and bodily being, aspects that are so pervasive as to be nearly invisible. Gadamer (1982) writes, "History does not belong to us, but we belong to it. Long before we understand ourselves through the process of self-examination, we understand ourselves in a self-evident way in the family, society and state in which we live. . . . The self-awareness of the individual is only a flickering in the closed circuits of historical life" (p. 245).

Gadamer (1982) points out that there is a dialectic or mutual influence between the subject of interpretation and the interpreter in which, as the horizons of each coparticipate, meaning is generated in that particular dyadic pair at that particular time and place. What is known is always known by a knower situated within history and society, and therefore interpretation is always conditioned and influenced by the tradition and the horizon of understanding within which one operates. Gadamer proclaims that one should not attempt to overcome the "prejudices" that constitute our sociohistorical vantage point, because no technique and method can ever secure absolute objectivity in interpretation (see HERMENEUTICS).

Gadamer (1982) defines horizons as the limits to our vantage point, the limits of our empathy. In order for the ideas of another person to become intelligible, we must dis-cover the standpoint and horizon of that person. Furthermore, horizons are always changing as we live and develop, so whenever we investigate we cannot disregard ourselves. This investigation, says Gadamer, is not primarily empathy (here he differs sharply with Kohut) but the forming of "a higher universality" (p. 272), a fusion of horizons. The search for truth, then, has to do with a dialogue between what is handed down to us and our willingness to test and risk our prejudices.

References

Gadamer, H. (1982). *Truth and Method,* trans. G. Braden and J. Cumming. New York: Crossroad.

Heidegger, M. (1962). *Being and Time,* trans. J. Macquarrie and E. Robinson. New York: Harper & Row.

HORIZONTAL SPLIT

In *The Analysis of the Self,* Kohut (1971) presents his concept of the vertical and the horizontal split (see his important diagram on p. 185 [Kohut 1971]). In this unfortunate use of geometry Kohut relates the vertical split to what Freud in a different context thought of as disavowal. The vertically split-off sector, or the disavowed part of the personality, is manifested in narcissistic personality disorders by openly displayed infantile grandiosity, which alternates with the patient's usual personality. This openly displayed grandiosity, says Kohut, is "related to the mother's narcissistic use of the child's performance" (p. 185). Yet, on the other side of the vertical split, the patient may show most of the time a low self-esteem, shame propensity, and hypochondria. Psychotherapy begins by dealing with the vertical split because it is usually possible to help the patient develop examples of the vertically split-off sector from his or her conscious everyday thinking and behavior. This reduces the openly displayed infantile grandiosity and increases the pressure from the repressed material hidden by the horizontal split.

The low self-esteem, shame propensity, and hypochondria represent a reaction formation to what is hidden by the horizontal split, which seems analogous to the repression barrier. Under the horizontal split are repressed, unfulfilled, archaic narcissistic demands, representing the emerging true self of the child that should have been acknowledged by the gleam in the mother's eye or facilitated by the soothing of a mature parent, but were rejected by her. By blocking the disavowed expression of infantile narcissism, the pressure of these archaic narcissistic demands is increased and the archaic grandiosity begins to appear. This fosters the development of what Kohut (1977) calls selfobject transferences (see TRANSFERENCE).

References

Kohut, H. (1971). *The Analysis of the Self.* New York: International Universities Press.
_____ (1977). *The Restoration of the Self.* New York: International Universities Press.

HORNEY, KAREN (1885–1952)

In general, Karen Horney is insufficiently appreciated today. Her ideas still remain extremely controversial and cannot yet be judged in perspective. First, she (1967) contended that Freud was wrong in his postulates about female psychology (see FEMALE PSYCHOLOGY); second, she emphasized the subject of self-realization much more than he did.

Kelman (1971) and others (see Quinn 1987) give a detailed exposition of Horney's life, which included a number of rather unpleasant episodes. She was born in Germany, near Hamburg, in 1885. Her father was a sea captain, a Norwegian who had become a German citizen, and her mother was Dutch, seventeen years younger than her husband and of a different temperament. He was morose and devoutly Protestant, given to long silences and bouts of Bible reading, while she was attractive and possessed a taste for worldly living. Karen Horney and her elder brother remembered as children seeing many parental explosions. Her father was away much of the time on ocean voyages, and she both admired and feared him; she felt that her mother favored her good-looking older brother.

At the age of 12 Horney decided on medicine as her future profession and was supported in this by her mother, who helped her obtain an education, even though her father adamantly opposed her career plans. The family turmoil ended with both mother and daughter leaving home; when Horney began medical school, her mother stayed with her.

Horney married and had two daughters, in 1911 and 1913, the same year she received her medical degree; a third daughter was born in 1915. She began as a neurologist and under the influence of Karl Abraham became involved with the Berlin Psychoanalytic Institute. Her first psychoanalytic paper was published in 1917 and already showed some disagreement with Freud.

Horney acquired a reputation for outspokenness, a trait that did not endear her to most of her colleagues, although she rose steadily at the Berlin Institute. She traveled frequently, leaving her husband, a lawyer, behind at home. He began to drink and gamble, and the marriage ended in 1926.

In 1932, on the invitation of Franz Alexander, Horney became the assistant director of the Chicago Institute for Psychoanalysis. But Alexander and she did not get along very well, and in 1934 she moved to the New York Psychoanalytic Institute.

Horney's ideas were presented in her first and most popular book, *The Neurotic Personality of Our Time* (1937). The appearance in 1939 of Horney's *New Ways in Psychoanalysis* led to the ugly episode of a complete break between herself, together with four others who supported her, and the rest of the New York Psychoanalytic Institute. She went on to form the Association for the Advancement of Psychoanalysis and, a year later, a training institute, the American Institute of Psychoanalysis. There were further administrative clashes, which in 1943 resulted in the departure of Harry Stack Sullivan, Erich Fromm, and Clara Thompson for the William Alanson White Psychiatric Foundation in New York. Horney remained at the head of the institute until her death in 1952.

Horney, like Alfred Adler, resisted compartmentalization of the personality into instincts and forces, and thus basically rejected both the Freudian instinct theory and the Freudian structural approach. For her, the purpose of psychotherapy is definitely not release from repression of specific infantile sexual material of continuing dynamic importance. In *The Neurotic Personality of Our Time,* she lays down the principles of her approach, attempting to explain neurotic phenomena not primarily in terms of the Oedipus complex but in terms of what she called basic anxiety, a feeling of being small, insignificant, helpless, endangered, in a world that is out to abuse, cheat, attack, humiliate, betray, envy.

References

Horney, K. (1937). *The Neurotic Personality of Our Time.* New York: Norton.

_____ (1939). *New Ways in Psychoanalysis.* New York: Norton.

_____ (1967). *Feminine Psychology.* New York: Norton.

Kelman, H. (1971). *Helping People: Karen Horney's Psychoanalytic Approach.* Northvale, NJ: Jason Aronson.

Quinn, S. (1987). *A Mind of Her Own: The Life of Karen Horney*. New York: Summit Books.

HOSPITALISM

Spitz (1945) published some remarkable studies of children up to 18 months old who underwent a prolonged stay in a hospital-type institution completely separated from their mother. The investigation found disorders involving retardation of development, of body mastery, of adaptation to the environment, of linguistic capacity, and in the most serious cases a loss of resistance to disease, which terminated in wasting and death. Spitz concluded that the effects of hospitalism are long term and in some cases not reparable. He thought of hospitalism as a total emotional deprivation and tried to distinguish it from what he called anaclitic depression, which he viewed as the consequence of a partial affective deprivation in a child who previously enjoyed a normal relationship with its mother.

What is clinically important is to realize that hospitalism in a less extreme form has taken place in the early lives of some of our adult patients. In my clinical experience a certain subgroup of apparently neurotic patients have at their core some of the symptoms of hospitalism, and these appear after a sufficient period of regression in the psychoanalytic situation. A sense of helplessness and hopelessness with despair and apathy characterize this syndrome, along with an impairment of ego functioning in several spheres, including linguistic confusion, self-defeating "mistakes," and even disorientation. Such phenomena should raise a suspicion in the mind of the therapist that an early period of utter maternal deprivation has been covered over due to perhaps more successful later parenting from the father or other family members. This has allowed the patient's development to continue but has left the patient vulnerable, especially in interpersonal relationships. The latter are always under a cloud because the patient is unable to allow the regression in the service of the ego that is vital to the development of true intimacy with another person. Because of this, there are difficulties in marriage and friendship that puzzle the patient as well as the partner. The resurfacing of these problems in the analytic setting begins to unravel the core of the patient's difficulties and reveals what has made it impossible for the patient to relate successfully. Such patients are sometimes labeled schizoid; usually they are able to hide their problems behind an apparent facade of effective functioning. The treatment of these patients is quite difficult, proceeds very slowly, and often ends unsatisfactorily (see BEYOND INTERPRETATION).

Reference

Spitz, R. (1945). Hospitalism—an inquiry into the genesis of psychiatric conditions in early childhood. *Psychoanalytic Study of the Child* 1:53–74. New York: International Universities Press.

HUMANENESS

Samuel Johnson (1773) defines "humane" as kind, civil, benevolent, and good natured (p. 974). The great ethologist Konrad Lorenz (1987), writing about the imminent destruction of our environment and the human species, as well as the decline of attributes that constitute humanity, transformed the adjective "humane" into the noun "humaneness." He describes the waning of humaneness as a malady and recommends close contact with nature as an important antidote to the problem. His work has not received the attention from psychotherapists that it deserves. The effects of the waning of humaneness are seen constantly in our clinical work.

Lorenz agrees with Freud's drive theory, for as a naturalist he observed how stimuli spontaneously surge up "with great force" (p. 129) when there is no situation for release (see DRIVE). For Lorenz, as for Freud (1930), this makes the stress of culture due to an encumbrance on the drives that each person must bear. In our society, Lorenz explains,

> one of the most dangerously vicious circles menacing the continued existence of all mankind arises through that grim striving for the highest possible position within the ranked order, in other words, the reckless pursuit of power which combines with an insatiable greed of neurotic proportions that the results of acquired power confer. I have already noted that the quantity of what is collected intensifies the drive to collect; the most evil of the reciprocally augmenting intensities occurs between the acquisition of power and the unquenched thirst for power. [p. 107]

Lorenz appropriately describes the "draining away of meaning" (p. 197) as combining with the increased technological frenzy in our society to produce the waning of humaneness. He points out that young people who grow up in materialistic environments do not see in their successful and comfortably situated fathers any exemplary models worthy of imitation, "especially when they also notice that such successful men are on the verge of heart attacks, are under constant stress and are not really happy at all" (p. 197).

It is important for psychotherapists to keep in mind the profound influence in our culture of the waning of humaneness on the production of psychopathology. In fact, some of the most important traits of adaptation to a culture such as ours, which Lasch (1978) has labeled "the culture of narcissism," may be the very aspects of the individual's personality that are causing the individual the most personal unhappiness. This poses some very thorny problems in making clinical decisions and interventions in psychotherapy.

References

Freud, S. (1930). Civilization and its discontents. *Standard Edition* 21:59–145.

Johnson, S. (1773). *A Dictionary of the English Language.* Beirut, Lebanon: Librairie du Liban, 1978.

Lasch, C. (1978). *The Culture of Narcissism.* New York: Norton.

Lorenz, K. (1987). *The Waning of Humaneness.* Boston: Little, Brown.

HUMAN SCIENCES (DILTHEY)

The human sciences include psychiatry, psychology, linguistics, education, economics, social science, administration, penology, philosophy, and politics. Although these have been modeled on the physical sciences, there is much argument today as to whether the method to use in the human sciences ought to be the same as that of the natural sciences. For example, the German philosopher Wilhelm Dilthey (1831–1911) distinguished the natural sciences, the rigorous and empirical sciences that observe the human *qua* natural object, as in behavioristic psychology, from *Geisteswissenschaften,* or the human sciences. The method used by *Geisteswissenschaften* is different and left somewhat vague by Dilthey, who labeled it as empathy, or *Verstehen.* One must remember that Dilthey's (1978) manuscripts were in fragments, but his main point was that there exist two "standpoints" of experience, two ways of experiencing the world: (a) standing back separately and observing a world conceived as composed of natural objects, and (b) living in the world—we cannot ever live and interact with people and things without adopting a stance toward them, an inextricable involvement.

To these there correspond two ways of being aware of experience, which Dilthey (1978) called (a) *Erklären,* "knowledge of the laws of the causal order of natural phenomena" (p. 246), rigorous scientific knowledge; and (b) *Verstehen,* knowledge of the inner mental life of humans, a function of our worldview, or system of value-laden and meaningful experience, and a consequence of our being-in-the-world. For Dilthey, "We explain nature, we understand mind" (p. 246).

Dilthey tried to establish *Verstehen* as a method by using the so-called hermeneutic circle: beginning with a preliminary notion of the whole, one then moves to an ever-more probing analysis and synthesis of the parts, which in turn leads to an evolving, ever-changing concept of the whole. This affords an increasingly internalized and thought-through understanding of the whole (see HERMENEUTICS).

From this Dilthey attempted to develop a method of understanding in human sciences that involved a kind of empathic reliving of the culture or the historical epoch that produced whatever was being studied. To put it another way, according to Dilthey a radically different method from that utilized in the natural sciences was required, one based on an empathic identification with the subject under study rather than on an attempt to remain separate and "objective." Although his theories have been criticized from many directions, they still present in outline a debate between whether the psychological study of humans should be carried on in a natural sciences fashion or through the method of hermeneutics and empathy. Authors disagree, some stressing one pole and some the other, and some trying to make the methods complementary and therefore synergistic—which is very difficult to do because their premises contain a basic epistemological opposition.

Reference

Dilthey, W. (1978). *The Critique of Historical Reason,* trans. M. Ermarth. Chicago: University of Chicago Press.

HYSTERIA

The extremely difficult nosological problem of what we mean by severe hysteria still persists. Lazare (1971) reminds us that Freud's early cases dealt with such symptoms as blindness, convulsions, contractures, and disturbances in sensation. The character traits usually associated with hysteria involving increased excitability, instability of mood, histrionics, and suggestibility were mentioned only in passing. Hysteria was used as a diagnostic term for those various symptoms of psychological, not neurological, origin believed related to disturbed sexuality.

The term "conversion" in Breuer and Freud's (1893–1895) studies on hysteria is used in the case of Emmy von N. (although it was first introduced elsewhere) to mean the transformation of psychical excitation into chronic somatic symptoms. Conversion (see CONVERSION) remains mysterious, and many authors still speak of the inexplicable leap from the mind to the body. The question of whether conversion exists solely in cases of hysteria or throughout the realm of psychopathology remains a matter of debate (Rangell 1959). Certainly the ubiquitous presence and the unpredictable shifts of conversion symptoms form one of the most dramatic manifestations in the realm of psychopathology, and the removal of conversion symptoms by the use of hypnosis or barbiturates is often a convincing demonstration to beginners of the influence of mental processes on body phenomena.

Florid conversion symptoms today are rarely found away from rural communities. The disappearance of dramatic classical conversion symptoms seems to be related to the growing sophistication about sexuality in our society and to the acceptance of the sexual needs of women. Perhaps the preponderance of florid conversion symptoms among nineteenth-century women can partly explain Freud's unfortunate disparagement of women (see FEMALE PSYCHOLOGY). This disparagement was partly due to Freud's Victorian mentality, and partly to the then prevailing theory that hysteria involved some kind of degeneracy or inferiority in the nervous system, a theory Freud gradually abandoned.

The early studies of Breuer and Freud (1893–1895) attempted to establish a therapeutic goal of compelling split-off ideas to unite once more with the conscious stream of thought. Freud remarked that, strangely enough, success does not run with the amount of work done; only when the last piece of work is completed does recovery take place. Freud postulated in these patients the existence of ideas marked by great intensity of feeling but cut off from the rest of consciousness. The essence of therapy is to get rid of the ideas and their associated affect, which was, so to say, "strangulated," a principle that remains one of the pillars of psychotherapeutic effort. Even in the case of Emmy von N., Freud already recognized that suggestion and abreaction are not enough, and he demonstrated the need to analyze down to causes in a deterministic way. Only then, he felt, can one use the abreaction technique successfully (see ABREACTION). Freud at that time believed hysteria was due to childhood sexual traumata of a passive nature and imposed on the child quite early. He soon changed his mind as a result of his self-analysis as revealed in *The Interpretation of Dreams* (1900), and his emphasis shifted from the effect of actual childhood traumata to constructed memories or fantasies (see FANTASIES).

Freud believed that the nucleus of hysterical disorders was always in an improperly resolved oedipal conflict. He divided hysterias into conversion hysterias or anxiety hysterias. Today the latter are more often labeled phobias. In addition to the innumerable possible bodily symptoms of conversion hysteria, there is often the appearance of an apparent indifference to the nature of the situation known as *la belle indifférence*. There may be episodic shifts in mental states with quite theatrical hysterical spells or "seizures" that may involve the dissociation of certain mental functions, producing such histrionic situations as multiple personalities, fugue states, and somnambulism.

Although repressed incestuous wishes were long thought of as basic to hysterical phenomena, there has been an increasing recognition of the effect of preoedipal conflicts in many cases of hysteria. Hysterical symptoms express in a form of body language the specific unconscious fantasies that the patient has developed as a compromise in the conflict between an instinctual wish that provokes anxiety and the defense against that wish. Both the instinctual wish and the defense against it are reenacted in the symptom, and the disability often represents a masochistic punishment for the partial gratification of the instinctual desire hidden in the forbidden fantasy. Some authors distinguish between conversion hysteria as a psychoneurosis and the so-called hysterical character, who acts out theatrically or histrionically exhibitionistic, seductive, and flirtatious behavior, with extremes of mood prevailing, but in intimate relationships is actually quite fearful and inhibited.

Treatment of hysteria with psychoanalysis has turned out to be much more difficult than originally believed. Chronic cases often include much secondary gain and so patients cling tenaciously to their symptoms or quickly develop new ones. More recent onset of symptoms has a better prognosis but the success depends on the relative preponderance of oedipal and preoedipal pathology. The "good," that is treatable, hysteric has primarily an unresolved Oedipus complex and has only recently regressed from an intolerable life situation to the oedipal fixation point (see FIXATION) and formed symptoms. She (or he) is young, highly motivated for treatment, psychologically minded, has the time and money for psychoanalysis, and shows little secondary gain from the illness.

References

Breuer, J., and Freud, S. (1893–1895). Studies on hysteria. *Standard Edition* 2:1–335.

Freud, S. (1900). The interpretation of dreams. *Standard Edition* 4,5:1–625.

Lazare, A. (1971). The hysterical character in psychoanalytic theory. *Archives of Psychiatry* 25:131–137.

Rangell, L. (1959). The nature of conversion. *Journal of the American Psychoanalytic Association* 7:285–298.

I

ID

In *An Outline of Psychoanalysis,* Freud (1940) tells us that the "core of our being, then, is formed by the obscure *id,* which has no direct communication with the external world and is accessible even to our own knowledge only through the medium of another agency" (p. 197). For Freud, the id plays the role that the noumenal world plays for Kant. Freud then proceeds to tell us about this obscure, unknowable id in his discussion of the primal organic instincts, as he calls them, that operate within it (see DEATH INSTINCT).

The id arises from and represents the biological furnace of the body. From the id emanates the fury and the passion of the organism. At its base we conceive of an energy system, arising from the body's biochemical processes, that requires the body to replenish itself and to maintain physiologic equilibrium. The id may be thought of as containing all that is inherited and fixed in the constitution. It may be thought of as a cauldron of seething excitement or chaos. It represents all the somatic processes of the body reflected on a psychological level; that is, eventually all the important somatic processes of the body have a psychic representation in the id.

The characteristics of the id are as follows:

1. The id is completely unconscious and always remains so. It consists of images in chaos, a cauldron of seething biologically driven excitement.
2. The id is that part of the mind that contains everything inherited, especially the instincts, or drives. The drives fill the id with energy and press for immediate satisfaction. The id has no organization and no will. Its only purpose is to satisfy the drives (see DRIVES).
3. There is no negation in the id, only desires, which demand satisfaction.
4. The id knows no values, no good, no bad, no evil, no morality.
5. Contradictory impulses may occur in the id, and they may exist independently side by side—love and hate, for example. Such contradictory impulses do not detract from one another, nor can they cancel each other.
6. The processes of the id are not related to reality; they are subject only to what we call the pleasure principle, which may be described as "I want what I want when I want it."
7. The processes of the id are timeless; that is, an unfulfilled need remains unchanged and unful-

filled if nothing has been done, regardless of the passage of years.

8. The id is subject to the mechanism of displacement. Images from it often appear in a disguised condensed form in dreams.

Freud took his concept of the id from Groddeck (1961), an extremely intuitive, dramatic, and imaginative man who attributed an overwhelming power to the "It" in both organic and psychic life. Groddeck has been neglected by psychotherapists, but his work deserves careful study. It abandons the distinction between the mental and the organic, although Groddeck was primarily an internist who later labeled himself a "wild analyst" (Grossman and Grossman 1965). For the extremist Groddeck, the It shapes our lives. Diagnosis is simply a label from a physician, but it is the all-powerful It that chooses the disease and allows it to heal. For Groddeck, in a sense we are lived by the It, a concept picked up by Lacan (see LACAN), but Lacan does not use Freud's structural theory, which includes the concept of the id.

A more traditional discussion of the id is found in Schur (1966), who conceives of the id as containing not only psychic energy but also psychic contents. The pleasure principle predominates in the id as well as the unpleasure principle, which regulates the necessity to withdraw from excessive stimuli. For Schur, thought is organized according to primary or secondary process on a continuum from the id to the ego.

The id is the reservoir of the psychic representatives of the drives and of all the phylogenetic acquisitions. According to Freud, it comprises the total mental apparatus at birth; in development the ego and the superego become differentiated from the id. Freud (1933) tells us that instinctual cathexes seeking discharge are all that the id contains. This encompasses the mental representations of the instinctual drives but does not include all the contents of the system unconscious from Freud's earlier topographic theory.

The concept of the id is controversial. There is considerable disagreement as to whether the id has any mental contents at all or is simply composed of biological forces. Should repressed unconscious memories and fantasies be assigned there, or only what has never reached consciousness or achieved representability? Slap and Saykin (1984) point out that the recent psychoanalytic literature has no references with the term "id" in the title. Without this concept, however, the entire structural theory has no meaning, just as in the philosophy of Kant, the noumenal world is assumed to be the unknowable basis of our mentation and experience. I (Chessick 1980) have elsewhere tried to demonstrate this shift toward a Kantian position in Freud's thought as he moved from the topographic to the structural theory. This shift contains the same metapsychological weaknesses as the metaphysical weaknesses in Kant's philosophy and leaves many problems unresolved.

References

Chessick, R. (1980). *Freud Teaches Psychotherapy.* Hillsdale, NJ: Analytic Press.

Freud, S. (1933). New introductory lectures on psychoanalysis. *Standard Edition* 22:57–80.

_____ (1940). An outline of psychoanalysis. *Standard Edition* 23:141–207.

Groddeck, G. (1961). *The Book of the It.* New York: Mentor Books.

Grossman, C., and Grossman, S. (1965). *The Wild Analyst: The Life and Work of Georg Groddeck.* New York: George Braziller.

Schur, M. (1966). *The Id and the Regulatory Principles of Mental Functioning.* New York: International Universities Press.

Slap, J., and Saykin, J. (1984). On the nature and organization of the repressed. *Psychoanalytic Inquiry* 4:107–123.

IDEALIZATION

Idealization occurs in both of Klein's basic positions, the paranoid-schizoid and the depressive, as a defense against sadism and destruction in phantasy (Segal 1974, 1980) (see PHANTASY). Internalized bad objects are no longer projected in the depressive position, nor are they reintrojected; instead, the total object is experienced and the bad objects remain, forming the basis of the primitive superego, which attacks the ego or self with guilt feelings. Good internal objects attenuate this attack.

This idealization of good internal objects leads to problems because the standards set by or the demands coming from the idealized good internal objects become, when combined with sadistic superego precursors, cruel demands for perfection leading to an unremitting harshness of the superego. This is complicated in cases where there is much sadism from the need to protect the good objects in the superego by excessive idealization.

Idealization represents an unrealistic exaggeration of a subject's personal attributes. It may occur in both the transference and narcissistic neuroses. Idealization is related to the state of being in love (see LOVE). In the transference neuroses, idealization does not lose touch entirely with the realistic features and limitations of the object. In typical neurotic situations, idealization can represent a projection of the analysand's idealized superego onto the analyst and can form a part of the positive transference, or defensive idealizations can form against transference hostility (see IDEALIZING TRANSFERENCE).

In the narcissistic disorders, the unconscious is fixated on an idealized selfobject for which it continues to yearn, according to Kohut's (1977) theory (see SELF PSYCHOLOGY). Persons with such disorders are forever searching for external omnipotent powers from whose support and approval they attempt to derive strength. In the narcissistic idealizing transferences, there is a sense of a vague idealization that becomes central to the material. This can lead to the extreme belief that the therapist is divine. The therapist, then, is not able to relate to the patient as one human being to another, but rather must deal with an eerie quality of unreasonable exaltation coming from the patient. The therapist reacts with embarrassment and negativism if he or she does not understand the material. The intensity of the distortion gives the therapist an idea of how desperate the patient is. The greater the desperation, the greater the requirement for soothing from the therapist (see IDEALIZING TRANSFERENCE). The big debate between the followers of Klein or Kernberg and the followers of Kohut involves the question of whether idealization as it appears in the transference is defensive or represents the breaking through of archaic unresolved narcissistic needs for an idealized parent imago (see GRANDIOSE SELF).

Idealization of the parents is important in the formation of the superego and can continue throughout life, becoming an especially important growth-promoting feature during adolescence. Freud originally discussed idealization as part of the sexual overestimation of the love object, but the term has been used in a more general sense to deal with narcissistic needs in which some of the self-love of the child is transferred or displaced onto a substitute that becomes the ego-ideal or superego and is looked upon as the possessor of all perfections (see EGO-IDEAL).

References

Kohut, H. (1977). *The Restoration of the Self.* New York: International Universities Press.

Segal, H. (1974). *Introduction to the Work of Melanie Klein.* New York: Basic Books.

———— (1980). *Melanie Klein.* New York: Viking.

IDEALIZED PARENT IMAGO (SEE GRANDIOSE SELF)

IDEALIZING TRANSFERENCE

As a consequence of developmental arrest and failure to integrate the archaic structures of the grandiose self and the idealized parent imago, characteristic selfobject transferences (Kohut 1977) occur in the treatment of narcissistic personality disorders. These transferences are the result of the amalgamation of the unconscious archaic narcissistic structures with the psychic representation of the analyst under the pressure of the need to relieve the unfulfilled narcissistic needs of childhood. It remains questionable whether they are to be called transferences in the strict sense. They are not motivated by the need to discharge instinctual tensions, nor are they produced by cathecting the analyst with object libido. One may wish to think of them as transferencelike phenomena, but following Kohut's (1977) later writing we will refer to them as selfobject transferences.

The goal of the idealizing selfobject transference is to share, via a merger, in the power and omnipotence of the therapist. Occurring as the result of therapeutic mobilization of the idealized parent imago are two basic types of such transferences, with a variety of gradations in between. The most obvious type is a later formation, usually based on a failure of idealization of the father, that stresses the search for an idealized parent to which the patient must be attached in order to feel approved and protected. A more archaic type of selfobject transference may appear or be hidden under the other types; this transference is usually related to a failure with the mother, in which the stress is on an ecstatic merger and mystical union with the godlike idealized parent.

Once such a transference has been formed, clinical signs of its disturbance are a cold, aloof, angry, raging withdrawal, which represents a swing to the grandiose self; feelings of fragmentation and hypochondria due to the separation; and the creation of eroticized replacements by frantic activities and fantasies, especially those involving voyeurism, with many variations. The typical countertransference to the idealizing selfobject transferences (Kohut 1971) occurs through the mobilization of the archaic grandiose self in whatever unanalyzed residue is present in the therapist. This leads to an embarrassed and defensive straight arming of the patient by denying the patient's idealization, joking about it, or trying vigorously to interpret it away. Such countertransference produces in the patient the typical signs of disturbance and retreat to the grandiose self just mentioned.

References

Kohut, H. (1971). *The Analysis of the Self.* New York: International Universities Press.

_____ (1977). *The Restoration of the Self.* New York: International Universities Press.

IDENTIFICATION, INTROJECTION, INCORPORATION

There are three terms that have been mixed up repeatedly and that represent subclasses of the classical mechanisms of internalization. They must be understood in order to distinguish them from Kohut's (1971) "transmuting internalization." Identification is the most mature of these mechanisms (for a review of the concept, see Compton 1985). It is less directly dependent on the drives, is more adaptively selective, and is the least ambivalent. It represents a modeling process, such as the original modeling we do on our parents. Identification is an automatic and usually unconscious mental process whereby an individual becomes like another person in one or several aspects. At times it can become consciously and deliberately employed. It is part of the learning process, but it can also be part of adaptation to a feared or lost object, or an attempt to improve one's skills in society. Identification is growth promoting and leads to better adaptation, a crucial clinical point. Some authors use the term to denote a defense mechanism operating unconsciously by which an individual patterns himself or herself after another. An example is Anna Freud's (1946) "identification with the aggressor," which plays a major role in the development of the superego. For such authors, the conscious process of identification is sometimes labeled "imitation" to distinguish it from unconscious identification.

Avoiding the subtle arguments and differentiations among these various processes of internalization, we turn next to incorporation and introjection, archaic prototypes of identification in which the mental process is sometimes even experienced as a bodily one, such as ingesting, devouring, or keeping something inside oneself. Introjection was originally used by Freud (1917) as a process in which the lost object is taken in and retained as part of the psychic structure. He later used it as a mechanism to explain the taking in of the parents' demands as if they were one's own in the formation of the superego at the time of the resolution of the Oedipus complex. Introjection does not simply copy selected aspects of the object, as in identification; it is more encompassing. The original definition assumed a solid repression barrier, a cohesive sense of self, and a functioning ego. This was Freud's use of the term.

Incorporation is a form or model of introjection, a taking into the mind the attributes of another person, which in fantasy follows the model of oral ingestion and swallowing. Introjection, when it is accomplished by incorporation, implies change by fantasied cannibalism. It is primary process ideation, a form of object relatedness, a primitive kind of interpersonal relations fantasy. At one time it was thought that this fantasy accompanies all in-

trojection, but now this is not believed to be correct.

Schafer (1968) defines introjection as "the process whereby object representations are constituted as introjects or are changed into them" (p. 16). An introject, he explains, is an inner presence with which one feels in continuous or intermittent dynamic relationship. The characteristics of introjects are the following:

1. They may be conceived as a personlike thing or creature.

2. They may be unconscious, preconscious, or conscious.

3. They may be experienced as exerting a pressure or influence on the subject's state or behavior independently of conscious efforts to control it.

4. They do not copy external objects, since they are shaped by "fantasies, projections, symbolizations, misunderstandings, idealizations, depreciations, and selective biases originating in the subject's past history and present developmental phase in dynamic position" (p. 73).

5. Once formed, introjects diminish the influence of the external object. This is a crucial clinical point. Introjects are formed due to a severe ambivalence or to disappointment in the attempt to modify distressing relations with an external object. Good introjects are also needed and formed to counteract and protect a patient from the bad.

6. Once formed, introjects alter the relationship with the external object in a way not correctable by

experiences with the external object, since the external object's influence is diminished by the patient's attention turning toward the introjects.

7. Introjection is an event, a change in psychic organization and in the psychic status of an object representation. Notice the active role of the mental processes in this, a capability assumed even of the infant. This is a highly controversial point.

8. Introjection represents or expresses a regressive modification of the boundaries and reality-testing function of the ego. Introjection perpetuates neediness and ambivalence, displacing it to the inside. It is not growth promoting per se. It is a passive mode of mastery and not adaptive in itself.

There is tremendous confusion in the literature about these three terms, and they are used in many different ways by different authors. For example, Campbell (1989) notes, "Some writers use incorporation synonymously with *identification* and *introjection*. Others equate incorporation with introjection and define both as the mechanism by which identification takes place. Others differentiate between them on the basis of the phase or level of psychic organization and development at which the assimilation of the object takes place" (p. 364). I have attempted to offer the definitions above as a useful starting point for the working clinician, but there is an enormous amount of metapsychological argu-

ment and confusion about their exact meanings.

References

Campbell, R. (1989). *Psychiatric Dictionary*. New York: Oxford University Press.

Compton, A. (1985). The concept of identification in the work of Freud, Ferenczi, and Abraham: a review and commentary. *Psychoanalytic Quarterly* 54:200–233.

Freud, A. (1946). *The Ego and the Mechanisms of Defense*. New York: International Universities Press.

Freud, S. (1917). Mourning and melancholia. *Standard Edition* 14:237–258.

Kohut, H. (1971). *The Analysis of the Self*. New York: International Universities Press.

Schafer, R. (1968). *Aspects of Internalization*. New York: International Universities Press.

IDENTITY

This concept is more psychosocial than psychoanalytic. It was stressed very much in the work of Erik Erikson (1959). Identity refers to the individual's self-image with respect to particular functions or roles in the family or society, such as gender, class, and work identity. It is very much shaped by environmental and social events in interaction with the patient's intrapsychic compromises. There are certain periods of time when the individual's sense of identity becomes challenged, and Erikson has labeled these identity crises. Such crises are characteristic especially of adolescents and include the so-called mid-life crisis of adults. This term and what it implies is based on a superficial social or interreactional view of psychic functioning and ignores the powerful underlying infantile fantasies that drive our personalities. A great many popular psychology texts have been devoted to this topic, with little benefit except to the bank account of the authors and lecturers.

Abend (1974) reviews the concept of identity and reminds us how Erikson emphasizes social values, roles, and ideals, rather than the internal sense and the body image. Abend distinguishes between personal identity, which makes the individual feel unique with respect to the world, and identity, which is a set of self representations that define the individual in social contacts. The sense of identity is subjective and fluctuating. Our sexual identity, a set of self representations about our sexual role and function as well as our genitals, forms a central aspect of ourselves. An identity problem occurs when there are disturbances in the stable social, sexual, and professional roles that we play and/or in our ideals, values, beliefs, and special interests.

An interesting twist is given by Joseph and Widlöcher (1983), who edited a collection of articles dealing with the identity of the psychoanalyst. For example, King points out how the esteem of colleagues is even more important than money to the professional because it enhances identity and self-esteem. She views 45 to 65 years of age as the peak creative period for an analyst, and she warns of the vocational danger of becoming isolated. The analyst must mourn what is not possible and must reassess where he or she stands with

respect to theory, as well as redefine continuously goals, lifestyle, and ideals. Grinberg decries the "pseudoidentity" of the analyst who adheres to the latest fashionable author and whose work is meaningless and not integrated into his or her personal life. Anna Freud interprets the identity of the psychoanalyst as based on a curiosity about what makes others function. This curiosity, she says, should carry through the whole of the professional life of the analyst. She asks candidates, "What have you read? What have you done in your life?" (p. 261). Even from this it should be clear that Erikson's (1959) fifth stage of human development, which he labels identity versus role diffusion, is not confined to late adolescence and early adulthood, but is a problem that exists throughout life.

Gender identity is the basic sense of maleness or femaleness, and it rests on a strong conviction developed very early in life that one is either male or female. It is usually clear by the age of 2 and relatively impossible to modify by the age of 4. There is no agreement to what extent biological factors contribute to gender identity, and it is important to distinguish between gender identity and "gender role"; the latter is a much more sociological concept and is formed by society's expectations.

References

Abend, S. (1974). Problems of identity: theoretical and clinical applications. *Psychoanalytic Quarterly* 43:606–637.

Erikson, E. (1959). *Identity in the Life Cycle.* New York: International Universities Press.

Joseph, E., and Widlöcher, D., eds. (1983). *The Identity of the Psychoanalyst*. New York: International Universities Press.

IDEOGRAPHIC

The German philosopher Wilhelm Windelband (1848–1915) distinguished studying an object from a nomothetic or from an ideographic standpoint. Nomothetic studies concentrate on general laws, such as the descriptions of empirical natural science. Ideographic studies stress specific and unique individuality. This distinction is used by Meissner (1971), who describes Freud's psychoanalysis as a scientific hybrid resting on and trying to combine two poles: (a) nomothetic—using rules, laws, mathematical physics, and energy, and (b) ideographic—representing ideas by symbols that are unique, characteristically human, and have subjective meaning.

Many authors argue that the human sciences by their very nature must be such a hybrid (see HERMENEUTICS and HUMAN SCIENCES). The contemporary psychiatrist cannot ever, by virtue of his or her subject matter, the human mind, be purely a medical specialist. This is because if he or she tries to be, the very subject of the study, the human being, will disappear and the psychiatrist will end up studying a thing, a machine, an apparatus. This is one of the extraordinary paradoxes of our profession and it means that regardless of advances in neurophysiology and neurochemistry, the psychotherapist and psychiatrist will never be able to escape from the effect of psychological and cultural factors in shaping the patient, the treatment, and even the psychiatrist or psychotherapist.

Reference

Meissner, W. (1971). Freud's methodology. *Journal of the American Psychoanalytic Association* 19:265–309.

IDOLS

Any method contains within it presuppositions about truth and falsity and about how these are determined that cannot be established by the method itself and so represent "prejudices" of the investigator (see HERMENEUTICS). Francis Bacon (1620) is usually credited as first delineating the principles of the inductive method in the natural sciences, principles that are more often honored in the breach than the observance, but are even today given lip service by naive investigators. His concept of idols, however, is rarely brought to the attention of modern medical students. Bacon distinguished "idols of the tribe," which represent unreasonable expectations in human observers, such as expecting that every effect must have an identifiable single natural cause; "idols of the cave," which represent cultural prejudices, such as chauvinism, feminism, and racism, and vastly distort the interpretation of data; "idols of the marketplace," which point to our immersion in language and the impossibility of getting away from current linguistic practices in trying to describe meanings and interpretations; "idols of the theater," in which an appeal is made to established authority, such as systems of philosophy that have become famous because they are "classical"; and, finally, "idols of the schools," in which appeal is made to authoritative rules rather than reason and judgment.

Reference

Bacon, F. (1620). *Novum Organum.* In *The English Philosopher from Bacon to Mill,* ed. E. Burtt, pp. 24–123. New York: Random House, 1939.

IMAGINARY ORDER (SEE LACAN)

IMAGO

Rycroft (1968) defines imago as follows: "Word used by Freud to describe (unconscious) OBJECT-REPRESENTATIONS. Not to be confused with an insect after its final metamorphosis" (p. 69). Frazier and colleagues (1975) add, "In Jungian *psychology,* an *unconscious* mental image, usually idealized, of an important person in the early history of the individual" (p. 65). The reader may choose between these definitions.

References

Frazier, S., Campbell, R., Marshall, M., and Werner, A. (1975). *A Psychiatric Glossary:* *The Meaning of Terms Frequently Used in Psychiatry.* Washington, DC: American Psychiatric Association.
Rycroft, C. (1968). *A Critical Dictionary of Psychoanalysis.* New York: Basic Books.

IMPASSE

There is a need in the psychoanalytic literature for further studies on the problem of the treatment that has reached an impasse. An impasse is an insidious arrest of the psychoanalytic process. As discussed by Etchegoyen (1991), "It tends to perpetuate itself; the setting is preserved in its basic constants; its existence is not obvious as incoercible resistance or technical error; it is rooted in the patient's psychopathology; and it involves the analyst's countertransference" (p. 786).

An impasse occurring even in one single case is very serious for the conscientious psychoanalyst because it forces the analyst to review his or her entire professional choice, theoretical orientation, and discipline. It is not the same as failure or interruption of treatment, which usually can be traced to relatively obvious personal and recognizable faults in both the patient and the analyst. The impasse, on the other hand involves a very subtle interaction between the analyst and the patient so that it may go on for months or even years before the analyst realizes what has happened. In fact, the patient who is suffering the impasse not only often does not mention it, but will resolutely deny it if it is suggested by the analyst. It is complex and multidetermined and the countertransference is always deeply and subtly involved. In my clinical experience, when the analyst realizes that an impasse has occurred, it may be a shocking and humiliating experience and requires serious self-analytic study (see the concept of countertransference structure in COUNTERTRANSFERENCE).

Reference

Etchegoyen, R. (1991). *The Fundamentals of Psychoanalytic Technique*. Trans. P. Pitchon. New York: Karnac Books.

INCORPORATION (SEE IDENTIFICATION, INTROJECTION, INCORPORATION)

INFANTILE FANTASY (SEE FANTASY)

INSTINCT (SEE ALSO DEATH INSTINCT AND DRIVE)

Probably no other concept has caused as much confusion and difficulty for students of Freud than his notion of instinct *(Trieb)*. Freud (1920) himself described instinct as "at once the most important and the most obscure element of psychological research" (p. 34). The main reason for this obscurity is that Freud's "instinct" refers us to the unresolved issue of the borderline between the mind and the body. Freud (1905) at the start defined it as "the psychical representative of an endosomatic, continuously floating source of stimulation" (p. 168), a concept lying on the frontier between the mental and the physical. In this early definition he did not distinguish between an instinct and its "psychical representative," but in later work he drew a sharp distinction between them. In his (1915b) later views an instinct can never become an object of consciousness; only the idea *(Vorstellung)* that represents the instinct can become conscious. Even in the unconscious an instinct cannot be represented by other than an idea: "When we nevertheless speak of an unconscious instinctual impulse or of a repressed instinctual impulse . . . we can only mean an instinctual impulse the ideational representative of which is unconscious" (p. 177).

The differentiation between an instinct (in Freud's sense of the word) and its ideational representative in the psyche contains within it the unresolved problem of the relationship between brain and mind. The most helpful suggestion to the reader is to remember that Freud conceives of instinct in a looser and less precise manner than is denoted by the current dictionary term, which implies an inherited behavioral trait or pattern, especially of animals. Jones (1955) explains that other words, such as "urge," "impulsion," or the American expression "drive," have been suggested as translations, but he

regards none of them as entirely satisfactory. Some contemporary authors wish to completely do away
with the instinct portion of Freud's
contribution, claiming it is inconsistent with modern biology. Numerous substitutions have been suggested, but none have found general
acceptance.

This vagueness in one of the fundamental concepts of Freud's psychodynamics has been unfairly used
to criticize the whole scientific foundation of the psychoanalytic approach. Freud (1915a) himself anticipated and answered this criticism in
the opening paragraph of "Instincts
and Their Vicissitudes," which contains one of Freud's basic statements
on the philosophy of science and reminds us that no science, not even the
most exact, begins with entirely clear
and sharply defined basic concepts:

> The true beginning of scientific ac-
> tivity consists rather in describing
> phenomena and then in proceeding
> to group, classify and correlate
> them. Even at the stage of descrip-
> tion it is not possible to avoid ap-
> plying certain abstract ideas to the
> material in hand, ideas derived from
> somewhere or other, but certainly
> not from the new observations
> alone. Such ideas—which will later
> become the basic concepts of the sci-
> ence—are still more indispensable as
> the material is further worked over.
> [p. 117]

Freud (1915a) maintains that
these ideas must necessarily possess
some degree of indefiniteness, and
strictly speaking they are in the nature of conventions, "although everything depends on their not being
arbitrarily chosen but determined by
having significant relations to the
empirical material, relations that we
seem to sense before we can clearly
recognize and demonstrate them" (p.
117). After thorough investigation
and observation in the field, we formulate these basic scientific concepts
with increased precision and pro-
gressively modify them, yet they still
remain basic postulates.

One such postulate is that of instinct. Freud (1915a) goes on to delineate the concept more clearly, first
separating it from a stimulus that
represents a single impact that can be
disposed of by a single expedient action (e.g., flight from the source of
stimulation). Thus instinct does not
arise from the external world but
from within the organism itself, and
it operates as a constant force rather
than as a momentary impact. "Moreover, since it impinges not from
without but from within the organism, no flight can avail against it" (p.
118).

We cannot actually tell what an
instinct is; we can only define it op-
erationally. Freud's definition rests
on the principle of constancy, which
he calls a biological postulate and describes thus: "The nervous system is
an apparatus which has the function
of getting rid of the stimuli that reach
it, or of reducing them to the lowest
possible level; or which, if it were
feasible, would maintain itself in an
altogether unstimulated condition"
(p. 120). This postulate as a mode of
mental functioning is quite contrary
to the findings of Piaget and many
recent investigators (Lichtenberg
1983, Stern 1985), which imply that

the mental functions even in the most primitive state seek out stimulation and thrive on mastery if the stimulation is not too overwhelming. It is clear that the notion of instinct as an explanatory casual hypothesis is highly controversial and fraught with philosophical difficulties; perhaps it is easier now to understand why Freud revised his instinct theory four times.

Although most psychoanalysts find Freud's final version of the theory of instincts unsatisfactory, it is important to have a working knowledge of his notion of instinct and his four theories in order to avoid becoming confused in reading his works. For a thorough metapsychological review of the whole topic, see Compton (1983a,b).

One of the earliest ways in which the organism distinguishes between the inner and outer world is through the discovery that muscular action can avoid certain noxious stimuli; one can take flight from the outer world but not from the inner world. The formation of the ego and the mechanisms of defense is given its primary impetus by the need to develop protection against the constant instinctual forces from the inner world that cannot be avoided by the muscular action of flight. Freud (1915a) sees an instinct as the "psychical representative of the stimuli originating from within the organism and reaching the mind, as a measure of the demand made upon the mind for work in consequence of its connection with the body" (p. 122). Each instinct is characterized by a pressure (Drang), which is a measure of force or the demand for work and represents the "very essence" of an instinct. The aim (Zeil) of an instinct is "in every instance satisfaction, which can only be obtained by removing the state of stimulation at the source of the instinct" (p. 122). The object (Objekt) of an instinct is the thing in regard to which or through which the instinct is able to achieve its aim; the source (Quelle) of an instinct lies in the somatic-chemical or mechanical aspects of the body. Freud (1915a) claims that the study of the sources of instincts lies outside the scope of psychology: "In mental life we know them only by their aims" (p. 123).

The difficulties multiply with Freud's question, "What instincts should we suppose that there are, and how many?" (p. 123). It is well known that Freud had a compelling need to keep the instincts divided into two homogenous groups. The original grouping was between the sexual instincts and the ego-preservative instincts, with very little attention paid to the latter since Freud at the time was so busy dipping into the id and uncovering the infantile sexual wishes. In 1905, in Three Essays on the Theory of Sexuality, the libido was first explicitly established as an expression of the sexual instinct; in a short paper on psychogenic disturbances of vision, Freud (1910) introduced the term "ego instincts," which he considered self-preserving.

In "On Narcissism" (1914), this duality broke down when the notion of ego-libido was introduced as a natural stage of development called primary narcissism. It then became necessary to distinguish between originally nonlibidinal ego instincts and libidinal ego instincts. Sexual energies flowing within the ego made it impossible to separate sexual and ego instincts; the "alibidinous" part remained poorly defined and not in balance with the libidinal ego instincts. The great danger at this point was in falling into Jung's solution of using libido to represent all instincts, a monistic theory that rendered the whole concept of instincts and libido meaningless.

A third and transitional theory of the instincts was suggested indirectly in the paper "Instincts and Their Vicissitudes" (1915a). Although the division between ego instincts and sexual instincts is preserved, a consideration of the relations between love and hate led Freud to the conclusion that hate was to be regarded as a nonlibidinal reaction of the ego. This implies that the important aspect of the nonlibidinal ego instincts is the aggressive or sadistic aspect. Freud suggests two kinds of sadism: (a) moral sadism, the drive for power or the control of the environment for self-preservation; and (b) sexual sadism, which appears in certain perversions and frustrations of the sexual instinct. Freud maintains that the impulses to assert, control, and aggress upon can be separated from libidinal impulses, but the argument is not convincing since if sadism is found at every level of sexual development, why can it not be considered a part of the libidinal instincts? In this theory sadism is considered partly sexual and partly nonsexual aggressiveness, with the nonsexual aggressive strivings for power and so on representing the nonlibidinal part of the instincts.

In the final theory of the instincts, as described in *Beyond the Pleasure Principle* (1920), Freud elevates aggressiveness to an independent status of its own and abandons the notion of ego instincts entirely. Aggression becomes a vicissitude of primary masochism. The instincts are finally divided into Eros, the libidinal or sexual instinct, and the death instinct—representing a tendency to disorganization and an expression of the inertia of living matter, of the organic to become inorganic, dead, inanimate. As libido represents the energy of the sexual instincts, so "destrudo" or "mortido" represents the energy of the death instincts (terms added by Freud's followers). This postulation of a primary death instinct is not generally accepted today, but it must be pointed out that no better formulation has been offered (see DEATH INSTINCT).

To claim that outwardly directed aggression is the primary instinct parallel or polar opposite to the sexual instincts forces one to postulate that man has an innate powerful, destructive, aggressive drive. Such a postulate leads to the confusing question of why, since aggression is a component of all sexual stages of development, a separate aggressive instinct at a polar opposite to the sexual instincts should be postulated. Either the libidinal and aggressive instinctual phenomena start from something that is common to both and only become differentiated in the course of development, or each has a different origin and follows separate though at times intersecting lines of development. The first of these views is a monistic one like that of Jung; Freud tried to sidestep this view by separating out the aggressive aspect of the ego-preservative functions from the problem of erotic sadism. The final step was to remove aggressiveness from the ego instincts and give it an independent status as an instinctual group with an aim of its own. The ego is now thought of as being obliged to struggle with aggressiveness exactly as it is obliged to struggle with libido; it could give way to it, sublimate, repress, develop reaction formations, neutralize it by adding libidinal elements, or direct the aggression onto itself. The logic of the hypothesis seemed to force Freud to postulate the death instinct. If the libido is the energy of the sexual instincts and is primarily and originally directed upon the self, we must similarly postulate that the energy of the aggressive instincts was originally directed upon the self—the stage of primary masochism.

In Freud's view, the vicissitudes of an instinct have a defensive connotation. These vicissitudes are: (1) reversal into its opposite, which can involve either a change from active to passive aim or a reversal of the content of the instinct; (2) a turning around upon the subject; (3) repression; and (4) sublimation, which Freud later says is not a vicissitude but a way of healthy discharge. These tendencies are all opposed to

the instinctual pressure for explosive straightforward discharge, regardless of reality.

In a turning around upon the subject, the first and second vicissitudes coincide in that both the aim and the object of the instinct sometimes change. For example, the wish to exercise violence or inflict pain on another person proceeds to a change of object to the self; this may also change the aim of the instinct from active to passive, and so the self is substituted as an object to take over the role of the other person. This is the situation of masochism (see MASOCHISM); thus sadism always precedes masochism in the third instinct theory (see above). In reversal into the opposite, the active aim to look at or torture, for example, is changed into the passive aim to be looked at and to be tortured, and this usually involves a turning around on the subject.

Freud's discussion of love and hate prepares the way for the final instinct theory. There is no polarity between love and hate, for love is not an instinct; according to Freud, it is an elaboration of the sexual instinct, whereas hate is an instinct and a primal emotion. For Freud, love is a higher-order reaction resulting from sexual satisfaction. Thus speaking of a reversal from love to hate is not a description of the vicissitude of an instinct. Freud (1915a) explains, "The case of love and hate requires a special interest from the circumstance that love refuses to be fitted into our scheme of the instincts" (p. 133). He insists that love and hate "spring from different sources, and had each its own development before the influence of the pleasure–unpleasure relation made them into opposite" (p. 138). Hate at this point is conceived as springing from the aggressive component of the nonlibidinal ego instincts. Thus sadism is the aggression of the ego instincts with vicissitudes of its own, although there is also a sexual sadism. The sadism of the ego instincts is a will to power or dominance. According to Freud, when the will to cruelty or torture is added, we have the infusion of the sadism of the ego instincts with sexual sadism.

This distinction between sexual sadism as a part of the libidinal instincts and hate or moral sadism as a vital component of the ego instincts is unsatisfactory and demanded revision, as Freud obviously understood. It is fascinating to see how Freud reached his final revision of the instinct theory and to study the various aspects of his personal and intellectual life that were at play when he created the polarity of the life and death instincts.

Why can we not postulate the two primary groups of instincts as libidinal and aggressive? The answer, as we have seen, is because we also postulate that the primary state of the organism involves these instincts infusing the self. So, in primary narcissism, the original investment of the libido is on the self. To be consistent we would have to postulate a primary masochism in which the original investment of the aggression was also on the self. One cannot logically avoid the consequences of Freud's final revision of instinct theory—like Freud, we are forced to accept this revision by the logic of our theoretical formulations. The only way to avoid this situation is to throw out his theory of instincts entirely. Compton (1983a) demonstrates that when one moves to structural theory, there is much confusion in the use of drives, regulatory principles, and objects. He claims that the concept of narcissistic libido is untenable.

References

Compton, A. (1983a). The current status of the psychoanalytic theory of instinctual drives: I. Drive concept, classification, and development. *Psychoanalytic Quarterly* 52:364–401.

——— (1983b). The current status of the psychoanalytic theory of instinctual drives: II. Relation of the drive concept, to structures, regulatory principles, and objects. *Psychoanalytic Quarterly* 52:402–425.

Freud, S. (1905). Three essays on the theory of sexuality. *Standard Edition* 7:125–243.

——— (1910). The psycho-analytic view of psychogenic disturbance of vision. *Standard Edition* 11:209–218.

——— (1914). On narcissism: an introduction. *Standard Edition* 14:67–102.

——— (1915a). Instincts and their vicissitudes. *Standard Edition* 14:109–140.

——— (1915b). The unconscious. *Standard Edition* 14:159–215.

——— (1920). Beyond the pleasure principle. *Standard Edition* 18:3–64.

Jones, E. (1955). *The Life and Work of Sigmund Freud: The Formative Years and the Great Discoveries 1856–1900.* New York: Basic Books.

Lichtenberg, J. (1983). *Psychoanalysis and Infant Research.* Hillsdale, NJ: Analytic Press.

Stern, D. (1985). *The Interpersonal World of the Infant: A View from Psychoanalysis and Developmental Psychology.* New York: Basic Books.

INTELLECTUALIZATION, ISOLATION

Isolation represents a mechanism of defense in which affect and idea are separated. In the typical clinical situation, the affect may appear with no ideation attached to it, or the idea may appear with no affect that one would expect attached to it. Intellectualization represents the concentration on abstract and speculative ideas. It becomes a defense when, as in adolescence, it is used to exert control over anxiety and reduce tension. The abstract discussions and "little groups of serious thinkers" that characterize college dormitories utilize intellectualization and isolation as ways of dealing with the tensions that are produced by physical proximity and the upsurges of the hormones during adolescence.

Although there has been considerable attention paid to the appearance of isolation in clinical material, not enough attention is paid to intellectualization. This is a special problem if one has a practice in a university community, or where other mental health practitioners are one's patients. The tendency for educated individuals to use defensive intellectualization must be watched for constantly, and the defensive use by one's patients who are mental health practitioners of all sorts of theories and speculations must be noted and interpreted properly. Nothing is more destructive to an uncovering psychotherapy than getting involved in intellectual, abstract, or theoretical discussions with patients. These kinds of interventions are invariably countertransference unless they are done for the very specific purpose of supportive therapy. The pitfall in the practice of psychotherapy is to be seduced by the patient's intelligence or intimidated by the patient's superior knowledge of psychiatric or psychological theory, a knowledge that is useless when one is a patient. The gravest problem with intellectualization is that it produces an unemotional atmosphere and hides the real affects and important aspects of the transference.

In my supervisory experience, insufficiently analyzed therapists are especially prone to becoming involved in intellectualization with patients as a form of countertransference or to being unaware that a patient is using intellectualization as a principal means of defense. The reason this is so seductive is that it produces a very pleasant and academic ambience in the therapy hour, allowing tension reduction in both parties.

INTERPRETATION, LISTENING (SEE ALSO LISTENING)

The goal of an interpretation is to help the patient become consciously aware of the meaning of some element in his or her mental life. This involves the patient's recognizing mental contents that were previously unconscious and defended against. Interpretation therefore acts as a tool chiefly in an insight-directed treatment; it is less commonly used in supportive treatment. Only some of the highlights of the technique of interpretation can be brought out here. It is both a skill and a delicate art that develops gradually as the therapist's self-knowledge, clinical experience, and maturity increase.

Every other procedure prepares for interpretation, amplifies the interpretation, or makes an interpretation effective (see INTERVENTIONS). To interpret is to make unconscious or preconscious psychic content conscious, to give it meaning and causality. The reasonable and conscious ego is made aware of something to which it had been oblivious. This usually requires more than a single intervention; hence, the need for working through (see WORKING THROUGH).

The therapist must use his or her own conscious mind, empathy, intuition, and fantasy life, as well as intellectual and theoretical knowledge, to arrive at an interpretation. By interpreting the therapist goes beyond what is understandable and observable by ordinary conscious and logical thinking. The patient's responses are necessary to determine whether the interpretation is valid or not.

All successful interpretation is based on adequate listening. If one cannot listen, one cannot possibly arrive at correct interpretations. Dewald (1964) approaches this subject by discussing the therapist's activity in listening, which is a good deal more than a passive recording of the material verbalized by the patient. The therapist takes note of the pattern and the sequence of the material presented, the "temporal juxtaposition" of the material, what material has been omitted by the patient and tries to observe his or her own personal reactions to the patient and to the patient's material. The therapist uses himself or herself as an exploring instrument, on the basis that personal reactions to the patient may indicate some of the effects that the patient produces in other people with whom he or she interacts. This gives the therapist a better understanding of the patient's interrelationship to his or her environment outside the treatment.

In many ways the therapist has to use his or her self as a stethoscope. At the same time, the therapist must adopt an attitude of evenly suspended attention (Freud 1912), in which he or she does not limit the self to specific ideas, thoughts, or feelings produced by the patient at that particular moment but rather attempts to let thoughts and associations range freely over the material. As the therapist listens and observes, he or she may be reminded at times of similar phenomena—general patterns or particular instances of human behavior and experience. This may enable the therapist to bring in new ideas and new understanding of the material that would not be noted if he or she had adhered to rigid listening and recording of the exact data from the patient.

It follows that the skilled therapist must have a superior capacity to listen. A certain lack of rigidity, a sensitivity, and an empathy with the patient as he or she presents thoughts and describes experiences are necessary. In addition, empathy involves the therapist in making a partial and transient identification with the patient, putting himself or herself into the patient's shoes. If the therapist does not have the capacity to listen with evenly suspended attention or empathize with the patient (or, in more technical terms, to regress in the service of the ego and oscillate between such a regression and the secondary-process capacities of putting the information received in this regression into terminology that can then be expressed to the patient), the therapist will fail.

The material presented by the patient produces in the therapist an empathic identification and understanding through resonance after evenly suspended attention. Considerable debate remains in the literature regarding the emphasis on empathy by Kohut and his followers (see EMPATHY). Balter and Spencer (1991) insist that Kohut's use of empathy and introspection represents a fundamental change in listening stance from that of Freud's free association and evenly suspended attention. This would, they claim, inevitably lead to a different theory and approach. Each psychotherapist must ponder this unresolved issue.

The therapist needs to rationally understand and organize the material in a way that makes it comprehensible to the patient. The therapist must also decide how and when to present what has been understood to the patient. For example, if the therapeutic session is almost over, it may be tactically wiser to wait for another

time, since the end of a session is not the best time to present the patient with new ideas.

Another way of approaching the problem of the taxing and difficult procedure of listening is to attempt to set out a series of rules that the therapist can use to help in understanding unconscious material. Saul (1958) gives a series of rules that I have found useful in my own clinical work and teaching. To paraphrase:

1. Keep close to the material; do not introduce your own associations; do not swing wide and far away from the material in your ideas about it.
2. Look for the major themes first, rather than the subsidiary themes and details.
3. Keep to the level of consciousness of the material. Do not mix levels. This is extremely important in the art of interpretation. If a patient is dealing with material in the area of resistance, it is very important to keep interpretation in the area of resistance and not interpret content when the patient is not ready for it. Or, if the patient is presenting deep, pregenital, unconscious material in sexual-genital form, it is important not to make probing interpretations of the pregenital material before the patient is ready for it. This is a common example of wild analysis (see WILD ANALYSIS) and is a grave mistake because it simply mobilizes defenses.
4. Distinguish dynamics from content. No matter how unintelligible associations and dreams

may be, at least the main topics and tendencies, the emotional forces, and something of their interplay are usually discernible. If the therapist finds himself or herself throughout even a single session totally lost and with no understanding of the material at all, there may be a problem with a lack of training or a counter-transference problem, or both. The only solution is self-analysis and consultation. For a therapist of any integrity, this will come as a command, self-instigated. In general, there are far too few consultations. Many disasters could be avoided by this simple device.

5. Keep separate what is current in the present life situation from the transference and from the past or childhood.

6. Be alert to the effects on the material of current stimuli in the patient's life and also from the transference. In psychotherapy one always has to keep a sharp eye on what is going on in the reality situation of the patient at any given time. Ignoring the reality situation soon makes of therapy a sterile intellectual process that gets nowhere and usually causes the patient to feel rejected and, correctly, misunderstood.

7. Review the material both in terms of the libidinal motivations directed toward self and others and the hostile motivations. Look for manifestations of fight and flight. Try to understand material in terms of the ego, id, and superego rather than emphasize any one of these realms of mental functioning. All material contains ego motivations and sexual as well as aggressive motivations.

8. Pay close attention to the sequence of associations and dream elements. The beginning of the hour often expresses the theme of the session; the end of a dream represents solutions, or lack of them, to conflicts.

9. Watch for those associations connected with the greatest emotional response. One of the ways to avoid getting bogged down in a great deal of apparently incomprehensible material is to concentrate on those areas that seem to be associated with the most feeling and those that seem to be associated with the least. Sometimes the patient isolates the material from the affect, and material that seems to be presented in the coldest manner can be the most important (see INTELLECTUALIZATION, ISOLATION).

10. Look for the positive progressive forces in the patient, as well as the regressive ones. In an eagerness to understand unconscious material, the therapist may forget that the patient is changing and improving. The patient has a progressive force toward health, which can be influencing the material.

11. Study the interpersonal relations of the patient for his or her object relations—persons whom he or she loves, hates, is dependent

on, and so forth—for identifications and projections.

12. Finally, be very cautious about interpreting symbols, slips, errors, and so forth on an *ex cathedra* basis. Look for what the patient accepts and acts upon in the material. Saul (1958) calls this "a prognostic guide" to what the person is really capable of accepting and acting on in real life. One of the most common beginner's errors is to attempt to impress the patient with wild analysis. This almost invariably has a paradoxical effect, and represents a countertransference problem.

Alexander (1956) points out that in analytic therapy our main allies are the striving of unconscious forces for expression and the integrating tendency of the conscious ego. Alexander maintains that even if we do nothing else but not interfere with these two forces, we will be able to help many patients. He continues,

> Interpretations which connect the *actual life situation* with *past experiences* and with the *transference situation*—since the latter is always the axis around which such connections can best be made—are called *total interpretations*. The more that interpretations approximate this principle of totality, the more they fulfill their double purpose: they accelerate the assimilation of new material by the ego and mobilize further unconscious material. [p. 68]

Certain factors can be kept in mind that will help in developing the art of interpretation. First, the patient must be ready to receive an interpretation, and there must be preparation for interpretation by the understanding of unconscious material. Then, interpretation should be as total as possible, and it should refer to major emotional forces and not bog down in too many intricate masses of detail. Interpretation should be realistic and in the clear, simple, and everyday language of the patient. It should never be wild. It should be presented in a matter-of-fact way, in a friendly and practical manner, and should be brought out almost casually so that the patient can accept and think about it without feeling put upon or forced to accept it.

Correct interpretations obviously also help the therapeutic alliance. They demonstrate an ability on the therapist's part to understand accurately the patient's unconscious and the central emotional forces in the material at hand. The correct interpretation is based on a great deal of evidence, focuses on main issues and not side issues, is presented in a nontechnical fashion, and is narrowed down to the presenting material. The therapist should wait until he or she has enough material and information so that the patient is almost making the interpretation by himself or herself. The only exceptions to this are emergency situations where the therapist feels that the whole therapy is in danger unless some form of resistance is stopped. The therapist may then have to interpret widely and deeply in an attempt to put a stop to therapy-threatening or even life-threatening behavior.

Glover (1955) distinguished between "incomplete" and "inexact" interpretations. An incomplete interpretation is simply a step in technique in which the therapist gets the patient to move closer to the unconscious material, but the interpretation is not total. It is based on lack of sufficient clinical material and problems with resistance.

An inexact interpretation has a different purpose, although at a given moment it might seem to be the same. An inexact interpretation is deliberately offered as providing a definitive meaning to a certain arrangement of material, a meaning that in the unstated opinion of the therapist actually falls short of the truth. The therapist has judged that the complete truth would be dangerous or intolerable to the patient. The patient seizes the inexact interpretation eagerly, because it helps to continue to repress the truth. The process at work here is effectively one of displacement. It is fostered by the therapist to bolster the patient's defenses when uncovering psychotherapy is contraindicated.

Tarachow (1963) notes that it is important for the therapist to realize the difference between an inexact interpretation and a wrong interpretation. An inexact interpretation is deliberately handed to a patient to enable the patient to shore up ego structure and to maintain stability of defenses. A wrong interpretation is simply a mistake by the therapist that the patient eagerly jumps on to shore up the forces of resistance. This will generally cause some difficulty in the progress of the therapy, unless the therapist is alert to the patient's responses and realizes that a mistake has been made.

The best test of an interpretation is in the response that it receives from a patient. If the interpretation is utilized in making a psychic change (e.g., the removal of a resistance, or an improved life adaptation) it is meaningful and useful. It is obvious that an important measure of the therapist's success in the technique and practice of psychotherapy is in his or her capacity to produce meaningful and useful interpretations. This capacity is partly intuitive and partly developed by study and clinical experience. Above all, it is enhanced by the personal integrity of the therapist and genuine dedication to self-understanding and understanding the patient.

References

Alexander, F. (1956). *Psychoanalysis and Psychotherapy: Developments in Theory, Technique, and Training.* New York: Norton.

Balter, L., and Spencer, J. (1991). Observation and theory in psychoanalysis: the self psychology of Heinz Kohut. *Psychoanalytic Quarterly* 60:361–395.

Dewald, P. (1964). *Psychotherapy.* New York: Basic Books.

Freud, S. (1912). Recommendations to physicians practicing psycho-analysis. *Standard Edition* 12:109–120.

Glover, E. (1955). *The Technique of Psychoanalysis.* New York: International Universities Press.

Saul, L. (1958). *The Technique and Practice of Psychoanalysis.* Philadelphia: Lippincott.

Tarachow, S. (1963). *An Introduction to Psychotherapy.* New York: International Universities Press.

INTERSUBJECTIVE FIELD

This term was introduced by Brandchaft and Stolorow (1984) and by Atwood and Stolorow (1984) to refer to the fact that diagnosis and meaning in a therapy situation are primarily a function of the mutual interchange between therapist and the patient. It is a variant of the hermeneutic approach (see HERMENEUTICS) and is introduced in order to contrast it with the classic positivist notion of the neutral realistic and relatively healthy therapist confronting the emotionally disturbed and pathological patient and making an "objective" diagnosis, a concept analogous to the medical evaluation of a patient with a physical disease. It again raises the unresolved important issue of whether the method in the human sciences (see HUMAN SCIENCES) can be adopted from that used by the physical and biological sciences or whether a unique method, such as phenomenology (see PHENOMENOLOGY) must be used.

This approach carries the risk of assuming that diagnoses have no objective validity and are simply a function of the intersubjective field. This is clearly wrong since there is now suggestive evidence for biological and constitutional factors that go into the formation of psychopathology. Brandchaft and Stolorow are well aware of this and have been falsely accused of an untenable position. Stolorow and colleagues (1987)

have developed their position at greater length, shown its relationship to self psychology, and given clinical illustrations of their approach.

An even more radical view has been presented by Natterson (1991), who proclaims that the idiosyncratic subjectivity of the therapist "is a basic motivational source and structuring influence in the therapeutic process" (p. 223). In this view there must be continuous self-monitoring by the therapist of his or her individual desires, fears, and perspectives brought to the treatment situation, inevitably and constantly exerting a shaping and constituting influence on the transference and the treatment process. This is beyond countertransference because it is in addition to it, since it is not stirred up simply by the patient's transference or personality, but by a whole host of other factors in the external life and past history of the therapist.

References

Atwood, G., and Stolorow, R. (1984). *Structures of Subjectivity: Explorations in Psychoanalytic Phenomenology.* Hillsdale, NJ: Analytic Press.

Brandchaft, B., and Stolorow, R. (1984). The borderline concept: pathological character of iatrogenic myth? In *Empathy II,* ed. J. Lichtenberg, M. Bornstein, and D. Silver, Hillsdale, NJ: Analytic Press.

Natterson, J. (1991). *Beyond Countertransference: the Therapist's Subjectivity in the Therapeutic Process.* Northvale, NJ: Jason Aronson.

Stolorow, R., Brandchaft, B., and Atwood, G. (1987). *Psychoanalytic Treatment: An Intersubjective Approach.* Hillsdale, NJ: Analytic Press.

INTERVENTIONS (SEE ALSO INTERPRETATION)

Some authors use intervention as a generic term for all the analyst's communications to the patient, including instructions, explanations, and reconstructions. There are four classical types of interventions that take place in psychoanalytic psychotherapy. The first three of these are questions, clarifications, and confrontations.

Clarification focuses on conscious and preconscious mental processes and is an intervention that presumes the patient has access to the material, although he or she may not have expressed it or have been fully aware of it. Confrontation is used to direct the patient's attention to something conscious or preconscious that has already been expressed but on which the patient's attention is not focused at the moment. Reconstructions and explanations gain special importance in self psychological analysis (Kohut 1984) and contain a certain mode of gratification (see RECONSTRUCTION).

The most important and most commonly emphasized intervention in psychoanalytic psychotherapy is interpretation. Moore and Fine (1990) define genetic interpretations as connecting present material with the past; they include reconstructions under genetic interpretations. Dynamic interpretations clarify current conflicting mental trends that result in current behavior, feelings, and so forth. Transference interpretations deal with the therapeutic relationship as it is affected by the transference (see INTERPRETATION).

References

Kohut, H. (1984). *How Does Analysis Cure?* Chicago: University of Chicago Press.
Moore, B., and Fine, B. (1990). *Psychoanalytic Terms and Concepts.* New Haven, CT: Yale University Press.

INTROJECTION (SEE IDENTIFICATION, INTROJECTION, INCORPORATION)

J–K

JEALOUSY

How curious that jealousy, which we have all experienced at one time or another, is not defined in Samuel Johnson's dictionary! It is an important concept for psychotherapists because it appears in a morbid form in paranoia, and also because it must be distinguished in Kleinian theory from envy. The morbid form of paranoid jealousy is the delusion that the marital or sexual partner is unfaithful. The classical example of this is in Shakespeare's *Othello*. Such jealousy may be accompanied by endless arguments and interrogations of the partner and even torture and violence, including homicide. There is a form of chronic alcoholism associated with pathological jealousy. Jealousy in psychotic conditions takes a delusional form.

In classical psychoanalytic theory envy, rivalry, and jealousy are not clearly differentiated and there is an overlap of jealousy and the concept of narcissistic wounding. The emphasis in classical theory is on the oedipal desire for exclusive possession of the parent of the opposite sex and the rivalry and jealousy with the siblings and the other parent when the desired parent shows any attention to them.

All this is in sharp contrast to the theory of Melanie Klein (1957), who introduced the concept of envy (see ENVY) as primary and constitutional. At a slightly later developmental time jealousy crystallizes out of this constitutional or primary envy. Primal envy, which contains the attack on people with special advantages and qualities simply for the sake of their goodness, is gradually modulated to jealousy and greed, and then hopefully to a more mature state of competition. According to Hinshelwood (1989), envy is a fantasy of forced entry and destructive attacks on the good object. There may be an equally omnipotent fantasy of taking the object in with a damaging violence so that the object is spoiled through a violent form of possession and control. This is defined as greed and may result in an accumulation of damaged objects inside, "each provoking a greater demand and hunger for a good object to be taken in to alleviate the steadily worsening internal state" (p. 171).

Jealousy is based more on love and aims at the possession of the loved object and the removal of the rival, pertaining to a triangular relationship at a time of life when objects are clearly differentiated from each other. Envy is more primary, more dyadic, and involves the wish to attack and destroy as a primitive and fundamental emotion aimed at spoiling the goodness of the object in order to remove the source of envious feelings. Because of the spoiling aspects of envy, it has the least libidinal components and the strongest suffusion with the death instinct (see DEATH INSTINCT); greed has a stronger libidinal component and is again more concentrated on possessing the goodness of the object through internalization.

References

Hinshelwood, R. (1989). *A Dictionary of Kleinian Thought.* London: Free Association Books.

Klein, M. (1957). Envy and gratitude. In *Envy and Gratitude and Other Works 1946–1963,* pp. 176–235. New York: Dell.

JUNG, CARL (SEE MID-LIFE CRISIS)

KERNBERG, OTTO (SEE SPLITTING)

KLEIN, MELANIE (1882–1960)

Melanie Klein, born in Vienna, was the youngest of four children from the second marriage of a Jewish doctor who was over 50 when she was born. She was closer to her much younger mother and became a humanities student, always regretting she had not studied medicine. She married at 21 and had three children. Her husband found work in Budapest and she began analysis with Ferenczi, who encouraged her to analyze children. In 1921, after separating from her husband, she moved to Berlin and began analysis with Abraham. But 14 months later he died and in 1927 she moved to England. There she engaged in a longstanding and often acrimonious debate with the followers of Anna Freud, who did not believe children could be psychoanalyzed. Segal (1974, 1980) offers the best overall review of Klein's life and thought. Her work is collected in four volumes (Klein 1932, 1961, 1975a, 1975b); a recent review of her basic concepts is presented by Petot (1990, 1991).

There are five crucial notions in Klein's system. First, she believed that stages of the Oedipus complex and superego formation exist in early infancy, which implies that the infant has the capacity for some very complex perceptions, emotions, and mental integrations. Second, she postulated that the early postnatal operation of introjection and projection build the infant's inner phantasy world; introjection and projection are based on dealing with the death instinct as the initial problem of life.

Third, Klein postulated two critical "positions," a difficult term that is different from Freud's developmental phases (oral, anal, genital). The paranoid–schizoid position deals with ambivalence by splitting and projection and occurs during the first three or four months of life; it is characterized by persecutory fears and anxiety over survival. During this position the good (gratifying) breast produces a feeling of love when the infant is satisfied. This is projected and experienced as the good breast loving the infant, who then internalizes this sense of being loved as a protection against the death instinct. The infant's oral sadism springing from the death instinct and from the bad (frustrating) breast imagined when the infant is frustrated produces hate. This is projected and experienced as the bad breast hating the infant. This bad breast is also internalized in order to control it (Klein 1946). The basic implication is that the infant can feel supported or attacked from within itself. Furthermore, the hate and love can be reprojected or reintrojected, so that if the hate is reprojected or reintrojected a vicious cycle of an increased sense of persecution from within or without is produced; if love is reprojected and reintrojected, a cycle of increased well-being is begun.

Klein introduced confusion through the use of her term "part-object" (see OBJECT). Kernberg (1980) points out that she used this term in two ways. First, Klein meant to represent a partial anatomical aspect of a real person, such as the breast, which the infant perceives as if it were the object to which the infant is relating. The second sense—predominantly used by Kleinian authors—is explained by Kernberg thus: "As a result of splitting, part-objects constitute either part of persons or total persons perceived in a distorted, unrealistic way under the influence of the projection of pure libido or aggression, so that those objects are either all good or all bad" (p. 882).

The second half of the first year of life, according to Klein, is marked by the depressive position (see DEPRESSIVE POSITION), emerging as self and object differentiation becomes possible in a cognitive sense. Splitting into part objects is less present; as a result, anxiety occurs over the loss of good objects without and within, ushering in the depressive position. This is a consequence of the capacity for internalizing whole objects, which Klein says begins in the second quarter of the first year of life. The infant fears that its own destructive, greedy impulses will destroy the good breast, which is later expressed as the child's fear that the parent may die. The destructive impulses can destroy the good breast by appropriating it; this is sometimes distinguished from the destruction of the breast due to envy, to be discussed shortly. At any rate, a state of sadness is ushered in and becomes the key hurdle in ordinary development. If it is too painful, a regression to the paranoid-schizoid position or a defensive swing to the manic state occurs, and the psychological groundwork is laid for the psychoses.

The good and bad breasts in the paranoid-schizoid position are forerunners of the benign and harsh superego. For Klein, the oedipal triangle begins in the oral stage, and there is an inborn knowledge of the genitals of both sexes. Thus there is a long and complex prehistory before Freud's oedipal stage, involving combinations of parents, splitting, projections, and internalizations. There may be a premature advance into oedipal material due to the use of genital love mobilized against prege-nital aggression.

The fourth set of Kleinian concepts are introjective identification and projective identification. Intro-jective identification results from the introjection of the object. Projective identification is a hybrid concept that is used differently by every subse-quent author (see PROJECTIVE IDENTIFICATION).

The fifth basic concept was in-troduced by Klein in her seventies as a major addition and produced new storms of protest against what she assumed was possible in the mind of the infant. She believed that there was an early infantile form of envy, also based on the death instinct, that was aimed at the destruction and possession of the envied good breast (or in treatment, the imagined serene analyst); furthermore, that there was a constitutional variation in the amount of envy and aggression present in each individual (see ENVY and JEALOUSY).

Oral sadism is the first critical manifestation of the death instinct (see DEATH INSTINCT and SA-DISM). Oral sadism varies with con-stitutional strength and is the key to understanding human development and pathology. It is first projected, resulting in persecutory fears and the fear of annihilation by the destruc-tive devouring breast. The first source of anxiety arises when pro-jected oral sadism threatens to de-stroy and invade the ego or self (again, not carefully differentiated by Klein). Oral sadism also produces envy, which appears first; the breast is experienced as willfully withhold-ing, and there is a wish to scoop out, destroy, and possess it. Later deriva-tions of envy are greed, which is a more sophisticated form of envy and arises from it, and jealousy, a later emotional development character-istic of triangular situations, such as the oedipal conflicts. Here a third person is hated because that person preempts the desired love. It follows that constitutionally excessive ag-gression would foster a great deal of splitting and denial of reality in order to deal with these affects, and their associated fantasies, constituting envy, greed, and jealousy.

Conversely, the projection of "good" inner objects onto new ob-jects forms the basis of trust in later life. Gratitude comes from good ex-periences, decreases greed, and leads to a healthy generosity in contrast to what Klein calls "reactive generosi-ty," a defense against envy that even-tually ends in feelings of being robbed.

Splitting originally occurs in good objects which are introjected and bad ones which are projected, but a secondary splitting can take place when aggression is strong and there is a related predominance of bad objects. These bad objects are then further split into fragments and when these fragments are projected we get the multiple persecutors or the so-called "bizarre objects" de-scribed dramatically by Klein's analysand and follower, Bion (1963, 1967).

Narcissistic internal structures and narcissistic object relationships arise in an effort to escape persecutory fears by an excessive dependence on an idealized object and by the use of others to confirm one's grandiosity. The idealization of external objects in the paranoid-schizoid position is marked by fantasies of unlimited gratification from these objects, which protects the individual against frustration, denies any need for aggression, and protects the individual against persecutory fears from the objects.

The idealization of internal objects in the depressive position protects the individual against unbearable reality. The denial of internal and external reality represents the denial of aggression and is a form of hallucinatory wish fulfillment at the cost of reality testing. The aggression of both the bad inner and outer objects is denied.

Sexual promiscuity or sexual conquests, seen commonly in the narcissistic disorders, may represent the turning from one idealized object to another in a desperate attempt to escape imagined inner and outer persecutors. Hypochondriasis is explained as the projection of persecutory bad objects to parts of one's own body; the fear of poisoning and of pathological control from the outside is based on a combination of persecutory paranoid and hypochondriacal fears.

In the depressive position the fear shifts from that of a persecutory fear to one of harming the good internal object, and idealization is used here to protect against aggression toward the good internal object. Depressive anxiety or guilt about the survival of good inner and outer objects is critical, so the object is idealized in the depressive position to protect against aggression to it and to remove guilt over this aggression. In contrast to Kohut, idealization is used in both of Klein's basic positions as a defense against sadism and destruction in fantasy (Segal 1974, 1980). Internalized bad objects are no longer projected in the depressive position, nor are they reintrojected, because now the total object is experienced. Therefore, the internal bad objects remain, forming the roots of the primitive superego that attacks the ego or self with guilt feelings. Good internal objects attenuate this attack.

The standards set by or the demands coming from the idealized good internal objects become, when combined with sadistic superego precursors, cruel demands for perfection leading to an unremitting harshness of the superego. This is complicated, in cases where there is much sadism, due to the need to protect the good objects in the superego by excessive idealization. The result is that the standards of the superego become extremely high.

Etchegoyen (1991) presents a complete textbook of psychoanalysis utilizing the Kleinian system, which is very popular in South America.

References

Bion, W. (1963). *Elements of Psycho-Analysis.* New York: Basic Books.

_____ (1967). *Second Thoughts: Collected Papers on Psychoanalysis.* London: Heinemann.

Etchegoyen, R. (1991). *The Fundamentals of Psychoanalytic Technique,* trans. P. Pitchon. New York: Karnac Books.

Kernberg, O. (1980). Melanie Klein. In *Comprehensive Textbook of Psychiatry,* 3rd ed., ed. H. Kaplan, A. Freeman, and B. Sadock, pp. 441–451. Baltimore: Williams & Wilkins.

Klein, M. (1932). *The Psycho-Analysis of Children.* London: Hogarth.

_____ (1946). Notes on some schizoid mechanisms. In *Envy and Gratitude and Other Works 1946–1963,* pp. 1–24. London: Hogarth.

_____ (1961). *Narrative of a Child Psycho-Analysis.* London: Hogarth.

_____ (1975a). *Love, Guilt and Reparation and Other Works 1921–1945.* New York: Free Press.

_____ (1975b). *Envy and Gratitude and Other Works 1946–1963.* London: Hogarth.

Petot, J. (1990). *Melanie Klein.* Vol. 1: *First Discoveries and First System, 1919–1932.* Madison, CT: International Universities Press.

_____ (1991). *Melanie Klein.* Vol. 2: *The Ego and the Good Object, 1932–1960.* Madison, CT: International Universities Press.

Segal, H. (1974). *Introduction to the Work of Melanie Klein.* New York: Basic Books.

_____ (1980). *Melanie Klein.* New York: Viking.

KOHUT, HEINZ
(SEE SELF PSYCHOLOGY)

L

In their guide to the maverick French psychoanalyst Lacan's (1977) *Ecrits,* Muller and Richardson (1982) explain how Lacan translates the topographic theory of early Freud into linguistics. Free association is thought of as the flow of "Signifiers," a term borrowed from the linguistic theory of Saussure (1986). Each Signifier refers not to an individual "signified" mental concept of desire, but to another Signifier in the chain of free associations. The subject, as he or she develops and becomes articulated with language, increasingly alienates primary unconscious desire in the Signifier chain. As Lacan puts it, we end up with the wanderings of true desire caught in the net of Signifiers; It is the It that speaks.

Freud's condensation aspect of primary process, according to Lacan, is actually metaphor, a linguistic process in which one phrase stands for a set of others suggesting a likeness; for example, "a volley of oaths." Condensation in Freud's theory is therefore a series of Signifiers connected through metaphor. Freud's displacement is metonomy, a linguistic process in which one contiguous element stands for another; for example, "a good table" for good food. When Lacan makes his most famous statement that the unconscious is structured like a language, he means that the unconscious consists of repressed early Signifiers of desire connected by the rules of metonomy and metaphor. The unconscious consists entirely of early Signifiers that had to be further linguistically disguised due to the demands of fitting into the cultural order. There are no drives and no instincts; no biology is involved.

According to Lacan, the phase of inaugural primary narcissism (unbounded phase) occurs first in human development. Next comes the imaginary or mirror stage, which is preverbal, presymbolic, and forms a false ego. This is described at length in Lacan's (1968) famous 1953 speech delivered in Rome and forms the basis of his disagreement with traditional psychoanalytic structural theory (see MIRROR STAGE). Then, in a brief transitory stage, the child comes up against the "forbidden." This results in the symbolic stage as the child acquires language; there is a split between the inner and outer world, between a false "I," (a false ego) and the outer world. To resolve this, the child must identify with the father's laws and cultural order and enter the quest for objects in a manner ever further removed from its original desire. (Later, Lacan calls these stages perceptual orders, since they can exist simultaneously.)

The child originally desires to be a phallus in union with the mother. It is the desire to be the desired of the mother, to be the mother's phallus. Lacan sometimes uses the word "phallus" here as a symbol; he is not using it only specifically to mean the penis. It represents what the mother wants the most, that which would bring her fulfillment. To understand Lacan, one must be familiar with Hegel, who held that "desire" is to be the desired of the other person (see DESIRE). As one develops toward adulthood, the chain of Signifiers moves further from the originally signified desire and from one's true self and, consequently, from understanding the meaning of one's own speech. The adult individual knows less about what is really meant by his or her linguistic expressions when speaking to another person.

There are three fundamental ideas in Lacan. First, the individual is constituted by language. The individual has no essence, center, or instincts. The unconscious consists only of the earliest Signifiers, which are structured like a language. Second, discourse embodies society; politics is embedded in our language and we are all caught up in it, since the human being is only an individual subject because of language and membership in society. Third, there is no such thing as an autonomous ego. This is a false notion, an *ex*

post facto explanation, says Lacan. Lacan maintains that the ego is always false and stands in the way of knowledge of our true desires.

For Lacan, desire is the driving human force, not libido. It comes from animal demand, the demand of the brute, as he calls it. The infant begins in a dual symbiosis with the mother, the realm of primary narcissism. As this ruptures, the infant realizes that it is not the mother. At this point human want begins to appear, the human form of desire. The human desires the paradise of fusion with the mother, to be what the mother desires most and in a fusion with her. Lacan uses for this the symbol "phallus," which is the Signifier of this desire for perfect union with the mother.

For Lacan, a primordial castration has occurred when this fusion is inevitably disrupted by the vicissitudes of development. Following Heidegger, the first experience of human limit occurs when this union is ruptured. Lacan does not distinguish between male and female earliest development. The dialectic of desire, based on Hegel's theory, occurs next. The ultimate quest is to be recognized and desired by the desired. This is closely related to the "gleam in the mother's eye" that Kohut mentions. Indeed, for Kohut (1971) there is also a "mirror stage" (p. 124) of preverbal beginnings, but there the similarity ends, for Kohut's mirror stage involves the mirroring and confirming response of the archaic selfobject to the emerging self of the infant and does not involve either mirrors or imaginings. Kohut is referring to an experience, not an image. For Lacan, the child wants to be the desired of the mother, her fullness, her phallus, but must end up expressing only culturally legitimate desires through endless derivative Signifier chains, multiple displacements in language.

It is impossible to become the desired of the mother because the father, who has the phallus, is there. When Lacan uses the term "father," he means three things: the real father, the imaginary father, and the law of the father. For Lacan, the father is a spoilsport. He says to the infant, you cannot sleep with your mother. He says to the mother, you cannot reappropriate your product. So the oedipal struggle is in having to forgo the original desire and channel it through the symbolic cultural order, expressing it in some way through words. It is interesting to compare this with the traditional drive-conflict psychoanalytic view of the resolution of the oedipal struggle. For example, Loewald (1980) describes the father as representing "castrating reality." He explains, "The longing for the father, seeking his help and protection, is a defensive compromise in order to come to terms with his superior, hostile power" (p. 9). For Lacan, to identify with the father is to find legitimate Signifiers, which means accepting the culture, the facts of life, and human finitude. This is a process that Lacan calls oedipization, by means of which one enters the social order. When one has accomplished this, the oedipal struggle is resolved; from then on in one's language, a chain of Signifiers

occurs in which the signified desire becomes hidden, sliding incessantly under the chain of Signifiers.

This concept of the signified "sliding" under a chain of Signifiers is central to Lacan's theory of treatment. For Lacan, psychoanalysis is hermeneutics. It brings out underlying contexts and structures from the unconscious. It reveals a personal code. The past is hidden by the linguistic transformations that occur because the individual must fit into the symbolic order. Historical reconstruction in psychoanalysis is not important, for psychoanalysis is a discourse with the other. It brings to light the desires that are hidden in the metaphors and tropes, for the human subject is endlessly displaced and reconstituted by the symbolic order of desire through which language passes. This study of the patient's language, says Lacan, can guide the patient back to insatiable, unconscious desires.

"Repression" for Lacan is simply a set of linguistic transformations using metaphor and metonomy that the child must use to fit into the symbolic order during oedipalization. In this sense, according to Lacan, "Man is a marionette of his culture." The enemy is the ego that is born in the mirror phase, a false notion that the individual has of the self as an entity.

In summary, Lacan decenters the self. Everyone has a divided self, says Lacan; from the mirror stage on we are all alienated from our true self. There is no autonomous ego or center to a person. Lacan changes the focus of theory from biology or instincts to language, and from mechanisms to tropes. There is no original instinctual unconscious, only chains of Signifiers in the unconscious. In psychopathology the person loses his or her grip on the chain of Signifiers, and the analyst must restore discourse to its owner. Psychiatric labels are useless, for each person's unique narrative is crucial.

For Lacan (1978), psychoanalysis or psychoanalytic psychotherapy is a reversal due to the "dummy" (le mort) analyst. The silence of the analyst causes a two-fold regression: backward among the chains of Signifiers "undoing the secret knots," as Lacan puts it, toward the unconscious primal Signifiers of desire that constitute the unconscious; and to the loss of false narcissistic images by which the ego is constituted in the mirror stage. This regression is caused by the frustration of the patient's desire in the psychoanalytic situation. The dummy of the analyst frustrates the patient's demand. Through transference, the chain of Signifiers retrogresses until it reaches the truth of the patient's desires and restores full speech to the patient. Ça parle, the it speaks, much more directly when that has been achieved, says Lacan (see LACAN'S "LE MORT").

References

Kohut, H. (1971). *The Analysis of the Self.* New York: International Universities Press.

Lacan, J. (1968). *Speech and Language in Psychoanalysis,* trans. A. Wilden. Baltimore: Johns Hopkins University Press.

———— (1977). *Ecrits: A Selection,* trans. A. Sheridan. New York: Norton.

———— (1978). *The Four Fundamental Concepts of Psycho-analysis,* trans. A. Sheridan. New York: Norton.

Loewald, H. (1980). *Papers on Psychoanalysis.* New Haven, CT: Yale University Press.

Muller, J., and Richardson, W. (1982). *Lacan and Language: A Reader's Guide to Ecrits.* New York: International Universities Press.

Saussure, F. (1986). *Course in General Linguistics,* trans. R. Harris. La Salle, IL: Open Court.

LACAN'S "LE MORT" (THE DUMMY)

Portrayed here is a clinical model from Lacan's (1977) *Ecrits.* In "The Direction of the Treatment and the Principles of Its Power," presented in 1958, Lacan compares the practice of psychoanalytic psychotherapy to a game of bridge involving four players (p. 229). The analyst's crucial role is that of the silently listening bridge "dummy" (le mort), and the purpose of the treatment is to induce the Other of the patient (the patient's unconscious, in Lacan's terms) to speak. The four "players" would be the consciously speaking patient, the patient's unconscious Other, the speaking analyst, and the silent, "dummy" analyst.

For Lacan (1968), psychoanalysis stresses "distracted listening" for the "return of truth" in the patient's discourse in the form of figures of speech or tropes, allusions, puns, equivocations, slips, and dreams, always concealing desire; the material is heard like polyphonic music. The goal of treatment is to move from "empty speech" to "full speech," in which the analyst reflects the message of the "it" to the subject. There is no offering of the therapist as a model for identification, no strengthening of the ego, no holding or nurturing or repair of structural deficits; there is, however, a de-emphasis on interpretation of resistances and defenses.

Lacan (see LACAN) posited four stages or, as he later referred to them, "perceptual orders" in human development: (1) the inaugural primary narcissism or unbounded chaotic fragmented stage; (2) the imaginary or mirror stage, which is preverbal and presymbolic and forms a false ego distinct from the truth about the subject (this claim that the ego is a false and alien image—as described in Lacan's [1968] famous speech delivered in 1953—is the basis of his disagreement with traditional psychoanalytic structural theory); (3) the brief transitory stage, when the child comes up against the "forbidden"; and (4) the symbolic stage, which is constituted as the child acquires language and produces a split between the inner and outer world. In order to do this, the child must identify with the father's laws and cultural order and enter the quest for objects in a manner further and further removed from its original desire. For Lacan, this original desire is to be a phallus in union with the mother (i.e., it is the desire to be the desired of the mother, for which the phallus is the primal signifier). As one moves in the chain of verbal signifiers from the originally signified desire, one moves away from one's individual truth, one's true wishes, and from understanding the meaning of one's

own utterances. So the maturing adult individual knows less and less about what he or she really means to say when he or she speaks to another person.

The past is hidden by linguistic transformations as a result of having to fit into the symbolic and cultural order. The psychoanalytic process brings to light the desires that are hidden in the metaphors and tropes, for the human subject is endlessly displaced and reconstituted by the symbolic order of language through which desire must pass, and then be translated and communicated. This study of the patient's language, says Lacan, can guide the therapist and patient back to the patient's unconscious desires. The main advantage of Lacan's approach is in his stress on the informed doctor who relates to a patient as an autonomous specific individual human subject and tunes in to what the patient is uniquely saying—the central goal of psychoanalytic listening.

One way this is accomplished is through the silence of the "dummy" analyst, which induces a twofold regression in the patient: (1) backwards along the chains of signifiers to the unconscious primary signifiers of desire that constitute the unconscious; and (2) to the loss of false narcissistic images by which the ego is constituted, starting in the fragmented stage, consolidated in the mirror stage, and continuing throughout life. What causes this regression is the frustration of the patient's desire in the psychoanalytic situation as the "dummy" analyst does not respond to the patient's demand. This generates a backward motion along the patient's chain of signifiers. Through transference it reaches what Lacan calls the truth of the patient's desires, and restores full speech to the patient.

In Lacan's bridge-game model of psychoanalytic psychotherapy, the patient's conscious speaks first; but contained in this speech are the desires from the patient's Other, hidden in metaphors or tropes, allusions, jokes, equivocations, slips, and dreams. These are addressed toward the "dummy" analyst, who is relatively silent because it is the analyst's professional obligation to keep his or her own desires unvoiced in the treatment; otherwise, explains Lacan, "the game will proceed without anyone knowing who is leading" (p. 230).

The conscious-speaking analyst has the option, as Lacan puts it, to play either to the right or to the left of the opening player (the patient). If the analyst's self intervenes before the patient experiences the "dummy" analyst, for example by responding to the conscious spoken demands of the patient in some way such as attempting to offer a model for identification, "strengthen the ego," support, hold, nurture, advise, or repair the patient, then the patient's Other will never be stimulated to speak in expressions containing more and more regressed and original chains of the signifiers of desire. If the analyst's conscious subject plays after the patient has experienced the "dummy" analyst and has responded, then the analyst is in a position to return the voice of the patient's Other back to the patient and restore the patient to fuller speech.

References

Lacan, J. (1968). *Speech and Language in Psychoanalysis,* trans. A. Wilden. Baltimore, MD: Johns Hopkins University Press.
———— (1977). *Ecrits: A Selection,* trans. A. Sheridan. New York: Norton.

LAING, R. D. (SEE MYSTIFICATION, ONTOLOGICAL INSECURITY, SCHIZOID SCHIZOPHRENIA)

LEISURE

Samuel Johnson (1773), surely a man who never experienced it himself, defined leisure as "freedom from business or hurry; a vacancy of mind; power to spend time according to choice" (p. 1133). This somewhat ambivalent definition underestimates the extreme importance of leisure as the basis of culture, and the use of leisure as a measure of a person's maturity. It is important in taking a psychiatric history to ask patients specifically whether they experience leisure and how they employ leisure; this information can tell a great deal about the patient's lifestyle, superego, level of maturity, and intrinsic energies.

There have been very few good references on the subject. In a diary note on October 7, 1962, I reviewed an unusual new book by DeGrazia (1962), as follows:

> [DeGrazia] chooses Aristotle's definition of leisure as part of the contemplative life and sharply separates it from "free time" which is merely for recuperation from work. Leisure is a great rarity these days and there is a certain snobbish implication by DeGrazia that those who live the leisurely life are better. He notes that leisure requires sacrifice and is a state of being in which an activity is performed for its own sake or its own end. . . . He suggests music, and contemplation, and friends chosen for their own worth.

DeGrazia presents statistics to show that work and work-oriented free time are in about the same proportion as they always have been, but leisure time is even less available than before. He warns how advertising has moved in to utilize free time, reducing the share of time that can be devoted to leisure, and he discusses the history of time, concluding, "to have leisure one must be free of the clock" (p. 328). The question of leisure, DeGrazia notes, is the question of whether "parcels of time" can be put aside for a person to be alone with himself or herself. Truth comes in leisure, claims DeGrazia, and he warns that democracy tends to seduce people away from leisure.

Three reasons why people don't utilize leisure are: first, there is often no tradition of it, as in our culture; second, television and the advertising industry are opposed to leisure and bring in a different tradition—

that of consumption; third, according to DeGrazia, leisure is beyond the capacity of most people. Culture is *paideia,* surely something one absorbs as a child. Many people do not have the intelligence, or the temperament, to enjoy leisure, says DeGrazia. He divides the world into two classes of people: the great majority and "the leisure kind." The latter love ideas and imagination—which provides them with both a blessing and a torment—and they create culture. It should be noted that these classes are not related to the "leisure class" discussed in Veblen's (1931) famous book dealing with conspicuous consumption.

DeGrazia claims that the great majority envies the leisure kind; also, each of these two classes has their own literature. He urges political action as necessary to encourage the growth of the leisure class and ends with an exhortation for us to live a life of good quality. He warns that design on the world fractionizes one's view and unsettles the mind: "The crowding of desires, one upon the other, can shake a man's head until it rattles" (p. 420).

A sort of sequel to this work appeared eight years later in Linder (1970). The motto of his work is *Horas non numero nisi serenas* (Only the quiet hours count). For Linder, cultivation of the mind and spirit is "generally accepted" as a supreme goal, and increased consumption reduces the time available for this. Self-discipline, concentration, achieving excellence, and even reading a book intelligently are all lost due to the pressures of time. He divides time into four kinds: ordinary work time; personal work time, which involves the maintenance of the body and one's property; consumption time for using these material goods; and culture time, which Russell (1972) calls "idleness." There is, of course, a fifth kind of time, which Linder labels "true idleness," that occurs in poverty and has nothing to do with leisure.

The pursuit of money and prestige is not compatible with the goal of having quiet hours. The enemies of leisure are the wish for money and ambition, a harsh punitive driving superego, or, using self psychology, an unconscious clamor for archaic grandiosity and exhibitionistic mirroring.

Rybczynski (1991) presents a rather upbeat discussion of how the weekend became a very important temporal institution in modern times. This is primarily an historical study, but Rybczynski recognizes that so-called free time can be gobbled up by a whole series of weekend chores even more strenuous than one's work during the week: home repairs, gardening, shopping, athletics, and the weekend trips on the crowded highways. A whole series of new tasks have arisen in our day that might be called "weekend work," such as working at one's golf swing, to say nothing of jogging, weight lifting, and all the other tortures that overfed Americans impose upon themselves. Add to that a good deal of unwanted but obligated Friday and Saturday night socializing and one has a weekend nightmare rather than a weekend of leisure. Rybczynski does not recognize

this, nor does he deal with the problem of boredom on the weekend, to say nothing about the brainstultifying effect on those unfortunate individuals who can find nothing better to do than lie in an overstuffed chair in front of the TV. He sees the weekend as a chance to create work that is more meaningful, but in my experience that is not what the great majority do with their free time.

None of these well-crafted discussions of leisure take up the realistic issues of the individual swept up by the materialistic values of our civilization, or the patient driven by a relentless superego or an unconscious archaic grandiosity. These are serious clinical problems and because this drive often results in financial or political success, they are sometimes overlooked in our patients. Today we are living in a civilization with material wealth far greater than that ever dreamed of, yet we have less true leisure than the lowest ancient shepherds, who could play the lute and give names to the constellations. As Livingstone (in Hutchins 1936) comments: "The Greeks could not broadcast the Aeschylean trilogy, but they could write it" (p. 25n). Schor (1991) points out that, contrary to all expectations, Americans enjoy less leisure today than at any time since the end of World War II, and she documents this unanticipated decline in leisure both at work and in the home. Schor argues that only in the eighteenth and nineteenth centuries did workers in Western countries have longer and more arduous work schedules than we have today, so that there is a trend as old as the industrial revolution in which leisure time has been eroded in favor of the strong preference of employers and of employees for longer hours and more money.

The major factor accounting for this is the great stress our civilization has placed on the acquisition of material wealth; as the value on goods increases, the competition for them becomes keener and the tempo of life speeds up. In addition, our new industrial state has all the communication techniques at its disposal to manufacture and expand our wants. When this is coupled with the fact that work in such a state is less backbreaking, in the literal sense of the word, due to technological progress, it is not hard to see why the hours of "work" would tend to be increased in an effort to satisfy all the new wants and to service and "enjoy" all the new gadgets and machines, from electric pencil sharpeners to snowmobiles.

An additional paradox quickly unfolds with a little observation. Greater affluence does not lead to more happiness or even to a more relaxed pace of life; the contrary is true. As the physician, for example, works his way up from the impoverished resident or intern to the middle-aged "pillar of the community," life does not tend to become easier, and expenses seem constantly to rise faster than income. This law as a generalization has been formulated by the clever C. N. Parkinson.

We are faced with a form of slavery, the danger of psychosomatic breakdown, increasing economic pressures, and unhappiness, all amazingly enough in the face of constantly rising personal affluence. The solution to this dilemma is to live a life of good quality. As Pieper (1952) said, we must find a way to substitute for restlessness (at the bottom of which there sometimes appears to be a fanatical and even ultimately suicidal activity) the capability of seeing life as a whole and the world as a whole, and to act in accordance with this extended viewpoint. This can only be done by provision for an intelligent use of leisure time. Pieper (1952) states:

> The point and justification of leisure are not that the functionary should function faultlessly and without breakdown, but that the functionary should continue to be a man—and that means that he should not be wholly absorbed in the clearcut milieu of his strictly limited function; the point is also that he should continue to be capable of seeing life as a whole and the world as a whole; that he should fulfill himself, and come to full possession of his faculties, face to face with being as a whole. [p. 57]

There are many other ways of posing the problem. For example, Schopenhauer saw men as driven by an unconscious will of imperious desire, always striving, never satisfied. As long as the consciousness is filled by the will, there can be no happiness and no peace, only at best a respite from pain, which itself is often felt as boredom. He (in Durant 1926) writes:

> To see how short life is, one must have lived long. . . . Up to our 36th year we may be compared, in respect to the way we use our vital energy, to people who live on the

interest of their money; what they spend today they have again tomorrow. But from the age of 36 onward, our position is like that of the investor who begins to entrance on his capital. . . . It is the dread of this calamity that makes love of possession increase with age. [p. 356]

Although insanity and suicide are discussed by Schopenhauer as ways of relief from the world of the strivings of "will," he also allows the possibility of relief through use of the intellect to achieve wisdom and enjoy the arts: "A man who has no mental needs is called a Philistine; he does not know what to do with his leisure—*difficilis in otio quies* (Quiet in leisure is difficult); he searches greedily from place to place for new sensations . . ." (p. 359).

The ultimate deliverance from servitude toward the "will" and material interests is found in the contemplation of art, according to Schopenhauer. His pessimism about man's captivation by the "will" would certainly be borne out by the recent trends in modern civilization toward worship of the material goods of life. The intelligent use of leisure is a significant mark of psychological maturity (see CORRUPTION).

References

DeGrazia, S. (1962). *Of Time, Work and Leisure.* New York: Twentieth Century Fund.

Durant, W. (1926). *The Story of Philosophy.* New York: Simon and Schuster.

Hutchins, R. (1936). *The Higher Learning in America.* New Haven, CT: Yale University Press.

Johnson, S. (1773). *A Dictionary of the English Language.* Beirut, Lebanon: Librairie du Liban, 1978.

Linder, S. (1970). *The Harried Leisure Class.* New York: Columbia University Press.

Pieper, J. (1952). *Leisure, the Basis of Culture.* New York: Pantheon.

Russell, B. (1972). *In Praise of Idleness and Other Essays.* New York: Simon and Schuster.

Rybczynski, W. (1991). *Waiting for the Weekend.* New York: Viking.

Schor, J. (1991). *The Overworked American: The Unexpected Decline of Leisure.* New York: Basic Books.

Veblen, T. (1931). *The Theory of the Leisure Class: An Economic Study of Institutions.* New York: Random House.

LIBIDO

Most authors agree that, along with *The Interpretation of Dreams,* Freud's (1905) *Three Essays on the Theory of Sexuality* represents his greatest work. The three essays present an elaboration of nosological considerations based on Freud's theory of the sexual etiology of psychogenic disorders. Freud's basic libido theory was set down in these three essays and in various later contributions; a thorough review of the subject is presented by Nagera (1969).

Freud was interested in the vicissitudes of the instincts as the individual grows up (see INSTINCT), particularly the sexual instinct. The "energy" of the sexual instinct is defined as the libido. Sexual life does not begin at puberty but starts with clear manifestations soon after birth. It is necessary to distinguish sharply between the concepts of sexual and genital. The former is the wider concept and includes many activities that have nothing to do with the genitals.

Sexual life comprises the obtaining of pleasure from certain zones of the body, an activity that is subsequently brought into the service of reproduction. In Freud's early thinking these zones (see EROTOGENIC ZONE) represented areas from which libido arose or that were stimulated by certain chemical or hormonal changes to bring forth certain urgent impulses. Later they were thought of as areas of pleasure through which libido could be discharged.

The first of the zones to appear is the mouth. During the oral period, the infant experiences pure pleasure around the mouth. Not only does it suck in the milk that is necessary for life, but it also enjoys stimulation of this erotogenic zone and subsequent libido discharge.

The first half of the oral period, the first six months of life, is thought of as essentially passive in Freud's libido theory. The infant desires to be given to and passively receive through the mouth. It wishes to suck and satiate, to fall asleep at the mother's breast, to be devoured and returned inside the mother.

The next six months of life, characterized by the development of teeth, is an active, or sadistic, oral stage. Here a new pleasure is found, that of biting. Anger or rage experienced in the oral period is reacted to by a hallucinatory fantasy of biting, chewing, and devouring the frustrating object. This may originally be a very pleasant retaliation fantasy, but it often has to be deeply repressed by the ego because the frustrating object is most often the mother. There would be danger if the mother

were to be devoured and destroyed since she is also the source of life for the infant.

Between the ages of 1 and 2 a new erotogenic zone becomes important, the anus. Many of the conflicts and problems of the 2-year-old revolve around toilet training and the production or withholding of bowel movements. The anal stage of development is divided by some into an active, or sadistic, and a subsequent passive, or retentive, period. The active period appears first; the appearance of the retentive period heralds the beginning of true object love. In the active anal or anal-sadistic stage, the predominant fantasy is to expel and to get rid of objects. Having a bowel movement is conceived of as the hostile expulsion of a bad object, which gives a pleasant sensation. During the passive anal stage, the wish to retain is predominant. The child may enjoy the sensation of control over the full rectum, and battles may ensue between the child and the mother as to where and when it should have the bowel movement. In the act of defecation and the mother's wiping and cleaning, libido is discharged through the anal erotogenic zone.

Around the age of 4 the erotogenic zone shifts to the genitalia. This has been called the phallic and subsequent oedipal phase of development. The object of the libido at the age of 5 is the parent of the opposite sex, and the parent of the same sex is seen as a rival. The fantasy is that of possessing sexually the parent of the opposite sex and destroying or getting rid of the parent of the same sex.

Here again, although the fantasy may be pleasant, it often has to be repressed because of the fear of retaliation, especially in the boy, who fears castration as retaliation for the desire to possess the mother.

The oedipal phase is followed by a so-called latent phase, in which no new erotogenic zones are developed, and finally by adolescence. So Freud often speaks of the biphasic nature of sexual urges. The first great increase in sexual urge occurs around the age of 5. It then falls off with the passing of the Oedipus complex and reappears again in adolescence. This is a biological phenomenon, part of the process of maturation.

As the individual advances through the various stages of psychosexual development, a tendency to attach certain quantities of libido to earlier erotogenic zones and associated fantasies is left behind. Fixation depends on two factors: the amount of overindulgence a person has had at a given stage of development and the amount of deprivation a person has had at this period of development. There is always some fixation in everybody at all stages of development (see FIXATION).

Later, when difficulties in living arise, there is a tendency to regress to earlier points of fixation in development (see REGRESSION). A price has to be paid for this regression, for it results in a revival of problems that were unsolved and unmastered in the earlier stage. These problems give rise to anxiety because they involve the pressing for expression of unsatisfied infantile impulses and needs that are unacceptable to the ego; this forces the ego to use additional defense mechanisms to aid repression. Often the defense mechanisms used in this situation are of a drastic nature and exaggerated quantity, causing the individual much difficulty in life and leading to the development of the clinical picture we call neurosis (see NEUROSIS). Furthermore, guilt about the regression tends to increase the complications and stress of the situation and encourage more regression.

The case of Little Hans (Freud 1909) illustrates the application of Freud's theories of infantile sexuality to clinical situations. The symptoms of neuroses develop as a converted expression of impulses, which in a broader sense might be designated as perverse if they could manifest themselves directly in purely conscious fantasies and acts. The polymorphous perverse disposition is the primitive and universal disposition of the human sexual impulse from which normal sexual behavior develops as a consequence of maturation, organic changes, and psychic repression. At this point in his work, Freud imagined libido as a quantum of sexual energy arising from all over the body; the psychic representative of this is ego libido. Libido is accessible to study only when invested in objects; libido can be given, removed, suspended, or invested in the self. In psychotherapy we study the vicissitudes of libido in the individual's life history and via the transference.

In his later work Freud (1914, 1915) more formally described the libido theory, in which the investment of libido in various mental representations was called cathexis (see CATHEXIS). Libido can be discharged when there is drive gratification or be dammed up if it is not discharged, which Freud thought led to the formation of certain forms of psychasthenia. Libido cathected to one's self representation Freud called ego libido, and libido cathected to various object representations Freud referred to as object libido.

Freud (1937) described individuals whose libido is readily attached to the object representation of the analyst and so easily form transferences as having plastic libido. Those who cannot make such cathexis and who cling to a heavy investment in archaic object representations he described as having adhesive libido. (see ADHESIVENESS OF THE LIBIDO). Unfortunately, the concept of adhesive libido has been used all too often as an excuse for the failure of psychoanalytic treatment. It should be kept in mind that this is a hydrodynamic theory in which libido is conceived of as analogous to energy, but the entire theory is a metaphor rather than a quantitatively measurable hypothesis. As such, it has been criticized from all sides, and some psychoanalysts have advocated its abrogation (see METAPSYCHOLOGY).

References

Freud, S. (1905). Three essays on the theory of sexuality. *Standard Edition* 7:125–243.
_____ (1909). Analysis of a phobia in a five-year-old boy. *Standard Edition* 10:3–149.
_____ (1914). On narcissism: an introduction. *Standard Edition* 14:67–102.
_____ (1915). Instincts and their vicissitudes. *Standard Edition* 14:109–140.
_____ (1937). Constructions in analysis. *Standard Edition* 23:255–269.
Nagera, H. (1969). *Basic Psychoanalytic Concepts on the Libido Theory.* New York: Basic Books.

LIMIT SITUATIONS (BOUNDARY SITUATIONS)

Boundary situations represent the crises in human existence in which conflict and its meaning become poignantly and tragically clear. Jaspers (1932a,b,c) emphasizes death, suffering, struggle, chance, guilt, and the uncertainty of the world, and two more general boundary situations—that of the particular historical determination of the individual's existence and that of the relativity of all that is real. Other authors sometimes refer to those as limit situations.

Limit or boundary situations, such as the knowledge of our impending death, bring us, says Jaspers, to illumination of our *Existenz* (if we let them). This leads to our grasp of transcendence, which is known only indirectly by what Jaspers calls "ciphers," such as myths or religions. The key point for psychotherapists is that the human is always more unknowable and indescribable than what is known and described.

Jaspers argues for what he calls "philosophical faith," pointing out that if one is unwilling to have philosophical faith, then one must hold that the immediate world is all there is, that the individual's destiny is fully determined, that humans are imperfectable and alone, and that the world is self-supporting. He (1962, 1966) tries to illustrate through study of the lives of the great philosophers how they have dramatically struggled with existential questions and boundary situations, and how by their actual lives and active philosophizing they have illuminated the various concepts he is trying to get across.

How an individual deals with limit situations is extremely important in psychotherapeutic work. An old Japanese saying reminds us that only when an individual is extremely desperate can we become acquainted with that person's true core. This is quite true both in our clinical work and in our assessment of ourselves and others.

References

Jaspers, K. (1932a). *Philosophy,* vol. 1. Chicago: University of Chicago Press, 1969.
_____ (1932b). *Philosophy,* vol. 2. Chicago: University of Chicago Press, 1970.
_____ (1932c). *Philosophy,* vol. 3. Chicago: University of Chicago Press, 1971.
_____ (1962). *The Great Philosophers,* vol. 1. New York: Harcourt, Brace and World.
_____ (1966). *The Great Philosophers,* vol. 2. New York: Harcourt, Brace and World.

LISTENING

Freud's (1912) technique of listening with evenly suspended attention constitutes an effort not to prescind from the patient's material, in order to prevent the therapist from making any selection out of preconceived expectations. Freud wishes to avoid the danger of the therapist never finding anything out that he or she does not already know, and distorting what is perceived to fit experience-distant theoretical preconceptions.

The question of whether one can really give such equal notice to everything communicated by the patient has often been raised, but only recently has it been answered increasingly in the negative. Many experienced therapists by now have learned that everyone approaches the data of the patient's free associations and behavior as manifested in the treatment with a certain mental set, one that is based on either conscious or preconscious theoretical and philosophical conceptions. This mental set determines what is perceived and what is selected, *regardless* of the therapist's effort to listen with evenly suspended attention. All a stance of evenly suspended attention can do is to try, in a deliberately conscious fashion, to reduce the influence of this mental set. It is obvious that this stance is enhanced greatly if the therapist is aware of his or her preconceptions and how these influence all aspects of perception of the patient.

A typical example of how such preconceptions or preoccupations interfere is the insistence on taking full notes on or even recording a patient's material. It is far better to take notes immediately after the session with the patient. Or, if one has a memory as prodigious as Freud's, to write these things down from memory, after work is over.

Recording invariably interferes

with the production of the patient's material. It represents an unwarranted intrusion into the individual's privacy and encourages exhibitionism on the part of the patient, as well as suspicion that the material the patient produces is being used for purposes other than the therapy itself—which is usually the case.

Freud (1912) offers the famous telephone receiver analogy:

> [The therapist] must turn his own unconscious like a receptive organ towards the transmitting unconscious of the patient. He must adjust himself to the patient as a telephone receiver is adjusted to the transmitting microphone. Just as the receiver converts into sound waves the electric oscillations in the telephone line which were set up by sound waves, so the doctor's unconscious is able, from the derivatives of the unconscious which are communicated to him, to reconstruct that unconscious, which has determined the patient's free associations. [pp. 115–116]

He goes on to maintain that "if the doctor is to be in a position to use his unconscious in this way as an instrument in the analysis," he must have "undergone a psycho-analytic purification" (p. 116). Otherwise the inevitable and innumerable "complexes of his own" (p. 116), even if the therapist is apparently a successful person, disqualify the therapist from practicing intensive psychotherapy. Freud says: "There can be no reasonable doubt about the disqualifying effect of such defects in the doctor; every unresolved repression in him constitutes what has been aptly described by Stekel as a "blind spot" in his analytic perception" (p. 116).

It is clear from Freud's writing that an important focus of psychoanalytic listening, if one includes both verbal and nonverbal communication, is to become aware of the nuances of the development of transference. As Freud repeatedly remarks, the success or failure of a psychoanalytic therapy rests primarily on the identification and management of transference phenomena.

In the process of psychoanalytic listening Freud (1914) suggests that the therapist not attempt, at least at the beginning of treatment, to bring any particular moment or problem into focus: "He contents himself with studying whatever is present for the time being on the surface of the patient's mind, and he employs the art of interpretation mainly for the purpose of recognizing the resistances which appear there, and making them conscious to the patient" (p. 147).

One of the most difficult resistances to deal with in intensive psychotherapy and psychoanalysis, says Freud (1914), occurs when the patient, instead of remembering what has been repressed, acts it out either within or outside the analytic situation: "He reproduces it not as a memory but as an action; he *repeats* it, without, of course, knowing that he is repeating it" (p. 150). This is a common way for patients to "remember" previous relationships. It is the task of the therapist, by careful listening, to become aware of what is being repeated in the course of the treatment, either in the relationship with the therapist or in the development of relationships with others outside treatment (see ACTING OUT). Thus all descriptions on the part of a patient about current relationships, as well as dreams, need to be listened to carefully for allusions to the relationship with the therapist, and for the repetition or displacement of disavowed aspects of this relationship outside the consulting room. Very important aspects of the transference often appear in this manner and are easily overlooked.

I have proposed elsewhere (see Chessick 1989) that we approach the data of psychoanalytic communication from five more or less psychoanalytic models in turn, without definitively assigning major preeminence to any one model in any given clinical situation until after we have been at least open to examining the data in detail from five points of view. Without this approach, no material can be convincingly understood as falling under the rubric of a given model.

Clinical experience unfailingly demonstrates two principles. The first is that a psychoanalytic model is the only acceptable kind of model for achieving depth understanding of a person. The second is that one neglects Freud's drive/conflict/defense orientation at one's peril. Many alternative approaches have been devised over the years to get away from Freud's emphasis on sexuality and aggression as ultimately constituting the infantile core or fantasy life or even the psychic reality of the adult, as well as from his central focus on the Oedipus complex. Many cases flounder when alternative stances are used by the therapist for defensive purposes. To avoid this, the primary model in approaching any patient material should be Freud's "drive/structure" model (Greenberg and Mitchell 1983); furthermore, Freud's dicta for psychoanalytic listening should be followed whenever possible. Any departure from this channel should be tentative, and the problem of possible defensive collusion should constantly be kept in mind.

We can begin listening from the channel of Freud's drive/conflict/defense orientation, staying carefully tuned for derivatives of core unconscious infantile fantasies that are expressed in the material both through verbal and nonverbal manifestations. At the same time, we can allow ourselves to be open to what Husserl (1913) would call "imaginative variations" in our minds, tentatively trying to fit the material into the orientations of the other listening channels. The material itself usually suggests what channel is most suitable for understanding what the patient is trying to communicate. This affords a temporary fusion of horizons with the patient, as Gadamer (1982) would characterize it (see FUSION OF HORIZONS), and helps us to frame our interventions in a language the patient will understand. But we must always keep in mind that sooner or later we are going to return to the drive/conflict/defense model as the patient develops trust in our empathy and reveals more and more of himself or herself to us. Further-more, if the therapy is to be truly psychoanalytic, we are ultimately going to focus on the core infantile fantasy derivatives as they are ex-pressed in the transference.

Our understanding of the pa-tient gained from these various chan-nels of psychoanalytic listening can then be translated into rational inter-ventions. With careful listening, the patient's response to our interven-tions may serve as validation or ne-gation of the correctness of our un-derstanding.

Each proposed channel of psy-choanalytic listening carries a stance about psychological development, a view of psychic change, and assump-tions about the curative factors in intensive psychotherapy. These stances contradict each other in important, philosophically funda-mental ways and cannot at present be reconciled, since they reflect pro-found disagreement about the nature of humans and the nature of knowl-edge itself.

The first model was presented by Freud and focuses on the Oedipus complex and the inevitable emer-gence, in a properly conducted psy-choanalysis, of the need for drive sat-isfaction in the transference. This enables us to study the patient's in-fantile conflicts and their subsequent vicissitudes in terms of defenses against the instinctual drives and the resulting crucial compromise forma-tions produced by the ego in dealing with its three harsh masters—the su-perego, the id, and external reality. At the core are the patient's child-hood or infantile fantasies, deriva-tives of which repeat themselves over and over again in the patient's mental life and behavior (Arlow 1985). On this channel we carefully listen for the derivatives of these fan-tasies and look for them to be reen-acted or reexperienced in the trans-ference.

The second channel utilizes the perspective of the so-called object-relations theory for its model. The work of Klein and Bion focuses on the earliest projective and introjec-tive fantasies of the patient as they appear in the object relatedness man-ifest in the transference and in the process of projective identification as it occurs in the analytic process (see KLEIN). Bion (1963, 1967) empha-sizes the "toilet function" of the an-alyst, in which the analyst must re-ceive, metabolize, and give back in acceptable form the unacceptable fantasies and affects and expressions of these coming from the patient (see REVERIE). This is of enormous im-portance, especially in the treatment of borderline patients (Waldinger 1987).

A study of projective identifica-tion operating in the therapeutic pro-cess emphasizes the patient's earliest internalized object relations and yields data about how the patient as an infant (if one follows Klein) or as a preoedipal child organized these re-lations into self and object represen-tations and then projected and rein-trojected various aspects of these images (see PROJECTIVE IDENTI-FICATION). Understanding of these processes clarifies the patient's relationships in the present because all such relationships are perceived and reacted to through the spectacles of these early organized self and object representations. Klein's assumption is that the infantile ego is capable of such organization.

A third channel, which focuses on the patient's being-in-the-world, is the phenomenological point of view. Here an attempt is made to grasp the facts of the patient's life "phenomenologically," that is, without other theoretical preconceptions to organize the data. This approach was elaborated in philosophy by Husserl and then differently by Heidegger, and taken up especially by the pioneer psychoanalysts Boss (1963) and Binswanger (1963).

The notion of phenomenology (see PHENOMENOLOGY) has been used in many ways and is very confusing. Husserl (1913) first used the term in 1900. For him the phenomenologic method was a way of doing philosophy. A phenomenon is whatever appears for us immediately in experience. Husserl's method rests on what he calls transcendental-phenomenological reduction; he does not permit the selection out of experience of certain specific sensations, feelings, and so on, since this already assumes classificatory principles about the world. Thus phenomenologic statements cannot be called empirical in the traditional sense since empirical statements are already about assumed "things" out there. Phenomenologic statements attempt what Husserl calls presuppositionless inquiry—no theories, just descriptions of the phenomena as they present themselves to an unprejudiced view.

From the point of view of the psychotherapist, the phenomenologic stance is just to react to what is simply there in a felt experience; one does not disconnect or isolate or interpret aspects of this experience. *Epoché,* phenomenological reduction, or the bracketing of being demand refrainment from judgment about morals, values, causes, background, even the subject (the patient) and objective observer (the therapist). One pays special attention to one's own state of consciousness in the presence of a patient, for example, "the feel" of a schizophrenic, the ambience such an individual creates.

The point of this stance is to keep looking and listening in the so-called phenomenologic sense, staying right with the material of the patient and taking everything the patient has to say at face value rather than searching for hidden processes. This is derived from the practice of phenomenological reduction. Phenomenologists argue that a distance is opened between the doctor and the patient by the analytic technique of free association, a gap that may be filled unproductively by abundant verbal material and analytic ideas, conceptions, and theories; instead, they advise proceeding by emotional interchange based on staying strictly with the phenomena and the manifest appearance that the patient presents. Phenomenological reduction of the emotional distance between the patient and the therapist, then, is the crucial procedure leading, hopefully, to a true meeting or encounter (Jaspers 1972).

The fourth listening stance is

that of self psychology (Kohut 1971, 1977, 1984), which focuses on the state of the patient's self as it is empathically grasped by the analyst (see SELF PSYCHOLOGY). Important originators of this approach were Fairbairn and Winnicott, who introduced the notion of the true and the false self. Although there were numerous versions of the self already utilized in philosophy and psychology, it was Kohut who brought the focus on the self into a systematic and elaborate psychoanalytic theory. Significant alterations in this theory have been offered by Gedo (1979, 1984). Although he rejects some of Kohut's premises, Gedo's establishment of hierarchies of self-organization represents a further elaboration and movement away from traditional psychoanalytic metapsychology, and his discussions contain arguments and proposals with which every therapist ought to be familiar (see BEYOND INTERPRETATION).

We can distinguish between cognitive observations and empathic observations. Cognitive observations are of verbal and nonverbal behaviors as well as of subjective reactions of the therapist, and are capable of being consensually validated by other objective observers. Empathy, on the other hand, is defined by the self psychologists Muslin and Val (1987) as "a mode of observation that attempts to capture the subject's inner life" (p. 5) and requires the observer to draw out of himself or herself a state or experience that somewhat approximates that of the subject. These assessments allow the therapist to answer such questions as "What is the patient experiencing?" and "Where are these reactions coming from?"

The complexity and controversial aspects of the empathic approach to data gathering have been much discussed in philosophy and in the psychotherapy literature. The systems of self psychology and traditional psychoanalysis are basically incompatible. Reed (1987) warns that the "classical analyst who listens only to resistance and the self-psychologist who listens only to material relating to the empathic failure of a self-object are listening to theory, not to the patient" (p. 437). But all authors agree that the essential task is listening. Listening requires the therapist to be free from the urges to do or to say something, which runs contrary to much of medical training and to our prevailing pragmatic culture. It leaves the problem of validation of empathic observations to the internal process of the treatment.

The final listening stance on which to organize the transmission from the patient might be termed the interactive, which focuses on the countertransference of the therapist or, more generally, on the here-and-now factors in the treatment, emphasizing the role of the analyst's participation. Many of the conflicting points of view placed under this rubric have been developed as a response to our increasing understanding of the patient's need for an experience and not just an explanation in the treatment. Modell (1976) offers the notion of the psychoanalytic process in the early phase of the treatment of narcissistic or schizoid patients as providing a "cocoon," a holding of the patient until he or she is ready for self-exploration. Langs (1982) emphasizes the presence of delineated interactive fields in which the data coming from the patient are loaded with allusions to the therapist's participation, and even to the therapist's mental state. In this extreme but carefully worked out view, the patient's unconscious is capable of perceiving the therapist's personal difficulties, thus allowing the therapist to be cured so that he or she may in turn cure the patient.

Gill (1982), in a less radical approach, emphasizes the importance of the therapist's participation in determining the particular transference manifestations that develop in a given treatment. He also focuses his interpretations on the here-and-now interaction between patient and therapist. Gill's view is close to Sullivan's (1947, 1953) more extreme "interpersonal" theory of psychiatry, which erroneously eschews Freud's crucial concept of "psychic reality" and attempts to study a scientifically delineated interaction in the treatment, one in which the therapist both participates in and observes the interaction. Sullivan's approach suffers from a certain metapsychological shallowness because of its emphasis on the interactional without sufficient study of the filtering mechanism constituted by intrapsychic fantasy configurations through which the patient inevitably experiences this interaction. Sullivan's concept of parataxic distortion attempts

to make up for this, but it has not received widespread acceptance.

Focus on the current interaction between the patient and the therapist reveals that Freud's early advocacy of neutrality and opacity to the patient represents a theoretical impossibility. It can be demonstrated easily that even in his own work Freud did not follow these precepts. It is likely that Freud's papers on technique were aimed at preventing massive acting out by incompletely analyzed or even unanalyzed therapists with their patients, as was common in the early days of psychoanalysis and remains all too common with much less justification today.

My view differs significantly from that of Gedo and Goldberg (1973) in that their principle of "theoretical complementarity" (p. 4) assumes that the different frames of reference, or models of the mind, operate only as long as no internal contradictions arise among the various parts of the theory. They believe that even Freud did not intend to dispense with his older conceptions as he went forward to propose new ones, and that the changeover from one set of Freud's concepts to another did not have to indicate that one replaced or superseded the other.

However, in my approach, theoretical orientations are being utilized that directly conflict with each other and cannot be thought of as complementary because the basic premises that underlie them, both their epistemological foundations and their basic assumptions about human nature and its motivations, collide (Chessick 1992). This forces a radical discontinuity as we shift from channel to channel in our receiving instrument, rather than, as we would all prefer to do, sliding back and forth between theoretically consistent positions, or at least complementary positions that are consistent with each other.

The worst mistake a beginner in psychoanalytic listening can make at this historical point in the development of psychoanalytic theory is to assume that in some fashion these five standpoints can be blended into some supraordinate theory that can generate all of them. Careful examination of the premises of these standpoints reveals that this is impossible in our current state of knowledge. If we use this shifting of systems, we are forced to accept the radical discontinuities, much in the way the early physicists had to accept the fact that certain data involving light rays were better explained by a wave theory whereas other data were best explained by a corpuscular theory, and these two theories were radically incompatible in the prevailing state of scientific understanding at the time. The problem in the human sciences is even more profound, and some thinkers such as Foucault (1973) have claimed that in principle no agreement can ever be reached on a single theoretical model for scientific understanding of all human mentation and behavior.

Other clinicians may insist that certain theoretical approaches should be added to these channels. The most important requirement of a model is that it be suggested by the very data the patient produces rather than be superimposed on the data by experience-distant or arbitrary or mystical or dogmatic prior conceptions in the mind of the therapist. This is a relative concept because no theory is truly experience-near, since it is impossible to approach data without some prior conceptions. Our only hope is that our conceptions are not too abstract, generalized, and divorced from the specific material, and that they are capable of being validated by a study of how the patient responds to interventions. Even this may be difficult, as it is all too human to hear what we wish to hear. Hence the value of consultation and of the presentation of the details of therapist–patient exchanges in case reports.

The hardest part in using this approach is to be willing to keep discontinuous and conflicting models in one's mind. This, however, offends the natural and very dangerous human tendency for a neat, consistent, and holistic theoretical explanation of all material, even if it is wrong. Kant (1781) called this mental tendency the regulative principle of reason, Bacon called it "idols of the tribe" (see IDOLS), and Freud would have based it on the powerful synthesizing function of the ego. Tolerance and flexibility on the part of the listener, as well as a certain maturity, are required, and this can be very difficult to achieve.

The advantage is a greater understanding of the patient and a capacity to render interpretations and interventions suitable to the developmental stage and point of view of the patient at any given time. As the patient experiences the therapist's understanding and communication at a level he or she finds meaningful, trust is increased and the ego is strengthened, allowing the patient to communicate more derivatives of the infantile fantasy life and receive greater depth of psychoanalytic understanding.

References

Arlow, J. (1985). The concept of psychic reality and related problems. *Journal of the American Psychoanalytic Association* 33:521–535.

Binswanger, L. (1963). *Being-in-the-World,* trans. J. Needleman. New York: Basic Books.

Bion, W. (1963). *Elements of Psycho-Analysis.* New York: Basic Books.

_____ (1967). *Second Thoughts: Selected Papers on Psycho-Analysis.* London: Heinemann.

Boss, M. (1963). *Psychoanalysis and Daseinanalysis,* trans. L. Lefebre. New York: Basic Books.

Chessick, R. (1989). *The Technique and Practice of Listening in Intensive Psychotherapy.* Northvale, NJ: Jason Aronson.

_____ (1992). *What Constitutes the Patient in Psychotherapy.* Northvale, NJ: Jason Aronson.

Foucault, M. (1973). *Madness and Civilization,* trans. A. Smith. New York: Vintage.

Freud, S. (1912). Recommendations to physicians practicing psychoanalysis. *Standard Edition* 12:109–120.

_____ (1914). Remembering, repeating, and working through. *Standard Edition* 12:145–156.

Gadamer, H. (1982). *Truth and Method.* New York: Crossroad.

Gedo, J. (1979). *Beyond Interpretation.* New York: International Universities Press.

_____ (1984). *Psychoanalysis and Its Discontents.* New York: Guilford.

Gedo, J., and Goldberg, A. (1973). *Models of the Mind: A Psychoanalytic Theory.* Chicago: University of Chicago Press.

Gill, M. (1982). *Analysis of the Transference,* vol. 1. New York: International Universities Press.

Greenberg, J., and Mitchell, S. (1983). *Object Relations in Psychoanalytic Theory.* Cambridge, MA: Harvard University Press.

Husserl, E. (1913). *Ideas: General Introduction to Pure Phenomenology,* trans. W. Gibson. New York: Macmillan.

Jaspers, K. (1972). *General Psychopathology,* trans. J. Hoenig and M. Hamilton. Chicago: University of Chicago Press.

Kant, I. (1781). *Critique of Pure Reason,* trans. N. Smith. New York: St. Martins Press, 1965.

Kohut, H. (1971). *The Analysis of the Self.* New York: International Universities Press.

_____ (1977). *The Restoration of the Self.* New York: International Universities Press.

_____ (1984). *How Does Analysis Cure?* Chicago: University of Chicago Press.

Langs, R. (1982). *Psychotherapy: A Basic Text.* New York: Jason Aronson.

Modell, A. (1976). "The holding environment" and the therapeutic action of psychoanalysis. *Journal of the American Psychoanalytic Association* 24:285–308.

Muslin, H., and Val, E. (1987). *The Psychotherapy of the Self.* New York: Brunner/Mazel.

Reed, G. (1987). Rules of clinical understanding in classical psychoanalysis and self psychology: a comparison. *Journal of the American Psychoanalytic Association* 35:421–446.

Sullivan, H. (1947). *Conceptions of Modern Psychiatry.* Washington, DC: White Foundation.

_____ (1953). *The Interpersonal Theory of Psychiatry.* New York: Norton.

Waldinger, R. (1987). Intensive psychodynamic therapy with borderline patients: an overview. *American Journal of Psychiatry* 144:267–274.

LOVE

Although Samuel Johnson (1773) offered fourteen definitions of love, Freud (1930) mused that human love is the only thing that may make sense out of the absurd condition of the existential world. Yet for Freud love was essentially a derivative of sex. According to Freud (1930), "Normally, there is nothing of which we are more certain than the feeling of our self, of our own ego" (p. 65). In passionately falling in love, however, ego and object libido cannot be distinguished: "At the height of being in love the boundary between the ego and object threatens to melt away. Against all evidence of his senses, a man who is in love declares that 'I' and 'you' are one, and is prepared to behave as if it were a fact" (p. 66).

Viederman (1988) tells us, "One of the most powerful aspects of a new passionate relationship is the formation of a new sense of self" (p. 9). He claims that the love experience helps us to understand what we can expect from our body and what we can expect our body to do. He believes that the unconscious illusion of at least some gratification of early infantile wishes occurring in requited love allows an individual to approximate aspects of the ego-ideal from childhood.

Many authors, including Freud, seem to agree that in the experience of passionate love there is a temporary intense gratification, or at least the illusion of potential gratification, of powerful archaic infantile desires that have long been frustrated and repressed. This leads to what Viederman (1988) calls "a euphoric sense of fullness," (p. 10) or what other authors have described as the sense of power and extraordinary exaltation that goes along with achieving requited passionate love.

Viederman also notes that passionate love allows one to escape the constraints of reality as one finds oneself in a passionate embrace.

Viederman stresses the illusion aspects of passionate love, but he does not wish to devalue it on this account, because he admits that once it is experienced and reciprocated, it is the closest thing to what he considers ever-elusive happiness. This is close to the Freudian concept that the greatest happiness consists of the preferably sudden gratification of long dammed up infantile wishes. To this Viederman adds the importance of being able to be one's true self in the lover's presence and of having one's true self accepted by the lover. This intense mirroring obviously has a powerful effect on the cohesion of the self.

One unanswered question is whether falling in love and being in love can be explained metapsychologically as a formation expressing the sexual drive. Certainly it is a complex experience and definitely not just a pathological regression in order to achieve the "oceanic feeling" and a sense of blissful fusion with the mother of infancy.

Passionate love can be set in motion by the state of flux and instability indigenous to the late adolescent phase, but somewhat paradoxically also in middle age by the relentless and leaden repetition of experience. For the middle-aged individual, says Viederman (1988), "It is easy to see how the search for change, the search for the new, the search for mystery can lead to a passionate experience that will act as a powerful antidote to frustration, disappointment, and repetition" (p. 12). Looking at the matter from the point of view of self psychology (Kohut 1977), the search for a passionate love experience in middle age is better explained by the increased narcissistic wounding that inevitably takes place as the individual realizes that he or she is not going to reach cherished goals and ideals. Passionate love can restore the damaged narcissistic equilibrium in these situations by achieving a fusion with the projected infantile ego-ideal, even if it is an illusion and only temporary. As Kohut (1977) writes, "There is no love relationship without mutual (self-esteem enhancing) mirroring and idealization" (p. 122n). I (Chessick 1985, 1989a, 1990b) believe this to be an important clue in understanding the sad situation of the aging therapist "falling in love" with his or her patient, as described, for example, by Dahlberg (1970).

For Viederman (1988), passionate love must inevitably diminish, yet it can be a growth experience. He views it as "an entirely personal and a subjective experience" (p. 13), one that depends on the individual's fantasies, wishes, and memories. Thus no accurate general definition of passionate love can be obtained: "When one experiences passion one is never sure of how much it approximates the experience of the partner" (p. 13). This has important clinical ramifications, since a patient's declaration of love for the therapist may have an entirely different meaning than what the therapist assumes.

One of the most remarkable phenomenological descriptions of the state of falling in love has been presented by the Italian sociologist Francesco Alberoni (1983). He points out the close relationship between the great collective movements of history and falling in love. The forces they liberate involve similar experiences of solidarity, joy and life, and renewal. There is the birth of a new collective "we" constructed out of two or more individuals, as when two people fall in love. In an existing social structure this may divide whoever was united and unite whoever was divided to form a new collective subject: "The forces that operate in both cases have the same violence and the same determination" (p. 6).

Alberoni (1983) points out the distinction between "ordinary sexuality" in our everyday life and the "extraordinary sexuality" that appears in the situation of passionate love. This distinction has not been stressed sufficiently in the literature. During the sexual activity of passionate lovers, a new vital energy is often released and there are new explorations of "the frontiers of the possible, the horizons of the imaginary and of nature" (p. 13). The lovers are in what Alberoni calls a "nascent state," in which "eros overflows the structures and floods prohibited territories" (p. 23).

Alberoni, like many other authors, stresses the long preparation period before this occurs, which may be characterized by increasing depression and a slow deterioration in relations with previous love objects. He insists that the experience of falling in love originates in an extreme depression, an inability to find something that has value in everyday life, the well-known existential malaise, "the profound sense of being worthless and of having nothing that is valuable and the shame of not having it" (p. 69). This can happen at any age and is characterized by the "irreparable loss of something in the self, a feeling that we will inevitably become devoid of value or degraded, compared with what we have been" (p. 69). The experience of romantic love becomes one of liberation, fullness of life, and happiness, in which all alienation is temporarily extinguished. Thus, for example, when a creative person falls in love, he or she becomes more and more creative and increases his or her capacity to enrich life with the fruits of imagination. Alberoni points out that "artists, poets and scientists live in the imaginary universe they have created, and when they fall in love, they tend to transport the person they love to this world of theirs" (p. 65).

The mystery of passionate love is that it does not go with marriage, but rather, historically speaking, it is often associated with thoughts of death or at least the longing for death. Thus, although passionate love may represent at some level the wish for union with incestuous objects and the overcoming of one's infantile sense of inferiority to the parental objects, there still seems to be an ultimate goal—permanent fusion in some eternal fashion in another world—consistently associated with it. This points to the deeper preoedipal roots of passionate love

or to evidence of man's inherent search for transcendence.

Bergmann (1982) emphasizes Freud's (1905) statement that "all finding is refinding" (p. 202). By this Freud meant the inevitable finding in adult love of the infantile love object. Freud mistrusted sexual passion as a basis for marriage. So, for example, in 1931 he claimed that first marriages, based on falling passionately in love, are often disappointing, while second marriages, assumed to be more dispassionately chosen and more practically determined, turn out better. Whether this is true or not remains highly debatable.

For Freud, tender feelings are always transformed sexual feelings. But Bergmann (1982) adds, "In real life many traumatized patients fall in love not with the person who reminds them of their parent, but with the person they hope will heal the wound the parental figures have inflicted. To fall in love with the rescuer or the person one has rescued is a frequent theme of romantic love. It is also an important source of transference love" (p. 107).

Hitschmann (1952) notes that Freud discusses love 130 times in his collected writings, yet he is not consistent about the subject and seems therefore basically ambivalent and uncertain about the matter of passionate love. Freud (1912) explained that the affectionate and sensual currents had to become properly fused to produce the normal attitude in love. For Freud, both of these currents are derived from the sexual instinctual drives: the affectionate current has aim-inhibited goals and the sensual current an openly erotic intent. Altman (1977) emphasizes the ego and superego aspects of the experience of love and points out that love requires good ego and superego functioning—it is far more than the discharge of libido.

Altman agrees with Freud (1921) that there is a hostile residue, repressed, in each love affair that can cause considerable difficulty. He (1977) also believes that behind the wish to die "is the unconscious wish for, expectation of, and belief in life everlasting in reunion with the love objects of childhood" (p. 44). This points again to the ceaseless effort to make good the loss of the preoedipal object, which, as Bak (1973) explains, results in a never-ending quest for love. Altman believes that such love is doomed since it is founded on depression and the unconscious wish for a reunion with the mother of infancy.

Freud (1921) describes the idealization of the love object, which he believed to diminish with each sexual satisfaction. For Freud, being in love is based on the simultaneous presence of directly sexual impulses and of sexual impulses that are inhibited in their aims, while the object draws a part of the subject's narcissistic ego libido to itself.

Bergmann (1988) summarizes Freud's views on love into three theories. The first, expressed in the *Three Essays on Sexuality* (Freud 1905), stresses the finding of the love object as a refinding of the infantile love object. The second, in the paper "On Narcissism" (1914), describes love as a massive transformation of

narcissistic libido into object libido with a subsequent depletion of the ego-ideal. The third, in the paper "Instincts and Their Vicissitudes" (1915), deemphasizes the instinctual component and depicts love as a relation of the "total ego" to its object, without any clear definition of "total ego."

An important correction to Freud's discussion of the problem of love has been made by a number of authors, such as Chasseguet-Smirgel (1970). Contrary to Freud's pronouncement, one's ego-ideal is not depleted, but there is an increased libidinal investment of the self that accompanies the experience of being in love, as even Robert Louis Stevenson (1988) remarkably described it:

> It seems as if he had never heard or felt or seen until that moment; and by the report of his memory, he must have lived his past life between sleep and waking. . . . a very supreme sense of pleasure in all parts of life—in lying down to sleep, in waking, in motion, in breathing, in continuing to be—the lover begins to regard his happiness as beneficial for the rest of the world and highly meritorious in himself. [pp. 8–9]

Person (1988) points out that the capacity for passionate love is inherent in human nature, and that both females and males seek to achieve this extraordinary state. Flashes of the possibility of a passionate love developing with this or that individual that crosses our path keep occurring to us, similar to flashes of sexual desire or fantasy. Passionate love is "a perpetual possibility waiting to be born" (p. 264), but these flashes are usually immediately discounted by the realistic situation in which there is not only no chance of reciprocation but usually the danger of a humiliating rejection. Unless there is some hope that one's love may encounter a less stringent response, the flashes suffer the same fate as fleeting sexual fantasies.

In the psychoanalytic situation, where the analyst is neither encouraging nor rejecting, and certainly does not condemn or belittle the patient for his or her feelings, passionate love can be allowed to flourish and does so much more frequently than in ordinary life. This gives us an opportunity to study the patient in depth if the proper empathic and analytic stance is maintained by the therapist.

Person locates the source of passionate love in our early lives, following Freud, and sees it as related to the play of the imagination and the springs of our creativity. She views it as potentially transforming and transcending the self, but opines that a mysterious leap is involved in falling in love, similar to a religious conversion. When this "leap" occurs, there is always a heightened drama and sense of self-awareness and, when the love is reciprocated, we experience a sense of intermittent transcendence and merger, with the "oceanic" feeling as a typical result.

When this happens, values and priorities may become reordered, new projects undertaken, new responsibilities assumed. This profound change in the self may last even after the passionate love affair has passed (Chessick 1992). Thus Person emphasizes the creative and positive potential of passionate love, a state that is discontinuous with the rest of our lives and can be a major agent of change even outside the transference love of psychoanalytic experience. Some people manage to allow such love to flourish for a long period, especially if there are obstacles to its consummation, which permit the individual to experience intervals of merger and surrender while at the same time preserving autonomy. On the whole this approach to love views it as an ego function, an act of the creative imagination, in contrast to Freud's more id-related explanation involving a refinding of incestuous objects. But it also preserves the concept of a "mysterious leap," a leap that is better understood by other authors quoted above, beginning with Freud.

This mysterious leap occurs when certain conditions are met. The first of these is indeed the safety requirement of not anticipating the certainty of serious narcissistic wounding if one manifests one's love. The totally inappropriate appearance of passionate love suddenly in a situation that clearly indicates it will be rejected, often cruelly and scornfully, demonstrates very poor reality testing in the lover. At best, such declared infatuation indicates a severe masochistic disorder; at worst, it is not uncommon in schizophrenia.

The second condition is some association in the lover's mind of the beloved with either an incestuous love object or an object from childhood invested with healing and soothing power—a selfobject, or both, as in the case of Tristan and Isolde (Chessick 1990a). Or at least there is the imaginative hope that the beloved will transform into such an object, given the proper persuasion and seduction. Arlow (1980) elaborates on this condition, maintaining that "in every love relationship the individual acts out some form of complicated unconscious fantasy rooted in early vicissitudes of drive and object experience, a fantasy that ultimately determines, but only in part, the pattern of loving and the specific person or types of persons that will correspond object choice" (p. 27).

The third condition is that of the activity of the creative imagination. There has to be a problem situation that calls for creative imagination, such as a loss that must be ameliorated or a depletion of middle age that is becoming unbearable. The leap, then, is one of the imagination where the illusion is created that the beloved object will be able to perform all these roles, and passionately, so there will be a sudden release of dammed up narcissistic and sexual tensions that have accumulated sometimes for many years. This creative leap triggers the idealization and obsession with the beloved, and explains the exaltation and ecstasy when the love is reciprocated.

Kohut (1978) points out, "People whose self is in need of sustenance, whether because of the energic drain and anxiety during a creative spell or for other reasons,

will tend to establish narcissistic relationships to archaic selfobjects—whether in the form of one of the varieties of a mirror transference or through a merger with an idealized imago" (p. 813n). He convincingly demonstrates that in periods of intensive creativity a similar archaic selfobject transference occurs to those seen in the psychoanalytic situation, a "transference of creativity" (p. 814). It follows from this that creativity enhances the tendency to idealization needed in falling in love, and falling in love enables the actualization of one's potential for creativity since it lends strength to a self that would otherwise be enfeebled by the creative process.

This is not so mysterious, and can be depicted in metapsychological terms. Furthermore, the length of the passion can be understood as a function of the capacity of the lover to maintain the illusion in his or her creative imagination for an indefinite length of time, and of the degree of their proximity and time spent together. Some of us have a greater capacity to regress in the service of the ego than others, to maintain illusions and idealizations longer, and to engage in a play space in our fantasy-lives. Freud already pointed out that with each sexual act the degree of idealization of the loved one diminishes—perhaps he was speaking from his own experience. But certainly familiarity makes it harder and harder to maintain idealization, whereas partings and obstacles fan the flames of illusion by keeping the reality of the beloved in a shadow and making it easier to project our wishes and fantasies onto him or her. That is why passionate love is often thought of as incompatible with marriage, and often fades after the familiarity of marriage into either an enduring affection or a parting of ways. In Freud's terms, the passionate or "lyrical" phase of love is replaced by a calmer, more rational, more durable "epic" phase.

Similarly, in the state of heightened creative imagination and expanded play space during passionate love there is an enhanced potential to create in other areas of one's life (Gediman 1975). New values, projects, dreams, even artistic compositions may abound. The increased cohesiveness of the self as a function of the mirroring from the beloved can also lead to better ego functioning, greater achievement, heightened joy in life, and an enhanced sense of being alive. This transformation is no mystery and can be understood in metapsychological terms, stressing ego apparatuses and self psychology. The debatable assumption I (Chessick 1989b) am making in this formulation is that ego psychology and self psychology can comfortably or uncomfortably exist side by side (see SELF PSYCHOLOGY).

But what of the longing for death at the moment of ecstatic union? Why is the long-awaited consummation often associated with death rather than life and companionship? Could this be due to guilt over breaking the incest barrier? Or would the final consummation of life secretly longed for be, indeed, the return to the inorganic? Was Freud right after all that the quest for nirvana is the fundamental human impulse and beyond the pleasure principle?

Falling in love cannot simply be explained as a refinding of incestuous parental objects, although this is always an important basic element in falling in love and object choice, as Freud said. What makes falling in love unique for each individual is the specific ego functions involved in the act of creative imagination that each person uses, falling in love in a specific way to solve specific intrapsychic difficulties. Falling in love represents a creative effort to find a solution for unbearable narcissistic and libidinal tensions, often in an emergency situation of object loss or narcissistic wounding. Depending on the nature of this effort, the falling in love can be a constructive, helpful, and forward-moving event, or it can lead to destruction and tragedy. But no generalizations can be made about the function of falling in love beyond the fact that it tends to occur when there is a serious problem to be solved. These problems of unbearable tension can range from the revived Oedipus conflict that occurs in normal adolescence, as well as from the preoedipal pathology that suffers a resurgence in adolescence, to old age, where problems of loss, loneliness, and despair can predominate. Any variety of these problems is a challenge for solution by the ego; one of the solutions that is possible is the creative, imaginative act of falling in love.

The phenomenon of falling in love only becomes intelligible when one views it as motivated by libidinal energies and narcissistic disequilibrium and molded into a compromise that is consistent with the historical and cultural horizons of the individual, so that it clearly incorporates the unique superego- and ego-functioning aspects of that individual. This is true even if one emphasizes the "oceanic feeling" or altered consciousness or "aberrant" experience in requited passionate love. Werman (1986) convincingly argues that such experiences in the adult cannot be simple replays of an infantile experience, but instead represent "a complex phenomenon that derives from all aspects of the psyche, including the subject's value system and the influences of his culture" (p. 123). With self psychological understanding of the problems in maintaining narcissistic equilibrium, the extreme exaltation accompanying requited passionate love is no longer a mysterious or quasi-psychotic phenomenon; rather, it represents both Freud's concept of rapid gratification of long dammed up infantile wishes, or at least the illusion of such gratification, and a powerful force toward the cohesion of the sense of self with the accompanying joyful experience that such improved cohesiveness of the self brings to the individual.

The mystery of falling in love lies only in the debate about the relationship between passionate love and death. If the preoedipal roots of falling in love are represented by the need to fuse with the mother of infancy in some eternal union, then we have an alternative and metapsychological explanation to the mystery of passionate love, which stands in contrast to viewing it as an aspect of the search for transcendence.

References

Alberoni, F. (1983). *Falling in Love.* New York: Random House.

Altman, L. (1977). Some vicissitudes of love. *Journal of the American Psychoanalytic Association* 25:35–52.

Arlow, J. (1980). Object concept and object choice. *Psychoanalytic Quarterly* 49: 109–133.

Bak, R. (1973). Being in love and object loss. *International Journal of Psychoanalysis* 54:1–8.

Bergmann, M. (1982). Platonic love, transference love, and love in real life. *Journal of the American Psychoanalytic Association* 30:87–112.

——— (1988). Freud's three theories of love in the light of later developments. *Journal of the American Psychoanalytic Association* 36:653–672.

Chasseguet-Smirgel, J. (1970). *Female Sexuality.* Ann Arbor: University of Michigan Press.

Chessick, R. (1985). *Psychology of the Self and the Treatment of Narcissism.* Northvale, NJ: Jason Aronson.

——— (1989a). The two-woman phenomenon revisited. *Journal of the American Academy of Psychoanalysis* 17:293–304.

——— (1989b). *The Technique and Practice of Listening in Intensive Psychotherapy.* Northvale, NJ: Jason Aronson.

——— (1990a). On falling in love. I: the mystery of Tristan and Isolde. In *Psychoanalytic Explorations in Music,* ed. S. Feder, R. Karmel, and G. Pollock, pp. 465–483. New York: International Universities Press.

——— (1990b). In the clutches of the devil. *Psychoanalysis and Psychotherapy* 7:142–151.

——— (in press). On falling in love and creativity. *Journal of the American Academy of Psychoanalysis.* 20:347–373.

Dahlberg, C. (1970). Sexual contact between patient and therapist. *Contemporary Psychoanalysis* 6:107–124.

Freud, S. (1905). Three essays on the theory of sexuality. *Standard Edition* 7:125–243.

_____ (1912). On the universal tendency to debasement in the sphere of love. *Standard Edition* 11:177–190.

_____ (1914). On narcissism: an introduction. *Standard Edition* 14:67–102.

_____ (1915). Instincts and their vicissitudes. *Standard Edition* 14:109–140.

_____ (1921). Group psychology and the analysis of the ego. *Standard Edition* 18:67–143.

_____ (1930). Civilization and its discontents. *Standard Edition* 21:59–145.

_____ (1931). Female sexuality. *Standard Edition* 21:223–243.

Gediman, H. (1975). Reflections on romanticism, narcissism, and creativity. *Journal of the American Psychoanalytic Association* 23:407–423.

Hitschmann, E. (1952). Freud's conception of love. *International Journal of Psychoanalysis* 33:421–428.

Johnson, S. (1773). *A Dictionary of the English Language*. Beirut, Lebanon: Librairie du Liban, 1978.

Kohut, H. (1977). *The Restoration of the Self.* New York: International Universities Press.

_____ (1978). *The Search for the Self,* ed. P. Ornstein. New York: International Universities Press.

Person, E. (1988). *Dreams of Love and Fateful Encounters: The Power of Romantic Passion.* New York: Norton.

Stevenson, R. (1988). *The Lantern-bearers and Other Essays,* ed. J. Treglown. London: Chatto and Windus.

Viederman, M. (1988). The nature of passionate love. In *Passionate Attachments: Thinking About Love,* ed. W. Gaylin and E. Person, pp. 1–14. New York: Free Press.

Werman, D. (1986). On the nature of the oceanic experience. *Journal of the American Psychoanalytic Association* 34:123–140.

M

Manic Defense

This represents a set of fantasies or a type of behavior that can protect the individual from anxiety, guilt, and depression. Denial is the principal means of defense, often accompanied by a fantasy of omnipotent power and control with a euphoric affect. The individual may identify with sources of power and project undesirable aspects of himself or herself onto others. The price of the manic defense is a superficiality of thought and personality and a loss of the capacity to emphasize with other people.

In Kleinian theory manic defenses characteristically appear during the depressive position (see DEPRESSIVE POSITION). The pain of the depressive position can occur throughout life and the manic defense can be utilized at any time to relieve this pain; this is often observed in clinical work. Denial, disparagement, contempt for what is lost, a false sense of control, and idealization accompanied by identification with the idealized object may result in a sense of triumph over the situation. Klein (1975) stated that the manic defenses evolved out of obsessional defenses that were employed to bind persecutory anxiety. She wrote, "I wish to stress the importance of *triumph,* closely bound up with contempt and omnipotence" (p. 351).

For Klein, mania represents a triumph in phantasy over the loss of the object, the basic fear of the depressive position. Mania is characterized by omnipotence, which represents a denial of need for the object and of any attacks on it; an identification with a sadistic superego in which the external objects are depreciated with contempt or devaluation by projection of bad parts; object hunger—life is a feast, so who cares if a few are eaten; triumph over a dead and dying universe of depression; or even an exaltation in which there is extreme idealization and identification with idealized internal and external objects leading to messianic states. In patients with manic and depressive symptoms no secure good internal object has been established. The various mechanisms described are all used to preserve the shaky, good internal object and protect it from destruction by aggression of bad internalized objects. There is a consequent failure to work through or resolve the depressive position.

The use of manic defenses, which are quite common and appear repeatedly in psychotherapeutic work, should not be confused with the presence of a bipolar disorder. The diagnostic criteria for a bipolar disorder are outlined in DSM-III-R (1987), and the treatment of bipolar disorders usually requires psychopharmacological intervention. The temporary appearance of mild manic defenses does not require immediate psychopharmacologic intervention but is an indication for interpretive work. It is assumed that the practicing psychotherapist, regardless of his or her basic training, is thoroughly conversant with the standard disorders as they are delineated by DSM-III-R and will not mix up the presence of these standard disorders with various transitory regressive maneuvers that occur in the normal course of intensive psychotherapy or psychoanalysis.

References

Diagnostic and Statistical Manual of Mental Disorders (1987). 3rd ed.-rev. Washington, DC: American Psychiatric Association.
Klein, M. (1975). The Writings of Melanie Klein: 1. Love, Guilt and Reparation and Other Works, 1921–1945. London: Hogarth Press.

MASCULINITY

Since the earliest times there has been a general assumption that a collection of anatomical and personality traits are characteristic of each sex; for Samuel Johnson (1773), to be masculine meant to be "virile." It has usually been assumed that this collection of personality traits is correlated with anatomy and is biological in origin. Freud equated masculinity with activity and femininity with passivity, but he recognized eventually that this equation was a false generalization. At present it seems uncertain and controversial as to whether any of the personality characteristics that have been labeled "masculine" and "feminine" are biological in origin or whether individuals develop their sense of identity in response to the gender role that is assigned to them from birth by the particular culture in which they live (see FEMALE PSYCHOLOGY).

These terms are included in the present dictionary because whenever they are used they are usually misused, and any contention that there is a certain masculine psychological core correlated with the possession of a penis and a feminine core correlated with female anatomy remains highly debated. This is inextricably mixed up with the issue of discrimination against women in society and until it can be removed from that issue, calm discussion of the matter will probably not be possible. Moore and Fine (1990) advise us that beside the anatomical and hormonal distinction between the sexes there are three major psychological differences: core gender identity, the sense of being a member of one or the other sexes that is established by the end of the third year of life; sexual behavior and fantasies involving the choice of sexual object and the type of activity preferred; and culturally determined attributes, including identifications with the parents and the assumption of a gender role or rebellion against it.

References

Johnson, S. (1773). *A Dictionary of the English Language*. Beirut, Lebanon: Librairie du Liban, 1978.

Moore, B., and Fine, B. (1990). *Psychoanalytic Terms and Concepts*. New Haven, CT: Yale University Press.

MASOCHISM

Leopold Von Sacher-Masoch was a nineteenth-century Austrian novelist whose characters derive sexual pleasure from being cruelly treated. For example, his *Venus in Furs* (1947) is the story of a man whose major desire was to be the cruelly tortured slave of the woman he adores, with the ultimate end to achieve the sensation of being whipped by a successful rival before the eyes of the adored woman. To this character, a whipping rather than sexual mastery of the woman was the primary drive of his life. The author argues that every woman is cruel in love and always between man and woman, one will be the hammer and one the anvil. The furs are the symbol of tyranny and cruelty that is the essence of woman.

Freud (1919, 1924) distinguished three kinds of masochism. Moral masochism is an unconscious trend to seek pain and enjoy suffering as the result of a desire for punishment that is a guilty reaction to forbidden wishes from the ego. Feminine masochism is the unconscious wish in women to be sexually abused and impregnated against their will. Erotogenic masochism is a form of sexual gratification and remains as a residue of the death instinct.

Feminine masochism was described by Freud as a characteristic passivity and receptivity of the feminine nature, but his followers (see Roazen 1975) extended this to a more extreme wish for rape, impregnation, and parturition. According to Lampl-de-Groot, Brunswick, and Deutsch, the essence of women consists of masochism, passivity, and the wish for a baby as a substitute for a penis. Elsewhere I (Chessick 1984) have suggested that these conclusions were based on the study of pathological women and represent an unwarranted generalization about women in general. The whole concept of feminine masochism is questionable and may well be an unwarranted concept.

In pathological situations, it is preoedipal envy and aggression against the mother and sometimes the father that makes later penis envy (see ENVY) critical and disturbs the girl's oedipal period (Blum 1976). Guilt or fear of retaliation over this aggression may even inhibit the libido entirely. This guilt is bypassed in rape fantasies, and the aggression is discharged in masochistic fantasies, commonly seen in the patients of Freud and his "pioneer" women psychoanalysts. The mistake was to generalize from this to statements about normal feminine development, as Horney and even Jones immediately objected (see FEMALE PSYCHOLOGY).

Kohut (1978) maintained that there is no general validity to the idea that a woman's wish for a child is reducible to her wish for a penis. He argued that the healthy woman's wish for a child is a manifestation of her nuclear self, her central ambitions and ideals, channeled toward motherhood when a convergence of biological and cultural factors gives this defined content to a woman's self-expressive needs. So the healthy self-esteem of a female baby mirrored empathically by the adult selfobject leads ultimately to the joyful wish of the grown woman to have babies, depending on whether hormonal stimulation and the cultural milieu support this wish or not.

In the not-empathically-responded-to depressed female baby, older girl, and ultimately woman, the wish for a baby represents the attempt to stimulate herself in order to feel alive and so represents a striving to cure a disturbance of her self. The failure to have a baby in such cases is experienced as shortcomings of body parts—no penis—and the frustration of "drives." Behind penis envy lies the child's experiences of the flawed personalities of the selfobjects who were unable to respond empathically to the needs of her self in its early formation.

For Kohut, the so-called drive characterized as penis envy represents an attempt to fill in the structural defects that form as a consequence of the lack of responses, by turning to hypercathexis of body parts to be stimulated and to feel alive. The craving for a penis here represents an intense need to fill in a structural defect in the self consequent on early narcissistic injury and deprivation of necessary empathic mirroring acceptance. The lowered self-esteem and chronic bitterness and rage arise out of this. The tendency is then to blame gross events, such as the discovery of the lack of a penis, which serve as crystallization points for future pathology.

In men, masochism is generally more disguised and less acceptable in fantasy, but masochistic perversions are more commonly reported in males. There is no evidence that innate masochism is greater in women than in men, and the appearance of it in female fantasies or male perversions carries no messages about "essences" of male or female. In general, the roots of later sadomasochism lie in pregenital conflicts and heightened aggression associated with infantile trauma and disturbed object relations (Panel 1956, Schafer 1974).

Freud's earliest hypothesis was that masochism represented a turning of sadism against the self, but his later hypothesis was that it represented a residue of the death instinct (see DEATH INSTINCT). In the latter view, Freud (1924) contended that there was a primary erotogenic masochism, most of which was removed by projecting a portion of it out towards objects in the external world in the phenomenon of sadism. This is a forerunner of the whole structure of Kleinian theory; both Freud and Klein agreed that sometimes the projected sadism was introjected, leading to a form of secondary masochism in which the sadism is turned on the self.

Reik (1941), agreed with Freud that masochism is based on the death instinct. Reik observed a special significance to fantasy that is crucial in both the masochist and exhibitionist, a ritual quality to the rigid rule and order that govern the masochistic scene and establish its erotic value. He noted the importance of a voluptuous expectation of pain that vacillates between pleasure and anxiety. In a sense, anxiety becomes an element of the pleasure. The masochist masters the anxiety by flight toward the future, argued Reik; to escape fear of punishment and humiliation, the masochist arranges them himself or herself. Reik noted the relation between exhibitionism and masochism, since the suffering is often displayed, and between sadism and masochism, since the individual tries to force another person to be cruel.

The area of greatest agreement in the unresolved issue of masochism is that forms of moral masochism certainly are clinically common. In fact, the need for punishment out of unconscious guilt may form a serious resistance to success in intensive psychotherapy or psychoanalysis and must be carefully watched for and analyzed when it appears. The well-known negative therapeutic reaction can be a function of this, in which a correct interpretation is followed not by relief, but by an exacerbation of the presenting symptomatology and suffering (see NEGATIVE THERAPEUTIC REACTION). It is a common clinical error to blame relapses or increased severity of the patient's symptomatology on a negative therapeutic reaction, but the therapist must be careful not to overlook the possibility that he or she has made a wrong interpretation or in some way has injured or humiliated the patient that could account for a malignant turn in the treatment. It is also clinically important to distinguish between masochism as a sexual perversion and masochistic elements in behavior that are much more widespread and subtle.

Freud believed that moral masochism rests on a wish for punishment at the hands of the father. This is a regressive distortion of the wish to have a passive or feminine sexual relationship with the father. According to Freud (1928), Dostoevsky's very strong destructive instinct, especially his aggression toward his father, might easily have made him a criminal. Instead it was directed mainly against his own person. Freud regarded Dostoevsky's epilepsy as hystero-epilepsy, not a truly organic epilepsy. This reaction is at the disposal of the neurosis and attempts by somatic means to get rid of amounts of excitation that it cannot deal with psychically. Dostoevsky's affective epilepsy began with feelings of impending death, which Freud interpreted as punishment for his death wish to his father and identification with the hopefully dead parent. The seizures, which were punishment for the death wish, stopped in Siberia when the czar administered the unconsciously needed punishment.

This analysis also explains Dostoevsky's masochistic identification with criminals and his need to ruin himself by compulsive gambling. For Freud, the gambling further represented a manifestation of Dostoevsky's urge to masturbate, an urge connected with his latent sexual wishes toward his father. Scholars today generally agree that the story of the "murder" of Dostoevsky's father on which Freud's argument rests is, at best, unproven; most scholars (Snow 1978) agree that his father died of apoplexy (see DIALOGUE).

Freud's (1919) important paper that involves the issue of masochism is entitled "A Child Is Being Beaten." From his experience Freud believed that this fantasy begins in boys who have a masochistic wish to be beaten by the father; as in Freud's (1918) case of the Wolf-Man, this wish represents a defense against homoerotic wishes for the father. This may shift into the fantasy of a boy being beaten by a woman (mother). In girls, three phases are involved. The first and originally conscious desire is the girl's nonsexual wish that her father beat another child of whom the girl was jealous. This is followed in the unconscious by a change to the masochistic pleasurable fantasy of the girl herself being beaten by the father; finally, in the conscious fantasy that emerges, a child is being beaten by a stranger. Thus the beating affords punishment to absolve the guilt for the incestuous wish and also provides a regressive substitute for it (see BEATING FANTASY).

The fantasy, sometimes accompanied by masturbation, begins to appear even before school age. It is clearly connected to the genesis of perversions. The Wolf-Man also, before the onset of the phobia, developed a behavior disorder; its primary aim was to provoke the father into beating him. This represented a masochistic form of gratification that rested on the same premises as the "child is being beaten" fantasy.

The sadistic aspect is important. Thus in the first phase of the girl's beating fantasy, the real phrase should be "My father is beating the child whom I hate." This switches in the second phase to the masochistic "I am being beaten by my father." A third phase is simply the vague conscious derivative "A child is being beaten," while the patient looks on. The first phase gratifies the child's jealousy and represents the assurance that father loves only her. The second phase represents the girl's sense of guilt over her incestuous love for her father and includes a regressive substitute for that love. Freud claims that in the third phase, the fact that the child being beaten is inevitably a boy indicates that in girls there is a wish to identify with the boy and to possess a penis.

In his paper Freud expresses the hope that the origins of all perversions in childhood can be found through study of the vicissitudes of the Oedipus complex (see OEDIPUS COMPLEX). He writes, "In this way the beating-fantasy and other analogous perverse fixations would also only be precipitates of the Oedipus complex, scars, so to say, left behind after the process has ended, just as the notorious 'sense of inferiority' corresponds to a narcissistic scar of the same sort" (p. 193). In this passage and in a further paragraph Freud recognizes the narcissistic aspect of the perversions.

He describes how repression transforms sadism into masochism in three ways: "It renders the consequences of the genital organization unconscious, compels that organization itself to regress to the earlier sadistic-anal stage, and transforms the sadism of this stage into masochism, which is passive and again in a certain sense narcissistic" (p. 194).

It is interesting to compare this statement to Kohut's (1971) discussion of phase-inappropriate disappointment in the idealized parent imago during the late preoedipal stage of development. The narcissistic blow consequent to this disappointment leads to a resexualization of pregenital drives and derivatives, leading to the formation of perversions in fantasy, or as acted out, or both. On this theory, which postulates a separate line of development for narcissism, the appearance of the "child is being beaten" fantasy in the preschool child would in some cases be a signal of narcissistic injury of a phase-inappropriate magnitude in the late preoedipal stage of development, rather than a vicissitude of a pathological resolution of the Oedipus complex itself.

Before the wolf dream, in addition to behavior designed to provoke beating by the father, the Wolf-Man had fantasies in which boys were beaten, especially on the penis. That the administrator of the beating was a woman is not mentioned by Freud (1918) in his case report; this substitution has been explained as a distortion so that the fantasy may attain acceptance in the conscious mind. In the final conscious fantasy, then, the boy changes the sex of the person doing the beating so that a woman is beating a boy; the girl changes the sex of the person being beaten so that a man is beating a boy.

Freud's (1917) comment on "A Childhood Recollection" from Goethe's *Dichtung und Wahrheit* indicates, as in the "child is being beaten" fantasy, the bitterness children feel about the expected or actual appearance of a rival sibling. In this case, Goethe's memory of having thrown all his dishes, pots, and pans out the window is interpreted by Freud as a violent expression of the wish to get rid of the hated rival sister or brother. This behavior has a similar motivation to that of the beating fantasy in girls, in the first phase of which another child is being beaten. Many other acts of naughtiness or destructiveness in children can be interpreted in the same way: as reflecting the wish to be the undisputed darling of the mother and father. Freud (1917) adds, "If a man has been his mother's undisputed darling he retains throughout life the triumphant feeling, the confidence in success, which not seldom brings actual success along with it" (p. 156); one wonders if he is talking about Goethe or Freud, especially since he first said this in a footnote added in 1911 to *The Interpretation of Dreams* (Freud 1900). At any rate, it is clear that the Wolf-Man's rivalry with his sister was intense, and an additional explanation of his naughty behavior certainly lies in this rivalry. The privileged status of being Professor Freud's famous patient represented the Wolf-Man's ultimate triumph over his sister.

References

Blum, H. (1976). Masochism, the ego ideal, and the psychology of women. *Journal of the American Psychoanalytic Association* 24:157–192.

Chessick, R. (1984). Was Freud wrong about feminine psychology? *American Journal of Psychoanalysis* 44:355–368.

Freud, S. (1900). The interpretation of dreams. *Standard Edition* 5:339–751.

————— (1917). A childhood recollection from *Dichtung und Wahrheit. Standard Edition* 17:145–156.

————— (1918). From the history of an infantile neurosis. *Standard Edition* 17:3–122.

————— (1919). A child is being beaten. *Standard Edition* 17:175–204.

————— (1924). The economic problem of masochism. *Standard Edition* 19:157–170.

————— (1928). Dostoevsky and parricide. *Standard Edition* 21:175–196.

Kohut, H. (1971). *The Analysis of the Self.* New York: International Universities Press.

————— (1978). *The Search for the Self,* ed. P. Ornstein. New York: International Universities Press.

Panel (1956). The problem of masochism in the theory and technique of psychoanalysis. *Journal of the American Psychoanalytic Association* 4:526–538.

Reik, T. (1941). *Masochism in Modern Man.* New York: Farrar & Rinehart.

Roazen, P. (1975). *Freud and His Followers.* New York: Knopf.

Sacher-Masoch, L. (1947). *Venus in Furs.* New York: Sylvan.

Schafer, R. (1974). Problems in Freud's psychology of women. *Journal of the American Psychoanalytic Association* 22:459–485.

Snow, C. (1978). *The Realists.* New York: Scribners.

MASTERY, INSTINCT FOR

A number of authors (Hendrick 1948) have attempted to get around the arguments Freud presents for the death instinct (see DEATH INSTINCT) by postulating instead an instinct for mastery. This is an effort to explain the repetition compulsion as an innate need to master a situation by repeating it over and over again (see COMPULSION TO REPEAT). Although the concept has a superficial appeal, it is totally inconsistent with the rest of Freud's psychoanalytic theory and actually has some similarity to the work of Adler, which is generally discredited as superficial and simplistic. Adler's writings represent a wrongful concretization of Nietzsche's metaphysical concept of the "will to power."

The concept of an instinct to mastery is not consistent with any of Freud's definitions of "instinct" (see INSTINCT), and should not be appealed to in psychoanalytic theory.

Reference

Hendrick, I. (1948). *Facts and Theories of Psychoanalysis.* New York: Knopf.

MASTURBATION

Masturbation is a conscious or preconscious self-stimulation of the genitals that may or may not produce orgasm but does produce sexual pleasure. It is universal and occurs at all ages in both sexes. The earlier difficulties with masturbation in clinical work referred mainly to the tremendous guilt that it raised in various individuals who were brought up to believe that masturbation was morally wrong, would cause them some physical damage, or would lead to insanity. The latter two ideas were strongly supported by many impressive medical "experts" in the nineteenth century.

Largely through the influence of Freud, discussion of masturbation has become much more open in clinical work and masturbation has become a more acceptable form of behavior in private, either individually or between consenting individuals. Still, many individuals object to masturbation on religious grounds. On the other hand, compulsive masturbation has little to do with sexuality and is primarily aimed at relief of depression and anxiety or the reassurance that in the case of the male castration has not occurred.

The focus in psychoanalytic treatment today is on the issue of the fantasies that accompany the masturbatory act. There is no longer much discussion of the guilt over masturbation except perhaps in religious individuals and among adolescents, but an understanding of the specific nature of masturbation fantasies is very important as part of the "royal road to the unconscious" that is traditionally constituted by dreams. Masturbation fantasies, like all others, represent a compromise formation between the instinctual drives and the defensive activities of the ego; they are highly erotized and often give an indication of the levels

of psychosexual development where there have been difficulties or fixations, or they point to the level of development to which the patient has regressed.

The topic of masturbation and the masturbation fantasies must be approached with great tact in psychotherapeutic work. Investigation of the patient's masturbatory activities and masturbation fantasies can constitute a mode of acting out on the part of the therapist who has voyeuristic or sadistic tendencies. This can lead to narcissistic wounding and retaliatory negative reactions. Casual questioning on the topic while taking an initial history often gives a clue as to how comfortable the patient will be in discussing the matter. Of course, there are certain therapy situations in which it is extremely difficult for the patient to discuss these matters. The most obvious example is that of an adolescent of one sex with a therapist of the other, or with a therapist, such as a pastoral counselor, who is seen as a representative of religious authority.

The patient's willingness to reveal masturbation fantasies and activities is a good measure of how deeply the patient is able to trust the therapist, providing the patient is not using these revelations in the interest of seducing or misleading the therapist. One of the most difficult aspects of this subject is that a number of patients will reveal masturbatory activity but insist they have no fantasies to go with it, so the information produced is not very useful. Here the question needs to be about what is blocking the patient's fantasy life, for example, the incest taboo or, in some cases, the knowledge that these fantasies ought to be shared with the therapist. Sometimes the fantasies involve the therapist, which makes it even more difficult for the patient to reveal them.

MEMORY

One of the basic tenets of psychoanalysis introduced by Freud (Breuer and Freud 1893–1895) was the importance of the recovery of repressed memories. The issue of whether these memories are of actual events, represent fantasies that in themselves are compromise formations between drives and defenses, or are screen memories remains unresolved and very difficult, varying from one patient to another. A screen memory employs one memory to conceal a deeper and more important memory. Again, the term "memory" may refer to actual events or the child's distortions or even fantasies of such events. The standard goal of psychoanalysis is to bring into the conscious mind both the repressed ideational content and the repressed affect that these memories constitute.

Breuer and Freud believed that the symptoms of the hysterical patient symbolized these repressed memories, which could not be recalled because of the intense affect associated with them. Hence Freud's famous statement that hysterical patients suffer from "reminiscences." The theory was that when the unconscious ideation and affect were enabled to come to the conscious mind, memory would replace the symptoms. The discharge of the affect was labeled abreaction (see ABREACTION). Memory and its recall, in Freud's final structural theory, is a function of the ego.

It is generally conceded that precise memories of such traumatic events as the primal scene are often not recalled even in a successful psychoanalysis, and often reconstructions must take place based on indirect evidence that has the best plausibility. This shifts modern psychoanalytic treatment to the realm of hermeneutics and exegesis, where specific historical truth is often difficult to ascertain and conflicting interpretations may predominate, depending on the personalities and theoretical orientation of different therapists and different patients. Freud would not have been happy with this shift because he insisted repeatedly that psychoanalysis was a natural science; the first cornerstone of it was the recovery of repressed memories that were thought to be of events etiological in the genesis of neurotic symptoms. Many hysterical patients, after traumatic memories have been made conscious, develop a new set of symptoms, which is not consistent with Breuer and Freud's original, more optimistic contentions. It became increasingly clear even in Freud's lifetime that the factors involved in successful psychoanalytic treatment are much more complex.

The dramatic revelations of child abuse over the last decade have also brought into question whether the early memories were actual traumata or fantasies based on the patient's wishes. The answer to this probably varies from individual to individual. Sometimes it is not possible to determine whether we are dealing with fantasies or literal events or a combination of the two. Thus we will not be able to get away from the hermeneutic aspect of psychoanalytic treatment (see HERMENEUTICS).

Reference

Breuer, J., and Freud, S. (1893–1895). Studies on hysteria. *Standard Edition* 2:1–335.

METAPSYCHIATRY

This term is commonly used in the professional psychiatric literature to represent issues involved in mysticism, transcendental meditation, and various esoteric phenomena known as parapsychology. I (Chessick 1991) defined it differently: the task of metapsychiatry is to ask certain questions: (a) What is the position of psychotherapy in Western philosophical tradition? (b) To what extent can psychotherapy be said to be a science and yield scientific knowledge? and (c) To what extent is it a philosophy or art?

An outstanding example of metapsychiatry in the sense that I use it is provided by Kohut (1971). In deciding whether a specific form of psychotherapy is primarily scientific or primarily inspirational, Kohut suggests asking three important questions: (a) Do we have a systematic grasp of the processes involved

in therapy? (b) Can the treatment method be communicated to others, learned, and practiced without the presence of its originator? (c) Does the treatment remain successful after the death of its creator? This latter question frequently separates out therapies that primarily depend on the charisma of their originators.

One of the most important areas of metapsychiatry to have generated controversy and needless acrimony is in the conceptualization and understanding of what goes on in psychotherapy between patient and therapist, often labeled therapeutic interaction. I (Chessick 1983) have attempted to reduce this metapsy chiatric controversy by putting various partial claims in perspective in a "special theory of psychotherapeutic interaction." Much further investigation remains to be done on these topics.

References

Chessick, R. (1983). *Why Psychotherapists Fail.* New York: Jason Aronson.
———— (1991). *The Technique and Practice of Intensive Psychotherapy.* Northvale, NJ: Jason Aronson.
Kohut, H. (1971). *The Analysis of the Self.* New York: International Universities Press.

METAPSYCHOLOGY, MENTAL APPARATUS

Pruyser (1978) argues that clinical theory and metapsychology in Freud's work coexist and are kept in a fructifying tension with each other. They cannot be separated. He argues that we must tolerate this tension because the only alternative is what he calls "clinicism," which is positivistic and therefore cannot really eliminate metatheory. Psychoanalysis for Pruyser is an "outlook," in a view exactly opposite to that of Gill (1978) in the same volume. Gill claims that metapsychology is irrelevant to psychoanalysis because psychoanalysis is the science of human meanings, dealing with goals, aims, and intentions. Metapsychology, he says, is not meant as a metaphor. Freud tried to make it a natural science of the mind based on force, structure, energy, and mechanisms. But Gill claims psychoanalysis is self-contained and needs no such natural science of the mind. He insists that we should not sharpen or replace metapsychology but simply dump it out as an excrescence, an unnecessary "neuropsychology."

Metapsychology represents the highest level of abstraction in the continuum from clinical observation to psychoanalytic theory (Waelder 1962). Freud described it as having a dynamic, economic, and structural viewpoint. Dynamics refer to various conflicting forces within the mind associated with varying energies and objects. The economic aspect concentrates on these energies and their distributions in the mental apparatus. The structural theory organizes the mind into the id, ego, and superego. Because these are experience-distant concepts, they have lent themselves to attack. The whole issue of whether metapsychology is worthwhile and whether any agreement can be reached on what it constitutes remains unresolved.

Metapsychology, for Freud, is a causal explanatory system substituting psychological explanations for missing organic explanations of mental processes. Freud insisted that his construction of a mental apparatus was justified by his clinical observations, but Basch (1973) makes it clear that philosophers have agreed that no hypothetical theory can be abstracted directly from observation. For Basch, Freud's mental apparatus is a bogus or pseudo-entity, one whose potential existence can never be proven or disproven. He argues that nothing can be learned about the nature of thought through the psychoanalytic method. Freud (1933) said, "First I must admit that I have tried to translate into the language of our normal thinking what must in fact be a process that is neither conscious or preconscious, taking place between quotas of energy in some unimaginable substratum" (p. 90).

On the premise of psychophysical parallelism (see MIND), Freud attempted to construct a mental apparatus of a psychological nature only, totally extricating himself from the problem of what simultaneously goes on in the brain. Thought, for Freud, consists of two components. The first of these is judgment, in which the system Pcpt.-Cs. compares an emerging word presentation linked to a thing presentation with successive memory traces to determine correspondence to reality. Second is trial action, which for Freud represents an experimental way of acting, using small bits of energy cathexis without involving the motor apparatus; we commonly refer to this as thinking about the subject. Basch (1975a,b) points out many difficulties in this. For example, a basic epistemological premise maintained throughout Freud's writings is the assumption that perceptions are endowed with sensory quality and are therefore primarily conscious, while instinctual drives are not of a sensory nature and can become conscious only by becoming united with perceptual residues. But Klein (1959) reviews the impressive body of evidence validating the fact that the brain registers and utilizes stimuli from the external world, stimuli that would never exist in subjective awareness; this contradicts Freud's fundamental postulate equating perception with consciousness in the system Pcpt-Cs. Klein (1976) thus calls for the elimination of many aspects of metapsychology from psychoanalysis.

Since metapsychological concepts cannot be said to be directly inferred from clinical work, they are subject to revision without affecting the clinical findings and clinical practice of psychoanalytic psychotherapy. Metapsychological constructs are for the purpose of explaining clinical findings, and insofar as these formulations fail to achieve this explanation and are directly contradictory to independent evidence gathered by other valid methods of scientific investigation, Basch (1973, 1976a) argues that they should be replaced.

The major early presentation of Freud's metapsychology is generally agreed to be found in chapter 7 of *The Interpretation of Dreams* (Freud 1900). Basch (1976b) subjects this chapter to a careful epistemological analysis, pointing out that it is replete with such undefined terms as "mental process" and "psychical acts." For Freud, even such terms as "mind" and "mental apparatus" were self-evident. In his psychophysical parallelism Freud equates the mental apparatus with the brain; in so doing, he presents a study of thought formation in general psychology. In this study the concept of brain as a physical entity is replaced with the concept of "mental apparatus," essentially a brain without anatomical properties, carrying out mental functions.

Freud's idea of perception was simplistic, assuming the sequence "stimulus – perception – memory." We now know that perception does not antedate conception. On the contrary, conception creates a perceptual set that determines how stimuli are perceived. In Freud the Cartesian dualism reasserts itself in the implication that thought, mind, and mental apparatus are somehow something different and beyond the physical. The term "mental apparatus" cannot be defended as a way of categorizing psychological phenomena in the manner that biologists make classifications, because "mental apparatus" has been given a generative capacity with causal substantive explanatory value. For Freud the clinical observation that some mentation is conscious, some preconscious, and some unconscious became expanded into reified systems: the generative entities Ucs., Pcs., and Pcpt.-Cs. of the topographical theory.

Those like Holt (1981) or Gill (1978) who wish to throw out metapsychology entirely are the philosophical opponents of Ricoeur

(1970, 1977). But Meissner (1971) points out: "The methodology that Freud employed was an open-ended and dynamic process, constantly involved in a return to dialectical interpretation of the data of experience and observation. His concepts were tentative, changing and evolving, always subject to the mutative and clarifying influence of new data based upon clinical observation and experience" (p. 285).

It seems to me that this description is unassailable. Meissner (1971) says Freud developed a method that embraced both objective and subjective data, making psychoanalysis a "scientific hybrid—a scientific approach to human subjectivity" (p. 305). Meissner concludes that Freud viewed psychoanalysis as standing closer to the ideographic pole rather than to the nomothetic pole in the continuum of sciences, for it is based on the uniqueness and individuality of meaning of the individual's life history and experiences.

The vicissitudes of the transference are central to the understanding and practice of psychoanalytic technique according to Gill (1982). The recurrences of these transference configurations, as Modell (1978) points out, constitute observable clinical data of a natural science— these are the "facts" of psychoanalysis, and they permit intersubjective validation. But Modell disagrees with Gill (and Klein), in that he objects to a fundamental disjunction between clinical theory and metapsychology. For example, the concept of superego is "eminently clinical," says Modell, and it should also be noted that claims of such a disjunction are contradicted by Meissner's description of Freud's view and method as described above.

Steele (1979) and Holt (1981) present directly conflicting opinions on the subject. For Steele, psychoanalysis is "unquestionably a form of hermeneutics" (p. 409). He emphasizes the congruity of Freud's ideas with those of modern hermeneutics on self-reflection, meaning, and validity. For Holt (1981), psychoanalysis is in principle exactly like all other sciences, but Grünbaum (1983, 1984) would vigorously disagree. Metapsychology, for Holt, is an inconsistent mess and is dying; what is needed is a scientific and testable clinical theory, which is just as possible for psychoanalysis as for any other natural science. This view is also strongly supported by Edelson (1984), who attempts to outline the requirements of such a theory. The problem remains unresolved.

References

Basch, M. (1973). Psychoanalysis and theory formation. *Annual of Psychoanalysis* 1:39–52.

——— (1975a). Perception, consciousness and Freud's project. *Annual of Psychoanalysis* 3:3–20.

——— (1975b). Toward a theory that encompasses depression. In *Depression and Human Existence,* ed. E. Anthony and T. Benedek. Boston: Little, Brown.

——— (1976a). Psychoanalysis and communication science. *Annual of Psychoanalysis* 4:385–421.

——— (1976b). Theory formation in chapter VII: a critique. *Journal of the American Psychoanalytic Association* 24:61–100.

Edelson, M. (1984). *Hypothesis and Evidence in Psychoanalysis.* Chicago: University of Chicago Press.

Freud, S. (1900). The interpretation of dreams. *Standard Edition* 4,5:1–625.

———— (1933). New introductory lectures on psychoanalysis. *Standard Edition* 22:3–182.

Gill, M. (1978). Metapsychology is irrelevant to psychoanalysis. In *The Human Mind Revisited*, ed. S. Smith, pp. 349–368. New York: International Universities Press.

———— (1982). *Analysis of the Transference*, vol. 1. New York: International Universities Press.

Grünbaum, A. (1983). Freud's theory: the perspective of a philosopher science. *Proceedings of the American Philosophical Association* 57:5–31.

———— (1984). *The Foundations of Psychoanalysis: A Philosophical Critique.* Berkeley: University of California Press.

Holt, R. (1981). The death and transfiguration of metapsychology. *Journal of the American Psychoanalytic Association* 25: 835–872.

Klein, G. (1959). Consciousness in psychoanalytic theory. *Journal of the American Psychoanalytic Association* 7:5–34.

———— (1976). *Psychoanalytic Theory.* New York: International Universities Press.

Meissner, W. (1971). Freud's methodology. *Journal of the American Psychoanalytic Association* 19:265–309.

Modell, A. (1978). The nature of psychoanalytic knowledge. *Journal of the American Psychoanalytic Association* 26:641–658.

Pruyser, P. (1978). "A child is being beaten": metapsychology as the whipping boy. In *The Human Mind Revisited*, ed. S. Smith, pp. 369–396. New York: International Universities Press.

Ricoeur, P. (1970). *Freud and Philosophy: An Essay on Interpretation*, trans. D. Savage. New Haven, CT: Yale University Press.

———— (1977). The question of proof in Freud's psychoanalytic writing. *Journal of the American Psychoanalytic Association* 25:835–872.

Steele, R. (1979). Psychoanalysis and hermeneutics. *International Review of Psycho-Analysis* 6:389–411.

Waelder, R. (1962). Psychoanalysis, scientific method, and philosophy. *Journal of the American Psychoanalytic Association* 10:617–637.

MID-LIFE CRISIS (JUNG)

Popular psychology blames a whole host of difficulties that occur in middle age on the "mid-life crisis," which is a term that explains nothing and describes very little. It is useful to remind psychotherapists that professional concentration on the middle period of life began with the work of Carl Jung (1875–1961). Jung believed that the unconscious contains creative as well as "monstrous" impulses and expresses itself by means of symbols. Most of his theorizing is simply mysticism, which appeals to those with a certain temperament. But Jung (1933) did make a sharp distinction between what he called the youth period, where all of Freud's theories hold and which is marked by rebellion and the wish to remain a child, and the afternoon of life, in which there is nothing left, and as the wine of youth becomes turbid, there is an increasing incidence of depression.

Jung disagrees with what he calls Freud's idea that humans should be interpreted exclusively in the light of their defects, and he labels Freud's work the psychology of the sick mind. He attributes a positive value to all religions as symbolic expressions of the unconscious and carriers of moral teachings and he rejects sexuality as a basic driving force. Jung argues that we must rediscover the life of the spirit and underlines the profound uncertainty of modern humans who cannot decide to accept the inner reality of the psyche, which leads to profound tensions. For Jung, a psychoneurosis is the suffering of a human being who has not discovered what life means, and in middle age it is necessary to find a religious outlook that helps the person hold his or her own against unconscious forces.

As vague and mystical as this is, Jung must be credited with noting that human being is being-toward-death. The considerations of the middle-aged and aging individual, although they are much contaminated by unresolved problems of childhood, must be referred increasingly to issues involving death and failing to live up to one's hopes, plans, and ideals. Much later Kohut (1971, 1977) reemphasized these issues, which are predominantly narcissistic problems and explain the incidence of narcissistic pathology in middle age. The term "midlife crisis" should be eliminated because it is not a necessary concomitant of middle age and has been used to "explain" a variety of phenomena that are not related to each other or to the aging process.

References

Jung, C. (1933). *Modern in Search of a Soul.* New York: Harcourt Brace.

Kohut, H. (1971). *The Analysis of the Self.* New York: International Universities Press.

_____ (1977). *The Restoration of the Self.* New York: International Universities Press.

MIND, MIND–BODY PROBLEM

There is a vast literature on this topic and a variety of professional positions, neatly summarized by Churchland (1984). The most common view of the mind in solutions to the mind–body problem is generally known as dualism, or psychophysical parallelism. Substance dualism is the famous philosophy of Descartes, stating that each mind is a distinct nonphysical thing, a nonphysical substance independent of any physical body to which it may be temporarily attached. Popular dualism viewed the mind as a sort of ghost in a machine, where the machine is the human body and the mind is some sort of spiritual or psychic substance unlike physical matter and inside the brain in intimate contact with it. Property dualism, for example, epiphenomenalism, sees the mind as containing special properties that emerge when the brain passes a certain level of complexity, which do not in turn affect the brain. Interactionist property dualism differs in that interactionists in this school assert that mental properties do indeed have causal effects on the brain and behavior. Churchland (1984) reminds us, "Any property dualist makes the further claim that mental states and properties are *irreducible,* in the sense that they are not just organizational features of physical matter . . . they are said to be novel properties beyond prediction or explanation by physical science . . . this last condition—the irreducibility of mental properties—is an important one, since this is what makes the position a dualist position" (p. 12).

In contrast to these dualist positions is philosophical behaviorism, which denies any ghostly inner states and claims there are just potential patterns of behavior, or reductive materialism, more commonly known as identity theory, claiming that mental states are physical states of the brain. In this view each mental process is one and the same thing as a physical state or process in the brain or central nervous system. In a modification, the view of functionalism, each mental state is thought of as definable only with respect to other mental states so that relational properties of the mind are the crucial ones. The difference from behaviorism is that functionalism claims mental states cannot be defined solely in terms of environmental input and behavioral output but always require an ineliminable reference to a variety of other mental states. Functionalists say a reductive definition of mind solely in terms of publicly observable inputs and outputs that the behaviorists use is not possible.

In the view of "eliminative materialism," there never will be a match-up between the common sense concepts of popular psychology and the concepts of theoretical neuroscience "because our common-sense psychological framework is a false and radically misleading conception of the causes of human behavior and the nature of cognitive activity" (Churchland 1984, p. 43). Furthermore, popular psychology is a misrepresentation of our internal states and activities. This old popular framework will be dropped out as neuroscience improves, argue the eliminative materialists.

The issue of whether artificial intelligence is equivalent to the mind also remains extremely controversial. Searle (1984) argues that mental phenomena, which are conscious, intentional, subjective, and seem to have mental causation, are caused by brain processes but have their own existence and can influence the brain. He combines naive mentalism with naive physicalism and argues that the mind is not just a computer program. For Searle, the natural sciences are not the same as the social sciences because social and psychological phenomena are mental. Thinking, he says, is not just simple manipulation, and understanding is not like a computer program.

The answer to this argument will probably come from whether or not experts in artificial intelligence can develop computers that are indistinguishable from minds! Recently the first Turing test, an experiment proposed 42 years ago by the British mathematician Alan Turing, took place in Boston (Markoff 1992). Turing proposed that the question of whether a machine could ever be built equivalent to the human mind would be answered if persons communicating with the machine could not tell whether it was a computer or a human being. The results were mixed, although for the most part the judges were able to distinguish computers from humans. But the trend seems to be that ultimately computers will not be distinguishable from humans in the Turing test. This will enormously complicate the issue of deciding what constitutes the human mind and make dualists quite hard pressed to maintain their theories. However, many experts on both sides of the debate reject the Turing test as providing a valid answer to the question of the equivalence of minds and computers.

A similar and overlapping debate exists over the mysterious nature of consciousness (see CONSCIOUS), where Freud himself stumbled and was forced to abandon his 1895 neurological "Project for a Scientific Psychology" (Freud 1950), and which often constitutes the central issue in arguments about the nature of mind. Reductionists, such as Jaynes (1976) and Dennett (1991), see consciousness as evolving in biology or history and constituting merely physical events in the brain, whereas Searle (1992) and Penrose (1990) take an opposing point of view as does also, rather surprisingly, the famous neurosurgeon Penfield (1975). I believe the extraordinary breakthrough in computer technology that is taking place at the turn of the twenty-first century will enable us to discuss and explore these problems at a much higher level of scientific sophistication. For a brief introduction to this increasingly technical and difficult subject see the debate over artificial intelligence in *Scientific American* 262:25–37, 1990, between Searle and the Churchlands.

References

Churchland, P. (1984). *Matter and Consciousness.* Cambridge, MA: MIT Press.

Dennett, D. (1991). *Consciousness Explained.* Boston: Little, Brown.

Freud, S. (1950). Project for a scientific psychology. *Standard Edition* 1:283–397.

Jaynes, J. (1976). *The Origin of Consciousness in the Breakdown of the Bicameral Mind.* Boston: Houghton Mifflin.

Markoff, J. (1992). Ideas and trends. *New York Times,* January 12, Sec. 4, p. 5.

Penfield, W. (1975). *The Mystery of the Mind.* Princeton, NJ: Princeton University Press.

Penrose, R. (1990). *The Emperor's New Mind: Concerning Computers, Minds, and the Laws of Physics.* New York: Oxford University Press.

Searle, J. (1984). *Minds, Brains and Science.* Cambridge, MA: Harvard University Press.

———(1992). *The Rediscovery of the Mind.* Cambridge, MA: MIT Press.

MIRROR STAGE

Lacan (1968) defined personality as a psychic synthesis that adapts the human to the milieu of society. It is formed first by the image in a mirror stage, an imaginary hallucinatory phase of development, and then by the milieu, which he calls "the name-of-the-father," or the symbolic order of society (see LACAN).

The mirror stage, which occurs from about age 6 to 18 months, is one in which the infant jubilantly identifies with its reflection, a reflection that promises unity, mastery, and stature. This image is a rigid idealized totality. For Lacan, it begins the opposition of the ego versus the true self. Lacan (1978) calls this a *Spaltung,* a splitting of the subject, which is required before the entrance into the cultural milieu, so that when one enters the milieu there is something to label as "I" in discourse. There is no empirical evidence for such a stage, but Lacan (1977) at times seems to argue that the mirror stage is only a metaphor, so he would not expect evidence for it from infant research. The mirror stage for Lacan is a misrecognition, a form of bad faith, and it forms the ego that is a false unity of the subject.

References

Lacan, J. (1968). *Speech and Language in Psychoanalysis,* trans. A. Wilden. Baltimore: Johns Hopkins University Press.

———— (1977). *Ecrits: A Selection,* trans. A. Sheridan. New York: Norton.

———— (1978). *The Four Fundamental Concepts of Psycho-analysis,* trans. A. Sheridan. New York: Norton.

MIRROR TRANSFERENCE

In Kohut's (1977) self psychology (see SELF PSYCHOLOGY), as a consequence of developmental arrest and the failure to properly integrate archaic structures, characteristic "selfobject transferences" take place. These transferences are the result of the amalgamation of the unconscious archaic narcissistic structures (grandiose self and idealized parent imago) with a psychic representation of the analyst, under the pressure of the need to relieve the unfulfilled narcissistic needs of childhood. They are not motivated by the need to discharge instinctual tensions, nor are they produced by cathecting the analyst with object libido. One may wish to think of them as transferencelike phenomena, since they do not fit Freud's metapsychology of transference.

Among these selfobject transferences are three forms of mirror transferences, the result of the therapeutic mobilization of the repressed and unintegrated archaic grandiose self. The purpose of these transferences is to share with the therapist the patient's exhibitionistic grandiosity, either by participating with the therapist in the imagined greatness of the patient or by having the therapist reflect and confirm the greatness of the patient. In the archaic merger type of mirror transference, the patient experiences the therapist as part of the patient, expects the therapist to know what is on the patient's mind, and demands total control of the type one demands from one's own arm or leg.

In the alter-ego or twinship type of mirror transference, the patient insists that the therapist is like or similar to the patient psychologically or that the therapist and the patient look alike. Kohut (1984) later separated this as a third form of selfobject transference.

In the third type of mirror transference, or mirror transference proper, the patient recognizes that the therapist looks and is different, but insists on assigning to the therapist the sole task of praising, echoing, and mirroring the patient's performance and greatness. Kohut relates this to the gleam in the mother's eye' as she watches her baby. It becomes very difficult at times to tell which type of selfobject transference has formed, especially in the less primitive transferences, where it is hard to distinguish between the grandiose demand for mirroring and the demand for approval from the idealized parent.

Disturbance of mirror transferences leads to a sense of crumbling self, hypochondria, and hypercathexis of isolated parts of either the body, various mental functions, or activities. Compulsive sexuality, characterized by exhibitionism and other sexual varieties and perversions, often appears to combat the sense of deadness and an empty self; its purpose is to magically restitute the sense of self and of being psychologically alive.

Typical countertransference reactions to mirror transferences (Kohut 1971) are boredom, lack of involvement with the patient, inattention, annoyance, sarcasm, and a tendency to lecture the patient out of the therapist's counterexhibitionism, or to obtain control by exhortation and persuasion.

References

Kohut, H. (1971). *The Analysis of the Self.* New York: International Universities Press.
_____ (1977). *The Restoration of the Self.* New York: International Universities Press.
_____ (1984). *How Does Analysis Cure?* Chicago: University of Chicago Press.

MULTIPLE FUNCTION

For Waelder (1936), humans are driven impulsively by the id and purposefully by the ego. Every one of a person's actions is an attempt by the ego to solve a problem; even an apparently impulsive act is such an attempt. The ego must deal with (a) the claims of instinct, (b) the compulsion to repeat, (c) the superego commands and prohibitions, and (d) the outer world. It not only has to mediate among each of these, but it has its own disposition to dominate and overcome them and to join them to its organization by active assimilation. So each of the four poses two problems for the ego. Thus Waelder arrives at his principle of multiple function: any solution of one of the eight problems represents simultaneously an attempted solution of all the others. Each psychic act, to some degree, attempts to solve all the problems, although it always represents a compromise. Because of this, says Waelder, all people are perpetually dissatisfied.

Overdetermination means that several trends are expressed by, and there is a multiple meaning to, every action, symptom, and psychological expression (see OVERDETERMINATION). Multiple function implies that a definitive number of solutions are always expressed. Even in character formation, says Waelder, the solution must gratify the instinct as well as defend against it. A neurosis attempts solutions of all the problems. Every solution must be for the claims of the outer world, for instinctual pressure, for superego demands, and for the pressure of the compulsion to repeat, as well as for the attempt to master and assimilate all of these. Symptom formation and the neuroses are seen as having multiple meanings, multiple functions, and an overdetermination of meanings.

This enormously complicates

the interpretive process and also allows us to understand why there is such resistance to alteration of the ego, a resistance even Freud (1937) recognized when he pointed out that the ego treats recovery as a danger. If so many things are being solved by any given symptom, a great deal is lost when the compromise formation is given up, and a whole Pandora's box of unresolved intrapsychic tensions is reopened.

References

Freud, S. (1937). Analysis terminable and interminable. *Standard Edition* 23:209–253.
Waelder, R. (1936). The principle of multiple function. observations on overdetermination *Psychoanalytic Quarterly* 5:45–62.

MUTATIVE INTERPRETATION

A major step in understanding the factors that lead to change in psychoanalytic therapy was taken by Strachey (1934). His work is based on Kleinian theory and represents a direction followed by Kleinians and neo-Kleinians in their characterization of factors that produce therapeutic change. Strachey begins by pointing out that 1912 to 1917 was the era of "resistance analysis," represented by Freud's papers on technique and chapters 27 and 28 of the *Introductory Lectures on Psychoanalysis* (Freud 1915–1917). Resistance analysis is derived from the early concepts described in *Studies on Hysteria* (Breuer and Freud 1893–1895), which assume that if one makes the unconscious conscious by an interpretation, the symptoms will disappear. When the symptoms did not disappear, this was explained as due to resistance, or due to the fact that the insight was only intellectual. The problem became one of how to get rid of the resistance. The idea at the time was that this would be a function of the will to recovery in the patient, of arguing with the patient about the importance of removing the resistance, and above all, of the transference, which allowed the analyst to influence the patient.

Strachey claimed that the part of the ego Freud wished to modify was the superego, the analyst taking the place of the superego (see SUPEREGO). In the Kleinian view, the neurotic superego is sadistic and savage due to cycles of introjection and projection. The introjected image of the analyst is kept separate from the savage superego and functions as an auxiliary superego. The danger of this is that the arrangement can break down at any time, in which case there is a projection of the sadistic superego on the analyst that leads to a sudden negative transference, a common clinical phenomenon.

A mutative interpretation, said Strachey (1934), calls attention at this highly affectually charged point to the difference between the reality of the analyst and what the patient is projecting onto the analyst. It breaks the vicious cycle, as what is now introjected will be more realistically benign and less hostile. Repeatedly, the harsh superego and the projection of it onto the analyst leads to a cycle of rage, projection, defense, and more rage. This is broken up by mutative interpretations involving these aspects of the transference. By the analyst's interpretation of primitive id impulses, the patient comes to realize that these are at an archaic fantasy object, not at all the "real" analyst. So small doses of reality modify the patient's superego through the internalization of the analyst, better perceived as a benign object, into the superego.

Strachey described two requirements for a mutative interpretation. First the patient must be able to realize that a quantity of id energy has been directed to the analyst; second, the patient must be able to distinguish between the real analyst and a fantasy object. Of course, this assumes that the analyst avoids behavior that confirms the projection. Reassuring and encouraging the patient to see the analyst as good—affect-laden active approaches, such as those of Ferenczi—are of no help because, according to the Kleinians, the good object is then just introjected to defend against the bad object, and so the negative impulses will never appear, never be projected, and cannot be analyzed.

An important factor producing change in psychoanalytic therapy, said Strachey, is that every mutative interpretation must be at the emotional point of urgency and made deeply in spite of anxiety. According to the Kleinians, this is the safest way to eliminate the anxiety. The interpretation must be specified, detailed, and concrete. Reassurance, inexactness, and vagueness all blunt the mutative effect. Abreaction does not bring about alterations in the ego or superego (see ABREACTION). Ex-

tratransference interpretations are not to the point of urgency and the object is not present, so the patient cannot compare the real and fantasy object. For Strachey, therefore, extratransference interpretations, at worst, can represent wild analysis; at best, they are less effective but less risky and so can be essential, but they are not mutative.

The crucial factor in the therapeutic action of psychoanalysis, according to Strachey, is the modification of the superego by innumerable small steps through mutative interpretations. This approach, which rests on Kleinian theory and conceives of the analyst being internalized as a temporary new object, is still based on the notion that cognitive insight leads to an alteration of the ego. It implies an affect-laden interaction between the patient and the therapist, in which the therapist is the arbiter of reality and is responsible for pointing out "distortions of reality" to the patient.

References

Breuer, J., and Freud, S. (1893–1895). Studies on hysteria. *Standard Edition* 2:1–335.

Freud, S. (1915–1917). Introductory lectures on psychoanalysis. *Standard Edition* 15,16.

Strachey, J. (1934). The nature of the therapeutic action of psychoanalysis. *International Journal of Psycho-Analysis* 15:117–126.

MYSTIFICATION (LAING)

One of the most important clinical contributions of R. D. Laing (1969) is the concept of mystification, also discussed at length in a little-known article by Laing (1965) that should be a classic for study by all mental health professionals. The concept of mystification actually comes from Marx, for whom it means "plausible" misrepresentation of what is going on in the service of the interests of one socioeconomic class over another. In *The Politics of Experience* (Laing 1967), mystification is illustrated by exploitation of third world countries being presented by the imperialists as benevolent, in which the Europeans view themselves as God's gift to the world. So when exploitation is made to seem benevolent, it appears to be bad or mad to think of rebellion. More generally, driving a person crazy means making it impossible for the person to tell who he or she is, who the other is, and what situation they are in. A common example would be a parent with a child or a therapist with a patient, who is in a situation where it is forbidden to gratify aroused sexual desire, yet subtly sexually stimulates the child or patient.

What keeps the child or patient in the mess is the shared ideology or fantasy system of the family, or of the therapist–patient dyad, which makes it impossible for him or her to see the problem clearly. As Laing (1969) says, the more untenable a position is, the more difficult it is to get out of it. An untenable position is a situation in which feelings are denuded of validity, acts are stripped of motives, and the situation itself is robbed of meaning. Emergence from a shared fantasy system is felt as bad, evil, and selfish. Mental illness is seen as the way out that the free organism in its total unity invents in order to be able to live through this intolerable situation. Laing points out that every preschizophrenic was in a highly mystified state before a breakdown.

Laing carries this further, because in the politics of the family or society to mystify means to befuddle, cloud over, or confuse what is going on by substituting false for true constructions of what is being experienced, done, or occurring, and by the substitution of false issues for actual issues. The purpose of mystification is to maintain stereotyped roles, such as political ideology, family roles, and "pseudomutuality" in the family. The state of mystification is one of being muddled and confused; however, a mystified person may not consciously feel confused but rather falsely calm, or, alternatively, conflicted over false issues. The therapist must decide what is the central issue, even if this is disjunctive with the perceptions of family members.

References

Laing, R. D. (1965). Mystification, confusion and conflict. In *Intensive Family Therapy*, ed. I. Boszonmenyi-Nagy and J. Framo, pp. 343–363. New York: Harper & Row.

———— (1967). *The Politics of Experience*. New York: Pantheon.

———— (1969). *Self and Others*. New York: Pantheon.

N

NARCISSISM

Freud's "On Narcissism: An Introduction" (1914) is one of the most famous and important of his writings. It had a revolutionary impact on his followers not only because it revised old ideas and introduced some new concepts, but because it introduced some serious new confusions and difficulties. Freud's main polemical point in this paper was his attempt to restrict the meaning of the term "libido" to sexual energy; Adler had attempted to regard it as a force or striving for power, and Jung had widened it to mean the energy behind all life processes (see LIBIDO). In order to stick to his original conception of the libido, Freud had to make important theoretical revisions, the most fundamental of which was a change in his theory of instincts (see INSTINCT).

Freud's famous U-tube analogy of the flow of libido is presented, beginning with the premise that in development all libido is first collected in the ego. We define its outward flow as the situation of object love—love for other objects than the self. However, it can flow back again or be withdrawn into the ego (not differentiated from self here) under various situations, such as disease, an accident, or old age, where this tendency for self-preoccupation and self-love is especially obvious. When the libido is attached to the ego, the situation is defined as narcissism and narcissistic personality features predominate. In the early phase of life this situation is normal, according to Freud; he labeled it primary narcissism. Secondary narcissism occurs in later stages of life, when the libido is withdrawn again to the ego.

What Jones (1955) calls the disagreeable aspect of this theory is the fact that Freud was hard put to demonstrate nonnarcissistic components of the ego. To say there is reason to suppose the ego is strongly invested with libido is not the same as saying it is composed of nothing else, Jones contends, but that "something else" is difficult to pin down and opens the theory to criticism of being a monistic libidinal conception of the mind. This theoretical aspect of narcissism is still not adequately resolved; considerable controversy rages about the entire subject (see Sandler et al. 1991). Clearly, at this point Freud conceived of two kinds of ego energies, the libidinal and the nonlibidinal.

Freud (1914) begins by stating that narcissism is not a perversion (see PERVERSION), but rather "the libidinal complement to the egoism of the instinct of self-preservation, a measure of which may justifiably be attributed to every living creature" (pp. 73–74). The U-tube theory is then introduced. Another analogy offered by Freud is that of the body of an amoeba related to the pseudo-podia that it puts out and withdraws. Just as one observes the pseudopodia under the microscope, so libido can either flow out to objects or flow back to the ego. This phenomenon of ego–libido spoils the neat dualistic early instinct theory that divides all drives into sexual or egoistic (self-preservative).

Freud immediately emphasizes the importance of the concept of narcissism in understanding schizophrenic phenomena; the megalomanic aspect of schizophrenic patients is explained as a consequence of secondary narcissism. Most of the libido is directed to the self, especially as seen in paranoid grandiosity. The converse phenomenon, where the most libido possible is directed to an object, is defined as the state of being in love (see LOVE). Freud does not distinguish between self and ego in this essay, using the term "ego" as the term "self" is used in ordinary discourse. Later, of course, he defined ego as an agency of the mind, a set of apparatuses or functions. The student will be less confused if "ego" in Freud's paper is thought of as "self-representation."

A period of autoerotism is postulated as the very beginning phase of life, even before the nuclei of the ego have coalesced. Once the ego has begun to develop, the libido is in-vested in it; this is the phase of primary narcissism, according to Freud.

The second section of Freud's paper begins with a discussion of hypochondria, in which the clinical phenomena of hypochondriasis are seen as the result of flooding of the ego with libido that has been withdrawn from objects. The flooding of the ego with libido appears in the psyche as megalomania, and an over-loading (or damming up) of this withdrawn libido is felt as the disagreeable sensations of hypochondriacal anxiety. No explanation is available as to why the libido-flooded ego should feel these disagreeable sensations, but an analogy is drawn to the so-called actual neuroses (see ACTUAL NEUROSIS), where dammed up libido due to inadequate discharge leads to the disagreeable sensations of neurasthenia. In the case of hypochondriasis, the libido flooding the ego comes from outside objects to which it has previously been cathected and is now being withdrawn; in the case of the actual neuroses, the libido comes from inside the individual and has been inadequately discharged.

Freud distinguishes three groups of phenomena in the clinical picture of schizophrenia: (a) those representing what remains of the normal or neurotic state of the individual; (b) those representing detachment of libido from its objects, leading to megalomania, hypochondriasis, and regression; and (c) restitutive symptoms in which an effort is made once again to attach the libido to objects or at least to their verbal representations. These distinctions form the foundation of Freud's theory of schizophrenia.

Another clinical application of the concept of narcissism, the distinction between anaclitic and narcissistic choices of love objects, concludes the second section of this paper. The anaclitic object choice attempts to bring back the lost mother and precedes developmentally the narcissistic object choice. The latter is a form of secondary narcissism in which the person chosen to love resembles one's own self. For Freud, in early development primary narcissism comes first. Then, due to inevitable frustration, anaclitic object choice occurs, with the mother as the first object. Therefore, narcissistic object choice, when it appears, represents a form of secondary narcissism in which the person loves what he himself is or was, what he would like to be, or what someone once thought of as a part of himself.

The final section of the essay begins with an extremely important sentence: "The disturbances to which a child's original narcissism is exposed, the reactions with which he seeks to protect himself from them and the paths into which he is forced in doing so—these are themes which I propose to leave on one side, as an important field of work which still awaits exploration" (p. 92). Kohut's work may be understood as emanating from this statement (see SELF PSYCHOLOGY).

In this essay, the aggressive instincts in Freud's formulation should not be considered purely or basically as sadism, since he conceived of them here primarily as the will to power, control, and dominance, which only in certain cases involve a secondary need to inflict pain. Looking at it in this way we may say that when the ego instincts are flooded by a libidinal complement from the sexual instinct, we have the clinical state of narcissism; when the sexual instincts are infused by an aggressive component from the ego instincts, we have the clinical situation of sexual sadism.

What is missing here is the structural theory involving the id, ego, and superego. A step in this direction is present in the essay on narcissism, where in the third part Freud introduces the notion of the ego-ideal. In the course of development the ego-ideal becomes infused with the subject's primary narcissism: ". . . what he projects before him as his ideal is the substitute for the lost narcissism of his childhood in which he was his own ideal" (p. 94). This substitution is differentiated from sublimation, in which the aim of the instinct is changed, with an accent upon deflection from sexuality.

It follows from these considerations that the ego becomes impoverished of libido by either object love or ego-ideal formation, and enriched by the gratification of object love or fulfilling its ideal. Self-esteem arises out of either of these enrichments and contains three components: (a) the leftover residue of primary infantile narcissism; (b) the sense of omnipotence corroborated by experiencing the fulfillment of the ego-ideal; and (c) satisfaction of object libido by an input of love from the love object. Thus loving, insofar as it involves longing and deprivation, lowers self-regard, "whereas being loved, having one's love returned, and possessing the loved object, raises it once more" (p. 99). Whether the self representation is impoverished, as Freud thought, or is actually enhanced by falling in love remains highly controversial (see Sandler et al. 1991).

Besides explaining a variety of easily observable everyday phenomena, these conceptions have an important bearing on the practice of intensive psychotherapy. It follows from them that if an individual is unable to love, that is to say, if there is a repression of the libidinal drive, only one source of self-regard is left—that of idealization, or that of "fulfilling the ego-ideal." As Freud puts it, such persons tend to attach themselves to individuals who have achieved what the patient's ego-ideal clamors for, who possess the excellences to which the patient cannot attain. This represents a cure by love and is the kind of expectation that often directs patients into psychotherapy. For certain patients, then, an important unconscious motivation for seeking therapy is to develop an attachment to the assumed successful person of the psychotherapist, who has achieved the aims of the patient's ego-ideal. This carries the temptation to form a crippling and permanent dependence on the psychotherapist, and also contains the further danger that when some capacity to love is developed through the psychotherapy the patient will withdraw from the treatment and choose a love object still permeated by the patient's ego-ideal, a phenomenon that Freud calls a cure by love. The disadvantage of this is that the crippling dependence is then transferred to this new love object, and we observe the clinical phenomena that Odier (1956) called the neurosis of abandonment (see ABANDONMENT NEUROSIS).

A final important hint leading to the work of Kohut is presented at the end of this essay, in which it is noted that an injury to self-esteem or self-regard—what today we would call a narcissistic wound—is often found as the precipitating cause of paranoia. The reason for this, from the above considerations, would be that any falling short of the ego-ideal, or any disappointment or depletion in the libidinal complement of the ego, would cause a withdrawal of the libido from objects, with the subsequent clinical phenomena of hypochondriasis and megalomania.

Freud's theory distinguishes between primary narcissism, which precedes loving others, and secondary narcissism, which results from a withdrawal of love that was previously invested in external objects. A certain amount of primary narcissism remains invested with the ego and is healthy and necessary. A narcissistic wound is an injury to self-esteem; narcissistic supplies are behaviors and statements and fantasies that enhance self-esteem. Freud regarded the clinical states of depression and schizophrenia as "narcissistic neuroses," by which he implied that patients with these conditions could not form a transference. This has subsequently been disproved, so the separation of narcissistic neuroses as opposed to transference neuroses or psychoneuroses has been dropped.

There are various contradictions in Freud's theory. For example, in his later writings, such as *The Ego and the Id* (1923), he stated that in the beginning all libido is stored in the id and therefore whatever is drawn into the ego as narcissism is secondary. By this theory there would be no such thing as primary narcissism, although Freud continued to refer to it. There is also further confusion in that at various times in later writings Freud implied object love to be most primary and the most primitive type of relationship to the environment, while at other times he stated narcissism was characteristic of the most primitive type of relationship. The general trend in Freud's development (Greenberg and Mitchell 1983) was toward an increasing emphasis on object relations early in life and away from the notion of a primary autistic and primary narcissistic phase. Etchegoyen (Sandler et al. 1991) claims that "the proposition of a primary narcissism as the starting point of psychic life is at the root of the fundamental controversies of psychoanalysis today" (p. 54).

Klein defines narcissism as identification with the good object and the denial of any difference between one's self and the good object. There is no "primary" narcissism (Greenberg and Mitchell 1983). This definition is used to explain the clinical phenomena of narcissism and should be distinguished from narcissistic internal structures and narcissistic object relationships, which are based on projective identification. Segal (1980) calls attention to Klein's differentiation between narcissistic states, which are states of identification with an internal ideal object and correspond to what Freud described as autoerotism, and the postulated complex narcissistic object relationships of the infant, which contain the internal phantasies of introjection and projection as described above. Each relationship is based primarily on an interaction between the individual and projected aspects of that same individual, which the individual experiences as belonging to another person. In addition to splitting, idealization preserves "all good" internal and external objects; when this breaks down, there appears the fear of destruction from within as well as destruction from without.

Kohut (1971) at first postulated a separate line of development for narcissistic libido. In fact, the term "narcissistic" has been employed in the literature to denote a sexual perversion, a state of development, a type of libido, a method of object choice, a mode of relating to the environment, a personality characteristic, and a reference to the state of one's self-esteem. In clinical use I think it best to confine this term to the last of these usages and to especially avoid using it in a pejorative sense. The problem of depleted self-esteem and the person's defenses against it or compensations for it is one of the most common and important clinical problems in psychoanalytical treatment today. It is to the credit of the self psychologists that they have focused our attention on this matter. Whereas classical psychoanalysts view narcissistic phenomena either as a fixation at an early developmental stage or as a defense against anxieties associated with instinctual strivings, self psychologists view narcissistic phenomena as manifestations of an enfeebled self resulting from important selfobject failures or as a defense against anxieties associated with the expression of selfobject needs.

References

Freud, S. (1914). On narcissism: an introduction. *Standard Edition* 14:67–102.

———— (1923). The ego and the id. *Standard Edition* 19:3–66.

Greenberg, J., and Mitchell, S. (1983). *Object Relations in Psychoanalytic Theory.* Cambridge, MA: Harvard University Press.

Jones, E. (1955). *The Life and Work of Sigmund Freud, 1856–1900: The Formative Years and the Great Discoveries.* New York: Basic Books.

Kohut, H. (1971). *The Analysis of the Self.* New York: International Universities Press.

Odier, C. (1956). *Anxiety and Magic Thinking.* New York: International Universities Press.

Sandler, J., Person, E., and Fonagy, P., eds. (1991). *Freud's "On Narcissism: An Introduction."* New Haven, CT: Yale University Press.

Segal, H. (1980). *Melanie Klein.* New York: Viking.

NARCISSISTIC RAGE

Kohut's (1978) most remarkable single clinical paper, "Thoughts on Narcissism and Narcissistic Rage," was first published in 1972. Kohut begins by reminding us of Heinrich Von Kleist's story "Michael Kohlhaas," which was written in 1808 and describes the insatiable search for revenge after a narcissistic injury. In this story, as in the novel *Moby Dick,* written in 1851, the protagonist is "in the grip of an interminable narcissistic rage" (Kohut 1978 p. 617) and thirst for revenge that eventually results in the destruction of everybody.

For Kohut, aggression is a function of narcissistic rage and can actually be most lethal when carried out in the form of orderly and organized activities. Narcissistic rage ranges from fleeting annoyance when a greeting is not reciprocated or a joke not appreciated to catatonic furor or the murderous grudges of a paranoiac. The crucial aspect of narcissistic rage is the obsessive need for revenge, to undo a hurt by whatever means, and an unrelenting compulsion to pursue this aim that gives no rest to those who have suffered a narcissistic injury.

Narcissistic injuries, such as ridicule, contempt, conspicuous defeat, and insult, may sometimes be undone psychologically by the use of identification with the aggressor. In this situation the wounded individual begins to inflict on others those injuries the person is most afraid of. For example, one observes sadism in a patient treated sadistically by his or her parents or a psychoanalyst who is sarcastic and sadistic toward his patients, who was so treated by his parents or by his training analyst.

In narcissistic rage there is a total lack of empathy for the offender, an unforgiving fury. Even psychotherapy or psychoanalysis can be experienced as a narcissistic injury and give rise to the most severe narcissistic resistances in such patients because it implies either that the patient is not in full control of his or her mind or that the therapist knows something the patient does not know, or is not totally available to the patient.

Abraham (1919) was the first psychoanalyst to point out how there are some patients for whom every psychoanalytic insight represents a humiliation. They identify with their physician and want to do the treatment all by themselves; the aim of cure retreats to the background. Abraham relates this to narcissism and points out how quickly these patients are disappointed at any imperfection in the analyst. He recommends an exhaustive analysis of their narcissistic problems.

The most lethal situation of all is chronic narcissistic rage. If acute narcissistic rage does not subside, the ego becomes more and more pulled in to reestablish control over the world. The whole personality and its functions gets pulled into this effort. Reasoning capacity becomes surrendered to rationalizing persistent insistence on limitless power. Failures are not seen as due to limits but as due to the malevolence and the corruption of uncooperative selfobjects, a malevolence and corruption that must be overcome at all costs.

Kohut suggests that when chronic narcissistic rage is blocked from being directed at the offending selfobject it may shift its focus and aim at either the self or the body self. The former leads to a self-destructive depression and self-destructive behavior that is chronic in nature, and the latter may lead to psychosomatic illness after a chronic period.

References

Abraham, K. (1919). A particular form of resistance against the psychoanalytic method. In *Selected Papers,* trans. D. Bryan and A. Strachey, pp. 303–311. New York: Basic Books, 1954.

Kohut, H. (1978). *The Search for the Self,* ed. P. Ornstein. New York: International Universities Press.

NARRATIVE TRUTH

Spence (1982) reminds us that the data of psychoanalysis are not self-evident. Putting images and pictures into words is such a complex process that it involves choice and creation, the work of the poet, artist, and aesthetician. Given this, how can psychoanalytic explanation and research occur?

A narrative must be persuasive and search for coherence and meaning. Each interpretation, claimed Freud, contains a kernel of historical truth, and this is why it works. Spence argues that the unconscious is not language but rather experiences waiting expression. Listening to narratives is what we do. A shared language develops over time *pari passu* with the analyst's active listening search for meaning. The analyst watches for thematic unity, significant meanings, manifestations of transference, and multiple meanings, and also attempts to be empathic with the patient. But the analyst is always making decisions based on this search.

The narrative truth of an interpretation is marked by clinical parsimony, the idea that a similar form suggests a similar content, and implies a pattern match of cause and effect. Why do these interpretations work? According to Spence, the narrative truths of interpretations help patients "see" by the right words, present a coherent account, remove responsibility, and have no evidence against them. An undocumented assertion acquires a life of its own. Therefore, for Spence, all interpretations are "inexact" and some are more creative than others. In all interpretations we exchange narrative truth for historical truth. Spence stresses the interpretations' "poetic value" and concludes that each psychoanalyst "hears" material in his or her own way (see LISTENING). For Spence, historical truth is unimportant in psychoanalysis, for psychoanalysis is not a science.

Reference

Spence, D. (1982). *Narrative Truth and Historical Truth.* New York: Norton.

NEGATIVE THERAPEUTIC REACTION

This concept is often blamed when a poor interpretation is followed by a deterioration of the patient's condition. However, this is not a negative therapeutic reaction and, if it is so labeled, the therapist is indulging in a form of self-justification.

The correct meaning of a negative therapeutic reaction is a paradoxical deterioration in the patient's condition as the consequence of a proper interpretation, a situation in which one would expect to see improvement rather than deterioration. There are two common reasons for this to occur. First, the patient may be suffering from moral masochism (see MASOCHISM) so that getting well is interfered with by the patient's unconscious guilt and need to stay sick and be punished. Second, the patient may be humiliated; a correct interpretation indicates that the therapist knows more than the patient. The content of the interpretation is not heard, and instead is simply experienced as a narcissistic wound, generating narcissistic rage.

There are some patients who can express their aggression only by stalemating or defeating the treatment. This may manifest itself in the negative therapeutic reaction, as Freud (1923, 1924) described it. Negative therapeutic reaction should be carefully distinguished from negative transference. In the negative transference, the patient is so angry at the therapist that he or she automatically rejects anything the therapist may have to say. In addition, the patient may manifest a strong need to puncture, wound, and defeat the therapist.

References

Freud, S. (1923). The ego and the id. *Standard Edition* 19:3–66.

_____ (1924). The economic problem of masochism. *Standard Edition* 19:157–170.

NEUROSIS

This term dates from the second half of the eighteenth century, when it was considered a disease of the nerves; in the nineteenth century it was used to describe diseases believed due to functional physiological disturbances of the nervous system without any identifiable structural change in the tissue.

Freud gave new life to the meaning of neurosis in his early work. He (1895a) attempted to distinguish the actual neurosis (see ACTUAL NEUROSIS) from psychoneuroses on the basis that in the former, the symptoms were due to unhealthy sexual practices in which there was a "damming up" of libido due to an inadequate sexual discharge. The psychoneuroses, on the other hand, arose as the result of mental conflict. The term "neurosis" was dropped from *DSM-III-R* (1987) in order to avoid the implication of a psychodynamic etiology that Freud emphasized.

From the clinical point of view, the neuroses are disorders in which ego-alien and distressing symptoms such as anxieties, phobias, obsessions, compulsions, hysterical conversion, dissociative phenomena, and other manifestations appear.

Some authors divided neurotic patients into those who have neuroses in which the symptoms are "autoplastic" and those who have neurotic character disorders, in which the symptoms are alloplastic (see ALLOPLASTIC). The latter are usually today referred to as *DSM-III-R* personality disorders.

Using Freud's (1926) mature signal theory of anxiety (see ANXIETY), the psychoneuroses are thought to develop somewhat as follows: A serious stressful, traumatic, or frustrating situation is endured by the patient. This leads to regression to earlier levels of psychosexual development in which the patient was either fixated due to overindulgence or unable to resolve due to lack of proper gratification. The regression to an earlier stage of development stirs up the early infantile wishes connected with that stage of development. These wishes conflict strongly with the superego, as well as with the reality of the patient's adult life. This conflict generates anxiety, the signal for the ego that the repression of these early infantile wishes is inadequate. To remove anxiety, the ego must produce a compromise formation using the mechanisms of defense that permits a distorted expression and partial gratification of the infantile wishes but also contains a punishment. There is often a secondary gain from being ill. (For details see Alexander 1948.)

In the psychoanalytic process the wishes that are central to the particular neurosis being treated become aimed for discharge at the object representation of the psychoanalyst and cross the repression barrier in this fashion. This constitutes the transference (see TRANSFERENCE), and through analysis the patient can become aware of the disturbing infantile wishes. Such wishes can now be dealt with by the adult ego so that better compromise formations can be formed, thus allowing the patient a relief of symptoms and a better level of adaptive functioning. Freud believed that certain types of neurotic disorders, the psychoneuroses, readily formed transferences.

In his early work Freud (1895b) believed that a neurosis has multiple causation:

1. hereditary disposition;
2. specific cause—factors without which the neurosis cannot occur;
3. contributory or ancillary causes—any other factors that may or may not be present and contribute toward overloading the nervous system;
4. exciting or releasing cause: the traumatic events immediately followed by the appearance of the neurosis.

This formulation represents Freud in transition from a neurological to a purely psychological understanding of the neuroses. The specific cause determines more than anything the type of neurosis; whether a neurotic illness occurs at all depends on the total load on the nervous system in relation to its capacity to carry this load.

The early classification based on this formulation is as follows:

ACTUAL NEUROSES (due to organic causes)

1. Neurasthenia proper—due to inadequate "abnormal" discharge of sexual excitation (e.g., masturbation).
2. Anxiety neurosis—due to blockage of sexual discharge and deflection into morbid anxiety (e.g., abstinence or coitus interruptus).

TRANSFERENCE NEUROSES (psychoneuroses)

1. Hysteria—due to childhood sexual traumata of a passive nature, imposed on the child quite early.
2. Obsessive-compulsive neuroses (including phobias)—due to the above plus later a superimposed, more pleasant aggressive sexual activity in childhood.

NARCISSISTIC NEUROSES

1. Depression
2. Paraphrenia (a term Freud preferred, loosely representing schizophrenia).

Certain other types of neurosis have been labeled in the literature. In the fate neurosis, for example, the individual, because of unconscious guilt, always seems to fail. The neurosis of abandonment has been described elsewhere (see ABANDONMENT NEUROSIS). Since Freud's day the term "neurosis" is attached to many other conditions and has acquired a loose and general meaning, implying an emotional illness that is less severe than a psychosis because reality testing is better preserved, and with autoplastic symptoms predominating, in contrast to the personality disorders, where alloplastic symptoms are typical (see DEPRESSION, HYSTERIA, MASOCHISM, NARCISSISM, OBSESSIONAL NEUROSIS, and PANIC DISORDER).

The clinician must pick and choose among these definitions. There is little reason to retain Freud's concept of the actual neuroses. We now know that depressions, schizophrenias, conversion hysterias, phobias, obsessive-compulsive disorders, narcissistic disorders, and anxiety disorders are all situations in which the patient is capable of forming a transference of one kind or the other. I personally prefer to retain the concept of neurosis for all of these but the psychotic disorders because it reminds me that there is an orderly sequence of intrapsychic events that takes place resulting in the formation of a neurosis, and it helps in the search to unravel this sequence of events. The *DSM-III-R* use of substitute terminology for these conditions, on the other hand, emphasizes the organic possibilities for etiology of these conditions and suggests psychopharmacologic treatment for short-term symptomatic relief. Much of the choice is based on the preferences, temperament, and orientation of the psychiatrist in these matters and will be reflected in the therapist's approach to his or her patients. It is both inappropriate and dangerous for a therapist to embark on the long-term intensive psychotherapy or psychoanalysis of neurotic patients without a thorough personal psychoanalysis.

References

Alexander, F. (1948). *Fundamentals of Psychoanalysis.* New York: Norton. *Diagnostic and Statistical Manual of Mental Disorders* (1987). 3rd ed.-rev. Washington, DC: American Psychiatric Association.

Freud, S. (1895a). On the grounds for detaching a particular syndrome from neurasthenia under the description "anxiety neurosis." *Standard Edition* 3:87–117.

———— (1895b). A reply to criticisms of my paper on anxiety neurosis. *Standard Edition* 3:121–139.

———— (1926). Inhibitions, symptoms, and anxiety. *Standard Edition* 20:77–172.

NEUTRALITY

It has always been recommended that the analyst be neutral with respect to his or her approach to the patient and refrain from value judgments. It is wise to keep in mind Anna Freud's suggestion to try to remain equidistant from the patient's id, ego, and superego. For the therapist, neutrality involves a physicianly vocation and a stance of professional commitment to the patient, at the same time, the therapist should not become overly detached or overly involved in the patient's life (see PHYSICIANLY VOCATION).

Neutrality has sometimes been confused with a cold withdrawal from the patient's suffering that usually results in an iatrogenic narcissistic neurosis in the patient or, if the patient is borderline, explosions of rage and acting out. This is simply a reaction to the analyst's counter-transference and is not a correct understanding of neutrality. It most commonly occurs in frightened beginners who are trying to imitate some kind of caricature of Freud that they have in mind. Freud was anything but cold and withdrawn with his patients, and a careful study of his case histories shows how professionally he was able to interact on a warm basis with his patients yet for the most part maintain a professional distance and neutrality with respect to their struggle and demands (Lipton 1977, 1979). Neutrality should not be confused with the rule of abstinence (see ABSTINENCE).

The great value of neutrality is that it encourages the patient's free association and expression of many embarrassing and very private thoughts and fantasies. It is not too much to say that an orderly psycho-analytic psychotherapy cannot occur if the therapist is unable to maintain a position of professional neutrality. It is fitting that Freud (1915) first used the term in his paper on transference love. Of course, neutrality also requires the analyst to be reasonably neutral with respect to religious, ethical, and social values; he or she must not direct the treatment according to some personal ideals and is expected not to read particular idiosyncratic meanings into the patient's free association according to his or her theoretical preconceptions. It is generally recognized that no therapist can be completely neutral, yet it is also agreed that neutrality is a most im-

portant goal for the therapist to strive to maintain.

De la Torre (1977) points out that the more treatment departs from a psychoanalytic framework, the less neutrality can be preserved. The successful achievement of neutrality pivots on the analyst's self-analysis and understanding of his or her countertransference. For De la Torre, it involves three components: abstinence, anonymity, and the proper balance of passivity and activity. Leider (1983, 1984) presents a thorough review and discussion of analytic neutrality.

References

De la Torre, J. (1977). Psychoanalytic neutrality. *Bulletin of the Menninger Clinic* 41:366–384.

Freud, S. (1915). Observations on transference love (further recommendations on the technique of psycho-analysis III). *Standard Edition* 12:157–171.

Leider, R. (1983). Analytic neutrality: a historical review. *Psychoanalytic Inquiry* 3: 655–674.

────── (1984). Panel report on the neutrality of the analyst in the analytic situation. *Journal of the American Psychoanalytic Association* 32:573–586.

Lipton, S. (1977). The advantages of Freud's technique as shown in his analysis of the Rat Man. *International Journal of Psycho-Analysts* 58:255–273.

────── (1979). An addendum to "The advantages of Freud's technique as shown in his analysis of the Rat Man." *International Journal of Psycho-Analysis* 60:215–216.

NEUTRALIZATION

Hartmann and colleagues (1949) described the process by which infantile sexual and aggressive energies are desexualized and deaggressified. The result is neutralized energy that can then be used for the autonomous functions of the ego. This concept, which is highly metapsychological, has fallen into disuse in the literature as ego psychology has become less fashionable and drive psychology has been challenged.

Hartmann and colleagues offer a splendid discussion of aggression from the drive psychology point of view, and their work has considerable clinical importance. For example, "the capacity to neutralize large quantities of aggression may constitute one of the criteria of 'ego strength' or of the high capacity of the ego for integration. Alternatively, the internalization of nonneutralized aggressive energy in the ego may be the hallmark of a weak, or eventually of a masochistic, ego" (p. 24). The authors also point out the important clinical phenomenon that occurs in regression, a breakdown of this neutralization and disruption of the balance of libidinal and aggressive energies.

Reference

Hartmann, H., Kris, E., and Loewenstein, R. (1949). Notes on the theory of aggression. *Psychoanalytic Study of the Child* 3:9–36. New York: International Universities Press.

NIRVANA PRINCIPLE

Freud (1920) adopted this term in "Beyond the Pleasure Principle" to denote the presumed tendency of the psychic apparatus to reduce the quantity of excitation in itself to zero or to as low a level as possible. This concept, which Freud went on to use in his arguments for the death instinct, has turned out to be wrong as demonstrated by both neurophysiological and infant research. It is now clear that from birth the mental apparatus seeks a certain optimal level of stimulation; when that level is too high, there is a malfunctioning, but when that level is too low, there is an active seeking for stimulation. So, for example, neglected infants who receive an abnormally low level of required stimulation may spend their time banging their heads on the crib or chewing on their own skin, and so forth, in an effort to feel alive and stimulated. The chronic masturbation often observed on the neglected back wards of mental hospitals is another example of attempts at self-stimulation when the level of tension in the mental apparatus becomes too low. Nobody at the present time believes that the nirvana principle is a correct neurophysiological description of the functioning of the nervous system.

The nirvana principle often becomes confused with the constancy principle. This, according to Freud, refers to a homeostatic mechanism that attempts to maintain excitation at as constant and low a level as possible. The constancy principle for Freud evolved into the pleasure principle, which assumed that pleasure is produced by the discharge of psychic energy. This is simply inconsistent with clinical observation since, for example, sexual behavior involves a pleasurable accumulation of energy that is deliberately withheld from discharge for a certain period of time to accentuate the pleasure. Freud never satisfactorily resolved this inconsistency, mentioning that perhaps another factor, such as the rhythm of accumulation and discharge, could be operative.

Removing the metapsychological aspect of this concept, which is clearly obsolete, an important clinical fact still remains. The most intense pleasure that a human being is capable of having, as Freud pointed out, is the preferably sudden discharge of long-dammed-up infantile wishes often in their most primitive and archaic form. There are some marvelous literary examples of this in which an individual who has led an ascetic and carefully organized life suddenly is seduced and becomes utterly dependent on this incredibly intense pleasure. Clinical work with addicts often flounders on the fact that the ordinary sublimated pleasures of civilization are pale compared to the sudden rush of pleasure that is experienced upon the ingestion of an addicting substance.

Life, very much as Freud de-scribed it, becomes a matter of having to trade off the intense pleasures of sudden discharge of dammed-up archaic wishes for more modest pleasures and sublimations, which carry with them far less of a destructive potential to the individual. In hedonistic or narcissistic or Alexandrian cultures this becomes almost impossible for many people; it is a vexatious burden for the ego even under the best of circumstances. Yet the survival of interpersonal civility, indeed all civilization, depends on it. The power of Freud's drive theory and of Spengler's (1962) description of the phases of cultures (see CORRUPTION) to explain the realities of our lives and our history tends to be ignored because these theories are not fashionable today. That does not mean they are wrong.

References

Freud, S. (1920). Beyond the pleasure principle. *Standard Edition* 18:3–64.

Spengler, O. (1962). *The Decline of the West.* New York: Knopf.

NOMOTHETIC (SEE IDEOGRAPHIC)

O

OBJECT, OBJECT REPRESENTATION, TRANSITIONAL OBJECT

The term "object" has been used in many senses in the literature. Generally, it denotes that toward which action or desire is directed. In Freud's theory every instinct has a source, an aim, and an object, where the object is interchangeable as long as it serves a suitable purpose for the discharge of the instinct. One of the biggest arguments in the field today is over whether the infant is or is not object-related at birth. If it is, then there are certain specific objects, primarily the mother, that become required for the infant's satisfactory existence. The concept of the infant as a bundle of instincts has been replaced by such approaches as Winnicott's (1965a) notion of the "nursing couple" (p. 15).

A careful review of the concept "object" in psychoanalysis (Compton 1986) reveals it to be ambiguous. A whole object is recognized as a person, while a part object (Klein) is part of a person (e.g., breast, penis) treated as a need-satisfying object. A "bad" object is one that the infant hates or fears and/or is experienced as malevolent either directly or by pro-jection. A "good" object is experienced as loving and gratifying and is required to neutralize experiences or internal representations of "bad" objects. Internal objects are phantasies* of whole or part objects, rather concretized by Kleinians (see KLEIN) in contrast to others who use the term "object representation" for a similar concept.

There is considerable confusion in the literature between "object" and "object representation." An object representation is the mental representation or image of an object. If metapsychology is to be followed properly, all cathexes are to the object representation, not the object itself. Otherwise one would have to imagine mental energy being attached to structures outside the psychic apparatus. Similarly, object love represents libidinal energy attached to an object outside the individual, but more precisely to the psychic representation of that object.

The transitional object was described by Winnicott (1953, 1965a,b, 1971) and refers to some literal physical object that the child treats as an extension or substitute for the mother. It is usually a piece of

*The British spelling "phantasies" is used to indicate the unconscious nature of the psychic process in Kleinian theory.

cloth that the child uses as a comforter and stands midway between the narcissistic love of the mother as a selfobject (what Winnicott calls a "subjective object") and the actual capacity for mature object love. For Winnicott, this emphasizes the infant's use of illusion in an intermediate area between psychic reality and objective reality, of great importance for healthy development.

References

Compton, A. (1986). The beginnings of the object concept in psychoanalysis. In *Psychoanalysis: The Science of Mental Conflict* pp. 177–189. Hillsdale, NJ: Analytic Press.

Winnicott, D. (1953). Transitional objects and transitional phenomena: a study of the first not-me possession. *International Journal of Psycho-Analysis* 34:89–97.

————— (1965a). *The Family and Individual Development*. London: Tavistock.

————— (1965b). *The Maturational Processes and the Facilitating Environment*. New York: International Universities Press.

————— (1971). *Playing and Reality*. New York: Basic Books.

OBJECT RELATIONS THEORY

Object relations theory conceives of the earliest relationships between the infant and its caretakers as forming certain mental representations and models of interaction that tend to be repeated with other people. These internalized object relations take the place of biological instincts and are seen as somehow having a motivating power of their own. Whether the relatedness is thought of as instinctually based or not, the focus is shifted from vicissitudes of instincts to vicissitudes of relatedness. The most extraordinary original proponent of a complete object relations theory was Melanie Klein (see KLEIN).

In Freud's early work, a part object is that part of the mother, such as the breast, where there is immediate discharge of instinctual energy. Only later does the child develop the capacity to attach libido to the whole object. In Klein's theory, either part or whole objects can be internalized, but here the notion of object is mixed with object representation. There are many object relations theories developed after Klein (see Greenberg and Mitchell 1983). Most popular among traditional psychoanalysts today is the modified Kleinian theory of Kernberg (1976, 1980).

Freud introduced the terms "narcissistic object choice," which is based on identification with an object similar to one's self, and "anaclitic object choice," which is based on passive dependent needs. The narcissistic object choice is based either on the subject's self (what he or she is, was, or would like to be), or on someone experienced as part of one's self (see NARCISSISM).

There is confusion in the literature about the notion of object constancy. This term was introduced by Hartmann in 1952 to describe the constancy that a child achieves when the relationship to its love object remains stable. Prior to this, the object is simply "need-satisfying." This requires object permanence, in which a mental representation of the object persists in the object's absence, a cognitive achievement of the first year of life.

The confusion arises over the interchangeable use of terms like libidinal object, libidinal object constancy, and object constancy. The important distinction to keep in mind is between object permanence, which develops early in life and is a cognitive achievement, and object constancy, which probably develops during the end of the second year of life and is a precursor of the capacity to love another person in a stable fashion, regardless of the state of one's needs.

From my point of view, the important aspect of object constancy is this: by the end of the second year of life there is established in the psyche of the child a relatively benign object representation of the mother that serves as a sense of security for the child. This has very important clinical ramifications in the treatment of preoedipally disturbed patients. For example, Adler (1980) claims that the hallmark of the borderline patient's transference is the rapid disintegration of the selfobject transference as soon as gratification is not forthcoming; this is blamed on the problem the borderline patient has with maintaining mnemonic images. Adler and Buie (1979) argue that the core of borderline pathology is the failure to develop the type of mental representation that captures positive experiences with nurturant caretakers. They call these representations holding or soothing introjects. They stress the loss of evocative memory and distinguish evocative memory

from recognition memory; that is to say, under stress, borderline patients lose evocative memory capacity for previously important objects, although they still may recognize these objects if confronted with them. A thorough review of object relations theories from the point of view of self psychology is presented by Bacal and Newman (1990).

References

Adler, G. (1980). Transference, real relationship and alliance. *International Journal of Psycho-Analysis* 61:547–558.

Adler, G., and Buie, D. (1979). Aloneness and borderline psychopathology: the possible relevance of child development issues. *International Journal of Psycho-Analysis* 60:83–96.

Bacal, H., and Newman, K. (1990). *Theories of Object Relations: Bridges to Self Psychology.* New York: Columbia University Press.

Greenberg, J., and Mitchell, S. (1983). *Object Relations in Psychoanalytic Theory.* Cambridge, MA: Harvard University Press.

Hartmann, H. (1952). The mutual influences in the development of ego and id. In *Essays on Ego Psychology*, pp. 155–182. New York: International Universities Press, 1964.

Kernberg, O. (1976). *Object Relations Theory and Clinical Psychoanalysis.* New York: Jason Aronson.

_____ (1980). *Internal World and External Reality.* New York: Jason Aronson.

OBSESSIONS, OBSESSIONAL NEUROSIS, OBSESSIONALISM

Freud (1909) wrote a classic paper on obsessive-compulsive neuroses. He stressed the magical thinking and personal superstitions in these disorders, the omnipotence of thought (a relic of the megalomania of infancy), obsessive ideas (formations of long-standing representing distortions, uncertainty, and doubt) that draw the patient away from reality to abstract subjects, ambivalence with much repressed sadism, displacement of affect and of ideas, isolation—both temporal and spatial—of the idea from the affect and from the world to the isolated life of abstractions, and regression, wherein preparatory acts become the substitute for final decisions and thinking replaces acting. Thus an obsessive thought, for Freud, is one whose function is to represent an act regressively.

In the obsessional neuroses the complex is often retained in the consciousness but with a dissociation of its affect. The starting point of a neurosis may be mentioned by the patient in a tone of complete indifference since he or she is unaware of the significance of the material. The two cardinal symptoms of obsessional neuroses are the tendency to doubt and the recurring sense of compulsion. A deep ambivalence dominates the patient's life—significant people in the patient's existence are both intensely loved and intensely hated. In the obsessional neuroses, these emotional attitudes are sharply separated. Freud saw the doubting as a result of this ambivalence, and the sense of compulsion as an attempt to overcompensate for the doubt and uncertainty. The omnipotence of a patient's thoughts, the belief in the power to make thoughts come true in some magical way, was applied by Freud (1907) to various primitive beliefs in magic and to religion. Just as

he believed infantile sexuality to be the root of hysteria, so Freud stressed infantile sexuality as leading to a nuclear complex in the obsessional neuroses. As in the cases of hysteria, he believed that the unraveling of these nuclear complexes would automatically lead to a resolution of the neuroses (see NEUROSIS).

Patients with obsessive-compulsive neuroses, which we now know to be sometimes not far psychologically from schizophrenia, are very good at the intellectual game of interpreting symbols. I have seen a number of patients recover from an acute schizophrenic reaction only to develop a serious obsessive neurosis sometimes complicated by moderate depression. These depressed obsessive states remain stable for many years and seem to protect the patient from another outbreak of schizophrenia.

The best phenomenological description of patients with "obsessionalism" has been presented by Sullivan (1956). These patients are extremely difficult to treat by the psychoanalytic method, and Sullivan is very helpful in his down-to-earth understanding of how to approach them. His work is based on his well-known interpersonal theory of psychiatry, in which the patient's self-dynamism (in this case, obsessionalism) functions primarily to avoid anxiety. Sullivan's (1956) great clinical insights into this condition are among the most valuable sources for the understanding and psychotherapeutic treatment of obsessions.

Recently there have been claims that such psychopharmacologic drugs as Prozac and Anafranil reduce the intensity of obsessive-compulsive symptoms. None of this refutes the original concept, however, that the obsessional neuroses are aptly called "guilt neuroses," as Moore and Fine (1990) explain: "The superego is severely turned against the impulses, affects, and ideas involved. These conflicts, along with ego mechanisms of defence . . . result in compromise formations manifested by the neuroses and character traits described" (p. 133).

There is no better clinical example than that of our friend Samuel Johnson, a person with many serious obsessive-compulsive symptoms. He admitted that "the great business of his life was to escape from himself" (p. 121), as his noted biographer W. Jackson Bate (1977) reports and then explains, "The part of himself from which he needed to escape was the remorseless pressure of 'superego' demand, of constant self-criticism, and all the unconscious ruses of insistent self-punishment" (p. 121).

DSM-III-R (1987) downplays the term "obsessive-compulsive neurosis" and substitutes "obsessive compulsive disorder" under the anxiety disorders (p. 245), and "obsessive compulsive personality disorder" (p. 354). The study of these disorders is in much ferment today, and there is considerable unresolved controversy about the etiology and treatment of the conditions.

References

Bate, W. J. (1977). *Samuel Johnson*. New York: Harcourt Brace Jovanovich.

Diagnostic and Statistical Manual of Mental Disorders (1987). 3rd ed.-rev. Washington, DC: American Psychiatric Association.

Freud, S. (1907). Obsessive acts and religious practices. *Standard Edition* 9:115–127.

———— (1909). Notes upon a case of obsessional neurosis. *Standard Edition* 10: 153–318.

Moore, B., and Fine, B., eds. (1990). *Psychoanalytic Terms and Concepts*. New Haven: Yale University Press.

Sullivan, H. (1956). *Clinical Studies in Psychiatry*. New York: Norton.

OCEANIC FEELING

In his correspondence with Sigmund Freud about the source of religious sentiment the writer Romain Rolland suggested as a religious source the "oceanic feeling," a wonderful sensation in which one feels essentially fused with the universe in a kind of transcendental sense of timelessness. Rolland was trying to use this feeling as evidence that there are more things in heaven and earth than are dreamed of in Freud's philosophy. Freud (1930) insisted this simply represented a regression to an early state of infantile narcissism during which everything seems coextensive with the ego of the infant. Werman (1986) convincingly argues that such experiences as the oceanic feeling in the adult cannot be simple replays of an infantile experience but instead represent "a complex phenomenon that derives from all aspects of the psyche, including the subject's value system and the influences of his culture" (p. 123).

There are three categories of approaches to religious experiences or mystical subjects. The psychoanalytic approach attempts to explain them in terms of inner psychodynamics, using various theoretical concepts. The philosophical approach (e.g., Jaspers 1932) views religious or mystical or ecstatic experiences as "ciphers" that point to transcendence as a possibility. Believers, such as William James (1929), who have had such experiences or followers of various religions are convinced of their suprarational source. It is interesting that the psychoanalytic orientation requires us to explain the choices of each of these categories as representing in each person a compromise formation provided by the ego in dealing with its "three harsh masters" (Freud 1933)—the id, the superego, and· reality—or, alternatively, having a role in maintaining the cohesion of the person's self. The reason for this situation was given by the nonbeliever Bertrand Russell, when asked what he would say to God if he found after death that an after-life existed. The answer: "Lord, you did not give us sufficient evidence." Freud's point was that the oceanic feeling and other mystical or ecstatic experiences are not sufficient evidence, except for those who already have faith.

References

Freud, S. (1930). Civilization and its discontents. *Standard Edition* 21:59–145.
———— (1933). New introductory lectures on psycho-analysis. Ch. 31. *Standard Edition* 22:57–80.
James, W. (1929). *The Varieties of Religious Experience.* New York: Modern Library.
Jaspers, K. (1932). *Philosophy,* vol. 3. Chicago: University of Chicago Press, 1969.
Werman, D. (1986). On the nature of the oceanic experience. *Journal of the American Psychoanalytic Association* 34:123–140.

OEDIPUS COMPLEX

This term represents a characteristic group of largely unconscious ideas and feelings universally manifest during the phallic phase (from about 3 to 6 years of age) that remain of central importance throughout life. The drives, aims, fears, and identifications are associated with the child's striving for a sexual union with the parent of the opposite sex and wishing for the death and disappearance of the parent of the same sex. The specifics of the sexual union wish vary from child to child depending on the particular theory of sexual union that pervades the child's mind at the time.

The central importance of the Oedipus complex as the nucleus of all psychoneuroses was stressed by Freud, who discovered it during his self-analysis conducted after the death of his father. He revealed this to his friend Fliess and then first published some material from his self-analysis in *The Interpretation of Dreams* (Freud 1900). The emphasis on the Oedipus complex as central to the psychoneuroses became a fundamental shibboleth of orthodox psychoanalysts at least through the 1960s. With the widening scope of psychoanalysis, the importance of the Oedipus complex has been increasingly debated, especially in the light of knowledge gained through attempts to psychoanalyze various personality disorders and other disorders that are not included under Freud's classical psychoneuroses.

Kohut (1984) maintained that although there was an oedipal phase of development, an enduring Oedipus complex did not occur unless the patient was already suffering from a disorder of the self. The lust and aggression manifest in the Oedipus complex, for Kohut, are already disintegration products of a damaged sense of self, not a universal phenomenon. This is an important disagreement with the work of Freud, but it should be pointed out that Kohut's earlier writings deal predominantly with narcissistic disorders, which Freud thought were not amenable to psychoanalysis. Later, Kohut (1984) extended his self psychology to explain many other forms of psychopathology (see SELF PSYCHOLOGY).

A nice review of varying conceptions of the Oedipus complex is to be found in Mullahy (1948). He compares the writings of Freud, Adler, Jung, Rank, Horney, Fromm, Sullivan, and others on the topic. Every psychoanalyst in the early years of the discipline gave central attention to the role of the Oedipus complex as they conceived of it in their clinical work.

Coexisting with the Oedipus complex is an entity called the negative Oedipus complex, in which the child wishes to sexually possess the parent of the same sex and destroy the parent of the opposite sex. It is assumed that if this holds sway in the child's personality, a homosexual orientation may develop. But it should be stressed that everyone goes through a combination of these phases.

The power of the Oedipus complex lies in the fear that it engenders. For the boy, the fear is clearly that of castration; for the girl, it is a less specific injury to the genitals (see FEMALE PSYCHOLOGY). But these fears are later versions of the child's most infantile fears of loss of the love of a parent or loss of the parent itself.

Resolution of the Oedipus complex takes place by identification with the parent of the same sex and a partial renunciation of the parent of the opposite sex, with the later rediscovery of the imago of that parent in the earliest love objects of adolescence and adult life. The Oedipus complex is very important because the resolution of it establishes the superego through an identification with the values and commands of the chosen parent. Lacan extends this even further in using the term "oedipization" to denote a process in which the child enters the symbolic order of speech through identification with the parent of the same sex, and in so doing becomes a member of the cultural milieu (see LACAN).

Some authors use the term *oedipal phase* as synonymous with the phallic phase of development, while others reserve it for the end of the phallic phase when the Oedipus complex is well formed. It is thought that in the early part of the phallic phase narcissism predominates, and in the latter part the first manifestations of what will become adult or mature object love appear.

Klein, on the other hand, argued that the Oedipus complex arises before the genital phase, and that Oedipal manifestations are always present, even during the first year of life (see KLEIN). Moreover, she maintained, when the depressive position is not worked through, there is a reprojection of the sadistic superego in order to deflect intolerable guilt outside, which in turn requires a regression to the paranoid–schizoid position. This, however, reinforces persecutory anxiety and leads to the greedy absorption of supplies as a protection against the dangers of threatening external attack. All of this may be prematurely sexualized as an attempt to deny pregenital sadism through genital love.

The longing for the "good breast" out of displaced oral dependency may be experienced as the longing for the father's penis and lead to homosexuality in males and hysteria in females. The "bad breast" out of displaced aggression may be experienced as the fear of the destructive penis. Similarly, the primal scene receives the projection of oral sadism characterized by the devouring phallic mother with the "vagina dentata" and the sadistic father. Due to this projection, an imagined sadistic father interferes with normal oedipal identification in males, while the imagined devouring phallic mother interferes with normal oedipal identification in females. According to Klein, penis envy is derived from oral envy and is therefore not a critical feature of female sexuality (see PENIS ENVY). Conversely, sexual inhibition arises from defenses against sadistic impulses that are infiltrating sexual urges. Klein conceptualized oral drives and conflicts as fueling and infiltrating oedipal developments everywhere.

The early fantasy life of the pregenital child contains many indications of incipient oedipal tendencies with marked aggression and sadism attached to them. Work with borderline patients often reveals enormously sadistically charged oedipal relationships. It is often very difficult to decide whether a borderline patient has retreated from a nuclear Oedipus complex to pregenital sadistic drives, or whether the Oedipus complex in the patient is loaded with unresolved pregenital sadistic elements.

Kohut (1982) correctly pointed out that the story of *Oedipus Rex,* from which Freud took the concept of the Oedipus complex, does not begin with the slaying by Oedipus of his father and subsequent marriage to his mother, but with the earlier action by Oedipus's father in which he puts the child out to die in spite of the lamentations of the mother. In this play we see how a massive failure in early pregenital parenting rebounds during the oedipal period in highly sadistic oedipal fantasies and behavior. Even the classical cases studied by Breuer and Freud (1893–1895) show many elements of serious pregenital damage, and some authors (Reichard 1956) have maintained that at least some of their cases of hysteria were actually borderline or schizophrenic patients.

The psychotherapist who neglects the importance of the patient's Oedipus complex does so at the serious peril of a successful psychoanalytic therapy. A number of theoretical psychotherapy orientations have evolved that can be used in a collusion between the therapist and the patient to avoid facing the powerful emotions that center on the Oedipus complex. The presence of these powerful emotions, and their concomitant guilt and fear of retaliation, is one of Freud's most important discoveries and is rediscovered in one's clinical practice over and over again with patients of every age group. The question of the centrality of the Oedipus complex in the various disorders treated in outpatient psychoanalytic therapy remains one of the most debated topics in the literature today. In my opinion, it should be assumed as significant in every case until overwhelming clinical evidence is produced that contradicts this assumption.

References

Breuer, J., and Freud, S. (1893–1895). Studies on hysteria. *Standard Edition* 2:1–335.

Freud, S. (1900). The interpretation of dreams. *Standard Edition* 4,5:1–625.

Kohut, H. (1982). Introspection, empathy, and the semi-circle of mental health. *International Journal of Psycho-Analysis* 63:395–407.

———— (1984). *How Does Analysis Cure?* Chicago: University of Chicago Press.

Mullahy, P. (1948). *Oedipus, Myth and Complex.* New York: Hermitage Press.

Reichard, S. (1956). A re-examination of *Studies on Hysteria. Psychoanalytic Quarterly* 25:155–177.

ONTOLOGICAL INSECURITY (SEE ALSO SCHIZOID)

Laing (1969) borrowed the term *ontological insecurity* from the theologian Paul Tillich, for whom it was the universal human condition. For Laing, it is the special problem of the schizoid. In the state of ontological insecurity there is no sense of continuity and no cohesion of the self in time, as illustrated in the literary works of Samuel Beckett. The problem the schizoid patient has is to preserve the self, as compared to neurotics and normal individuals, who wish to gratify the self.

The cause of ontological insecurity is the lack of mirroring of the true self, according to Laing, the absence of the smiling notice and appreciation of the patient's self as a child. He (1969) writes that the development of a self requires "the loving eye of the mother" (p. 125). This is required for ontological autonomy, Laing says. Such patients, however, do not suffer from unconscious conflicts. Their problem is "beyond the pleasure principle." Gratification is not the issue for patients with ontological insecurity.

There are three forms of anxiety that manifest themselves in ontological insecurity. The first of these is anxiety of engulfment, the fears of being overwhelmed and of the loss of the self in a merger with the other. This is prevented by isolation from people and a deliberate effort to confuse others and to be misunderstood. The second is labeled anxiety of implosion. This is a sense of persecution from reality, a fear that it will crash in and obliterate the person, who already feels empty. A third form of anxiety and ontological insecurity is of petrifaction. This represents becoming a thing or a robot. To defend against petrifaction the patient uses depersonalization; that is, he or she stops responding when the other individual is tiresome or disturbing. This destroys the other person's subjectivity. It "petrifies the other," but it leads to more ontological insecurity, since one's ontological security depends on an enlivened reaction from the other. Thus a vicious circle becomes activated.

In patients with ontological insecurity, dependency on the other is substituted for genuine mutuality. The schizoid patient oscillates between merger and isolation, not, as in the normal person, between relatedness and separation. The patient splits into a secret true self and a body associated with a false self. All of us reversibly do this under stress, for example, at a boring party, under torture, during a painful or embarrassing medical examination, or during painful dental work; but in the schizoid individual, a definitive split occurs between the true self and a false self system, in which the false self system becomes the manifest personality. This definitive split becomes a basic and irreversible schizoid style. The patient, in a common clinical picture, tries to do everything for himself or herself in isolation. The advantage of this is that it protects the patient from ontological insecurity and the anxieties described above as associated with ontological insecurity.

It should be pointed out that the term *ontological insecurity* is a dreadful misnomer and a mixture of levels of discourse between the metaphysical and the clinical. This does not detract from the fact that Laing's (1969) description of the development of the schizoid style is one of the best in the literature.

Reference

Laing, R. D. (1969). *The Divided Self.* New York: Pantheon Books.

OPTIMAL FRUSTRATION, OPTIMAL RESPONSIVENESS

Kohut's conceptual shift from viewing transmuting internalizations, based on dynamics and energetics in Freud's metapsychology, as curative in psychoanalytic therapy to viewing empathy as curative represents a change from a focus on mechanisms to a focus on the experiential and the transactional in the treatment. Terman (1989) points out that self psychologists can be classified on the basis of this shift. The explanatory-interpretive group claims that the curative process in psychoanalytic therapy occurs when a self psychologist recognizes and interprets the vicissitudes of the selfobject transference. This transference undergoes its vicissitudes because of the inevitable provision of optimal frustration by the therapist. The assumption is that change will occur on the basis of interpretation of these transference vicissitudes alone. The crucial function of the analyst is to articulate archaic affect states for the patient. Terman explains, "The weight of emphasis, then, is on the explanatory-interpretive aspects of the therapeutic process—not as they facilitate a different experience in a relationship nor as they permit internalization of functions, but as they foster intercognitive transformations" (p. 92).

Terman calls the other self psychologists the relationship or experiential group, in which he includes himself. This group believes that a happy archaic transference enables development to resume. It emphasizes optimal responsiveness, not optimal frustration, as crucial. The experience of a new relationship becomes central to the patient's resumption of development. So even among self psychologists, the same polarization occurs as among "traditional" psychoanalysts, between those who emphasize cognition and articulation as crucial factors in altering the ego and those who emphasize experience, relationship, and interaction. One of the disadvantages of self psychology is that neither group presents a very convincing specific metapsychological formulation of how the self is altered either by optimal frustration with transmuting internalization or by optimal responsiveness and empathy. This refinement remains for the future (see SELF PSYCHOLOGY).

Reference

Terman, D. (1989). Therapeutic change: perspectives of self psychology. *Psychoanalytic Inquiry* 9:88–100.

OVERDETERMINATION

Any symptom, dream, fantasy, or behavioral item is always overde-termined. That means it has more than one meaning and expresses drives and conflicts derived from more than one level or aspect of the personality. It provides a solution to a number of problems and expresses a number of convergent tendencies (see MULTIPLE FUNCTION). All these things are overdetermined in the sense that it is possible to interpret all of them as the result of compromises formed at various levels of psychological development. It remains necessary, then, for the therapist to decide what is the central focus of the material and what is the theme going through the particular set of free associations in that particular session (Saul 1958). This is a clinical judgment and depends on the sense of continuity between the present session and previous sessions. Interpretations are optimally aimed at whatever level is central to the patient's focus at the time they are made.

It does not follow from this that any dream or symptom may be interpreted in an infinite number of ways, but rather that a certain limited set of various possible interpretations are permitted. Ambiguity is dispelled by the context, verbal intonation, material of previous sessions, and nonverbal expressions. This implies that in good psychoanalytic practice it is sometimes possible to come back to an important dream months later and reinterpret the dream in a different way. This would not mean that the original interpretation was wrong, but that it was simply at a different level not as deep as the current one. The achievement of depth in a patient's material over time is one of the most important signs of whether a psychoanalytic treatment is truly psychoanalytic; if an increasing depth and primitivity of the material does not appear, the treatment should be reevaluated and consultation should be requested.

Reference

Saul, L. (1958). *The Technique and Practice of Psychoanalysis*. Philadelphia: Lippincott.

P

PANIC DISORDER

Panic disorder, unlike generalized anxiety disorder, comes on suddenly, is very acute in its symptomatology, and exhibits relative calm between episodes. Panic attacks are characterized by hyperventilation, a fear of going crazy, a sense of intense terror and impending doom, and a conviction that one is about to die from some organic catastrophe, such as a heart attack. These attacks may last several minutes or more than an hour. *DSM-III-R* (1987) differentiates among panic disorder with concomitant agoraphobia, panic disorder without agoraphobia, and agoraphobia without panic disorder.

Panic attacks have been under intensive biochemical investigation. There are claims in the literature that such drugs as Xanax (alprazolam) are effective in preventing their onset. Other authors suggest the use of tricyclic antidepressants, often in combination with benzodiazepines. From the psychodynamic point of view, the panic disorder is a form of anxiety disorder (see ANXIETY).

The proper approach to panic disorder, it seems to me, would be first supportive psychotherapy with the use of psychopharmacologic agents. A current textbook of psychopharmacology should be consulted for details, but only a person properly qualified and experienced in the use of these agents should administer them. If there is no response to this form of treatment, or if the patient desires more than palliative measures, psychoanalysis should be considered. Vanggaard (1989) reports details of a case of panic disorder treated successfully by psychoanalysis, although his technique is rather unorthodox.

References

Diagnostic and Statistical Manual of Mental Disorders (1987). 3rd ed. rev. Washington, DC: American Psychiatric Association.

Vanggaard, T. (1989). *Panic: The Course of a Psychoanalysis,* trans. J. Vanggaard. New York: Norton.

PARAMETER

Eissler (1953) used the term "parameter" to mean any intervention in psychoanalysis other than interpretation. This assumes that in classical psychoanalysis interpretation is the exclusive technical tool. A parameter is introduced only if the treatment process would otherwise come to a standstill; furthermore, the parameter must be dispensable and analyzable. The interpretation of the meaning of the parameter to the patient is very important in this extremely strict theoretical position.

In actual practice there are many parameters introduced and they cannot be avoided. The very physicianly vocation (see PHYSICIANLY VOCATION) of the psychotherapist requires them, and they prepare the patient to be receptive to properly timed interpretations. Unfortunately, the term "parameter" has a pejorative implication for any interventions other than interpretations that the analyst may make. An interaction with another person that consisted solely of interpretation, however, would be intolerable to all but masochists.

Probably the most extreme view is found in the work of Langs (1979, 1982). The issue is whether interventions other than interpretations do irreparable damage to the analytic process, or whether, since they are unavoidable, they may be permitted as part of establishing a reasonable ambience in the therapeutic situation. The danger of an extremely arid relationship characterized only by interpretations is that of an iatrogenic narcissistic regression on the part of the patient. Self psychologists have made much of this issue and would consider an attempt to restrict the relationship solely to interpretations as a gross failure of empathy on the part of the therapist. Langs, on the other hand, would consider any interventions other than interpretation as examples of acting out, projective identification, and psychopathology on the part of the therapist, which the patient would then pro-

ceed to attempt to cure. There are some unusual implications about the patient's unconscious in Langs' views (see Chessick 1982).

References

Chessick, R. (1982). Psychoanalytic listening: with special reference to the views of Langs. *Contemporary Psychoanalysis* 18: 613–634.

Eissler, K. (1953). The effect of the structure of the ego on psychoanalytic technique. *Journal of the American Psychoanalytic Association* 1:104–143.

Langs, R. (1979). *The Therapeutic Environment.* New York: Jason Aronson.

———— (1982). *Psychotherapy: A Basic Text.* New York: Jason Aronson.

PARANOIA, PARANOID

Paranoia has been known to the western world from the earliest Greek literature, although it has never been clearly or consistently defined. A sensible use of the term appears in *DSM-III-R* (1987). Delusional paranoid disorder is characterized by delusions "involving situations that occur in real life, such as being followed, poisoned, infected, loved at a distance, having a disease, being deceived by one's spouse or lover" (p. 202). This has to last at least one month; apart from the delusions there is no grossly bizarre or flagrantly psychotic behavior. Depending on the kind of delusional material, *DSM-III-R* distinguishes erotomanic, grandiose, jealous, persecutory, somatic, and unspecified types of delusional paranoid disorders. The essential abnormality is usually a persecutory or grandiose set of delusions.

The older literature conceived of paranoia as an encapsulated condition in which a very complex and intricate delusional system develops outside the patient's everyday life and is often kept secret from those around the patient. Paranoid delusional disorder and paranoia differ from paranoid schizophrenic disorders in that in the former the delusions are usually organized into a coherent, internally consistent system. All too often the patient may be prepared to act on that system, which may lead to very serious consequences for the patient and others. Paranoid individuals are often extremely dangerous and are very difficult to work with in intensive psychotherapy.

Here is a case of delusional paranoid disorder. A middle-aged philosophy professor came to see me after what appeared at first to be a standard mid-life crisis: his children were grown and married, and his wife was getting tired of the role of housewife and nurturant supporter. She was beginning to indicate that she wished to have a life and career and self of her own, thus disrupting a rather long-standing arrangement and cozy empathic support matrix for my patient.

My patient had noticed about six months prior to treatment the onset of peculiar sensations, suggesting an inner change in him that he had difficulty explaining. These feelings especially occurred when he was in a small office with two or three of his male colleagues working closely together on some philosophical project.

After a while it seemed to him that these changes, which had led to a puzzling sense of estrangement of various parts of his body, did indeed have an identifiable source. He felt that their origin was from certain electric currents emanating from a specific focus in his body, a focus that he gradually recognized to be his right testicle.

As these sensations continued, he became convinced this focus in his testicle was not really a part of himself but was a source within him that was not actually him, a source that he eventually identified as some kind of radioactive material that had been placed there in some mysterious fashion, perhaps while he slept.

The feeling of inner change began to continue even at night. As he would fall asleep, he would begin to see images in which the world took on a kind of distorted appearance; vague shadows would flit across his visual field. He became aware that the source of radiation was not autochthonous but he was the receptor of messages sent from outside himself. At first, he thought that these messages were transmitted to the focus in his testicle through some sort of gas, electron beams, X rays, or cosmic radiation of an unidentified source.

Eventually, as he reflected on the experiences, it became clear to him that this unidentified external source that exerted such influence on him was not friendly. It was also apparently making changes in his wife and children without their knowledge.

This unidentified source was both revealing itself to him but also concealing itself, in that it was vague and mysterious; to his wife and children it was completely concealed, so that he was in the privileged position of having stumbled into a clearing in which he could get a glimpse of a cosmic process that seemed more and more to him to pervade the entire being of himself and his family.

Gradually a certain clarification took place regarding the nature of this cosmic process. He realized that everything being done to him, even his very existence and life experiences, was transmitted and regulated by this unseen influencing apparatus, a machine of obscure construction containing large and unimaginable parts, far beyond the grasp of any normal mortal to understand. As time passed, it became apparent that this remarkable machine served as the ground of the being of all the entities with which the patient had to interact, and determined the very mode of their existence and the way in which they experienced the world and communicated these experiences to him.

His final revelation came when in a lightning flash he realized that behind this enormous machine was a group of unidentifiable enemies, all men, perhaps male demons, who were operating the machine. The impression grew stronger and stronger that these male demons bore a suspicious resemblance to the very men that he was working with in his university office. In a way, these male colleagues seemed to him to have been created in the image of the male demons.

The details of my patient's influencing machine have been described before (Tausk 1933). Since it was capable of producing the world of visual reality for the patient, everything he saw was generated by the machine. It could produce as well as remove moods, thoughts, and feelings by means of waves or rays or mysterious forces that the sophisticated philosopher, with all his knowledge of modern physics, was unable to explain. It produced all the motor phenomena of his body, including erections and other body movements, through the use of air currents, electricity, magnetism, or X rays. It was responsible for all physical occurrences in the patient's body, such as skin eruptions and abscesses. The machine also created indescribable sensations, sometimes ecstatic, that were even strange to the patient himself and that he had never felt before. A constant concern of the patient was that, as his therapist, I too was under the influence of the apparatus, although it was not clear whether I was allied with the conspiracy of demonic enemies who were driving this apparatus or was simply another victim of it, like the patient and his family. Obsessed with his discovery, the patient reminded me that Nietzsche was right when he wrote, "A philosopher is a man who never ceases to experience, see, hear, suspect, hope, and dream extraordinary things. . . . Philosophy is a voluntary living amid ice and mountain heights."

The great psychoanalyst and pediatrician Donald Winnicott (1968) postulated that good-enough holding facilitates the formation of a psychosomatic partnership in the infant:

> This contributes to the sense of "real" as opposed to "unreal." Faulty handling militates against the development of muscle tone, and that which is called "coordination," and against the capacity of the infant to enjoy the experience of body functioning, and of Being. [p. 19]
>
> If the environment behaves well, the infant has a chance to maintain a sense of continuity of being; perhaps this may go right back to the first stirrings in the womb. When this exists the individual has a stability that can be gained in no other way. [p. 28]

Searles (1960) claims that

> there is within the human individual a sense, whether at a conscious or unconscious level, of *relatedness to his nonhuman environment,* that this relatedness is one of the transcendentally important facts of human living, that—as with other very important circumstances in human existence—it is a source of ambivalent feelings to him, and that, finally, if he tries to ignore its importance to himself, he does so at peril to his psychological well-being. [p. 6]

Searles argues that a chronic inability during infancy and early childhood to relate oneself to a relatively stable, relatively realistically perceived, relatively simple world of inanimate objects may have much to do with one's inability in adult life to find fundamental, graspable realities and a tangible meaning in life. Conversely, a mature relatedness with the nonhuman environment is very fruitful in the assuagement of anxiety, the fostering of self-realization, the deepening of feeling of one's reality, and the fostering of one's appreciation and acceptance of others.

Searles quotes Fromm and Tillich in describing the repercussions in various areas of human living that result from disjointedness in the individual's relationship with his nonhuman environment. He describes the most important result of this disjointedness as causing the person to deal with his or her fellow humans in a noncherishing manner. Human relations and material possessions are experienced in ways that are similarly impoverished of a sense of meaningfulness.

Freud (1914) argued that metaphysical speculation was based on self-observation, which he also regarded as the basis of the self-criticism of conscience. He called self-observation a kind of "internal research, which furnishes philosophy with the material for its intellectual operations" (p. 96). In paranoid patients this self-critical function becomes projected, says Freud, and their delusions of being watched and criticized by external "voices" has the same psychodynamic root as their "characteristic tendency to construct speculative systems" (p. 96). He views the "heightening" of the activity of this critically observing agency as the basis of both conscience and philosophic introspection.

A voluminous literature has developed around Freud's (1911) interpretation of the Schreber case. Freud believed that homosexuality is at the basis of paranoid thinking. Defensive denial, reaction formation, and projection yield a formulation in which the unconscious loving wish for the man is denied ("I do not love him, I hate him") and returns to consciousness as a projected hatred coming from the individual the patient secretly loves. This gives rise to what is sometimes called paranoid anxiety, in which the terrified patient anticipates an attack by the individual on whom the projection has been made and may even kill that person in an attempt to prevent the attack. Whether it is possible, as Freud did, to postulate homosexuality at the basis of every paranoid delusion remains undecided and much debated. Even traditional psychoanalysts are divided between those who believe that there is a homosexual element in every case of paranoia and those who do not follow Freud on this matter.

It is possible that a confusion between homosexuality and pseudohomosexuality has led to this controversy (see PSEUDOHOMO-SEXUALITY). Ovesey (1969) attempted to reinterpret Freud's theory by claiming that anxiety about homosexuality has at least three motivational components. The first component is the sexual. The true homosexual seeks sexual gratification with a member of the same sex as a goal. The second and third of these components are dependency and power motives, in which the individual seeks nonsexual goals through the use of the genitals. Ovesey defines worry about such strivings as pseudohomosexual anxiety. He maintains that paranoid projection is a common defense against pseudohomosexuality, but he concedes that all three motives are present in various degrees in all homosexuality (see HOMOSEXUAL-ITY). Ovesey's main contribution is to remind us that the patient can misinterpret his own power and dependency strivings as feminine, or dream or conceive of them in homosexual terms. This leads to anxiety about being a "homosexual," which can then lead to paranoid defenses. The question of why the patient chooses genital expression of his power and dependency strivings is unanswered.

A similar concept is presented by Kohut (1978). He describes the regression that takes place during a therapist's vacation when the patient, who is seeking an idealized parent imago, becomes involved in a homosexual episode. The sexualization provides a sense of aliveness, self-cohesion, gratification, and mastery over a situation in which the patient feels in serious danger of fragmentation of the self (see SELF PSYCHOLOGY).

Melanie Klein used the concept of paranoid position in a very special way (see KLEIN). She postulated a fluctuating process in which paranoid fears and suspicions are reinforced as a regressive defense against the anxieties associated with depressive position. Meissner (1978) gives an elaborate neo-Kleinian interpretation of paranoia with only passing reference to Kohut's theories.

References

Diagnostic and Statistical Manual of Mental Disorders (1987). 3rd ed.-rev. Washington, DC: American Psychiatric Association.

Freud, S. (1911). Psycho-analytic notes on an autobiographical account of a case of paranoia (dementia paranoides). *Standard Edition* 12:3–82.

———— (1914). On narcissism: an introduction. *Standard Edition* 14:67–102.

———— (1917). Mourning and melancholia. *Standard Edition* 14:237–258.

Kohut, H. (1978). *The Search for the Self*, ed. P. Ornstein. New York: International Universities Press.

Meissner, W. (1978). *The Paranoid Process*. New York: Jason Aronson.

Ovesey, L. (1969). *Homosexuality and Pseudohomosexuality*. New York: Science House.

Searles, H. (1960). *The Nonhuman Environment in Normal Development and Schizophrenia*. New York: International Universities Press.

Tausk, V. (1933). On the origin of the influencing machine in schizophrenia. *Psychoanalytic Quarterly* 2:519–556.

Winnicott, D. (1968). *The Family and Individual Development*. London: Tavistock.

PARAPHRENIA

Kraepelin (1904) originally used this term to refer to chronic psychoses characterized by grandiosity and megalomanic delusions, but not accompanied by intellectual deterioration. Freud used the term to denote paranoid schizophrenia. He preferred it because it differentiated paranoia from schizophrenia, which he believed had a different fundamental etiology. He thought that homosexual wishes were at the basis of paranoia (see PARANOIA), but he did not think that schizophrenia was grounded on such wishes. For Freud, schizophrenia represents a massive regression to an early narcissistic state, although he used the terms "paraphrenia" and "schizophrenia" interchangeably and inconsistently. For example, in his (1914) essay on narcissism the term "paraphrenia" denotes both paranoia and schizophrenia, yet he refers to schizophrenia as "paraphrenia proper." This term is perhaps best relegated to the history of psychiatry.

References

Freud, S. (1914). On narcissism: an introduction. *Standard Edition* 14:67–102.

Kraepelin, E. (1904). *Lectures on Clinical Psychiatry*, trans. T. Johnstone. New York: Hafner, 1968.

PART OBJECT (SEE OBJECT)

PATIENCE

In one of his most beautiful definitions, Samuel Johnson (1773) defines patience as "the power of suffering; calm endurance of pain or labour . . . the quality of expecting long without rage or discontent . . . perseverance . . . the quality of bearing offences without revenge or anger" (p. 1411). Of all the qualities required of the psychoanalytically oriented psychotherapist, this is perhaps the most important. Again and again patients fear that the therapist, like the patient's busy, harassed, and overwhelmed parents, will run out of patience either with the demands or the complaints voiced in therapy sessions. Or they fear that the therapist, like the narcissistic parent, will demand immediate improvement and instant gratification, so that the patient not only will have to flatter and love the therapist but will have to bring the therapist proof that his or her interpretations are correct.

The therapist has to maintain patience in spite of a patient's complaints that no cure is taking place. He or she must often tolerate pressure from the patient's own family, including insinuations that the therapist is out to cheat, exploit, or brainwash the patient. Perhaps hardest of all, the therapist must bear with the clamor of third-party payers for documentation and proof that the treatment is necessary and should continue. The therapist, by example and by proper interpretation, has to help the patient develop tolerance toward these pressures and has to maintain a certain conviction that the process will ultimately prevail and be worthwhile.

The importance of the silent manifestations of the therapist's patience, experienced over years of therapy, has not been given the attention in the literature that it deserves. The occasional reported cases of analyses with Freud as he grew sicker, older, and more irascible indicate that at times he ran out of patience, sometimes abruptly terminating the treatment, to the detriment of the patient. Kardiner (1977), although a questionable source, since his report is essentially a failed six month's analysis with Freud, quotes Freud as saying in 1921 at the age of 65, "I have no patience in keeping people for a long time. I tire of them, and I want to spread my influence" (p. 69).

The work of Kohut (see SELF PSYCHOLOGY) has perhaps made it easier for therapists to be patient, because the apparently self-centered or narcissistic demands made on the therapist day after day become more understandable in the light of archaic grandiosity and the search for an idealized parent imago. This allows the therapist to accept these demands without meeting them, but also without arguing with the patient's interpretation of "reality" and without moralizing or condemning the patient.

One must never forget that each psychotherapy or psychoanalysis is unique, and because of adhesiveness of the libido (see ADHESIVENESS OF THE LIBIDO) or fixation to an archaic self/selfobject bond (Muslin 1989), or other factors, each patient unfolds on his or her unique timetable even with the best of therapists. Attempts to hurry this are not only unempathic, they are unwise and counterproductive. The therapist must tune in to the rhythm of the patient.

But even the best analyzed and insightful therapist will find his or her patience taxed at times, and will have to deal with the empathic lapses that inevitably result. This is an important test of the therapist's continuing self-analysis and therapeutic skills, and often the success or failure of a long-term treatment hinges on it. As one matures, one becomes more patient, and this should manifest itself both in the life of the therapist and the patient. Patience can be understood either traditionally as the capacity of a strong ego to span time and withstand frustration, or as a manifestation of a strong cohesive sense of self that is not thrown into disequilibrium by the inevitable narcissistic wounds that a long-term psychotherapy entails.

References

Johnson, S. (1773). *A Dictionary of the English Language.* Beirut, Lebanon: Librairie du Liban, 1978.

Kardiner, A. (1977). *My Analysis with Freud: Reminiscences.* New York: Norton.

Muslin, H. (1989). Analysis terminable and interminable revisited: on self/selfobject fixations. In *Dimensions of Self Experience,* ed. A. Goldberg, pp. 143–167. Hillsdale, NJ: Analytic Press.

PATRON

Johnson's (1773) famous definition of a patron as "a wretch who supports with insolence and is paid with flattery" (p. 1412) is worth remembering when we consider to what extent third-party payers and insurance companies are involved in the financial support of treatment. The difficulty becomes even more complex when we remember that many young patients, especially adolescents, are having their bill paid by parents or other relatives. This always poses a considerable danger to the psychotherapy or psychoanalysis.

Third-party payers and insurance companies do not demand flattery, but they do have the insolence to demand a great deal of very personal information about the patient before they are willing to make payments. This places the patient in a terrible dilemma because there is no reasonable way to be assured that this information will remain private, even though the insurance companies or third-party payers maintain they will use caution. This becomes especially acute when insurance claims have to be filed through the insurance office at the patient's place of employment. I have often treated patients who were entitled to insurance payments but who refused to file the claims because they were certain that the insurance office at the patient's place of employment would use their case material for other purposes. I was not in a position to prove that this behavior was paranoid or to reassure the patients that it would not happen. The problem has reached a scandalous proportion in our country.

The flattery aspect of Johnson's definition is also pertinent; a serious countertransference involvement can take place between the therapist and the patient's family members who are paying for the treatment. Because they pay for the treatment, family members often demand the right to either interfere with the therapy or to have the therapist share with them all sorts of private information. They also use withholding of payment as a way to punish the therapist or even to punish the patient for changing. This enormously complicates good psychoanalytic or psychotherapeutic work.

In my clinical experience, it is often better to allow the patient to pay a very small fee for the sessions than to take a large fee from relatives who, however well meaning, can entangle the patient and therapist in a web of control and manipulation. The integrity of the therapist and the therapist's serious dedication to the patient's best interests are often demonstrated by how the therapist deals with patrons, and by what sacrifices the therapist is willing to make in order to protect the patient from the interference of patrons.

Reference

Johnson, S. (1773). *A Dictionary of the English Language.* Beirut, Lebanon: Librairie du Liban, 1978.

PENIS ENVY (SEE ALSO ENVY, FEMALE PSYCHOLOGY)

Freud (1925) wrote, "A little girl . . . makes her judgment and her decision in a flash. She has seen it and knows that she is without it and wants to have it" (p. 252). What is penis envy? Is it a defensive act, as Clower (1979) has said, a turning away from the mother "too far" so as to deny the longing for her? Is it a two-stage development of feminine identity, as Greenacre (summarized by Tyson 1982) believes? Or is penis envy just an invention of chauvinistic male psychoanalysts, as Horney (1967) thought—a view that some feminists still endorse? In Greenacre's theory, the first phase of penis envy is thought to take place in the middle of the second year and is frequently experienced by the girl as a normally transient narcissistic wound. However, some authors believe that this new awareness functions as a psychic organizer and, in normal development, leads to an increased feminine identification with the mother and a consequent firming of a healthy sense of femaleness.

In the second phase, at around the age of 3, after the foundations of female gender role identity have been laid, genital masturbation and exhibitionism increase. During this early phallic phase, penis preoccupation and penis envy reign supreme in what Greenacre (1953) refers to as the "second peak of the experience of envy" (p. 33). Resolution of this allows the girl to identify more fully with the mother's femininity and further consolidates the female gender identity, after which the girl is ready to enter into a true oedipal love relationship with the father.

Arlow (1986) describes a case illustrating the classical current psychoanalytic view of a woman's persistent unconscious wish for a penis. Other authors view penis envy as a function or expression of the narcissistic wounding from unsuccessful competition between girls and boys in our male-oriented culture. For Tyson (1982), rather than castration issues, "it is with little girls and boys alike, that the threat of narcissistic mortification and resulting loss of self-esteem at continuing oedipal failure provides an essential motivation for relinquishing oedipal wishes" (p. 79). Research on pathological resolution of the Oedipus complex is also much needed.

What light does self psychology throw on these problems? Elsewhere (see Chessick 1983) I discussed Marilyn Monroe's wish to have a baby as a pathological attempt to heal a defective self, as compared with the normal assertive feminine wish to have a child, as described by Kohut (1978). Schafer (1974) points out that there is a curious lack of interest in Freud's writings about the background of the so-called castration shock in girls. Schafer says this is due to Freud's evolutionary model, his preoccupation with the organs of reproduction in nineteenth-century biology. For Freud, a woman above all must yearn to reproduce and be prepared to love the child, or the species will not survive.

References

Arlow, J. (1986). Interpretation and psychoanalytic psychotherapy: a clinical illustration. In *The Transference in Psychotherapy,* ed. E. Schwaber, pp. 103–120. New York: International Universities Press.

Chessick, R. (1983). Marilyn Monroe: psychoanalytic pathography of a preoedipal disorder. *Dynamic Psychotherapy* 1:161–176.

Clower, V. (1979). Feminism and the new psychology of women. In *On Sexuality,* ed. T. B. Karasu, and C. Socarides, pp. 279–315. New York: International Universities Press.

Freud, S. (1925). Some psychical consequences of the anatomical distinction between the sexes. *Standard Edition* 19: 243–258.

Greenacre, P. (1953). Penis awe and its relation to penis envy. In *Emotional Growth,* New York: International Universities Press.

Horney, K. (1967). *Feminine Psychology.* New York: Norton.

Kohut, H. (1978). *The Search for the Self,* ed. P. Ornstein. New York: International Universities Press.

Schafer, R. (1974). Problems in Freud's psychology of women. *Journal of the American Psychoanalytic Association* 22: 459–485.

Tyson, P. (1982). A developmental line of gender identity, gender role, and choice of love object. *Journal of the American Psychoanalytic Association* 30:61–86.

PENSION

Johnson (1773) defines pension as follows: "An allowance made to anyone without an equivalent. In England it is generally understood to mean pay given to a state hireling for treason to his country" (p. 1424). His notorious definition should cause us to pause and reflect on the effect of offering psychotherapy or psychoanalysis for nothing or for a fee next to nothing. The patient experiences the psychoanalytic work being done as a gift, and is therefore most reluctant to feel or express rage at the therapist in the transference. The therapist has an inevitable sense of resentment, which sooner or later manifests itself in countertransference difficulties, no matter how well meaning the therapist may be. In those cases where the therapist is a student and works under supervision, and the patients know they are getting a reduced fee because of this, the situation is more honest and such problems are less likely to arise. But a therapist who accepts a long-term psychotherapy or psychoanalytic patient at a very low fee should seriously question himself or herself regarding secret or unconscious motivations. Self-analysis is required, lest there be treason to the patient.

Reference

Johnson, S. (1773). *A Dictionary of the English Language.* Beirut, Lebanon: Librairie du Liban, 1978.

PERVERSION

Johnson (1773) defines perversion as a corruption, a "change to something worse" (p. 1438). So the term has come to represent "something worse" than the normal genital heterosexual act; it connotes all sorts of judgmental terms such as "abnormality, aberration, distortion, dysfunction; any deviation from the correct, proper, expected, or normal range" (Campbell 1989, p. 534). A perversion refers to some deviation from the normal heterosexual means of reaching genital orgasm, see *DSM-III-R* (1987) for a classification.

Many of the so-called perversions are found to be part of normal sexual foreplay, although not all of them. The difference is that in the case of perversion, the behavior brings about genital orgasm, whereas in normal heterosexual behavior the act is only a minor part of foreplay leading to increasing sexual excitement. The activity of the perversion becomes an end in itself.

Freud (1905) believed that neuroses were the opposite of perversions. He argued that all children are polymorphously perverse in both their behavior and their fantasies, and that lying at the root of psychoneuroses and perverse behavior were these fantasies from the various stages of child psychosexual development. The fantasies themselves must be viewed as compromise formations among the id, the superego, and the demands of reality developed by the patient's ego. In the perversions the libidinal investments in certain behaviors are carried directly into adult life and not repressed, whereas in the psychoneuroses these wishes and behaviors are repressed and appear in the form of neurotic symptoms.

It should be remembered that the perversions are also compromise formations and have complex and multidetermined functions. An important unconscious fantasy that is crucial in many perversions is the denial of castration; at some deep level many patients with perversions attempt to disavow the anatomical distinction between the sexes. It has been recognized that perversions serve many other functions. For example, the exhibitionist is really assaulting women and expressing a hatred of and aggression toward them, beside reassuring himself by a woman's shock that he does have a penis.

Due to the long-standing negative connotations of the term "perversion," these disorders are often referred to as paraphilias or sexual deviations. In a paraphilia, what excites the patient is some unusual object or quality of the object; in a sexual deviation, behavior during sexual activity is clearly abnormal or is that usually seen only to a minor extent during foreplay.

The literature is replete with case examples of perversions, but it must be kept in mind that we may never see in the office a great many patients with perversions, given the proper partner and a not-too-dangerous perversion. Perversions are extremely difficult to treat and are often accompanied by a great many other neurotic and sometimes psychotic symptoms. I have treated a number of cases of perversion in which the particular perversion was stopped because it was extremely dangerous to the career or life of the patient or his or her partner, but this often resulted in a serious exacerbation of neurotic or paranoid symptoms. The neurotic or paranoid symptoms caused the patient great difficulty but threatened less danger from society and consequently appeared to the patient as a reasonable tradeoff. This is another way of saying that when the compromise formation that constitutes a perversion is broken up, the ego must find other compromise formations and the patient is far from cured. Kleinians in particular emphasize the sadistic nature of the perversions, and many tend to regard all perversions as a manifestation of the death instinct (see DEATH INSTINCT).

References

Campbell, R. (1989). *Psychiatric Dictionary*. New York: Oxford University Press.

Diagnostic and Statistical Manual of Mental Disorders (1987). 3rd ed.-rev. Washington, DC: American Psychiatric Association.

Freud, S. (1905). Three essays on the theory of sexuality. *Standard Edition* 7:125–243.

Johnson, S. (1773). *A Dictionary of the English Language*. Beirut, Lebanon: Librairie du Liban, 1978.

PHALLUS

The phallus, or male genital, has been used to connote a great many things, both in literature and in psychoanalysis. Freud used the concept of phallic phase to refer to a period beginning at about 2 or 3 years of age and lasting through the oedipal phase of development. During this period the phallus becomes the primary erogenous zone for both sexes. Also during this phase the psychosexual development of boys diverges from that of girls.

A "phallic woman" has been pejoratively defined as a woman who has so-called phallic personality traits involving aggression, assertiveness, and strength, characteristics usually associated with masculinity. A woman who asserts herself professionally or even socially, unfortunately is often so labeled.

Phallic narcissism refers to an overestimation of one's penis and a preoccupation with so-called phallic behavior or traits, as defined above. This often can become fixed into the phallic character disorder, which is now included under the narcissistic personality disorders in *DSM-III-R* (1987). Patients who suffer from phallic narcissism are traditionally viewed as dealing with unconscious castration anxiety. (Self psychology views narcissism quite differently; see NARCISSISM.) The so-called macho man is the classic example of this, but it should be pointed out that women can exhibit phallic narcissism by unconsciously equating their entire body as a phallus and displaying their body with the same abandon as "macho" activities. In such patients there is usually a strong unconscious dependency and attempt to deny this dependency by exhibitionism and aggressive activities. These aggressive activities may also be based on a concept of the penis as a sadistic or attacking weapon, and indeed, sexual behavior in a phallic narcissistic individual often has a sadistic component and conveys a depreciation of members of the opposite sex. At the extreme end of the interpretations of phallic narcissism and of the phallic character is the Kleinian theory (see OBJECT RELATIONS THEORY). Klein postulated an unconscious equation of the penis with the "bad breast" seen as a penetrating, destructive, and poisonous implement. Out of anxiety the patient identifies with the feared aggressor.

The concept of phallocentrism has been introduced recently by feminists to remind us that Western culture tends to exaggerate the importance of the phallus and of what is attributed to masculinity in the Western value system. Traits often attributed to femininity, such as passivity, masochism, and dependency, are often treated disparagingly.

Lacan (1978) labels the phallus as the signifier of the patient's basic desire, to be desired by the other, a notion he borrowed from Kojève's (1969) reading of Hegel. He sometimes uses the term to represent this general signifier and at other times to refer specifically to the penis, so the implication would be that the basic desire of the patient's mother is to have a penis. This is a form of very classical Freudianism, but it also involves a disparagement of women, which is found in many of Lacan's writings (see Mitchell and Rose 1982).

An outmoded term, the "phallic mother," represents a woman who is endowed in fantasy with a phallus. The image of a woman equipped with male sexual organs is often met with in dreams and fantasies.

References

Diagnostic and Statistical Manual of Mental Disorders (1987). 3rd ed.-rev. Washington, DC: American Psychiatric Association.

Kojève, A. (1969). Introduction to the Reading of Hegel: Lectures on the Phenomenology of the Spirit. Ithaca, NY: Cornell University Press.

Lacan, J. (1978). The Four Fundamental Concepts of Psycho-analysis, trans. A. Sheridan. New York: Norton.

Mitchell, J., and Rose, J., eds. (1982). Feminine Sexuality: Jacques Lacan and the Ecole Freudienne. New York: Norton.

PHANTASY (SEE ALSO FANTASY)

The term "phantasy" is used in the British psychoanalytic literature, especially in the writing of the Kleinians. For them, phantasy has a very specific and object-related meaning involving whole or part objects (see

OBJECT and OBJECT RELA-TIONS THEORY). These archaic self and object representations are imaginative activities underlying all subsequent thought and feeling (e.g., in the paranoid-schizoid and depressive positions).

Unconscious fantasies are very important, and the disagreement is only on the type and kind of fantasies that develop in the earliest years of life. For the Kleinians, "phantasies" are direct expressions of the death instinct and necessarily involve objects or part objects. For American ego psychologists, fantasies are compromise formations developed early in childhood to deal with the demands of the id, external reality, and the superego. Once these compromise formations are developed, they have a profound effect on the patient's further perceptions, judgments, and activities (see FANTASY).

PHANTOM LIMB (SEE ALSO ALLON)

An exploration of the concept of the phantom limb offers an excellent opportunity to consider the value of phenomenology to psychiatry and, in particular, the work of the phenomenologist-psychiatrist Erwin Straus (1891–1975). (For a concise review, see Melzack 1992.)

The phantom limb phenomenon represents a feeling an individual has that an extremity that has been lost is really present. This does not necessarily have to be an extremity of the body per se; for example, I noticed that when I stopped smoking a pipe I had the constant sensation that the pipe, which I used to have continuously in my hand or mouth, was still there. I often found myself reaching for it to light it or start to smoke it. Clearly, objects like a pipe or the violin of the professional violinist become closely associated with one's body image. The body is perceived through external tactile sensations and internal sensations of depth sensibility. The body representation in the phantom limb phenomenon becomes placed in the foreground because the patient has great difficulty in correlating it with the objective reality of the absence of an extremity.

As is well known to neurologists, the phantom gradually shrinks and the body image changes in due course in normal individuals. In most cases, it disappears into the stump. The remarkable ubiquity of this phenomenon indicates that it is not by itself abnormal or neurotic; only the prolonged persistence of it or the investment of the phantom limb with pain indicates emotional disturbance.

Straus (1966) emphasizes the way in which each human being organizes his or her experiences of the environment in perception and inner experience history. At the same time, he does not recognize the role of the unconscious, especially unconscious fantasy processes, in affecting an individual's perspective and experiences of the environment, as well as his or her organization of those experiences. Many concepts in psychoanalysis have their roots in physicalistic thinking, such as the environmental influences affecting the developing human being in self psychology and the influences of the parents and the child's internal representations of them in object relations theory. Straus insists that mental existence must be studied as an individual conscious historical continuum. Here his thinking is closer to that of Sartre (1981) in his studies of Flaubert. I think Straus would approve of the kind of progressive/regressive method used by Sartre in an effort to totalize the inner conscious continuum of the mental experiences of an individual that reflect what Sartre labels that individual's basic project.

Straus proposed to make a science of the life-historical experience of subjectivity the theoretical foundation for psychoanalysis, a historiological foundation emphasizing subject-centered experience. Whether psychoanalysis should be characterized as a hermeneutic of the historical stream of experience that Binswanger (May et al. 1958) called the "inner life history" or not, remains highly controversial.

One of the weaknesses of Straus's work for the American psychiatrist and psychoanalyst is that his terminology has become obsolete since the advent of DSM-III-R (1987). Furthermore, it has been shown that the "phobic neuroses" and panic disorders discussed by Straus in phenomenological terms can be in some cases traced to biochemical imbalances and respond relatively rapidly to proper psychopharmacological and/or behavioral treatment. My experience with Straus convinces me he would have welcomed this development and would have been eager to work it into his holistic biological theory, just as he did for patients with general paresis in his efforts to understand their inner life experience. More important for American psychoanalysts is the fact that, as Bräutigam (Straus 1982) explains, "Straus was more sympathetic with the luminous surface than with the deeplying passions and the human instinctual world, more at home with the real conflicts and existential wrong-attitudes than with the sexual and aggressive motives arising from the archaic depths" (p. 9).

This forms an unbridgeable gap between the work of Straus and the current work of many depth psychologists and psychoanalysts. Straus tended to stay meticulously with the conscious surface because he did not appreciate or concede the power of unconscious fantasy process in determining the patient's inner subjective life history. At the same time, Straus deserves credit for being one of the first thinkers to observe that Freud's metapsychology, based on a hydrodynamic model and utilizing such concepts as energy and cathexis, was really a vague notion that tended to produce a reductionism and obscurity rather than an understanding of the individual patient's experience. There has been a general acknowledgment that Freud's metapsychology represents an inadequate model of human mentation, and few psychoanalysts adhere strictly to it today (see METAPSYCHOLOGY).

There is an interesting affinity between the approach of Straus and that of Kohut's self psychology (see SELF PSYCHOLOGY). In both instances, there is an exceptional effort to get in touch with the way the patient is experiencing the world. The self psychologist does this through empathy and vicarious introspection, while the phenomenologist does this through meticulous study of the patient's conscious reports (see PHENOMENOLOGY).

It is clear that Straus (1982) was also much influenced by Husserl when he refers to the "natural attitude" (p. 26). He clearly opposes the Cartesian distinction between subject and object, which I think remained a stumbling block in the work of Husserl. One of the most important contributions of Straus was his attempt to develop an awareness in practicing psychiatrists and psychoanalysts that an understanding of the patient's inner experiences may be achieved through phenomenology. Both the methods of phenomenology and of self psychology are complementary to the more reductionistic or traditional psychoanalytic viewpoint.

One of the main gaps between the epistemology of psychoanalysis and the phenomenology of Erwin Straus is in his concept of the "existential-neurosis" (1982, p. 30). The traditional view sees neuroses as based on conflicts and compromise formations, but Straus emphasized the problems involved in various forms of human existence, a much more conscious psychology, again more akin to the approach of Sartre than to the approach of Freud. Depending on whether a neurosis is thought of as a conflict neurosis or an "existential-neurosis," the therapist's interventions will be quite different, so a major incompatibility arises.

The phenomenologist will concentrate on examining the meticulous details of the patient's lived experience, while the traditional psychoanalyst will rely on free association and interpretation to uncover unconscious conflicts and their concomitant fantasy processes. It should be clear from this why Straus's approach is more easily acceptable in the examination of organic syndromes, and much more controversial when it is applied to the neuroses or character disorders commonly seen in the outpatient work of a psychoanalyst.

References

Diagnostic and Statistical Manual of Mental Disorders (1987). 3rd ed.-rev. Washington, DC: American Psychiatric Association.

May, R., Angel, E., and Ellenberger, H., eds. (1958). Existence: A New Dimension in Psychiatry and Psychology. New York: Basic Books.

Melzack, R. (1992). Phantom limbs. Scientific American pp. 120–126.

Sartre, J-P. (1981). The Family Idiot: Gustave Flaubert, 1821–1857, trans. C. Cosman. Chicago: University of Chicago Press.

Straus, E. (1966). Phenomenological Psychology: The Selected Papers of Erwin Straus, trans. E. Eng. New York: Basic Books.

_____ (1982). Man, Time, and World: Two Contributions to Anthropological Psychology, trans. D. Moss. Pittsburgh, PA: Duquesne University Press.

PHENOMENOLOGY

Phenomenology may be thought of as a style of thinking that suspends traditional scientific explanation and attempts to get in touch with the primordial experiences underlying all our more mature constructions of the world. Edmund Husserl (1913) first introduced his phenomenological method as a way of doing philosophy in the early 1900s. His pupil, Martin Heidegger, took up this method, although he completely changed Husserl's orientation. Heidegger applied it to investigating the human condition, his so-called existential analytic, in his most famous and influential work, *Being and Time* (1962). This remarkable work spawned a school of psychiatric treatment on the European continent whose most prominent practitioners were Ludwig Binswanger and Menard Boss, among others. All of these in turn, however, presented a hodgepodge of approaches, each of which differed from Husserl's original method and intent (Kockelmans 1967). Their publications pose formidable difficulties for United States psychiatrists, who as a rule are not familiar with philosophy, in spite of Galen's (1952) famous treatise entitled "That the Best Physician Is Also a Philosopher," written about 160 A.D.

Phenomenology received a brief flurry of interest in the 1950s in the United States when a small school of "existential psychiatrists" claiming an affinity to phenomenology appeared. It is only after two further developments that the phenomenological approach has again claimed attention here in psychiatry. The first of these was Kohut's (1971, 1977) psychology of the self, with its emphasis on the sense of self as it appears at birth and emerges with vicissitudes throughout various phases of development. This led to a resurgence of interest in infant research among psychiatrists, although Kohut confined his work to the clinical situation. Infant research lends itself nicely to a phenomenological approach, a description of the observed infant experience without prior logical or conceptual categories, since whatever is observed is prelinguistic. This is not to be confused with the pioneering work of Mahler and her colleagues (1975), who approached their infant observations with strongly held theoretical preconceptions (Brody 1982, Tanguay 1977). The second development came from a new generation of psychiatrists in Europe, mostly German, who took their starting point from the extensions and modifications of Heidegger's work by Gadamer (1982; see HERMENEUTICS).

Phenomenology requires the psychiatrist and psychotherapist to be tolerant of unfamiliar terms and ways of stating things, of difficult new concepts that are not easily and immediately grasped but require prolonged thought, and of ways of approach and presentation that, springing from the European and especially the German philosophical tradition, are different from the pragmatic tradition of the United States.

Since we all tend to stay with the familiar and the comfortable, a certain effort will be required from the psychiatrist or psychotherapist to wrench himself or herself from routine thinking and to concentrate in a different manner. This effort is made more difficult by the current trend toward "medicalization" of psychiatry, which tends to lose vital information about the total patient that phenomenology attempts to retrieve.

The Greek word φαινόμενον (phainomenon) comes from the verb φαίνευθαι (phainesthai), which means "that which shows itself." Phenomenology attempts to return to the primordial data of experience, that which shows itself in the manner in which it shows itself. Phenomena are always prior to our theories and concepts; they are immediate data but they are not simply "appearances," for appearances are always appearances of something, whereas phenomena are that something which shows itself. They are primary, they are what is.

The most important feature of phenomenology is that it is in some ways a nonempirical science. It does not describe empirically observable matters of fact, and it does not lend itself to what Heidegger called the "calculative thinking" that pervades our time. Thus phenomenological statements are not considered true if they correspond to the observation of facts thought of as "out there" in "reality"; they are considered true if they accurately describe phenomena experienced, and false if they do not. The phenomenologist does not frame theories; instead, he or she examines and describes phenomena as they present themselves to a relatively unprejudiced view.

Husserl (1913) believed that phenomenology offers us a presuppositionless form of inquiry, since it insists on no prior theoretical commitment and demands a dedication to try to operate without any unexamined assumptions. Husserl's main idea was that the examination of the phenomena yielded the truths of phenomenology directly—it brought us to the things themselves. Using his method, Husserl believed, things speak for themselves; that is to say, instead of understanding through controlled experiments based on scientific hypotheses, understanding is through an undergoing of experience.

The confusing method of phenomenology was originally developed by Husserl under the influence of Franz Brentano (1838–1917), a philosopher-psychologist who developed the notion of "intentionality": all acts of consciousness are directed toward some intentional object. That consciousness is always a consciousness of something became a fundamental theme of Husserl's philosophy. According to Jones (1953), Freud attended Brentano's seminar in philosophy once a week for a couple of years, and some of his teleological thinking may be traced to Brentano's influence. Husserl first used the term "phenomenologic method" in 1900, and for him it was a way of achieving philosophic certainty. Husserl's (1913) final method attempts what he called transcendental-phenomenological reduction; as a starting point, he did not permit the selection out of experience of certain specific things, sensations, and feelings, since to do so would assume classificatory principles about the world. Thus phenomenological statements cannot be called empirical, because empirical scientific statements are about already assumed "things" out there. Phenomenological statements attempt what Husserl called presuppositionless inquiry—no theories, just descriptions of phenomena as they present themselves to an unprejudiced view.

Husserl defined this starting point for phenomenological reduction as the "bracketing of experience," or *epoché*, the unbiased contemplation of phenomena without intellectual preconsiderations. Then, in a controversial methodological step, he proposed the use of "imaginative variations" to intuit the essence of the phenomena. So for Husserl, phenomenological statements are not empirical; they are ultimately statements about the intuited essence of the phenomena, and in this way they lead to philosophical certainty. Most subsequent proponents of phenomenology have rejected this further step, a rejection that caused Husserl great disappointment.

From the point of view of the psychotherapist, the phenomenological stance is to examine one's reaction to what is simply there in a felt experience; the therapist does not disconnect, isolate, or interpret aspects of this experience. *Epoché*, or the bracketing of experience, demands refrainment from judgment about morals, values, causes, background, and even from separating the subject (patient) and objective observer (therapist). One pays special attention to one's experience or state of consciousness in the presence of a patient. The therapist must continue to observe and listen, staying with the patient's material and directly experiencing the patient rather than searching for hidden processes.

Phenomenologists warn that a distance can be created between the therapist and the patient by the standard interviewing technique, a gap that may be unproductively filled by abundant verbal material and analytic ideas, conceptions, and theories. They advise focusing on the emotional interchange, staying strictly with the phenomena presented by the patient and concentrating on the experienced interaction with the patient.

Phenomenological reduction of the cognitive and emotional distance between the patient and the therapist, then, is the crucial procedure, leading to a true meeting or encounter (Jaspers 1972). The application of phenomenology to psychotherapy raises the valid question of whether we as therapists can be sure that we are seeing and hearing our patients as they really are, rather than as projections of our theories about them. The aim of phenomenological study is to rediscover the whole living person and how being in the world is experienced by that person and those around him or her (see Van Den Berg 1955).

All the modes of human lived experience can be described phenomenologically and are interlocked with our constituted self (Chessick 1992), so that no hidden essences or entities are postulated. This eliminates the whole infrastructure of metapsychology, the disease classifications of *DSM-III-R,* and, above all, the classical notion of an independent neutral subject (e.g., the psychiatrist) observing the outside world (e.g., the patient) through collecting data and developing empirical and quantitative laws of cause and effect.

Phenomenology has a useful application in psychiatry and psychoanalysis. We know that the phenomena of the encounter between one person and another, including that between the therapist and the patient, always are interactively or dialectically constituted, and that diagnoses and the postulation of psychic entities, commonly made on the basis of the phenomena generated in that encounter, are therefore relative to both the observer and the observed, or the therapist and the patient. This is consistent with quantum physics and the whole postmodern approach in philosophy and hermeneutics.

The famous Husserlian slogan, *Zu den Sachen selbst!* (To the things themselves) reflected Husserl's goal, to intuit the essences of the things themselves. Although not many philosophers still follow his methodology for that purpose today, *Zu den Sachen selbst!* could be taken as a slogan to admonish us to concentrate on treatment of the whole patient, examining and describing the whole of the phenomena the patient presents, including the phenomena of our interaction with the patient as we experience it. This *is* the patient.

In Husserl's terminology, the act of experiencing contains two phases. The first of these is *noesis* or the *noetic phase,* in which sense data are constituted as meaningful by the subject. In order to do this, a second or *noematic phase* is necessary, in which the "objects" of experience are constituted by the intentionality of the experience. Such "objects," invested with the subject's meaning and emotions, are called *noemata* (a single such "object" is called *noema*). Human sciences must be built not on so-called natural objects, which are abstractions from *noemata* in which the intentional component is suspended, but on the *noemata* themselves. Otherwise we lose the vital human component and end up with less than the full experienced reality. We also must know what kind of noematic world the person constitutes around himself or herself that makes his or her choice of behavior appropriate.

As a clinical example, Pao (1979) urged us to consider the diagnosis of schizophrenia not so much on the basis of Bleuler's famous criteria, but as a function of the kind of ambience the therapist experiences, that peculiar sensation of relating to someone who is both there and not there, which generates our considerable personal discomfort. We might extend this further by employing Kohut's (1971) method of empathy (see EMPATHY), to identify the self-experience such a patient has by using trial identification, trying to see how we feel if we can put ourselves in the place of a patient who has to relate to us in this matter. Although Kohut's method goes beyond phenomenology, one cannot help but focus on the self-experience that is so central to Kohut's approach.

Phenomenologists ask, What self-conception or self-image would make suicide seem like a reasonable alternative for dealing with personal problems? How can we make sense of paranoia as a way of being in the world—what experiences led the person to constitute the objects (noemata) of his or her experience in this manner?

A phenomenological approach to patients commonly labeled borderline is, in my opinion, more fruitful than a pejorative diagnosis, which immediately shifts the interaction into an adversarial mode. Atwood and Stolorow (1984) have tried to apply their version of "psychoanalytic phenomenology" to this condition. R. D. Laing (1960) called diagnosis a "political act," referring to what it means to have the diagnostic label of schizophrenia pinned on one—what it means to the world of the patient and to the very therapy itself. It is more useful therapeutically if we try to articulate the phenomenology of the experience with the patient and convey an empathic understanding of it rather than try to "scientifically" explain it by postulating and interpreting, especially in the early phase of treatment.

Phenomenology with subsequent hermeneutic exegesis hopefully leads to better recognition for patients as to how others may experience them and how their difficulties in living come about through the generation of maladaptive interactional phenomena. It also removes the onus of being diagnosed as having secret malevolent representations carried about in one's psyche like some sort of poison that threatens to contaminate those around one. It allows the patient to preserve self-esteem during the investigation rather than to feel primitive and contemptible. It preserves the humanity of the patient and the vital sense of wholeness or autonomy of the self, even during the investigation.

Husserl, Heidegger, Sartre, Merleau-Ponty, and such existential psychotherapists as Binswanger and Boss use a different conception of phenomenology, as do modern investigators (see Edie 1965, 1967, 1969). They share very little in common, which, along with much obscure writing, accounts for some of the confusion in the field. For each investigator we must decide what is their phenomenological method and try to evaluate the method by the way the investigator actually applies it and by what information it provides us that is complementary to and enhances what can be obtained by the standard scientific approach. Unfortunately, sometimes a maximum of jargon conceals a minimum of information.

References

Atwood, G., and Stolorow, R. (1984). *Structures of Subjectivity: Explorations in Psychoanalytic Phenomenology.* Hillsdale, NJ: Analytic Press.

Brody, S. (1982). Psychoanalytic theories of

infant development and its disturbances: a critical evaluation. *Psychoanalytic Quarterly* 51:526–597.

Chessick, R. (1992). *What Constitutes the Patient in Psychotherapy.* Northvale, NJ: Jason Aronson.

Edie, J., ed. (1965). *An Invitation to Phenomenology.* Chicago: Quadrangle Books.

———— (1967). *Phenomenology in America.* Chicago: Quadrangle Books.

———— (1969). *New Essays in Phenomenology.* Chicago: Quadrangle Books.

Gadamer, G. (1982). *Truth and Method.* New York: Crossroad.

Galen (1952). *Selections.* In *Great Books of the Western World,* vol. 10, ed. R. Hutchins, pp. 107–215. Chicago: Encyclopedia Britannica.

Heidegger, M. (1962). *Being and Time,* trans. J. Macquarrie and E. Robinson. New York: Harper & Row

Husserl, E. (1913). *Ideas: General Introduction to Pure Phenomenology,* trans. W. Gibson. New York: Macmillan, 1952.

Jaspers, K. (1972). *General Psychopathology.* Chicago: University of Chicago Press.

Jones, E. (1953). *The Life and Work of Sigmund Freud,* vol. 1. New York: Basic Books.

Kockelmans, J., ed. (1967). *Phenomenology.* Garden City, NY: Anchor.

Kohák, E. (1978). *Idea and Experience.* Chicago: University of Chicago Press.

Kohut, H. (1971). *The Analysis of the Self.* New York: International Universities Press.

———— (1977). *The Restoration of the Self.* New York: International Universities Press.

Laing, R. (1960). *The Divided Self.* New York: Pantheon Books.

Mahler, M., Pine, F., and Bergman, A. (1975). *The Psychological Birth of the Human Infant.* New York: Basic Books.

Pao, P. (1979). *Schizophrenic Disorders.* New York: International Universities Press.

Tanguay, P. (1977). Review of "The Psychological Birth of the Human Infant." *Journal of the American Academy of Child Psychiatry* 16:542–544.

Van Den Berg, J. (1955). *The Phenomenological Approach to Psychiatry.* Springfield, IL: Thomas.

PHYSICIANLY VOCATION

Stone (1961) is convinced that the nuances of the therapist's attitude can determine the difference between a lonely vacuum and a controlled but warm and human situation. He defines physicianly vocation as a kindly and helpful, broadly tolerant, and friendly interest in one's patients. Physicianly vocation is a manifestation of maturity on the part of the therapist, of his or her sense of identity, of a lifelong vocation, of the capacity for a commitment and a real relationship to another individual. It is not role playing. If there are excessively severe deficits in human response on the part of the therapist, human responses that the patient may reasonably expect or require, there are going to be very serious transference distortions and the therapy will flounder. Greenson (1968) echoes this thought, when he writes: "The patient will be influenced not only by the content of our work but by how we work, the attitude, the manner, the mood, the atmosphere in which we work" (p. 212).

The ambience we offer greatly affects the patient whether we like it or not. The patient may react to and identify with precisely those aspects of us that are not necessarily conscious to us. For example, if a patient's child is seriously ill and she comes in crying and worrying about it, and the therapist insists on continuing without discussing the matter at all and shows no concern, this will have a profound effect because it represents a lack of normal human response. It will insure a deleterious and destructive reaction sooner or later in the therapy situation.

Baudry (1991) identifies the analyst's beliefs and attitudes, personal style, and characteristic reactions as crucial components of his or her technique. He defines the analyst's character as "the complex organization of stable recurrent traits, behaviors, and attitudes which define him" (p. 918). A derivative of this is the analyst's style, which denotes the "behavioral components of the analyst's professional identity" (p. 919). Patients are intimidated by aspects of our style and behavior, "which they sense is invested with a certain sense of pride and is not open to question; this is often conveyed in nonverbal ways" (p. 926). The sicker and more repressed patients are most influenced by these factors, and they show up especially when it is not clear how to proceed, for example in the introduction of so-called parameters (see PARAMETER). Certain character traits are designed to evoke particular types of responses in others in order to actualize a wished-for relationship existing in fantasy. These styles and character traits of the analyst have a profound effect in determining the analyst's day-to-day clinical decisions and interventions and in facilitating or stalemating the treatment, as well as in influencing consequent transference–countertransference interactions.

As the scope of psychoanalytic treatment has expanded, we see a variety of transference–countertransference interactions that can no longer be accounted for by simply postulating the revival of oedipal wishes now aimed across the repression barrier at the representation of the analyst. In patients with substantial preoedipal damage, more archaic phenomena manifest themselves, thought by some to be an indication of an ego deficit and by others to be the result of intrapsychic conflict and compromise formation. These archaic phenomena pose an immediate challenge to the character and style of the analyst. The clinician will have to decide in each case what is the optimal response, using evidence provided by the patient's history and unfolding transference.

Unfortunately, there are a number of individuals who try to become psychotherapists because they are unable to relate in a normal way to other people. In the situation of psychotherapy, the psychotherapist has a privileged and controlling position, and people with schizoid anxieties sometimes become psychotherapists in order to maintain that privilege and control in their relationships with others. Because of this, the lack of human response profoundly affects the course of the treatment and often results in treatment failure, stalemate, or massive acting out by the patient alone or by the patient together with the psychotherapist.

The best example of the proper human response to patients is provided by Freud himself in some of his case histories. For example, Lipton (1977, 1979) discusses Freud's behavior and stance to Paul Lorenz, as described in Freud's (1909) case history of an obsessional neurosis.

The lack of a physicianly vocation is one of the most common and serious reasons for the failure of intensive psychotherapy and psychoanalysis. The most valuable contribution of the psychology of the self (see SELF PSYCHOLOGY) has been to focus on the physicianly vocation and the empathy it implies as an important healing element in psychoanalytic and psychotherapeutic treatment.

References

Baudry, F. (1991). The relevance of the analyst's character and attitudes to his work. *Journal of the American Psychoanalytic Association* 39:917–938.

Freud, S. (1909). Notes upon a case of obsessional neurosis. *Standard Edition* 10:153–318.

Greenson, R. (1968). *The Technique and Practice of Psychoanalysis.* New York: International Universities Press.

Lipton, S. (1977). The advantages of Freud's technique as shown in his analysis of the Rat Man. *International Journal of Psycho-Analysis* 58:255–273.

_____ (1979). An addendum to "The advantages of Freud's technique as shown in his analysis of the Rat Man." *International Journal of Psycho-Analysis* 60:215–216.

Stone, L. (1961). *The Psychoanalytic Situation.* New York: International Universities Press.

PLASTICITY OF THE LIBIDO

This is essentially the opposite of adhesiveness of the libido (see ADHESIVENESS OF THE LIBIDO). In some ways, too much plasticity of the libido can lead to difficulties in the treatment because the transference is often fleeting and thus the transference interpretations cannot be based on any strong trend. Patients with too much plasticity of the libido will have difficulty forming relationships of any but the most superficial nature. Freud did not use this term as commonly as he used adhesiveness of the libido.

POSITION (SEE OBJECT RELATIONS THEORY)

PREJUDICE (SEE HERMENEUTICS)

PRIMAL REPRESSION (SEE REPRESSION)

PRIMAL SCENE

The term *primal scene* is used ambiguously in the psychoanalytic literature. At times it refers to the child's actual observation of parental intercourse. More accurately, it refers to the child's conception of the parents having intercourse, a combination of reality and important fantasy. The resulting conception is a compromise formation formed by the immature ego to deal with the id, superego, and external world.

The child's fantasies or recollections of parental intercourse woven together often contain a sadomasochistic component. It is often impossible to determine in psychoanalysis whether the patient as a child actually witnessed parental intercourse or whether much of the material around the primal scene represents the child's primitive conception of what parental intercourse is like. This makes very little difference as far as the great importance of primal scene material in determining the patient's relationships with people and sexual activity is concerned. Psychic reality is what counts in the unconscious, and, as Arlow (1985) explains, "Patients whose free associations, symptomatology, and life history clearly reflect the effects of a primal scene experience rarely recover the memory of the event" (p. 533).

Whether or not primal scene material will be traumatic for the child usually depends less on the nature of what has been observed than on the child's basic relationship with the parents. One can generalize that when primal scene material seems to have been very traumatic for the child, there was probably a basic difficulty in those relationships. Further evidence for this is in the fact that in many societies where children frequently and openly witness parental intercourse there are no observable consistent psychopathological effects. Arlow (1985) concludes, "What constitutes trauma is not inherent in the actual, real event, but rather in the individual's response to the disorganizing, disruptive combination of impulses and fears integrated into a set of unconscious fantasies" (p. 533).

Reference

Arlow, J. (1985). The concept of psychic reality and related problems. *Journal of the American Psychoanalytic Association* 33: 521–535.

PRIMARY IDENTIFICATION

Freud (1917) described this as a form of internalization that occurs before one can speak of object loss because it takes place prior to the infant's clear differentiation between the self and the object. It is an immediate and direct early form of internalization. Primary identification must be distinguished from later forms of incorporation, identification, or introjection, all of which postulate the capacity to distinguish between the internal and the external world (see IDENTIFICATION, INTROJECTION, INCORPORATION). Some authors refer to the latter as secondary internalizations.

According to LaPlanche and Pontalis (1973), Freud does not use the term very often, but when he does, he (1921, 1923) means it as a boy's identification with the father. Freud considers this a direct and immediate identification that takes place earlier than any love-object cathexis. But other authors use the term to represent the infant's bond to the mother, the first relationship before the differentiation between the ego and the external world has been firmly established. It is still thought of, as Freud (1921) says, as "the original form of emotional tie with an object" (p. 107). Although it is not an easy concept to articulate, it is clear that primary identification is extremely important. It has to do with the infant's feeling of fusion or oneness with the mother before it has discovered that others and objects are separate from it.

In preoedipal cases, where there is a primary identification with a pathological mother, extreme difficulties arise in achieving the very basic skills of adaptation. These "apraxias," as Gedo (1988) calls them, may be global or specific in nature, depending on the pathology of the mother (see BEYOND INTERPRETATION).

In an early discussion of the management of archaic transferences Gedo (1981) writes as a case example, "I persisted, in spite of the lengthy rages provoked by this policy, in consistently pointing out the disavowed magical ideation at the root of the patient's behavior, including the enactments in the analytic situation. Only the cognitive grasp of the actualities of her performances permitted the patient to gain insight into their sources in the identification with her mother" (p. 113). As Gedo explains, somewhere around 18 months of age, the prevalence of the magical ideation in the patient "will be decisively influenced by the quality of the familial matrix." He continues, "I think it is entirely likely that grandiose fantasies may not be 'endogenous' at all but are entirely *learned*" (p. 112).

The appearance of archaic demands, says Gedo, are compensatory efforts to patch over developmental deficits, skills that the patient lacks. He calls these deficits an accumulation of functional handicaps produced by early developmental vicissitudes. Gedo (1981) believes that "in such cases, psychoanalysis must be attempted to correct the structuralization of maladaptive patterns" (p. 57), a kind of repair job applied to the early background practices that constitute the fore-understanding of the individual.

Gedo goes so far as to insist that selfobject needs, claimed by Kohut to be present throughout life, "may well disappear if patients succeed in mastering psychological skills they failed to acquire in childhood" (p. 175), a contention that places him in direct opposition to Kohut's theories. For Gedo, the selfobject transferences described by Kohut really represent an attempt to mask inadequacies at presymbolic levels of functioning through the adaptive use of external assistance. Thus, for Gedo, "Everyone to a large extent determines his own unfavorable destiny" (p. 30), and rationalizations cover the self-restrictive or self-damaging enactments "that could be stopped if only patients recognized that options are open to them" (p. 30).

In a clinically valuable comment, Gedo points out that people with overwhelming psychological deficits can reach adulthood and adapt adequately by learning to imitate the behavior of other adults, "although they usually feel imposturous and fraudulent while doing so" (p. 61). Or they may adapt through a symbiosis to a selfobject; even their use of the couch is primarily for a holding experience. Interpretations are heard as soothing proof of caring, regardless of their content, which is ignored (Feinsilver 1983).

There seems to be a congruence between Heidegger's (1962) emphasis on background practices, which cannot be fully articulated and which form the grounding of all meaning and experience, and Gedo's attribution of psychopathology to failures in the proper inculcation of these practices. This has extremely important ramifications for the practice of intensive psychotherapy with borderline and other preoedipally damaged patients. The congruence of findings in these two separate methods of investigation lend support to the conclusions of each and form a fascinating field for the future investigation of primary identification and its consequences.

References

Feinsilver, D. (1983). Reality, transitional relatedness, and containment in the borderline. *Contemporary Psychoanalysis* 19: 537–569.

Freud, S. (1917). Mourning and melancholia. *Standard Edition* 14:237–258.

———— (1921). Group psychology and analysis of the ego. *Standard Edition* 18: 67–143.

———— (1923). The ego and the id. *Standard Edition* 19:3–66.

Gedo, J. (1981). *Advances in Clinical Psychoanalysis.* New York: International Universities Press.

———— (1986). *Conceptual Issues in Psychoanalysis: Essays in History and Method.* Hillsdale, NJ: Analytic Press.

———— (1988). *The Mind in Disorder: Psychoanalytic Models of Pathology.* Hillsdale, NJ: Analytic Press.

Heidegger, M. (1962). *Being and Time,* trans. J. Macquarrie and E. Robinson. New York: Harper & Row.

Laplanche, J., and Pontalis, J. (1973). *The Language of Psychoanalysis,* trans. D. Nicholson-Smith. New York: Norton.

PRIMARY LOVE

Balint (1952) defines primary love as object love beginning in early infancy. He denies that there is such a thing as primary narcissism and argues that the infant reaches out with object love for the mother from the beginning of life. Thus narcissism in children as well as adults would all be of a secondary nature, because it involves one's love for and gratification of one's self. What is basic is active object love, a primary direct love for the mother—which of course is an egoistic way of loving originally and exclusively directed at the mother.

Furthermore, says Balint, maternal love is the instinctual counterpart of the infant's primary love. Just as the mother is to the child, so the child is to the mother an object of gratification. This concept of primary love, an object love, and not narcissism as characterizing the beginning of life is a revolutionary reorientation from Freud's basic theories (see INSTINCT and OBJECT), although in his later work (Greenberg and Mitchell 1983) Freud seems to have shifted toward the notion of primary object relatedness occurring very early in life.

References

Balint, M. (1952). *Primary Love and Psycho-Analytic Technique.* New York: Liveright.
Greenberg, J., and Mitchell, S. (1983). *Object Relations in Psychoanalytic Theory.* Cambridge, MA: Harvard University Press.

PRIMARY NARCISSISM (SEE NARCISSISM)

PRINCIPLE OF CONSTANCY (SEE ALSO NIRVANA PRINCIPLE)

The principle of constancy is defined by Freud (1920) as: "The mental apparatus endeavors to keep the quantity of excitation present in it as low as possible or at least to keep it constant" (p. 9). A common confusion tends to occur between Freud's notion of the pleasure principle and the principle of constancy (which Freud later labeled the Nirvana principle) since at the beginning Freud himself assumed that these two principles were either closely correlated or identical. This is one of those subjects on which Freud changed his views several times; the appropriate references for his various viewpoints are given in "Instincts and Their Vicissitudes" (1915).

Since conditions, such as sexual excitement, in which there is a state of increasing tension can be pleasurable, it seems clear that the principle of constancy and the pleasure principle cannot be identical. Freud's final conclusion rests on the suggestion that the pleasurable or unpleasurable quality of a state may be related to a rhythm of the changes in the quantity of excitation present. In "Beyond the Pleasure Principle" (1920) he regards the pleasure principle as a modification of the principle of constancy (the Nirvana principle). In his final speculation he maintains that the principle of constancy comes from the death instinct, and its modification into the pleasure principle is due to the influence of the life instinct (see DEATH INSTINCT). The principle of constancy has been largely discredited by recent research on the physiology of the brain, the psychological functioning of infants, and sensory deprivation experiments (Lichtenberg 1983).

References

Freud, S. (1915). Instincts and their vicissitudes. *Standard Edition* 14:109–140.
———— (1920). Beyond the pleasure principle. *Standard Edition* 18:3–64.
Lichtenberg, J. (1983). *Psychoanalysis and Infant Research.* Hillsdale, NJ: Analytic Press.

PROJECTION, PROJECTIVE IDENTIFICATION

The infant has little in the way of a barrier against the internal impulses of its id. One of the ways it can deal with these primitive impulses is to perceive them as coming from outside itself. This early and primitive attempt to deal with unacceptable discomfort evolves into the defense mechanism of projection.

In projection one's own ideas or impulses are cast upon another. When used to an extreme, projection interferes with reality testing. It is the predominant mechanism in patients with paranoia (see PARANOIA). Freud (1911) described it in connection with Schreber's delusions of persecution, the result of denial, projection, and reversal.

Klein (1975) developed the concept of projective identification, which has been defined differently by different authors and has given rise to a vast literature. For Klein, projective identification had two aspects, one intrapsychic and the other interpersonal. First, projective identification is characterized by a forceful, aggressive evacuation in fantasy, consisting of a penetration into the object and a reinternalization of the object that was injured, which may lead to depression, or a reinternalization of the object that was rendered hostile, which may lead to persecutory hypochondria. It also represents a very primitive means of communication, and leads to "beyond the countertransference" distress in the therapist and to interpersonal interaction. So Klein inconsistently conceived of projective identification both as a fantasy and as an interpersonal relationship, an interactional process.

Kernberg (1975, 1976, 1980) views projective identification as solely intrapsychic; for him, it represents an incomplete projection. He presents three case illustrations of projection and projective identification that are worthy of serious study (Kernberg 1987). In projection there is first the repressing of the intolerable, then the projecting of it onto the object, and finally the "separating or distancing [of] oneself from the object to fortify the defensive effort" (p. 796). In projective identification, which Kernberg views as more primitive, there is a similar projection of the intolerable onto the object, but the patient maintains a relationship with the object, now experienced as what has been projected, and "tries to control the object in a continuing effort to defend against the intolerable experience, and, unconsciously, in an actual interaction with the object, leads the object to experience what has been projected onto him" (p. 796).

At the basis of projective identification, patients are thought to place into the analyst whatever self or object representations they wish to place there, a view leading to more therapeutic focus on preoedipal fantasies and processes. A study of projective identification operating in the therapeutic process emphasizes the patient's earliest internalized object relations and yields data on how the patient as an infant organized these relations into self and object representations and then projected and reintrojected various aspects of these images. Understanding these processes clarifies the patient's relationships in the present because all such relationships are perceived and reacted to through the spectacles of these early organized self and object representations (see Ogden 1979).

The assumption here is that the infantile ego is capable of such organization; recent research on infants

(Stern 1985) suggests that this is unlikely. Empirical investigation of infants carries the hope that, as we come to understand the capacities and limitations of the mind of the infant and child, we will have better criteria on which to choose or reject psychoanalytic models (Lichtenberg 1983).

References

Freud, S. (1911). Psycho-analytic notes on an autobiographical account of a case of paranoia (dementia paranoides). *Standard Edition* 12:3–82.

Kernberg, O. (1975). *Borderline Conditions and Pathological Narcissism.* New York: Jason Aronson.

_____ (1976). *Object Relations Theory and Clinical Psychoanalysis.* New York: Jason Aronson.

_____ (1980). *Internal World and External Reality.* New York: Jason Aronson.

_____ (1987). Projection and projective identification: developmental and clinical aspects. *Journal of the American Psychoanalytic Association* 35:795–819.

Klein, G. (1975). *Envy and Gratitude and Other Works, 1946–1963.* New York: Delta.

Lichtenberg, J. (1983). *Psychoanalysis and Infant Research.* Hillsdale, NJ: Analytic Press.

Ogden, T. (1979). On projective identification. *International Journal of Psycho-Analysis* 60:357–373.

Stern, D. (1985). *The Interpersonal World of the Infant: A View from Psychoanalysis and Developmental Psychology.* New York: Basic Books.

PROJECTIVE COUNTERIDENTIFICATION

When excessive projective identification occurs (see PROJECTION), the psychotherapist may deal with it in several ways. He or she may immediately and equally violently reject what the patient is attempting to project, may use other personal defense mechanisms, may postpone or displace the reaction to other individuals, or may counteridentify with the projection. As described by Grinberg (1962), the analyst is not consciously perceiving the projection but "may have the feeling of being no longer his own self and of unavoidably becoming transformed into the object which the patient, unconsciously, wanted him to be" (p. 202). This situation of projective counteridentification may be brief or may persist for a long time, with the ensuing possibility that "the analyst will resort to all kinds of rationalizations in order to justify his attitude or his bewilderment" (p. 203). For those who accept the existence of this Kleinian mechanism in the psychotherapeutic interaction, the analyst is described as then behaving "as if he had *really and correctly* acquired, by assimilating them, the aspects that were projected on to him" (p. 205).

Reference

Grinberg, L. (1962). On a specific aspect of countertransference due to the patient's projective identification. In *Classics in Psychoanalytic Technique,* ed. R. Langs, pp. 201–206. New York: Jason Aronson, 1981.

PROTECTIVE SHIELD (REIZSCHUTZ)

Freud (1920) used the term *Reizschutz,* or stimulus barrier, in *Beyond the Pleasure Principle* to account for a protection of the infant against external excitation. Freud points out that there is no similar protective shield within the infant against stimulation coming from within. One way of dealing with internal stimuli is to experience them as coming from without the organism and then protect one's self by the use of the protective shield (see PROJECTION). The notion of *Reizschutz* has a physiologic implication in Freud's work, but it seems to me that the most important *Reizschutz* for the infant, metaphorically speaking, is the mother.

The mother has the function of intuitively protecting the infant from excessive stimulation from the external world. It is painful, tragic, and excruciating to watch a situation in which the mother does not perform this function. The infant is clearly overwhelmed by the external stimuli and, in my own observations, seems to put itself into a sort of stupor; I have even noticed this in dogs who are exposed to intense stimuli. I think in a household where the infant is not properly protected against external stimuli as, for example, where there is marital skew and the father is excessively intense and even overtly physical with the infant and the mother does nothing to prevent it, the chronic exposure to overwhelming stimuli damages the infant's psychic apparatus. In other households the infant is exposed and unprotected from the continual quarreling among siblings and parents, and the blaring of a TV set that is on at high volume for much of the day and night.

I believe this may well account for some of the difficulty that underprivileged children in the third world or in the United States have with socialization and learning when they reach school age. These children have taught themselves to live in a chronic stupor or perhaps even in an autistic world, and they emerge from this stupor only with excessive pressure, all too quickly returning to it when the pressure is relieved. I believe that these children enter school already with a serious handicap because the mother has not performed an important protective function for them. The notion of *Reizschutz* deserves more attention in the current literature.

Reference

Freud, S. (1920). Beyond the pleasure principle. *Standard Edition* 18:3–64.

PSEUDOHOMOSEXUALITY

Ovesey (1969) attempts to distinguish between homosexuality and pseudohomosexuality. He argues that anxiety about homosexuality has three motivational components: sexual (seeking homosexual gratification), dependency, and power. Anxiety about dependency and power-striving when expressed sexually are defined by Ovesey as pseudohomosexual. The psychodynamics of paranoia as described by Freud (1911) can be applied to either deep latent homosexual or pseudohomosexual strivings, since as far as the patient is concerned, all are experienced in the same way (see PARANOIA).

Ovesey's views have great clinical importance. He explains, "The desire for dependency through the paternal love of a father-substitute is the most superficial form of the dependency fantasy. The same fantasy on a deeper unconscious level is integrated in a more primitive fashion through the equation *breast* = *penis*. The patient who resorts to this equation attempts to gratify his dependency needs through the oral or anal incorporation of the stronger man's penis" (pp. 62–63). On the other hand, "The power-driven male tries to dissipate his weakness in a compensatory fashion through a show of strength, and to this end he is continuously engaged in competition with other men. There is no discrimination about this competition; it is about anything and everything. Unfortunately, his conviction of inadequacy is so strong that he concedes defeat in advance. The result is a chronic pseudohomosexual anxiety" (pp. 57–58).

Ovesey's main contribution has been to point out that the patient can misinterpret his frightening power and dependency strivings as feminine, or conceive of them in homosexual terms. This leads to anxiety about being a homosexual (pseudo-homosexual anxiety), which can then lead to paranoid defenses. The question of why the patient chooses genital expression of his power and dependency strivings remains unanswered in Ovesey's formulation.

The critical question that each psychotherapy must answer is whether, given a case of developing paranoia, this is based on an outburst of homosexual libido or on power or dependency problems appearing in the patient's mind in a genitalized or sexualized homosexual form. There simply is no agreement on this subject at the present time. My clinical experience is that in cases of paranoia one can always trace this development to the longing for the love of a man, in the case of males—and less easily, in the case of females, to the longing for a female. Although Ovesey argues that the pseudohomosexual conflict develops in men who fail to meet successfully society's standard of masculine performance because of an inhibition of assertion, I am inclined to agree with Freud (1911), especially with respect to men, that "what lies at the core of the conflict in cases of paranoia among males is a homosexual wishful fantasy of loving a man" (p. 62).

References

Freud, S. (1911). Psycho-analytic notes on an autobiographical account of a case of paranoia (dementia paranoides). *Standard Edition* 12:3–82.

Ovesey, L. (1969). *Homosexuality and Pseudohomosexuality.* New York: Science House.

PSYCHIC DETERMINISM

This is one of the most difficult, controversial, and philosophical issues embedded in Freud's psychoanalytic system. It holds that every mental phenomenon and all current psychic acts and events are the result of previous forces at play within the psyche (see MULTIPLE FUNCTION). This apparently plunges Freud directly into the age-old disputed philosophical issue of free will versus determinism. Indeed, Freud's work constitutes a philosophical system. He never wavered in his attitude of belief in a regular chain of mental events, including the thoroughgoing meaningfulness and determinism of even the apparently most obscure and arbitrary mental phenomenon. His view on the subject of free will was that apparently free choices are decided by our unconscious but we claim conscious credit for the outcome; therefore, when unconscious motivation is taken into account, the rule of determinism still holds.

Freud's version of determinism is retroactive; that is to say, he believed that given any psychic event or process one can work backwards in the chain of free associations and find previous events that led to the current event. The opposite procedure is not implied, however; namely, that given a knowledge of all the current psychic forces, one can predict what the outcome of the interaction of these forces will be. This is an important distinction philosophically speaking, and it fortunately places Freud outside of the issue of pure free will versus pure determinism; he is not a "hard determinist" in philosophy. His interest was solely in working backwards, not in predicting the future.

The great value of Freud's approach shows itself when we use the method of free association. By patient listening we discover that the most apparently disconnected thoughts and fantasies turn out eventually to have a major unconscious connecting determinant. This is one of Freud's most dramatic and valuable discoveries.

PSYCHOANALYSIS

Psychoanalysis is in some ways very simple to define and in other ways very difficult. All psychoanalytic models have the same conceptual base, the dynamic unconscious, although they may differ in certain fundamental ways. All deal with transference and countertransference and use the method of free association. All view infantile and childhood experiences as crucial and stress preoedipal and oedipal factors to one degree or another. All in various ways and to different degrees emphasize repetition, the role of the analyst, and the importance of interpretation. Although one neglects Freud's drive/conflict/defense orientation at one's peril, many "alternative" approaches have been devised over the years to avoid both Freud's emphasis on sexuality and aggression as constituting the infantile core of the adult and his central focus on the Oedipus complex.

Psychoanalysis is thought by some to be a branch of natural science as Freud described it and by others to be a form of hermeneutics. Leavy (1980) attempts to move psychoanalysis in the direction of hermeneutics and argues against it as a natural science. His argument rests on the fact, as he sees it, that there are no objective data in psychoanalysis with which we can put nature to question. Others would disagree with this, arguing that the transference constitutes the most important objective data of psychoanalysis.

Leavy is influenced by Lacan, who views transference as a misrecognition of the other in the dialogue based on desire (see LACAN). For Lacan (1978), the purpose of the psychoanalytic dialogue is to achieve greater self-knowledge, that is, knowledge of one's desire, not the lifting of repression or the releasing of energy for the use of the ego. Psychoanalysts who view psychoanalysis as a natural science and/or are members of the ego psychology school would strongly disagree with this.

For Leavy and Lacan, interpretation begins with marveling at tropes. Metaphor leads to the discovery of latent structure, the message, and desires. So in the therapeutic process we move from utterances to images to preverbal wants. Unconscious fantasies, for Leavy and Lacan, represent a signified desire that we reach via language. For hermeneuticists, repression is a linguistic transformation and psychoanalytic validity is a function of the coherence of memories. For Leavy and Lacan, this cuts psychoanalysis loose from objective reality and science and focuses only on the dialogue (see DIALOGUE). This means that for Leavy, as for Spence (1982), we have only narrative truths in psychoanalysis.

The standard view, on the contrary, envisions psychoanalysis as a natural science, a method of investigating the mind, and a modality of therapy for psychopathology. But arguments remain as to what are the essentials of a psychoanalytic treatment. A traditional view holds that the external trappings of the treatment (e.g., very frequent sessions and the use of the couch) are vital to the definition, while an opposing extreme view maintains that psychoanalysis is whatever psychiatric treatment is practiced by psychoanalysts. A middle view might be that psychoanalysis takes place when there is a sufficient regression in the service of the ego so that a stable and interpretable transference forms. The interpretation of this transference, along with the patient's actual experience of the interaction with the therapist (i.e., a new object relation; see Loewald 1980), is the crucial curative factor in the treatment.

For the self psychologists, the important aspect of the relationship with the therapist is empathy, and what is interpreted are the patient's reactions to perceived disturbances in the therapist's empathy. For traditional psychoanalysts, what is interpreted is a transference in which instinctual desires cross the repression barrier and are attached to the representation of the analyst. It is true that the use of the couch and very frequent sessions tend to facilitate regression in the service of the ego, but such regression and the formation of an interpretable transference can occasionally occur even in a less frequent treatment.

What makes the procedure a

psychoanalysis is when the transference is given a total interpretation. That is to say, the current situation and the patient's perception of it are tied convincingly to the patient's childhood situation and his or her perception of that. This latter perception usually takes the form of compromise formations, which are essentially early psychic fantasies that become reenacted or reexperienced in the transference. When there is a consistent formation and interpretation of a significant transference this interpretive work, if properly carried out, should lead into the depths of the patient's personality and developmental stages so that, layer by layer, one eventually reaches in an orderly fashion the core unresolved psychic conflict.

My position is that empathy with the patient that allows the self-object transferences to arise is a vital way of beginning the treatment (see EMPATHY). Along with the physicianly vocation of the analyst (see PHYSICIANLY VOCATION), empathy sets up an ambience that is optimal for the integration of interpretations and for the development of a new object relationship. This object relationship, as it arises out of the proper ambience of the treatment, continuously provides the motivation for the patient to develop, whether one wishes to view it with Freud as love for the analyst or with Loewald (1960) as a developmental reaching out toward higher levels of integration.

The setting of the analytic treatment with the patient on the couch and doing most of the talking promotes regression. The rule of abstinence (see ABSTINENCE), properly applied, promotes the resurgence of yearnings for old objects, the appearance of fantasy activity, and the subsequent development of the transference. If the patient is excessively gratified, the transference does not appear, but if the patient is irrationally or sadistically ungratified in the treatment, the reaction will be one of iatrogenic narcissism and rage, which cannot properly be called transference. Everything depends on the maturation, skill, and clinical judgment of the analyst.

The interpretation of the transference and of extratransference situations should aim at focusing on the central core of the patient through the continuous analysis of derivatives of that core. The patient's observing ego must engage with the analyst and eventually take over the search for the crucial infantile fantasies and/or traumata and identify them. However, as Arlow (1985) points out, events such as the primal scene (see PRIMAL SCENE) are rarely directly remembered. What counts as the patient's psychic reality is a basic core of fantasies or traumata in some combination of intensity, woven into a unique special fantasy activity; in some patients the material will be almost purely fantasy, and in others the most serious kind of abuse and exposure to real horror and death has taken place. Still, no matter how great the traumata, it is the basic fantasy activity woven around traumata that has the primary effect on all the patient's subsequent behavior and capacity to relate to other people.

If this vital core can be reached, identified, and worked through with the patient, the past can recede and no longer pervade the present. The ghosts can become ancestors (Loewald 1960). This offers the ego new options, new choices, and new compromises in dealing with the id, the superego, and reality. Thus, although change can occur in psychoanalytic therapy through a new object relationship or an empathic experience with an understanding analyst, a basic structural change that does not simply consist of identification or internalization of a more benign object can only come about, in my opinion, when there has been a thorough understanding of the early infantile fantasy activity that forms the background mental set of the patient's perceptual and motor system, the core of the patient's psychic reality. Derivatives of these fantasies can be found in every aspect of the patient's choices, behavior, and relationships in later life and persist to an amazing degree even into old age. Hence the wise saying, "If you do what you've always done, you'll get what you've always got."

It has also been my experience that some analyses are aborted as this core is approached; the treatment is covered over by a superficial and premature turn toward increased integration and maturation, giving the impression that the patient has made a recovery and suggesting termination. The uncovering of these fantasies is vigorously defended against,

as they represent some kind of crucial compromise formation in an attempt to master infantile anxieties, traumata, and conflicts. To expose them renders the patient vulnerable to re-experiencing the intense dread of annihilation and overwhelming fragmentation the infant suffered at a time when it was as yet extremely incapable of dealing with such powerful affects. This, in my judgment, forms the bedrock of analytic treatment; if the patient cannot bear to have this core exposed, the treatment will abort and remain a psychotherapy even though an apparently superficial improvement in the patient may take place. This leaves the patient vulnerable to continual pervasion of his or her behavior and choices by the core infantile fantasy activity, so that the improvement is maintained only as long as the internalization of the therapist continues.

Fenichel (1941) wrote a classic on standard psychoanalytic technique. For him, the psychoanalytic tool is the unconscious of the analyst, which intuitively comprehends the unconscious of the patient. The aim of the treatment is to lift this comprehension out of intuition into scientific clarity. We try to influence the ego by strengthening it to help defend against the instincts and by bringing the ego to give up less suitable defenses and replace them by more suitable ones. For Fenichel, all psychoanalysis is ego analysis. We are told to always start at the surface with interpretations: the patient must determine the subject matter of the hour, and interpretation of resistance (see RESISTANCE) must precede the interpretation of content. We are to avoid too deep or too superficial interpretations. The libidinal strivings of the analyst are less dangerous than his or her narcissistic needs and defenses against anxiety. The patient should always be able to rely on the humaneness of the analyst; neither can isolate psychoanalysis from life. The task of analysis is confrontation of the ego with that which was warded off, and the effective factor is the patient's own rediscovery of this material. One can see even from these brief descriptions of Fenichel's technique how different the traditional or natural sciences view of psychoanalysis is from that of the hermeneuticists discussed above. There is no agreement; each side rejects the views of the other, and Grünbaum (1984) rejects both sides.

References

Arlow, J. (1985). The concept of psychic reality and related problems. *Journal of the American Psychoanalytic Association* 33:521–535.

Fenichel, O. (1941). *Problems of Psychoanalytic Technique.* New York: Psychoanalytic Quarterly.

Grünbaum, A. (1984). *The Foundations of Psychoanalysis: A Philosophical Critique.* Berkeley: University of California Press.

Lacan, J. (1978). *The Four Fundamental Concepts of Psycho-analysis,* trans. A. Sheridan. New York: Norton.

Leavy, S. (1980). *The Psychoanalytic Dialogue.* New Haven, CT: Yale University Press.

Loewald, H. (1960). On the therapeutic action of psychoanalysis. In *Papers on Psychoanalysis,* pp. 221–256. New Haven: Yale University Press, 1980.

Spence, D. (1982). *Narrative Truth and Historical Truth.* New York: Norton.

PSYCHONEUROSIS (SEE NEUROSIS)

PSYCHOSIS

Frosch (1983) presents a thorough review of the psychotic process utilizing a basic traditional ego psychology. For Frosch, ego defects, such as the loss of reality testing, are brought into service as a defense against basic anxiety. This anxiety is the fear of dissolution and disintegration of the self. But due to regressive dedifferentiation, this defense carries the possible loss of the self and so actually increases the anxiety in a circular process. Consequently, the ego is invaded by unneutralized aggressive and libidinal id derivatives (see NEUTRALIZATION). There is a strong primary process influence due to the regression, and so marked ambivalence occurs. In the patient's superego archaic precursors predominate; these exist *pari passu* with superego lacunae and the consequent impulsive breakthrough of unacceptable behavior and harsh reactions, with subsequent severe guilt and depression.

For Frosch, the defects in psychotic patients are already in the ego and are exploited for the purpose of defense. Frosch reviews a variety of other theories of psychoses, ranging from the purely organic to the purely psychoanalytic. All of these definitions are probably true, depending on which psychosis one is talking about.

What is common to the psychoses? Probably the most important mark of each psychosis is the failure in reality testing. A psychosis in a sense has a sociological definition because the patient's reality testing is measured against the reality testing of the psychiatrist, who is assumed to be sane. Since a psychosis renders a person unable to adapt or integrate into his or her immediate culture and environment, another sociologic definition is implied. Because of this, Foucault (1973) argues that "psychosis" is always a relative term and in a sense cannot be scientifically defined. Such views are, of course, extreme views, because in general it *is* possible to determine when an individual has a flagrant psychosis, whether it be organic, psychogenic, or both.

The classification of psychoses remains unsatisfactory and is always being questioned by one author or another, but there seems to be a general consensus that many psychoses are best treated by a combination of psychopharmacologic agents, supportive psychotherapy, and manipulation of the environment in various ways. Psychotic patients do form transferences, although these are archaic (see ARCHAIC TRANSFERENCES AND EGO STATES). They are amenable to interpretation but, because of the severe disruptions in reality testing and gross and bizarre behavior that are based on disrupted reality testing, additional measures are usually necessary in the treatment of the psychoses.

Those psychotherapists who attempt to treat the psychoses without these additional measures leave themselves open to possible malpractice suits. Because of this, there has been a certain neglect of attempts to psychoanalyze patients with psychoses these days, as compared to the wonderful work of Sullivan (1947, 1953, 1956) and Fromm-Reichmann (1950). This is unfortunate, because residents and students today no longer have the opportunity to listen to psychotic patients who are not thoroughly tranquilized. Psychotic patients can teach us a great deal about the unconscious mind and also have a wonderful capacity to teach us about ourselves; unfortunately, they always teach us about the most unpleasant and repressed aspects of ourselves, so most psychotherapists are only too happy to tranquilize them. Listening to the psychotic patient is a unique experience and is one of the best ways to convince a student of the power of the unconscious and of psychodynamic factors because the psychotic patient often lays these out before the therapist with very little in the way of "resistances."

References

Foucault, M. (1973). *The Order of Things*. New York: Vintage.

Fromm-Reichmann, F. (1950). *Principles of Intensive Psychotherapy*. Chicago: University of Chicago Press.

Frosch, J. (1983). *The Psychotic Process*. New York: International Universities Press.

Sullivan, H. (1947). *Conceptions of Modern Psychiatry*. Washington, DC: White Foundation.

_____ (1953). *The Interpersonal Theory of Psychiatry*. New York: Norton.

——— (1956). *Clinical Studies in Psychiatry.* New York: Norton.

PSYCHOSOMATIC

The psychosomatic approach may be defined as the study of the influence of emotional factors in any disease and the investigation of the coordination of somatic and psychological factors with each other. In the chain of causal events leading to certain illnesses, some of the links can be described only in psychological terms, and these are what we look for in classical psychosomatic studies.

There are three types of influence of psychological processes on body functions, which constitute the three areas commonly studied in psychosomatic medicine: coordinated voluntary behavior, the motivational background of which can be described only in psychological terms; Darwin's (1965) "expressive innervations," the purpose of which is to bring about a discharge of emotional tension; and possibly adaptive responses that take place in the visceral organs, involving neither direct goals, conscious motivations, nor the immediate discharge of emotional tension. Cannon (1953) explained these responses as changes in the body economy under the influence of emotions and introduced the idea of an adaptive preparation for fight or flight.

For example, the wish to receive food, if sustained, has certain typical physiologic responses associated with it, such as the secretion of gastric juices. These responses become pathological only in situations of stored tension over a long period of time. Thus, when no relief from the emotional problem or conflict by voluntary activity is possible, the organic difficulty begins to occur. When the voluntary behavior that would relieve the emotional tension never takes place—due, for example, to conflicts about this behavior—the perpetuation of the wish leads to organic pathology. This approach stresses the chronicity of the situation.

The early literature on psychosomatic illness (Alexander 1950) attempted to demonstrate that patients with such diseases as bronchial asthma, peptic ulcer, ulcerative colitis, rheumatoid arthritis, hypertension, neurodermatitis, and hyperthyroidism had common specific features of personality. This work has been largely discredited. It is not necessary to postulate specific complex psychological drive/conflict constellations in explaining each of the psychosomatic disorders. For example, narcissistic psychosomatic disorders (Chessick 1985) may be defined as pathological, altered body conditions secondary to certain chronic narcissistic personality and behavior patterns. These patterns, like narcissistic personality and narcissistic behavior disorders, arise out of basic defects in the structure of the self that produce a state of chronic narcissistic disequilibrium superimposed on a faulty self-soothing apparatus. The patterns, along with their physiological concomitants, represent failed efforts at restoring narcissistic equilibrium, are repetitive and chronic in nature, and are accompanied by narcissistic rage secondary to the failures—which imposes an additional chronic burden on the already faulty drive-channeling and drive-controlling capacities and increases the disequilibrium, leading to a vicious pathological spiral and possible chronic physiological self-destruction. The "type-A" personality that accompanies coronary artery disease is a well-known example. In addition, there are always multiple genetic and constitutional factors involved.

Of course, psychosomatic disorders have to be distinguished from conversion reactions and organic diseases. Anyone who attempts psychotherapy with such disorders must be thoroughly trained in medicine and psychiatry or work very closely with a consultant. It is extremely dangerous when misdiagnosis takes place or early signs of exacerbation of the psychosomatic illness are overlooked.

References

Alexander, F. (1950). *Psychosomatic Medicine.* New York: Norton.

Cannon, W. (1953). *Bodily Changes in Pain, Hunger, Fear and Rage.* Boston: Branford.

Chessick, R. (1985). *Psychology of the Self and the Treatment of Narcissism.* Northvale, NJ: Jason Aronson.

Darwin, C. (1965). *The Expression of Emotion in Man and Animals.* Chicago: University of Chicago Press.

PSYCHOTHERAPY

Psychotherapy is based on a paid professional relationship undertaken by the patient for the purpose of the relief of mental suffering, the various syndromes of which are delineated in *DSM-III-R* (1987). The patient assumes that the psychotherapist has had a thorough training in diagnostic and treatment techniques and a personal psychoanalysis that will maximally ensure against countertransference acting out and enable the psychotherapist to listen to what the patient is trying to communicate. Symptom removal attempted primarily under the influence of some sort of relationship is known as supportive psychotherapy. If the focus is on allowing the transference to develop and interpreting it when it does so, then the usual uncovering techniques that define the psychoanalytic approach can be used (see PSYCHOANALYSIS).

Heraclitus said that "character is the demon in man," by which he meant, I believe, that the driving force of a person's behavior, the motor behind success or difficulties in living, is our basic characterological structure. This character, or personality, is formed in the first few years of life in a series of epigenetic layers, beginning with a unification of the sense of self and laying down of self-soothing techniques or apparatuses, proceeding to the development and integration of narcissistic structures, and consolidating upon the resolution of the Oedipus complex. After that, with a renewed phase of flux and consolidation in adolescence and a series of tasks and experiences that can be growth-promoting later in life, such as marriage and parenting (and grandparenting), further modifications of character are possible but less likely, in a fundamental sense.

The findings of almost one hundred years of psychoanalytic investigation have provided a solid base of understanding of at least the outlines of character formation and personality functioning. Although several theories present alternate views on the details, the usual assortment of Freudian drive/conflict/defense, object relations (whether Kleinian or neo-Kleinian), and self psychological approaches and theoretical formulations serve in practice to define the basis of our conceptualization of what has happened to produce the individual we are trying to help. Some authors like myself (Chessick 1989) also like to call on the "phenomenological" and the "interactive" points of view, especially when they are stumped.

This theoretical basis defines our approach to the patient in terms of setting goals, techniques, and practices. After careful listening to the patient, a decision needs to be made as to whether the psychotherapy offered will be primarily for the purpose of uncovering or support.

If supportive therapy is the primary mode, then, providing the presuppositions just mentioned are correct, any technique that is pleasing both to the therapist and to the patient is acceptable. This includes a whole variety of therapies, whether group, family, or individually oriented, that are described in sections of any standard textbook, sometimes with the founder's name attached and sometimes not. The point of

support is to improve the cohesion of the patient's sense of self by offering either mirroring techniques or an idealizable figure for identification, validation, permission, and education. Regardless of the technique used, from the point of view of psychoanalytic psychotherapy manipulation of the transference is the method employed to bring about change. Hence the advantage of beginning with a psychoanalytically trained and oriented psychotherapist.

If uncovering psychotherapy is the primary mode, then only the psychoanalytic orientation offers an escape from conscious or unconscious collusion with the patient to avoid facing the truth of the patient. This method requires special techniques and capacities in the psychotherapist in order to let the material emerge in a relatively undisturbed fashion and to facilitate the development of transference manifestations. Interpretation of these transference manifestations offers the patient insight into his or her mental suffering and the basic functioning of his or her character (see ANALYTIC THERAPY).

Psychoanalytic psychotherapy and psychoanalysis are currently regarded in the United States as unfashionable, unpleasant, and economically questionable. A certain level of sophistication is required for a patient to be able to rise above the popular opinion; usually this develops only after the patient has tried a variety of other simpler, cheaper, and more enjoyable and appealing techniques, of which there seem to be no end, and which come and go in fashion.

Karl Jaspers (1972), philosopher and psychiatrist, said that the doctor is the patient's fate. A lot depends on the doctor to whom the patient is referred, a referral that often depends more on the capacity of the doctor to develop and nourish referral sources than on the validity of his or her technique. Patients able to accept only supportive psychotherapy are not harmed by this unless the presuppositions of proper training and personal psychoanalysis mentioned above are not met.

Uncovering psychoanalytic psychotherapy has many pitfalls. It is long, time-consuming, and expensive. There are not many good studies either validating or invalidating it, which works to the advantage of insurance companies and business corporations who wish to minimize employee benefits for mental illness; they claim it is not proven to be "cost-effective." This uncertainty and lack of coverage causes many problems for the patient and his or her family. Yet such therapy often prevents much more expensive hospitalization and collapse, as demonstrated in a number of studies, even as early as 1958 by Hollingshead and Redlich.

The assessment of a long-term uncovering psychotherapy is extremely difficult for an outside party since it is primarily a two-person relationship and stands or falls on the basis of what happens in that relationship. Even recording of such therapies has proven unsatisfactory because it profoundly interferes with the treatment itself (no matter how much collusion there is to pretend it does not matter, it represents an unempathic invasion of privacy) and because so much data are gathered that it is extremely difficult to develop criteria and techniques to "analyze" the data for anything really relevant, although advanced computer techniques hold at least the theoretical hope that this problem can be overcome.

Training of psychotherapists is in a very poor state, with all sorts of programs designed to produce the various medical, nonmedical, and paramedical professionals who offer "psychotherapy" to the public. There is no coordination and no agreed-upon standards of training. To do effective intensive psychoanalytic psychotherapy requires the most meticulous training and most complete analysis on the part of the therapist. Therefore most "psychotherapists" today avoid the whole thing. A once-a-week psychotherapy for a year or two is *not* a personal training psychoanalysis. It does not prepare a student to practice psychotherapy. As a result, a whole variety of acting out goes on, leading to many messy situations in which the patient runs the risk of being exploited or retaliated against or forced into dependent compliance.

Psychoanalytic psychotherapy in an uncovering mode carried out by an untrained psychotherapist poses the greatest risk to the patient; it is analogous to brain surgery carried out by a barber. So the major disadvantage of my approach is in the demands it makes on the therapist. In an age that values fast-fast-fast relief above all, the tendency is to bypass these slower techniques or to present a mine of misinformation or "wild psychoanalysis" (see WILD ANALYSIS) to the patient, sometimes even over the telephone or on a radio or TV talk show. It is easy to make a mockery of intensive psychoanalytic psychotherapy, and there is always a patient who is eager to enter into collusion with such "therapists" in order to avoid facing the truth.

A serious problem manifests itself among psychoanalytic psychotherapists themselves, even those with proper training. There is a long-standing tradition, beginning with Freud's experience, of professional schisms and theoretical disagreements degenerating into the formation of opposing groups, who then proceed to malign each other publicly in a most immature fashion. There is no commonly accepted "truth" among psychoanalytic sys-

tems at this time, although some clearly have greater clinical validity and capacity to be empirically tested in the psychoanalytic consulting room than others. A lack of tolerance among opposing theoreticians for each other personally, and a lack of civilized dialogue and exchange of ideas on an academic plane, make it harder to examine and resolve apparently irreconcilable theoretical stances and add to the chaos in the field for no acceptable reason. In some instances even angry litigation has been initiated between opposing professional groups, to the cost and detriment of everybody.

References

Chessick, R. (1989). *The Technique and Practice of Listening in Intensive Psychotherapy.* Northvale, NJ: Jason Aronson.

Diagnostic and Statistical Manual of Mental Disorders (1987). 3rd ed.-rev. Washington, DC: American Psychiatric Association.

Hollingshead, A., and Redlich, F. (1958). *Social Class and Mental Illness.* New York: Wiley.

Jaspers, K. (1972). *General Psychopathology,* trans. J. Hoenig and M. Hamilton. Chicago: University of Chicago Press.

Q-R

QUASI-INDEPENDENCE (FAIRBAIRN)

W. R. D. Fairbairn (1889–1964) formed his theories in reaction to Melanie Klein's work because he felt that the so-called biological or id basis of her theories should be eliminated. For Fairbairn, the individual begins with a pristine ego that out of its inherent energy strives for self-development. His work gets into difficulty because he assumes that the ego becomes split in all development, normal as well as pathological. The precise metapsychological meaning of Fairbairn's split-up psychic self is not clear; for example, it employs the undefinable notion of "internalized object." Fairbairn uses ego in his theories to mean the psychic self (Guntrip 1974). The struggle of this split-up psychic self to cope with the outer world is the problem, rather than the struggle, of the ego with the id. In Fairbairn's view, there is no id. Fairbairn thus differs fundamentally with Freud and presents an entirely different metapsychology (Rangell 1985).

Fairbairn, Winnicott, and Balint emphasize the primacy of the environment and the mother's influence. Unless "good enough mothering" (Winnicott 1958) occurs, the infant increasingly frequents the inner world of fantasy objects, but the ego always seeks and needs objects and always stands in some relationship to them. The ego is never regarded as an abstract set of functions or subsystems. Libido, for Fairbairn, in a totally non-Freudian definition, is always object-seeking rather than seeking discharge; libido is the energy of the search for good objects, which makes ego differentiation and growth possible. As in the subsequent work of Kohut, Fairbairn views aggression not as an instinct, but as a reaction to the frustration of libidinal drive.

Fairbairn (1954) attempted to replace the classical concept of psychosexual development that Freud (1905) began with three developmental stages of object relations based on the vicissitudes of dependence on the mother. In the infantile dependence stage the infant is literally dependent on the actual breast as a biological object. There is an incorporation of the object in this stage rather than the libidinal investment of the mouth, resulting in internalization of the breast. These are primary identifications that Fairbairn postulated as representing fusion with an object not yet fully differentiated from the self.

In the quasi-independence stage there is a transitional situation in which partial independence of the breast is achieved by means of certain transitional techniques. These constitute an organization of the internal world with the internal representations of the objects, accompanied by extrusion of the "bad" parts of the object. During this stage, Fairbairn says, an "excretory attitude" is manifest, but not related to Freud's concept of libidinal investment of the anal zone.

The stage of mature dependence is marked by the give-and-take relationship with whole objects and a complete differentiation of the self from the object. This last phase has some superficial resemblance to the later work of Kohut, who emphasizes the "empathic matrix" needed by all adults. All this differs from classical theory in that the stages of development are defined not in terms of erotogenic zones, but in terms of the relation to an object. Also, the various neuroses are not regarded as regressions to different levels of libidinal development, but as pathological solutions to the problem of achieving detachment from the breast.

Fairbairn (Guntrip 1974) presents a threefold split in the psychic self and an internal struggle that he calls "internal ego-object relations." The infantile libidinal ego (analogous to Freud's id) in a state of dissatisfaction is related to an internal bad object that Fairbairn calls the "exciting object," which excites but never satisfies the child's needs. This "libidinal ego-exciting object" is illustrated clinically in the dream of a male patient who follows a woman who constantly retreats from him.

The next sector of the self is the infantile antilibidinal ego (the sadistic part of Freud's superego), which represents the identification with rejecting objects; it is turned against the individual's own libidinal needs. A clinical example of this aspect of the self, "the antilibidinal ego-rejecting object," is presented in the dream of a female patient: "I was a little girl who saw you and thought 'If I get to him, I will be safe.' And I began to run to you . . . but another little girl smacked my face and drove me away" (see SABOTEUR, INTERNAL).

The third aspect of the self or the central ego (Freud's ego) is the conscious self of everyday living attempting to deal with reality, and in so doing idealizing the parents (the ideal object, the moral aspect of Freud's superego). Thus "the central ego-ideal object" struggles to preserve good relationships with the parents for the purposes of strength and adaptation.

Guntrip, the analysand and pupil of Fairbairn, adds an ultimate split in schizoid patients postulated to be in Fairbairn's infantile libidinal ego itself. This aspect splits into a clamoring, orally active hysteric libidinal ego and a deeply withdrawn, passive schizoid libidinal ego. This latter "regressed ego" is experienced by the patient as a compulsive need to sleep, exhaustion, feelings of being a nonentity, a sense of having lost part of the self, of being out of touch—the commonly reported phenomena of schizoid states, such as feeling that there is a sheet of plate glass between one's self and the world. Guntrip (1974) points out that the patient may protect against this sense of annihilation by remaining chronically angry and fighting in order to maintain the energy level. This should be compared with Kohut's (1977) later theory in which the patient produces a pseudodramatization of everything in order to defend against the unbearable subjective sense of a depleted, empty self.

Fairbairn (1963) published a one-page summary of his complex views. Guntrip (1974) attempts to explain this theory, which, as stated, rests on an apparently metapsychologically untenable notion of internalized objects. Kernberg (1980) offers some stimulating ideas on the use made by Guntrip of Fairbairn's theory, and he criticizes them both from his own point of view. Klein and Tribich (1981) denounce Kernberg's criticism of Fairbairn severely; they seem to prefer Fairbairn's object relations theory over that of Kernberg. The psychology of the self movement (see SELF PSYCHOLOGY) shares with Fairbairn, Balint, and Winnicott the emphasis on the mother–infant interaction ambience as crucial to the formation of the basic personality.

Robbins (1980) reviews the current controversy in object relations theory, pointing out the striking resemblance between the views of Kohut and the ideas of Fairbairn. Robbins contrasts the views of Fairbairn and Kohut with those of Klein and Kernberg, which he feels are also closely related to each other.

According to Robbins, Fairbairn's terminology is confusing because Fairbairn uses the ego ambiguously to signify a primary self rather than simply an intrapsychic structure. Robbins criticizes Fairbairn because the latter's theory assumes capacities to differentiate among part objects and affects, and to introject, segregate, and structure experience, all of which may be beyond the capacity of the infant. He adds:

> His core ideas are harbingers of Kohut, particularly his de-emphasis of libido, his conception of aggression as a disintegration product, and his focus on the primary relationship between the self as a dynamic structure and an empathic self-object. When such a relationship fails or disappoints, both Fairbairn and Kohut describe the expression of rage, the development of perverse, auto-erotic phenomena, and an overall picture of detachment and apathy. [p. 484]

References

Fairbairn, W. (1954). *An Object-Relations Theory of the Personality.* New York: Basic Books.
——— (1963). Synopsis of an object-relations theory of the personality. *International Journal of Psycho-Analysis* 44:224–225.
Freud, S. (1905). Three essays on the theory of sexuality. *Standard Edition* 7:125–243.
Guntrip, H. (1974). Psychoanalytic object relations theory: the Fairbairn–Guntrip approach. In *American Handbook of Psychiatry,* vol. 1, 2nd ed., ed. S. Arieti, pp. 828–842. New York: Basic Books.
Kernberg, O. (1980). *Internal World and External Reality.* New York: Jason Aronson.
Klein, M., and Tribich, D. (1981). Kernberg's object-relations theory: a critical evaluation. *International Journal of Psycho-Analysis* 62:27–43.

Kohut, H. (1977). *The Restoration of the Self.* New York: International Universities Press.

Rangell, L. (1985). The object in psychoanalytic theory. *Journal of the American Psychoanalytic Association* 33:301–334.

Robbins, M. (1980). Current controversy in object relations theory as an outgrowth of a schism between Klein and Fairbairn. *International Journal of Psycho-Analysis* 61:477–492.

Winnicott, D. (1958). *Collected Papers: Through Paediatrics to Psycho-Analysis.* New York: Basic Books.

RECONSTRUCTION, CONSTRUCTION

Traditional views of reconstruction in analysis are presented by Blum (1980) and Greenacre (1981). But Arlow (1991) reminds us that, for Freud, reconstruction is inferred from derivatives. As Freud (1937) said, "Quite often we do not succeed in bringing the patient to recollect what has been repressed. Instead of that, if the analysis is carried out correctly, we produce in him an assured conviction of the truth of the construction which achieves the same therapeutic result as a recaptured memory" (pp. 265–266).

Arlow warns us of Hartmann's "genetic fallacy," in which the therapist forces on the patient's associations an interpretation based on a concept of pathogenesis using a preconceived model. Derivatives appear in the associations and dreams of the patients and in compromise formations, not just in a repetition of events; similarly, the transference is not just a repetition of the past,

claims Arlow. Arlow objects to any object relations theory (see OBJECT RELATIONS THEORY) that assumes that in later life there is simple repetition of early object relations formed in the first three years of life. He argues that this assumes too much beyond the infant's capacity for memory and structure. He is very skeptical of preverbal reconstructions and finds it obsolete to request the recall of very early precise events. Accurate reconstructions, according to Arlow, synthesize and produce further material.

Arlow argues that what appears to be repetition in the transference "most often constitutes repetitions of earlier experiences that, even in childhood, were derivative, acted-out manifestations of the unconscious fantasy, elaborated in connection with a traumatic experience or relationship" (p. 547). The child's capacities for symbolization, structuralization of memory, and fantasy formation in the preverbal period are quite limited compared to what develops in the second and third year of life. Arlow objects to the idea that specific sets of early interactions with objects come to have a dynamic thrust of their own so they are compulsively repeated in later life, even in situations in which they are inappropriate. He insists on a drive investment in any object relationship and claims, "It seems impossible for the memory and the significance of early object relations not to undergo some transformation in the course of time" (p. 557).

Because psychoanalytic formulations usually do not exactly replicate earlier events they are thought of as constructions (Freud 1937) rather than reconstructions. These constructions lead to important insights and help to understand the background of the patient's current behavior.

References

Arlow, J. (1991). Methodology and reconstruction. *Psychoanalytic Quarterly* 60: 539–563.

Blum, H. (1980). The value of reconstruction in adult psychoanalysis. *International Journal of Psycho-Analysis* 61:39–52.

Freud, S. (1937). Constructions in analysis. *Standard Edition* 23:255–269.

Greenacre, P. (1981). Reconstruction: its nature and therapeutic value. *Journal of the American Psychoanalytic Association* 29: 27–46.

REGRESSION

Regression is a well-known defensive process that involves reversion to an earlier state or mode of functioning. Unfortunately, it compels the individual to reexperience the anxieties and conflicts that fit the stage to which the individual has regressed. Since regression involves going to a developmentally more immature level of mental functioning, it usually interferes with adaptation and even reality testing (see NEUROSIS).

Readers of Freud may be confused by the fact that he uses the concept of regression in several different ways: (a) temporal regression, defined as returning to earlier reaction patterns or to temporally earlier modes of psychic functioning; (b) formal regression, involving a change from general and abstract symbols to visual imagery as in dreams; and (c) topographical regression, representing a change from organized secondary process thought and behavior to primary process thought. A thorough discussion of this difficult subject is presented by Arlow and Brenner (1984).

Reference

Arlow, J., and Brenner, C. (1984). *Psychoanalytic Concepts and the Structural Theory.* New York: International Universities Press.

RELUCTANT COMPLIANCE

This is one of the most controversial aspects of the psychology of the self (see SELF PSYCHOLOGY). "Reluctant compliance with the childhood wish" (Kohut 1978, p. 507) denotes a situation in which the analyst feels that, at least in some instances, gratification of a childhood wish has to be provided, usually in the early part of the treatment, to facilitate the beginning of selfobject transferences that the patient could not otherwise tolerate. This came up in the treatment of Miss F., Kohut's seminal patient, who made him aware of her never-ending demand for mirroring (see MIRROR TRANSFERENCE). She wanted him only to summarize or repeat what she had already said. Whenever he went beyond this and offered an interpretation, the patient furiously accused him in a tense, high-pitched voice of undermining her. No interpretations based on an oedipal level made any difference whatsoever. Ultimately, the high-pitched tone of her voice, which expressed in the tone of a very young child such utter conviction of being right, led Kohut to recognize that he was being used for mirroring purposes in the patient's effort to replace missing psychic structure. He offered this mirroring that the patient missed from the mother as a corrective emotional experience so that the patient's self-object transference formation could proceed.

It should be noted that Kohut is not advocating reluctant compliance with the childhood wish as a curative factor but only as an unavoidable method in setting the stage for the ultimate working through and interpretation of the transference by traditional means. This approach has sometimes been used as an excuse for all sorts of acting out by insufficiently analyzed psychotherapists, for which one cannot blame Kohut.

The concept of optimal frustration (see OPTIMAL FRUSTRATION) means that a certain amount of compliance with patients' wishes is necessary if the treatment of narcissistic disorders is not to degenerate into a hostile confrontation with accusations and counteraccusations. For example, if the patient enters the office early in the treatment and wants to show a picture of someone to the therapist, it is usually better to look at the picture and then discuss the matter rather than to refuse to look at the picture, which the patient rather appropriately experiences as an insult. A very strict orthodox ambience in the treatment can produce a counterproductive iatrogenic narcissistic withdrawal.

The problem that confronts the analyst and is a challenge for his or her self-analysis is the extent to which this reluctant compliance with the childhood wish should be permitted. Too much compliance generates the desire for more and usually precludes a successful resolution of the treatment process. The same is true if there is not enough of it. This is very tricky, and depends on the therapist's capacity to empathically grasp what the patient is experiencing, and with what intensity, at any given time.

Reference

Kohut, H. (1978). *The Search for the Self,* ed. P. Ornstein. New York: International Universities Press.

REPARATION

Reparation is a Kleinian concept defined as reducing guilt by making good the imagined harm that has been done to an ambivalently invested object. For Klein, all creative activity is reparative and reparation is an important mechanism of defense used in the depressive position (see OBJECT RELATIONS THEORY). The forms of reparation mentioned by Klein (1975) are (a) manic reparation, which is a reversal of the child–parent relationship causing humiliation to the parents and a sense of triumph in the child; (b) obsessional reparation, consisting of compulsive repetitions of undoing actions designed for magical placation;

and (c) truly creative reparation grounded in love and respect for the object.

In the depressive position, (see KLEIN and DEPRESSIVE POSITION) reparation becomes the repair of the internal world through repairing the external world and so supplies great energy for creativity. It is called out by the anxieties of the depressive position and comes out of a real concern for the whole object: "Powerful reparative urges are often responsible for lives devoted to humanitarian ends and lived in great hardship. It is a phantasy that may be acted out with external objects—for instance through going into one of the helping professions" (Hinshelwood 1989, p. 399). If reparation fails, or is interfered with by manic defenses, the patient may suffer serious depressive anxiety about harming and about destructive impulses. This can interfere with normal child development and even in adult life cause a regression back to the paranoid-schizoid position.

The point is that although reparation is concerned with the good object in the internal world, it is expressed in action toward objects in the external world that represent the phantasied damaged internal object. It is this that makes it a force for constructive action in the external world and enhances a love relationship, since it focuses on the repair of the troubles or difficulties of the loved object.

References

Hinshelwood, R. (1989). *A Dictionary of Kleinian Thought*. London: Free Association Books.

Klein, G. (1975). *Envy and Gratitude and Other Works, 1946–1963*. New York: Delta.

REPETITION COMPULSION (SEE COMPULSION TO REPEAT)

REPRESSION

Repression was the initial and most important mechanism of defense described by Freud. It functions to render and keep an unacceptable impulse or idea unconscious. Freud (1914) declared that the theory of repression is the cornerstone on which the whole structure of psychoanalysis rests, and his concept of repression goes back historically to the very beginning of psychoanalysis. Since Freud's notion of repression changed gradually, the reader sometimes becomes confused as to what he means by the term repression.

Freud's (1915b) brief paper on repression is one of his early works on metapsychology and begins by defining repression as an instinctual vicissitude, one of the resistances that seeks to make an instinctual impulse inoperative. Repression is a preliminary stage of condemnation, "something between flight and condemnation" (p. 146). According to Freud, repression is not a defense mechanism present from the very beginning and cannot arise until a cleavage has occurred between conscious and unconscious mental activity. When the need to avoid pain is greater than the pleasure of gratification, repression occurs, and its essence "lies simply in turning something away, and keeping it at a distance, from the conscious" (p. 147). Before the mental organization achieves the cleavage between conscious and unconscious mental activity, the task of fending off unacceptable instincts is dealt with by the other vicissitudes that instincts may undergo, such as reversal into the opposite or turning around upon the subject's own self.

Freud then introduces one of the most difficult of his concepts, that of primal repression, in which the ideational representative of the instinct is from the beginning denied entrance into the preconscious or conscious. At this point, astute psychiatric residents (in those few training programs that still study Freud) usually ask how there can be ideational content to an instinct if it never reaches the preconscious or consciousness. Primal repression is a hypothetical construct that seems to confuse the theory. One way to look at it is to realize that Freud is talking about unstructured rudimentary ideational material or pre-ego impulses that are simply left behind or outside consciousness as the ego develops, and thus can never be subjected to secondary process. However, this answer is not very satisfactory.

At this point, even more astute residents may ask how such material can be kept in repression if there is no countercathexis. Here again we must say that this rudimentary unstructured material is simply left out as the ego forms its structure. Philosophers immediately argue that this is one of those concepts that cannot be proven and can never be known, since if it could be known, by definition it would not be in a state of primal repression. In Freud's early notion of primal repression, we are dealing fundamentally with a metaphysical concept, a target for Ockham's razor.

Freud (1915b) next defines repression proper, in which mental derivatives of repressed instincts or associated with repressed instincts are expelled into the unconscious. He insists that this material must be connected to primally repressed material, which has a magnetic attraction and draws its derivatives into the id: "Repression proper, therefore, is actually an after-pressure" (p. 148). Repression proper occurs not only because of a repulsion that operates from the direction of the conscious upon the unacceptable instinct; "quite as important is the attraction exercised by what was primally repressed upon everything with which it can establish a connection" (p. 148). Freud believes that repression would probably fail in its purpose if there were not something previously repressed ready to "receive" what is repelled by the preconscious.

Not everything that is related to what was primally repressed is withheld from the conscious; some derivatives get through, but they are far enough disguised and removed. Repression can even receive a transitory lifting, as, for example, in jokes.

Freud (1915b) proceeds to make one of his most important clinical observations. Repressed instinctual representatives proliferate in the dark, as he puts it, and take on extreme forms of expression that seem alien to the patient and actually frighten him or her by posing the picture of extraordinary and dangerous strength of instinctual forces: "This deceptive strength of instinct is the result of an uninhibited development in fantasy and of the damming-up consequent on frustrated satisfaction" (p. 149). In the neuroses there is great fear of various repressed instinctual derivatives, but when they have become exposed to the light in intensive psychotherapy they appear silly and relatively harmless. It is a serious failure of empathy on the part of the psychotherapist to assume that apparently minor wishes of an infantile nature should be as ridiculous to the patient as they obviously are to the therapist, and to ridicule such infantile desires. To the patient these are threats of the greatest magnitude coming from within, and much of his or her personality has been developed to protect against what he or she considers to be explosive or catastrophically destructive ideation and wishes. It is only after a successful treatment that patients can look back on their unconscious ideation and regard it as a harmless set of infantile phenomena. In fact, when patients begin to snicker at their own infantile wishes we know that they are often making good progress in the psychotherapy.

The entire notion of dynamic psychiatry rests on the concept of repression. Freud (1915b) explains that the repressed (repression proper) exerts a continuous pressure in the direction of the conscious that must be balanced by an unceasing counter pressure; thus the maintenance of repression involves an uninterrupted expenditure of force, and its removal results in a saving of energy. Similarly, whenever an unacceptable idea acquires a certain degree of energy or strength, this activation leads to repression; thus a substitute for repression would be a weakening, by indirect discharge, of what is distasteful. Notice that both the energic charge of affect and the ideational presentation of the instinct undergo a fate—the former is transformed and the latter is repressed. At this point Freud still thought of anxiety as the result of the transformation of these affects into anxiety. Two other possible fates for the affect are either total suppression so that no trace of it is found or "it appears as an affect which is in some way or other qualitatively colored" (p. 153), that is diluted or altered.

The implication of this theory seems to be that ordinary ideas always go first through the unconscious and then move into the higher integrated areas of conscious mental function. The lower systems of mentation must therefore cathect the higher ones for the perception of an idea—or even of an external stimulus—to reach consciousness. The id thus retains or attracts certain perceptions where the cathexes are, and much elaboration has to occur before conscious perceptions take place (see CONSCIOUSNESS). Freud (1915b) explains, "The mechanism of a repression becomes accessible to us only by our deducing that mechanism from the *outcome* of the repression" (p. 154). In this theory, symptoms are substitutive formations that represent the return of the repressed, and thus the mechanism of forming symptoms is not the same as that of repression. The paper concludes with examples of symptom formation in the various psychoneuroses.

The distinction between repression and disavowal, or denial (*Verleugnung*), was first made in Freud's (1927) paper on fetishism. Disavowal as the ego's reaction to an intolerable external reality was further developed in some of Freud's (1940) later writings, especially chapter 8 of *An Outline of Psychoanalysis*. Recent studies of preoedipal pathology and narcissistic personality disorders have brought this distinction into focus. (see DENIAL, DISAVOWAL).

Brenner (1957) distinguishes four stages at which Freud made important innovations in or significant additions to the concept of repression. In the first stage (1894–1896), repression was thought of as a pathological mental process in which memories of a painful nature were suppressed in individuals who had a sexual experience in childhood—an experience that, "though pleasurable at the time it occurred, had been later considered bad or shameful and whose memory had consequently been repressed" (p. 23).

In the second stage (1900–1906), repression was thought of as occurring in normal as well as neurotic individuals, and infantile (primal) repression was a consequence of sequences in the maturation of the psychic apparatus and was the precondition of later repressions. Thus a store of infantile memories and wishes that never had been and never would be accessible to the preconscious constituted the infantile core of the repressed. Brenner (1957) explains, "This formulation was in accord with Freud's experience that infantile memories and wishes were not recoverable or rememberable as such in later years and that their existence has to be *inferred* from their effects on mental life, notably in dreams and neurotic symptoms" (p. 27). As explained above, this store of inaccessible memories was thought to be the precondition of all later instances of repression; the conscious has to turn away from any derivatives of such infantile memories. A vague notion of an organic factor in repression was introduced at this time but was largely neglected in Freud's later writings.

The theories of the third stage (1911–1915) were put forward in the paper on repression described above and in "The Unconscious" (1915a). Here, repression is still seen as an immature mechanism that is replaced in the process of psychotherapy or psychoanalysis by conscious judgment and condemnation of unacceptable impulses.

The final stage (1923–1939) was necessitated by the introduction of the structural theory of mind and the signal theory of anxiety (see ANXIETY). Anxiety is now thought of as the predecessor and motive for repression; the signal of anxiety arises as the anticipation of danger from intrapsychic conflict and of flooding due to the intensity of stimuli. Although Freud did not make a full final statement on the subject, upon shifting to the structural theory he seems to have concluded that of several defense mechanisms, repression is the one the ego immediately employs against an instinctual drive that is the source of anxiety. The mechanism of repression is now seen as the establishment of a countercathexis by the ego, and therefore a substantial degree of ego development must take place before this can occur. The notion of primal repression shifts to represent early infantile repressions that occur by the same mechanism and are quite basic; later repressions are by and large repetitions or consequences of the infantile ones. The earlier conceptual distinction between primal repression and repression proper fades away.

Brenner (1957) mentions certain other aspects of the later theory of repression. Between the repressed drive and the countercathexis of the ego an equilibrium is established that may shift, for example, when (1) the defenses of the ego are weakened, as by illness or sleep; (2) when drives are strengthened, as in puberty or chronic frustration; and (3) when there is "a correspondence between the content of current experience and of the repressed drive" (p. 45). Repression is potentially pathogenic in that it produces a crippling of the instinctual life and a constriction of the sphere of influence of the ego, as well as a continuing drain on the ego's store of available psychic energy.

References

Brenner, C. (1957). The nature and development of the concept of repression in Freud's writings. *Psychoanalytic Study of the Child* 12:19–45. New York: International Universities Press.

Freud, S. (1914). On the history of the psychoanalytic movement. *Standard Edition* 14:3–66.

———— (1915a). The unconscious. *Standard Edition* 14:159–215.

———— (1915b). Repression. *Standard Edition* 14:141–158.

———— (1927). Fetishism. *Standard Edition* 21:149–157.

———— (1940). An outline of psychoanalysis. *Standard Edition* 23:141–207.

RESISTANCE

Resistance represents the opposition encountered to the psychoanalytic work of making unconscious processes conscious. Patients may oppose the analyst's interpretations or behave in such a way as to make the work difficult or take certain attitudes toward the treatment, including avoiding free association.

Resistance is understood as a function of the ego's defensive efforts to keep in repression unacceptable childhood wishes, fantasies, and impulses. In his early work (Breuer and Freud 1893–1895) Freud conceived of resistance as an obstacle to be overcome by every method the doctor had at his disposal, including suggestion, authority, persuasion, and the power of the relationship. The removal of resistance was from the beginning considered the central task of psychoanalytic treatment. In *Minutes of the Vienna Psychoanalytic Society* (Nunberg and Federn 1962), Freud is noted by Rank as saying, "There is only one power which can remove the resistances, the transference. The patient is compelled to give up his resistances to *please us*. Our cures are cures of love. . . . The vicissitudes of the transference decide the success of the treatment" (pp. 100–102). Freud regarded the notions of resistance and transference as the conceptual hallmarks of psychoanalysis. We now understand that transference can be a source of resistance (see TRANSFERENCE).

Once a patient has agreed to the basic contract and has attempted to express whatever comes to mind, certain phenomena soon appear that interrupt and interfere with the steady flow of thoughts, associations, feelings, and memories. These various phenomena are collectively termed resistance. Acting out is a particularly pernicious form of resistance because it can break up the therapy. Freud (1900) defined resistance as anything that interrupts the progress of analytic work. He (1926) distinguished five kinds of resistance and classified them according to their source:

1. The resistance of repression (the resistance of the ego's defenses).
2. Resistance of the transference. Since transference is a substitute for memory and is based on a displacement from past objects onto present objects, Freud classified this resistance as also derived from the ego.
3. The gain from illness, or secondary gain, was also placed by Freud under ego resistance.
4. The repetition compulsion (see COMPULSION TO REPEAT).

Freud at first attributed this to adhesiveness of the libido (see ADHESIVENESS OF THE LIBIDO) and considered it as stemming from the id. Later he explained id resistance as a function of the death instinct (see DEATH INSTINCT).
5. Resistances that arise from unconscious guilt and a need for punishment. These originate in the superego.

It is useful to divide resistances into ego-alien and ego-syntonic. The ego-alien resistances appear foreign, extraneous, and strange to the patient's reasonable ego; as a consequence, such resistances are relatively easy to recognize and work with. In contrast, the ego-syntonic resistances are characterized by their seeming familiarity, rationality, and purposefulness to the patient. The patient does not sense the resistance function of the activity under scrutiny. Such resistances are harder to recognize and more difficult to work with. They are sometimes called defense transferences. Greenson (1968) explains that they usually represent well-established habitual behavior patterns of the patient and character traits, sometimes of social value. He places reaction formations, acting out, character resistances, counterphobic attitudes, and screen defenses in this category.

The working through of ego-syntonic resistances is difficult. Such resistances must first be made ego-alien for the patient before they can be dealt with. The therapist's task, notes Greenson, will be first to help the patient establish a reasonable ego in regard to the particular resistance. When the patient can understand the historical reasons for the origin of the resistance defense, the patient will be able to differentiate past needs for that defense and the present inappropriateness of the defense.

It is clear that the psychotherapy must deal first with the patient's resistances and only second with content, and it is surprising how frequently this is violated. Unless resistances are removed first, interpretations of content will lead to nothing. It is usual to begin with ego-alien resistances. Although the ego-syntonic resistances are present from the beginning, it is pointless to begin by attacking them, since the patient will simply deny their significance or give lip service to understanding.

Transference resistance may take the form of defenses against awareness of the transference. When the transference becomes conscious, wishes and attitudes may become so intense that they disrupt the treatment. A transference defense represents the establishment of a transference with its set of wishes and attitudes as a defense against another transference with an even more unacceptable set of wishes and attitudes (see TRANSFERENCE). Transference is often considered a form of resistance because it expresses the wish for direct gratification and acting out rather than the proper task of analysis, i.e., remembering and analyzing the origins of the transference in past relations.

Resistances in intensive psychotherapy or psychoanalysis are understood differently by self psychologists (Kohut 1984). Self psychologists interpret resistances as manifestations of the patient's fear of "humiliation or rejection or some other form of depreciation," and this fear makes them "sensitively cautious" against self-revelation, explains Wolf (Stepansky and Goldberg 1984, p. 152). This caution does not represent defense against the drive but against selfobject failures that may fragment the self. Wolf calls these "measures of obligatory self-protection." He feels that a patient should not be labeled borderline until there have been trials of analysis "by more than one or two analysts" (p. 153), because he believes the disruptions in the treatment of these patients can often be brought to an end "by interpretation and explanation" (p. 155), allowing a stable selfobject relationship to form eventually. The skill and emphatic attunement of the analyst are very important.

There are at least two potential traumas to which the self is exposed: the loss of a needed selfobject response and the intrusion of the selfobject across its boundaries into its own core. Wolf explains that "the more fragile the self structure, the more vulnerable the self and the more distorted the self's defensive maneuvers against the potential danger" (p. 152). From the point of view of self psychology, the more the therapist learns about his or her patient-assigned function as a selfobject in the treatment, the better the therapist will be at practicing psychotherapy, and the more "resistances" can be understood and analyzed correctly.

References

Breuer, J., and Freud, S. (1893–1895). Studies on hysteria. *Standard Edition* 2:1–335.

Freud, S. (1900). The interpretation of dreams. *Standard Edition* 4,5:1–627.

—— (1926). Inhibitions, symptoms, and anxiety. *Standard Edition* 20:77–174.

Greenson, R. (1968). *The Technique and Practice of Psychoanalysis.* New York: International Universities Press.

Kohut, H. (1984). *How Does Analysis Cure?* Chicago: University of Chicago Press.

Nunberg, H., and Federn, E., eds. (1962). *Minutes of the Vienna Psychoanalytic Society,* vol. 1. New York: International Universities Press.

Stepansky, P., and Goldberg, A., eds. (1984). *Kohut's Legacy: Contributions to Self Psychology.* Hillsdale, NJ: Analytic Press.

REVERIE (BION)

Wilfred Bion (1897–1979), an extraordinarily intuitive analysand and follower of Klein, described the state of mind that an infant requires of the mother as "reverie" (Bion 1967). This is a state of calm receptiveness established to contain the infant's feelings. Through projective identification the infant inserts into the mind of the mother a state of anxiety that it is unable to make sense of and is considered intolerable. Mother's reverie allows the alpha function (see ALPHA FUNCTION) to operate, translating confused and projected sense data, or beta elements, from the infant into some sort of meaning. By introjecting this receptive understanding mother, the infant begins to develop the capacity for reflection and ego structuring.

If the mother is incapable of reverie, the infant cannot receive a sense of meaning from her and experiences instead a sense of meaning having been stripped away with a terrifying sense of the ghastly unknown that Bion (1967) calls "nameless dread." Beta elements then accumulate, and the mind develops into an apparatus for getting rid of these accumulations rather than for thinking. This is important to an impressive understanding of schizophrenia offered by Bion.

If the mother's mind is cluttered with other worries, she is absent for the infant and is inadequate as an external object or container. But the infant's own envy may cause it to attack the very containing function upon which it depends. Too much envy may be projected into the mother and render her an envious container, an unfortunate phantasy that deprives what the mother has to offer of any meaning. Finally, as any pediatrician knows, the mother may be a fragile container of projections and collapse under the force of projective identifications from the infant.

The analytic situation could be described as an endeavor to provide a bounded calm world or container where meaning (the contained) can be developed or found (Bion 1962). This is sometimes thought of as a "toilet function" of the analyst, but it also involves returning the projected elements in a metabolized and articulate form, similar to the mother's alpha function.

Etchegoyen (1991) offers an excellent review of Bion's container-contained theory. Transferring this to the psychoanalytic process itself, he views the analyst at one stage of the treatment as a container of the analysand's anxieties: "The fundamental analytic task at this stage is the analyst's containment and interpretation of the patient's anxiety. To the extent that this process is carried out, if the patient deposits or, rather, *evacuates* his anxiety . . . and the analyst is able to bear it, a type of relationship is established in which the patient feels the analyst as an object whose function is to contain him" (p. 611). Etchegoyen approves of Meltzer's idea that as this containing function or "toilet-breast" operates in the analyst, the analysand will develop a growing confidence and gradually introject this function. When this occurs the patient now has within an object where he or she can deposit his or her anxieties. It is interesting to compare this explanation of the growing capacity of the patient for tension regulation with Kohut's concept of transmuting internalization (see SELF PSYCHOLOGY).

References

Bion, W. (1962). "Learning from experience." In *Seven Servants,* pp. 1–111. New York: Jason Aronson, 1972.

––––––– (1967). *Second Thoughts: Selected Papers on Psycho-Analysis.* London: Heinemann.

Etchegoyen, R. (1991). *The Fundamentals of Psychoanalytic Technique,* trans. P. Pitchon. New York: Karnac Books.

REVERSIBLE PERSPECTIVE

Bion (1963) introduced this concept to denote a drastic attempt to destabilize the analytic situation through a remarkable reversal of the processes of thought on the part of the patient. Etchegoyen (1991) offers an excellent summary of this maneuver, which has great clinical importance and does not receive the attention that it deserves. Etchegoyen reworks the concept to apply to borderline and even severely neurotic patients, whereas Bion thought of it as pertaining more to psychotics. In my clinical experience, I have found it in borderline and severe character disorders.

The patient silently, either consciously or unconsciously, experiences the entire psychoanalysis from a different set of premises than those held by the therapist. The analytic contract is actually violated, although the patient appears on the surface to be cooperating with the treatment. A mental disposition underlying reversible perspective has to do with these premises. Etchegoyen explains, "He [the patient] is continuously reinterpreting the analyst's interpretations so that they can blend with his own premises, which is also a way of saying that the analyst's premises have to be silently rejected—silently, because between analyst and analysand there is manifest accord and latent discord, of which the analyst usually becomes aware only when he realizes that the process is completely stagnant" (p. 759). The clinical example Etchegoyen offers is that of a homeopathic physician who ostensibly came seeking psychoanalytic treatment for anxiety and crises of depersonalization as well as hoping for a modification of the psychological factors contributing to his bronchial asthma. Actually, the patient was guided by professional rivalry and not by any desire to be cured. He simply wanted to reassure himself that the method of homeopathic medicine was superior to the method of psychoanalysis.

Reversible perspective is often operative in patients who are chronically late. Such patients are often using the psychoanalytic process to prove something rather than for the purpose of cure. In those situations, as Etchegoyen explains, "To interpret at the level of defense mechanisms is not enough. Because as long as one interprets lateness or silence in terms of fear, frustration, revenge, envy, Oedipus complex, castration anxiety, omnipotent control or whatever, one has not reached the level at which the conflict is rooted" (p. 766).

The reversion of perspective should be suspected when everything seems to be going well in the treatment but no change is taking place in the analysand. This is not an infrequent occurrence in training analyses, where the analyst thinks he is helping the patient to resolve neurotic difficulties but the patient, a candidate analyst, is simply intending to use the training analysis as a source of borrowed knowledge and accreditation. This is an example of reversible perspective that often appears in narcissistic personality disorders; the most extreme example is the patient who enters analysis not in order to be cured of neurotic difficulties but to demonstrate to the analyst that he or she does not need analysis! One sometimes sees a similar situation when analyzing colleagues in the mental health profession who attempt to use the analysis to "teach" the analyst that the analyst's theoretical orientation is incorrect and to persuade the analyst to adopt the analysand's theoretical orientation!

References

Bion, W. (1963). Elements of psycho-analysis. In *Seven Servants,* pp. 1–110. New York: Jason Aronson, 1977.

Etchegoyen, R. (1991). *The Fundamentals of Psychoanalytic Technique*, trans. P. Pitchon. New York: Karnac Books.

RULE, FUNDAMENTAL (SEE FREE ASSOCIATION)

RULE OF ABSTINENCE (SEE ABSTINENCE)

S

This is Fairbairn's term for what he later calls the "antilibidinal ego," one of the three aspects into which the original pristine ego becomes split (see QUASI-INDEPENDENCE for an outline of Fairbairn's theories). For Fairbairn, the individual begins with a pristine ego that out of its inherent energy strives for self-development. His work gets into difficulty because he assumes that the ego becomes split in all development, normal as well as pathological. Fairbairn uses the term "ego" to mean the psychic self. The struggle of this split-up psychic self to cope with the outer world is the problem, rather than the struggle of the ego with the id. In Fairbairn's view, there is no id. Fairbairn (1963) thus differs fundamentally with Freud and presents a unique metapsychology.

The sector of the self called the infantile antilibidinal ego (the sadistic part of Freud's superego) that Fairbairn originally named the "internal saboteur" represents the identification with rejecting objects; it is turned against the individual's own libidinal needs.

Reference

Fairbairn, W. (1963). Synopsis of an object-relations theory of the personality. *International Journal of Psycho-Analysis* 44: 224–225.

SADISM, SADOMASOCHISM (SEE ALSO MASOCHISM)

The Marquis de Sade (1740–1814) described in great detail the pleasures he obtained in his fantasy life of inflicting cruelty on others. He is mentioned by a number of thinkers, such as Foucault (1973), as one of the "mad artists" that herald the breakdown of our era. The term *sadism* comes from his name.

Sadism is easy to define, but there is considerable controversy as to its source or sources. It can be thought of as a sexual perversion in which pleasure comes from inflicting pain on the object or more generally, pleasure in cruelty. The sexual significance of sadistic wishes or behavior may not be consciously known to the individual. Some authors speak of "oral sadism," most manifest during the second half of the first year of life, during which the teeth develop and the infant gets pleasure in biting, and anal sadism, a phase during the early second year of life in which there is pleasure in smearing, dirtying, and directly inflicting pain.

The debate about sadism is over whether it is the manifestation of an instinctual drive or whether it arises only secondarily as a disintegration of normal assertiveness due to frustration. This argument is actually an outgrowth of an old theological controversy, which may be found not only in early Christianity but even among the followers of Confucius, as to whether or not humans are innately evil. Freud (1920) explained sadism in his later work as a manifestation of the death instinct turned outward (see DEATH INSTINCT). Although Freud was not consistent about this, Melanie Klein based her entire theories on it (see KLEIN). Kohut (see SELF PSYCHOLOGY) was convinced of the opposite, that sadism when it appears is an indication of fragmentation of the sense of self and is a disintegration product rather than anything indigenous to the individual or a primary drive. This view was shared by Fromm, Fairbairn, and others who came before Kohut.

The classic interpretation of sexual sadism was that it defended the individual against castration fears. This would then be a form of secondary sadism, a derivative from conflict, and would have to be differentiated from some sort of primary primitive instinctual destructive urges postulated to reside in the id and originally turned against the individual as the death instinct. Not all of the death instinct is turned toward others, according to Freud, and some of it remains within the organism as a sort of primal sadism, the source of erotogenic masochism. Some authors use the concept of phallic sadism, in which the phallus becomes associated with aggressive and violent impulses during the phallic phase of development. Many manifestations of this are found in the never-ending stream of movies dealing with overcoming castration fears by overexaggerating the penis or employing penis symbols as powerful and aggressive weapons of violence and destruction.

For psychotherapists, the most important aspect of sadism is in the so-called sadistic superego (see SPLITTING). The early precursors of the superego are infused with oral and anal sadistic drive derivatives. Patients with depressions and obsessive-compulsive disorders exhibit an extremely punitive, rigid, and destructive superego that drives them relentlessly.

The standard attempt to modify this superego comes from mutative interpretations (see MUTATIVE INTERPRETATION). The essence of this technique is the hope of replacing the harsh punitive superego of the patient with an introjection of the more benign and tolerant aspect of the therapist. This comes about, theoretically speaking, through the projection of the harsh punitive superego onto the therapist and then proper interpretation, which brings the patient to an awareness of the reality of the situation and an understanding of what has been projected. This leads to improved reality testing and an incorporation of the therapist as a benign introject. In actual practice this is much more difficult than it appears to be, because this harsh primitive superego often consolidates in the first year of life or may even be a primary identification (see PRIMARY IDENTIFICATION) that the patient cannot imagine being without.

One of the most important contributions of Melanie Klein was her emphasis on the early development of sadistic superego precursors before the oedipal period. This is of special importance in the treatment of the rampant preoedipal disorders that we see in today's clinical work. In Kleinian theory the harsh sadistic superego precursors are a manifestation of the child's own infantile primordial sadistic phantasies and strivings, turned against the individual in order to preserve the maternal object.

Klein was shocked by the amount of violence she discovered in children's play during her early psychoanalytic play therapy explorations. She was also influenced by Abraham (1949), who described the oral and anal sadistic phases of development. Klein soon became convinced that extreme cruelty is a basic instinctual endowment of human beings. She tried to link this to Freud's death instinct (see DEATH INSTINCT) without achieving general agreement on the topic.

According to most theories, sadism and masochism always exist together. In classic psychoanalytic theory they represent fusions of the libidinal and the aggressive drives. The term "sadomasochism" has been used to emphasize this fact. Freud (1905) coined the term "sadism proper" for situations in which there was an association between violence against others and sexual orgasm; he used "sadism" more loosely to refer to hostile and aggressive behavior or fantasies. There is a certain ambiguity in the term in the psychoanalytic literature, where "sadism" is sometimes used to mean violent fantasies and behaviors accompanied by sexual orgasm (a perversion), or simply violent and aggressive fantasies and behavior.

Perhaps the most interesting issue is whether or not sadism is a built-in feature of humans. Some may argue that one's viewpoint on this is simply a projection of one's own pessimistic or optimistic orientation toward life. It is not clear at the present writing how this argument could ever be resolved, but certainly the history of the twentieth century, culminating in the Holocaust, strongly suggests aggression and destructiveness as a core feature of the human psyche, a psyche that easily erupts when the thin veneer of civilization is erased by various socioeconomic conditions or, as in the situation of war, by group consent (see CORRUPTION).

References

Abraham, K. (1949). *Selected Papers on Psychoanalysis.* London: Hogarth Press.

Foucault, M. (1973). *Madness and Civilization,* trans. A. Smith. New York: Vintage.

Freud, S. (1905). Three essays on the theory of sexuality. *Standard Edition* 7:125–243.

———— (1920). Beyond the pleasure principle. *Standard Edition* 18:3–64.

SCHIZOID (LAING)

This term is used differently by different authors. The British psychoanalysts tend to use it in place of what United States' psychoanalysts would call "narcissistic." When British psychoanalysts write about schizoid patients, they are often discussing what *DSM-III-R* (1987) calls narcissistic personality disorders. Whether there is a spectrum of disorders ranging from the schizoid personality disorder described in *DSM-III-R,* through borderline schizophrenia and schizo-affective disorders, to schizophrenia, remains a matter of dispute and a subject of genetic research.

In the United States the term "schizoid" brings to mind the shy, sensitive, aloof, introverted type of individual who is easily offended and sometimes has persecutory preoccupations. When the latter become predominant, the condition shades into the paranoid personality disorder. These patients are often withdrawn and suspicious, and tend to have a vivid fantasy life. This fantasy life may enable them to engage in considerable creative activity in spite of their schizoid or paranoid traits; some of the greatest artists in history have clearly been schizoid or paranoid personality disorders.

The defenses typically involved are splitting, disavowal, introjection and projection. Melanie Klein (see KLEIN) postulates a normal "paranoid–schizoid" position early in infancy. She originally conceived of this as a "paranoid position" but was influenced by Fairbairn's concept of the "schizoid position" in early infancy which results in the infant's splitting of the ego into three parts (see QUASI-INDEPENDENCE). It should be noted, however, that Klein's and Fairbairn's theories are not compatible and that the use of the term *schizoid* as both a normal descriptive and psychopathological adjective leads to confusion. Klein conceived of the paranoid-schizoid position as turning the death instinct outwards and thus preserving the infant's life; Fairbairn argued that frustration during early development led to a split in the ego, and no biological instincts were involved. Bleuler (1911) introduced the term *schizoid personality* to indicate what he thought to be the typical premorbid personality style of patients who ultimately develop schizophrenia. Today we know that many patients with schizoid personality disorders or borderline personality disorders never go on to develop schizophrenia, and a substantial portion of patients with schizophrenia were not schizoid personality disorders before their schizophrenia appeared.

From the point of view of the practicing psychotherapist, the best understanding of the schizoid individual is provided in the early work of R. D. Laing (1927–1989). According to Laing (1969a), the schizoid individual is split in two ways. With respect to the world, he or she is not at home in the world, but rather alienated, split off, and alone. The second split is within the patient's own self. The true self is split from the false self; the latter remains associated with the body. Such a patient often speaks of his or her body in the third person, a clue that this split has taken place. For Laing, this is "tragic man" and represents a double alienation, as he calls it.

Laing borrows the term *ontological insecurity* from the theologian Paul Tillich, for whom it was the universal human condition. In the state of ontological insecurity there is no sense of continuity and no cohesion of the self in time. For Laing, it is the special problem of the schizoid. The schizoid patient seeks to preserve the self, as compared to neurotics and normal individuals, who wish to gratify the self (see ONTOLOGICAL INSECURITY).

The cause of ontological insecurity is the lack of mirroring of the true self, according to Laing, the absence of the smiling notice and appreciation of the patient's self as a child. He (1969a) writes that the development of a self requires "the loving eye of the mother" (p. 125). This is required for ontological autonomy, Laing says. Patients exhibiting such insecurity, however, do not suffer from unconscious conflicts. Their problem is "beyond the pleasure principle." Laing gives a case example of agoraphobia based on the well-known unconscious fantasy of being a prostitute. But the patient's sexual fantasy used sex as a way of recognition, to create the illusion of being looked at and desired. It was not based primarily on a defense against incestuous desires. Gratification is not the issue for patients with ontological insecurity,

says Laing. This resembles Kohut's (1984) version of self psychology, although the terminology is quite different.

The schizoid patient oscillates between merger and isolation and psychologically splits into a secret true self and a body associated with a false self (see FALSE SELF). All of us reversibly do this under stress, for example, at a boring party, under torture, during a painful or embarrassing medical examination, or during painful dental work; but in the schizoid individual, a definitive split occurs between the true self and a false self system, in which the false self system becomes the manifest personality.

This definitive split engenders the schizoid style. The patient, in a common clinical picture, tries to do everything for himself or herself in isolation. This protects the patient from ontological insecurity and the anxieties associated with ontological insecurity (see ONTOLOGICAL INSECURITY), but it is impossible since we all need other people; isolation of one's self leads to despair and a sense of emptiness and alienation from the world. The common schizoid existential complaint of the futility and meaninglessness of life arises from this. The patient longs to get into life, and suffers a dread of the increased emptiness and dissolution that develops as the patient feels more and more isolated and vulnerable. This is a problem, says Laing, which begins in infancy. He (1969a) writes, "The more the self is defended this way, the more it is cut off and destroyed" (pp. 80–81). There is no exit for this mode of being-in-the-world, similar to Sartre's (1949) concept of "no exit," hell as an eternal trap with no way out.

The true self is never revealed by the schizoid individual. It is hidden by compliance, which, as Kohut (1984) pointed out, is the hardest resistance of all to deal with in any treatment. In the famous terms of Martin Buber (1958), there is for the healthy person an I-Thou or creative relationship, in which the mutual potentiation of ourselves with the world around us and others take place. Laing compares this with the Quasi-it (compliant false self)-It (petrified or depersonalized other) relationship, a sterile relationship in which both the person and surrounding individuals are impoverished. As Laing (1967) writes, if you don't live in the world with people, "something dies inside" (p. 144).

In these patients the inner true self breaks up into subsystems or fragments. It hates itself and becomes preoccupied with fantasies and memories that get more and more unrealistic, since the individual is not in contact with others and the world for correction. Clinically the patient complains of a world in ruins and the self as dead, impoverished, and empty. There is no frantic activity that can bring it to life again, although the patient may try everything.

Such a person never really marries. He or she is perpetually alone, and never commits himself or herself fully to anything in the world, as this would reveal the true self. The patient is filled with longing, envy, and hatred of the self and the world, and is guilty over duplicity, fearing at the same time his or her own destructiveness or fragmentation, which Laing calls "going crazy."

The typical clinical problem of the schizoid patient is a morbid self-consciousness. This assures the patient that he or she exists. The patient is apprehensive and hypervigilant, sensing a danger that is felt everywhere as a consequence of the patient's ontological insecurity. This poses a dilemma, since the patient wishes to be seen and to have his or her self confirmed but at the same time wishes to be invisible, since it is a threat to the self if the patient is seen.

Persecutory delusions or ideas of reference represent an attempt to mirror one's self. They represent some form of imagined responding, says Laing. The cold gaze of the mother now comes inside and is projected in an attempt at self-mirroring. Laing (1969a) presents the dramatic case of Peter, who was always treated by his family literally as not being there. This patient was overwhelmed with chronic anxiety and ontological insecurity, typical of the schizoid tragedy.

References

Bleuler, E. (1911). *Dementia Praecox or the Group of Schizophrenias,* trans. J. Zinkin. New York: International Universities Press, 1950.

Buber, M. (1958). *I and Thou.* New York: Scribner.

Diagnostic and Statistical Manual of Mental Disorders (1987). 3rd ed.-rev. Washington, DC: American Psychiatric Association.

Kierkegaard, S. (1946). *The Concept of Dread,*

trans. by W. Lowrie. Princeton, NJ: Princeton University Press.

Kohut, H. (1984). *How Does Analysis Cure?* Chicago: University of Chicago Press.

Laing, R. D. (1967). *The Politics of Experience.* New York: Pantheon.

———— (1969a). *The Divided Self.* New York: Pantheon Books.

———— (1969b). *Self and Others.* New York: Pantheon Books.

Sartre, J-P. (1949). *No Exit and Three Other Plays.* New York: Vintage.

SCHIZOPHRENIA (SEE ALSO SCHIZOID)

This term was introduced by Bleuler (1911) to describe the group of psychoses separated out by Kraepelin as dementia praecox and differentiated from manic-depressive disorders. The earliest distinction among the schizophrenias was of three varieties: the hebephrenic, the catatonic, and the paranoid. *DSM-III-R* (1987) uses a somewhat amended classification. (The reader is referred to the APA manual for an overall description of schizophrenia.)

The truth is there is very little consensus on or understanding of this condition. Bleuler thought of it as representing a splitting of the mind that resulted in four fundamental symptoms: inappropriate affect, ambivalence, autism, and, above all, a disturbance in the normal associational processes of thought. A vast literature has developed on the subject of schizophrenia and numerous theories abound. There seems to be general agreement that some sort of genetic predisposition to the disorder must exist for it to appear. Depending on the strength of this disposition, there will also be certain unfavorable environmental factors in the etiology that precipitate the disorder. Earlier in this century much focus had been placed on the role of the so-called schizophrenogenic mother and the passive, relatively impotent father. This resulted in an unfortunate phase of "mother-bashing" in the literature. Today the emphasis is more on genetic factors, but the problem is that there is no consensus on what constitutes the essence of the group of schizophrenias, which makes all forms of research extremely difficult.

This problem was recognized by Freud (1911), who was not impressed with the term "schizophrenia" because he felt that it prejudiced the issue by making the splitting a central characteristic. Instead he used the term "paraphrenia" (see PARAPHRENIA), but this did not receive general acceptance.

Freud (1914) thought of schizophrenia as involving three groups of phenomena: (a) those representing what remains of the normal or neurotic state of the individual; (b) those representing detachment of libido from its objects, leading to megalomania, hypochondriasis, and regression; and (c) restitutive symptoms in which an effort is made to attach the libido to objects or at least to their verbal representations. These distinctions form the foundation of Freud's theory of schizophrenia.

Freud (1915) postulated that schizophrenics have given up the cathexis of objects with libido; they return this libido on the soma in the formation of hypochondriasis, and on the self in the formation of megalomania. In schizophrenia words are subjected to the same process as that which makes dream images out of latent dream thoughts. Thus words undergo condensation and displacement and indeed, a single word may take over the representation of a whole train of thought. However, there is an essential difference between dream work and schizophrenia: in schizophrenia the words themselves, in which the preconscious thought was expressed, become subject to modification; in dreams, it is not the preconscious thoughts or words that are modified, but what Freud calls the "thing presentations" in the unconscious. In schizophrenia the link between word presentations in the preconscious and thing presentations in the unconscious is broken, so that the schizophrenic is forced to be content with words instead of external things because of withdrawal of libido from the outside world. The hypercathexis of word presentations is an effort to regain the lost thing presentations from both the external and internal world. The schizophrenic confuses these two worlds and ends up embedded in the word presentations of each.

At this point it is best to think of the schizophrenias as a heterogenous group of disorders that no single theory can explain. The loss of reality testing is, of course, the most serious aspect of schizophrenia and invariably causes grave problems. Hallucinations, delusions, and regression to very primitive levels of intrapsychic and interpersonal functioning are characteristic of schizophrenia, especially in the acute phases.

Today psychopharmacologic agents are commonly used to treat schizophrenia. This treatment can make the patient more amenable to hospital management or even home care, but it has the disadvantage of quieting the patient's communications and making it harder for the therapist to learn from the patient about his or her difficulties. In addition, there are problems associated with overmedication, including neuroleptic malignancy syndrome and tardive dyskinesia. Some side effects are not reversible even after the medication has been stopped. The advantages of psychopharmacologic treatment, however, outweigh the disadvantages.

Psychosis develops from the situation of a false self system, according to Laing (1969; see SCHIZOID). The schizoid solution fails, anxiety increases, and more desperate measures are needed. The inner world becomes more and more unreal; deadness and hate increase. The false self system expands and becomes autonomous, and the individual begins to feel that he or she has a mechanical body that belongs to others. The patient tries to use magic, to touch, to feel, or even to steal, somehow to fill the emptiness; this dynamic is found in many cases of bulimia. The schizophrenic's last hope may be in such extreme activities as child molestation, promiscuity, homosexuality, or perversions.

Again, this is similar to Kohut's (1977) description of fragmentation of the self.

The true self may suddenly emerge, manifesting all its unrealistic fantasies, and we discover, says Laing, that our carefully recorded "psychiatric history" has been the history of the false self system. The "cure" here, using drugs, milieu therapy, and so forth, would be to get the patient back to manifesting the false self system. The patient either decides to go back to the false self system or murders the self in such activities as self-mutilation, suicide, or homicide (killing the projected "bad" part of the self). This preserves any sense of being alive and reduces anxiety because the patient says, paradoxically, "If I am dead I cannot be killed." In chronic schizophrenia the self breaks up into fragments or *archetypal agencies,* to use Laing's term. The final result is the disintegrated dilapidated hebephrenic.

In treatment we must always remember that a true self exists somewhere in every patient. We try to contact this. When we do, the patient feels understood and schizophrenia abates. Thus, for Laing, schizophrenia is a smoke screen for protection and the physician must fight to get through it to the true self. Diagnosis is based on the "praecox feeling"; that is, the physician is in the presence of another person, yet feels that nobody is there. It is a life-in-death existence.

One of the great pioneers in the understanding and psychotherapy of schizophrenic patients was Harry Stack Sullivan (1892–1949), who developed a psychological explanation for schizophrenic disorders and demonstrated that schizophrenic processes were never very far from the normal processes of living. In contrast to prevailing theories, Sullivan (1947, 1953, 1956, 1962) showed that schizophrenia can develop as the direct outgrowth of psychological issues and that it can occur in any individual. He saw schizophrenia as a personality distortion emerging from a complicated and warped series of interpersonal relations, and he documented this in innumerable case histories and studies. (See Chessick 1991 for a brief review of Sullivan's psychodynamic theories.)

By demonstrating the roots of schizophrenia in the distortions of personality development, Sullivan greatly stimulated the hope of a possible psychotherapeutic resolution of this disorder. He felt that the most peculiar behavior of the acutely schizophrenic patient was made up of interpersonal processes that were in essence the same as those found in every person. He felt that the core of the schizophrenic state was a failure of the self-system and that the schizophrenic change was due to an inability to maintain dissociation. The best detailed explanation of this is in Sullivan's *Clinical Studies in Psychiatry* (1956), which consists of material contained in lectures given in 1943.

A typical concept of Sullivan is the notion of the *malevolent transfor-*

mation. As Sullivan (1953) conceives of it, this occurs as a miscarriage of the need for tenderness, in which a child discovers that manifesting the need for tenderness toward figures around him or her leads to anxiety rather than to relief. The child learns that it is highly disadvantageous to show any need for tender cooperation from authority, in which case he or she shows a basic malevolent attitude, the attitude that one really lives among enemies. This causes a situation in which the child makes it practically impossible for anyone to feel tenderly toward him or her. The patient outwits the caretakers by the display of his or her attitude, which is a manifestation of the early discovery that any need for tenderness would bring anxiety or pain. This serious distortion of what might be called the fundamental interpersonal attitude Sullivan (1953) defines as the malevolent transformation: "Once upon a time everything was lovely, but that was before I had to deal with people" (p. 216).

Sullivan (1947) did not regard the capacity for interpersonal relations as completed during any point of development, which was another important disagreement that he had with basic Freudian concepts. Sullivan's view of schizophrenia is not generally shared, and only a mere handful of schizophrenic people receive psychotherapy today. The main reason for this is not so much the theoretical argument about the meaning of schizophrenia as the lack of motivation or financial resources to maintain long-term intensive psy-chotherapy of any patients, particularly schizophrenics.

The best application of Sullivan's work to the treatment of schizophrenia is found in the writing of Fromm-Reichmann (1950, 1959) and Pao (1979). These authors should be studied carefully and their knowledge and suggestions thoroughly mastered before any attempt is made to do intensive psychotherapy with a schizophrenic patient. Schizophrenic patients are notorious for raising the anxiety level of therapists, and therefore a very thorough and in-depth personal psychoanalysis is required for any psychotherapist who attempts to work with them.

References

Bleuler, E. (1911). *Dementia Praecox or the Group of Schizophrenias,* trans. J. Zinkin. New York: International Universities Press, 1950.

Chessick, R. (1991). *The Technique and Practice of Intensive Psychotherapy.* Northvale, NJ: Jason Aronson.

Diagnostic and Statistical Manual of Mental Disorders (1987). 3rd ed.-rev. Washington, DC: American Psychiatric Association.

Freud, S. (1911). Psycho-analytic notes on an autobiographical account of a case of paranoia (dementia paranoides). *Standard Edition* 12:3–82.

———— (1914). On narcissism: an introduction. *Standard Edition* 14:67–102.

———— (1915). The unconscious. *Standard Edition* 14:159–204.

Fromm-Reichmann, F. (1950). *Principles of Intensive Psychotherapy.* Chicago: University of Chicago Press.

———— (1959). *Psychoanalysis and Psychotherapy.* Chicago: University of Chicago Press.

Kohut, H. (1977). *The Restoration of the Self.* New York: International Universities Press.

Laing, R. D. (1969). *The Divided Self.* New York: Pantheon Books.

Pao, P. (1979). *Schizophrenic Disorders.* New York: International Universities Press.

Sullivan, H. (1947). *Conceptions of Modern Psychiatry.* Washington, DC: White Foundation.

_____ (1953). *The Interpersonal Theory of Psychiatry.* New York: Norton.

_____ (1956). *Clinical Studies in Psychiatry.* New York: Norton.

_____ (1962). *Schizophrenia as a Human Process.* New York: Norton.

SCREEN MEMORIES

A screen memory is defined by Freud (1899) as a recollection whose value lies in the fact that it represents, in the reported memory of impressions of a later date, events that are associated either by symbolic or other links from an earlier date in a person's life. Freud distinguished between the simpler type of screen memory, in which the preserved memory is but a part of a more significant whole that has been repressed, and a more complex type, in which the memory is a construction combining the memory of a certain event in early childhood with a repressed memory of an event in adolescence. The earlier memory is not necessarily untrue but is a harmless substitute for the later, unacceptable memory. The autobiographical screen memory described by Freud is of this complex type, one in which an early memory is used as a screen for the memory of later events. This kind of screen memory is not mentioned as often in subsequent literature.

Freud (1901) points out that in earliest childhood recollections we possess not the genuine memory but a later revision of it. This revision is subjected to influences of a variety of later psychic forces; thus memories presented by patients as from early childhood acquire the same significance as screen memories. This explains why a person's earliest childhood memories frequently seem to have preserved what is indifferent and unimportant, and why some seem even odd and unintelligible. The usual processes of condensation and displacement with respect to both time and place are at work here just as in the formation of dreams: "The indifferent memories of childhood owe their existence to a process of displacement: they are substitutes, in (mnemic) reproduction, for other impressions which are really significant" (p. 43).

The indifferent memories of childhood that are reported owe their preservation to an associative relation between their content and another memory that is repressed—in this sense, they are screen memories. Similarly, mistakes in recollection cannot be attributed to simply a treacherous memory, for motives are present that make the distortion and the displacement of the experience necessary: "Strong forces from later life have been at work on the capacity of childhood experiences for being remembered—probably the same forces which are responsible for our having become so far removed in general from understanding our years of childhood" (p. 47).

Freud's screen memory work implies the importance of asking patients for their earliest memories, the content of which is usually referred back to the period between ages 2 and 4. The most frequent content of the earliest memories involves occasions of fear, shame, physical pain, and such important events as illnesses, deaths, fires, and the births of siblings. Such memories must be regarded as disguised representations of more fundamental psychological interactions with significant people in the past, or even better, as representations of the atmosphere of early childhood. As such, they are important clues to what will appear in the transference and in the uncovering of significant childhood interactions and events. It should be added that such "events" may never have happened at all and the screen memories may be reports of childhood fantasies (see FANTASY).

In my clinical experience, the best way to treat a screen memory and to understand it is as one would understand a dream. The memory covers or screens other associated wishes, fantasies, or recollections that would be disturbing and emotionally painful if recalled. Free associations (see FREE ASSOCIATION) are often helpful in understanding screen memories. Often the earliest memories provided by a patient in the initial interviews contain a clue to the nucleus of the patient's neurosis.

References

Freud, S. (1899). Screen memories. *Standard Edition* 3:301–322.

_____ (1901). The psychopathology of everyday life. *Standard Edition* 6:1–310.

SELF, SENSE OF SELF (SEE ALSO BIPOLAR SELF)

Self is one of the most difficult terms to define because it is used in so many ways by so many authors. Even Samuel Johnson (1773) devotes two pages of quotations to trying to get the notion clear, after stating that the primary signification of the term "seems to be that of an adjective; very; particular; this above others; sometimes, one's own" (p. 1737). No two authors use this term exactly the same way. A thorough review of the concept of self in psychoanalytic theory and its philosophical foundations is presented by Kirshner (1991), and a study of this review indicates the complexity and conceptual problems involved.

Perhaps the best-known use of the term "self" is that of Mead (1962), a pragmatist who tried to eliminate the parallelism between the mind and the body by seeing the mind and the self as arising out of social interaction and having no innate separate existence. For Mead, the self was a social self that formed in two stages. At first, the individual's self is constituted simply by an organization of the attitudes of others toward both the individual and one another in the specific social acts in which the individual participates with them. Then, at the second stage, there is added "an organization of the social attitudes of the generalized other or the social group as a whole to which he belongs" (p. 158). For Mead, the mind or self is formed by "reflexiveness" from social experience, a view that influenced Sullivan (1953) in forming his interpersonal school of psychiatry and a view that represents "social behaviorism," an attempt to extend empiricism to the psychology of the mind or the self.

Thus most authors used the term "self" as a social construction until it came to be employed by psychoanalysts. Freud did not distinguish between the self and the ego. In current object relations theory (see OBJECT RELATIONS THEORY), such as that of Kernberg, the term "self" really means "self-representations."

Kohut (1977) maintained that the self in its essence cannot be defined, and concentrates his work on the "sense of self." There is no agreement, even among self psychologists, on a strict definition of "self." Kohut (1978) claimed that the fundamental advance of psychoanalytic fact-finding is to step into a new methodology by which the therapist vicariously introspects with the patient and experiences the inner self and the world around the patient in a manner congruent to that of the patient. This yields important data about the state of the patient that cannot be obtained in any other manner of approach (see SELF PSYCHOLOGY). Kohut's (1971) early notion of the sense of self comes from the therapist's empathic identification with the patient's sense of self at any given time. It is in truly understanding how the patient's

sense of self waxes and wanes, or coheres and fragments, that we gain an explanation of why and how the patient perceives the inner and outer world around him or her and behaves accordingly.

This is more experience-near than Freud's metapsychology, because additional apparatuses or structures are not postulated as homunculi within the head of the individual determining the outcome of his behavior; the patient's perception and behavior are directly attributable to the patient's sense of self. This approach sidesteps what Freud (1937, p. 225) called the witch metapsychology, but understanding then depends fundamentally on the capacity of the therapist to empathize with the patient's inner state at any given time.

The parallel between Kant's (1781) noumenal self, which lies behind our synthetic unity of consciousness in our inner states as phenomenally perceived, and Kohut's self, which lies behind empathically perceived psychological manifestations, steadily expands as Kohut matures in his views. Kohut (1977) writes in *The Restoration of the Self:*

> We can collect data concerning the way in which the set of introspectively or empathically perceived inner experiences to which we later refer as "I" is gradually established, and we can observe certain characteristic vicissitudes of this experience. We can describe various cohesive forms in which the self appears, can demonstrate the several constituents that make up the self—its two poles (ambitions and ideals) and the

area of talents and skills that is interposed between the two poles—and explain their genesis and functions. And we can, finally, distinguish between various self types and can explain their distinguishing features on the basis of the predominance of one or the other of their constituents. We can do all that, but we will still not know the essence of the self as differentiated from its manifestations. [p. 311]

Here the self is "a generalization derived from empirical data," and like Kant's noumenal self, has both a stimulating and a synthesizing set of functions. The kind of empirical data from which it is derived, the data of vicarious introspection, differs from the empirical data used by Kant (introspected inner states that Kant says lead up to the limiting concept of the noumenal self), but the concept of the underlying and unknowable self is the same.

Later, Kohut at times, like Kant, slips into the concept of self in the positive sense, as when he speaks of it as empty and depleted, or as "yearning" for mirroring or merger. The self in these situations is used as an "as-if" concept, and the anthropomorphic language has been criticized. For example, in a footnote to Kohut and Wolf (1978) the criticism of the psychoanalyst Nathaniel London is mentioned: "He thinks our language often suggests an anthropomorphization of the concept 'self', in the same way that 'ego' used to be anthropomorphized" (p. 415n); in essence, Kohut and Wolf plead guilty to the accusation but claim

that it is "in the service of evocativeness and conciseness" (p. 416n).

Kohut (1971, p. 130) mentions that the cohesive experience of the self in time is the same as the experience of the self as a continuum, which seems to be the same as Kant's notion of inner states; in the same paragraph Kohut mentions the "breadth and depth" of cohesiveness of the self, but without definition.

Kohut's (1971) concept of the fragmentation of the self (see FRAGMENTATION) is equated with psychoticlike phenomena, at which time reality testing and contact even with the therapist is in danger of being lost. It is characterized as a regressive phenomenon, predominantly autoerotic, in contrast to the state of the cohesive self, "the growth of the self experience as a physical and mental unit which has cohesiveness in space and continuity in time" (p. 118).

Kohut's (1971) original notion of the cohesiveness of the self has to do with a "firm cathexis with narcissistic libido" (p. 119), leading to a subjective feeling of well-being and an improvement of the functioning of the ego. In later writings this metapsychological explanation is dropped; signs of fragmentation of the self then have to do with a subjective feeling of self-state anxiety, and of objective and subjective signs of deteriorating ego function. Thus fragmentation of the self, which Kohut calls "the dissolution of the narcissistic unity of the self" (pp. 120–121), is manifested by certain characteristic subjective sensations, such as hypochondria and frantic activities, "in order to stem the tide of regression." Kohut sees a regression from the cohesiveness of the self to its fragmentation as parallel to a regression from narcissism to autoerotism. A clinical description of this is based on the self as an organizing center of the ego's activities. When the self fragments, the personality that has not participated in the regression attempts to deal with the central fragmentation, but "the experience of the fragmented body-mind-self and self-object cannot be psychologically elaborated" (p. 30).

In *The Restoration of the Self* (1977), Kohut conceives of the self as a supraordinate concept and elaborates on its bipolar nature (see BIPOLAR SELF). In this work metapsychological energic concepts are dropped out, and the self is now seen as occupying the central position within the personality. Kohut also writes about a core self present early in life: "This structure is the basis for our sense of being an independent center of initiative and perception, integrated with our most central ambitions and ideals and with our experience that our body and mind form a unit in space and a continuum in time" (p. 177).

Kohut, then, first presents the self as an experience-near abstraction from psychoanalytic experience. As his work evolves, he focuses more and more on the self, finally placing the self "into the center of our being from which all initiative springs and where all experiences end" (Kohut 1978, p. 95). This emphasis on the self would be the same as Kant's noumenal self used to explain free will—again, a center of our being from which all initiative springs and where all experiences end. When Kohut moves to the bipolar self and its constituents he introduces a new concept. The self is no longer a depth-psychological concept that can be metapsychologically defined using classical terminology, and the self is no longer thought of as either within the mental apparatus or even as a fourth "agency" of the mind. "The area of the self and its vicissitudes," as Kohut (1978, p. 753) calls it, is essentially a separate science from Freud's psychoanalysis, just as the study of the phenomenal world in the *Critique of Pure Reason* is a separate discipline from the study of the noumenal world in the *Critique of Practical Reason* (Chessick 1980).

Kohut (1978) himself labels his work "the science of the self" (p. 752n), and the conclusion is inevitable that he has attempted to found a new science. Kohut, like Kant, although he claims to maintain an experience-near definition of the self, relies more and more on the definition of the self as a supraordinate concept, which more resembles Kant's noumenal self as an explanatory concept. We see the evolution of this in Kohut, beginning, for example, in his 1972 presentation (chapter 31 in *The Search for the Self* [1978]), in which he definitely offers the earlier definition, and moving toward his focus on the self in *The Restoration of the Self* (1977) as a supraordinate concept that solves the philosophical dilemma regarding the phenomena of free will. The turning point in this shift is labeled by Kohut (1978) himself as coming first in 1974 in his essay, "Remarks about the Formation of the Self" (chapter 45 in *The Search for the Self*).

The original concept of the self of Kohut as a simpler experience-near abstraction, marked in its fragmentation by certain clinical phenomena, is certainly consistent with traditional psychoanalytic theory. Kohut's later use of the self, however, is not consistent with this theory, because although he continues to derive his concepts from psychoanalytic experience, postulating the self as a center of initiative implies that a mysterious something besides the instinctual drives—either instead of them or in addition to them—is a main energic spring of human behavior and thought. Indeed, Kohut regards manifestations of the drives as "disintegration products" rather than as fundamental parts of human nature.

Stern (1985) cites evidence that a sense of an emergent self is present from birth to 2 months of age. As Basch (1991) puts it: "It is the very activity of extracting meaningful information from a multitude of stimuli and experiencing the dependable rhythms that make up [the infant's] existence that allows a sense of self to emerge" (p. 6).

From 2 to 6 months of age there is an observed sense of core relatedness and an apparent separation of the infant's notion of its own body from its notion of others. This is the development of a sense of a core self,

the point at which the baby learns to experience itself as a center of activity and perception. Basch writes, "Now the infant begins to organize and generalize experience into practical action schemas, which it then repeats when seemingly similar conditions of experience arise. In this way, the infant encodes rules for behavior that greatly increase his or her effectiveness; and, the more effective, the stronger the infant's cohesive self" (p. 7).

From 7 to 15 months Stern emphasizes the sense of a subjective self, which actually develops out of the intersubjective exchange or affect attunement between the mother and the infant, probably the most vital psychological nutrient.

The sense of a verbal self appears after 15 months and before that time Stern believes there are no enduring specific intrapsychic representations, since these require the development of language. Basch writes,

Infancy ends and childhood begins when reflection and evocative recall become a possibility. The infant lives in the present, he accommodates to the immediate situation, and assimilates what he learns from experience into patterns of expectation with which he meets the next event. The unique capacity of human beings for unlimited reflection, made possible by symbolic representation of events, makes possible evocative recall and fantasy and the concepts of past and future. Words are especially powerful symbols that can be used to recreate the past and to plan for the future. An inner reality or private world can be created that may enhance actual experience, falsify it through fantasy, or forecast a reality that has not yet been experienced and may never be experienced. [pp. 8–9]

Basch also mentions a sense of a narrative or consensually validated self after the age of 36 months that is not discussed by Stern (1985). This seems close to Sullivan's (1947) notion of consensual validation, but it includes the contribution of privately thinking over as well as sharing with others one's plans, activities, and sense of what is real.

Some self psychologists, such as Wolf (1988), think of the self as if it has a "structure" (p. 38), which changes slowly and is made of parts either well put together (cohesive) or easily fragmenting. Wolf uses this bipolar structure definition metaphorically, but runs the danger of causing confusion with Freud's (1923) structural theory and with Jung's archetypal self (Jacoby 1990). The reader must decide; my predilection is for Kohut's earlier emphasis on the sense of self as explored by the therapist's vicarious introspection, which keeps it more experience-near.

It should be remembered that the self in self psychology is not an actual essence or contraption governing the mind, like Freud's psychic agency ego, but is a bipolar organization of experiences and needs that may be classified as mirroring, idealizing, or twinship in nature, with some sort of tension among these poles. To avoid confusion, I prefer the term "self configuration" rather than "self structure" (Wolf 1988). Using "self configuration" when discussing the psychology of the self rather than

"self" or "self structure" provides a sharper connotation of the term "self" as it is used in self psychology, separates it more clearly from Freud's structural theory, and avoids some of the Kantian inconsistencies as described above.

References

Basch, M. (1991). Are selfobjects the only objects? Implications for psychoanalytic technique. In *The Evolution of Self Psychology: Progress in Self Psychology*, vol. 7, ed. A. Goldberg, pp. 3–15. Hillsdale, NJ: Analytic Press.

Chessick, R. (1980). The problematical self in Kant and Kohut. *Psychoanalytic Quarterly* 49:456–473.

Freud, S. (1923). The ego and the id. *Standard Edition* 19:3–66.

――― (1937). Analysis terminable and interminable. *Standard Edition* 23:209–253.

Jacoby, M. (1990). *Individuation and Narcissism: The Psychology of Self in Jung and Kohut*, trans. M. Gubitz. London: Routledge.

Johnson, S. (1773). *A Dictionary of the English Language*. Beirut, Lebanon: Librairie du Liban, 1978.

Kant, I. (1781). *Critique of Pure Reason*, trans. N. Smith. New York: St. Martin's, 1965.

Kirshner, L. (1991). The concept of the self in psychoanalytic theory and its philosophical foundations. *Journal of the American Psychoanalytic Association* 39:157–182.

Kohut, H. (1971). *The Analysis of the Self*. New York: International Universities Press.

――― (1977). *The Restoration of the Self*. New York: International Universities Press.

――― (1978). *The Search for the Self*, ed. P. Ornstein. New York: International Universities Press.

Kohut, H., and Wolf, E. S. (1978). The disorders of the self and their treatment: an outline. *International Journal of Psycho-Analysis* 59:413–425.

Mead, G. (1962). *Mind, Self, and Society*. Chicago: University of Chicago Press.

Stern, D. (1985). *The Interpersonal World of the Infant: A View from Psychoanalysis and Developmental Psychology*. New York: Basic Books.

Sullivan, H. (1947). *Conceptions of Modern Psychiatry*. Washington, DC: White Foundation.

———— (1953). *The Interpersonal Theory of Psychiatry*. New York: Norton.

Wolf, E. (1988). *Treating the Self: Elements of Clinical Self Psychology*. New York: Guilford.

SELF-ANALYSIS

Freud's self-analysis, through his letters to Fliess and as manifested in *The Interpretation of Dreams* (1900), was heralded correctly as a gigantic breakthrough in methodology, and as an act of personal courage, daring, and devotion to truth. As early as 1910 Freud recommended self-analysis for anyone who wished to do analytic work. Fleming (1971) traced the development of the training analysis from this original recommendation and identified the many changes over time in the theory and practice of training analysis. She added that one major objective of training analysis is to encourage a lifelong process of self-analysis through introspection, empathy, and interpretation.

Freud at first expected spontaneous self-analysis to occur after the termination of training analysis (Tyson 1986), but later he (1937) became rather pessimistic about the psychoanalytic process and recommended periodic formal reanalysis for psychoanalysts every five years. This recommendation, although it is based on a formidable argument by Freud, is largely ignored for practical and other reasons, and has been replaced by general agreement that those practicing psychoanalytic therapy will feel a professional obligation to engage in self-analysis whenever they become aware of the interference of countertransference difficulties. This vague expectation is seldom documented or spelled out in the literature; it is just assumed that everyone who has finished a training psychoanalysis successfully, which implies achieving a sense of professional psychoanalytic identity and personal integrity, will somehow carry out this function as a normal part of everyday psychoanalytic work.

Until recently the difficulties involved in self-analysis have tended to be glossed over, and very few authors have presented data for study. Elsewhere I (Chessick 1990) have reviewed the literature and presented data from my own self-analysis. Wheelis (1956) cautioned that, training analysis notwithstanding, analysts also employ defensive mechanisms and are personally affected by the nature of analytic work. Kramer (1959) concentrated on the so-called continuing self-analysis, and tried to compare and review the forces operating in self-analysis with those in a formal psychoanalysis, singling out the positive transference, the reexperience of old conflicts in the transference situation, and the function of the analyst as interpreter. She claimed that transference feelings in self-analysis are directed toward other objects and emphasized the importance of identification with one's psychoanalyst as interpreter, so that the same procedure is followed as during one's formal psychoanalysis "with the important difference of being patient and analyst at the same time" (p. 19).

Freud (Tyson 1986) recognized this difficulty as early as 1897, and Fleming (1971) agreed that "the experience of resistance is more intense in self-analysis than with an external analyst present" (p. 30). But, she added, "We know it can be overcome with persistent effort and in time" (p. 31). However, she presented no data to support her contention.

Kramer (1959) tried to draw the distinction between methodical active efforts at self-analysis and an "autoanalytic ego function" that involves "seemingly spontaneous experiences" (p. 19), in which material that was previously impervious to active attempts at self-analysis spontaneously, forcefully, and convincingly broke through into her conscious mind. She left open the question of whether active self-analytic efforts stimulate this autoanalytic ego function. No other author has attempted to maintain this distinction between active self-analysis and the autoanalytic ego function because the two occur together. Kramer's most important contribution was to contend that, upon losing the analyst as an object at the termination of one's analysis, a replacement takes place through identification; the analyst and his or her demand to analyze are set up in the ego-ideal. Thus, according to

Kramer, the positive transference as an incentive to face inner conflicts comes from the superego and ego-ideal demand and approval.

Myerson (1960) utilized a framework similar to that of Kramer and described an autobiographical episode that he attempted to analyze by a method he considered a step-by-step repeat of the analytic process. He conceded, however, that discoveries in self-analysis may "serve to cover deeper and more threatening meanings" (p. 155). For him, as for Kramer, the analytic ego-ideal formed from an identification with one's analyst comes to function as a "permanent part of the post-analytic personality" (p. 150).

A different approach to the study of self-analysis was presented by Ticho (1967), who carried out discussions with an unspecified number of practicing analysts, all of whom had a personal psychoanalysis that was terminated not less than four to five years before they were questioned. Ticho believed that self-analysis depends on the development of a new skill that evolves during one's formal psychoanalysis, a skill based on the formal psychoanalytic functions of "free association, objective and respectful listening, and interpretation" (p. 309), but the final organization of these functions into a unified whole is achieved by each analysand on his or her own.

Ross and Kapp (1962) offered a specific technique for self-analysis of countertransference by using the psychoanalyst's visual images in response to the narration of the patient's dreams (see COUNTER-TRANSFERENCE). The analyst then associates to his or her visual images and applies self-analysis in this fashion. Their technique, although it is quite clever, stumbles on the same problem of how one validates the insights gained; a sudden change in level of tension, a sudden feeling of understanding the self better, and a spurt in the progress of the patient's analysis, as Ross and Kapp conceded, can occur with both correct and inexact interpretations. These authors suggested a process utilizing a supervisor to cross-check the validity of the insight, but this would not be practical for an ongoing self-analysis.

Calder (1980) described his deliberate self-analysis over a period of fifteen years. He wrote down certain data and his associations to the data, then attempted to understand the primary data on the basis of the associations, the written record permitting comparisons at different times. The primary data were dreams, followed by memories, daydreams, and symptoms. Calder found his dreams to be too complex and less useful than expected. Memories and daydreams were much more useful, and symptoms both more frequent and more useful than anticipated. A similar technique was first proposed by Pickworth Farrow (1926) and used by Freud (1926), who also told Jones (1953) that he devoted the last half hour of each day to self-analysis. Considering the incredible length of Freud's working day, one would like to know a lot more about this rather cryptic remark.

Implicit in Calder's discussion is the important differentiation between one's formal psychoanalysis and self-analysis in the absence of an analyst as the object of transference. Contrary to Kramer (1959), who, as mentioned above, reported the transference in self-analysis taking place to "other objects," Calder claimed that insight in self-analysis can be achieved by means other than the analysis of transference. Calder (1980) concluded that, "self-analysis is a labor of love" (p. 19); there is clearly an important narcissistic factor at work.

Indeed, Warner (1980), in his study of the misalliances formed by Guntrip with both of his analysts, noted that self-analysis during a formal psychoanalysis can be a formidable resistance. Abraham (1919) first pointed this out, and Warner provided a striking case illustration. In fact, Pickworth Farrow's (1926) self-analysis was brought about by his failures in psychoanalysis. It is in this area of the narcissistic aspects of self-analysis that the greatest potential deceptions of the procedure clearly lie.

Beiser (1984) attempted a systematic self-analytic approach somewhat like Calder's, but did not have the "patience or persistence" involved and soon gave it up. Her final technique was similar to that of Myerson (1960), using the self-analytic process in situations of anxiety or distress. An example of the most intensive self-analysis arising in a situation of acute stress or the sudden appearance of a symptom is presented by Engel (1975), who proceeded to focus his self-analysis on that situation and its anniversary (in Engel's case, the death of his twin brother). Beiser, Myerson, and Engel, in contrast to Calder, call up self-analysis only in specific extraordinary situations rather than as a nonspecific ongoing methodical process.

Kohut (1984) suggested that the diminution of conscious self-analysis taking place in some psychoanalysts as they mature in their profession is not necessarily deleterious, and could be evaluated as a positive sign indicating that the total functioning of the analyst qua analyst has improved. He asked, "Has [the analyst] replaced plain self-analysis, consciously undertaken, with more nuanced reactions that proceed silently?" (p. 224). Indeed, for Kohut the continuous deliberate exercise of self-analysis represents "the need to reinstate the functions of the selfobject analyst in the form of a conscious exercise of self-analysis" (p. 170). This view seems to cast doubt on the motivation for regular methodical self-analysis, seeing self-analysis appropriate only as a nuanced reaction to countertransference, and suggesting that the decline of self-analytic activity could be a manifestation of increasing maturity and smoother preconscious personality functioning.

Because of the ever-present danger of defenses and resistances in self-analysis already recognized by Freud (1935), it is not possible to resolve the issue of whether self-analysis can reveal genuinely new insights or consists primarily of reworking unfinished material from one's training psychoanalysis. It also seems evident that theoretical issues such as choices between self-psychological interpretations and traditional oedipal interpretations as applied to psychoanalytic data cannot be resolved by self-analysis; one's employment of various theoretical orientations is so multiply determined that it cannot be separated convincingly from defenses and compromise formations.

Above all this stands the most important goal of self-analysis: the understanding of one's countertransference reactions. This is especially important in the treatment of seriously disturbed patients who become disruptive, and thus are labeled borderline, often as a response to unconscious countertransference manifestations from the analyst that are experienced in the selfobject transference as failures in empathy. For the psychoanalytic therapist, therefore, it seems mandatory that some process of self-analysis be continued throughout his or her professional life.

References

Abraham, K. (1919). A particular form of neurotic resistance to the psychoanalytic method. In *Selected Papers on Psychoanalysis,* trans. D. Bryan and A. Strachey pp. 303–310. New York: Basic Books, 1954.

Beiser, H. (1984). An example of self-analysis. *Journal of the American Psychoanalytic Association* 32:3–12.

Calder, K. (1980). An analyst's self-analysis. *Journal of the American Psychoanalytic Association* 28:5–20.

Chessick, R. (1990). In the clutches of the devil. *Psychoanalytic Psychotherapy* 7: 142–151.

_____ (1990). Self-analysis: a fool for a patient? *Psychoanalytic Review* 77: 311–340.

Engel, G. (1975). Ten years of self-analysis—reaction to the death of a twin. *International Journal of Psycho-Analysis* 56:23–40.

Fleming, J. (1971). Freud's concept of self-analysis. In *Currents in Psychoanalysis*, ed. I. Marcus. New York: International Universities Press.

Freud, S. (1900). The interpretation of dreams. *Standard Edition* 4,5:1–625.

_____ (1926). Prefatory note to a paper by E. Pickworth Farrow. *Standard Edition* 20:280.

_____ (1935). The subtleties of a faulty action. *Standard Edition* 22:233–238.

_____ (1937). Analysis terminable and interminable. *Standard Edition* 23:211–254.

Jones, E. (1953). *The Life and Work of Sigmund Freud.* New York: Basic Books.

Kohut, H. (1984). *How Does Analysis Cure?* Chicago: University of Chicago Press.

Kramer, M. (1959). On the continuation of the analytic process after psychoanalysis (a self-observation). *International Journal of Psycho-Analysis* 40:17–25.

Myerson, P. (1960). Awareness and stress: post-psychoanalytic utilization of insight. *International Journal of Psycho-Analysis* 41:147–156.

Pickworth Farrow, E. (1926). A method of self-analysis. *British Journal of Medical Psychology* 5:106–118.

Ross, D., and Kapp, F. (1962). A technique for self-analysis of countertransference. *Journal of the American Psychoanalytic Association* 10:643–657.

Ticho, G. (1967). On self-analysis. *International Journal of Psycho-Analysis* 48: 308–318.

Tyson, R. (1986). Countertransference evolution in theory and practice. *Journal of the American Psychoanalytic Association* 34: 251–274.

Warner, S. (1980). A clinical note on auto-analysis as a narcissistic resistance. *Journal of the American Academy of Psychoanalysis* 8:279–286.

Wheelis, A. (1956). The vocational hazards of psycho-analysis. *International Journal of Psycho-Analysis* 37:171–184.

SELF DISORDERS

Kohut and Wolf (1978) present à nosology of disorders of the self. Borrowing from their paper and from Kohut (1977), self disorders can be divided into secondary and primary disturbances. The secondary disturbances of the self are reactions of a structurally undamaged self to the natural vicissitudes of life and health. This engenders a critical area of understanding for crisis intervention and adolescent adjustment problems. The psychotherapy of secondary disturbances provides a mirroring and idealizable selfobject so that the self automatically firms up (see SELFOBJECT). The patient's ego functions improve *pari passu*, and the difficulties and vicissitudes can be handled in an optimal, relatively brief fashion, without much interpretation.

Primary disturbances of the self may be divided into five categories. In *psychoses* there has been serious damage to the nuclear self, and no substantial or reliable defensive structures to cover the defect, whether biological or not, have been formed.

In *borderline states* there is the same defect as in psychoses, but it is masked by complex defenses with which it is unwise for the therapist to tamper except to improve their adaptability. This pessimistic outlook on borderline states has been challenged (see BORDERLINE).

Schizoid and paranoid personalities wall off the self and keep themselves at an emotional distance from others in order to protect against "a permanent or protracted breakup, enfeeblement, or serious distortions of the self" (Kohut 1977, p. 192) (see SCHIZOID and PARANOIA). Again, we are warned by Kohut (1971) not to be a bull in a china shop in trying to reach such patients. Here also I believe there is excessive pessimism. If the therapist is empathic and relatively patient, stable selfobject transferences are sometimes formed by these patients and much improvement can occur.

In *narcissistic behavior disorders* there are symptoms of perversions, addictions, and delinquency, but the self is only temporarily distorted or enfeebled. These patients have a significantly more resilient self than patients in the first three categories and are more amenable to treatment. However, they are not easier to treat than borderline or schizoid personality disorders.

In *narcissistic personality disorders* the problem is the same as the previous category with one exception. Instead of predominantly behavioral (see ALLOPLASTIC) symptoms, there are autoplastic symptoms of hypochondria, malaise, boredom, depression, and hypersensitivity to slights. According to Kohut, only narcissistic behavior and personality disorders are analyzable, as the self in the first three categories cannot withstand the reactivation of narcissistic needs without fragmentation. This is a kind of reverse definition and depends on whether or not stable narcissistic transferences form.

Kohut and Wolf (1978) review certain clinical syndromes in identifying disorders of the self. The *understimulated self* is due to a chronic lack of stimulating responsiveness from the selfobject of childhood. The individual shows a lack of vitality, boredom, and apathy, and may have to use any excitement to ward off painful feelings of deadness.

The *fragmenting self* occurs when the patient reacts to narcissistic disappointments, such as the therapist's lack of empathy, by the loss of a sense of cohesive self: disheveled dress, posture and gait disturbances, vague anxiety, time and space disorientation, and hypochondriacal concerns. In a minor way this occurs in all of us when our self-esteem has been taxed for long periods and no replenishing sustenance has presented itself, or after a series of failures that shake our self-esteem.

Kohut (1978) points out that a narcissistic blow can lead to regression of the self in which there are archaic but cohesive forms. It can also lead to empty depletion or enfeeblement, or to temporary fragmentation. Such regression can manifest itself by a shift from normal assertiveness to narcissistic rage, voyeurism in the search for an idealized parent imago, or gross exhibitionism in the search for mirroring confirmation of the grandiose self.

The *overstimulated self* is caused by unempathic excessive responses from the childhood selfobject, the intrusive overconcerned narcissistic excitement of neurotic parents. If the grandiose-exhibitionistic pole has been overstimulated, the patient is always in danger of being flooded by archaic greatness fantasies, which produce anxiety and spoil the joy of normal successes. Frightened by their intense ambition, these patients avoid normal creativity and productivity and avoid situations where they would attract attention.

If the ideals pole is overstimulated by parents displaying themselves to gain admiration from the child, internalization cannot occur and an intense merger need remains. Loss of healthy enthusiasm for normal goals and ideals results.

In the closely related *overburdened self* the childhood selfobject has not been calm. There has been neither merger with the calmness of an omnipotent selfobject nor development of an internalized, self-soothing capacity. A world that lacks soothing selfobjects is experienced as inimical and dangerous. When the therapist fails in empathy, the patient dreams of living in a poisoned atmosphere surrounded by snakes and other creatures and complains of the noises, odors, and temperature changes in the therapist's office (see EMPATHY).

Certain behavioral syndromes in the realm of the disorders of the self are also presented by Kohut and Wolf (1978). *Mirror-hungry personalities* thirst for selfobjects who will give them confirming and admiring responses. "They are impelled to display themselves and to evoke the attention of others, trying to counteract, however fleetingly, their inner sense of worthlessness and lack of self-esteem" (p. 421).

Ideal-hungry personalities are forever in search of others whom they can respect and admire for various idealized traits, such as prestige, power, beauty, intelligence, and moral or philosophical stature. Such patients can only experience themselves as worthwhile when they are related in some way to these idealized selfobjects.

Alter-ego personalities want others to experience and confirm their feelings, appearance, opinions, and values, but are capable of being nourished longer than mirror-hungry personalities and of forming friendships of a sort. These three types of narcissistic personalities are not primarily pathological, although they may be so if carried to an extreme.

Two other types of behavior represent psychopathology. *Mergerhunger personalities* have a compelling need to control their selfobject, are very intolerant of the independence of the selfobject, are very sensitive to separations, and demand the continuous presence of the selfobject.

Contact-shunning personalities are the opposite in that they avoid social contact and become isolated. The intensity of their need is so great that they are excessively sensitive to the slightest sign of rejection, which they prevent by isolation and withdrawal from others.

References

Kohut, H. (1971). *The Analysis of the Self.* New York: International Universities Press.

———— (1977). *The Restoration of the Self.* New York: International Universities Press.

———— (1978). *The Search for the Self,* ed. P. Ornstein. New York: International Universities Press.

Kohut, H., and Wolf, E. (1978). The disorders of the self and their treatment: an outline. *International Journal of Psycho-Analysis* 59:413–425.

SELF-ESTEEM (SEE ALSO NARCISSISM)

Self-esteem is believed by self psychologists to rest on successful childhood selfobject experiences. It fluctuates according to whether experiences in relations with others are gratifying or frustrating and whether an individual feels appreciated or rejected by other people. In traditional theory it is also dependent on the evaluation by the ego-ideal of how close one has come to one's goals and aspirations (see CORRUPTION, EGO-IDEAL). Self-esteem is related to pressures exerted by the superego on the ego; if the superego is highly sadistic, there is a continual lowering of self-esteem, regardless of the individual's successes. This represents aggression directed by the sadistic superego toward the ego. Kernberg (1991) explains that self-esteem may also be lowered by "lack of gratification of instinctual needs of both a libidinal and an aggressive nature, so that unconscious ego defenses that repress awareness and expression of such instinctual needs will impoverish the ego of gratifying experiences and thus 'deplete' libidinal self-investment and diminish self-esteem . . . the images in our mind of those we love and by whom we feel loved strengthen our self-love" (p. 143).

Freud (1914) maintains that there are three aspects to self-esteem. One part is "the residue of infantile narcissism," another arises out of the omnipotent experience of fulfilling one's ego-ideal, and a third part "proceeds from the satisfaction of object libido" (p. 100). Self-esteem can be thought of as a state of being on good terms with one's superego. The importance of self-esteem as a motivation for human action cannot be sufficiently emphasized, as La Rochefoucauld (1959) explained in his famous maxims written in 1665.

References

Freud, S. (1914). On narcissism: an introduction. *Standard Edition* 14.67 102.

Kernberg, O. (1991). A contemporary reading of "On Narcissism." In *Freud's "On Narcissism": An Introduction*, ed. J. Sandler, E. Person, and P. Fonagy, pp. 131–148. New Haven, CT: Yale University Press.

La Rochefoucauld, F. (1959). *The Maxims of La Rochefoucauld*, trans. L. Kronenberger. New York: Vintage.

SELFOBJECT

An object (see OBJECT) may be defined as a selfobject when it is experienced intrapsychically as providing functions in an interpersonal relationship that add to or maintain the cohesive sense of self. This includes affect attunement, consensual validation, tension regulation and soothing, recognition of one's autonomous potential, and restoration of a temporarily threatened fragmentation of the self through a variety of activities and comments. We have all experienced others as selfobjects, and Kohut (1984) maintains that we need selfobjects from the beginning to the end of life. Kohut mentioned both structure-building and structure-maintaining selfobject experiences. Developmental phase-appropriate and, later on, age-appropriate selfobject functions form the mainspring of an individual's self-love, self-esteem, and self-respect.

There remains a debate in the literature (Shane 1991) as to whether there is a difference between an object experience and a selfobject experience. An object experience might be thought of as a situation in which a cohesive self expresses itself affectively and tries to bring about a certain outcome or solve a certain problem. A selfobject experience involves a self that is threatened and requires a particular function to make up for an inadequacy or weakness in the self structure. Shane paraphrases Basch as maintaining that the difference relates "exclusively to the self state of the individual, whether the self state is cohesive or shaky" (p. 31).

Wolf (1988) presents a classification of age-appropriate selfobject needs, defined as "normally required selfobject experiences that fit the age-dependent requirements to sustain self-cohesion" (p. 56). An infant needs experiences with a real person who provides certain responses that fit the early stages of the emerging sense of self, as defined by Stern (see SELF). An adolescent needs selfobject experiences with peers, symbols, and the adolescent subculture. An adult needs selfobject experiences with other individuals or symbols, "such as [those] provided by art, literature, music, religion, ideas, which by their availability function as self-

objects for that particular adult. . . . These experiences are only partly conscious, but their effect on the self is powerfully strengthening" (p. 54).

References

Kohut, H. (1984). *How Does Analysis Cure?* Chicago: University of Chicago Press.

Shane, M. (1991). Selfobject or self-regulating other. In *The Evolution of Self Psychology: Progress in Self Psychology,* vol. 7, ed. A. Goldberg, pp. 31–36. Hillsdale, NJ: Analytic Press.

Wolf, E. (1988). *Treating the Self: Elements of Clinical Self Psychology.* New York: Guilford.

SELF PSYCHOLOGY (KOHUT)

Self psychology refers to the theory and practice of psychoanalysis advocated by Heinz Kohut (1913–1981). I (Chessick 1985) have described it in detail elsewhere and have referred to it under various concepts in this dictionary (see BIPOLAR SELF, FRAGMENTATION, GRANDIOSE SELF, HORIZONTAL SPLIT, MIRROR TRANSFERENCE, NARCISSISTIC RAGE, OBJECT, OPTIMAL FRUSTRATION, SELF DISORDERS, SELF, SELFOBJECT).

Our self-assessment becomes closer to the assessment of others as our narcissism matures through a series of developmental pathways. In response to stimuli from the environment and due to an epigenetic preprogramming involving our heredity, these developmental pathways lead from autoerotism, to primary narcissism—in which the infant blissfully experiences the world as being itself—and then, due to inevitable disappointment in such narcissistic omnipotence, the formation of the grandiose self and the idealized parent imago. The grandiose self implies the conviction of being very powerful, if not omnipotent, with a demand for mirroring confirmation by the selfobject; the idealized parent imago attributes all omnipotence to a magical figure, which is then viewed as a selfobject to be controlled and fused with this imago. By a series of microinternalizations in an appropriate environment, the grandiose self becomes incorporated into the ego or self as ambition (the ambitions pole of the self), a drive or push that can be realistically sublimated and is itself drive-channeling and drive-controlling, resulting in motivated enthusiastic activity. The idealized parent imago becomes infused into the ego-ideal (or, in the later theory, the other pole of the self; see BIPOLAR SELF), which attracts the individual toward certain goals and performs a drive-curbing function. The proper microinternalization of these formations leads ultimately by further transformations to a sense of humor, empathy, wisdom, acceptance of the transience of life, and even to creativity within the limitations of the individual.

As a consequence of developmental arrest and failure to properly integrate these archaic structures, characteristic "selfobject transferences" (Kohut 1977), previously called "narcissistic transferences" (Kohut 1971) occur as the result of the amalgamation of the unconscious archaic narcissistic structures (grandiose self and idealized parent imago) with the psychic representation of the analyst, under the pressure of the need to relieve the unfulfilled narcissistic needs of childhood. The goal of the idealizing selfobject transference is to share magically, via a merger, in the power and omnipotence of the therapist. Occurring as the result of therapeutic mobilization of the idealized parent imago are two basic types of such transferences, with a variety of gradations in between. The most obvious type is a later formation, apparently based on a failure of idealization of the father, that stresses the search for an idealized parent, which the patient must attach himself or herself to in order to feel approved and protected. A more archaic type of selfobject transference may appear, or be hidden under the other type; this transference is related to a failure with the mother, in which the stress is on ecstatic merger and mystical union with the godlike idealized parent.

Once such a transference has been formed, clinical signs of its disturbance are a cold, aloof, angry, raging withdrawal, which represents a swing to the grandiose self; feelings of fragmentation and hypochondria due to the separation; and the creation of erotized replacement by often frantic activities and fantasies, especially those involving voyeurism, but with many variations.

The typical countertransference to the idealizing selfobject transferences occurs through the mobilization of the archaic grandiose self, in whatever unanalyzed residue is present, in the therapist; this leads to an embarrassed and defensive "straight-arming" of the patient by denying the patient's idealization, joking about it, or trying vigorously to interpret it away. Such countertransference produces in the patient the typical signs of disturbance mentioned above.

Three forms of mirror selfobject transference are seen as a result of the therapeutic mobilization of the repressed and unintegrated archaic grandiose self (see MIRROR TRANSFERENCE for details). In the archaic-merger type, the patient experiences the therapist as part of himself or herself, expects the therapist to know what is in his or her mind and what he or she wants, and demands total control. In the alterego or twinship type of mirror transference, the patient insists that the therapist is like or similar to him or her psychologically or that the therapist and the patient look alike. This was later separated out by Kohut (1984) as a third form of selfobject transference. In the third type of mirror transference, or mirror transference proper, the patient recognizes that the therapist looks different, but insists on assigning to the therapist the sole task of praising, echoing, and mirroring the patient's performance and greatness.

In clinical work we can pick up certain signs that selfobject transferences have formed. We note that the patient reacts to our empathic lapses, or to cancellations and vacations, or even to the gap of time between sessions, with (a) perverse or other sexual acting out, (b) hypochondriasis, (c) irritable and arrogant behavior, (d) painfully depressive moods, and (e) a sense of emptiness and depletion. These signs may be understood as manifestations of partial fragmentation of the self due to the disruption of the selfobject transferences, and as attempts to restitute and discharge the painful tensions involved.

The purpose of the selfobject transferences is to relieve the unfulfilled narcissistic needs of childhood for the selfobject to joyfully accept and confirm the child's grandiosity, and for "an omnipotent surrounding," which Kohut and Wolf (1978) regard as healthy needs that had not been responded to in early life. When these responses are forthcoming, a temporary sense of narcissistic peace and equilibrium results.

Phase-inappropriate disappointment in the idealized parent imago that occurs very early in experiences with the mother leads to a need for optimal soothing from the idealized parent and a search for drugs, with a malfunctioning stimulus barrier. Such patients tend to become addicted to psychotherapy for just this reason. In the late preoedipal period, phase-inappropriate disappointment causes a resexualization of pregenital drives and derivatives, with a high incidence of perversions in fantasy or acts. In early latency the severe disappointment in the idealized oedipal object undoes the recently established and thus precariously idealized superego. This leads to the search for an external object of perfection, an intense search for and dependency on idealized selfobjects, which are conceived as missing segments of the psychic structure. For such patients, each success can give only transient good feelings but does not add to the patient's self-esteem because the patient is fixed on finding an idealized parent imago outside of himself—he is at a developmental stage such that he must have an outside source of approval.

In the neurotic transferences, idealization (see IDEALIZATION) does not lose touch entirely with the realistic features and limitations of the object. In other neurotic situations, idealization can represent a projection of the analysand's idealized superego onto the analyst and form a part of the positive transference, or defensive idealizations can form against transference hostility. In the narcissistic transferences, there is a sense of a vague idealization, which can lead to the extreme delusion that the therapist is godlike. An eerie quality of unreasonable exultation is present, to which the therapist reacts with embarrassment and negativism if he or she does not understand the material conceptually. The intensity of the distortion gives the therapist an idea of how desperate the patient is.

The grandiose self and idealized parent imago are either split off or repressed if the developmental line of narcissism is interfered with. If they are split off, one gets Kohut's (1971) "vertical split" in which there is a barrier between two conscious parts of the self that are not integrated. The

patient acts as if one aspect of the self does not know about the other.

If these primitive narcissistic structures are repressed, we observe reaction formations or the sudden emergence of many vague symptoms. Some of these are (a) fear of the loss of the real self to ecstatic merger with the idealized parent, God, or the universe; (b) fear of loss of contact with reality due to intense unrealistic grandiosity; (c) shame and self-consciousness consequent to dealing with the intrusion of exhibitionistic libido; and (d) hypochondriasis, which represents an elaboration by the ego as disintegration anxiety appears; body parts become crystallization points for hypochondriacal worry, an attempt to reconstitute and explain the incipient fragmentation of the self. In these disorders, acting out represents a partial breakthrough of the grandiose self and may be life-threatening.

In working with self disorders, the therapist must participate by dealing especially with responses to separation and disappointments in the transferences, and by staying nearer to everyday experiences rather than deep interpretations of the past. In fact, interpretations of the past may come as a narcissistic injury because the patient can't do much about it. The therapist takes a benign approach and fosters the development of the transference relationship by patient, craftsmanlike work. Minor disappointments in the narcissistic transferences, followed by characteristic reactions in the patient, must be calmly explained to the patient. Without this conceptual understanding, the temptation occurs to launch all kinds of extratherapeutic activities toward the patient. Some of these temptations are based directly on countertransference hostility and some are based on reaction formations to this hostility; but the principle remains that the therapist's temptation to step outside the role of the calm, benign craftsman is based on a misunderstanding of what is going on in the therapy and is motivated by countertransference. There is no end to the rationalizations that the unanalyzed psychotherapist may present to himself or herself to justify this exploitation of and retaliation toward the patient.

To protect themselves against rejection and further narcissistic wounding, patients with an insufficient ego-ideal tend to withdraw into grandiosity—which bothers and irritates people and produces further rejection, leading to further withdrawal. Clinically, narcissistic peace can be established with concomitant improved function when the idealizing transference occurs, but such transferences may also lead to a fear of loss of ego boundaries and fusion if the wish to merge with the idealized parent imago is so strong, and so may result in a negative therapeutic reaction. The patient must resist the threatened merging out of fear of loss of the autonomy of the self.

In Kohut's (1977, 1984) later "psychology of the self in the broad sense," a complementary role in development is given to the oedipal phase. Here, it is the response of the parents to the child's libidinal and aggressive and exhibitionistic strivings—their pride and mirroring confirmation of the child's development—that permits internalizations to occur smoothly. To clarify, in Freud's theory, for example, it is the boy's fear of castration by the father that causes him to identify with the aggressor and internalize the values of the father. For Kohut, it is at the same time the father's pride in the boy's emerging assertiveness, as it shows itself in the boy's oedipal strivings and imitative efforts, that softens the boy's disappointment of not possessing the mother and enables an internalization of the idealized parent imago as a nuclear pole of the self. If, for example, the father or mother withdraws from the child as a response to their horror of his oedipal strivings, this internalization cannot occur, and the child remains fixed in development on finding some individual outside of himself to which he attaches the idealized parent imago.

Some authors claim that Freud would not have considered Kohut's psychology of the self a complementary theory. Kohut's (1977) procedure is based on the Zeigarnik phenomenon, which postulates some kind of inner motivation of undeveloped structures to resume their development when given the opportunity; the energy behind this motivation has nothing to do with Freud's instinctual drives, and the origin of it is not explained. The basis of therapy in the psychology of the self assumes that proper understanding and development of "selfobject transferences," or transferencelike structures in the treatment, make it possible for this force to take over and thus for development of the self to resume via transmuting internalization; this is clearly fundamentally different from the resolution of conflicts via interpretation of a transference neurosis. Thus Slap and Levine (1978), in a rather extreme statement, write, "Although Kohut refers to it as a psychoanalysis, his therapeutic method depends on suggestion and learning, but not insight, conflict resolution, or making the unconscious conscious" (p. 507).

Bacal (1991) distinguishes five characteristics that separate self psychology from classical psychoanalysis: (1) instinctual motivation is not thought of as a central factor in development and pathogenesis; (2) there is a shift to a "multi-body psychology" (p. 38); (3) the subjective sense of self is placed consistently at the center; (4) the selfobject relationship is seen as a central significant form of relationship between the self and the other; and (5) there is a "transformation of the traditional perspectives on narcissism": narcissism (see NARCISSISM) is traditionally viewed as a fixation at an early stage of development or a defense against anxieties associated with object-instinctual strivings, whereas "self psychology regards narcissism as a self defect or self distortion resulting from a significant failure of selfobjects and the mounting of defenses against the anxieties associated with the expression of selfobject needs" (p. 38).

References

Bacal, H. (1991). Notes on the relationship between object relations theory and self psychology. In *The Evolution of Self Psychology: Progress in Self Psychology,* vol. 7, ed. A. Goldberg, pp. 36–44. Hillsdale, NJ: Analytic Press.

Chessick, R. (1985). *Psychology of the Self and the Treatment of Narcissism.* Northvale, NJ: Jason Aronson.

Kohut, H. (1971). *The Analysis of the Self.* New York: International Universities Press.

———— (1977). *The Restoration of the Self.* New York: International Universities Press.

———— (1978). *The Search for the Self,* ed. P. Ornstein. New York: International Universities Press.

———— (1984). *How Does Analysis Cure?* Chicago: University of Chicago Press.

Kohut, H., and Wolf, E. S. (1978). The disorders of the self and their treatment: an outline. *International Journal of Psycho-Analysis* 59:413–425.

Slap, J., and Levine, F. (1978). On hybrid concepts in psychoanalysis. *Psychoanalytic Quarterly* 47:499–523.

SELF-STATE DREAMS (SEE DREAMS)

SHAME

No one has improved on Samuel Johnson's (1773) definition of shame: "The passion felt when reputation is supposed to be lost; the passion expressed sometimes by blushes" (p. 1763). Piers and Singer (1953) produced a classic study of shame and guilt. Shame is felt when one does not live up to the standards of one's ego-ideal, whereas guilt is the affect experienced when one transgresses the rules and regulations of the superego. So transgressions of moral codes and laws result in the feeling of guilt; lack of tact and errors in taste produce shame.

The concept of shame is closely connected with the concept of narcissistic wounding (see NARCISSISM). Shame compels us to see ourselves through the eyes of others and may increase insight. Moore and Fine (1990) eloquently describe shame as referring to "embarrassment, humiliation, mortification, and disgrace—that accompany the feeling of being rejected, ridiculed, exposed, or losing the respect of others" (p. 181). Shame may be a warning of anticipated rejection of one's grandiosity or exhibitionism, or become part of one's character as a helpful defense against the expression of such wishes.

Psychotherapists should always remember that shame or humiliation is extremely painful, and patients unavoidably suffer a lot of these affects in the process of treatment.

References

Johnson, S. (1773). *A Dictionary of the English Language*. Beirut, Lebanon: Librairie du Liban, 1978.
Moore, B., and Fine, B. (1990). *Psychoanalytic Terms and Concepts*. New Haven, CT: Yale University Press.
Piers, G., and Singer, M. (1953). *Shame and Guilt*. New York: Norton.

SIGNAL ANXIETY (SEE ANXIETY)

SPLITTING (KERNBERG)

Splitting is a term used differently by authors in object relations theory (Pruyser 1975) (see OBJECT RELATIONS THEORY). It represents a failure in the synthesizing function of the ego, which Freud (1940) related to disavowal but which has come to have more preoedipal connotations. It is crucial to the turning away from reality in any condition, including dreams, perversions, neuroses, and psychoses, and it enables these processes to occur. The concept of splitting lies at the basis of Otto Kernberg's theories of development and is the concept central to his long experience with, understanding of, and treatment of borderline patients. At present Kernberg is Associate Chairman and Medical Director of The New York Hospital–Cornell Medical Center and Professor of Psychiatry at the Cornell University Medical College. He is also Training and Supervising Analyst of the Columbia University Center for Psychoanalytic Training and Research, and the recipient of many awards for his work.

Kernberg (1976) postulates five stages of development of internalized object relations. The first, or primary undifferentiated, stage resembles Mahler's (1975) phase of normal autism. Object relations theory lends itself well to the organization of direct observations of the initial preoedipal mother–infant dyad, during which there are no self or object representations (or images, as they are called by Kernberg). This stage lasts about a month or two and leads to the second stage, which corresponds to Mahler's symbiotic phase between the ages of 2 and 6 months, plus her first or "differentiation" subphase of separation-individuation from 6 to 9 months of age.

In this stage, there are representations, but these are roughly undifferentiated self and object constellations separated only into good and bad; consequently there is no differentiation between self and object. Kernberg here postulates a primary undifferentiated good self-object representation or constellation associated with pleasurable experiences (pure pleasure ego) and invested with libido, and a primary undifferentiated bad self-object representation associated with pain and frustration and invested with aggression. Kernberg's conception of "self-object-affect unit" should not be confused with Kohut's "selfobject," which is an experience-near conception coming from an entirely different methodology and theory (see SELF-OBJECT, SELF PSYCHOLOGY).

The third stage, which follows the first rumblings of separation-individuation that occurred from the age of 6 to 9 months, begins when the self and object representations have been differentiated within the two primary constellations (good and bad) that predominate in the second stage, as described above. It ends somewhere in the third year of life, with the eventual integration of good and bad self representations into an integrated self-concept and the integration of good and bad object representations into total object representations. The achievement of object constancy and the firm capacity to distinguish the inner from the outer world (stable ego boundaries) depends on this stage.

Kernberg (1976) postulates that "pathological fixation and/or regression to this stage of development of internalized object relations determines borderline personality organization" (p. 65). He explains that in this third stage, "the separation of libidinally invested and aggressively invested self- and object-representations becomes strengthened by active utilization of the mechanism of splitting, which is geared to protect the ideal, good relationship with the mother from 'contamination' by bad self-representations and bad representations of her" (p. 67). Normally this splitting decreases, but Kernberg continues with a statement meant to specifically delineate the intrapsychic pathology that predominates in the borderline personality: "The main objective of the defensive constellation centering on splitting in the borderline personality organization is to keep separate the aggressively determined and the libidinally determined intrapsychic structures stemming from early object relations" (p. 67). Although by the end of the third stage in normal development there is a firm self-concept differentiated from object representations, within the self-concept there is still some splitting of good and bad self representations. Similarly, within the object representations "at first only representing mother, and then also father, siblings, etc." (pp. 66–67), good and bad object representations coexist by splitting, which, however, is gradually diminishing.

The fourth stage, beginning in the latter part of the third year of life and lasting through the oedipal period, "is characterized by the integration of libidinally invested and aggressively invested self-representations into the definite self-system, and of libidinally invested and aggressively invested object-images into 'total' object-representations" (Kernberg 1976, p. 67). In this phase the ego and superego as intrapsychic structures are consolidated. The typical pathology in this stage is represented by the neuroses and the organization of character pathology Kernberg calls higher level, where "pathogenic conflicts typically occur between the ego and a relatively well-integrated but excessively strict and punitive superego" (p. 67).

One variant of character pathology forming at this stage is the narcissistic personality, which is, according to Kernberg, an abnormal consolidation, characterized by the formation of a pathological grandiose self, embedded in a defense organization "similar to that of the borderline personality organization" (p. 68), due to regression back to the third stage.

Thus, according to Kernberg, the coalescence of the good and bad self representations into a definite, integrated, relatively realistic overall self representation in the ego, and the coalescence of the good and bad object representations into a definite, integrated, relatively realistic overall self representation in the ego, is the task of the fourth stage, and fails in the borderline patient. This failure may be due to congenital ego defect or excessive aggression, fixing the patient in the third stage or causing regression back to it, and making the fourth stage impossible. This coalescence is related to Hartmann and colleagues' (1949) concept of neutralization (see NEUTRALIZATION), freeing energy for ego functioning and the higher level exercise of repression, that is, setting up countercathexes; if it fails, the weakened ego must utilize splitting as its principal defense, setting in motion a downward spiral of further weakness and more splitting.

The fifth and final developmental stage, from age 5 to 7, is the resolution of the oedipal phase, the consolidation of the superego, a diminished sharp opposition between the ego and the superego leading to more internal harmony, and finally the formation and consolidation of ego identity. Notice that in normal development, according to Kernberg, splitting begins around the third month, peaks several months later, and gradually disappears at the end of the second year and beginning of the third year of life, after which there is the development of repression and higher-level defenses.

In his conceptions of the superego and narcissism, Kernberg shifts from these more Kleinian concepts to a heavier reliance on the work of Jacobson (1964). However, Jacobson avoided rigid stepwise descriptions and "considered parental interaction with the child of crucial importance rather than those conflicts which go on between 'primitive introjects'" (Abend et al. 1983, p. 163).

According to Kernberg, the main components of the superego are built during the second to fifth year, earlier than Freud thought. They are integrated in the fourth to the sixth years and toned down and consolidated (depersonified and abstracted) during the fifth through seventh years. The earliest superego structure is from "the internalization of fantastically hostile, highly unrealistic object-images reflecting 'expelled', projected, and reintrojected 'bad' self-object representations" (p. 71). The stronger the pregenital frustration and constitutional aggression, the more predominant the sadistic superego forerunners; the sadistic superego peaks at the beginning of the fourth stage of development.

There is also a second primitive superego structure—the condensed, ideal, "all good" self and object representations that form the kernel of the ego-ideal through primitive idealization.

In the fourth stage of development these two aspects of the precursors of the superego are "integrated," leading to decreased defensive projection and permitting the internalization of more realistic demands and prohibitions of the parents during the oedipal period. Integration and internalization perform the function of toning down the superego from primitive and archaic to more modulated and reasonable functioning. In the fifth stage of development the toned-down superego becomes more integrated and harmonious with the ego, leading to consolidation of ego identity, and the superego becomes more abstract and depersonified.

In Kernberg's theory two types of superego failure can occur. In the first type, there is a failure in the integration of the sadistic precursors of the superego with the benign or primitively idealized precursors, which interferes with the internalization of more realistic oedipal parental images and so perpetuates the primitive sadistic superego forerunners and fosters excessive reprojection, leading to paranoia.

In the second type, as in the borderline personality, there is a similar type of failure of integration of these precursors due to a dangerous primitive idealization. External objects are seen as totally good in order to be sure they cannot be destroyed by projected bad objects. This phenomenon occurs too early and in too extreme a fashion as a result of the need to defend against so much aggression. Thus, again, idealization is seen as a defense against aggression. Furthermore, the internalization of primitively idealized early object-images creates impossible internalized demands, causing an impasse in which "a catastrophic fusion" between these unrealistic ideal objects and the "external persecutors," or projected bad objects, then forms. This leads to a sadistic superego nucleus that is perpetuated by reprojection and reintrojection. This also leads to an interference with the toning down of the superego by the internalization of more realistic parental prohibitions, with the integration of the superego itself, and with the development of harmony between the superego and the ego. The latter causes interference with the formation of ego identity, leading to the lack of a consistent solid integrated self-concept, one of the important *DSM-III-R* characteristics of the borderline patient (see BORDERLINE).

References

Abend, S., Porder, M., and Willick, M. (1983). *Borderline Patients: Psychoanalytic Perspectives*. New York: International Universities Press.

Freud, S. (1940). Splitting of the ego in the process of defense. *Standard Edition* 23:271–278.

Hartmann, H., Kris, E., and Loewenstein, R. (1949). Notes on the theory of aggression. *Psychoanalytic Study of the Child* 3:9–36. New York: International Universities Press.

Jacobson, E. (1964). *The Self and the Object World*. New York: International Universities Press.

Kernberg, O. (1976). *Object Relations Theory and Clinical Psychoanalysis*. New York: Jason Aronson.

Mahler, M., Pine, F., and Bergman, A. (1975). *The Psychological Birth of the Human Infant*. New York: Basic Books.

Pruyser, P. (1975). What splits in "splitting"? *Bulletin of the Menninger Clinic* 39:1–46.

STIMULUS BARRIER (SEE PROTECTIVE SHIELD [*REIZSCHUTZ*])

STRAUS, ERWIN (SEE ALLON AND PHANTOM LIMB)

STRUCTURAL THEORY (SEE EGO, ID, SUPEREGO, AND TOPOGRAPHIC THEORY)

SUBLIMATION

The concept of sublimation was originally suggested by Rousseau and given importance by Nietzsche, who actually named the process. Nietzsche argued that passion, not reason, controls and drives humans, but he always added that sublimations of passion is best. He was not an advocate of raw, crude passions, but he insisted that the body and the mind, or passion and reason, are inseparable. Even conflict can be good, he thought, because it generates growth (Nietzsche 1968).

In sublimation, as taken up by Freud (1915), the energy of an unacceptable impulse is diverted and directed to socially acceptable means and goals. Freud (1930) thought of sublimation as an extremely important mechanism in the building of civilization. He claimed that artistic creation and intellectual curiosity, which may have no apparent connection with sexuality, were motivated by the force of the sexual instinct through diversion to a new nonsexual aim and socially valued objects. Thus sublimation modifies an instinctual drive according to the demands of society but still allows some measure of gratification. It is an unconscious ego function in which, unlike the mechanisms of defense, the ego is not acting in opposition to the id but rather is helping the id to gain gratification in the external world. Therefore sublimation does not involve repression, although the original impulse is not conscious.

Sublimation is sometimes thought of as a form of deaggressivization or desexualization; this was the second way Freud tried to define it. Here, it represents a theoretically inferred concept rather than something that is clinically observable. Anna Freud (1946) viewed sublimation as a defense because it provides a progressive solution of infantile conflicts that might otherwise lead to neurosis.

There is general agreement that a complete theoretical understanding of sublimation has not been developed in psychoanalytic literature and that the concept remains somewhat shadowy. Levey (1939) reviews the theory and points out many unexplained loopholes and generalities. There is a certain mystery to the idea, since there is no clear explanation of how sublimation takes place and why it occurs in some individuals and in some forms rather than others. Loewald (1988) attempts to present a traditional psychoanalytic theory of sublimation. He warns us that neutralization is not the same as sublimation since passion is not absent in sublimation. Without sublimation, the transformation of the sexual instinct, there would be no understanding in metapsychological terms of the development of civilization as Freud conceived of it. Sublimation is

indispensable in human individual and collective life.

References

Freud, A. (1946). *The Ego and the Mechanisms of Defense.* New York: International Universities Press.

Freud, S. (1915). Instincts and their vicissitudes. *Standard Edition* 14:109–140.

――― (1930). Civilization and its discontents. *Standard Edition* 21:59–145.

Levey, H. (1939). Critique of the theory of sublimation. *Psychiatry* 2:239–270.

Loewald, H. (1988). *Sublimation.* New Haven, CT: Yale University Press.

Nietzsche, F. (1968). Thus spoke Zarathustra. In *The Portable Nietzsche,* trans. W. Kaufmann, pp. 103–439. New York: Random House.

SULLIVAN, HARRY STACK (SEE SCHIZOPHRENIA)

SUPEREGO (SEE ALSO EGO IDEAL)

Freud (1914) proposed two psychic agencies that function to preserve for the ego a sense of self-esteem. The first agent, or ego-ideal, represents the series of achievements that, when reached, lead to a state of imagined infantile perfection and narcissistic bliss. Freud differentiated this agent from the agent that had the function of observing the real achievements and comparing them with the ideal standards. Later he (1916) considered this self-criticizing faculty to be the same as the dream censor and as belonging to the ego, not the superego. In the next step,

Freud (1921) began to separate the "conscience" and ego-ideal from the ego. He conceived of the possibility of the ego-ideal-conscience as coming into conflict with the rest of the ego, and even raging with a critical cruelty against the ego. The extent of this cruelty, which can function unconsciously, was a major motivation for his (1923) development and presentation of the structural theory, in which the psychic apparatus is a tripartite model containing the id, superego, and ego.

Freud considered the development of the superego primarily as a consequence of the resolution of the Oedipus complex. He increasingly emphasized the punitive and cruel aspects of the superego rather than its benign, loving aspect. He (1926) thought of the threat from the superego as an extension of the castration threat. He (1933) came to view the superego as an internalized parental authority dominating the ego through punishment and threats of withdrawal of love.

The apparent paradox of the sometimes clinically observed contrast between the harshness of the superego imitation of the parents and the actual kindness of the parents in real life was explained as the borrowing by the superego of the child's own hostility to the prohibiting parents. Thus the superego is always thought of as having a direct connection to the id and is able to drain aggression from the id by turning it upon the ego.

Recent work has focused much more on the preoedipal aspects of superego development (see also OBJECT RELATIONS THEORY and SADISM). An outstanding example of this is in the work of Kernberg (see SPLITTING). A considerable aspect of the superego is unconscious. The heir of the Oedipus complex, as Freud conceived of it, the superego functions mainly unconsciously to approve or disapprove, to critically self-observe, to bring about self-punishment, to bring about reparation for perceived wrongdoing, and to establish or reduce self-esteem. See KLEIN for details of her views on the development of the superego, which are quite different from Freud's conception.

References

Freud, S. (1914). On narcissism: an introduction. *Standard Edition* 14:67–102.

———— (1916). Introductory lectures on psycho-analysis. *Standard Edition* 15,16: 3–496.

———— (1921). Group psychology and analysis of the ego. *Standard Edition* 18: 67–143.

———— (1923). The ego and the id. *Standard Edition* 19:3–66.

———— (1926). Inhibitions, symptoms, and anxiety. *Standard Edition* 20:77–174.

———— (1933). New introductory lectures on psychoanalysis. *Standard Edition* 22: 3–182.

SYMPTOM FORMATION (SEE NEUROSIS)

T

TERMINATION

There is little agreement on the subject of termination in psychoanalysis or in psychoanalytic therapy. Drawing on data from the Psychotherapy Research Project at the Menninger Clinic, Ticho (1972) attempted to formulate a reasonable set of indications for the inception of the termination phase of the treatment. These include such issues as whether the transference neurosis has been reduced, attenuation of the patient's symptoms and character pathology to the point where functioning is not impaired, a sense that the patient's treatment goals have been reached, a movement in the direction of equality between the analyst and the patient (including the patient's capacity to perceive the analyst more or less realistically), analysis of the patient's separation anxieties, infantile expectations, and so forth, with a consequent improvement in the patient's ego capacities, and an assessment of the residual transference and the patient's future capacities.

In general, when the therapist feels that termination is at hand on the basis of his or her assessment of these items, or on the basis of material from the patient indicating that the patient is at some level contem-

plating termination, the therapist often has to articulate this readiness and present it for discussion. When there is mutual agreement that termination is at hand, it is wise to set a termination date proper. Once the date is set it is not wise to change it because this can lead to a number of complications.

Firestein (1978) devotes a book to a study of case histories of termination followed by a summary of his viewpoint and a review of the literature. He believes that there is a specific termination phase characterized by many affects such as separation anxiety, grief, and rage. During this phase there is no particular change in the therapeutic alliance but certain communication becomes more blunt. He feels that in instances where there is too much gratification in the analysis or too many defensive anxieties and hostilities against the termination idea, it is very important for the analyst to introduce the subject of termination. One can check on how the patient experiences the analyst's vacations as an indication of how termination will go. Firestein concedes that the subject of termination is sometimes brought up as an intuitive maneuver. Attempts to "wean" the patient represent countertransference and not psychoanalytic therapy. The analyst should not change the frequency of the sessions or his or her style, or attempt to develop a friendship, nor should the patient sit up because these countertransference maneuvers may interfere with the postanalytic working-through process phase that follows termination.

Loewald (1988) regards mourning as the crucial aspect of the termination phase. In order to assess whether there are reasonable grounds or pathological motives behind a patient's wish to terminate, he suggests we examine whether termination is brought up during a hostile or friendly phase of the treatment, whether it constitutes a testing of the therapist's "love," how it is related to behavior of the therapist (such as the therapist's detachment from the patient for one reason or another), and whether themes of separation or loss followed by reunion are becoming manifest in the patient's material. He writes, "Most often the motives for the patient's inclination to terminate are mixed, and frequently it is no easy task for the therapist to assess the balance of forces. I would include here also the therapist's realistic appraisal of the weight of external factors that may favor or seem to compel termination" (p. 158). Loewald concludes, and I agree, that it is the therapist's responsibility as well as a measure of the therapist's competence, to make an objective assessment of the balance of motives in order to reach agreement or disagreement with the patient about termination although, of course, the final decision is always up to the patient.

In my clinical experience, I feel that the seriousness of bringing up the issue of termination to a patient has not been sufficiently stressed in the literature. I have treated some cases where therapists have, either out of incompetence or out of countertransference problems, raised the issue of termination prematurely, with the consequence of suicidal acting out by the patient. In general, readiness for termination usually suggests itself in a well-conducted psychotherapy or psychoanalysis and, with careful self-analysis, the therapist usually only needs to be a minor step ahead of the patient's material to recognize that the patient is ready for the termination phase. If this material does not appear at a time when the therapist feels it ought to be showing itself, it is an occasion not for confrontation with the patient or a demand for termination, but rather for the therapist to consult with a colleague.

I am also on the side of those who believe that the analytic work should continue to the very last day and that the relationship should remain professional to the very end. This leaves the door open for the patient to return if problems arise later and to resume treatment without having to deal with the contamination emanating from the therapist's countertransference. This countertransference typically consists of anxiety over separation from the patient or mourning over the loss of the relationship and can show itself in some very peculiar ways. Some of these that I have encountered are: giving the patient a farewell kiss, developing a personal friendship with the patient after the treatment, contacting the patient after termination for a variety of rationalizations, inquiring about subsequent activities of the patient from friends or acquaintances (of either the therapist or patient), and so forth. Both assessing the patient's readiness for termination and dealing with the termination phase up to the last minute of the treatment are important pitfalls for countertransference acting out.

References

Firestein, S. (1978). *Termination in Psychoanalysis.* New York: International Universities Press.

Loewald, H. (1988). Termination analyzable and unanalyzable. *Psychoanalytic Study of the Child* 43:155–166. New York: International Universities Press.

Ticho, E. (1972). Termination of psychoanalysis: Treatment goals, life goals. *Psychoanalytic Quarterly* 41:315–333.

THANATOS (SEE ALSO DEATH INSTINCT)

This rather unnecessary term was probably introduced by Federn (1952) to denote the death instinct. The idea was to draw a parallel to Eros, or the life instincts. It adds only obfuscation and is not in Freud's writings, although allegedly he used it in conversation (Jones 1957, p. 273).

References

Federn, P. (1952). *Ego Psychology and the Psychoses,* ed. E. Weiss. New York: Basic Books.

Jones, E. (1957). *The Life and Work of Sigmund Freud, 1919–1939: The Last Phase.* New York: Basic Books.

THERAPEUTIC ALLIANCE, WORKING ALLIANCE

Freud (1912) spoke of an "unobjectionable positive transference" as the basis for a therapeutic or working alliance to develop. There is considerable debate in the literature as to whether the so-called real relationship, or therapeutic or working alliance, is different from the unobjectionable positive transference. These are ambiguous and controversial ideas and have generated debate that currently is not resolved (Gill 1982).

The therapeutic alliance is thought of as a real and mature alliance with the conscious adult ego of the patient, encouraging the patient to be a scientific partner in the exploration of his or her difficulties. This can be extended to overlap with the whole concept of after-education, essentially thought of as correcting the blunders of the parents (Freud 1940).

For those who differentiate it from the unobjectionable positive transference, a working alliance is mandatory for any therapy to be successful. The concept of a working alliance was introduced by Zetzel (1956) and brought to the attention of the psychiatric community by Greenson (1965). Very often the key to understanding therapeutic stalemate is found in the failure of the patient to develop a reliable working relationship with the psychotherapist. This working relationship depends both on the patient and on the therapist. No matter what the patient is like, if the therapist does not meet the requirements of maturity, a sound working alliance cannot develop and the therapy is doomed from the beginning.

The patient also makes a contribution: he or she must have the capacity to form a working alliance. The best definition of a working alliance is that it is an alliance between the patient's reasonable or conscious or mature ego and the therapist's working or therapeutic or analytic ego. What makes this possible, claims Greenson, is the patient's partial identification with the therapist's approach as he or she attempts to understand the patient's behavior.

In simpler terminology, if the therapist is genuinely interested in the patient and genuinely concerned with understanding the patient, and if the patient has the ego capacity to develop a working alliance, then the patient will develop and exercise one of the unique functions of a human being—the capacity to stand off and observe one's self. The patient will take on the therapist's stance of non-anxious investigation. Hopefully, the patient will also identify with the therapist's tolerance.

It is possible to train the patient's ego in the therapy to the point where a working alliance can be formed, maintained, and improved. This is sometimes called preparation for psychotherapy, and is done by consistently focusing on the alliance in such a way as to reinforce those ego functions in the patient that contribute to the alliance and by attempting to stimulate the necessary ego functions that are inadequate. A mutual concern with the working alliance tends to enhance it. It is extremely difficult to separate the conditions of the working alliance from the conditions of the transference, and it is not even clear whether it is useful to attempt such a separation.

References

Freud, S. (1912). The dynamics of the transference. *Standard Edition* 12:97–108.

———— (1940). An outline of psychoanalysis. *Standard Edition* 23:141–207.

Gill, M. (1982). *Analysis of the Transference,* vol. 1. New York: International Universities Press.

Greenson, R. (1965). The working alliance and the transference neurosis. *Psychoanalytic Quarterly* 34:155–181.

Zetzel, E. (1956). Current concepts of transference. *International Journal of Psycho-Analysis* 37:369–376.

TOPOGRAPHIC THEORY

There are two major metapsychological theories introduced by Freud. Chapter 7 of Freud's *The Interpretation of Dreams* (1900) and his paper "The Unconscious" (1915) offer the basic concepts of the topographic theory. The structural theory, involving the psychic agencies ego, id, and superego (see EGO, ID and SUPEREGO) was introduced by Freud in 1923.

The early form of the topographic theory may be described as follows:

1. The mind is made up of two

parts: the system unconscious (Ucs.), or the infantile part, and the system preconscious (Pcs.), or the adult part.

2. The system unconscious contains wishes and seeks to reexperience the sensations of previous gratifications.

3. The unpleasure principle (later called the pleasure principle by Freud) governs the system unconscious. According to the pleasure principle, accumulated mental energy must be discharged as quickly as possible to bring the system back to the previous resting state. The system preconscious is guided by what Freud later called the reality principle.

4. The system unconscious is oblivious to reality and operates essentially by condensation and displacement of mental energies; mutually contradictory tendencies can exist side by side.

5. Mental energies are freely mobile in the system unconscious.

6. There is a dynamic interplay between the unconscious and the preconscious, introducing the thorny metapsychological problem of repression (see REPRESSION) as a major concept. The failure of the preconscious to have ever cathected a certain unconscious wish is called primal repression. This store of infantile wishes, "which has from the first been held back from the *Pcs.,* becomes a *sine qua non* of repression" (Freud 1900, p. 604).

If a preconscious wish or idea becomes associated with or cathected by an unacceptable unconscious wish, the preconscious cathexis will be withdrawn, in accordance with the unpleasure principle. This withdrawal of cathexis from a preconscious idea is called repression proper. As Freud conceived it, a strong instinctual drive associated with the repudiated idea may still try to force its way to the conscious, even if it has lost its cathexis from the Pcs. There then follows a defensive struggle, for the Pcs. in turn reinforces its opposition to the repressed thoughts (i.e., produces an anticathexis). The result may be the appearance of a compromise formation in the conscious. Notice that primal repression leads to a pulling of associated ideas into the unconscious; repression proper is a pushing out of the system preconscious.

7. The topographic theory is to be thought of as a functional, not a spatial theory.

8. Consciousness is like an eye, a sense organ for the perception of external or internal qualities.

The famous diagrams in chapter 7 of *The Interpretation of Dreams* are worthy of careful study. The notion of psychotherapy as a vehicle to bring the unconscious under the domination of the preconscious is presented first; the critical distinction between primary and secondary process is then established:

> The primary processes are present in the mental apparatus from the first, while it is only during the course of life that the secondary processes unfold, and come to inhibit and overlay the primary ones; it may even be that their complete domination is not attained until the prime of life. In consequence of the belated appearance of the secondary pro-

cesses, the core of our being, consisting of unconscious wishful impulses, remains inaccessible to the understanding and inhibition of the preconscious; the part played by the latter is restricted once and for all to directing along the most expedient paths the wishful impulses that arise from the unconscious. These unconscious wishes exercise a compelling force upon all later mental trends, a force which those trends are obliged to fall in with or which they may perhaps endeavor to divert and direct to higher aims. [pp. 603–604]

From this it appears that the system unconscious plays the same role for Freud as noumena did for Kant. Indeed, Freud continues, "The unconscious is the true psychical reality; in its innermost nature it is as much unknown to us as the reality of the external world, and it is as incompletely presented by the data of consciousness as is the external world by the communications of our sense organs" (p. 613). In this chapter of *The Interpretation of Dreams* the whole notion of psychodynamic psychiatry and its underlying philosophy is set down—the symptoms of mental illness are explained on a dynamic basis, as a result of the strengthening and weakening of the various components in the interplay of inner forces, so many of whose effects are hidden from view even while ordinary mental functions are apparently normal.

It should be noted that all the concepts of metapsychology have come under recent attack even from within the psychoanalytic community itself. In Freud's shift from the topographic theory to the structural theory, certain aspects of clinical material were insufficiently reinterpreted at the time in the light of the newer metapsychology, leaving an inconsistency in the formulation of the theory of mental functioning. Arlow and Brenner (1964) give a complete review of the topographic and structural theories and attempt to resolve the inconsistencies.

References

Arlow, J., and Brenner, C. (1964). *Psychoanalytic Concepts and the Structural Theory.* New York: International Universities Press.

Freud, S. (1900). The Interpretation of Dreams. *Standard Edition* 4,5:1–625.

_____ (1915). The unconscious. *Standard Edition* 14:159–215.

_____ (1923). The ego and the id. *Standard Edition* 19:3–66.

TRANSFERENCE, TRANSFERENCE NEUROSIS

The crucial concept of transference has a long history and there are innumerable articles on the subject; a detailed review of the background of this concept is presented by Orr (1954). The customary definition of transference is given by Fenichel (1945): "In the transference the patient misunderstands the present in terms of the past; and then instead of remembering the past, he strives, without recognizing the nature of his action, to relive the past and to live it more satisfactorily than he did in his childhood. He 'transfers' the past attitude to the present" (p. 29).

Transference is a form of resistance in which patients defend themselves against remembering and discussing their infantile conflicts by reliving them. It offers a vital and unique clinical opportunity to observe and experience derivatives of the past directly and thereby to better understand the development of the nuclear childhood conflicts. Wetzler (1985) points out that "in current practice transference analysis and reconstructive work go hand-in-hand," and that transference "offers the patient a sense of conviction that the narrative is about *his* life" (p. 190).

Arlow (1985) views the analyst's behavior as a stimulus, as a day residue, but it is through the stimulation of the patient's unconscious fantasy life that the reaction we call transference occurs. Even in the transference, at least at first, we see only derivatives of the persistent unconscious fantasy activity of childhood that governs the individual's life. At the core of every patient there resides a crucial fantasy activity, interwoven with early infantile experiences to a greater or lesser degree, depending on how traumatic these experiences have been. But Arlow (1985) explains, "What constitutes trauma is not inherent in the actual, real event, but rather the individual's response to the disorganizing, disruptive combination of impulses and fears integrated into a set of unconscious fantasies" (p. 533). Certain object relations and self psychology theories tend to minimize the role of this unconscious fantasy activity and emphasize the pathogenic effect of real events and interactions. But the indi-

vidual's experience, explains Arlow (1980), "is usually organized in terms of a few, leading, unconscious phantasies which dominate an individual's perception of the world and create the mental set by which she or he perceives and interprets her/his experience" (p. 131). Transference is not a repetition of the patient's actual early interactions with present objects, but expresses derivatives of the patient's persistent unconscious childhood fantasies, the "psychic reality" of these early interactions for the patient (see FANTASY).

Greenson (1967) points out that the term "transference" itself may be misleading. It is a singular noun, but transference phenomena are plural, multiple, and diversified. Greenson lists five important characteristics denoting a transference reaction. The outstanding trait that overrides all others and is included in all the others is inappropriateness: "It is inappropriateness, in terms of intensity, ambivalence, capriciousness, or tenacity which signals that the transference is at work" (1967, p. 162).

A transference can appear in many kinds of interpersonal situations and play a very important role. In psychotherapy we usually speak of a positive or negative transference. A positive transference implies reactions composed predominantly of love in any of its forms or in any of its forerunners or derivatives (see LOVE). Greenson (1967) writes: "We consider a positive transference to exist when the patient feels towards his analyst any of the following: Love, fondness, trust, amorousness, liking, concern, devotion, admiration, infatuation, passion, hunger, yearning, tenderness, or respect" (p. 225).

In the process of intensive psychotherapy we often do not worry as much about the appearance of positive transference as we do about the appearance of negative transference. In a negative transference we observe a series of reactions based on the various forms of hate. According to Greenson (1967), "Negative transference may be expressed as hatred, anger, hostility, mistrust, abhorrence, aversion, loathing, resentment, bitterness, envy, dislike, contempt or annoyance, etc." (p. 233). It is always present, although it is perhaps surprisingly often much more difficult to uncover negative transference than the manifestations of positive transference. There are many possible reasons for this clinical fact. The two most obvious are that patients don't like to become aware of transference hate and to express it and that therapists don't particularly enjoy being the object of transference hate and to have to deal with it or be exposed to it.

As a general rule of thumb, one may say that for an uncovering psychotherapy to be successful, there will have to be sharp manifestations of both positive and negative transference. To put it another way, therapists must be prepared to be exposed to powerful negative and positive emotional feelings coming from patients, often on a highly irrational basis. This exposure to such powerful feelings can lead to many mistakes, retreats, and confusions in psychotherapy, if therapists are not expecting them to appear, are not prepared to deal with them, or are so primarily preoccupied with their own needs and problems that they cannot perceive clearly what is going on. There is an all-too-human tendency in psychotherapy to deflect emerging manifestations of powerful erotic or negative transferences by various forms of interventions, resulting in a collusion (Langs 1979) to avoid these uncomfortable emotions. It is the responsibility of the therapist not to allow this to occur.

"Transference neurosis" was Freud's (1914) term for a clinical psychoanalytic situation in which the patient developed such intense transference feelings to the therapist that everything else in his or her life became of lesser importance. The classical conception of the transference neurosis has it that the infantile feelings and conflicts of the patient are focused almost exclusively on the analyst. The transference neurosis could also be thought of more generally as an extremely important—or even the patient's temporarily most important—object relationship, the affectual nature of which is determined predominantly by the patient's projection of repressed split-off self and object representations.

The concept of transference neurosis has run into difficulty because very often, even in a formal psychoanalysis, the classical transference neurosis simply does not appear. One sees a great many varieties of transference phenomena, but a focal, sharply defined transference neurosis cannot always be expected to take place. The reasons for this failure of transference neurosis formation are a matter of considerable debate, but it is not always just the result of poor technique. Because of this, many contemporary authorities, such as Brenner (see Kligerman's discussion in Pollock and Gedo, 1984), would like to eliminate the concept.

An issue of the *Journal of the American Psychoanalytic Association* (Calef 1971) is devoted almost entirely to the subject of the transference neurosis. At least certain basic premises can be agreed upon:

1. The transference neurosis revives the infantile neurosis.
2. It is created out of the frustrated demands for love that, in turn, arise out of the therapeutic situation as we structure it.
3. The symptoms of the transference neurosis are dynamic, shifting, and changing; it is not a static concept.
4. Important in the development of the transference neurosis are the mechanisms of regression and repetition—indeed, the transference neurosis can be thought of as arising out of the repetition compulsion.
5. In the transference neurosis, the old symptoms of the adult neurosis that the patient has come to complain about lose their libidinal force and seem to be much improved, for the patient is preoccupied with the transference.
6. The transference neurosis is not identical to and does not describe in a one-to-one manner the nature of the infantile relationships that have been transferred. There

is a process of layering of subsequent meanings on to infantile relationships and events that reflects current interests and conflicts. These layers coalesce into meaningful transference patterns.
7. Eventually, the transference neurosis itself becomes involved in a resistance to treatment. This is known as transference resistance (Gill 1982), a resistance to the resolution of the transference as manifested, for example, by refusal to see determinants in it from the past or by a demand for gratification of the transference wishes. If the therapist breaks Freud's rule of abstinence and provides such gratification, further insight becomes impossible and a stalemate usually results, with an interminable therapy.

The management of the transference neurosis, according to classical psychoanalysis, permits the undoing of repression and is the central issue of treatment. The concept of interpretation as primarily functioning to resolve the transference neurosis differentiates psychoanalysis from other forms of treatment. It is important to clarify this issue a little more. According to classical psychoanalysis, a full-blown transference neurosis develops in an orderly and manageable fashion. This is then interpreted, and such interpretation permits an undoing of the transference neurosis, which, in turn, frees the patient from the nuclear infantile conflicts by allowing the adult ego to resolve them in new ways. It is the preoccupation with the transference neurosis that differentiates psychoanalysis from other forms of treatment; the special efficacy of psychoanalysis is believed to be in the removal of the transference neurosis through interpretation, rather than through any other aspects of the treatment. The most recent thinking on the transference neurosis is in a panel reported by Shaw (1991).

The transference neurosis may also appear in psychotherapy. It is not necessary for a patient to come in four or five times a week and lie on the couch for a transference neurosis to appear. On the other hand, it is much more likely that, if the transference neurosis is going to appear, it will appear under the conditions of formal psychoanalysis. But it is very important for anyone doing intensive psychotherapy to understand the concept of the transference neurosis and to be aware of its appearance, if it does appear in the psychotherapy.

A transference neurosis can arise in situations wherein the patient has a very weak ego state and poor defenses. In such situations the patient cannot actually utilize the transference neurosis toward the working through of intrapsychic problems. If a profound transference neurosis seems to be developing in a psychotherapy, the therapist must be careful to ascertain the ego state of the patient and to determine by the use of interpretation whether the patient is actually capable of utilizing the developing transference neurosis. If the patient cannot utilize it, efforts should be made to break up the transference neurosis by decreasing the frequency of the treatment, by active interpretation and support, and so on.

It is often diagnostic of borderline patients that they develop highly negative or strongly eroticized transferences very early, even in a once-a-week psychotherapy (see BORDERLINE). These must be resolved by prompt interpretation, today usually based on Kernberg's (1975) modified Kleinian concepts of projected split-off all bad or all good self and object representations (see SPLITTING). Or, if self psychology is utilized, transferences powerfully infused with lust and aggression appearing early and suddenly in therapy are analyzed as manifestations of profound disappointment in the patient's expectations of empathy from the subjectively perceived self-object analyst. Failure to resolve such disruptive transference typically destroys the therapy. As Blum (1973) points out, for example, the incorrect response to a highly eroticized transference can deadlock the treatment in an unconscious conspiracy of mutual admiration and endearment.

A transference psychosis sometimes appears. This is always a very undesirable situation that resembles the strong transference neurosis, but the patient has absolutely no insight into it and denies completely that the phenomena he or she is experiencing are transference at all. Such situations as falling desperately in love with the therapist can be understood as a transference psychosis if this tremendous falling in love refuses to yield to any kind of interpretation; the patient insists that the love is genuine and based on the marvelous qualities of the therapist, and definitely refuses to see any transference phenomena involved in it. Clinical judgment is required here to distinguish between an object-instinctual transference that has exploded without insight and Kohut's (1971) narcissistic "idealizing transference." The latter contains a more eerie and vague form of idealizing of the therapist, and interpretations are met with rage because the patient needs such a transference and experiences the therapist's attempts to break it up by interpretation as a severely disappointing failure of empathy and understanding (see SELF PSYCHOLOGY).

The transference often becomes a part of the patient's resistance maneuvers in a further effort to avoid undoing the forces of repression. This leads to terminological confusion because all transference can be thought of as a form of resistance to remembering. The difference is that transference as a resistance maneuver arises more specifically in certain situations in psychotherapy that call it forth and then functions as a resistance to further psychotherapy. An example would be the patient's sudden demand for gratification and refusal to concentrate on anything else.

In a transference defense, or "defensive transference reaction" (Greenson 1967), just as the patient would be expected to arrive at a certain insight out of the material that is being presented, there suddenly appears instead a powerful transference reaction, most typically a negative transference. The sudden and sometimes dramatic appearance of strong transference manifestations at a sharp point in a psychotherapy session gives rise to the possibility that the patient is using the transference to defend against feelings, memories, or emerging insight that must be denied at the time. The therapist also must be vigilant and constantly aware of the appearance of transference manifestations that can show themselves either in small or subliminal ways, as well as in dramatic explosions.

Some authors (Schlessinger and Robbins 1974) use the term "defense transference" as a transference that forms to defend against awareness of a deeper, more important transference. They write, "It is the characterological defensive organization, evident at the onset of an analysis, which serves as a shield against the transference neurosis, and as a major coping mechanism of the ego in the face of conflict" (pp. 547–548). For example, a highly idealized transference commonly develops as a defense against the awareness of a hidden negative transference. Here one form of transference is habitually used to defend the patient from the emergence of another more intense and upsetting transference—or even of the transference neurosis—into awareness, and so the defense transference serves the function of tension regulation (Schlessinger 1984).

Other authors (Greenson 1967) refer more specifically to character transference phenomena. These character transference phenomena can be thought of as hidden in the patient's more general behavior patterns. The term is somewhat misleading and confusing, but what distinguishes this form of transference from others is that the reaction to the therapist is part of the patient's habitual, representative, and typical responses to people at large, and the transference behavior is characteristic of the patient's relationships in general. It is this quality of the nonspecific behavior that has led to the term "character transference." The important point is that the patient may be reacting to the therapist with his or her habitual reactions to a different kind of person than the therapist actually is. This is what the therapist has to be aware of in watching for character transference phenomena.

Much recent work has been presented in the literature on the so-called archaic transferences (Gedo 1977, Gunther 1984) (see ARCHAIC TRANSFERENCES), stimulated by the work of Kohut (1971, 1977, 1978). Kohut describes the well-known mirror and idealizing transferences found in narcissistic personality disorders, which are not transferences in the technical sense because they do not involve instinctual wishes that cross the repression barrier. They are instead a demand for a "selfobject" in order to fill in intrapsychic defects and allow, in the treatment, a resumption of development from the preoedipal narcissistic stages (for details, see SELF PSYCHOLOGY). More generally, the archaic transference is marked in preoedipal disorders by an intense and overt demand for gratification,

making the psychotherapist feel almost like a prisoner and forced away from the analytic analyzing attitude. Refusal to comply is often followed by seriously disruptive rage and chaos. Certain authors (Gunther 1984) feel that some gratification is necessary, but should always be followed by interpretation. This remains a controversial technical area. Adler (1980) points out that the hallmark of the borderline patient's transference is the rapid disintegration of the selfobject transference as soon as gratification is not forthcoming, and recommends the use of one's best judgment about how much deprivation is tolerable in such situations. Therefore the instability of the transference is an important hallmark of an archaic transference, and it poses extremely difficult problems for the therapist.

Kleinian therapists (Spillius 1983) characterize this as projective identification (see PROJECTIVE IDENTIFICATION) in the transference, marked by interpersonal pressure placed on the therapist to *do something,* which, of course, represents an obstruction to understanding. But Greenson (1974) complains that the Kleinians emphasize this concept of projective identification in the transference in all cases, blurring the distinction between neurotic, narcissistic, and archaic transferences. The identification and handling of archaic transferences becomes a specialized aspect of intensive psychotherapy, requiring the willingness to work with very primitive and disruptive patients.

An especially central role involving the transference in both psychoanalysis and psychotherapy is presented by Gill (1982, 1984). Gill is especially concerned with the therapist's here-and-now behavior as profoundly influencing the transference that develops, so for him transference is the result of the interaction between the patient and analyst and is therefore always present. It may be most commonly manifested by allusions to it in dreams and associations, and the therapist must continuously look for it, clarify the contribution of the analytic situation to it, interpret the patient's resistances to awareness of it, and finally translate the disguised and displaced expressions of it into direct experience and discussion. In such resolution of the transference, Gill emphasizes the corrective emotional experience that is involved, since by such a procedure the analyst behaves quite differently from what the patient has come to expect and even provokes from others. The most controversial premise of Gill's view is the assumption of the centrality of the transference in all material.

The therapist must be aware of the serious danger of the acting out of the transference outside the therapist's office. So all reports by the patient of interactions outside therapy, even dreams containing such interactions, must be closely examined for veiled allusions to the transference.

The most serious flaws in the handling of transference reactions are from the subtle, chronic, unrecognized ones that go on for years without being detected. These flaws usually stem from two main sources:

countertransference reactions and incorrect understanding of the patient for reasons other than countertransference.

One of the most common causes of stalemate or failure in psychotherapy is the lack of awareness on the part of the therapist to the manifestations of transference. This is often due to the therapist's own lack of proper training psychoanalysis or ongoing self-analysis.

References

Adler, G. (1980). Transference, real relationship and alliance. *International Journal of Psycho-Analysis* 61:547–558.

Arlow, J. (1980). Object concept and object choice. *Psychoanalytic Quarterly* 49: 109–133.

———— (1985). Some technical problems of countertransference. *Psychoanalytic Quarterly* 54:164–174.

Blum, H. (1973) The concept of eroticized transference. *Journal of the American Psychoanalytic Association* 21:61–76.

Calef, V. (1971). Concluding remarks. *Journal of the American Psychoanalytic Association* 19:89–97.

Fenichel, O. (1945). *The Psychoanalytic Theory of Neurosis.* New York: Norton.

Freud, S. (1914). Remembering, repeating and working through. *Standard Edition* 12:145–156.

Gedo, J. (1977). Notes on the psychoanalytic management of archaic transferences. *Journal of the American Psychoanalytic Association* 25:787–803.

Gill, M. (1982). *Analysis of the Transference,* vol. 1. New York: International Universities Press.

———— (1984). Psychoanalysis and psychotherapy: a revision. *International Review of Psychoanalysis* 11:141–179.

Greenson, R. (1967). *The Technique and Practice of Psychoanalysis.* New York: International Universities Press.

———— (1974). Transference: Freud or Klein. *International Journal of Psycho-Analysis* 55:37–52.

Gunther, M. (1984). Archaic transferences—a prototype. In *Psychoanalysis: The Vital Issues,* vol. 2, ed. G. H. Pollock and J. E. Gedo, pp. 69–95. New York: International Universities Press.

Kernberg, O. (1975). *Borderline Conditions and Pathological Narcissism.* New York: Jason Aronson.

Kohut, H. (1971). *The Analysis of the Self.* New York: International Universities Press.

―――― (1977). *The Restoration of the Self.* New York: International Universities Press.

―――― (1978). *The Search for the Self,* ed. P. Ornstein. New York: International Universities Press.

Langs, R. (1979). *The Therapeutic Environment.* New York: Jason Aronson.

Orr, D. (1954). Transference and countertransference: a historical survey. *Journal of the American Psychoanalytic Association* 26:311–330.

Schlessinger, N. (1984). On analyzability. In *Psychoanalysis: The Vital Issues,* vol. 2, ed. G. Pollock and J. Gedo, pp. 249–274. New York: International Universities Press.

Schlessinger, N., and Robbins, F. (1974). Assessment and follow-up in psychoanalysis. *Journal of the American Psychoanalytic Association* 22:542–567.

Shaw, R. (1991). Report on panel: concepts and controversies about the transference neurosis. *Journal of the American Psychoanalytic Association* 39:227–239.

Spillius, E. B. (1983). Some developments from the work of Melanie Klein. *International Journal of Psycho-Analysis* 64:321–332.

Wetzler, S. (1985). The historical truth of psychoanalytic reconstructions. *International Review of Psycho-Analysis* 12:187–197.

TRANSIENCE

The eleventh-century Persian poet Omar Khayyam (1941) in the latter half of the 11th century wrote (p. 52, p. 155),

. . . One thing is certain, that Life flies;
One thing is certain and the Rest is Lies;
The flower that once has blown forever dies.

Whether at Naishápúr or Babylon,
Whether the Cup with sweet or bitter run,
    The Wine of Life keeps oozing drop by drop,
The Leaves of Life keep falling one by one.

I have included this item in the dictionary for two reasons. In the first place, Freud wrote a beautiful paper on the subject in November 1915, about a year after the outbreak of the First World War. This essay shows him as a man of letters at the height of his powers, and stands with any collection of the great essays of the Western world. It also shows that in 1915, in spite of the war, he was not a pessimistic man. The essay demonstrates a lifelong capacity in Freud to appreciate what is available to appreciate in spite of the gloom and difficulties of his situation.

The other reason for including this item is that patients often complain of the "transience" of human life, even of its finest moments of enjoyment and beauty. As Freud (1915) points out, it is typical of young melancholy poets to give voice to this kind of complaint. It is also typical of patients who are depressed, lonely, or feeling alienated or isolated to dwell on the transience of everything in human life. In our psychotherapeutic work we do not respond the way Freud did to the young poet in the essay. His response was on a summer walk with the young and famous poet and "a taciturn friend" (p. 305), who has never been identified. On such summer walks Freud's beautiful response is appropriate, but in psychotherapeutic work we listen to this material but attempt to link it, as Freud does, to a sense of depression or mourning. Freud interprets the concern over transience as an attempt to escape the necessity of mourning over the decease of beautiful or enjoyable times because the mind "instinctively recoils from anything that is painful" (p. 306). In my clinical experience, these concerns about transience have more to do with what Bion (1967) has called *attacks on linking*. These patients cannot allow themselves to become deeply committed in any enduring fashion to anything or anybody, because they are afraid of their own needs and afraid to be vulnerable to loss or narcissistic wounding.

It is the task of psychotherapeutic work to do with the developmentally damaged individual what Freud hopes for after World War I: "We shall build up again all that war has destroyed, and perhaps on firmer ground and more lastingly than before" (p. 307).

References

Bion, W. (1967). *Second Thoughts: Selected Papers on Psycho-Analysis*. London: Heinemann.
Freud, S. (1915). On transience. *Standard Edition* 14:303–307.
Khayyam, O. (1941). *Rubaiyat of Omar Khayyam*, trans. E. Fitzgerald. New York: Pocket Books.

TRANSITIONAL OBJECT (SEE OBJECT)

TRANSMUTING INTERNALIZATION (SEE SELF PSYCHOLOGY)

TWO PRINCIPLES OF MENTAL FUNCTIONING

"Formulations on the Two Principles of Mental Functioning" (Freud 1911) has become one of the classics of psychoanalysis even though it is extremely difficult, condensed, and was badly received when first presented. It represents a turning point in Freud's interests and begins a series of papers on metapsychology, which in turn were conceived as the first part of a book on the subject that was later abandoned.

The basic point of it is to introduce the distinction between the pleasure principle, which dominates the primary processes of mental life, and the reality principle, which dominates secondary process thought. Primary processes are unconscious mental processes striving, under the domination of the pleasure principle, for the realization of wishes and a yield of pleasure as well as to avoid unpleasure; with the introduction of the reality principle, which occurs gradually, fantasy and daydream are split off and conscious thought guides the person to strive for what is useful and to guard against the imagination. Repression or flight is, to some extent, replaced by judgment and sublimation.

This setting up of the reality principle leads to some basic changes in the psychic apparatus. The perceptual apparatus must be expanded in order to be aware of external as well as internal states, and the sense organs become more directed toward the external world. Consciousness becomes more interested in sensory qualities in addition to the qualities of pleasure and unpleasure, "which hitherto had been alone of interest to it" (p. 220).

A special function is instituted to search the external world; the activity of this function meets the sense impressions halfway instead of awaiting their appearance. This searching function is defined as a "tension" by Freud. At the same time, a system of "notation" is introduced to lay down the results of this periodical activity of consciousness, part of what Freud calls "memory." Ideas leading to pain and which therefore have previously been shut out by repression are now subjected to judgment. In this paper, drawing back from pain and shutting out reality is defined as repression, which may confuse the reader; some authors suggest the word "disavowal" as more suitable for this function.

Motor discharge, which was initially under the pleasure principle for the purpose of unburdening the mental apparatus of accretions of stimuli, now shifts under the reality principle to action in changing the environment. Restraint upon action or motor discharge becomes necessary and is provided by means of the process of thinking, which is defined here as "an experimental kind of acting, accompanied by displacement of relatively small quantities of cathexis together with less expenditure (discharge) of them" (p. 221). Thus thought makes it possible for the mental apparatus to support an increase in tension with the delay of discharge, and thought becomes an experimental way of acting.

The ego permits small quanta of primary process energy to pass through; such quanta are then transformed by the ego into secondary process energy, using memory, and are more in tune with reality. This is Freud's conception of thought—the change of unbound primary process energy into secondary process energy—an experimental way of acting with comparison to memory and the modification and synthesis into secondary process.

The clinical point of this discussion is the explanation of pathological thought, which occurs when the instinct itself is discharged in thought. Thus obsessional thought is a discharge, but a regressive one, and the instinct is not discharged through the motor apparatus as instincts should be, but rather in a substituted discharge of rumination or obsessional thinking.

The reality principle governs the process of thought, which contains judgment—in which there is a comparison of external reality with the conceivably successful memory traces, and finally a form of trial action as described above—an experimental way of acting using small amounts of energy. This process also makes the original impulse easier to deal with, since some of its energy has been borrowed and discharged in the thought process. Under this theory, such thinking as that employed in pure mathematics, which does not have action as its end result, would have to be defined as regressive. If a serious block of discharging energy in the operation of the motor apparatus is erected by the superego, then all the energy is dammed up, floods backwards, and hypercathects the thought systems, leading to a drainage through obsessive rumination (Freud 1909).

References

Freud, S. (1909). Notes upon a case of obsessional neurosis. *Standard Edition* 10: 153–318.

———— (1911). Formulations on two principles of mental functioning. *Standard Edition* 12:213–226.

TWO-WOMAN PHENOMENON

Weiss (1987) published an important clinical paper describing what he named "the two-woman phenomenon." A man who shows this syndrome retains his commitment to his wife but is also passionately in love with another woman (see LOVE). He appears in the clinician's office only when a conflict occurs because one or the other woman must be given up due to the vicissi-

tudes of life. Such a patient usually got married early in life to a woman from a background similar to his own. The new woman is usually from a different background and her age is not of obvious significance. This is not the same man who divorces his wife in mid-life and begins over with a younger woman (see MID-LIFE CRISIS); rather, he is devoted and conscientious. Reciprocally, the wife is depicted as a devoted and conscientious woman who takes good care of the home and children. Unfortunately, she does not stimulate passion or excitement in the man. He in turn indulges in sex with his wife infrequently and out of duty. In fact, it is often reported that sexual relations occur mainly because the man does not wish his wife to become suspicious that he has another woman. The man believes, often correctly, that his wife is not interested in his work, except possibly for the money and prestige that it brings to her.

Weiss adds that the man is not promiscuous and sets high standards of functioning for himself and others. When the man considers having to give up the other woman, he speaks sadly of life "returning, once again, to the colorless, dull, daily routine, devoid of any pleasure" (p. 274), usually accompanied by a profound fear that his creative functioning will also be lost.

These relationships involving two women can go on for a long time. The crisis occurs when a decision must be made, in which the individual must choose between his terrible guilt involved in deserting a devoted, conscientious wife of long standing on the one hand, and the terrible despair involved in losing a woman who has enhanced his creative functioning and brought excitement and happiness into his life, on the other. An additional factor in coercing the man to give up the other woman, if he is forced to decide, is the fear of this usually successful individual that he will otherwise be shunned by his colleagues and his career will be ruined. Such an individual often views or imagines his wife as powerful and destructive and believes that the new woman is devoted to enhancing his masculinity, autonomy, pleasure, and creativity.

A cardinal psychodynamic agent in these cases is a primitive superego that wants to extinguish all sexual pleasure, aggression, and autonomy, and demands a central emphasis on self-sacrifice and hard work for never-ending success. This leads to an intense unconscious conflict between powerful id wishes for instinctual gratification and the prohibition by the superego with its never-ending demands for more and more performance. Weiss explains the two-woman phenomenon as a compromise formation. At home the man remains true to his superego requirements but with a smoldering anger toward his wife; outside the home he experiences success and pleasure but at the same time a fear of devastating punishment if he commits himself to the new woman.

Patients who present this two-woman phenomenon do not fall into any one diagnostic category. A considerable degree of psychodynamic variation was manifest in the cases

that Weiss investigated, from those with significant preoedipal pathology and an archaic superego to others in which the two-woman phenomenon is an analyzable defensive style. There is such a complicated mixture of preoedipal pathology often present in these patients, Weiss explains, that they present difficulties in evaluating analyzability and treatment strategy.

I (Chessick 1989) have suggested that what has occurred is a gradual accumulation of anger, which tends to peak in middle age as the needs of such men are sharply enhanced by the self-depletion problems of middle age. The wife is not hated or regarded as all bad. She is appreciated and loved, in a way. She does not stimulate passion anymore because of the man's accumulating anger that she cannot and will not function as a nursing mother, an archaic selfobject (see SELFOBJECT)—which he regressively needs more and more as he grows older and more depleted. The perception of the wife as powerful or destructive is a projection of the man's own anger and vulnerability in needing her, not a projection of an "all bad" archaic maternal representation. When the man returns to his wife he does not return to a hated object but to an empty, colorless, dull, daily routine, a reflection of his empty, depleted self. He feels regressively weak and passive in her presence and, in Weiss's report, even thinks of suicide or death as the way out. This is the picture of a disappointed, deeply humiliated, narcissistic person who has a dim awareness of his increasing neediness and his increasing desire for support, mirroring, and empathy as he ages.

Weiss's notion that the maternal image is split into a good and bad image as a defense against the Oedipus complex does not seem to fit the actual development of the two-woman phenomenon as I have observed it clinically. I think it is an escape from the superego and from a depression that intensifies as narcissistic goals are not reached in middle age and the individual rages at himself for his failures and suffers from an empty depletion. The two-woman phenomenon represents a reaching out again, a regressive reidealization of an external figure to make amends for the depletion in failing to attain unreachable ego-ideals, and then a reassuring erotic fusion with this idealized person, which restores narcissistic equilibrium.

The clinically observable split is between an idealized woman on the one hand, and a sought for wife-mother on the other, who is feared but who is still viewed as good. Escape from the rigid superego and its threats of punishment and unbearable humiliation for failing in middle age to live up to youthful and romantic narcissistic ideals, in my clinical experience, is the central issue. Suicide is another such escape.

With the new woman there is the pleasure of uncomplicated orgasm with which nothing can compare because it is unambivalent as far as the idealization is concerned; there is no smoldering anger to interfere with libidinal arousal. For the wife there is a sense of duty and a felt requirement to deliver an orgasm to her, which dilutes the man's sexual pleasure by increasing his rage, since this duty is not consistent with his unconscious demand that she function as an archaic selfobject—always giving and always present, with no needs of her own. The other woman wishes to please the man and gives narcissistic gratification, whereas the wife sets adult requirements, has demands, and makes often realistic criticism.

The man is healthy enough not to commit himself completely to the other woman because he knows at some level that if he did, eventually the idealization of her would suffer the same fate that his idealization of his wife has suffered, and he would not end up in a better situation than he is already in. The bilateral arrangement, while it is stable, functions well as a compromise. It allows the man to receive the mirroring that he needs and to enjoy the illusion of archaic selfobject functioning from the other woman, while at the same time obtaining the needed maternal devotion of a conscientious wife who makes him a reasonable home. That is why such patients come into treatment only when they have to choose between one or the other woman. They desperately need both.

References

Chessick, R. (1989). On falling in love: the two-woman phenomenon revisited. *Journal of the American Academy of Psychoanalysis* 17:293–304.

Weiss, S. (1987). The two-woman phenomenon. *Psychoanalytic Quarterly* 56:271–286.

U-Z

UNCONSCIOUS

There is considerable confusion about the concept of the unconscious, a notion that has a long history before Freud. Authors such as Nietzsche and Schopenhauer used this concept; Ellenberger (1970) produced a complete scholarly discussion of the unconscious as it evolved or was "discovered."

Freud used the term "unconscious" either as an adjective or as a realm in the topographic theory (see TOPOGRAPHIC THEORY). The special characteristics of the unconscious as a realm are discussed in Freud's (1915) essay on the unconscious, section 5. These are:

1. The unconscious is made up of ideational representatives of the instincts, which are exempt from mutual contradiction. Thus there is no negation in the unconscious.
2. Thought processes in the unconscious behave according to primary process. That is to say, one idea may surrender to another all its cathexis (the motility of cathexis), a process known as displacement. One idea may appropriate the whole cathexis of several ideas, a process known as condensation.

3. The unconscious has no conception of time. Ideas and impulses from different chronological ages are telescoped together, and only the present exists.
4. The unconscious has no sense of outer-world reality. A sense of psychical reality replaces our sense of external reality so that a wish for something is equated with the actual happening. Thus unconscious processes are subject merely to the pleasure principle (see TWO PRINCIPLES OF MENTAL FUNCTIONING) and operate according to displacement and condensation, which are the laws of primary process thought.

The unconscious as a realm allegedly contains inherited mental formations, as well as what has been discarded in childhood in the process of ego formation. Jung (Campbell 1977) emphasized the archaic or collective aspect of the unconscious, but Freud did not. The unconscious as a noun refers to a dynamic system in the topographic theory, and the unconscious as an adjective refers to mental content not available to the conscious mind even with prolonged concentration. If prolonged concentration does bring material to the conscious mind, we define this mate-

391

rial as having existed in the precon-scious. The tendency today is to use "unconscious" more as an adjective, in describing not only the id of the structural theory (see ID) but also important aspects of the ego and su-perego.

References

Campbell, J., ed. (1977). *The Portable Jung.* New York: Penguin.

Ellenberger, H. (1970). *The Discovery of the Unconscious: The History and Evolution of Dynamic Psychiatry.* New York: Basic Books.

Freud, S. (1915). The unconscious. *Standard Edition* 14:159–215.

VERTICAL SPLIT (SEE SELF PSYCHOLOGY)

WILD PSYCHOANALYSIS (SEE ALSO PSYCHOANALYSIS)

Wild psychoanalysis was first described by Freud (1910). In Freud's case vignette, a middle-aged lady has been told by her doctor that the cause of her anxiety is lack of sexual satisfaction and has been ad-vised to either return to her husband (whom she had recently divorced), take a lover, or masturbate. Freud begins with the important clinical caution that one should not accept as true what patients report that their physicians have said or done to them.

Physicians, especially psychiatrists, easily become the target of their pa-tient's hostile feelings and often be-come, by projection, responsible in the patient's mind for the patient's own repressed wishes. Whether or not the doctor in Freud's case vi-gnette actually gave his patient such poor advice, the scientific errors in misunderstanding the meaning of sexual life and in the notion that sexual abstinence produces mental disorders are obvious. As Freud ex-plains, "If knowledge about the un-conscious were as important for the patient as people inexperienced in psychoanalysis imagine, listening to lectures or reading books would be enough to cure him. Such measures, however, have as much influence on nervous illness as a distribution of menu-cards in a time of famine has upon hunger" (p. 225). Wild inter-pretations or attempts to rush the patient by brusquely telling him or her about the unconscious not only do not work, they usually inspire the patient's hearty enmity and may eliminate any further influence by the physician. Freud also points out that one may be wrong in such early surmises, and that one is never in a position to discover the whole truth.

In certain situations the patient may wholeheartedly accept early and premature interpretations as a way of sidetracking the therapist and avoiding any depth understanding. One variant of this is in the training candidate who eagerly accepts every interpretation of his or her training analyst in the secret hope of getting through the analysis and graduating from the institute as quickly as possible (see REVERSIBLE PERSPECTIVE).

It is not possible for any psychotherapist or psychoanalyst to practice anything but wild psychoanalysis if the therapist has not received a thorough personal psychoanalysis of his or her own. Otherwise the therapist's "insights" and "interpretations" will be unconsciously aimed at reducing the anxiety of the therapist in the psychoanalytic situation. One of the most frequent causes of wild analysis lies in unresolved narcissistic problems in the therapist, who attempts to dazzle the patient with his or her remarkable knowledge of the unconscious. This is a form of exhibitionism.

An argument exists as to whether the early and deep Kleinian interpretations made by the members of that school (see KLEIN) are legitimate psychoanalysis or represent wild analysis. There is no agreement on this question. Most psychoanalysts agree that early deep interpretations are experienced by the patient as an assault and may have an important effect on the therapeutic alliance, either fracturing it or shifting it into a sadomasochistic relationship. Conversely, sadistic psychoanalysts tend to make early deep wild interpretations.

Granting the psychoanalyst has had a thorough personal psychoanalysis, the question often arises as to what extent his or her technique represents an identification with his or her own training psychoanalyst. To even further complicate the matter,

one must admit that wild psychoanalysis sometimes works! It is a form of charismatic therapy. Groddeck (1961) labeled himself a "wild analyst" somewhat to the perturbation of Freud, and was able to accomplish considerable improvement in various psychosomatic disorders by his deep charismatic and "wild" interpretations. This is no longer psychoanalysis, but a form of suggestion therapy in which the patient forms an idealizing transference with the charismatic doctor and feels better, protected, and in the hands of an omnipotent healer.

For a current view of this controversial topic, see Schafer (1985).

References

Freud, S. (1910). Wild psycho-analysis. *Standard Edition* 11:219–227.

Groddeck, G. (1961). *The Book of the It*. New York: Mentor Books.

Schafer, R. (1985). Wild analysis. *Journal of the American Psychoanalytic Association* 33:275–300.

WINNICOTT, DONALD W.

At the beginning of this century, Freud established the ubiquity of the role of unconscious instinctual wishes and conflicts in the development of the human individual. He also invented a therapeutic setting and process, which he named psychoanalysis, in which these conflicts could be discovered, explored, and resolved. The emphasis was upon knowing and insight. In England Donald W. Winnicott (1897–1971), a pediatrician before becoming a psychoanalyst, from his deep involvement with infants and their caretaking mothers, took the next logical step and enlarged the scope of the psychotherapeutic task to include realization of and meeting the need of the patient as a person. Winnicott had a long and distinguished career as a fellow of the Royal College of Physicians, a fellow of the British Psychological Society, president of the British Psychoanalytical Society, and president of the pediatric section of the Royal Society of Medicine. He was awarded the James Spence Medal for Pediatrics in 1968. His researches in this area have had a momentous impact on the whole nature of the therapeutic undertaking, in which, according to Winnicott, the therapist patiently waits for the patient's own creative unfolding from formlessness to reintegration.

Winnicott models his clinical orientation to the patient largely on an "ordinary and devoted mother's" holding care of her infant. He writes of the "average expectable environment" as essential to the growth of the health and personality in the child, and the important element in it is the "good enough mother." The capacity of the secure mother to provide security for her baby is described by Winnicott as primary maternal preoccupation. Winnicott (1965) introduces his important concept of "basic ego relatedness." This conceptualizes what a good-enough mother–infant relationship does for the child in terms of an experience that lasts for a lifetime and of a foundation upon which all the child's

later growth can take place. The sense of belonging, of being securely in touch that grows in the baby from the mother's loving reliability, becomes an established property of his psyche.

Winnicott (1968) believes that, apart from interpersonal relations, an ego or true self never develops at all. He concentrates on the beginnings of the ego and argues that the differentiation of subject and object out of the state of primary identification stimulates the beginning of specific ego development. The growth of the experience of basic ego relatedness, and therefore of the capacity both to enter into object relations and also to be alone without anxiety and insecurity, is based on the early relationship between the mother and the infant— "the nursing couple."

In chapter 3 of *The Maturational Processes and the Facilitating Environment* (1965) Winnicott presents his theory of the parent–infant relationship. He argues that infant development is facilitated by good-enough maternal care and is distorted by maternal care that is not good enough. The infant ego can be said to be weak, but in fact is strong because of the ego support of maternal care. Processes in the mother and the father bring about a special state in which the parent is oriented to the infant and thus in a position to meet the infant's dependence.

Winnicott's concept of "holding" is defined as a protection from physiologic insult that takes account of the infant's skin sensitivity and includes the whole routine of care throughout the day and night. It is not the same with any two infants because it is part of the infant and no two infants are alike. Also, it follows the minute day-to-day changes belonging to the infant's growth and development, both physical and psychological.

In *The Family and Individual Development* (1968) Winnicott explains how if the environment is not reliable, a hidden true self forms. All we can see, however, is a false self engaged in the double task of hiding the true self and of complying with the demands that the world makes from moment to moment. When there is very early failure in the holding stage of infancy, the tremendous anxiety provoked by this experience is followed by the building up of a false self in order to save the infant from total disintegration. In other cases, the false self disguises the true self which exists only as a potential and is allowed a secret life. In health the false self is represented by the whole organization of the polite and mannered social attitude, something that is adaptable.

Winnicott's view of the basic psychotherapeutic relationship rests squarely on his concept of the maturational processes and the facilitating environment. Only the mother who is capable of primary maternal preoccupation and identification with her baby is capable of giving it a sound start in ego development. This view plants human personality squarely in the soil of personal object relationships as the starting point of all human living. It is clear, then, that the earlier the cause of trouble is in the patient, the more fundamental is

his or her ego weakness, and the more profoundly important is the quality of the therapeutic personal relationship.

Winnicott distinguished between psychoanalysis for oedipal cases and "management" for preoedipal cases, where initial good-enough mothering cannot be taken for granted. For these sicker patients, Winnicott takes the mother–infant relationship as the model for and the basis of psychotherapy. Our personal knowing of the patient, working by empathy and intuition, seems to be the essence of the therapy. Winnicott's idea is that patients who have suffered serious disturbances of the mother–child symbiosis early in life will not get well unless the therapist "behaves." (Of course, this concept of the therapist behaving is a shibboleth and covers a great deal of the patient–therapist interaction, as described at length by Winnicott [1958] in chapters 22 and 23 of the *Collected Papers*.) Winnicott divides Freud's classical psychoanalysis into two parts. First, there is the technique as it is gradually developed and in which the material presented by the patient is to be understood and to be interpreted. Second, there is the setting in which this work is carried through. Winnicott enumerates in some detail certain points which seem obvious but tend to be overlooked about the setting.

Three of Winnicott's papers have vital implications for the therapeutic relationship. The importance of hate in the countertransference and the countertransference itself are discussed in detail in two classic papers (*The Maturational Processes and the Facilitating Environment,* chapter 14, and *Collected Papers,* chapter 15). Winnicott's most famous paper is "Transitional Objects and Transitional Phenomena" in the *Collected Papers,* chapter 18 (see OBJECT).

References

Winnicott, D. (1958). *Collected Papers: Through Paediatrics to Psycho-Analysis.* New York: Basic Books.

_____ (1965). *The Maturational Processes and the Facilitating Environment.* New York: International Universities Press.

_____ (1968). *The Family and Individual Development.* London: Tavistock.

_____ (1971a). *Playing and Reality.* New York: Basic Books.

_____ (1971b). *Therapeutic Consultations in Child Psychiatry.* New York Basic Books.

WORKING ALLIANCE (SEE THERAPEUTIC ALLIANCE)

WORKING THROUGH

Freud (1914) discussed the problem of "a trial of patience" for the therapist during the working through of resistances. The first step in overcoming resistance, he said, is made by uncovering the resistance and at least acquainting the patient with it intellectually. However, "One must allow the patient time to become more conversant with this resistance with which he has now become acquainted, to *work through* it, to overcome it, by continuing, in defiance of it, the analytic work according to the fundamental rule of analysis" (p. 155). In these situations a sense of growing impatience in the therapist is an important manifestation of countertransference (see PATIENCE).

Working through means going over the same insights again and again, applying them to more and more situations, and helping the patient make significant and lasting changes as a consequence of new compromise formations. These new compromise formations occur as a result of interpretations which acquaint the patient with older unconscious and maladaptive compromise formations, giving the patient another chance. Sedler (1983) points out how repeating enslaves the ego. Remembering through interpretation can lead to working through, which gives distance to the search for repeating and leads to increased autonomy in the patient.

Freud explained the resistance to interpretations after they have been made as "id resistance" (see ADHESIVENESS OF THE LIBIDO and RESISTANCE). He had in mind that compromise formations which were in place for decades rarely collapsed and were replaced by new ones simply on the basis of an interpretation. This is why considerable time and effort is required to expand and modify interpretations until they become maximally effective in achieving change in the patient. Thus working through is a crucial aspect of the psychoanalytic process, and raises the issue of to what extent this prolonged process represents suggestion out of the intersubjective experience of the patient and the analyst. In effective psychoanalytic work this problem seems less apparent because interpretations during the working through process consist chiefly in showing how the interpretation applies in many different contexts of the patient's thoughts, fantasies, and behavior, rather than in persuasion, and is carried out by a calm craftsperson, not a rhetorician.

Nevertheless, working through is dependent on the character and orientation of the psychoanalyst who cannot wholly avoid being a teacher, a definer of reality, an exemplar of a value system, and hence an influence on the patient. This leaves working through as somewhat ill defined and usually attached to periods of the analysis where little progress is being made. When interpretations seem to be having little effect, the idea of id resistance comes up and the necessity of working through is offered as an effective means of countering it. But this id resistance or adhesiveness of the libido really represents the fact that patients have their own internal timetable of integrating and applying interpretations in a way that produces lasting structural change. Patients cannot be hurried.

Of course, there is also the possibility that the analyst has failed to discover hidden transference situations that impede the acceptance of interpretation. An example of this is the humiliation certain patients feel upon hearing any interpretation, since it means the analyst knows more than the patient. As a revenge the patient may resist and object to the interpretation, or refuse to work with it, or to apply it to his or her thinking and life. What would be necessary in this situation would be a recognition of the patient's sensitivity, and further interpretation and discussion of the patient's reaction to narcissistic wounding.

Working through can all too easily degenerate into the therapist's "hammering" on a given interpretation or point of view until the patient surrenders or undergoes a massive introjection of the therapist as an identification with the aggressor. This may lead to a rigid identification with the therapist, which was a common problem in the early days of training psychoanalyses. Highly charged clinging to the therapist's personality traits and theories as a result of poor or incomplete training analysis partly accounts for the early tendency of splits to occur in psychoanalytic organizations, with little groups of followers or "disciples" clustered around each charismatic training analyst (see CORRUPTION).

Working through can be looked at as a necessary and time-consuming process based on the inherent timetable of the patient, or it can be looked at as having to do with the patient's resistance to the therapist's interpretation, requiring further psychoanalytic efforts. Depending on one's definition of resistance (see RESISTANCE), both of these can be true. Working through can be thought of constructively or pejoratively. Samuel Johnson (1773) defines working as "to labor; to travail; to toil" (p. 2263), and that is the essence of working through.

For a thorough review of the development of this concept from 1914 to 1984 see Brenner (1987).

References

Brenner, C. (1987). Working through: 1914–1984. *Psychoanalytic Quarterly* 58: 88–108.

Freud, S. (1914). Remembering, repeating and working through. *Standard Edition* 12:145–156.

Johnson, S. (1773). *A Dictionary of the English Language.* Beirut, Lebanon: Librairie du Liban, 1978.

Sedler, M. (1983). Freud's concept of working through. *Psychoanalytic Quarterly* 52: 73–98.

Index

◆